FROM FRAGMENTS TO OBJECTS

Segmentation and Grouping in Vision

ADVANCES IN PSYCHOLOGY

130

Editor:

G. E. STELMACH

ELSEVIER
Amsterdam – London – New York – Oxford – Paris – Shannon – Tokyo

FROM FRAGMENTS TO OBJECTS

Segmentation and Grouping in Vision

Edited by

Thomas F. SHIPLEY
Department of Psychology
Temple University
Philadelphia, PA, U.S.A.

Philip J. KELLMAN
Department of Psychology
University of California
Los Angeles, CA, U.S.A.

2001
ELSEVIER
Amsterdam – London – New York – Oxford – Paris – Shannon – Tokyo

ELSEVIER SCIENCE B.V.
Sara Burgerhartstraat 25
P.O. Box 211, 1000 AE Amsterdam, The Netherlands

First edition 2001

Library of Congress Cataloging in Publication Data
A catalog record from the Library of Congress has been applied for.

ISBN: 0 444 50506 7
ISSN: 0166-4115 (Series)

Printed and bound by Antony Rowe Ltd, Eastbourne
Transferred to digital printing 2005

This book is dedicated to all who have taught me, I return but a little piece. To Wendy for the present, to Noah and Anne for the future — Noah thee was there for the beginning and Anne thee made it in time for the end, and to Gamu (how many people get to edit a book with authors who cite their mother) and Grandfather for our past.

-TFS

This book is dedicated to those who inspired it. To a century of researchers who discovered and pursued the problems of perceptual organization, we owe a debt that can be paid only by continuing the work. In this effort, I thank my teachers and students for the privilege of being a link between them. For inspiration of many kinds, I dedicate this book to my wife Pam, and to my daughters Julie, Laura and Kim.

-PJK

Contents

Acknowledgements		ix
List of Contributors		xi
I.	**Philosophy and History of Perceptual Unit Formation**	1
1	The Concept of an "Object" in Perception and Cognition *Robert Schwartz*	3
2	Balls of Wax and Cans of Worms: The Early History of Object Perception *Margaret Atherton*	19
II.	**Development**	35
3	Perceptual Unit Formation in Infancy *Martha E. Arterberry*	37
4	Perceptual Units and Their Mapping with Language *Barbara Landau*	71
III.	**Attention**	119
5	An Object Substitution Theory of Visual Masking *James T. Enns and Vincent Di Lollo*	121
6	Attention and Unit formation: A Biased Competition Account of Object-Based Attention *Shaun P. Vecera and Marlene Behrmann*	145
IV.	**Models of Segmentation and Grouping**	181
7	Geometric and Neural Models of Object Perception *Philip J. Kellman, Sharon E. Guttman, and Thomas D. Wickens*	183
8	Varieties of Grouping and its Role in Determining Surface Layout *Barbara Gillam*	247

9 Amodal Completion: A Case Study in Grouping 265
Allison B. Sekuler and Richard F. Murray

10 Perceptual Organization as Generic Object Recognition 295
David W. Jacobs

11 Simplicity, Regularity, and Perceptual Interpretations:
A Structural Information Approach 331
Rob Van Lier

12 Computational Neural Models of Spatial integration in Perceptual Grouping 353
Heiko Neumann and Ennio Mingolla

13 Part-Based Representations of Visual Shape
and Implications for Visual Cognition 401
Manish Singh and Donald D. Hoffman

V. Spatiotemporal Segmentation and Grouping 461

14 Gaze Control for Face Learning and Recognition by Humans and Machines 463
John Henderson, Richard Falk, Silviu Minut, Fred C. Dyer,
and Sridhar Mahadevan

15 The Visual Interpretation of Object and Human Movement 483
Maggie Shiffrar

16 Contours From Apparent Motion: A Computational Theory 509
William Prophet, Donald Hoffman, and Carol Cicerone

17 Breathing Illusions and Boundary Formation in Space-Time 531
Nicola Bruno

18 Perception of Occluding and Occluded Objects Over Time:
Spatiotemporal Segmentation and Unit Formation 557
Thomas F. Shipley and Douglas W. Cunningham

Author Index 587

Subject Index 605

ACKNOWLEDGEMENTS

The editors would like to acknowledge not only the wisdom of the contributing authors, but their patience. They held on through one birth and some creative interpretations of temporal intervals by the editors and last few contributors. We thank our publisher who stayed the course though numerous missed deadlines.

Object perception is a gratifying scientific area, not only because of its intrinsic fascination, but also because of the extraordinary creativity and camaraderie of those who have chosen to study it. The authors in this volume exemplify these attributes, and they are shared by many others who are not directly represented here. We thank all of these researchers for their ideas, enthusiasm and for being, as we are, thoroughly committed to trying to understand how we see and represent the world.

We are grateful to Sharon E. Guttman and Jennifer L. Vanyo for compiling the author index and for expert general assistance. Editing this book was supported in part by research grants from the National Science Foundation (BNS 91-20919) and the National Eye Institute (R01 EY13518) to Thomas F. Shipley and grants from the National Science Foundation (SBR-9496112) and the National Eye Institute (R01 EY13518) to Philip J. Kellman.

List of Contributors

Martha E. Arterberry
Department of Psychology, Gettysburg College, Gettysburg, PA 17325 USA

Margaret Atherton
Department of Philosophy, University of Wisconsin-Milwaukee, Milwaukee, WI 53201 USA

Marlene Behrmann
Department of Psychology, Carnegie Mellon University, Pittsburgh, PA 15213 USA

Nicola Bruno
Dipartimento di Psicologia, Università di Trieste, via S. Anastasio 12, 34134 Trieste Italy

Carol Cicerone
Department of Cognitive Science, University of California, Irvine, CA 92697 USA

Douglas W. Cunningham
Max-Planck Institute for Biological Cybernetics, Spemannstrase 38, 72076 Tübingen Germany

Vincent Di Lollo
Department of Psychology, University of British Columbia, Vancouver V6RT 1Z4 Canada

Fred C. Dyer
Department of Zoology, Michigan State University, East Lansing, MI 48824-1117 USA

James T. Enns
Department of Psychology, University of British Columbia, Vancouver V6RT 1Z4 Canada

Richard Falk
Department of Psychology, Michigan State University, East Lansing, MI 48824-1117 USA

Barbara Gillam
University of New South Wales, School of Psychology, Sydney 2052 Australia

Sharon E. Guttman
Department of Psychology, University of California, Los Angeles, CA 90095-1563 USA

John M. Henderson
Department of Psychology, Michigan State University, East Lansing, MI 48824-1117 USA

Donald Hoffman
Department of Cognitive Science, University of California, Irvine, CA 92697 USA

David W. Jacobs
NEC Research Institute, 4 Independence Way, Princeton, NJ 08540 USA

Philip J. Kellman
Department of Psychology, University of California, Los Angeles, CA 90095-1563 USA

Barbara Landau
Department of Cognitive Science, The Johns Hopkins University, Baltimore, MD 21218 USA

Rob Van Lier
NICI, University of Nijmegen, PO Box 9104, 6500 HE Nijmegen, The Netherlands

Sridhar Mahadevan
Department of Computer Science, Michigan State University, East Lansing, MI 48824-1117 USA

Ennio Mingolla
Department of Cognitive and Neural Systems, Boston University, Boston, MA 02215 USA

Silviu Minut
Department of Computer Science, Michigan State University, East Lansing, MI 48824-1117 USA

Richard F. Murray
Department of Psychology, University of Toronto, Toronto, Ontario, M5S 3G3 Canada

Heiko Neumann
Fakultät für Informatik, Abteilung Neuroinformatik, Universität Ulm, 89069 Ulm Germany

William Prophet
Department of Cognitive Science, University of California, Irvine, CA 92697 USA

Robert Schwartz
Department of Philosophy, University of Wisconsin-Milwaukee, Milwaukee, WI 53201 USA

Allison B. Sekuler
Department of Psychology, McMaster University, Hamilton, Ontario, L8S 4K1 Canada

Maggie Shiffrar
Department of Psychology, Rutgers University, Newark, NJ 07102 USA

Thomas F. Shipley
Department of Psychology, Temple University, Philadelphia, PA 19122 USA

Manish Singh
Department of Psychology and Center for Cognitive Science, Rutgers University, New Brunswick, NJ 08903 USA

Shaun P. Vecera
Department of Psychology, University of Iowa, Iowa City, IA 52242-1407 USA

Thomas D. Wickens
Department of Psychology, University of California, Los Angeles, CA 90095-1563 USA

I.

PHILOSOPHY AND HISTORY OF PERCEPTUAL UNIT FORMATION

This book represents our attempt to marshal leading researchers in the area of object perception, have them review the current state of the field, and offer suggestions for future research. We encouraged authors to delve more deeply, and perhaps speculatively, than they might in preparing a manuscript for a journal. In this first section, Robert Schwartz takes the time to review what we mean by an *object*. Is there any such thing? Can the notion be made clear and coherent? This chapter generated, by far, the most debate among the author and editors. One may not agree with its conclusions. Who wants to be told their focus of study may not be coherent? Like Justice Stewart's criterion for recognizing obscenity, we all seem to think we know what an object is when we see one. Yet, as Schwartz suggests, the core notions are not at all simple or settled. Perhaps acquaintance with philosophical issues such as those raised by Schwartz should be required reading for anyone doing scientific research on object perception. Margaret Atherton provides us with some of the historical roots of issues in object perception. Readers of current journals could hardly be blamed for concluding that scant research in this area occurred prior to 1980. Here we see that central issues of object perception have been the subject of debate for a little longer than that.

From Fragments to Objects – Segmentation and Grouping in Vision
T.F. Shipley and P.J. Kellman (Editors)

1

THE CONCEPT OF AN "OBJECT" IN PERCEPTION AND COGNITION

Robert Schwartz, Department of Philosophy, University of Wisconsin-Milwaukee, Milwaukee, WI 53201 USA

> Object recognition ... is often taken as the primary goal of a visual system. Surprisingly, a significant obstacle in the path of understanding object recognition is that we lack a precise definition of what constitutes an object. Without such a definition, how can we possibly know where we are headed? Furthermore, any computational theory of object recognition becomes impossible, for what is to be computed?[1] (Whitman Richards)

In the theory of vision, object recognition has long been a topic of interest. For today's computational theorists it is a core area of study. As Richards indicates, this computational work has brought with it considerable pressure to find a precise definition of the notion of an "object". The last number of years has also witnessed an explosive growth of research in developmental psychology concerning the perception and conception of objects. Beautiful experiments have been conducted on ever younger infants attempting to determine their earliest awareness or appreciation of objects. The current trend has been to set the date closer and closer to birth. Many developmentalists assume, in fact, that the only way to account for the phenomena they have discovered is to assume the concept of an "object" is innate. But these developmental claims, like those of vision theorists, would seem to

[1] Richards (1988), p.17.

presuppose some acceptable characterization of objecthood.

What is it then to be an object? In turn, what is it for an organism to perceive or conceive of something to be one. Finding a precise, computationally satisfactory specification of objecthood has proven to be an elusive task for vision theorists. For example, even if it is agreed that a car is an object, is its radio also an object or is it only a part of the car? And what is the status of the radio's volume control knob or the left half of this knob? Do they each fall under the concept "object"? Similarly, consider the car's fender. Is it a part of an object when attached to the car but an object in its own right when on the warehouse shelf? And is the dent in the fender itself an object or merely a feature of one? To raise these questions is enough to see the extent of the difficulties, and this without pressing for answers to questions about the objecthood of non-solids (e.g. the gasoline in the tank), or two-dimensional items (e.g. decal emblems and the car's shadow), or conglomerations of non-continuous bits of stuff (e.g. the collection of the car's tires), or extended continuous surfaces (e.g. garage walls, the driveway on which the car now rests, and roads traversed).[2]

AN ANSWER

In light of the remarks above, it might be thought we lack any plausible account of what it is for something to be an object. Not so! There is a perfectly reasonable characterization of objecthood that is as simple and clear as it is unhelpful. From an ontological point of view, everything that is, is an object. And as W. V. Quine (1953, 1960) has forcefully argued, all it may mean to treat something as an object ontologically is to be willing to quantify over it in discourse. "To be is to be the value of a bound variable." is his motto.

Now there are those who rebel at the idea of granting existence and hence object status to non-spatial items, assuming that everything that is or exists must be material and observable. Herein lies the seeds of classic metaphysical debates over the ontological status of abstract entities, such as numbers and properties, or mental items, such as dreams or qualia. For our concerns these controversies can best be ignored. Little will be lost by stipulating that the objects of perception and conception are all material spatial things.[3]

---

[2] Related problems are involved in attempts to specify formally the notion "object part". It is not possible in this paper to discuss explicitly the complications this issue raises. For a non-technical account of the idea of "object part" in theories of vision, see Hoffman (1998).

[3] Whether holes, perforations, rainbows, clouds, molecules, or atoms are allowed in will depend on how one understands the agreed on restriction to spatial objects and to unresolved, if not unresolvable, issues about how and where to draw the line between the observable and the non-observable.

Still, this narrowed domain is not what theorists have in mind when they talk of the visual segmentation of the world into objects or attribute to newborns an awareness of objects. For the domain of the spatial includes gerrymandered parts and sums as well as temporal segments of the material world. Ontologically speaking, not only may a chair count as an object, but so can all of its pieces, from the atomic to the large. In addition, the spatially separated bits of carpet on which a chair stands, a chair plus a dachshund, or the compound of the tip of a dachshund's nose for two minutes and a chair for a moment before, may all be treated as objects of quantification. But if any assemblage of spatial material, or instantaneous temporal slices thereof, can be understood to be an object, the computational task of vision remains under-specified and the developmental importance of studying the onset of object awareness is obscure.

THE PROBLEM

As generally understood, the problem for psychology is not to explain whether, when, and how organisms perceive and conceive the full range of objects that may be said to have "ontological" status. Instead, the intuition underlying visual and developmental studies seems to be that there are real objects (e.g. individual chairs and particular dachshunds) and there are parts, sums, and temporal slices of what spatially exists (e.g. a chair plus dachshund, the dented portion of a fender, or the sum of scattered carpet pieces) that are not objects, or are spurious ones at best. The objects of perception and conception are the real ones, and the goal of psychology is to explain when and how we perceive and conceive of them.

This way of putting matters, however, is not entirely satisfactory. For we not only see individual chairs and dachshunds, we do see chairs together with dachshunds, we do see gerrymandered spatial sums and parts, we do see the separated bits of carpet where the chair's legs have left their impression, and we do see temporal slices of them all.[4] What's more, if asked, we can identify and label these things as such. So the idea can not be that we are only able to see and categorize "real" objects. It must be that although we can see the dimensions, respond appropriately, recognize, and even talk about spurious things, we do not perceive or conceive of them as objects. But what does it mean for something to be a real object and to be so taken?[5] And are volumes of gasoline, shadows, "natural" collections of real objects, and extended surface areas objects in this sense? Or are these items, like the gerrymandered,

---

[4] In fact, in one sense of the word 'see', at any given moment we can only see a temporal slice of an object

[5] In some of the literature the supposed real objects are said to be 'units' or 'things' or 'wholes'. Whatever the difference in terminology, the problems to be considered remain much the same.

not to be seen as objects?

Quine's criterion, by itself, is too wide to provide answers to these questions, since anything, including the spurious, can be an ontological object. The criterion also seems too narrow in that to quantify over an item in discourse (or partake in discourse best interpretable as so doing), presupposes having a reasonable degree of linguistic competence. Both vision theorists and devlopmentalists find this requirement unsuitable for their needs. For vision theorists, perception in general does not depend on having a language. Non-linguistic animals, human and non-human, are thought to perceive objects. Developmentalists, too, reject a language prerequisite. Their experiments with newborns would be pointless, if the appreciation of objects required infants to have relatively sophisticated linguistic skills. Thus, even if Quine is right about what it is to speak of objects, his criterion of ontological commitment does not seem to offer an acceptable analysis of the psychologically relevant notions of "perceiving" or "conceiving" objects. Still, I think more careful and detailed attention to Quine's concerns about reference and ontology can help illuminate the issues.

In fact, in his account of ontology, Quine finds it useful to introduce the notion of a "body," and this notion matches reasonably well with the intuitive concept of an "object" found in many psychological studies. According to Quine (1973), bodies are segregated, bounded, areas of the spatial-temporal environment that display "continuity of displacement, continuity of visual distortion, (and) continuity of discoloration" (p.55). Thus cars, chairs, and dachshunds are bodies, while gerrymandered parts and sums of them are not. Quine claims that our basic ontology is one of bodies, and that our initial and firmest grip on the whole idea of "ontology" is in connection with our commitment to physical bodies. Also, Quine readily admits that innate dispositions and Gestalt principles of perceptual organization probably make bodies salient and a major locus of early language acquisition.

Quine goes on to argue that an appreciation of the distinction between count and mass terms is most important in the context of these ontological matters. Mass terms, such as 'red' or 'water', function differently from the count terms 'car,' 'chair,' and 'dachshund'. Although 'red' and 'water' do apply to bounded areas of material stuff, the terms do not individuate or set the boundaries of the stuff to which they apply. The terms do not themselves divide into units the areas of the environment they refer to or denote. 'Red' applies to parts and sums of parts of a red car, as well as to the car's exterior surface as a whole. In contrast, 'car' denotes only individual cars, not their parts or sums. This distinction between count and mass terms, however, depends on use. Quine notes, for example, that the word 'lamb' in "Mary had a little lamb,' functions as a count term on the usual reading, but as a mass term when reporting Mary's dinner.

Similarly, 'body' may have both count and mass uses, exhibited perhaps in the distinction between 'more bodies' and 'more body'. As a count term 'body' individuates; it sets boundaries as to where one body leaves off and another begins. As a mass term it only attributes a property of "body-ness" to regions otherwise picked out or delineated.

Not surprising, count concepts are the ones needed for counting. All counting presupposes a unit to be counted, and for this it is necessary to divide reference. Mass terms do not provide units, since they themselves do not individuate among the parts of space-time they describe. Count terms, though, may denote "spurious" objects as well as "real"ones. 'Left half of a radio volume control knob,' 'fender dent,' and terms denoting gerrymandered spatial or temporal parts of chairs and dachshunds also divide reference, yet the items they pick out do not meet intuitive criteria for being a "body". Nevertheless, there is no problem in principle counting the spurious as well as the real.[6]

Quine realizes that his own rough and ready characterization of "body" is vague and its employment context sensitive. His characterization leaves considerable room for differences in interpretation and application, and provides no theoretical grounds for settling many of the problem cases earlier canvassed. But for his own purposes, Quine sees little reason to formulate a very precise definition. It is enough for him that cars, chairs, and dogs are representative examples of our untutored, everyday notion of an object. They serve as uncontested touchstones for what in the end is Quine's challenge to the very idea of there being any such thing as a referentially fixed, determinate ontology.

PERCEIVING BODIES PER SE

Suppose, for ease of exposition we identify the psychological notion of an "object" with Quine's idea of a "body". Nothing much hinges on adopting his characterization versus most of the others found in the vision or developmental literature. Suppose, too, we suspend worries about the linguistic focus of Quine's project, and consider what it might mean or

---

[6] The notions "object files" and "object file counters" have gained some prominence in recent work in perception and cognition. (See, for example, Scholl and Leslie, 1999) Space limitations prevent my giving this work the specific, in depth treatment it deserves. It us enough to note that this approach does not abnegate the need for schemes to divide reference, rather it is to be understood as a proposal about what the scheme and units may be in some cases. There is a vast and growing body of research purporting to show that very young infants can count. Elsewhere, I have expressed reservations about the claim that these studies demonstrate that the concept of number is innate (Schwartz, 1995). Accumulating evidence also seems to indicate that much of the experimental data on infant "number" behavior may be explained in terms of infants having an appreciation of amounts (e.g. area or volume) rather than an appreciation of cardinality (Mix et.al., in press). This is significant for our concerns in that such judgments of sameness and difference of amounts may presuppose only a rudimentary mastery of mass terms or concepts rather than a need for count categories to divide reference. (Schwartz, 1999). In any case, it should be clear that full fledged counting, whether counting cars, chairs, and dachshunds, or simply bodies (i.e. objects) does require count labels or concepts to provide units.

entail for a linguistically competent subject to perceive bodies. More does hinge on this assumption, but in order not to get bogged down, I wish to bracket my discussion here from the usual debates over the relationship between language and concepts. For me the linguistic focus serves to concretize the issues in more manageable terms. Those who cannot abide the approach may substitute their favored view of concepts or categories or internal representations, where I talk of words and what they denote. (Further comfort may also be found in the next section, "Object Perception Redux")

With language-speaking organisms, applying or perhaps being disposed to apply correctly a "body"-denoting term might seem the simplest and most obvious test of body perception. So formulated, however, the criterion is both ambiguous and problematic. First, the term "body' has both mass and count uses; the latter individuates, the former does not. It does not divide the world into entities. Second, words like 'car,' 'chair,' and 'dachshund' apply to bodies as much as the word 'body' itself does. Moreover, we may know or know how to use these words without either having learned the word 'body' or having any other term available meant to acknowledge that a given item falls into a category whose membership includes all and only bodies per se.

These considerations, in turn, raise questions about the role any explicit representation of something's being a "body" might play in object perception. After all, the count concept "body" is just one way to label or describe regions of space-time, and the need for and specific function of it remains unclear. Seldom, for example, does the task at hand require determining if or how many bodies per se are in the offing. More usually the task at hand is to perceive the kinds and properties of the bodies present. We need to know if what is in front of us is edible, sit-able, lift-able, weight bearing, alive, prey, predator, car, chair, or dachshund, not if it is a body per se.

Perhaps if the notion of a "body" actually plays a significant role in object perception, it is because such a concept is implicitly, rather than explicitly, involved in determining the kinds and properties of things in our environment. Perceiving cars, predators, edibles, and sit-ables must somehow require or reflect an appreciation of them as bodies. But how is this claim to be understood empirically? What does it means for the visual system to implicitly take something as a body?

Various of the problems explored above repeat themselves. Cars, predators, some edibles and some sit-ables are instances of bodies. It follows, then, that in perceiving them as such the visual system "marks out the boundaries" of whatever spatial regions are so described. This is all pretty tautologous. It says little more than that the processes of the visual system enable perceivers to discriminate those regions of the material world that contain cars, predators, edibles, and sit-ables from those that do not. What does not seem to follow is that in order for the visual system to make these discriminations it must first determine, represent, or otherwise render the information that there is an instance of the (count) property "body" present. And surely it does not follow that responding differentially to cars, predators, edibles and sit-ables entails an appreciation of the fact that the regions so discerned share membership in the class of bounded items that exhibit continuity of displacement, continuity of visual distortion, and continuity of discoloration.

OBJECT PERCEPTION REDUX

To some it may seem that I have changed, misunderstood, or avoided the issue of object perception as they conceive it. For them, the task of object perception concerns the visual system's encoding space time regions (STR's) as bodies and creating/assigning various descriptions or descriptors to them. Now granted that the level of analysis may be different, I think the issues raised above more or less carry over to this task specification as well. To appreciate this, make the following terminological replacements:

"encodes STR x as a body" for "perceives that the STR x is a body"

"assigns to STR x the description # or a # descriptor" for "perceives that the STR x is or is a #"

Nothing here assumes that descriptions or descriptors are previously established categories or that they are restricted to basic level shape categories or that segmentation cues only operate for familiar shapes. Nor does it preclude that the encodings and assignings are the work of relatively autonomous perceptual mechanisms. Also note that "functional" property descriptors such as weight-bearing, sit-able, and (in)edible and various "non-functional" property descriptors such as size, shape, texture, color, and composition are applicable to both bodies and non-bodies (e.g. shadows, fender dents, and driveways). And, as mentioned earlier, whatever analysis of the layout the visual system makes available does enable us to describe verbally and respond appropriately to "non" and "spurious" objects along with the "real".

That the visual system provides or affords information that guides the way we navigate, act, and react to the environment goes without saying. The issue, rather, is to understand better the sense in which the visual system must encode regions as bodies in order to do so. If in the end all the claim amounts to is that descriptors and descriptions are applied to regions of material space, there is little to debate. There does, of course, remain much to find out and debate about how the visual system actually accomplishes these tasks.

DEVELOPMENTAL CONSIDERATIONS

From a developmental perspective, it may seem there is more reason to suppose that some body-representation per se may be employed in perception and/or conception. After all, newborns do not divide the world into cars, chairs, and dachshunds, and their appreciation of which things are edible, sit-able, lift-able, and alive may not amount to much either. So it would not be surprising, if infants start out lumping all these different types of things into one big diffuse category, that of "bodies" (Shipley & Shepperson, 1990).

But again, there are problems understanding the exact content of such a claim. For example, it is generally agreed that quite early on in life infants can separate figure from ground and can distinguish spatially continuous bits of matter from disconnected pieces of stuff. They also respond differently to portions of their environment that move together and those that do not. And their appreciation of the layout, such as it is, can guide their activities. Does this mean, though, that they have and make use of a label (concept or representation) that serves to connote or denote all the things that are bodies or have the property "body"? If not, does it at least mean that their visual system makes implicit use of such a representation in the course of providing the infant information about the environment? Again, and for reasons similar to those canvassed in the previous section, I am not convinced a positive answer to either of these question is logically or empirically required.

Now some theorists seem content to let the evidence speak for itself. They are willing simply to call instances of figure/ground discrimination, Gestalt grouping phenomena, or perceptual tracking activities, whether by infants or adults, instances of or proof of object perception. And I have no qualms with this practice, as long as the nature and extent of the claims are kept in mind. For other theorists, perceptual discrimination, grouping, and tracking, are not taken to be sufficient for the attribution of object perception. The infant or adult must in some sense be cognizant of or represent the space-time regions isolated, grouped, or tracked as bodies. For them finding a satisfactory understanding or characterization of this richer demand remains an issue.

Past and Future Contingencies

Bodies have both spatial and temporal dimensions. Cars, dachshunds, edibles, and sit-ables not only occupy areas of space, they also have settled pasts and futures rife with threats and promises. Discriminating among regions of space that are so described, however, neither requires nor presupposes having knowledge of such life histories and prospects. It is one thing to be able to perceive correctly a wide variety of cars, dachshunds, edibles, and sit-ables under ideal and less than ideal conditions. It is another, to have perceptual constancy, to appreciate the sameness of particular shapes, sizes, textures, and colors when viewed under variable lighting and from different angles and distances. It is another to be able to perceive these shapes, sizes, textures, and colors when parts of the regions are occluded from view. And it is another still to have a firm grip or conviction about how things will be and look at much later dates.

Cars, dachshunds, edibles, sit-ables, indeed material substances in general, change in shape, size, color, coherence, and consistency as they age and interact with the world. Some of the changes can be reliably predicted, many can not, and the best scientifically sanctioned predictions will not always turn out as expected. Given the vagaries of life histories, we are thus much more likely to be accurate about how a currently observable temporal slice of our environment might look under certain different viewing conditions than about how future temporal slices will appear. Nonetheless, perhaps the most basic, general, and reliable prediction we make about our environment is that things do not change or go out of existence without cause. In addition, we assume that neither mere spatial displacement nor our observing and failing to observe the world are causes of physical change or annihilation.

Appreciation of persistence over time, independent of displacement and observation is at times referred to as 'object permanence'. The term can be somewhat misleading in that regions to which mass terms apply (e.g. red or water containing places), "non" objects (e.g. shadows, fender dents, or driveways) and "spurious" objects, likewise, do not change or go out of existence without cause. And they, too, are presumed by us to carry on their lives independent of our observation. So there is nothing special about the domain of bodies or "real" objects on this score. Undeniably, temporal slices of real, non, and spurious objects do go out of existence when their time is up and they are no longer observed, but this is by definition not by cause. Be that as it may, an appreciation of such persistence over time is what many theorists mean by perceiving or conceiving of the world as composed of objects.

THE OBJECT CONCEPT

Piaget argued that an infant's conception of reality is much different from our own. The newborn does not distinguish the world of experience from experience of the world. Conception of a world with enduring material objects existing independently of oneself comes later and requires construction. In addition, Piaget claimed that an infant's concept of reality is initially constructed in terms of his or her own actions and the immediate environmental effects or reactions they precipitate.

To support these contentions Piaget devised a variety of ingenious experiments intended to show that infants' responses to spatial and temporal transformations are not at all like those of older children and adults. Initially, Piaget contends, babies do not expect objects to persist over time and place. Hence, they do not, as we, search persistently for hidden objects, nor do they have the same expectations about what happens when things move behind and emerge from occlusions. For newborns, out of sight is not only out of mind, it is out of existence. Or put more accurately, newborns do not have a substantial conception of existence in and for which these distinctions make good sense. Eventually infants do begin to search intentionally for missing objects, but the searches are guided more by past patterns of interaction than by the available evidence. Infants expect to find an object at the place they found it before, rather than where they have just observed it being placed.

Piaget's pioneering work and theories set the stage for much contemporary discussion of the development of object perception and conception. A spate of recent experiments claim to demonstrate that Piaget may have underestimated young babies' prowess. Infants, it is maintained, do seem surprised when things hidden behind a screen are not there when the obstructing screen is removed. They seem to share with us some biases about the paths moving things will take, and they have some expectations about the full contours of simple shapes whose parts are occluded from view. In addition, their searches are not guided solely by past success but may take into account new conflicting evidence.

Now I have no desire to criticize these experiments, although issues of design and data have been raised (Haith & Benson 1998). My concern is how best to understand their implications and import. Earlier I raised questions about the proper interpretation and role a notion of a body per se might play in conceptual activities or in the encoding activities of the visual system. These questions and qualms, of course, do not preclude our having expectations. And I am willing to accept that the recent experimental evidence suggests infants may have richer sets of expectations at an earlier age than many, including Piaget, may have thought. Less clear is what these findings say about the perception and conception of objects.

In The Child's Conception of Reality, for example, Piaget allows that infants may have crude expectations of constancy, occlusion completion, and persistence that they use to accommodate their experiences. They may briefly search for the hidden, be surprised when something disappears without cause, and have wired-in visual pursuit schema for tracking movement. What Piaget denies is that these expectations and perceptual strategies extend much beyond the here and now. According to Piaget, infants do not have cognitively useful representations of the structures and patterns of events in the environment that enable them to place items in our ordinary "scheme of things" -- a stable world with its own independent past and future. But Piaget argues, an appreciation of permanence and persistence restricted largely to the here and now is not sufficient for the attribution of the object concept. A more enduring spatial/temporal framework is required (See Sugarman 1987). Is Piaget correct, though, about the real nature of objecthood, and are his more demanding criteria for attributing object perception and conception warranted?

Knowing how things can or will behave in and out of our presence makes up a large part of what we each know about the world. Some of this knowledge may be genetically inherited, some is readily attainable and commonplace (e.g. dropped objects tend to fall), most comes only with a good deal of experience or learning, and much remains exclusively within the purview of scientists or other experts (e.g. an accurate theoretical conception of space and time). Moreover, there is no plausible bound on what there is to know (what correct expectations we may have) about the possible or actual behavior of the animate or inanimate world and the events that can or will take place. It goes without saying that an infant's conception and understanding of the world is different from and impoverished compared to our own.

When, though, in the course of this development do infants first appreciate a world of objects? At what age or stage does a child first perceive or conceives of things as bodies? The analysis found in these pages suggests that this question may not be clear enough to answer or answer univocally. For neither everyday practice nor current psychological theory seems in a position to sanction a single privileged way to understand the claim. Furthermore, I am not sure what is at stake in settling on one. Is there, for example, a substantive difference between the claim that at a particular age infants do not perceive and conceive of objects and the alternative claim that infants do have an appreciation of objecthood, only their expectations and biases about the course of events are quite different from our own? But surely if infants' expectations and biases (or lack thereof) are radically different from our own, they can not be said to have our concept of an object. But what specifically is "our" concept of an object, and what role does it play in perception and conception?

IDENTITY OF KIND AND STRICT IDENTITY

Some of the controversy over object perception and conception is, I think, the result of conflating issues of constancy, permanence, and expectations with claims of identity. To determine that various space-time regions are or are segments of the "constantly" same/identical car, dachshund, edible, or sit-able is distinct from being able to appreciate the constancy of their sizes, shapes, textures, and even material compositions. Nor does it amount to having expectations about how such regions will look from other vantage points or when occlusions are removed. Judgements of identity require a determination of where a particular car, dachshund, edible or sit-able starts up and where it ends off. Identity involves linking segments, not merely describing them. It is a judgement that a space-time region here and there, before and now, go together in ways appropriate to sustain a claim that it is the very same car, dachshund, edible, or sit-able with which we are dealing.

Identity judgements of this sort often do assume sameness of body or bodily stuff in that in most contexts spatial-temporal regions are usually not said to constitute segments of the very same, car, dachshund, edible or sit-able unless their material makeup traces a more or less continuous path. But obviously the reverse does not hold. A set of space-time regions may continue as the same body or bodily stuff but lose its kind-identity. The same body is no longer identifiable as a car, when compressed into a lump of metal at the junk yard. And even if this lump is then reconstituted as a car, the resulting vehicle is unlikely to be considered the identical car as its pre-crushed embodiment. Similarly, being shown the pre and post crushed cars, but unaware of their history of transition, one may readily declare each such space-time regions to be bodies, i.e. segregated, bounded matter, perhaps of a particular size, shape, texture and composition. Yet one may have no idea that these different looking manifestations are actually segments of a single continuous lump of metal. And confuted expectations of persistence of size, shape, texture and color may be a main reason for the mistake.

Thus judgments of identity run deep. Appreciation of change whether expected or unexpected, entails neither a claim of identity nor one of non-identity. A cake cut into slices can for some purposes be considered the same cake, although the transformation into segments may not have been observed and the resulting spatial array unanticipated. In contrast, an identically looking intact substitute confection is not the same cake, although there may be no visually apparent differences to be discerned. Surprise at finding many pieces of cake when a screen is lifted, is compatible with judging the now non-contiguous pieces to constitute a stage in the life of the one cake hidden. The space-time regions before and after hiding count as segments of the same cake, relative to one way the term "cake" may be wielded to divide reference.

The situation is similar with the concept "body". Surprise at finding a distribution of matter not of the shape, color, or cohesion expected is compatible with a judgement of the identity of the constituting materials. Likewise, failure to notice any difference in bodily appearance between space-time regions is compatible with a denial that the regions so observed are parts of one and the same body. Body-identity is to be understood in terms of an evaluation of identity over space and time with respect to some particular individuating notion of a "body".

Identity, then, is a more abstract notion than phenomenal or physical indistinguishability. And for the most part, we get along on vague if plausible intuitions of sameness or difference of identity adjusted to context, salience, and need. If pressed for something firmer or fixed, we usually soon find out we have great difficulty coming up with criteria of identity in anything that approaches necessary and sufficient conditions. For example, is the car at hand, the same old car totally refurbished, or is what exists a new car, given that all the original parts have been changed? And would or should it matter, if the (re)building took place in a day, not over a decade? Alternatively, might it even make sense to think that the pre and post crushed cars previously alluded to are really temporal slices of one "transformed" car, since all the materials are the same? Centuries of philosophical puzzles about personal identity, the identity of a ships completely rebuilt one plank at a time, the metamorphosis of butterflies, and a mind boggling array of cases of object fission or fusion serve as further warning of the problems to be faced.

Another source of confusion in discussions of object perception and conception is the failure to keep in mind a distinction between two different kinds of identity judgements. The claim that a space/time region a and another space/time region b belong to one and the same car, dachshund, edible, sit-able, or body per se differs from the claim that a = b. The former says that a and b are parts of the same whole, relative to some way of individuating which wholes are to count. The latter says that the space/time region picked out by a and that picked out by b is the very same one. Thus, consider the much cited identity: the Evening Star = the Morning Star = Venus. This identity is not to be understood as a claim that certain evening spatial/temporal slices of the heavens and certain morning spatial/temporal slices are parts of the planet Venus. Instead, the claim is that the entity picked out by each of the three expressions is the exact same totality. Our use of 'star' and 'planet' to individuate and divide reference may play a role in fixing the reference of these labels, but the identity itself is not relative to either concept. Numerical identity is not identity with respect to an individuating category. In general, $x = y$, if and only, the objects referred to by the names, variables, or other singular terms are identical.

Neither part/whole nor numerical identity, however, simply inhere in Nature and the course of events. Quine, indeed, questions wherein the empirical content of identity claims is to be found other than in our use of general terms to divide reference and singular terms to name. For Quine, reification or commitment to a world of objects amounts to no more. It also demands no less, since what makes an entity the entity it is, is its identity. The linguistic focus of Quine's account of ontology and ontological commitment lies in this understanding of identity and reification.

Quine's more radical and controversial ideas lie elsewhere. They have to do with his views about language and about how language hooks up with the world. Quine maintains that there are incompatible ways to assign meanings and denotations to the terms of our language and no fact of the matter as to which among a set of observationally adequate assignments is correct. Therefore, ontology and attributions of ontology are themselves parochial, relative to the scheme of translation adopted (Quine 1960, 1969). Now this is no place to explicate, let alone defend, Quine's theses of indeterminacy of translation, the inscrutability of reference, and the implications they both have for his doctrine of ontological relativity. Suffice it to say Quine's ontological notion of perceiving and conceiving of objects is more abstract and linguistically focused than that of most psychologists, including Piaget.

CONCLUSION

My goal in this paper has not been polemical. I have attempted to sort out a number of theoretical issues central to discussions of the perception and conception of objects. As indicated, I believe many of the difficulties result from unclarities in the questions asked. Much of the controversy, too, lies in the fact that, matters of clarity aside, quite different questions are being asked. Hence quite different theoretical and empirical problems are raised. Not surprising, the answers offered are diverse and often incommensurable. At one extreme, all some theorists seem to mean by "taking something to be an object" is that the organism responds differentially to certain discrete pieces of the environment. For minimalist claims of this sort, the mere phenomena of figure/ground differentiation, occlusion completion, or perceptual tracking may fit the bill.

At the other end of the spectrum are the ontological issues that have been of philosophical concern since ancient times. Here the questions are more metaphysical, centering on accounts of identity and reification. And the answers offered have ranged from pinning entity-hood on some notion of "substance," the pure stuff in which the "essence" of individual things inhere, to accounts, like Quine's, that abjure the whole substance/essence framework. For Quine, science and other empirical study, not metaphysics, informs us about what there is and what is identical with what. Ontological commitment is reflected in how we group, categorize, and talk about our world. In the case of talk, reification shows itself primarily in the distinctions language draws between such statements as : (i) 'Something is red and something is a car' versus 'Something is a red car', and (ii) 'That (a) is a car and that (b) is a car' versus 'That and that are segments of the same car', and (iii) 'That segment a and that segment b are segments of one car.' versus 'a is identical to b'. These distinctions get reflected in symbolic logic notation as: (i) '(Ex)(Ey)(Rx & Cy)' versus '(Ex)(Rx & Cx)', and (ii) '(Ca & Cb)' versus '(Ex)(Cx & Sa,b,x)', and (iii) '(Ex)(Cx & Sa,b,x)' versus 'a = b'. Thus for Quine, ontological commitment is keyed to the use of variables, names, and other singular referring expressions.[7]

Although my goal in this paper has been expository not polemical, I think there are some issues the exposition does serve to highlight. Among these are:

1. Questions of constancy, occlusion completion, permanence, and identity are not peculiar to the perception of bodies or the properties of bodies *per se*. One can raise, I think with some profit, the same questions about non or spurious objects.

2. Mapping the course of development of vison and cognition from birth thereon has intrinsic interest. Attempting to determine when *the* concept of an "object" makes its first appearance, founders on fact that there is no unique object concept sanctioned either by ordinary use or present scientific theory.

3. Differential responses and manifestations of expectations met or frustrated are important tools for studying perception and conception. Nothing said in this paper is meant to decry or challenge their usefulness. But they can only take us so far. When it comes to richer, more abstract notions of "object," "identity," and "reification," whether those of Piaget, Quine, or those championed by other theorists, they may not be able to take us far enough.

---

[7] My sympathies lie with Quine in rejecting substance/essence metaphysics in either its old or newer guises. At the same time, I think it important in the study of perception and cognition to be less language oriented and to consider the role other forms of symbolization may play in informing thought and guiding behavior. In this, along with unease about Quine's privileging physics, I am more at home with Nelson Goodman's (1968 and 1978) constructivist views (Schwartz, 1996, 2000).

AKNOWLEDGEMENTS

I wish to thank Sidney Morgenbesser, David Rosenthal, and the editors of this volume for comments and helpful criticism.

REFERENCES

Goodman, N. (1968). *Languages of Art*. Indianapolis: Hackett Publishing.

Goodman, N. (1978). *Ways of Worldmaking*. Indianapolis: Hackett Publishing.

Haith, M. & Benson, J. (1998). Infant cognition. In W. Damon (Ed.). *Handbook of Child Psychology 5th Edition* (pp.199-254). New York: John Wiley.

Hoffman, D. (1998). *Visual Intelligence*. New York: W. W. Norton.

Mix, K., Huttenlocher, J., & Levine, S. (in press). *Math Without Words*. Oxford: Oxford University Press.

Piaget, J. (1954). *The Construction of Reality in The Child*. New York: Ballantine Books.

Quine, W. V. (1953). *From a Logical Point of View*. Cambridge: Harvard University Press.

Quine, W. V. (1960). *Word and Object*. New York: John Wiley.

Quine, W. V. (1969). *Ontological Relativity and other Essays*. New York: Columbia University Press.

Quine, W. V. (1973). *The Roots of Reference*. La Salle, IL: Open Court.

Richards, W. (1988). Image interpretation: Information at contours. In W. Richards (Ed.), *Natural Computation* (pp.17-35). Cambridge: MIT Press.

Scholl, B. & Leslie A.M. (1999). Explaining the infant's object concept: Beyond the perception/cognition dichotomy. In E. Lepore & Z. Pylyshyn *(Eds.), What is Cognitive Science?* (pp.26-73). Oxford: Blackwell.

Schwartz, R. (1995). Is mathematical competence innate? *Philosophy of Science, 62,* 227-240.

Schwartz, R. (1999). Counts, amounts and quantities, paper presented at Society for Research and Child Development. Albuquerque, New Mexico.

Schwartz, R. (1996) Symbols and thought. *Synthese 106,* 399-407.

Schwartz, R. (2000) Starting from scratch: Making worlds. *Erkenntnis,* 151-159.

Shipley, E. & Shepperson, B. (1990). Countable entities: Developmental changes. *Cognition, 34,* 109-136.

Sugarman, S. (1987). *Piaget's Construction of the Child's Reality,* Cambridge: Cambridge University Press.

From Fragments to Objects – Segmentation and Grouping in Vision
T.F. Shipley and P.J. Kellman (Editors)

2

Balls of Wax and Cans of Worms: The Early History of Object Perception

Margaret Atherton, Department of Philosophy, University of Wisconsin-Milwaukee, Milwaukee, WI 53201 USA

I am going to begin my attempt to reconstruct the early history of object perception, perhaps somewhat surprisingly, in the middle of the seventeenth century with Descartes. Descartes himself didn't write very much about object perception, but he might nevertheless be said to have invented the problem of object perception as a psychological problem, so he seems the right place to begin. Before Descartes there was no problem of object perception per se because the answer was taken to be obvious. The answer to Koffka's question, Why do things look as they do?, would have been assumed to be the one Koffka wanted to reject: Things look as they do because things are as they are.. An object is as it is and is the kind of thing that it is because of the intellectual and sensible forms that organize it, and by virtue of which things have the essential properties they do. We see and understand objects because we are built to be informed by these forms. While simple and intuitively attractive, this theory had the flaw that it failed to give a clear account of how the forms that make objects what they are also function psychologically to inform us of their nature, how they make the transfer from object to perceiver. In his *Optics*, Descartes pointed out that he was able to give an account of perception entirely in terms of his own impact physics, an account free from the substantial forms "flitting about" which had been so beloved by scholastics[1].

[1] For accounts of Pre-Cartesian theories of vision, see David C. Lindberg (1976) and Gary Hatfield and William Epstein (1979). Descartes's reference to "flitting forms" in the *Optics* is in the First Discourse (p. 68, Descartes, 1637/1965).

Descartes's account, with its freedom from flitting forms gained widespread currency, but it brought with it this problem: if our perceptual capacities are not informed by those self same organizational structures that make objects the kinds of things they are, then why *do* things look as they do? Why do we appear to open our eyes onto a world of discretely organized units, tables and trees, mugs and flowers? While it was Descartes who, as I shall discuss in a minute, identified this challenge, it was the group of canonical empiricists, Locke, Berkeley and Hume, who, in one way or another, took it up. Thus, the earliest attempts to raise and deal with issues surrounding our capacities to perceive a world of tables, trees, mugs and flowers are empiricist in nature. The positions developed and put forward by these early empiricists were not, however, identical with what had, by the end of the nineteenth century, hardened in the "empiricist" position, against which many psychologists even into the present have taken it as their task to argue. Instead, as I shall show, they are quite diverse and raise a number of issues. I will go back, therefore, to the early days of thinking about object perception, to see what has gone into constructing the problem.

1. DESCARTES

While flitting forms are no doubt universally regarded as a highly dispensable portion of perception theory, there is nevertheless something in an Aristotelian or scholastic account which is very satisfying to anyone of a realist bent. It says that we are so structured, perceptually and cognitively, to be able to pick up the basic categories, perceptual and cognitive, into which the world is organized. What Descartes found objectionable was the implication that the perceptual categories into which we divide the world we see constitute a group of ontologically basic substances, each different in their essential nature, out of which the world is made. Descartes found this view conflicted with what he took to be central to a proper understanding of physics, which requires us to see the physical world as sharing a single material nature. Rather than the more complicated approach in which each kind of thing's behavior and properties followed from its essential nature, Descartes developed a much simpler physics of extended matter in motion. The purpose of his optics was to show that perception was not dependent upon a variety of different sensible forms, but could be understood entirely in terms of the action of matter in motion on the material properties of the visual system. But in simplifying the physics of the world as he did, and in conceiving perception as the action of undifferentiated matter in motion, Descartes left it as a problem for psychology to explain why, if the physical world is essentially extended material substance in motion, we perceive it as a world of perceptually varied physical objects.

Descartes's approach to the perceptual world of objects is most familiarly expressed in the passage in the Second Meditation about the ball of wax. In this passage he considers a ball of wax as an example of those bodies we think ourselves to be most readily acquainted with --the bodies we touch and see. He asks which of the many sensory properties by means of which we think we know this ball of wax, its odor, color, shape, hardness, its sound when struck, etc., are those that continue to exist throughout the changes to which things like balls of wax are continually subject. Which properties can the ball of wax not lose without ceasing to exist, by virtue of which we can know the essence of the object? His answer is that it can be none of the sensible qualities of the wax, for we can imagine changes in all of these while the ball of wax remains. "It is of course", Descartes concludes" the same wax which I see, which I touch, which I picture in my imagination, in short the same wax which I thought it to be from the start. And yet, and here is the point, the perception I have of it is a case not of vision or touch or imagination--nor has it ever been, despite previous appearances--but of purely mental scrutiny; and this can be imperfect and confused, as it was before, or clear and distinct as it is now, depending on how carefully I concentrate on what the wax consists in" (p. 21, Descartes, 1641/1984). What Descartes is saying here is that we grasp what is essential to being a ball of wax when we understand that it is something extended. Such an understanding is abstract and theoretical in nature; it is in fact a piece of innate knowledge belonging to the mind alone. None of the qualities we perceive by means of the senses are essential to being a ball of wax because the wax can gain or lose any such properties without ceasing to be that ball of wax. Only if it ceased to be extended would it cease to be not just a physical body but that individual physical body. So the ball of wax is really and essentially a physical body, but there is nothing that is essentially true of it by virtue of which it is some *kind* of wax-like physical body. It is worth noting here that Descartes's criterion cuts the physical body or material thing category pretty broadly: anything that is extended or takes up space is included, and so this will include clouds, fog patches, shadows, and gasses, and other items which it is appropriate to include as part of the subject matter of physics, but which are dubiously physical bodies from a common sense point of view. Descartes is finally able to conclude that our knowledge of the physical world is entirely intellectual or theoretical (if largely inexplicit). Sense derived information is irrelevant to physics.

So, what the ball of wax passage tells us is that we can identify something as a physical body, a piece of material substance, by means of the understanding or the intellect. We subsume it under our conceptual understanding of what it is to be a material substance. What the ball of wax passage doesn't do is explain how we perceive the ball of wax as we do as a particular instance of extended material substance, with a particular extension, that is, particular spatial dimensions, where, moreover, a lot of different perceptual qualities such as color or hardness seem to be located. It is unfortunately the case that Descartes himself never appears to give a definite answer to the question, why do things look as they do, that is, of a particular shape, size and color? It is possible from various things Descartes says to reconstruct some positions he might be willing to endorse, although not to attribute any one position to him with confidence. One quite tempting possibility is to say Descartes thought that, starting with our concept of what it is to be a physical substance, we possess algorithms allowing us to form judgments about the spatial location and properties of the object, like the ball of wax, we are perceiving. But even if this is a claim Descartes is willing to endorse, it remains unclear how we would want to integrate these judgments with the sensory information present in any perceptual contact with a physical object. One thing that makes this problem especially pressing is that, while it seems clear that Descartes wanted to assert some kind of discrepency between the way spatial properties are registered by us and the way we judge them to be, it is by no means clear how he wanted to conceptualize the situation. For example, he writes: "And it is equally obvious that shape is judged by the knowledge or opinion, that we have of the position of various parts of the objects, and not by the resemblance of the pictures in the eye; for these pictures usually contain only ovals and diamond shapes, yet they cause us to see circles or squares" (p. 107, Descartes, 1637/1965). Descartes's subsequent discussion makes it very difficult to decide how he is thinking about a causal process in which ovals produced by circles cause us to see circles. Are his "pictures in the eye", pictures on the retina corrected by the visual system or are they pictures that are phenomenally present in the visual field that are corrected somehow by the judgment or the belief system of the perceiver?

2. LOCKE

Just as Descartes's rejection of the scholastic account of objects was fueled by his commitments to his physics, so Locke's contrary position derives in part from some reservations about the epistemological element of Descartes's physics. Locke thought while Cartesian impact physics might at the moment be the conceptually clearest theory available, it was Locke's somewhat prescient opinion that future developments in physics might lead us to give up the view that what is essential to material substance is extension. He was therefore dubious of the viability of assuming such a concept to be part of our innate intellectual equipment. At least a part of Locke's argument involves an investigation into the nature and limitations of our cognitive faculties by means of which we arrive at, among other things, our concepts of objects. In making his argument, Locke is striving in part to reverse the claim for which Descartes argued in the ball of wax passage, that our knowledge of objects is based on highly abstract and specialized knowledge. It is not the learned, Locke claims, but "yet those ignorant Men, who pretend not any insight into the real Essences, nor trouble themselves about substantial Forms, but are content with knowing Things one from another, by their sensible Qualities, are often better acquainted with their Differences; can more nicely distinguish them from their use;, and better know what they may expect from each, than those learned, quick-sighted Men, who look so deep into them, and talk so confidently of something more hidden and essential" (Section 3.6.24, Locke, 1690/1975). Locke's claim is that it is in fact perceptually based knowledge, especially in the hands of skilled practitioners, that is more informative than the specialized theoretical knowledge of the physicists.

For Locke, perceiving or conceiving an object requires a particular kind of complex idea of a substance. To call an idea complex signifies it is an idea the mind had to do something in order to have, it requires some sort of activity or mental processing. Complex ideas are to be distinguished from simple ones, which provide the materials or content for complex ideas. When Locke gives examples of simple ideas he lists sensory qualities, such as red, blue, hot, cold, hard, soft, and the like. There are two characteristics of simple ideas Locke stresses that help explain what constitutes a list like this and accounts as well for the importance of such a list to Locke. A simple idea presents a single, undifferentiable sense quality; its content, in Locke's words, is "a uniform appearance" (Section 2.2.1, Locke, 1690/1975). We should therefore refine the language of the list of sense qualities to understand it to be referring to a single shade of red or degree of hotness. Secondly, the mind is entirely passive in the reception of a simple idea. It is impossible to make a simple idea or to alter one. We can have only the simple ideas our senses have equipped us to have and with which our past experience has presented us. Ideas of the taste of an unknown fruit or colors to the blind are as nothing to us. In order to understand what Locke is getting at here it is important to be clear his claim is not ontological--he is not sayng that the world is made of single sense qualities. Rather, he says the qualities of the world exist all blended together, but it is in the nature of our senses that we apprehend distinct qualities, we feel the ice, for example, to be hard and cold. Nor is it the case that he thinks he is describing a sensory field as made up of atoms or mosaics of sense qualities. Instead, his goal is to describe how he takes our sensory processes to work. What our senses can do is passively register just noticable differences in qualities. They are passive apprehenders of just distinguishable, hence, simple qualities. So, as I sit in my room looking out of the window, my senses register distinguishably different senses qualities, but that I see such objects as a window and trees through the window is the work of the mind.

In describing the formation of a complex idea of a substance, Locke mentions two things the mind has to do. From all the simple ideas with which the mind is "furnished" Locke says it "takes notice also, that a certain number of these simple *Ideas* go constantly together" (Section 2.23.1, Locke, 1690/1975). Locke as it happens leaves vague what is involved in "going constantly together". He almost certainly means the simple ideas are spatially and temporally contiguous, but he doesn't specifically mention this characteristic as opposed to others that come up in the current literature, such as boundedness or common movement. It does seem, however, that, for Locke, object recognition is a matter of being able reliably to expect some qualities in the presence of other qualities, and is therefore a process taking place over time. He is not obviously interested in how we tell at a glance we are looking at an object as opposed to a non-object. It is also important to notice however that for Locke the complex idea isn't formed until the mind "takes notice." From this, it is possible to surmise, for Locke, what is more important than any particular set of relations among ideas that might be intended by "go constantly together" is the mental state of attending that singles out some set of properties as ones having a common history. Whatever relations might or might not obtain among simple ideas or sensations, until the mind takes notice there is no complex idea to which we give a single name.

The second part of the process Locke mentions takes place after the mind has taken notice of the qualities going constantly together. Then, he says, the mind appends an idea of substance to the set of qualities in order to explain why all the qualities go constantly together. Thus, it is the concept of substance that turns the set of qualities into a free-standing object, that expresses the idea all these qualities have a permanent and continuous existence. It is important to notice some things about Locke's account. First, the notion of a substance is for him close to being a dummy-concept. It is, he says, "a something-I-know-not-what" that gets added to the qualities that go constantly together. There is nothing further we learn about being an object from the concept of substance. Secondly, the concept of a substance is something the mind comes up with as an explanation for why some qualities go constantly together. We don't develop the concept of an object until after we have noticed sets of qualities to which we have given names. We are not, as it were, primed to look for objects as independent substances before we set out to find them. On Locke's account, we don't develop more general concepts, like body, until after we possess more specific ones, like tree or stone, from which we then abstract those qualities trees and stones share. Extension turns out to be one of those properties which happen to have gone constantly together with the other qualities of things we call bodies, like solidity or motility, but it does not constitute a preestablished essence of body. Further experiences of body may cause us to change our minds about which properties all bodies share.

Locke's discussion of the way in which we frame sortal concepts (a term he introduced into the literature) indicates how far he is moving from an account in terms of some set of essential properties. We sort, Locke tells us, by means of abstract ideas which are the "workmanship of the understanding".[2] While the urge to communicate tends to stabilize these abstract ideas to which we attach general names, each abstract idea is in fact individual and reflects the particular history of the person to whom it belongs. Each abstract idea has a developmental history. Locke opines that children attach a word to an idea containing very few qualities, so that, for example, a child will use the word 'gold' for anything of a characteristic color, most adults will include still more properties, but metallurgists still more. Thus what it is to be gold will vary from person to person and for a single person, from one time to another. Nevertheless, it is the abstract idea that provides an answer to Descartes's

[2] This is a phrase Locke uses more than once. See *Essay Concerning Human Understanding*, 3.3.13 and also 3.3.14. The same sentiment is put slightly differently in 3.3.11. Locke introduces the term "sortal" in 3.3.15.

question about the ball of wax, which qualities must a thing have and fail to lose in order to be what it is. Such abstract ideas, however, only separate things into sorts at a time, reflecting human interests and developmental states. They do not reflect those states or processes in the physical world that determine the existence of any *particular* set of properties. In order to be that particular, a thing can't lose *any* of its properties, but we can only ask what properties it must have in order to be a kind or sort of thing, as opposed to a particular thing, with respect to an abstract idea. Locke's conceptualism provides one kind of account of why things look as they do, developing Descartes's challenge that it cannot simply be that things are as they are.

Locke, then, has provided a kind of answer to the question, why do things look as they do? at a certain level of generality. He would not find particularly congenial an attempt to answer this question by trying to show why things look like objects or units. He does not think it necessary (or indeed intelligible) to suppose that humans bring an innate knowledge of the essence of objecthood to the perceptual task nor does he in fact think there is such a thing as the essence of objecthood, in the sense of properties all and only objects must have in order to be objects. Rather, he finds the idea of an object is a complex idea, framed like all complex ideas, by noticing which qualities go together. It is of course entirely true that, in both the case of the idea of a tree and in the case of the idea of a stone, that among the ideas that go constantly together are those that constitute the idea of an object. Locke does not, however, think that the complex idea of an object plays a formative role in the construction of ideas of trees of stones, but is instead abstracted from them and many others. These abstract ideas are not the ideas we notice or pay attention to as we look about us. In general, Locke thinks it makes very little sense to explain the particular in terms of something more abstract. If a child knows sweet is not bitter, there is no need to attribute to the child the knowledge that it is impossible for the same thing to both be and not be. It would seem then, for Locke, the question, why do things look as they do? is first and foremost a question about why things appear to us to be of various sorts and the answer is going to be in terms of the going together of qualities we happen to notice. Locke's procedure, moreover, suggests, although this implication is never explicitly drawn out, that he thinks the task of recognizing kinds of objects over time precedes recognizing something as an object at a time.

3. BERKELEY

Berkeley's account of how we arrive at complex ideas of objects, at least initially, differs very little from Locke's. Here is what he says at the beginning of *Principles of Human Knowledge*.

> By sight I have the ideas of light and colours with their several degrees and variations. By touch I perceive, for example, hard and soft, heat and cold,

> motion and resistance, and of all these more or less either as to quantity or degree. Smelling furnishes us with odours; the palate with tastes, and hearing conveys sound to the mind in all their variety of tone and composition. And as several of these are observed to accompany each other, they come to be marked by one name, and so to be reputed as one thing. Thus, for example, a certain colour, taste, smell, and figure and consistence having been observed to go together, are accounted one distinct thing, signified by the name *apple*.

The Lockean language of this passage is obvious.

Berkeley, of course, also differs from Locke in some significant respects. He doesn't think it is helpful to regard the stability of objects as captured by the dummy concept of substance, and instead wants to call attention to the lawlike regularities displayed by the qualities we experience, regularities which allow us to assign stable meanings to the items in our immediate experience. But, in addition, Berkeley's interest in the problems of vision and his insistence on the absolute difference of the ideas derived from sight and touch led him to raise some quite novel problems for object perception. Most striking is his argument that visual units neither resemble nor are demonstrably connected with tangible units and that we can never perceive something as stable as an object through vision alone. For Berkeley, talking about the perception of visual objects strictly means talking about perceiving by sight the visual properties alone of an object (which has other properties). By sight, we perceive the colors of a tree, which in turn suggest to us we are seeing something with characteristic colors, hardnesses, sounds, odors, etc. To Berkeley, the question, why do things look as they do? cannot be answered simply in terms of sight, since sight must be supplemented with other sensory information before we can see a world of trees and tables.

Berkeley's view that by sight we perceive only visual properties is further complicated by his dramatically restrictive ideas about our visual capacities to perceive spatial properties. It is a quite familiar piece of Berkeleian argument that distance is not the sort of thing that can be seen. The third dimension is not part of the visual scene, but must be constructed by the perceiver. In Berkeley's terminology, pictorial and other cues "suggest" distances, which are themselves rendered meaningful tangibly. Thus, when we turn to the task of recognizing objects in space, a part of what is involved in the problem is learning to take cues, such as occlusion, as signs for different distances. But Berkeley's famous claim about distance is in fact only a part of his argument. Berkeley is not actually claiming that the visual scene is rather like a two-dimensional picture into which we must learn to read the third dimension, although this is sometimes taken to be the lesson he is teaching. Instead, his view is there is nothing inherently spatial about vision, and we have to learn to construct, not just distance, but also size and shape, and what Berkeley calls situation, the position of what we see, up, down, to the right, to the left. Inasmuch as sight informs us of nothing more than unlocalized (and constantly varying) light and color, the task of object or unit perception for Berkeley is formidable.

The full thrust of Berkeley's theory can be seen in his explanation of his claim that there is no problem for vision theory in the fact that images on the retina are upside down and backwards. The most obvious response to this problem is to say that since we don't see the retina in the act of seeing, no properties of the retina, neither its flatness or the orientation of pictures on it, are relevant. But Berkeley's response is more complicated, since he thinks the tug of this issue as a problem reveals some interesting confusions. Using the image of a man born blind and made to see, Berkeley first points out that a blind man, before he had been made to see, would understand position terms like up and down tangibly in terms of the direction toward or away from gravitational pull. So, when such a blind man is made to see, the visual scene in front of him would look neither erect nor inverted, the man made to see would have no resources to make such identifications. In fact, Berkeley thinks we are all actually in the position of such a blind man: we learn the meaning of situation terms tangibly and then apply, for example, a term like 'up' to those portions of the visual field coming into focus when we turn our eyes up, which come to mean what we reach for when we raise an arm up, away from gravitational pull. A visual scene of a man looks erect, to us and to the man born blind, when we have learned to correlate and give meaning to what we see by reaching up to touch the head and down to touch the feet.

Berkeley answers what seems to be an obvious objection to this view in a very revealing way. It seems plausible to suppose that it is possible just to see whether the man we are looking at is erect or inverted, without resorting to touch, because we, or a man born blind when made to see, can tell whether there is a single or head blob above or below the two feet blobs. Berkeley's answer is that the man born blind would have no reason to correlate the colors he is now seeing in his newfound state with the texture qualities with which he used to feel and identify heads or feet. There are no inherent connections between them, since the two sets of properties are entirely different from one another. Nor could this blind man so much as tell there was one head and two feet until he had performed the mental act of forming them into units. Berkeley explains,

> Hence it follows that a man born blind and afterwards, when grown up, made to see, would not in the first act of vision parcel out the ideas of sight into the same distinct collections that others do, who have experienced which do regularly coexist and are proper to be bundled up under one name. He would not, for example, make into one complex idea, and thereby esteem an unit, all those particular ideas which constitute the visible head or foot. For there can be no reason assigned why he should do so, barely upon his seeing a man stand upright before him. There crowd into his mind the ideas which compose the visible man, in company with all these ideas of sight perceived at the same time: but all these ideas offered at once to his view, he would not distribute into sundry distinct combinations till such time as by observing the motion of the parts of the man and other experiences he comes to know which are to be

separated and which to be collected together. (Berkeley, 1709/1948).

By sight, we perceive only shifting light and colors. A head or a foot or a man comes to be identified as a stable unit only when those shifting lights and colors are combined with the more stable qualities perceived by touch. Berkeley's notion is that the project of perceiving objects by sight, like the project of perceiving distance, can only be accomplished through the cooperation of sight and touch. What Berkeley is introducing into the question of object perception is a claim that this is not a matter that can be settled by considering only one sense modality. He encourages the investigator to ask: What precisely is the content of the information available to the perceiver through vision? So long as at least a part of the content of concepts of an object or of particular objects involve information we do not and cannot learn through vision alone, the question of object perception cannot be translated without loss into a question about the visual perception of objects. The question, why do things look as they do? is not a question just about seeing.

4. HUME

David Hume concluded his *Abstract* of *A Treatise of Human Nature*, the short summary he wrote in the third person in order to make the nature of his argument in that book easier to understand, with the claim that the most novel invention of his book is the principle of the association of ideas. Hume writes:

> Thro' this whole book, there are great pretensions to new discoveries in philosophy; but if any thing can entitle the author to so glorious a name as that of an *inventor*, 'tis the use he makes of the principle of the association of ideas, which enters into most of his philosophy. Our imagination has a great authority over our ideas; and there are no ideas that are different from each other, which it cannot separate and join, and compose into all the varieties of fiction. But notwithstanding the empire of the imagination, there is a secret tie or union among particular ideas, which causes the mind to conjoin them more frequently together, and makes the one, upon its appearance, introduce the other....These principles of association are reduced to three, *viz., Resemblance*; a picture naturally makes us think of the man it was drawn for. *Contiguity*; when *St. Denis* is mentioned, the idea of *Paris* naturally occurs. *Causation*; when we think of the son, we are apt to carry our attention to the father. 'Twill be easy to conceive of what vast consequence these principles must be in the science of human nature, if we consider, that so far as regards the mind, these are the only links that bind the parts of the universe together, or connect us with any person or object exterior to ourselves. For as it is by means of thought only that any thing operates upon our passions, and as these are the

> only ties of our thoughts, they are really *to us* the cement of the universe, and all the operations of the mind, must, in a great measure, depend on them.[3]

It is worth pointing out, since the phrase 'association of ideas' has since become closely associated with the empiricist position generally, that Hume's use of the phrase represents the first occasion on which it was used non-pejoratively. Locke added a section to the *Essay* in order to warn against the ways in which habitual connections could mislead, and Berkeley used the much looser term, 'suggestion', which he elucidated in terms of an analogy with language: one idea suggests another to us as a written or spoken word suggests its meaning. It is Hume's proud boast that he is the first to have proposed that ideas are associated according to a few simple principles, so that if we perceive objects and not disconnected impressions, it will be because the complex ideas involved can be explained in terms of the relations of resemblance, continuity or causation. Hume has provided a revised version of Locke's claim that the mind "takes notice" that some qualities "go constantly together." On Hume's view, we are built to take ideas to go constantly together when they are like each other, or are spatially or temporally joined or are related through causal connections.[4]

While Hume was the first to claim that we perceive objects as we do through a process of association, his actual account of this associative process is extremely intricate, in part because, in Hume's hands, the question, why do we perceive bodies? reveals some hidden complexities. We have to explain not just why this or that collection of qualities is perceived as a body, but we need to explain why bodies are something that we take our selves to be perceiving at all. Under Hume's analysis this is not at all obvious. Hume takes the distinguishing characteristics of a body to be that it has a continued existence, whether or not anyone is perceiving it, and that it has an existence independent of any mind or perceiver. Thus, for Hume, to perceive something as a body is to perceive it as something continued and mind-independent. But the sensations we actually are aware of are not bodies, nor can they have these characteristics of bodies. Instead of continuously existing, our sensations are fleeting and changing at every moment as we look this way and that, and are, moreover,

---

[3] *An Abstract of a Book lately published, entitled A Treatise of Human Nature, etc. wherein the chief argument of that book is farther illustrated and explained* in David Hume, *A Treatise of Human Nature*, edited by David Fate Norton and Mary J. Norton, Oxford, Oxford University Press, 2000, pp. 416-417. The *Abstract* was first published in 1740 and the *Treatise* itself in 1739/40.

[4] Causality is itself of course a complicated notion to elucidate for Hume and was the source of considerable analysis. It was after Hume had given an account of relation of causality that he went on to make use of this, as he calls it, natural relation, one of the ways in which our mind just works, in order to develop an account of object perception.

widely assumed to be mind-dependent. Given that our sensations have quite opposite characteristics from those we ascribe to bodies, we have to account for what, on the face of it, looks like an inexplicable tendency to believe in bodies at all.

Hume's project is to use his natural associative principles to explain why we don't take our sensations to be emanating from ourselves but instead to be located outside of and independent of ourselves and why we take the qualities we sense to go on existing when we are no longer apprehending them. It is this latter problem that Hume sees as most demanding. He points out there is no way in which we can ascribe this belief to experience, that is, to custom or habit, since we never experience a sensation continuing to exist unperceived. Hume's explanation is quite complex. He first supposes that we perceive things causally, which leads us to ascribe a coherence to our experiences. Thus, when I hear a knock at the door, I am not surprised to find someone on the other side, because I fill in a causal chain from the effect I hear to its cause behind the door. But while a coherent world is an organized and understandable one, coherence alone does not explain why I take the things in the world to exist unperceived. To explain this, Hume turns to resemblance. We experience the world as constant when the sensations of the paper before me now closely resemble the ones I had a minute ago before I looked up. Hume supposes that, as my imaginative, associative faculties work overtime, I confuse the experience of constancy with that of identity, the experience of something continuing to exist unchanged through temporal changes, and for this reason, assume a continued and hence distinct existence to my discontinuous mind-dependent sensations. Hume's approach to the problem demands the recognition that explaining why things look as they do requires taking into account aspects of the problem that are sometimes taken for granted. That we believe there are objects in the world at all existing independent of perceivers is a part, for Hume, of what must be regarded as the problem.

5. Concluding Remarks

As should have emerged by now, seventeenth and eighteenth century empiricism is a very mixed bag, revealing a number of different approaches to problems of object perception. There are a couple of lessons, however, that I would like to draw from this sketch of a history. The first is that if there is a common focus to the various thinkers called empiricist, it is in fact a very traditional one. They all display a reluctance to employ anything like a Cartesian intellectualist or innate idea in their explanations of cognitive and perceptual capacities, in the sense of ideas or principles whose content is not derived from sensation. They all therefore start from a common starting point, the simple ideas or simple sensory impressions on which the content of our ideas and beliefs are held to be based. But while they all think that an analysis of our cognitive capacities must begin with an analysis of the ways in which our sense organs can function and of the nature of the content the sense organs deliver to us, there is no commitment as to some form in which the sensory field is organized or experienced. In particular, there is no commitment to the view that the sensory field is experienced as discrete units. Hume's view, for example, that the imagination can break down wherever it perceives a difference is not a claim that the original sense impressions arrive so broken down. Some of the important ways, therefore, in which gestalt views are often held to differ from earlier empiricist account, do not apply to these original empiricists. Similarly, attempts in the recent psychological literature, such as that of Elizabeth Spelke, to challenge empiricists by showing that infants do not experience a center-occluded object as two separate objects bears little relationship to positions maintained in the early modern accounts.[5] The claim that the early empiricists were willing to make, that the eye, for example, works by registering discriminably different shades of color is not a claim that the eye registers discrete units or mosaics of color. This early empiricist claim is indifferent to the question, Are infants perceiving a tableau of visual surfaces or an organized unit? To the extent that *this* question could be answered within the resources of early modern empiricist theory, the answer would be most likely to be, neither one. Neither Berkeley nor Hume, for example, thought that the original deliverances of the visual system constituted a tableau of any sort or of any organization.

On the other hand, there is much in this early theorizing that does bear quite directly on issues discussed today. Consider the following account of the problems to be solved in an account of object perception, also from Elizabeth Spelke.

> Human adults experience the world as a layout of physical bodies that endure through time. Our ability to do this is both mysterious and fascinating, because the information we receive about physical objects is potentially so misleading. Consider the case of vision. Objects are bounded, but the visual scenes in which they appear are continuous arrays of surfaces. Somehow, we must determine which of the many surfaces that touch or overlap in a visual array are connected to one another. Objects are also integral units, but they are only partly visible at any given time and their visible surfaces are often separated from one another by nearer occluding objects. Somehow, we must recover the integrity of each object from this mosaic of visible fragments. Finally, objects exist and move continuously through space and time, but they are frequently occluded and disoccluded by movements of surfaces or of the observer. Somehow, we must apprehend the continuous existence of an object from our sporadic encounters with it. Vision, moreover, appears to provide the richest

[5] I have in mind some of the claims made by Spelke in theoretical articles summarizing some of the empirical work of herself and her colleagues. See, in particular, Spelke (1988) and Spelke (1990).

> information for objects. The problems of apprehending objects only seems to increase when human explore by listening or touching (p. 197, Spelke, 1988).

Every issue in this admirable summary is one which had been touched on by one of the theorists whose ideas I have been describing, and frequently in ways which provide a different angle through which to look at the problem. For example, the issue of determining the boundaries of objects is not, according to Berkeley, precisely as Spelke has described it, because, in his eyes, we do not perceive surfaces, because we are not immediately presented with a visual field in two dimensions. The problem of locating the boundaries of objects requires locating them spatially as well as discriminating them from other surfaces. Locke has raised the possibility that the problem of assembling an object from its fragments is highly individual and and needs to be discussed in terms of attention. Hume suggests that the fact that our encounters with objects are sporadic requires us to deal with the question, how do we construct the concept of an object at all, given that the information we take in is fleeting and mind-dependent. And Berkeley again would suggest that once we understand the limited nature of the information available through vision, it is plausible to suppose that information from touch and kinesthesia is helpful is solving the problem of object perception. These are just a few examples. The general lesson that I would like to propose is that a Whiggish approach to the history of psychology, in which present day efforts with experimental know-how are thought to supplant earlier accounts is not the most productive use of the ideas of the past. When these earlier contributions are considered in their full complexity, they not only provide more worthy opponants, but they can even sometimes provide useful hints and suggestions.

REFERENCES

Berkeley, G. (1948). *Essay Towards a New Theory of Vision* in *Works*, edited by A A Luce and T E Jessop, vol I. Edinburgh, Nelson,, NTV 110. (Original work published in 1709)

Descartes, R., (1965). *Discourse on Method, Optics, Geometry, and Meteorology*, translated by Paul J. Olscamp, Indianapolis, The Bobbs-Merrill, Co, Inc. (Original work published in 1637)

Descartes, R., (1984). *Meditations on First Philosophy*, Second Meditation, *The Philosophical Writings of Descartes*, translated by John Cottingham, Robert Stoothoff, and Dugald Murdoch, Cambridge, Cambridge University Press. (Original work published in 1641)

Hatfield, G., & Epstein, W. (1979). The Sensory Core and the Medieval Foundations of Early Modern Perceptual Theory, *Isis*, 70, 363-84.

Lindberg, D. (1976). *Theories of Vision from Al-Kindi to Kepler*, Chicago, University of

Chicago Press.

Locke, J. (1975). *An Essay Concerning Human Understanding*, edited by Peter H. Nidditch. Oxford, Clarendon Press. (Original work published in 1690)

Spelke, E. S. (1988). Where Perceiving Begins: The Apprehension of Objects in Infancy. In A. Yonas, ed., *Perceptual development in infancy. The Minnesota Symposia on Child Psychology, vol. 20*, Hillsdale, NJ, Lawrence Erlbaum. pp. 197-234.

Spelke, E. S. (1990). Origins of visual knowledge. In D. N. Osherson et.al., *Visual cognition and action An invitation to cognitive science, vol. 2* Cambridge. MA. M. I. T. Press. pp. 99-127.

II.

DEVELOPMENT

How does object perception develop? Which segmentation and grouping processes come hardwired in perceptual systems; which unfold via maturation; and which are acquired through experience? How does object perception -- or the representations it produces -- tie in to other cognitive processes? These questions are important in their own right but also as key windows into our understanding of perceptual organization in general. The two chapters in this section take up these questions with two different objectives. Martha Arterberry examines what we have learned about the development of segmentation, grouping, and object perception processes from studies of young infants. This research informs experimental studies and modeling of adult abilities and is in turn motivated and informed by them. Barbara Landau reflects on the relation between object perception and language. Without compatible representations between perceptual knowledge and language, we could neither talk about what we know nor know what we are talking about. Although the mapping between these domains is subtle and complex, Landau uncovers both clear connections and important differences between the ways we encode objects (and their parts) and the ways in which we talk about them. Her discussion gives us reason to believe that object perception and language are more closely related than often realized, and that understanding in both areas will benefit from exploring these relationships.

From Fragments to Objects – Segmentation and Grouping in Vision
T.F. Shipley and P.J. Kellman (Editors)

3

PERCEPTUAL UNIT FORMATION IN INFANCY

Martha E. Arterberry, Department of Psychology, Gettysburg College, Gettysburg, PA 17325 USA

INTRODUCTION

Perceiving something that actually isn't visible, such as the hidden section of a partly occluded object or an illusory contour, may be considered a challenge because there is a lack of a one-one correspondence between stimulation and percept. In many contexts, observers must infer the nature of the object parts that are occluded. For adults, there may be several processes they can rely upon. Adults may use their knowledge and experience of the partly occluded object and come to a conclusion about its properties and features of the occluded part. For example, when perceiving a couch with a coffee table in front of it, adults may know that the center of the couch extends behind the table, even though the central region is not visible, because they know something about couches -- they know couches are long, solid, continuous objects often placed behind coffee tables. However, using knowledge about or previous experience with objects does not help the perceiver when confronted with a never-before-seen object. In this situation, observers must rely on more fundamental processes that take advantage of the available perceptual information.

Now consider a less experienced perceiver – an infant. The young perceiver may not have much experience with or knowledge of specific partly occluded objects. Continuing with the couch example, infants may not be able to acquire the knowledge that couches are continuous objects until they have had the chance to crawl or walk along the front of the couch, something babies usually do not do until 6 to 9 months of age because of the timing of the onset of self-produced locomotion. However, infants may be sensitive to perceptual information that specifies the nature of the occlusion and the properties of the occluded object, regardless of whether they have knowledge of or experience with the object. Thus, for both infants and adults, it is possible that perception of partly occluded familiar and unfamiliar objects can be achieved using perceptual processes that rely on features in the optic array, rather than on specific knowledge structures. This chapter focuses on the perceptual processes that enable young perceivers to parse their visual world into cohesive perceptual units. In doing so, this presentation will rely heavily on the theory of visual interpolation espoused by Kellman and Shipley (1991) to explain adults' perception of partly occluded objects and illusory figures.

Theory of Visual Interpolation

In the 1990s, Kellman and Shipley provided a theory of object perception that specifically addressed perception of partly occluded objects and illusory contours, and they conducted a number of elegant studies supporting their claims (Kellman & Shipley, 1991; Shipley & Kellman, 1992, 1993, 1994). The main construct of their theory is visual interpolation. They posit that through processes of edge detection, boundary assignment, and the relatability of the visible parts of objects, perceivers can interpolate features of an occluded object across the nonvisible areas in the array. Moreover, Kellman and Shipley (1991) claim that observers perceive illusory figures as complete units through similar processes. Although they were modest in terms of their claims – in fact, they claimed that their model "... may be incomplete in some respects and perhaps incorrect in some others..."(Kellman & Shipley, 1991 p. 159) – three postulates of their theory have stood the test of time and research. The three postulates are:

- Perception of the unity and boundaries of partly occluded objects and perception of illusory figures are the results of an identical unit formation process
- Static and kinematic perception of hidden object boundaries may depend on a single process
- The mechanisms of unit formation incorporate basic ecological constraints, specifically utilizing the information provided by spatial and spatiotemporal discontinuities in projected edges.

The first postulate suggests that the same processes underlying perception of illusory figures also underlie perception of partly occluded objects. Let's consider each case separately. Perceiving a partly occluded object as complete, such as the rod continuing behind the block in Figure 1A, requires interpolation of the rod across the gap produced by the block. Adults viewing such a display can achieve this interpolative process using several sources of information. First, the visible ends of the rod are relatable in that a smooth contour can connect the ends across the expanse of the block. Second, the depth cue of interposition specifies that the rod is located in a depth plane behind the plane of the block. Specifically, the intersection of the rod and the block form a T-junction, an important cue for the ordering

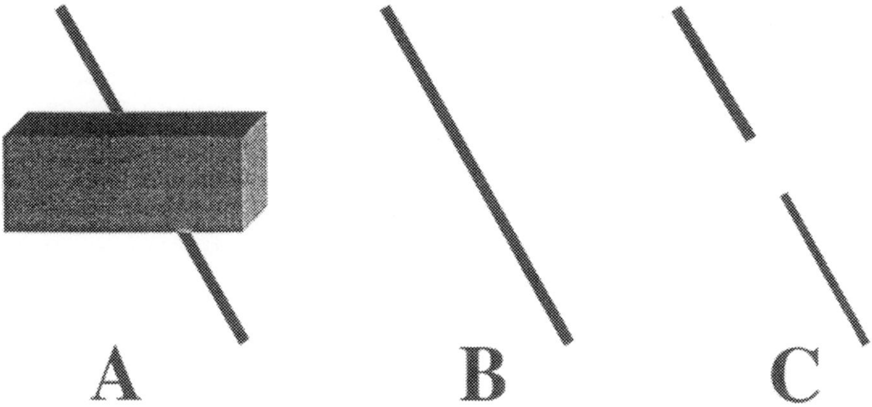

Figure 1. Three-dimensional rod-block display created with real objects was used by Kellman and Spelke (1983) as a habituation stimulus. The rod extended behind the block. B and C are the complete and broken rod test displays, respectively. When common motion is present, the rods in all three displays move.

of surfaces in depth. Third, edge detection and boundary assignment processes specify the block as a complete entity and as separate from the rod. If the rod moved behind the block, additional information provided by the common motion of the visible ends of the rod would further specify the rod's unity.

Perception of illusory figures, as illustrated in Figure 2A, can be explained by similar processes that explain perception of unity. Typically, this display is perceived as a white

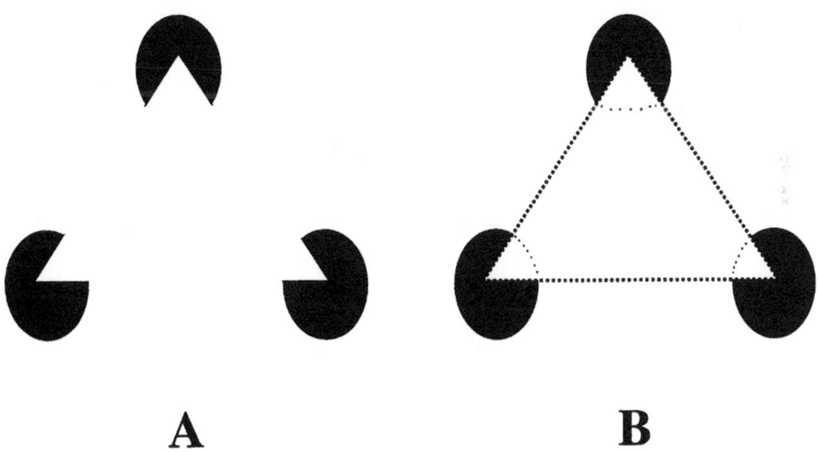

Figure 2. An example of an illusory figure (after Kanizsa, 1955). Typically, the illustration in A is perceived as a triangle in front of three circles. The dotted lines in B illustrate completion of the units.

triangle in front of three black circles, but it also can be perceived as three holes through which the triangle's vertices are visible. In the first interpretation, the circles are partly occluded objects and the triangle is the occluding object, similar to the rod and block, respectively, in the previous example. The occluded edges of the inducing elements (i.e., the black circles) can be interpolated across the gap produced by the triangle because the edges are relatable; a smooth contour can connect the visible edges of the circles across the triangle vertex to create complete circles (Figure 2B). In addition, the edges of the triangle can be interpolated across the gap between the inducing elements because these edges are relatable (Figure 2B). In contrast to the rod-block display, Figure 2A contains relatively little information for depth. The necessary T-junctions for interposition are not available, even with interpolation of the edges. Rubin (1915; cited by Kellman & Shipley, 1991) suggests that because a white field encloses the black circles, observers perceive them as figures. Thus the triangle must be in front. Because there is little depth information available for ordering the circles and triangle relative to each other, this display is bistable: At times it is seen as a triangle in front of three circles, and at other times it is seen as a triangle behind three circular holes. If the triangle rotated around a central axis, the kinematic information provided by the successive occlusion of the circles would provide additional information for the connectedness of the triangle, and the successive occlusion of the circles by the triangle vertices would provide adequate information for the separation of the circles and triangle in depth, resulting in a less ambiguous interpretation than the static display (Kellman & Cohen, 1984).

The suggestion that the processes underlying the perception of illusory contours and object perception are the same is supported by neuropsychological research (Peterhans & von der Heydt, 1989, 1991). When real edges at preferred orientations were projected, recordings of neurons in areas 17 and 18 of the visual cortex showed maximum firing. The firing rate varied as orientation was manipulated. When illusory contours were presented, neurons in area 17 did not fire, but neurons in area 18 did, suggesting that the illusory contours were treated as real edges at higher cortical levels, even though stimulus information (ie., a physical edge) was not present at lower levels.

The second postulate suggests that visual processes across space in static displays and across space and time in kinematic displays may derive from the same or closely related processes (Kellman & Shipley, 1991). The resulting percepts are clear object boundaries and perceived depth. How the object boundaries are specified and how depth is perceived in static and kinematic displays will differ because static and kinematic information operates differently and are supposedly governed by different neurological areas (e.g., Livingstone & Hubel, 1988), but the general principles are predicted to be the same. In other words, regardless of the specific type of input (static or kinematic information), the unit formation process is the same.

The third postulate addresses how the visual system determines where edge interpolation will occur. A crucial task in perception is making correct interpretations of discontinuities detected in the early stages of vision. In general, there are two types of discontinuities in images. One type arises from luminance changes, such as at the corners where planes of an object intersect or markings on a surface caused by changes in the surface material (e.g., wood grain). A second type of discontinuity results from disruptions in visible edges, such as when one object occludes another. This type of discontinuity provides possible sites for visual interpolation.

Kellman and Shipley (1991) proposed that spatial and spatiotemporal discontinuities are the primary source of information to perceivers about which parts of objects are occluded and where boundaries lie. Identification of such discontinuities relies on regularities in the environment. In static images, differences in luminances, surface color and/or texture, and regions of concavity are often correlated with different objects. When motion is involved, discontinuities need to be detected over time, and one object occluding another produces different optical changes than cases of nonocclusion (Shipley & Kellman, 1993).

Overview

In this chapter we will use these postulates as a framework for organizing the body of research on object perception in infancy, with particular emphasis on the research pertaining to infants' perception of partly occluded objects and illusory figures. The goal of this chapter is to provide an understanding of what we currently know about object perception in infancy, specifically what processes are used, what abilities infants may be born with, and what abilities develop with age. In addition, we hope to provide directions for future research with infants by identifying areas in need of further inquiry. First, we will begin with an overview of methodology typically used by researchers to answer questions about visual perception in very young children.

General Methodology

Much of the research that will be discussed in this chapter was conducted with infants between birth and 12 months of age, with an emphasis on the first 4 months of life. Unlike adults, infants are unable to provide clear responses to questions like "how connected does this object appear?" As a result, researchers must resort to inferring infants' perception from a limited set of behavioral responses. Most of the evidence discussed in this chapter has come from studies relying on visual attention in a habituation paradigm (e.g., Bornstein, 1985; Cohen, 1973), a paired-preference paradigm (Fantz, 1956), or a violation-of-expectation paradigm (Baillargeon, 1993).

In the habituation paradigm, infants are typically shown a display on repeated trials, such as the rod-block display illustrated in Figure 1A. Initially, infants typically show high levels of attention to such a display but across trials, their attention wanes. When their level of attention reaches a predetermined criterion (such as a 50% reduction from the first two trials), the display is changed (Figure 1B and C). In this post-habituation or test phase, infants view two or more displays on alternate trials, and one of the displays is the same as the habituation display and the other is a new or novel display. Using this method to determine whether infants perceive the rod as complete behind the block, infants would be habituated to Figure 1 A and then view Figures 1B and 1C. If infants perceive the rod as complete behind the block, then the complete rod without the block (Figure 1B) should be familiar or something they have seen before. Likewise, the broken rod (Figure 1C) should be novel because they have not seen a broken rod before. In this case, infants would show an increase in attention to the broken rod because infants usually show an increase in looking to a display that is new to them. In contrast, if infants perceive the rod in Figure 1A as two separate pieces and not continuing behind the block, then the broken rod (Figure 1C) should be familiar and the complete rod novel (Figure 1B). Increased looking to the novel compared to the familiar display is typically between 5 to 10 seconds when averaged across a sample of infants. It is possible that infants find both test displays equally novel or equally familiar. Equal looking to the two test displays is difficult to interpret and in the case of the rod-block displays, it is usually concluded that infants' perception of the habituation display was ambiguous with regard to the rod's connectivity.

A second procedure commonly used to study infant perception is the paired-preference paradigm. In this procedure, infants are familiarized to a particular stimulus (like the rod-block display in Figure 1A), but they are not required to reach a predetermined criterion for a reduction in looking. Instead infants receive a set number of familiarization trials. Following familiarization, infants view two displays on any given test trial (such as Figure 1B and 1C, presented side by side). The prediction is that infants will show a preference for one display over the other if they perceive a difference between the two and one as different from the display presented in the familiarization phase. Typically the results are reported in terms of a novelty preference (i.e., the percentage of time spent looking at the novel display as a function of total looking during the test phase). Thus, using the stimuli in Figure 1 as an example, infants who perceive the rod behind the block as unified will find the complete rod in the test phase more familiar and exhibit a looking preference for the broken rod that is significantly greater than chance (50%). Infants who perceive the rod in the rod-block display as broken will exhibit a significant looking preference for the complete rod. Such preference scores usually fall between 58-65%. Finally, if infants are unsure about the unity of the rod in the rod-block display, then they should show approximately equal looking to the complete and broken rod, resulting in a novelty preference that is not significantly greater or less than 50%.

A third method, originally designed to test infant cognition, also has been applied to questions of infant perception. The violation-of-expectation paradigm developed by

Baillargeon (see Baillargeon, 1993 for a review) consists of showing infants pairs of events. One event is "possible" or "expected" in that it follows certain laws or assumptions that adults (and possibly infants) have. For example, in the top frames shown in Figure 3, one might perceive the textured rectangle partially covered by a thin black panel. In the "complete object event" (the left side of Figure 3), the black panel moves to the side to fully reveal the complete rectangle. This event is expected because in the first frame the rectangle was perceived as complete, and this percept was confirmed as the complete rectangle was revealed. In the "broken object event" (the right side of Figure 3), the rectangle looks complete in the first frame, but as the thin black panel moves away the observer sees that the rectangle is actually two pieces -- an event that violates what was expected given the first frame. In studies using this methodology, it is predicted that infants will look longer at unexpected than expected events, and they typically do so on an order of 3-7 seconds.

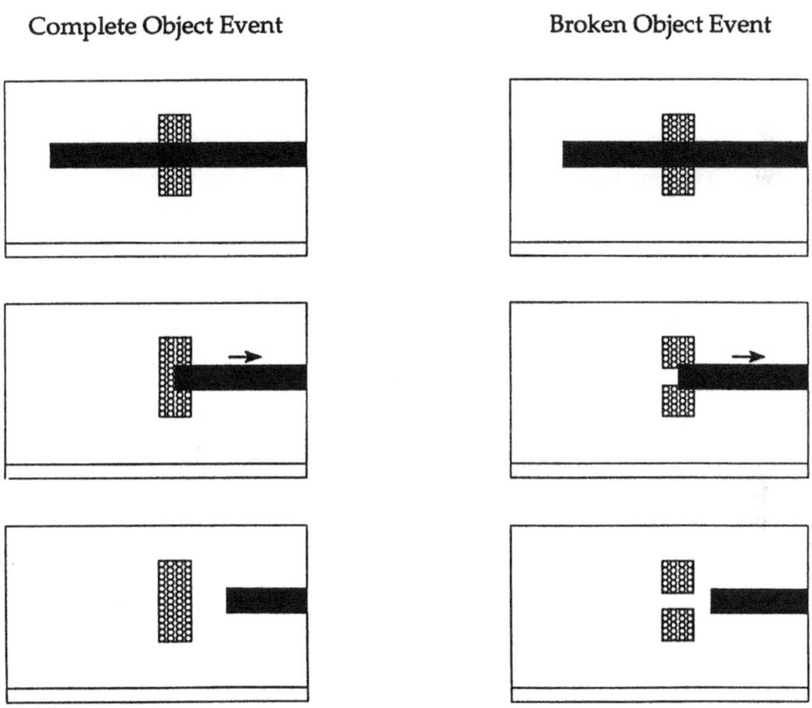

Figure 3. Two events used to test infants' perception of object unity in the violation-of-expectation paradigm (see text). From Craton, L. G. (1996). The development of perceptual completion abilities: Infants' perception of stationary, partially occluded objects. *Child Development*, *67*, 890-904. Copyright © 1996 by the Society for Research in Child Development. Reprinted with permission.

INFANTS' PERCEPTION OF PARTLY OCCLUDED OBJECTS AND ILLUSORY CONTOURS

The first postulate of Kellman and Shipley's (1991) theory of visual interpolation suggests that the same processes that underlie perception of partly occluded objects also underlie perception of illusory contours. Research has been conducted in both areas with infants. We begin with the more substantial body of work on infants' perception of partly occluded objects and then turn our attention to infants' perception of illusory contours.

Infants' Perception of Partly Occluded Objects

Infants' perception of partly occluded objects provides an intriguing developmental story. At risk of spoiling the ending, it appears that two processes can account for perception of unity of occluded objects -- a robust edge-sensitive process and a primitive edge-insensitive process (Kellman & Shipley, 1991). The edge-sensitive process depends on edge positions and orientations for perceiving both moving and stationary displays as unified, and it also provides information for object form. The edge-insensitive process is a lower level process that merely relies on common motion, and it provides information for object unity but not form. The data from infants suggest early reliance on the edge-insensitive process and later emergence of the edge-sensitive process (e.g., Kellman & Arterberry, 1998).

Much of the work on infants' perception of unity has been conducted with variants of the rod-block display described earlier and illustrated in Figure 1A. In general, 4-month-old infants perceive the rod as continuing behind the block only under conditions of common motion, that is when the visible ends of the rod move in the same direction (Kellman & Spelke, 1983; Johnson & Nanez, 1995). This common motion can be translatory in the horizontal and vertical planes or in depth (moving toward or away from the infant but still behind the block), and it can result from observer or object motion (Kellman & Spelke, 1983; Kellman, Spelke, & Short, 1986; Kellman, Gleitman, & Spelke, 1987). In addition, the common motion of the visible ends overrides other conflicting information, such as discontinuities in surface properties and the Gestalt principle of good form (the rod-blob configuration illustrated in Figure 4A; Kellman & Spelke, 1983).

However, unity is perceived by 4-month-olds only under conditions of common motion of the visible ends of the rod, not just motion or some other type of synchronous change in the display. For example, motion of the block does not yield the perception of unity of the rod, nor does motion of both the rod and block (Kellman & Spelke, 1983). Four-month-olds do not perceive unity when the visible ends of the rod rotates (Kellman & Short, 1985), but 6-month-olds do (Eizenman & Bertenthal, 1998). Moreover, a synchronous change in the absence of object motion, such as a color change in the visible ends of the rod, did not support the perception of unity (Jusczyk, Johnson, Spelke, & Kennedy, 1999).

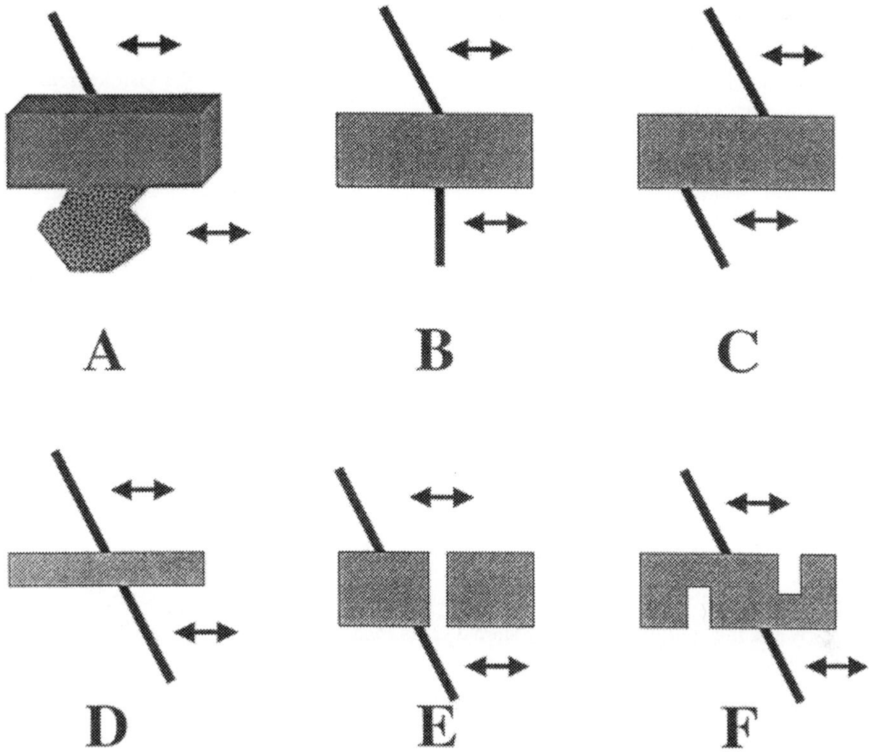

Figure 4. Displays used to test infants' perception of object unity when the visible ends of the rod moved in the same direction in the presence or absence of other variables. In A, the rod-blob display created with real three-dimensional objects, tests for whether common motion overrides differences in surface texture, color, edge unrelatability, and lack of alignment (after Kellman & Spelke, 1983). Displays B-F were two - dimensional representations presented on a computer screen. In B, the visible ends of the rod are relatable but not aligned, and in C the visible ends of the rod are not relatable nor are they aligned (after Johnson & Aslin, 1995). In D the size of the block was reduced, in E part of the center of the rod was visible in the central gap, and in F the complete rod was revealed over time (after Johnson & Aslin, 1996).

For 4-month-old infants, there appear to be two key variables, in addition to motion, that support the perception of object unity. One variable is adequate information for the depth separation of the block, rod, and background. In three-dimensional displays using real objects (Figure 1A, Figure 4A), infants have motion cues – such as the relative motion of the rod compared to the stationary block and the stationary background. In addition, binocular information may help separate the depth planes. In two-dimensional displays, such as those shown on a computer screen (Figure 4B-F), binocular information is not available. In these cases, infants appear to need additional information for separation of the depth planes, such as the presence of background texture (Johnson & Aslin, 1996). A second variable may be alignment of the visible ends of the object, at least when infants are presented with two-dimensional displays (such as those presented on a computer screen). Kellman and Shipley (1991) emphasize the requirement of relatability for adults' perception of object unity. Relatability is achieved if a straight line or a smooth curve can connect the visible areas, such as in Figure 4B but not 4C. Infants appear to require that the visible ends be aligned – producing the case in which the ends are most easily related, that is with a straight line (Figure 1A), when viewing two-dimensional displays on a computer screen. Infants presented with the rod-block display in Figure 4B looked equally to the broken and complete rods in the test phase. Infants presented with Figure 4C, a display lacking alignment and relatability, looked significantly more to the complete rod (Johnson & Aslin, 1996) suggesting that they saw Figure 4C as two separate pieces as it moved behind the occluder. In contrast is infants' performance with Figure 4A, the rod-blob display created with real objects. The rod and blob are neither aligned nor are the visible edges relatable; yet, infants looked significantly longer to a broken rod-blob test display than a complete rod-blob test display, suggesting that they perceived the rod and blob as unified behind the block.

Older infants perceive partly occluded objects as complete in the absence of kinematic information, thus relying on static information. Craton (1996) found that 6.5-month-olds perceived a static rectangle as unified when a bar occluded its center (see top frame of Figure 3). However, infants at this age provided no evidence of perceiving the shape of the occluded region. When the thin, black bar revealed a cross instead of a rectangle (the horizontal piece of the cross was hidden behind the thin black bar), and it was not until 8 months that infants looked longer at the "cross event" than at the "complete object event", suggesting that before 8 months infants expected the partially occluded rectangle to be a single unit but was agnostic regarding its specific form. Even when motion is present, such as the case of a rectangle peaking out from either side of a central occluder, infants' perception of unity appears to precede their perception of form (van de Walle & Spelke, 1996). In this case, 5-month-olds perceived the rectangle as unified but showed no evidence of knowing the shape of the occluded parts.

Research conducted with 2-month-old infants adds an additional piece to the developmental puzzle. When tested with a two-dimensional display of a rod moving behind a block, 2-month-olds showed equal looking to the complete and broken rod, suggesting a degree of ambiguity regarding the unity of the rod when it was partly occluded (Johnson & Aslin, 1995; Johnson & Nanez, 1995). When the occluder was more narrow than in traditional displays (26% of the rod occluded as opposed to 41%; Figure 4D), when infants were allowed to see more regions of the complete rod during translation (although the complete rod was never fully visible; Figure 4E), or when all parts of the rod were revealed over time during translation (Figure 4F), 2-month-olds showed a significant increase in looking to the broken rod in the test phase. The highest amount of looking to the broken rod was found with Figure 4D; marginally more looking to the broken rod was found with Figure 4F. This pattern of results is consistent with a view that infants at 2 months are able to perceive object unity in partial occlusion contexts using common motion, at least under certain conditions.

Newborn infants, in contrast to 2- and 4-month-old infants, show a consistent preference for the *complete* rod following habituation to moving rod-block displays (Figure 1A; Slater, Johnson, Brown, & Badenoch, 1996; Slater, Johnson, Kellman & Spelke, 1994; Slater, Morison, Somers, Mattock, Brown, & Taylor, 1990). This finding suggests that they perceived the rod as broken during the habituation phase, even though the size of the rod and depth separation of the rod and block was increased in comparison to that used with 4-month-olds (Slater et al., 1994) and when the block height was reduced and texture was added to the background to increase the available information specifying the depth relations (Slater et al., 1996). The implication of these findings is that newborns are making their perceptual judgments based on the visible parts of the displays, and they cannot make judgments about the parts of the visual array that are occluded.

This limitation in perceiving object unity in the newborn period is striking because it implies that babies begin life perceiving their world inaccurately, and the very young infant's first introduction to the world is fragmented. A world based on solely visible surfaces and objects would be a multi-colored and multi-textured mosaic from which relations among objects may be difficult to discern, a description that more closely matches James' "blooming, buzzing, confusion" than many infancy researchers would like to admit (e.g., Kellman & Arterberry, 1998).

If newborns are truly limited in their perception of unity of partly occluded objects, recent findings suggest that this limitation does not last for long. Kawabata, Gyoba, Inoue, and Ohtsubo (1999) have found at least one condition in which 3-week-old infants perceive a partly occluded region as complete. Instead of using the traditional rod-block display, they presented infants with drifting sine-wave gratings that were occluded by either a narrow or broad (wide) central occluder. When the spatial frequency of the grating was low (.04 cpd; i.e., the black and white bars were thick) and the occluder was narrow (1.33 deg; LN in Figure 5A), infants looked significantly longer to the broken test display (SG) illustrated in Figure 5B. This finding suggests that they perceived the low frequency grating as continuing behind the narrow occluder. In contrast, when the spatial frequency was high (1.2 cpd; i.e., the black and white bars were narrow) and the occluder was broad (4.17 deg; HB in Figure 5A), 3-week-olds looked significantly longer to a complete grating (CG in Figure 5B) as opposed to a broken grating (SG in Figure 5B). This finding suggests that they perceived the high spatial-frequency grating as two separate regions. Further manipulations revealed that there is an interaction between spatial-frequency and occluder width. Infants looked equally to the two test gratings when they viewed a high spatial frequency grating behind a narrow occluder (HN in Figure 5A) and when they viewed a low spatial frequency grating with a broad occluder (LB in Figure 5B). In both of these conditions, infants provided ambiguous results regarding whether they perceived the high-spatial frequency grating behind the narrow occluder and the

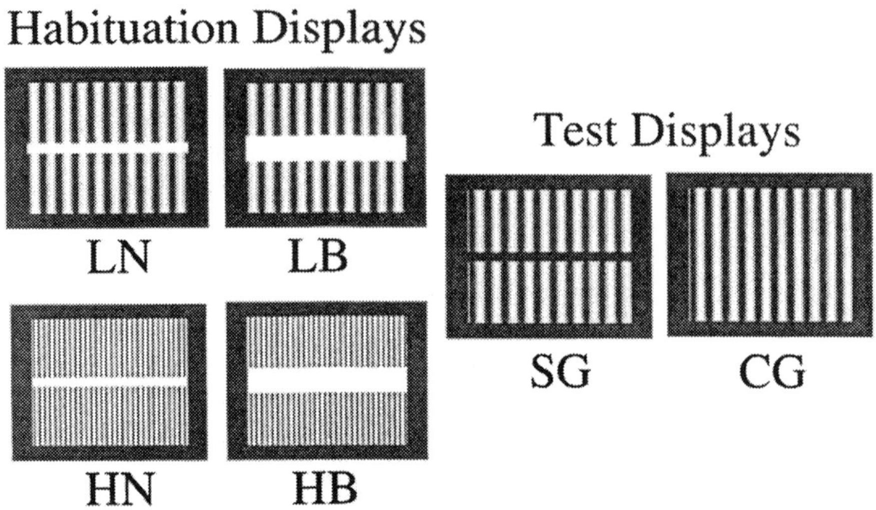

Figure 5. Habituation and test displays used to test 3-week-old infants' perception of unity. LN refers to low-spatial frequency display behind a narrow occluder. LB refers to low-spatial frequency display behind a broad occluder. HN refers to high-spatial frequency display behind a narrow occluder. HB refers to high-spatial frequency display behind a broad occluder. SG refers to "separate grating" (analogous to the broken rod in Figure 1C) and CG refers to "complete grating" (analogous to the complete rod in Figure 1B). Reprinted from *Vision Research*, volume 39, Kawabata, H., Gyoba, J., Inoue, H., & Ohtsubo, H., Visual completion of partly occluded grating in young infants under 1 month of age, pages 3586-3591, copyright ©1999, with permission from Elsevier Science.

low spatial-frequency behind the wide occluder as complete or broken.

The findings of Kawabata et al. (1999) provide some interesting insights into very young infants' perception of unity. Recall that their displays were quite different from the ones typically used to assess infants' perception of occluded objects. To infants, the low spatial frequency stimulus with the narrow occluder may have appeared to be a series of "rods", and infants' perceptual experience may be similar to looking through the bars of a jail cell or a crib with an object across the central region of the bars (a file or bumper pads, perhaps). Moreover, the rods were oriented vertically in Kawabata et al., rather than obliquely as in previous studies. Thus, there are two possible factors that might contribute to very young infants' perception of object unity under partial occlusion. One factor is object orientation. In other contexts, infants have shown a processing advantage with vertical stimuli over oblique stimuli (Bornstein & Krinsky, 1985). A second factor that might predict whether infants will perceive an occluded object as unified may be the ratio involving a parameter of the object and the occluding element. Shipley and Kellman (1992) found that the ratio of edge length to edge separation predicts perceived unity in illusory figures by adults. A similar function using the infant displays would consider the length of the rod and the height of the block; however, this does not explain the infant data. If this ratio were guiding infants' ability to perceive object unity, then Kawabata et al. should find infants perceive object unity in both the low and high spatial frequency displays when occluded by the narrow occluder. In both the LN and HN displays, the bars are the same length and the occluder is the same height; yet, LN was perceived as complete but the unity of HN was ambiguous.

There is another ratio, however, that may help explain the findings - object width to occluder height (Table 1). In their studies with 4-month-olds, Kellman and Spelke (1983) presented infants with a .75 deg wide rod behind a 7.9 deg high block, a rod to block ratio of .09. Johnson and Aslin (1995) found that 2-month-olds perceived the rod as unified when the block was narrower than the one typically used with 4-month-olds (Johnson & Nanez, 1995). Two-month-olds perceived a 1.4 deg wide rod as unified behind a 2.9 deg high block, a resulting ratio of .48. Kawabata et al. (1999) found evidence of unity perception in infants only when the grating was low spatial frequency (the bars of the grating were thick) and the occluder was narrow (a ratio of .75), but not when spatial frequency was high (i.e., the bars were thin) and the occluder was broad (a ratio of .14). In the latter case, infants perceived the occluded grating as broken -- just as newborn infants did (Slater et al., 1996). Even though newborn infants were presented with a narrow occluder, the rod/occluder ratio only reached .45. Comparison of these ratios reveals three findings. First, we have additional evidence that with age infants tolerate larger separations of the visible ends of partly occluded objects. Secondly, the amount of separation tolerated is not an absolute amount but rather is dependent upon the ratio of object and occluder size. Finally, the findings suggest that previous tests of

Study	**Display Features**	**Age / Perceived Unity?**	**Object width / Occluder height**
Kellman & Spelke (1983)	Thin rod, Broad block	4 months / yes	.09
Johnson & Aslin (1995)	Thin rod, narrow block	2 months / yes	.48
Kawabata et al. (1999)	Thin bars, Broad "block"	3 weeks / no	.14
Kawabata et al. (1999)	Thick bars, narrow "block"	3 weeks / yes	.75
Slater et al. (1996)	Thin rod, narrow block	42 hours / no	.45

Table 1. Ratio of object width to occluder height. Younger infants may require greater ratios in order to perceive unity of partly occluded objects.

newborn perception of partly occluded objects may have not used large enough objects and small enough separations. Youngest infants may not tolerate rod width/occluder height ratios that are less than about .75.

Summary. Together it appears that infants' perception of object unity and form is refined over the first 8 months of life. Infants begin perceiving the world as unified as long as some minimum stimulus requirements are met, such as presence of common motion, adequate depth information, and/or a sufficient object width/occluder height ratio. Poor performance with static displays suggests that young infants are not relying on edge information; hence, an edge-insensitive process appears to guide their perception. Reliance on edge information emerges later in development, as perception of the form of partly occluded objects emerges some time after 4 months of age. Infants perceive unity and form in static displays by 8 months of age, and it is unclear if perception of form in moving displays also emerges at this time, or some time between 5 and 8 months of age. Johnson & Aslin (1996; see also Johnson, 1997) suggest a threshold model for infants' unit formation, namely that veridical perception is achieved only when sufficiency of visual information matches the efficiency of perceptual and cognitive skills. In other words, if infants do not have sufficient cues, perception of object unity will fail, and infants at different ages may have different cue requirements -- 2-month-olds have a higher threshold than 4-month-olds and 4-month-olds have a higher threshold than adults.

What accounts for the different cue requirements at different ages is unclear, but it is likely that immaturities in the visual system may be a factor. The structure of the visual system is undergoing changes within the first months of life, and it is possible that changes in foveal density, mylenation, and/or synaptogenesis could account for increased stimulus requirements (see Kellman & Arterberry, 1998, for a review). Moreover, infants demonstrate some limitations in detection of motion and differential motion sensitivities (Wattam-Bell, 1996a, b), which could impact their use of common motion.

Infants' Perception of Illusory Contours

Compared to infants' perception of partly-occluded objects, infants' perception of illusory contours has commanded relatively little attention by researchers, and, as a result of the dearth of studies, the general findings and age trends are less clear. In contrast to the research on infants' perception of partly occluded objects, which concentrated primarily on kinematic information, to our knowledge, all of the published research on infants' perception of illusory contours has concentrated on static information[1].

---

[1] One paper on this topic is a conference presentation by Kaufmann-Hayoz, Kaufmann, & Walther (1988) but a full-published report of the work is not available.

The clearest evidence for infants' perception of illusory contours based on static information comes from a study in which 5- and 7-month-olds were tested for discrimination of the displays similar to the ones depicted in Figure 6A and B (Bertenthal, Campos, & Haith, 1980). Most observers describe Figure A as a square in front of four circles. When some or all of the circles (or "elements") are rotated, the illusory effect is diminished and perception of the square is less apparent or disappears all together (Figure 6B). Following habituation to an illusory square (Figure 6A), 7-month-olds showed an increase in looking to a display in which two of the four inducing elements were rotated (i.e., the top right and bottom left elements). Following habituation to Figure 6B, a display that preserves the symmetry of Figure 6A, but does not produce an illusory figure, 7-month-olds showed an increase in looking to the illusory square (Figure 6A). Finally, 7-month-olds looked equally to displays in which two or four elements were rotated, suggesting that even though the displays differed in the number of elements that were rotated, they were still perceptually similar. These findings were taken as an indication that infants at 7 months perceived the illusory square in Figure 6A, and when the inducing elements were rotated (either two or four of them), the display looked quite different from the illusory square.

Figure 6. Two displays used to test infants' perception of illusory contours in static displays. In A the inducing elements are oriented to create an illusory square. B represents a symmetrical display, like A, but all the elements have been rotated outward, thus eliminating any perception of illusory contours. Rotating two of the four elements in A also reduces the perception of an illusory square.

The results from younger infants are less clear. Five-month-olds showed an increase in looking to a two-rotated element display following habituation to the illusory square (Figure 6A). However, they showed no change in looking to the illusory square (Figure 6A) after habituation to the four-rotated element display (Figure 6B). Together, these patterns provide equivocal evidence of perception of illusory contours at 5 months.

Using displays similar to Bertenthal et al. plus another display in which the top left and bottom right elements were rotated, Ghim (1990) tested for illusory contour perception in 3- and 4-month-olds. Infants familiarized to an outline of a square showed a significant preference for the two figures with two rotated elements when paired with the illusory square (Figure 6A). However, infants did not show a preference for the symmetrical, four-rotated element display (Figure 6B) when it was paired with the illusory square. Similarly, when infants viewed successive trials of illusory squares created by three varieties of inducing elements (circles, squares, and octagons, each with a missing quadrant), infants showed a significant preference for the displays in which two of the elements were rotated over the illusory square, but they did not show a preference for the symmetrical, four-rotated element display over the illusory square. This result, specifically the lack of a preference for the symmetrical, four-rotated element display over the illusory square, is curious because when infants were tested for their ability to discriminate all four displays, they clearly showed discrimination of the two displays (Figure 6A and Figure 6B). Another curious finding was that infants discriminated Figure 6A when paired with a two-rotated element display with the top right and bottom left elements rotated but not Figure 6A when paired with a two-rotated element display with the top left and bottom right elements rotated. Both two-rotated element displays represent the same type of element rotation; the only difference is which elements are rotated.

Together Ghim's work provides some evidence that infants may perceive illusory contours younger than 7 months of age, but it is not wholly convincing. In each of Ghim's experiments, one predicted preference did not reach significance, and there was not a consistent pattern for which pairs did not reach significance. Ghim accounts for these "nuisance" findings as the result of sampling error and shows that they wash out by pooling the data across experiments (which, by the way, collapses data across different familiarization experiences). However, pooling the data may actually be hiding reality. It is possible that there is large sampling error because perception of illusory contours in 3- and 4-month-olds is tenuous, at least in static displays.

Summary. Illusory contours may be perceived as part of an enclosed form for infants as they are for adults; however, at what age is unclear. The most convincing evidence suggests that perception of static illusory contours is present by 7 months. Research with dynamic displays is needed to complete our understanding of infants' perception of illusory contours.

Conclusion

The above discussion has revealed that we know considerably more about infants' perception of object unity in partly occluded contexts than in illusory contexts. It is possible that with more research we will find similar developmental trends in these two areas. It is clear that motion plays a primary role in infants' perception of unity, and it is possible that a similar trend will be found in illusory figure perception. Alternatively, illusory figure perception may require edge sensitive processes, and thus infants may not perceive illusory figures, whether static or dynamic, until this process emerges (some time between 6.5 and 8 months of age).

More research will also answer questions about the parameters of infants' illusory contour perception in comparison to unity perception. For example, younger infants (eg., 2-month-olds) viewing rod-block displays require more narrow blocks than older infants, suggesting limitations in their interpolation processes. In a similar vein, it is possible that the distance between the inducing elements may also influence younger infants' perception of illusory figures. Also, relatability and alignment of the visible parts of an occluded object are important variables for infants' perception of object unity. If the processes are similar in illusory contour perception, then we should find degradation in the perception of illusory contours as the alignment and/or relatability of the inducing elements is reduced. Finally, another question to be explored regarding illusory figure perception is whether there is development between birth and 8 months of age. Systematic work with different ages is sparse and further work should include adequate tests for age differences.

STATIC AND KINEMATIC PERCEPTION OF HIDDEN OBJECT BOUNDARIES

We have seen that object unity can be perceived in the absence of object form. Infants viewing partly occluded objects can tell that the visible ends are unified before they know what the occluded parts look like (Craton, 1996; Kellman & Spelke, 1983; van de Walle & Spelke, 1996). In order to perceive both object unity and form, observers must interpolate edge information across space in static displays and across space and time in kinematic displays. Kellman and Shipley (1991) suggest that these interpolative processes may derive from the same or closely related processes, even though the specifying information may be quite different. As should be clear from our discussion of the first postulate, the infant data are not complete enough to discuss whether or not the same or different visual interpolation processes are available to infants depending on whether they have access to static or kinematic information. However, research in other areas provides an intriguing picture of how useful static and kinematic information is for babies. We already have seen an advantage for kinematic information in infants' perception of object unity. This advantage is also present in other areas of infant perception.

Infants' Sensitivity to Static vs Kinematic Information

Motion is ever present in the infants' environment, and the way objects move provides a wealth of information about what objects are, where they are, how they may function, and the like (E. J. Gibson, 1982; J. J. Gibson, 1979). Infants appear to take advantage of this rich information in the first months of life even though infant motion detection thresholds are suppressed compared to those of adults (Aslin & Shea, 1990; Dannemiller & Freedland, 1989), and directional sensitivity may not develop until 2 months of age (Wattam-Bell, 1996a, b). Not only does motion attract the attention of the young infant (Slater, Morison, Town, & Rose, 1985), use of kinematic information is effective in the perception of object shape, spatial layout, and in perceiving surface and object properties (see Kellman, 1995, and Kellman & Arterberry, 1998 for reviews).

Consider depth perception. There are multiple sources of depth information – some of which rely on the structure of our visual system (ie., binocular information such as stereopsis and convergence), others that rely on movement of the viewed object or observer, or both (i.e., kinematic information such as optical expansion, accretion and deletion of texture, motion parallax), and yet others that are available to the stationary, monocular observer (i.e., static monocular [pictorial] depth information such as familiar size, shading, interposition, texture gradient, linear perspective; see Kellman & Arterberry, 1998). Development of sensitivity to the three types of depth information varies by age. Kinematic information (such as optical expansion information) appears the earliest, at 3 weeks of age for some types of information (e.g., Nanez, 1988), whereas sensitivity to static-monocular information (such as interposition) emerges last, around 7 months of age (e.g., Granrud & Yonas, 1984). Binocular information emerges between the two; convergence develops at 3 months and stereopsis emerges around 4 months (e.g., Hainline, Riddell, Grose-Fifer, & Abramov, 1992; Held, Birch, & Gwiazda, 1980).

Similarly, kinematic information may be the primary source of information for young infants' perception of three-dimensional object shape (e.g., Arterberry & Yonas, 1988, 2000; Kellman, 1984, Kellman & Short, 1987). When 4-month-old infants were presented with displays of a continuously rotating three-dimensional object or a wire figure, they provided evidence of perceiving its shape. In contrast, when they viewed successive views of the object as it rotated, they provided no evidence of perceiving the shape of the object (Kellman, 1984). Similarly, 2- and 4-month-olds perceived three-dimensional structure from motion specified in kinetic random dot displays (Arterberry & Yonas, 1988, 2000). When infants are able to perceive object shape from successive static views of a rotating three-dimensional object is unknown, but it is likely after 8 months of age (Kellman, 1993).

Implications for Visual Interpolation

There are several implications for development of visual interpolation given the differential onset of sensitivity to static and kinematic information. First, early in infancy, at least prior to the onset of stereopsis (4 months) and static-monocular sensitivity (7 months), visual interpolation processes will best occur when kinematic information is available. In other words, visual interpolation first takes place over space *and* time. With age, infants develop sensitivity to information that will allow for interpolation across space, such as stereopsis or interposition. Initially, this might appear to be an odd design – a task involving two variables (space and time) may be harder than a task involving one (space). However, our visual system may have evolved to be maximally sensitive to discontinuities in space and time earlier than to discontinuities only in space. Some have argued elsewhere that this developmental progression may reflect an adaptive design (e.g., Kellman & Arterberry, 1998) because there are fewer ambiguities in perception under conditions of motion, either of the observer or the object (J. J. Gibson, 1979). Therefore, infants begin their perceptual life relying on the most accurate information.

For the edge-insensitive process, there may be little or no developmental story. Recall this process relies solely on common motion, and infants at least by 3 weeks of age (Kawabata et al., 1999) use common motion to perceive object unity under certain conditions, namely when the object was thick and the occluder was narrow. With age, infants tolerate larger gaps between the visible ends of objects; however, there is no change in the type of information they are using.

For the edge-sensitive process, there are at least two stories. Recall that the edge-sensitive process leads to perception of unity and form of partly occluded objects and it is possible that both static and kinematic information are involved.

The first story takes a maturational tone. Early in life infants perceive partly occluded objects and illusory figures using kinematic information. This information aids them in their perception of edges, boundaries, and cohesive perceptual units. As sensitivity to static information comes on line, infants are able to exploit the static features in the environment, and they can combine this information with the available kinematic information. In other words, infants use what information is available for perceiving their world, and when new information becomes accessible, it is readily utilized.

An alternative story emphasizes an interaction between kinematic and static information. It is possible that within the first 6-7 months of life infants form a foundation for parsing the world into perceptual units based on kinematic information. When sensitivity to static information emerges, infants are able to learn which static cues are helpful for discerning partly occluded objects, illusory figures, and the like. In other words, infants may learn about visual interpolation across space alone (static information) from the information gained earlier from interpolative processes across space and time (kinematic information). If this is the case, the learning process itself might be limited by other limitations in infants' spatiotemporal abilities. Early in the first year infants are able to integrate information across short periods of time (Johnson & Aslin, 1995; van de Walle & Spelke, 1996), but they cannot tolerate longer time frames until the end of the first year (Arterberry, 1993, 1995).

Conclusion

Infants' perception of partly occluded objects may be constrained by their ability to effectively use static and kinematic information. Early in life infants' sensitivity to motion carried information is robust and it supports the edge-insensitive process. At the same time, infants' sensitivity to static information, in general, is limited and this has a direct impact on the edge-sensitive process.

THE IMPORTANCE OF DISCONTINUITIES SPECIFYING EDGES

Kellman and Shipley (1991) argue that perception of partly occluded objects and illusory figures begins with finding boundaries. From this information the scene can then be parsed into meaningful units. Infants appear to be sensitive to both static and kinematic discontinuities specifying boundaries, but at different ages. We address each type of information in turn.

Infants' Sensitivity to Static Discontinuities

Boundaries specified by static information are often marked by discontinuities in luminance. Yet, surfaces also contain markings that are characterized by discontinuities in luminance. For example, the edge of a wooden table viewed against a white wall will create a sharp change in luminance, but the surface of the table may also be marked by luminance discontinuities that specify the grain of the wood, the location of a leaf extension, and, perhaps, a knot hole or two. In order for accurate object perception, a differentiation between surface markings and boundary edges must be made. Infants are able to accomplish such a task at least by 7 months of age (Yonas & Arterberry, 1994; Kavsek, 1999). Consider the cube in Figure 7A. In these relatively impoverished displays, the key information is the line junctions. Arrows indicate corners, Ys indicate vertices between three surfaces and I junctions (or a single line sharing two T junctions) indicate markings. When infants were habituated to a line drawing depicting a cube with surface markings (Figure 7A), they looked significantly longer to a display in which the boundary information specifying intersections of the planes had been removed but had preserved the markings (Figure 7B) than to a display that preserved the intersections but removed the markings (Figure 7C). Similar results were found with a line drawing display depicting two overlapping rectangles with markings (Yonas & Arterberry, 1994) and displays of cylinders (Kavsek, 1999).

In richer displays, the task of differentiating markings and boundaries may become easier due to an increase of information. In Figure 8A differences in surface markings and color provide information that the two curved regions are probably different objects. In addition, this conclusion is supported by the presence of the boundary edge between the two

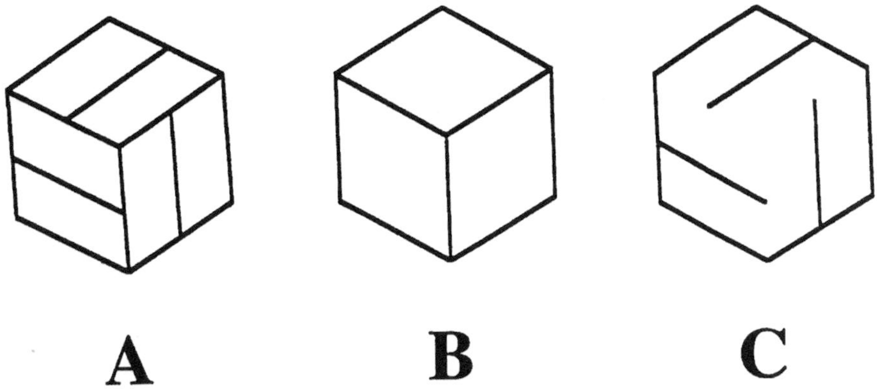

Figure 7. Line drawing of a cube that depicts boundary edges between surfaces and surface markings (A). In B the surface markings have been removed and in C the boundary edges have been removed. After Yonas and Arterberry (1994).

parts – again a discontinuity in luminance -- and the abrupt change in curvature along the top edge (e.g., Hoffman & Richards, 1984). In Figures 8B and C, the color and surface markings are now identical, but the central boundary and curvature discontinuity along the upper edge still specify the presence of two objects placed side by side. Infants at 4 months perceived the display in Figure 8C as disconnected, but not Figures 8A or B (Needham, 1999), suggesting that they were relying on the available visual information for segregation of the two surfaces, but only to a limited degree. One interpretation of these findings is that infants' segregation of the scene relied on edge discontinuities but not differences in surface color or markings (but see Diamond & Lee, 2001; Needham, 1999; Needham, Baillargeon, & Kaufman, 1997 for different interpretations). Also there are limits in terms of discontinuities in curvature that infants will tolerate: Both Figure 8B and C had clear discontinuities, at least for adults, but

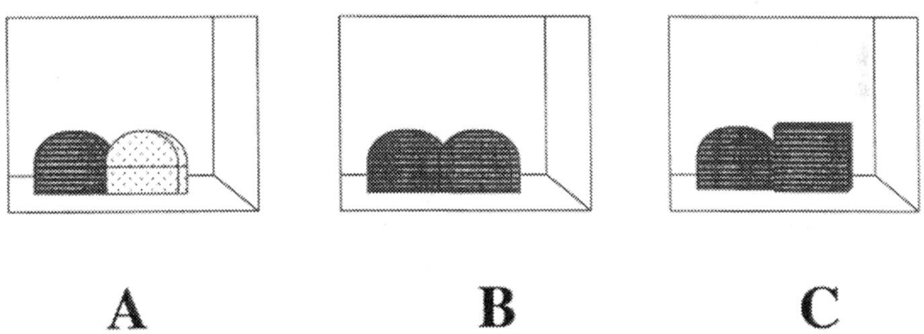

Figure 8. Adjacent surfaces with different surface features but similar shape (A), identical surface features and shape (B), and different surface features and different shape (C) similar to those used by Needham (1999) to test infants' segregation of surfaces.

only the display that contained the sharpest discontinuity led to infants' segregation of the surface into two parts.

In a similar vein, Spelke and her colleagues (Spelke, Breinlinger, Jacobson, & Phillips, 1993) found that with age infants rely on edge and surface features for perceiving object unity. In this experiment, infants saw a hand lift an object. The object was either lifted off the support surface as a single unit (middle column in Figure 9A and B) or the object broke into two pieces (right column in Figure 9A and B). For the homogeneous object, movement as a single unit was consistent with expectations about the composition of this object (i.e., "it's one piece"). Breaking into two pieces was inconsistent with this expectation. For the heterogeneous object, which looks like two stacked objects due to the surface features and edge information, the expectations are reversed. It is not at all unexpected that this object would break into two pieces if only the top portion were lifted; however, movement as a single unit (as in the center column in Figure 9B) would be unexpected.

Three-month-olds viewing these events looked longer to the event in which the object broke apart than to the event in which it stayed together, regardless of whether the object was homogeneous (Figure 9A) or heterogeneous (Figure 9B). In contrast, 5- and 9-month-olds looked longer to the break up of the homogeneous display, but they did not find the one-piece movement of the heterogeneous display novel. From 3 to 5 months, it appears that infants come to understand the information contained in edge boundaries that specify an object as being composed of one or two pieces. At three months, any object that broke apart was novel. At 5- and 9-months, when the object in Figure 9A came apart infants found this event

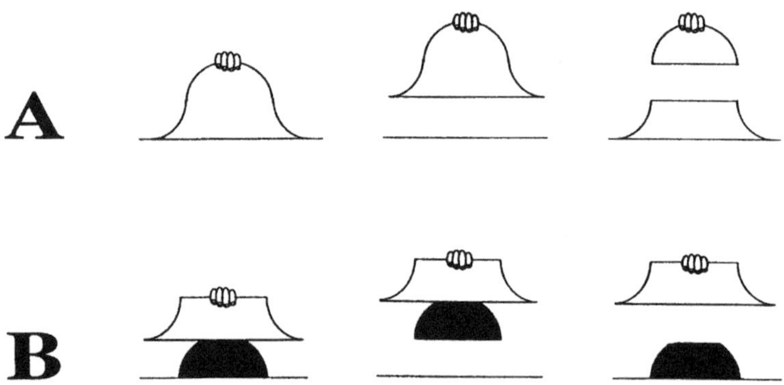

Figure 9. Homogeneous displays (A) and heterogeneous displays (B) and their one-piece and two-piece movements used to assess infants' segregation of surfaces. From Spelke, E. S., Breinlinger, K., & Jacobson, A. P. (1993). Gestalt relations and object perception: A developmental study. *Perception*, *22*, 1483-1501. Copyright © 1993 by Pion Limited, London. Reprinted with permission.

novel, suggesting that the infants originally perceived the object as one piece. The smooth edge in Figure 9A provides information for the object's unity. Five- and 9-month-old infants' use of edge information, however, is not complete. In Figure 9B, there are clear discontinuities among the external contours of the object (and surface differences), but infants did not find it novel when this display moved as a single unit.

Summary. There is some evidence that infants are able to use static discontinuities for perceiving boundaries between objects in the second half of the first year of life, and possibly earlier. Edge discontinuities appear to play a more primary role than differences in surface color or patterns. The superiority of edge discontinuities makes sense in light of the fact that surface color and patterns are changeable and only perceived via one modality; whereas, edge discontinuities are less likely to be ambiguous and can be perceived in several modalities, such as touch and vision.

Infants' Sensitivity to Motion-Induced Discontinuities

Motion-induced discontinuities arise when different objects or parts of an object move relative to each other. For example, as a waterbed undulates, neighboring surface texture elements change their position relative to each other. These small changes lead to the perception of changes in a surface, but different areas of the surface will still be perceived as part of the same object. Larger textural changes cause optical tearing, and the scene is parsed into two or more bounded surfaces (Shipley & Kellman, 1993). Shipley and Kellman (1993) call this process spatiotemporal boundary formation, and it is the process by which spatially and temporally separated changes in texture elements lead to the perception of boundaries. Spatiotemporal boundary formation is dependent upon displacements of texture that are registered as discontinuities.

One important source of information for spatiotemporal boundary formation is the accretion and deletion of texture. As an object moves in front of another object, surface texture on the closer surface covers surface texture on the more distant object (see Figure 10A). As the object continues to pass by, the surface texture on the more distant object reappears. In real viewing contexts, surface texture discontinuities are available in addition to static edge information. To isolate static information from dynamic information, researchers create displays in which there are no static boundaries – only discontinuities in texture are present when the display is in motion. Thus, the boundaries are created via the processes of motion. Infants as young as 5 months perceive the relative ordering in depth of two surfaces (Granrud, et al, 1984), 5-month-olds separate figure from ground (Craton & Yonas, 1990a) and 3-month-olds perceive object form (Kaufmann-Hayoz, Kaufmann, & Stucki, 1986) from the accretion and deletion of texture (see Figure 10A).

It is also possible to perceive boundaries without accretion and deletion of texture.

Yonas and his colleagues (Yonas, Craton, & Thompson, 1987; Craton & Yonas, 1990b) discovered that the cue of boundary flow was sufficient for specifying depth from merely the relative motions of texture elements. In their displays, regions of a display in which textural elements moved in the same direction were seen as part of the same surface and different from regions of the display in which textural elements moved in a different direction. However, texture did not appear or disappear (see Figure 10B). Adults and 5-month-old infants perceived the relative ordering of depth using boundary flow (Craton & Yonas, 1988, 1990b; Yonas, Craton, & Thompson, 1987).

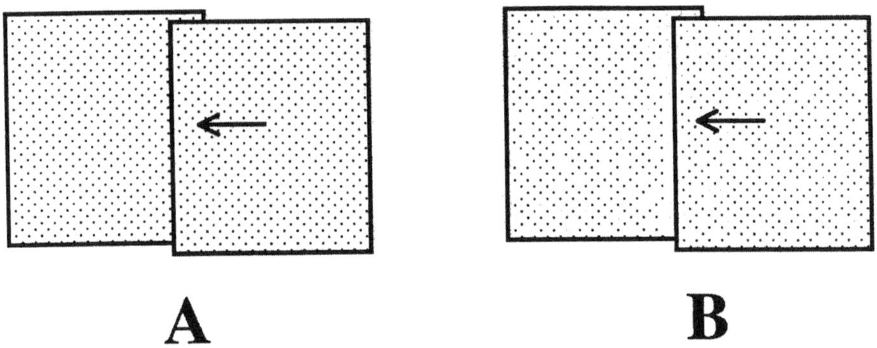

Figure 10. Schematic representations of the ordering of two surfaces in depth as specified by the accretion and deletion of texture (A) and boundary flow (B). In A, as one surface covers another, texture elements are occluded. In B, due to the sparseness of texture at the surface edge, no texture is deleted as the right surface covers the left. In both cases, adults report clear impressions of one surface located behind another.

A similar process may be operating when infants view kinetic random-dot displays. In these displays, there is no information for the boundaries between surfaces and when the displays are static, there is no form (Figure 11A). However, when the display is in motion, observers report a clear impression of a three-dimensional object, in this case a cube, and 2- and 4-month-olds look longer at a cube with a different shape following habituation (Figure 11B and C; Arterberry & Yonas, 1988, 2000). Infants as young as 2 months perceived three-dimensional structure from the relative motion of dots in the absence of static boundaries, suggesting sensitivity to kinematic discontinuities because the surfaces and their edges were *created* by the flow patterns (Figure 11D).

Conclusion

Clearly, infants within the first year of life are able to determine the boundaries of objects and surfaces and differentiate object boundaries from surface markings. Moreover, they are able to make use of multiple sources of information to do so. However, their ability to detect object boundaries from static information appears to be delayed compared to their

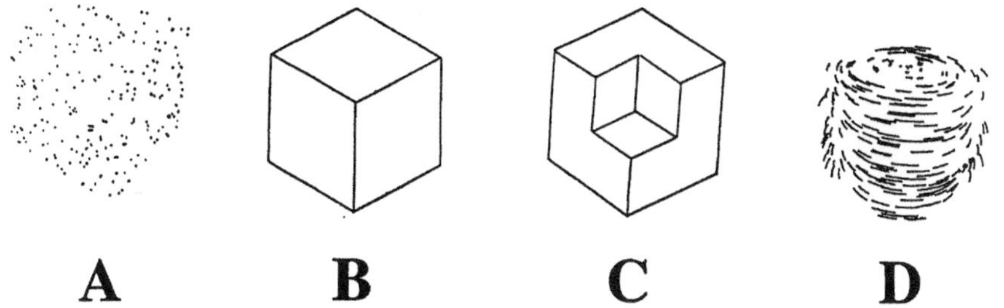

Figure 11. One frame of a kinetic random-dot display used to test infants' perception of three-dimensional shape (A). B and C depict a schematic representation of the display when the dots are in motion, and D is a time-lapse photograph of one oscillation of the display illustrating the flow field. After Arterberry and Yonas (1988, 2000).

ability to detect object boundaries from kinematic information. This trend is similar to the one we identified earlier: Kinematic sensitivity was found early, within the first few months of life, and static sensitivity was found later, after 6 months.

PERCEPTION OF DISUNITY IN PARTLY OCCLUDED OBJECTS

What information specifies separate or broken objects for infants? Disruption of the key variables discussed earlier, specifically alignment, relatability, lack of common motion, should convey to the perceiver that a partly occluded object is in fact two pieces. There are several clear pieces of evidence for infants' perception of "disunity". For example, when 4-month-old infants view a stationary broken rod in front of the block instead of behind it (Figure 12A), they look significantly longer to the complete than the broken rod in the test phase (Kellman & Spelke, 1983). Similarly, when the ends of the rod are visible above and below the block (Figure 12B), 4-month-old infants look significantly longer to the complete rod (Kellman & Spelke, 1983). In both these conditions, there was clear information for the disconnectedness of the rod, and infants showed a clear novelty response to the complete rod, even in the absence of motion.

However, there are instances when there is plenty of information specifying that the rod is broken, at least for adults, in which infants do not respond as if they perceived the rod as broken. In all of Johnson's studies utilizing rod-block displays (Johnson & Aslin, 1995, 1996; Johnson & Nanez, 1995) and in Experiment 1 of Kellman and Spelke (1983), control conditions were included. In these conditions, one visible end of the rod moved while the other end did not (Figure 12C), providing information that the rod was not a complete object from the *uncommon motion* of the two ends. In other displays, there were several sources of information for the lack of unity, such as no alignment (Figure 12D) and no visible region

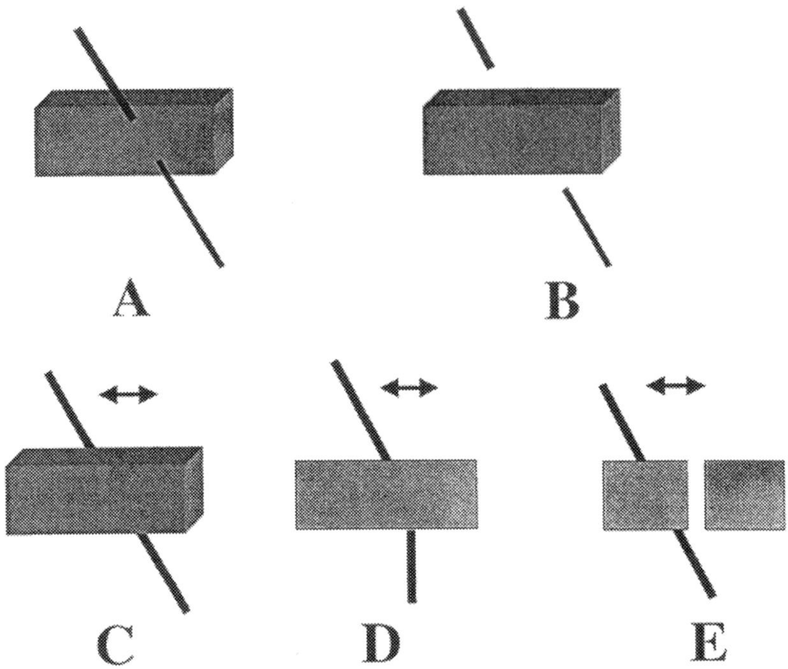

Figure 12. A and B illustrate two displays in which infants perceived the rod as broken (after Kellman & Spelke, 1983). It is unclear whether infants perceived the rod in C, D, and E as broken or complete. In C only the top portion of the rod moved, resulting in lack of common motion, alignment, and relatability of the two visible ends (after Kellman & Spelke, 1983). Similarly, D disrupts common motion, relatability and aligment (after Johnson & Aslin, 1996), and in E the rod did not appear in the gap as the top part passed behind it (after Johnson & Aslin, 1995).

appearing in the gap (Figure 12E). Infants viewing these and other displays showed equal looking to the complete and broken rods presented in the test displays. At least 9 control experiments have been conducted (5 with 4-month-olds; 4 with 2-month-olds), and not one group of infants looked significantly longer to the complete display. Instead, infants consistently looked equally to the two test displays suggesting that they perceived the connectivity of the rod behind the block as ambiguous despite the fact that there was plenty of information available for the disunity of the rod.

Why don't the infants show an increase in looking to the complete rod? It is unlikely that this finding is due to inherent preferences for the broken rod over the complete rod. All of the researchers were careful to rule out preferences for one test display over the other (e.g., Johnson & Aslin, 1995, 1996; Johnson & Nanez, 1995; Kellman & Spelke, 1983). Perhaps a closer look at the data is warranted.

A mean difference of zero could arise from the infants truly showing no preference for one test display over the other, resulting in a mean difference in looking times that is close to zero. But a mean difference of zero could result from half of the infants showing an increase in looking to the complete display and half showing an increase in looking to the broken display, and when the data are averaged across the group, the mean difference is zero. If the second case were true, then we would find that some infants perceived the rod in the habituation display as complete whereas others perceived it as broken.

The second outcome, namely that half of the infants saw the rod as complete and half saw the rod as broken, might suggest that the habituation displays were bistable. As the top rod moved back and forth, there would be a moment when the rod may have appeared complete – at least for an instant. As a result some infants may have relied on the information specifying the rod was broken whereas others may have relied on the information specifying the rod was complete. Alternatively, the fact that half the infants saw the rod as complete and half saw it as broken might mean that a developmental change is occurring at that age, and only half of the sample has some necessary ability allowing them to perceive the rod as unified. In other areas of perception, such as perception of form from binocular and kinetic information, 4-month-olds who have not yet developed sensitivity to binocular disparity do not recognize the equivalence of an object specified by binocular and kinetic information (Yonas, Arterberry, & Granrud, 1987). In other words, at the same age, 4-month-olds showed differential patterns of responsiveness due to the presence or absence of a necessary capacity. The nature of the capacity in perceiving unity in rod/block displays is unclear, and such an explanation would have to account for why both 2-month-olds and 4-month-olds show different patterns.

Currently, we cannot resolve the issue, but a theory that tells us how we perceive objects as unified also has to be effective in explaining how we perceive objects as separate entities. At this point we do not have a good explanation for infants' perception of disunity.

General Conclusions and Remaining Questions

The material presented in this chapter has addressed three interrelated topics -- perception of discontinuities at edges, use of static and kinematic information for perception of discontinuities, and use of these discontinuities for parsing the world into unified interrelated objects and surfaces. We have seen that infants' ability to find edges and perceive objects as unified may be dependent on the type of information available. In several areas of perception, there is an advantage for kinematic information over static information, and the present review suggests that the kinematic advantage also pertains to perceptual unit formation in infancy. Infants' perceive partly occluded objects and illusory contours as unified figures under conditions of motion, either by the observer or the object, before they do under static conditions.

Infants' unit formation abilities are limited in comparison to adults, but from relatively early in life infants appear to be able to perceive the unity of partly occluded objects. In the second half of the first year of life infants perceive the form of partly occluded objects and figures specified by illusory contours. Our review of the literature has shown that infants' stimulus requirements vary by age. For example, for the perceiving object unity, infants demand motion where adults do not, and younger babies need to see more of an occluded object than older babies. Many of the differences between adults' and infants' perception of partly occluded objects and illusory contours may be reflective of the immaturity of infants' perceptual system, particularly in the use of static information. Due to these immaturities, unit formation relies first on an edge-insensitive process, one that is dependent on common motion. With development, unit formation can be achieved using edge relations alone, but not before 6.5 months of age.

We need to learn more about infants' edge sensitive process in the context of dynamic displays, particularly with illusory contours. To evaluate Kellman and Shipley's (1991) claim that the identical process underlies perception of partly occluded objects and perception of illusory contours, we need more information about infants' perception of kinetic illusory contours. For example, what type of motion facilitates the ordering of objects in depth? Do infants need simultaneous occlusion of the inducing elements in order to perceive the illusory figure or can they integrate such information across time? Do limitations in processing sequential information found in other contexts apply to illusory figure perception (Arterberry, 1993, 1995)? These are but a few questions that will help guide future research on infants' perception of illusory contours.

A remaining issue about infants' perception of partly occluded objects is the interaction of edge relatability, alignment, and common motion and whether common motion is dependent upon these other two processes. Kellman and Spelke (1983) found perception of unity when common motion was present in the absence of edge relatability and alignment (Figure 4A), however Johnson and Aslin (1995) found that without alignment (Figure 4B) infants perceived the rod's unity as ambiguous. This difference in findings may be due to infants' limitations in unit formation, but it also could be an artifact of testing conditions. Real three-dimensional objects created the rod/blob display in Figure 4A and two-dimensional shapes created the images in Figure 4B for presentation on a computer screen. Other factors involved in perceiving two-dimensional displays as representations of three-dimensional objects may contribute to whether infants perceive object unity in two-dimensional displays. Thus, when designing studies and comparing results across research labs, we need to be sensitive to *all* factors that may influence unit formation processes.

Perceptual unit formation is all about finding boundaries, whether from kinematic or static information. In fact, Shipley and Kellman (1994) remind us that, "boundary perception is a growth industry" (p. 19). Perhaps the statement should be "boundary perception is a *necessary* growth industry". Boundary perception is the crux of object perception in all contexts -- partly occluded, illusory, and fully visible. Understanding the processes underlying boundary formation and their development will lead us to a better understanding of object perception in general.

ACKNOWLEDGEMENTS

During the preparation of this chapter, the author was a visiting scientist at the Child and Family Research Section of the National Institute of Child Health and Human Development. The author thanks Carolyn Tuckey for help with manuscript preparation and Lincoln Craton, Scott P. Johnson, and Phil Kellman for helpful comments on previous drafts.
Correspondence may be addressed to the author at the Department of Psychology, Box 407, Gettysburg College, Gettysburg, PA 17325 USA or via email: arterber@gettysburg.edu.

REFERENCES

Arterberry, M. E. (1993). Development of spatiotemporal integration in infancy. *Infant Behavior and Development, 16*, 343-363.

Arterberry, M. E. (1995). Perception of object number through an aperture by human infants. *Infant Behavior and Development, 18*, 359-362.

Arterberry, M. E., & Yonas, A. (2000). Perception of structure from motion by 8-week-old infants. *Perception and Psychophysics, 62*, 550-556.

Arterberry, M. E., & Yonas, A. (1988). Infants' sensitivity to kinetic information for three-dimensional object shape. *Perception and Psychophysics, 44*, 1-6.

Aslin, R. N., & Shea, S. L. (1990). Velocity thresholds in human infants: Implications for the perception of motion. *Developmental Psychology, 26*, 589-598.

Baillargeon, R. (1993). The object concept revisited: New directions in the investigation of infants' physical knowledge. In C. E. Granrud (Ed.), *Visual perception and cognition in infancy*. Hillsdale, NJ: Erlbaum.

Bertenthal, B. I., Campos, J. J., & Haith, M. M. (1980). Development of visual organization: The perception of subjective contours. *Child Development, 51*, 1072-1080.

Bornstein, M. H. (1985). Habituation of attention as a measure of visual information processing in human infants: Summary, systematization, and synthesis. In G. Gottlieb & N. A. Krasnegor (Eds.), *Measurement of audition and vision in the first year of postnatal life: A methdological overview* (pp. 253-300). Norwood, NJ: Ablex.

Bornstein, M. H., & Krinsky, S. J. (1985). Perception of symmetry in infancy: The salience of vertical symmetry and the perception of pattern wholes. *Journal of Experimental Child Psychology, 39*, 82-86.

Cohen, L. B. (1973). A two-process model of infant visual attention. *Merrill-Palmer Quarterly, 19*, 157-180.

Craton, L. G. (1996). The development of perceptual completion abilities: Infants' perception of stationary, partially occluded objects. *Child Development, 67*, 890-904.

Craton, L. G., & Yonas, A. (1988). Infants' sensitivity to boundary flow information for depth at an edge. *Child Development, 59*, 1522-1529.

Craton, L. G., & Yonas, A. (1990a). The role of motion in infants' perception of occlusion. In J. T. Enns (Ed.), *The development of attention: Research and theory* (pp. 21-46). Amsterdam: Elsevier North Holland.

Craton, L. G., & Yonas, A. (1990b). Kinetic Occlusion: Further studies of the boundary-flow cue. *Perception and Psychophysics, 47*, 169-179.

Dannemiller, J. L., & Freedland, R. L. (1989). The detection of slow stimulus movement in 2- to 5-month-olds. *Journal of Experimental Child Psychology, 44*, 255-267.

Diamond, A., & Lee, E. Y. (2001). Inability of 5-month-old infants to retrieve a contiguous object: A failure of conceptual understanding or of control of action? *Child Development, 71*, 1477-1494.

Eizenman, D. R., & Bertental, B. I. (1998). *Developmental Psychology, 34*, 426 -434.

Fantz, R. L. (1956). A method for studying early visual development. *Perceptual and Motor Skills, 6*, 13-15.

Ghim, H. (1990). Evidence for perceptual organization in infants: Perception of subjective contours by young infants. *Infant Behavior and Development, 13*, 221-248.

Gibson, E. J. (1982). The concept of affordances in development: The renascence of functionalism. In W. A. Collins (Ed.), *The concept of development: The Minnesota Symposium on Child Psychology* (Vol. 15, pp. 51-81). Hillsdale, NJ: Erlbaum.

Gibson, J. J. (1979). *The ecological approach to visual perception.* Boston: Houghton Mifflin.

Granrud, C. E., & Yonas, A. (1984). Infants' perception of pictorially specified interposition. *Journal of Experimental Child Psychology, 37*, 500-511.

Granrud, C. E., Yonas, A., Smith, I. M., Arterberry, M. E., Glicksman, M. L., & Sorknes, A. C. (1984). Infants' sensitivity to accretion and deletion of texture as information for depth at an edge. *Child Development, 55*, 1630-1636.

Hainline, L., Riddell, P., Grose-Fifer, J., & Abramov, I. (1992). Development of accommodation and convergence in infancy. Special Issue: Normal and abnormal visual development in infants and children. *Behavioural and Brain Research, 49*, 33-50.

Held, R., Birch, E., & Gwiazda, J. (1980). Stereoacuity in human infants. *Proceedings of the National Academy of Sciences, USA, 77*, 5572-5574.

Hoffman, D. D., & Richards, W. A. (1984). Parts of recognition. *Cognition, 18*, 65-96.

Johnson, S. P. (1997). Young infants' perception of object unity: Implications for development of attentional and cognitive skills. *Current Directions in Psychological Science, 6*, 5-11.

Johnson, S. P., & Aslin, R. N. (1995). Perception of object unity in 2-month-old infants. *Developmental Psychology, 31*, 739-745.

Johnson, S. P., & Aslin, R. N. (1996). Perception of object unity in young infants: The roles of motion, depth, and orientation. *Cognitive Development, 11*, 161-180.

Johnson, S. P., & Nanez, J. E. (1995). Young infants' perception of object unity in two-dimensional displays. *Infant Behavior and Development, 18*, 133-143.

Jusczyk, P. W., Johnson, S. P., Spelke, E. S., & Kennedy, L. J. (1999). Synchronous change and perception of object unity: Evidence from adults and infants. *Cognition, 71*, 257-288.

Kanizsa, G. (1955). Margini quasi-oercettivi in campi con stimolazione omogenea. *Rivista di Psicologia, 49*, 31-49.

Kaufmann-Hayoz, R., Kaufmann, F., & Stucki, M. (1986). Kinetic contours in infants' visual perception. *Child Development, 57*, 292-299.

Kavsek, M. J. (1999). Infants' responsiveness to line junctions in curved objects. *Journal of Experimental Child Psychology, 72*, 177-192.

Kawabata, H., Gyoba, J., Inoue, H., & Ohtsubo, H. (1999). Visual completion of partly occluded grating in young infants under 1 month of age. *Vision Research, 39*, 3586-3591.

Kellman, P. J. (1984). Perception of three-dimensional form by human infants. *Perception & Psychophysics, 36*, 353-358.

Kellman, P. J. (1993). Kinematic foundations of infant visual perception. In C. Granrud (Ed.), *Visual perception and cognition in infancy. Carnegie Mellon symposia on cognition.* (pp. 121-173). Hillsdale, NJ: Erlbaum.

Kellman, P. J. (1995). Ontogenesis of space and motion perception. In W. Epstein & S. Rogers (Eds.), Han*dbook of perception and cognition* (Vol. 5, pp. 327-364). New York: Academic Press.

Kellman, P. J. & Arterberry, M. E. (1998). *The cradle of knowledge: Development of perception in infancy.* Boston: MIT Press.

Kellman, P. J., & Cohen, M. H. (1984). Kinetic subjective contours. *Perception and Psychophysics, 35*, 586-593.

Kellman, P. J., & Shipley, T. F. (1991). Theory of visual interpolation in object perception. *Cognitive Psychology, 23*, 141-221.

Kellman, P. J., & Short, K. R. (1985, June). *Infant perception of partly occluded objects: The problem of rotation.* Paper presented at the Third International Conference on Event Perception and Action, Uppsala, Sweden.

Kellman, P. J., & Short, K. R. (1987). Development of three-dimensional form perception. Special Issue: The ontogenesis of perception. *Journal of Experimental Psychology:*

Human Perception and Performance, 13, 545-557.

Kellman, P. J., & Spelke, E. S. (1983). Perception of partly occluded objects in infancy. *Cognitive Psychology, 15*, 483-524.

Kellman, P. J., Gleitman, H., & Spelke, E. S. (1987). Object and observer motion in the perception of objects by infants. *Journal of Experimental Psychology: Human Perception and Performance, 13*, 586-593.

Kellman, P. J., Spelke, E. S., & Short, K. R. (1986). Infant perception of object unity from translatory motion in depth and vertical translation. *Child Development, 57*, 72-86.

Livingstone, M. S., & Hubel, D. H. (1988). Segregation of form, color, movement, and depth: Anatomy, physiology, and perception. *Science, 240*, 740-749.

Nanez, J., Sr. (1988). Perception of impending collision in 3- to 6-week-old infants. *Infant Behavior and Development, 11*, 447-463.

Needham, A., Baillargeon, R., & Kaufman, L. (1997). Object segregation in infancy. In C. Rovee-Collier and L. P. Lipsitt (Eds.), *Advances in infancy research* (vol. 11, pp. 1-44). Greenwich, CT: Ablex.

Needham, A. (1999). The role of shape in 4-month-old infants' object segregation. *Infant Behavior and Development, 22*, 161-178.

Peterhans, E., & Heydt, R. von der, (1989). Mechanisms of contour perception in monkey visual cortex. II: Contours bridging gaps. *Journal of Neuroscience, 9*, 1749-1763.

Peterhans, E., & Heydt, R. von der, (1991). Subjective contours – bridging the gap between psychophysics and physiology. *Trends in Neurosciences, 14*, 112-119.

Shipley, T. F., & Kellman, P. J. (1992). Strength of visual interpolation depends on the ratio of physically-specified to total edge length. *Perception and Psychophysics, 52*, 97-106.

Shipley, T. F., & Kellman, P. J. (1993). Optical tearing in spatiotemporal boundary formation: When do local element motions produce boundaries, form, and global motion? *Spatial Vision, 7*, 323-339.

Shipley, T. F., & Kellman, P. J. (1994). Spatiotemporal boundary formation: Boundary, form, and motion perception from transformations of surface elements. *Journal of Experimental Psychology: General, 123*, 3-20.

Slater, A., Johnson, S. P., Brown, E., & Badenoch, M. (1996). Newborn infant's perception of partly occluded objects. *Infant Behavior and Development, 19*, 145-148.

Slater, A., Johnson, S. P., Kellman, P. J., and Spelke, E. S. (1994). The role of three-dimensional depth cuesin infants' perception of partly occluded objects. *Early Development and Parenting, 3*, 187-191.

Slater, A., Morison, V., Town, C., & Rose, D. (1985). Movement perception and identity constancy in the new-born baby. *British Journal of Developmental Psychology, 3*, 211-220.

Slater, A., Morison, V., Somers, M., Mattock, A., Brown, E., & Taylor, D. (1990). Newborn and older infants' perception of partly occluded objects. *Infant Behavior and Development*, *13*, 33-49.

Spelke, E. S., Breinlinger, K., & Jacobson, A. P. (1993). Gestalt relations and object perception: A developmental study. *Perception*, *22*, 1483-1501.

Van de Walle, G. A., & Spelke, E. S. (1996). Spatiotemporal integration and object perception in infancy: Perceiving unity versus form. *Child Development*, 67, 2621-2640.

Wattam-Bell, J. (1996a). Visual motion processing in one-month-old infants: Preferential looking experiments. *Vision Research*, *36*, 1671-1677.

Wattam-Bell, J. (1996b). Visual motion processing in one-month-old infants: Habituation experiments. *Vision Research*, *36*, 1679-1685.

Yonas, A., & Arterberry, M. E. (1994). Infants' perceive spatial structure specified by line junctions. *Perception*, *23*, 1427-1435.

Yonas, A., Arterberry, M. E., & Granrud, C. E. (1987). Four-month-old infants' sensitivity to binocular and kinetic information for three-dimensional-object shape. *Child Development*, *58*, 910-917.

Yonas, A., Craton, L. G., & Thompson, W. B. (1987). Relative motion: Kinetic information for the order of depth at an edge. *Perception and Psychophysics*, *41*, 53-59.

From Fragments to Objects – Segmentation and Grouping in Vision
T.F. Shipley and P.J. Kellman (Editors)

4

PERCEPTUAL UNITS AND THEIR MAPPING WITH LANGUAGE

Barbara Landau, Department of Cognitive Science, The Johns Hopkins University, Baltimore, MD 21218

INTRODUCTION

Our phenomenal experience of the world is one of coherence and stability-- objects, motions, and events in a seamless tapestry evolving over time. Yet, as the other chapters in this volume discuss, our impression of coherence is far from a direct reflection of the physical input provided to our perceptual systems. Rather, it is the product of rich mental representations through which we construct the world that we experience. The constancy and coherence of objects and events is part of the perceptual world of the infant. Unlike the vision of infancy articulated by Bishop Berkeley and Williams James, we now know that the infant's world is three-dimensional, populated with objects that have constant shape and size, occupy specific locations in space, and travel over continuous paths through this space (see Kellman & Arterberry, 1997 for review).

Perhaps one of the most striking reflections of this unity and constancy is our ability to talk about what we see. Even in the earliest vocabulary of 12 month-olds, one sees the reflection of an organized world, including words for objects, paths, motions, and properties. As young children-- and as adults -- we regularly and easily talk about the objects around us, their motions, interactions, and relationships, without any conscious awareness that a translation or conversion has taken place. Our capacity to map aspects of our experience into language clearly differentiates us from other species, marking a distinctly human aspect of knowledge. But despite the ease with which this capacity manifests itself, the mechanisms by which it is accomplished are likely to be as complex as those by which our perceptual and cognitive systems construct a unified world. This is because the mapping between perception and language demands that two systems of knowledge with quite different format and nature be codified in some compatible format.

The purpose of this chapter is to explore the language of objects and object parts as case studies of such compatibility. As we will see, even for cases that might appear to be simple, the mapping between perception and language is surprisingly complex. Even our simplest use of language -- naming concrete solid objects-- engages not only the capacity to perceptually represent the individual object being named, but also the capacity to represent it as a unique entity whose identity endures over time, as a member of a group of similar objects, and as a simultaneous member of multiple categories in a taxonomy. In the case of object parts, naming sometimes engages clearly defined perceptual units; but in other cases, part names engage units that are quite abstract and appear to go beyond those particular units provided by perception. Considering both cases in which perception appears to serve as a critical foundation, and cases in which it plays a much less straightforward role can serve as a starting point for a comprehensive understanding of the mapping between language and perception.

In what follows, I will first present a general framework for thinking about language-perception mappings. Then this framework will be used to examine two case studies: Objects and object parts. For each case, there will be discussion of those aspects of language which are firmly supported by perception, and those aspects which are not.

1.0 GENERAL FRAMEWORK: CHARACTERISTICS OF LANGUAGE-PERCEPTION MAPPING

Many theorists have assumed that talking about objects and events in the world depends, in part, on our non-linguistic representations of the world. Because we can talk about aspects of our spatial experience, there must be some elements of linguistic and non-linguistic representation that are shared. This idea has been explored extensively by cognitive scientists including psychologists, computer scientists and linguists (H. Clark, 1973; Fillmore, 1975; Hayward & Tarr, 1995; Herskovits, 1986; Jackendoff, 1983; Landau & Jackendoff, 1993; Miller & Johnson-Laird, 1976; Regier, 1996; Talmy, 1983; see Bloom, Peterson, Garrett and Nadel, 1996, for recent views). In this chapter, we will be concerned with those aspects of spatial language that encode words for objects and object parts. Each of these entities can be represented by the spatial-perceptual systems, and they can also be expressed by language. They therefore present useful cases for examining the nature of the mapping between language and perception.

As a way of circumscribing our inquiry, we can first ask quite generally how much of our linguistic and non-linguistic representations are actually shared. We can then ask where, in our representational systems, the sharing occurs.

1.1 Some first guesses: How much is shared by non-linguistic representations of space and spatial language?

The idea of a language-space mapping assumes that spatial representations are a relevant part of the lexical representations of words. The correspondence might be one in which a word "points to" a spatial representation, or one in which some aspect of the spatial representation is actually encoded by syntax or morphology. An example of the former is the case of the word DOG, whose lexical representation might be linked to a spatial representation of the objects we normally would call "dog" (see Section 2 for discussion). An example of a spatial distinction that is encoded in syntax or morphology is the syntactic distinction between count and mass noun, which corresponds to individuated objects vs. non-individuated portions (Soja, Carey, & Spelke, 1991); the latter non-linguistic distinction might also be represented in the spatial / perceptual systems (Jackendoff, 1996). But how much of our representation of space is actually pertinent to the meanings of words in the spatial vocabulary? There are at least three possibilities.

1.1.1 Complete identity. Spatial terms might be a direct reflection of non-linguistic spatial representations, a relationship of identity (Figure 1a). This hypothesis is easily falsified by examining the general character of spatial language. Consider object names, which typically encode an object's category (e.g., dog, house, table). Each name encodes the object's membership in a category, regardless of the many distinctions that can be made by

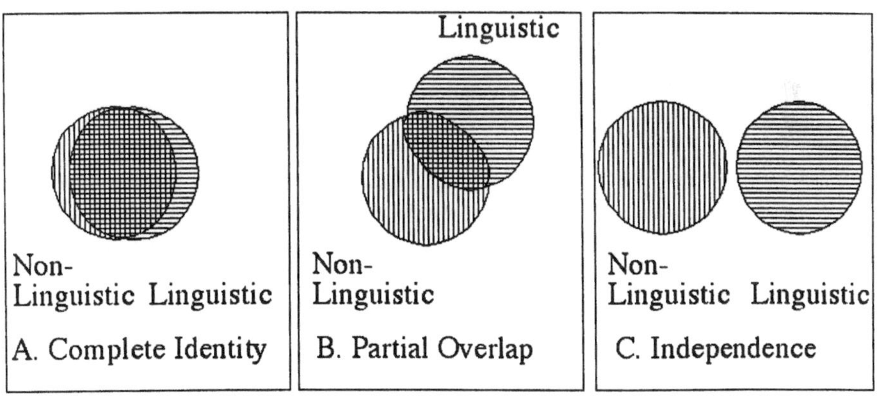

Figure 1. Three possible relationships between non-linguistic spatial cognition and spatial language.

the spatial- perceptual systems. For example, the same label dog applies to objects that vary substantially in size, color, and surface chateracteristics; the label is essentially "blind" to these distinctions, which are clearly made by the human perceptual system. This blindness may be attributable to the design of language: Lexical items encode categories at a level of detail coarser than that available to perception (Landau & Jackendoff, 1993). This is why a picture is worth a thousand words.

Note that properties that distinguish the individual object from others clearly are encodable by language-- we can talk about the big dog, the black dog, or the short-haired dog. But properties such as these are usually encoded in a separate stock of the language's terms (in English, often as adjectives), leaving the basic object names to encode membership in the category, which is agnostic with respect to the particulars of size or color. This characteristic of the lexicon-- the requirement to group many perceptually distinct entities under a single term-- applies to many (if not most) lexical categories.

Even in the case of spatial relational terms, the basic lexicon abstracts away from the many spatial properties that the spatial/ perceptual systems must encode at some level. For example, in order to compute size and shape constancy, or to accurately reach and grasp an object, metric information about the object, viewer, grasping hand, etc. are required; the latter continually change as the action is carried out. Such spatial representations, which are necessary for accurate motor control, are thought to be represented in the brain's dorsal stream (Milner and Goodale, 1995). Languages, however, do not have a stock of basic spatial terms that encode absolute metric distance or orientation (Talmy, 1983). Rather, English prepositions such as near or far (and equivalent terms in other languages) encode relationships that are blind to absolute distance. The encoding of metric distance is accomplished by the language's stock of metric terms (the measure terms plus number words) used in phrases. These, and many other examples, show that the basic terms of a language are highly selective in the properties they choose to encode and that these constitute only a subset of the properties available to the human spatial-perceptual systems.

1.1.2 Partial overlap. A second possibility is that language draws selectively on aspects of spatial representation, but that a language's basic spatial terms always correspond to some units in the non-linguistic spatial representation system (Figure 1b). That is, whenever a language has a basic spatial term, there should be a corresponding non-linguistic spatial representation that serves as its foundation. An example of this is the case of the word dog, which might be linked to an abstract spatial representation of things we normally call dogs. As discussed above, not all of the details of our visual representations of dogs would be pertinent to application of the word, but whatever aspects are pertinent should be found in non-linguistic spatial representations.

This view has two consequences. First, it would suggest that spatial language might be constrained by the nature of non-linguistic spatial representations-- spatial language would be capable of expressing only that which can also be found in the non-linguistic spatial system. A specific version of this hypothesis was proposed by Landau & Jackendoff (1993) who suggested that the functional bifurcation of non-linguistic representations into "what" and "where"might be responsible for a parallel bifurcation in the spatial semantics of words for objects and places. This general approach would suggest that we should use studies of perceptual and spatial representations to motivate and explain the nature of linguistic distinctions made by spatial terms.

A second consequence reflects the other side of the equation. If the basic spatial terms of a language always correspond to non-linguistic spatial units, then examining the nature of spatial language should also shed light on the kinds of elements one would expect to see in the non-linguistic spatial representational system. For example, as Landau and Jackendoff pointed out, although most theories of object representation (e.g. Biederman, 1987; Marr, 1982) treat objects as solid volumes, the lexicon includes many names whose referents may be better represented as thickened surfaces (e.g., record, slab, sheet, and lake), hollow containers (e.g., cup, bowl, box, jar), or "negative" object parts (e.g., hole, pit, groove, slot). If it is true that any spatial entity we can talk about also has corresponding non-linguistic representations, then our capacity to talk about geometric entities such as slabs and holes could provide a theoretical and empirical motivation for vision scientists to search for corresponding non-linguistic representations (see Willats, 1992).

1.1.3 Independence. A third possibility is that the distinctions made by spatial language do not arise from non-linguistic spatial representations; but rather, emerge independently, possibly under somewhat different constraints (Figure 1c). Kemmerer (1999) gives an interesting example. He describes in detail the distinction within pairs of so-called proximal and distal demonstratives such as this/that, here/there, near/far. He also reviews neuroscientific evidence showing that the brain has distinctly different mechanisms for representing two different kinds of space-- "near" (peripersonal) space, which surrounds the body and extends outward to the end of the arm's reach, and "far" (extrapersonal) space, which begins at the boundary of near space, and progresses outward. If spatial terms always correspond to non-linguistic distinctions, then the terms near/far (and the demonstratives) should correspond to the "near" and "far" spaces revealed by neuropsychological studies.

However, Kemmerer argues that the **linguistic** distinction within proximal/distal pairs of terms does not correspond to these spaces in any direct fashion. Rather, these terms encode relative distance, which can be contrasted within the peripersonal space, within the extrapersonal space, or across these spaces. For example, one can refer to "the pain here" vs. "the pain there", both on the lower part of the leg (hence within the peripersonal space), or to "the tree that is near" vs. "the tree that is far", both within extrapersonal space. Thus whereas language makes a binary relative distinction that is blind to metric distance, other cognitive systems also make a binary distinction but incorporate metric distance. Kemmerer concludes that terms such as these present a case in which there is no clear direct correspondence between non-linguistic spatial representations and the spatial representations relevant for the lexicon. In this case, the linguistic distinction pertinent to contrasting terms such as near/far or this/that may have emerged under constraints of its own, independent of those that apply to non-linguistic spatial representations.

Although Kemmerer argues for independence between linguistic and non-linguistic representations of space, we should note that just one aspect of distance is different in the two; this is the metric vs. non-metric distinction. Thus we might say that both systems make a binary and relative distinction, but that only one (non-linguistic) also encodes metric distance. As Talmy (1983) pointed out, languages are blind to this property (in their stock of basic terms). The non-metric aspect of language might or might not arise independently of non-linguistic spatial representations.

In sum, the two most plausible hypotheses about the relationship between non-linguistic and linguistic spatial representations are Partial Overlap and Independence. In either case, there will have to be means for binding spatial aspects of a word's meaning to other aspects of its representation that are more traditionally considered "linguistic".

1.2 More first guesses: Shared representations

A simple scheme assumes that a given word just "points to" a perceptual or spatial representation, with no consequences for other levels of linguistic representation pertinent to the word. For example, suppose we assume that the word dog is linked in some way to the spatial representations of things we recognize as dogs. In this scheme, the relationship between language and perception captures the fact that there is some regular relationship between the word dog and the visual system's representation of these objects. This is not a trivial fact (see Fodor, 1998 for discussion of the necessity of this rational relationship for word learning to occur.) However, the scheme does not really tell us how these two kinds of representation are bound together; the perceptual representations are essentially just appendages to the lexical representations.

Jackendoff (1994) has suggested that more is required, both to understand how spatial representations are related to other aspects of a word's representation and to understand how these different kinds of representations are bound together. Specifically, he has suggested that the binding is accomplished via an "interface"-- a separate level of description that expresses those properties that are shared between two or more different kinds of representation.

As Jackendoff points out, every level of linguistic representation (e.g. phonology, syntax) has its own privileged vocabulary. Because of this, there is inherent incommensurability across levels. However, there are also some partial equivalences across levels, and these could serve to bind together the different representation. As an example,

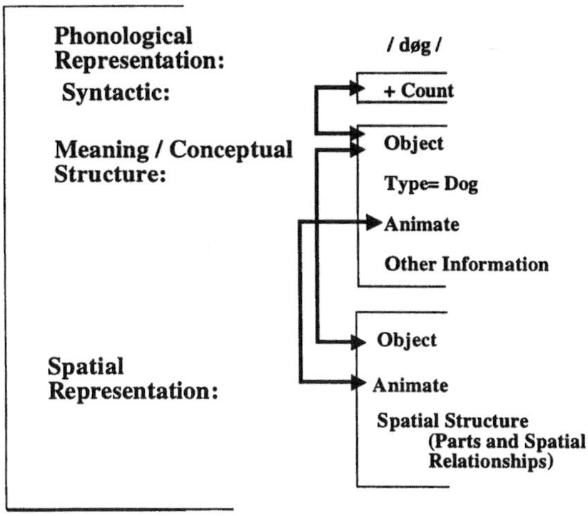

Figure 2. Different levels of representation for the lexical item "dog". Each level contains information specific to itself, but commonalities across levels permit binding for a unified representation of the word. (adapted from Jackendoff, 1996).

consider the word DOG (see Figure 2). Traditionally, this word's lexical entry will include specification of how the word sounds (its phonological representation), and the syntactic contexts in which it will occur (e.g. that it is a count noun), as well as others aspects of its meaning. In Jackendoff's scheme, much of the meaning is expressed in the word's "conceptual structure", a level of representation that is a universal level of conceptualization that maps to spatial representation on the one hand, and syntactic representations on the other. The information contained in this level includes, for example, that the concept DOG represents a **type** of object (not just an individual token), that it represents an **animate**, its taxonomic relationship to other types of object, and possibly other information about its category or "kind".

Jackendoff (1996; Landau & Jackendoff, 1993) has further suggested that words representing concrete spatial entities (such as objects or their parts) will also have a corresponding spatial representation. This representation describes the fact that the entity is an **object** or **part**, its spatial structure (as described by Marr, 1982; Biederman, 1987), and, in the case of a word such as dog, perhaps its geometry over motion, in this case, biological motion (Marr & Vaina, 1982). Thus, three levels of representation (aside from phonological) would be implicated in the representation of the word dog-- syntactic, conceptual structure, and spatial.

How are these different kinds of representation bound to each other? This is the role of the interface, which expresses those properties shared across levels. In the case of dog, the spatial representation encodes its status as an **object** (along with the particulars of its spatial structure), and an **animate**; conceptual structure also represents its status as **object type** and **animate**. Syntax then links to conceptual structure by formally encoding **objects** as **count nouns**. Binding the shared representations across different levels supports a unified representation for the word.

Note that the mappings are not direct, one-to-one correspondences across levels. As Jackendoff points out, if they were, this would amount to wholly redundant representation of the same information. The fact that the information **differs** over levels is precisely why we need an interface. For example, not all aspects of spatial representation are reflected in the other levels of representation: The typical spatial part-structure of dogs is not encoded in any other level of the representation. Similarly, other levels of representation encode aspects of meaning that never appear in the spatial representation: The conceptual structure and syntax both encode whether the word refers to a **type** (using the count noun, **a** dog) vs. a unique **token** (e.g. using the proper noun, Fido, which does not take determiners); but the spatial representation does not (in this scheme) have any means of encoding this distinction. The decision to represent certain properties in certain levels of representation must be dictated on a case by case basis, according to Jackendoff. For example, in the case of types vs. tokens, it seems unlikely that perception itself encodes the type/token distinction, hence this distinction would not be properly placed in the spatial representation (see Section 2.ii for discussion)[1]. The word dog might be linked to a typical kind of spatial configuration, but spatial configuration would not be encoded by the other, linguistically-relevant levels (unless, for example, we discovered that particular specific shapes are encoded by syntax or morphology ; for some interesting possibilities, see Levinson, 1992). Crucially, however, the connection between the conceptual and syntactic representations of dog and the spatial representations is made possible by the interface.

In sum, shared representations might be the mechanism by which spatial representations are bound to other levels of representation that are pertinent to the meaning and form of a word. In what follows, we will assume that such an interface exists for the domains of object names and part-terms. To the extent that spatial language-- in this chapter, words for objects and object parts-- engages non-linguistic spatial representations, we would theorize that these spatial representations are a proper part of the full word's meaning. Alternatively, where spatial language does not engage non-linguistic spatial representations,

---

[1] Evidence suggests that token information may be discarded when people recognize basic-level object types. For example, people name objects of a category (such as "plane") whether they are primed with toy propeller planes or full-size 747 jets. It is unclear, however, whether perceptual processes actually mark the distinction between types and tokens (see Section 2.ii for further discussion). I am grateful to Phil Kellman for pointing out the relevance of this evidence to me.

the meaning of the word would be restricted to its conceptual structure, syntax, and phonology. In these cases, spatial/ perceptual representations would provide no obvious foundation for spatial language. Finally, it is possible that different relationships will be true of different lexical items. The evidence that follows suggests that we can, in certain cases, find perceptual and spatial foundations for spatial terms; but in other cases, there is a surprising degree of independence between the units provided by perception, and those encoded by language.

2.0 CASE #1: OBJECTS AND THEIR NAMES

There is considerable evidence for the primacy of the object as a perceptual and cognitive unit during infancy. By four months of age, infants possess knowledge that objects are permanent, unitary entities that move along continuous paths through space (Baillargeon, 1995; Kellman & Spelke, 1983; Leslie et al., 1998; Spelke et al., 1995). Late during the first year, infants begin producing names for things. At first, these names are tied to individual exemplars that have been named, and are not freely generalized to other exemplars (Woodward, Markman, & Fitzsimmons, 1994; Smith et al., 2001). The child's vocabulary grows slowly during this period, increasing from 0 to 25 words over a period of several months, then from 25 to 50 words over the next several months. This early vocabulary is overwhelmingly composed of names for things: In a recent study, Smith, Jones, Landau, Samuelson, & Gershkoff-Stowe (2001) found that the vast majority of the words in children's earliest vocabulary were nouns that named objects, and 90% of these were names for solid objects. Just as in perception, the object is a principal unit in early language learning.

But the problem of linguistically encoding objects is much more complex than simply learning the correspondence between a given object and a name. Languages have the means to encode the very same object at many different levels: The same dog may be referred to as a dog, an animal, that dog, or Fido; although each expression refers to the same animal, each expression points to a different concept or meaning. This set of varying meanings thus would appear to go beyond what is afforded by perceptual/ spatial representations. In the process of learning, the child must determine which expressions go with which meanings, often in the context of viewing the same physical object.

What, then, is the correspondence between the infants' object perception and object knowledge, and his or her representation of objects for the purposes of naming? We consider several different aspects of object naming, and examine the implications for this correspondence.

2.1 Evidence, Part A: Where perception supports language

After acquiring roughly 50 words, children begin to generalize object names to new objects they have not heard named before. Often these generalizations are based on visual similarity, especially on similarity in shape (E. Clark, 1973). Although perceptual foundations surely include more than the perception of object shape (e.g. actions, functions, events are also important), shape would appear to provide one clear case in which perceptual organization could serve as an important foundation for early naming.

Although almost all developmentalists would agree that perceptual organization forms **part** of the foundation, there is considerable controversy over the extent to which perceptual similarity guides infants' and children's generalization of object names (see Landau et al., 1998; Woodward & Markman, 1998 for review). Many have observed that object names often refer to objects which do not share obvious perceptual similarities, even at the basic level (e.g. a digital desk clock and Big Ben are both called clock; see Bloom, 1996, for discussion). Thus, perceptual similarity is not necessary for assigning the same name to two objects in the language that the child must learn. Others have argued that the foundation for naming is never perceptual similarity, but rather, an object's category or "kind" (Mandler & McDonough, 1998; Markman, 1989; Soja et al., 1991; Waxman & Markow, 1995).

Unfortunately, invoking the notion of "kind" does little to answer the question of how the child comes to organize actual exemplars in the world into diverse kinds that he or she can name; nor does it provide any clear mechanisms for the child's knowledge of kinds to interface with perceptual representations of objects. Even if the child possesses mental categories which he will use to organize exemplars (say, basic ontological categories such as animal or artifact), how should he determine which objects go together into which categories? This aspect of the induction problem has been largely ignored in explanations of how children come to map names onto categories of objects. Yet there is abundant information provided by the perceptual systems that can help the learner solve this problem.

i. Infants are sensitive to rich and subtle kinds of perceptual similarity: shape and surface texture

Research in visual perception tells us that an object's 3-dimensional structure-- its shape-- is critical to adults' object recognition (Biederman, 1987; Marr, 1982). In some current theories, basic-level objects-- airplanes, cups, cars-- are recognized through decomposition into parts, either by analysis of contour minima (Hoffman & Richards, 1984; see chapter by Singh & Hoffman, this volume) or by encoding specific spatial arrangements of volumetric primitives (Biederman, 1987). Perhaps not coincidentally, the basic level seems to provide an easy entry point into object naming (Brown, 1958; Rosch, Mervis, Gray, Johnson, & Boyes-Braem, 1976; Waxman & Markow, 1995, but see Mandler & Bauer, 1988, for a different view). It seems plausible that infants and young children might be predisposed to use perceptual similarities-- in particular, similarity of object shape-- as one foundation upon which they can come to learn which names go with which sets of things in the world. Although less is known about categorization based on surface properties, the differences in surface texture between natural kinds and artifacts suggests that these distinctions could also support categorization.

Basic-level categories and shape. A remarkable study by Behl-Chadha (1996) suggests that even 4 month-old infants might recognize and encode complex shape-based distinctions betweeen objects in different basic level categories-- things such as chairs, couches, or tables. In Behl-Chadha's experiments, infants were habituated to a series of photographs of objects from one such category, e.g. a series of chairs, including, i.e. kitchen chairs, side chairs, stuffed chairs, in styles such as colonial, Victorian, and contemporary. Then they were tested for generalization to photographs of new objects from that same category (i.e. new chairs), compared to objects from a different complex category, i.e. a series of tables varying in style (including dining room tables, coffee tables that were round, oval, rectangular, and tables with either central pedestals or four legs). The results showed that infants did indeed distinguish between the two categories of objects, suggesting that complex perceptual similarities are computed well before the child learns names for things.

Related findings supporting the role of perception in infant categorization have been reported by Quinn and Eimas (1996), who examined infants' capacity to perceptually encode distinctions between cats and dogs. Four month-olds could distinguish between photographs of cats vs. dogs, but could not distinguish between photos of cats vs. female lions (which are arguably more perceptually similar to cats than are dogs). Further experiments showed that 7 month-olds could distinguish between cats and female lions, especially when the stimuli were presented in contrasting contexts (see Section 2.3.i for further discussion). These findings suggest that complex shape-based computations could support the infant's capacity to distinguish between members of contrasting basic level categories.

Superordinate categories and surface texture. Complex aspects of an object's surface structure may also support infants' capacity to categorize members of contrasting superordinate categories-- such as natural kinds vs. artifacts. Many investigators have observed that the textures which characterize natural kinds (e.g. plants, animals, rock formations) are qualitatively different from those that occur in man-made things (see Figure 3 for examples). Exceptions exist, of course. For example, objects may be designed specifically to "look natural" and natural substances may be used to create objects (e.g. a stone clock, a wooden table). In the latter cases, the natural substances are usually modified-- smoothed and polished-- to remove the relatively rough texture that naturally occurs in stone, wood, and the like. Mandelbrot (1982) specifically suggested that repeating self-similarity characterizes the surfaces of naturally-occurring objects. He contrasted this with the surfaces

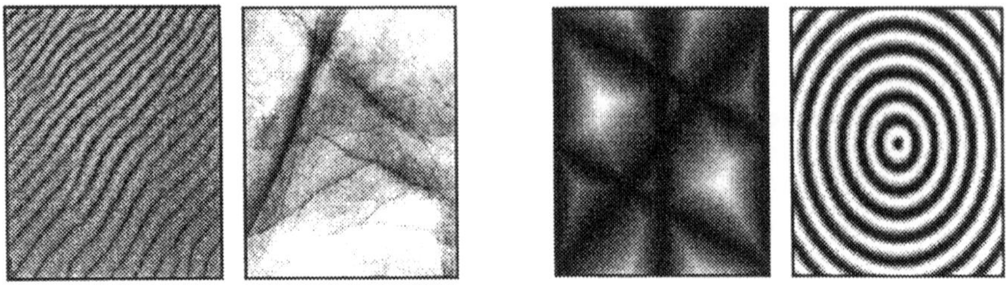

Figure 3. Natural kind objects and artifacts tend to have surface textures with unique characteristics. The surface textures in panel A are from natural entities (sand, skin), and exhibit characteristic regularities; the surface textures in panel B are from artifacts, and have quite different kinds of regularities. The differences between these kinds of surface textures could support infants' categorization of natural kind objects vs. artifacts. See text for discussion.

of manufactured objects, which usually are relatively smooth and do not exhibit the hierarchical "layering" characteristic of natural textures. Although the correlation between surface texture type and natural/ artifact status is not perfect (there are leather sofas and fur coats), statistical regularities could allow learners to use these perceptual characteristics as support in forming different kinds of categories.

Recent studies suggest that infants are sensitive to the distinctions among these different types of surface texture, and that such sensitivity might play an important role in early categorization-- especially categorization of superordinates, e.g. animals vs. vehicles. Mandler and Bauer (1988) first reported that infants can form categories at the superordinate level, specifically animals vs. vehicles. Smith and Heise (2000) took up this finding, asking whether pertinent distinguishing surface textural features might play an important role in infants' categorization. Using a habituation of looking time paradigm, Smith and Heise showed that 12 month-old infants were highly sensitive to the surface textural differences of toy models of animals and vehicles whose shape and surface textures clearly specified their different kinds. Furthermore, they showed that surface texture-- and not global shape-- was sufficient for distinguishing members of these two categories.

In their first two experiments, Smith and Heise habituated infants to two toys from a single category (e.g. two animals or two vehicles), then tested them on a novel toy-- either from the same superordinate category as the habituation toys or from the other superordinate category (e.g., a black and white boat if they had been habituated to animals, or a black and white cow if they had been habituated to vehicles). Infants looked longer at the toy from the different superordinate category, showing that they had initially habituated to the "category" of animal vs. vehicle.

Smith and Heise then proceeded to test which perceptual cues were crucial in supporting categorization. They systematically removed from the stimuli those properties hypothesized to be critical to the discrimination, testing each time to see whether the infants still habituated to one category and showed renewed attention to the novel category. With facial features of the toy animals removed, the pattern of results were the same as for the first two experiments: The infants still discriminated animals from vehicles. Now Smith and Heise removed information about global shape, but preserved surface textural difference. They did this by cutting up the toys, removing all eyes, mouths, or wheels, and remounting the pieces on a wheel. Infants still dishabituated to the member of the novel category, showing that they could perform the categorization task using only surface textural information. Finally, Smith and Heise removed this surface textural information, but preserved global shape. They did this by covering all intact toys with a thin layer of plasticine, to create smooth surfaces. Now infants showed **no** evidence of categorizing animals vs. vehicles. Note that these plasticine-altered objects were clearly recognizable by adults for what they depicted, because they were "animal" shapes or "vehicle" shapes. Yet the global shape differences between the animals and vehicles were not sufficient to support dishabituation to the members of the novel category. Thus, in the case of categorizing animals vs. vehicles, global shape information was not sufficient for infants to distinguish the two categories, but surface texture was.

The combination of experiments on basic level and superordinate categories strongly suggest that both shape and the surface properties of objects provide important information that infants can se to categorize objects prior to language. Shape appears to be especially important when the infant must categorize members from one basic level against those from another basic level; surface texture appears to be important for superordinate categorization. This makes sense, in view of the fact that (a) it is principally shape that distinguishes one basic level type of object from the next, and that (b) surface texture can distinguish one type of superordinate from the next. The human visual system is likely to be sensitive to important properties such as these, and hence detection of this information may play an important role in early categorization activities. The knowledge constructed from such activities will serve the toddler well once naming begins.

ii. Early object naming may rest on similarities in object shape

Direct evidence for the importance of object shape in naming can be found in numerous studies. The first pertinent observations were made by Eve Clark (1973), who found from diary data that children often generalize their earliest words on the basis of shape. For example, children might use the word ball to refer to all round objects, including, e.g. a face or a moon. Yet diary data-- the spontaneous productions of young children-- can be difficult to interpret. Is the child using the word ball because he thinks the moon is a ball, or because he is attempting to draw attention to the similarity in shape between balls and the moon? This difficulty in interpretation can be overcome to a degree by empirical study of children's generalization patterns in experimental contexts where they are introduced to novel objects having novel names, and then tested for how they generalize the novel name to other new objects.

Such investigations have been carried out in a series of studies by Landau, Smith, and Jones (Landau, Smith, & Jones, 1988; 1996; Smith, Jones, & Landau, 1992; 1996). Across a wide range of studies, Landau et al. found that young children show a pronounced tendency to generalize novel object names on the basis of an object's shape. For example, if shown a novel object (the "standard") and told "See this? This is a dax", children will later judge that objects having the same or similar shape also are called "dax" (see Figure 4A). This bias in favor of object shape begins rather weakly, around age 2, and becomes quite strong by around age 3. Surprisingly, it is strong in adults in certain contexts-- especially when the objects are novel and no further information about its category is available (Gentner, 1978; Landau, Smith, & Jones, 1996; see Section 2.2.1).

A. B.

Figure 4. When young children are shown a novel object and hear it named, they tend to judge that objects with the same shape are members of the same named category (panel A). In contrast, when children are shown the same novel object and do not hear the object named, they make similarity judgments on the basis of other properties, such as the object's size and/or texture (panel B). This pattern has been dubbed "the shape bias" (Landau, Smith, & Jones, 1988).

Importantly, the shape bias is reliably found in naming contexts, but not in contexts where the objects are not named (Figure 4B). Thus, if children are shown the same "standard" object as in the Name task, and hear only "See this?" (with no name given to the object), they will later judge objects to "go with" or "match" the standard on the basis of a variety of properties including color, texture, and size (Landau et al., 1988; Smith et al., 1992). The "shape bias" appears only in contexts of object naming. The presence of the shape bias in object naming tasks has been shown by a number of other investigators using novel objects as well as real objects (Baldwin, 1992; Imai, Gentner, & Uchida, 1994; Keil, 1994; Soja, 1992; Subrahmanyam, Landau, & Gelman, 1999; see Landau, Smith, & Jones, 1998, for review).

Note that young children do notice, attend to, and become engaged by other properties of objects-- so it cannot be argued, simply, that shape is just"salient" for young children. For example, when 3 year-olds are shown a novel object and told it is "food", they generalize to new objects on the basis of color (Macario, 1991). When 2 year-olds are asked to choose an object to pull a toy, they choose any object having an appropriate length and rigidity, regardless of specific shape (Brown, 1990; Landau et al., 1996). When they are asked to choose an object in order to "fix up" a doll's unkempt hair, they choose objects that are rigid and have prongs -- objects that are functionally similar to combs (Figure 5A). In this context, they do not choose flimsy paper objects cut out to look exactly like a comb (Landau et al., 1996). Yet at the same time, both 2 year-olds and adults alike pick out a flimsy paper object shaped like a comb when asked to find "a comb" (Figure 5B). Thus, young children's knowledge of objects is considerable, and their attention can be drawn to different properties

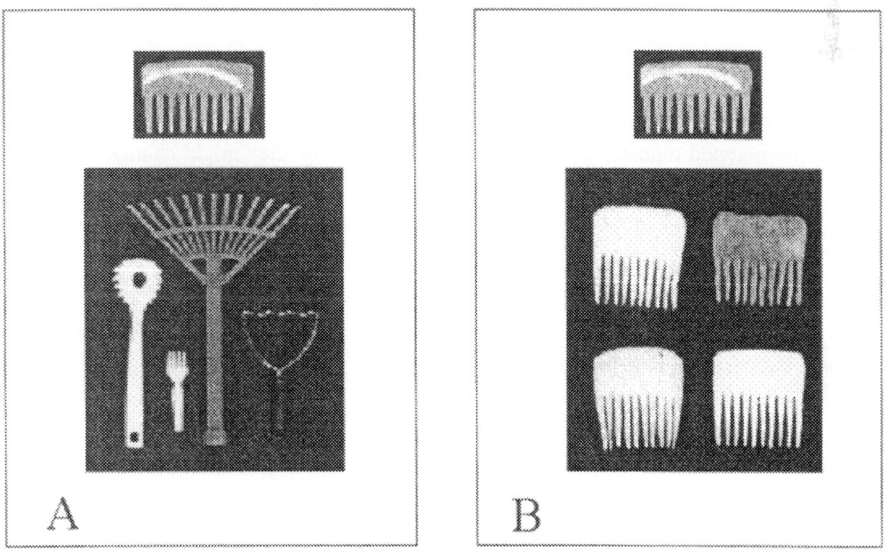

Figure 5. When shown a comb, and asked for another object that will "fix up" a doll's hair, children are likely to choose a different-shaped object that can carry out the same function as the comb (e.g. the objects in panel A) rather than objects of the same shape that are made of materials that will not allow them to carry out the function (e.g. the objects in panel B, which are shaped like the model comb, but made of flimsy paper or clay). In contrast, if they are asked for another "comb", they will choose the objects in panel B, not panel A.

on the basis of differences in the task she is asked to carry out. Clearly, the child's mental goal in solving the task varies as a function of what they are asked to do, and this goal guides her attention to different properties. The task of **object naming** in young children is selective, and solution to this task appears to engage representations of an object's shape.

If object shape provides a privileged kind of similarity in the early acquisition of object names, then many important questions follow. In what sense are the shapes of all cats or dogs similar? What level of detail is actually encoded for the purposes of object naming, and is this a different level of detail from that required for object recognition? How are such different scales of shape represented in the brain, and what are the connections between these representations and areas of the brain engaged during naming?

To date, most work on the visual perception of shape has focused on whether object recognition engages viewpoint-invariant or viewpoint-dependent representations of objects (e.g. Biederman, 1987; Tarr and Pinker, 1990; Tarr & Bulthoff, 1995). This work is critical in understanding how the visual system computes object shape. Yet, it is unlikely that solutions to this particular issue will be central to understanding the relationship between visual perception and object naming. Rather, a separate challenge to vision scientists is to construct theories of the way that object shape similarity is computed. Categories of "similar" shapes are likely to depend on rich perceptual representations of objects that are flexible and incorporate knowledge about the kinds of shape properties that covary in real-world objects (see Landau & Leyton, 1999, for discussion). Armed with an adequate theory of shape representation, developmentalists could then determine how perceived similarity and object naming are mapped together during development, and how they might change with learning (see Section 2.2.iii).

2.2 Evidence, Part B: Where more than perception is required

i. Named object categories go beyond the perceptual descriptions of objects: The roles of enriched knowledge and taxonomic structure

Despite the strong role of shape in early object naming, mature object naming surely engages other kinds of distinctions and other kinds of knowledge. First, in the mature system, named object categories often reflect similarities among objects that do not correspond to perceptual similarities (Soja et al., 1991; Keil, 1994; Woodward & Markman, 1998; Bloom, 1996). For adults, Big Ben and a digital clock are both definitely clocks. Whatever makes this so, it is not that they look alike, in any obvious sense. Similarly, for adults, what makes all dogs members of the named category dog is not only (or even necessarily) their perceptual similarity, but possibly, some "essence" which they share (Medin & Ortony, 1989; Putnam, 1977). This essence is not straightforwardly reflected in how a thing looks, but may be better predicted by characteristics such as an object's genetic lineage or its intended function.

Second, the mature lexicon organizes object names taxonomically; any single object can be named at multiple levels of this hierarchy. For example, the same thing may be called dog or animal, and we understand that dogs are sub-types of the type "animal". At any given taxonomic level, a category label stands for those objects that have in common many characteristics -- and these are not solely perceptual.

Thus there are two ways in which named object categories go beyond perceptual or spatial descriptions. One is in the enrichment of knowledge systems that enter into decisions about what a thing should be called. This knowledge is not clearly traceable to perceptual systems. The second is in the hierarchical structure into which object names become organized. This structure is unlikely to be found in the perceptual or spatial systems themselves, and hence must reside in some other level of representation (perhaps Jackendoff's 1990 "Conceptual Structure".)

Do young children's object names rest on a taxonomic structure? And does enriched knowledge enter into early object naming? Answers to these questions are now being vigorously debated in the naming literature.

Taxonomic structure. A number of investigators have argued that children's object naming does reflect taxonomic categories (Waxman and Markow, 1995; Mandler & McDonough, 1998) That is, when the child learns the word dog, he knows that objects sharing that label are in the same taxonomic category, which presumably implies representation of other levels of the taxonomy, and relationships among these levels. Strong evidence for such taxonomic organization would be the child's ability to label objects using multiple labels that respect class inclusion relationships. Waxman and Senghas(1992) found such evidence. They taught 2 year-olds different novel count nouns for each of two novel unfamiliar objects that were related to each other, for example a toy horn and a toy flute. The children were also taught a separate noun for a different object not at all related to the first two, e.g. a whisk. The teaching sessions took place on separate occasions. Toddlers then were tested for their generalization and use of the word.

The results showed that the children readily learned the names of each of the objects. More importantly, the children's patterns of generalization suggested a hierarchical organization among these newly-learned names. First, toddlers sometimes generalized the word for the related items (horn, flute) to the other member of the pair; but never generalized either of these words to the unrelated item (whisk). This indicates that they set up a partition between the related items and the unrelated item. Second, and most important as evidence for taxonomic hierarchical knowledge, the children's generalization within a related pair was asymmetric. For example, a child might call the horn and flute both by the name that was taught to him for the horn alone; but this child never called the flute by anything except its correct (i.e. taught) name. This suggests that the children assumed that the two related objects were members of one category (horns/flutes, akin to a superordinate), and that one of the objects also had a separate name, presumably its basic level name. Thus a single object was called by two different names, consistent with organization of the same object at multiple levels, which would imply at least rudimentary hierarchical structure in the object lexicon by the age of 2. Other studies by Waxman show that by 3 or 4 years of age, children definitely organize common nouns into hierarchical classes, including superordinate, basic level, and subordinate categories, each related to each other in a conceptual hierarchy (Waxman, 1990).

Enriched knowledge and naming. One line of research suggests that there are clear developmental trends in the degree to which enriched knowledge enters into object naming. Landau et al. (1996; Smith et al., 1996) observed that, for adults, an object's function is often more important to determining its name than its shape (see also Malt & Johnson, 1992; Miller & Johnson-Laird, 1976). For example, if asked what makes a chair a chair, adults often respond that it is "something you sit on"; a knife is "something you cut with", etc.

Landau et al. examined the developmental course which leads from a strong reliance on object shape to a reliance on function. They presented 2, 3, 5 year--olds and adults with novel objects, and either named the object (with a novel name) without saying more, or named the object while also describing its (fictional, but plausible) function. People then were tested for whether they would generalize the object's name to new objects that were either the same shape, but incapable of carrying out the designated function, or a different shape, but capable of carrying out the function (Figure 6). For example, people were shown an object that was made of sponge; those who heard its function were told that it was made to mop up water. The test objects included an object of a different shape, but made of sponge, and an object that was of the same shape as the target, but made of tightly woven glossy fabric-- which would only repel water. Subjects of all ages who were not told the objects' functions generalized on the basis of shape. However, for those who were told the objects' functions, there was a definite developmental trend: Two and three year-olds still generalized on the basis of shape, but 5 year-olds and adults generalized on the basis of function. Thus, as development progresses, enriched knowledge about object categories-- in this case, an object's function -- begins to guide naming generalization.

There are many other kinds of evidence showing that preschoolers and school-age children possess rich knowledge that guides judgments about what objects belong in what categories, and hence what they should be called. But the evidence suggests these are somewhat later developments-- that is, beyond the ages of 4 or so. For example, Keil (1989) described to children an object that had been altered in some way to change its outer appearance (e.g. a skunk that underwent surgery to look just like a racoon). Children then were asked whether this altered animal was still a skunk or was now a racoon (i.e. what it looked like). Preschoolers judged the resulting animal to be called a racoon, whereas second graders judged that it was a skunk that just looked like a racoon. In a separate study, Gelman and Wellman (1991) told 4 year-olds that they knew of a seed that came from an apple but was planted in a flower pot and grew with other flowers. They asked the children whether

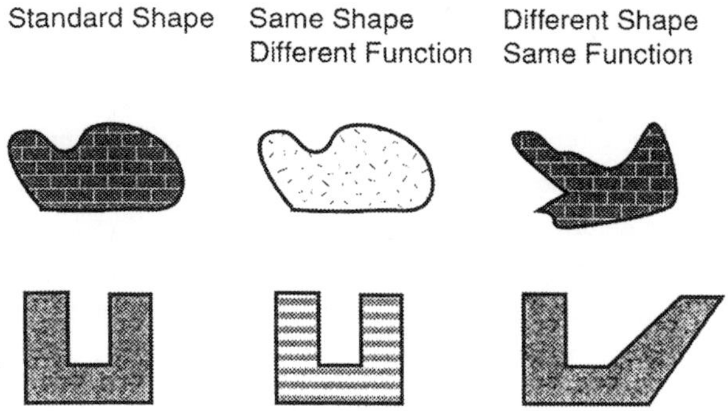

Figure 6. When young children are shown a novel object (the "standard") and hear it named, they will judge that objects having the same shape as the standard are also members of the same named category. If they are also shown the standard object's function (e.g. a sponge that is designed to soak up water), they will still select same-shaped objects as members of the named category, even if the objects cannot carry out the function (because they are made of different materials). In contrast, older children or adults who are shown the standard, hear it named, and are shown its function will select objects as members of the same named category only if they carry out the designated function (e.g., are made of the same material) even if they are of a different shape from the standard. Thus, enrichments in knowledge about object functions seem to enter into the process of object naming relatively late in development (from Landau et al., 1996).

they thought the seed would grow up to be an apple or a flower. Children judged that it would be an apple, suggesting that the child believed that the seed's innate potential-- and not its environment or current perceptual appearance-- determines what it really is.

The evidence from naming studies such as Landau et al. (1996) and conceptual judgment studies such as Keil (1989) and Gelman and Wellman (1991) show unequivocally that young children use a variety of kinds of knowledge to decide how to call a thing. Thus, the evidence-- both logical and empirical-- shows that similarity of shape is neither necessary nor sufficient for having the same name. Mature object naming entails considerably more than representing the similarity of two objects' shapes. But equally important, the evidence does not rule out a critical role of shape similarity in the early development of object naming. The most reasonable conclusion from these widely varying studies is that perceptual similarity-- in particular, object shape-- can serve as a rich foundation for children as they come to group objects into categories that will support early object naming. This early reliance on perceptual similarity as a guide to category membership is later enriched with additional knowledge, which may-- in some cases-- come to override the evidence of our perceptual systems.

ii. Types and tokens are distinguished from each other in language, but not in perception

As we observed earlier, the very same object can be encoded by language as a type (a dog) or a token of the category (that dog). Unique tokens often have proper names: My own dog is Fido. Yours may look identical to mine (and may even be its identical twin), but its uniqueness is marked by its having a different name, Rover. The distinction between types and tokens can also be encoded by determiners: Both types and tokens can be encoded by count nouns (e.g. a dog, referring to a member of the category or a particular dog; the dog referring to any member of the category or to a particular dog). In addition, tokens can be distinguished by other determiners (this dog, that dog, both referring to a particular dog). Unique animate tokens are distinguished by proper nouns, which do not take count determiners (e.g. one would not say *The Fido, except in highly unusual circumstances, e.g. Donald Trump referring to himself as "The Donald"). Because the type/token distinction is encoded both conceptually and syntactically, Jackendoff (1996) has proposed that it should be encoded as part of Conceptual Structure, by marking whether the item is to be coded as a [TYPE] or [TOKEN]. Corresponding syntactic/morphological distinctions then appear in the syntactic representation.

Is the type/token distinction encoded by perceptual systems? If so, we might look for correspondences between the perceptual and linguistic distinctions. If not, then this would appear to be a linguistic/conceptual distinction that emerges independently of perception.

A number of considerations suggest that perception encodes tokens, but not types. For example, Scholl and Pylyshyn (1999) found that adults have the capacity to track the simultaneous motions of up to about four individual objects-- or tokens-- at a time. In their experiments, people view an array of about nine identical balls on a computer screen, and see a number of them flash briefly. Each of the nine balls then moves around the screen for a period of time, along continuous but randomly directed paths. When the array stops, the viewer is to identify the same balls that had initially flashed. Adults find this an easy task, and Scholl and Pylyshyn suggest that a perceptual- attentional mechanism acts as if to hook an index to each of the balls that is to be tracked. Further experiments show that people can easily track targeted balls as they move behind faux-barriers on the screen, indicating that they retain a mental representation of the set of objects as tokens as they move through space. Thus, our perceptual system can track individual tokens-- a particular object that could later be called "this X".

A correlate of the object TYPE, however, is not apparent in perception, despite the fact that types are readily encoded by languages. That is, there is no obvious way for our perceptual system to encode the fact that a particular dog belongs to the category of DOG. Moreover, there does not appear to be any clear way for perception to encode that a given object **is** in fact a member of TYPE X: We can track an individual object's identity over time (though even this becomes complex, as described below); but only by tagging it in some non-perceptual format --such as conceptual structure-- can we represent the fact that it is a TYPE.

<u>iii. Tracking identity through language allows for longer persistence over space and time than identity tracked through perception</u>

If an object's identity is traced over time, it can be said to be the same unique object. The evidence reviewed above suggests that perceivers can track the identity of up to about four objects-- or tokens-- at a time over motion, even when the paths of motion are not continually visible (e.g. when objects move behind barriers). Pylyshyn and Scholl have suggested that relatively low-level attentional mechanisms guide such perception of identity over time; these mechanisms are assumed to be insulated from higher cognitive processes.

A rather different conception of how we track identity has been offered by Spelke (see Spelke et al., 1995). She proposes that humans have an innate core concept of "object", which guides our capacity to trace an object's persistence during events in which objects move in and out of sight. In this view, an object is an entity which follows a continuous path through space. Our understanding of physical events-- such as those in which objects move through space, whether visible or not--are guided by this core concept. Spelke presents evidence that infants infer a single object's existence when a physical event can be interpreted as consistent with a single object moving along a continuous path through space-- whether it is continually visible, or is occluded during a portion of its path. In this conception, unlike Scholl and Pylyshyn's, perception is guided by knowledge-- core knowledge, which is part of our innate capacity.

Which of these views could most adequately support the linguistic encoding of identity? It is clear that we can talk about an object's identity: For unique individuals, language provides a number of means of marking identity over time. One mechanism is the proper noun: Once we give an object a proper name, it is marked as unique, and thereafter, we can refer to this particular individual simply by its name. Although names are typically given to people and pets, they can also be given to favorite objects, such as one's car or computer. Another mechanism for marking identity uses determiners that can specify uniqueness, for example, <u>this</u> dog or <u>that</u> dog can be used to indicate a specific dog. Linguistic devices such as proper <u>vs</u>. common nouns, determiners, etc., can be used by children as young as 18 months of age to make inferences about the referent of a novel noun. For example, Katz, Baker, & Macnamara (1974) showed 18-24 month-olds a doll, and labelled it either "a dax" or "Dax". Children were subsequently shown the same doll plus another similar doll, and asked to point out either "a dax" or "Dax". Children who heard the proper name pointed only to the original doll, whereas children who heard the count noun pointed to either. More recent replications and extensions of this finding have shown that young children are particularly prone to assign proper nouns to animates (Gelman & Taylor, 1984; Hall, 1994). These findings suggest that types and tokens (both unique and non-unique) are conceptually represented by very young children and properly encoded in their early language.

Given that very young children understand at least some devices for encoding identity through language, it seems plausible that there is some correspondence between either the perceptual or conceptual foundation for tracing identity over time. It is interesting to observe that a conceptual foundation for identity-- one which could plausibly guide perception, in Spelke's view-- could be useful in accounting for a wide range of phenomena related to the tracing of object identity over space and time, whereas the perceptual foundation envisioned by Pylyshyn and Scholl can only account for tracing object identiy within relatively limited spatio-temporal confines. Even cases of temporary occlusion, in which we must infer an object's existence, would appear to require some **conceptual** notion of continuity.

The need for a conceptual foundation for tracing identity is especially clear in cases where perceptual tracing of identity cannot plausibly be invoked. One such case is the classic problem of the Ship of Theseus (Hobbes, 1672/1913), recently studied in detail by Hall (1998). In the original problem, one is asked to consider a ship owned by Theseus of Athens, which is sailed for years over the seas. With use, parts wear out and must be replaced. After a number of years, the ship consists of entirely new parts. The question is whether the ship, made of these new parts, is still Theseus' ship. If so, this would imply that temporal and spatio-temporal continuity are sufficient for maintaining the ship's identity.

In Hall's study, he posed pragmatically appropriate versions of this problem to children and adults, and discovered that spatio-temporal continuity often did suffice for judgments of identity, although this tendency was strongly modulated by considerations of particular object kind (stronger for animals than artifacts), by the nature of the causal mechanism by which the "parts replacement" was carried out (stronger for apparent natural biological causes of an animal's transformations than intentional human causes), and by the age of the participant (stronger for adults than children). Thus judgments of persistence and identity can be heavily affected by our knowledge of the world, and must in many cases, be governed by principles that go beyond those that can guide the perceptual tracking of identity. It would appear necessary, therefore, to posit a conceptual-- not perceptual-- foundation for the linguistic encoding of identity.

2.3 Evidence, Part C: Learning affects the perception/ naming relationship

Even in cases where perception may serve as a critical foundation for object naming, there is growing evidence that learning plays an important role in modulating what is grouped together under the same name. If perceptual representations of objects single-handedly determined what an object was to be called, then one would expect very little change-- either developmentally or over tasks-- in the kinds of grouped objects that would be considered similar enough to be called by the same name. Yet, changes do occur in what objects will be grouped together, and these changes depend on a variety of experiential factors.

i. Infants learn to make new perceptual and category distinctions

Before the emergence of object naming, infants categorize objects (Quinn & Eimas, 1996; Mandler, 1992), and some categorization reflects surprisingly subtle detection and comparison of perceptual similarities (see Quinn & Eimas for discussion). Even here, however, we can see effects of experience on modulating the infant's categories. For example, Eimas and Quinn (1994) asked whether infants' basic-level categories were identical to those of adults. They familiarized one group of infants with photographs of domestic cats, and then tested the infants' looking preference for novel cats vs. horses, tigers, and female lions. The latter are arguably the most perceptually similar to cats, but do not belong to the same adult basic-level category, i.e. they are not normally named cat. Eimas and Quinn found that 3-4 month-olds looked longer at the horses and tigers (instances of two novel categories) than the novel instances of cats (novel tokens of an old category), but did not look longer at the female lions than the cats. This indicates that the infants distinguished between cats vs. horses/ tigers, but did not categorize cats separately from female lions, despite the fact that, for adults, these belong to two different categories. By 6-7 months, infants in the same procedure looked longer at female lions than novel cats, indicating that the distinction between these two groups of animals (cats/ female lions) must have developed sometime in between. How could such a distinction develop, in the absence of language or formal tutoring?

Eimas and Quinn wondered whether they could provide familiarization experiences for 3-4 month-olds that would induce the infants to form two separate categories, distinguishing between cats and female lions. They reasoned that separating the two kinds into different categories would require some experience during which the two were directly contrasted with each other. Therefore, they presented infants with 12 instances of photos of cats alone, followed by 6 instances in which they presented pairs of familiar (just seen) cats together with (novel) female lions. They also included 2 pairings of familiar (just seen) cats, in order to highlight the difference between these completely familiar pairs and the familiar cat- novel lion pairs. Infants then were tested on their preference for novel cats relative to instances of two novel classes-- either novel dogs or novel female lions. The infants preferred both the dogs and the female lions, relative to the cats, indicating that they could distinguish female lions from cats. The induction of this category -- female lions-- from short-lived laboratory experience suggests that, as young as 3-4 months of age, the perceptual systems of the infant are subject to modulation in response to experience-- in this case, the experience stemming from direct contrast. Thus, whatever perceptually-based categories the infant begins with, early non-linguistic learning experiences can reshape these categories, at least to some degree.

ii. Toddlers learn that object shape is relevant for the names of solid objects

The evidence reviewed earlier shows that object shape plays a privileged role in early object naming. This makes sense on the view that the primate visual system recognizes objects in terms of their shape representations, rather than, say, color or texture. If shape is the preferred format for recognizing objects, then it follows that the child learning to name objects might naturally link names to such shape-based representations of objects.

As simple and appealing as this story might be, recent evidence strongly suggests that the child's tendency to name objects on the basis of shape is just as much a product of his experience with the vocabulary of objects represented in his language as a pre-potent tendency to represent objects in terms of their shape. Smith, Jones, Landau, Gershkoff-Stowe, and Samuelson (2001) carried out a series of experiments in which they examined the origins and growth of the shape bias in children at the earliest points in vocabulary learning-- beginning when children are producing fewer than 25 words. They found that the shape bias in object naming is not present at the beginning of language learning, but rather, is learned during the early course of acquiring object names.

First, Smith et al. examined children's productive vocabulary over the earliest stages of word learning, to determine whether a shape bias exists in natural language learning contexts (as opposed to the laboratory contexts in which the shape bias has usually been shown). Examining the first 100 words that children produce, Smith et al. found that the large majority were nouns-- specifically, words for solid objects. Of these, 90% were words for objects that -- according to adult judgments-- are well-organized by shape, for example, items such as cars, trucks, or balls. Not surprisingly, most of these were also artifacts, for which shape is typically important. Only 18% of the children's early noun vocabulary included words for objects that adults judge to be well-organized by material (e.g., banana) or color (e.g. crayon). The child's early productive vocabulary thus reflects a preponderance of words that represent objects for which shape appears to be important.

Subsequent studies examined whether this tendency to produce words from shape-based categories was present from the beginning of vocabulary learning, or learned as the child's vocabulary grows. Children in the early stages of vocabulary learning were brought into the laboratory over a period of several months, and were shown sets of objects in which one object (the "standard") was frequently labelled with a novel count noun. After several visits, the children were tested for their generalization of the novel label to new objects which varied from the original standard object in either shape, material, or color. Results showed that only children who had productive vocabularies over 50 words generalized on the basis of shape. Children who were not exposed to the object sets but were nevertheless tested for naming generalization did not show shape-based generalization.

Further experiments showed that this growing tendency to generalize novel object names on the basis of shape occured only in the context of naming (consistent with other findings, see Section 2.1.ii). A separate group of children was brought into the lab and shown a set of objects with a common shape, but did not hear the objects named. Their attention was drawn to the standard by holding it up and saying "Look at this!" Later, they were asked to generalize from the standard by asking them to "Give me another one". These children did **not** generalize the standard's label on the basis of shape, but **did** tend to spontaneously group objects by shape as they were playing with them. This shows that the experience of seeing sets of same-shaped objects presented together heightened their attention to shape without connecting it to the act of naming. Importantly, when a separate group of children was shown sets of objects having either a common color or a common texture (but heard no naming), they did not generalize the novel names on the basis of color or texture; nor did they spontaneously group objects by color or texture. Thus non-linguistic grouping of objects by shape resulted when the children merely saw sets of objects whose shapes were the same. But naming by shape resulted only when the children both saw the same-shaped objects and heard them named.

These findings lead to two conclusions. First, they show that shape is a pre-potent organizer for young children, since exposure to same-shaped sets of objects can promote spontaneous non-linguistic grouping by shape. The same is not true for color or texture. Second, the results show that the use of object shape as the basis for generalization depends both on this pre-potence of shape and on the exposure to naming in the context of such similarities. We can now see why the shape bias grows in potency as the child acquires vocabulary: The shape bias reflects a generalization that the child makes over his or her experiences hearing same-shaped objects named by the same name. Importantly, as the child hears the same name being applied to objects which share shape similarity, he or she comes to generalize that object shape, in general, is important to proper generalization of object names. Thus, when the child hears a novel name applied to a novel object, he generalizes this name on the basis of the object's shape.

iii. Learning different distributions of labels alters naming boundaries

Although languages show strong overlap in the kinds of objects that are named, there is also surprising cross-linguistic variation in the distribution of labels across a number of domains. Much research effort has focused on the domains of color and space, in which there are clear cross-linguistic differences (Bowerman, 1996; Davidoff, Davies, & Roberson, 1999; Heider & Oliver, 1972; Levinson, 1996; Munnich, Landau, & Dosher, 2001). Less activity has focused on the domain of objects, but a recent study by Malt, Sloman, Gennari, Shi, and Wang (1999) shows that cross-linguistic variability exists even in the domain of common artifacts. Any complete theory of the relationship between perception and naming will have to account for how this variability arises over languages, and how it is transmitted to generations of new speakers.

Malt et al. studied the naming of commonly used containers by native speakers of English, Chinese, and Spanish. Their naming patterns were compared to the patterns arising when independent groups of subjects made non-linguistic judgments of object similarity. In the naming task, people were asked to provide names (in their native language) for 60 different containers. The distribution of names for these containers carved up the space of exemplars in different ways across the three languages. For example, Chinese speakers used a single term to cover a variety of objects that were lexically distinguished by English speakers, specifically, 13 objects called bottle, 8 called container, and 19 called jar. Spanish speakers used a single term to cover 6 objects that English speakers called bottles, 3 they called containers and 19 they called jar.

In the non-naming similarity tasks, Malt et al. asked speakers of the same three languages to judge the objects in terms of their (a) physical similarity, (b) functional similarity, or (c) overall similarity relative to each other. Results from each of these tasks yielded spaces that were quite different from the naming task. Importantly, the judgments of overall and physical similarity corresponded extremely well across the three groups of speakers, and therefore did not predict the very different patterns of naming that had emerged when the objects were named. Judgments of functional similarity corresponded somewhat less well, and again, did not predict naming categories.

These results accord well with findings from early development that suggest strong effects of linguistic input on the organization of the child's lexical similarity space-- effects that do not necessarily show up in their non-linguistic similarity space. For example, the findings of Smtih et al. (2001) discussed in Section 2.3.ii show early growth of shape-based generalization in naming tasks, but not in non-linguistic similarity tasks. As another example, Bowerman (1996) reported evidence from spontaneous and elicited language that 24 month-old children learning English lexically group together the instances of the spatial relationships of "apple IN bowl" and "hand IN glove" (using the term IN), but that 24 month-old children learning Korean will lexically categorize these differently, in accord with their native language environment, using one verb for relationships of loose fit (such as "apple IN bowl" or "bowl ON table") and a different verb for relationships of tight fit ("hand IN glove" or "top ON pen"). Bowerman argues that the specificity of these acquisitions proves that linguistic input must play a strong role in learning.

These cases show that the range of psychologically natural categories receives further structuring from the number of terms in the language and their location relative to each other. It follows from this cross-linguistic variability that, regardless of how clearly the possible natural lexical categories might be served up by non-linguistic systems of knowledge, there must also be a powerful learning mechanism whereby the child comes to set up the right number of divisions based on the number of terms in her language and how they are distributed over the space of instances.

A recent study by Landau and E. Shipley (2000) shows that even short-lived experience can affect the child's assumptions about which exemplars belong in which named categories. Landau and Shipley showed two year-olds, three year-olds, and adults two "standard" objects, which were either named with the Same Label, two Different Labels, or No Label at all (see Figure 7A). Subjects then were asked whether objects morphed as

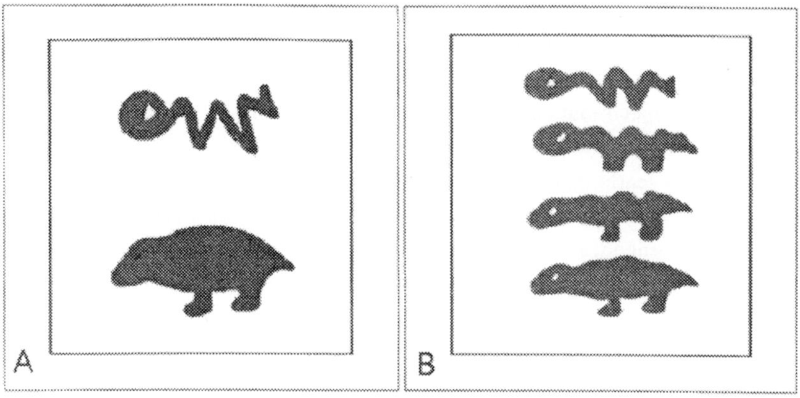

Figure 7. Children and adults were shown the two objects in panel A, and heard them named with the same name (e.g. "a dax"), two different names (e.g. a "dax" and a "rif"), or no name at all. When asked to judge whether the objects in panel B were also "daxes", children and adults in the Same Label condition judged that all objects were also called "dax". Children and adults in the Different Label condition judged that only about half of the objects were also called "dax", splitting the set of objects in half along lines of similarity to the standards. Children and adults in the No Label condition fell in between the other two groups (Landau & E. Shipley, 2000).

intermediates to these standards (Figure 7B) belonged to one of the labelled categories, or in the No Label condition, was "like" one of the standards. In the Same Label condition, children and adults generalized to all intermediates, whereas in the Different Label and No Label conditions, they showed division of the intermediates into two separate categories, with sharper division in the Different Label condition. Landau and Shipley suggested that two mechanisms might underlie this shaping of the lexical space: *Boosting* the equivalence of different exemplars by providing the same label to two exemplars, even if they are perceptually quite distinctive, and *differentiating* exemplars through differences in labelling, even if they are perceptually quite similar. These ideas are compatible with E.J. Gibson's (1969) theory of perceptual learning: Depending on the task at hand, we can learn to count or discount particular object features so as to result in "acquired equivalence" or "acquired distinctiveness" of individual properties and objects. Although the findings from Landau and E. Shipley do not tell us whether the underlying perceptual space has also been shaped by distribution of labels, the findings from Malt et al. and Smith et al. suggest that naming spaces can be shaped independently of other, corresponding non-linguistic spaces.

2.4 Summary of Case 1

The results reviewed here suggest that infants are well-prepared to use rich perceptual information as a foundation upon which to begin object naming. In particular, representations of objects in terms of their shape and surface texture may provide an important foundation for the beginning stages of object naming. However, the relationship between perceptual representations of objects and object naming is complex: Naming spaces may be built upon -- but are not identical to-- the perceptual spaces that support them. Perceptual foundations are modulated by early learning, both pre-linguistically and during language learning. The latter can result in distinctions that are particular to naming, and not other representational domains. Finally, language encodes some aspects of object knowledge that are not transparently encoded in the perceptual systems. These include the encoding of taxonomic structure, types vs. tokens, and the persistence of object identity over large scales of time and space.

3.0 CASE #2: OBJECT PARTS AND THEIR NAMES

Names for object parts appear in the child's earliest vocabulary, showing that children represent parts of objects as natural units upon which language can be built. However, in the early vocabulary, part names are much sparser than names for whole objects. Moreover, when names for parts do appear, they are first and foremost body parts-- a rather limited selection from the wealth of possible object part names. For example, Smith et al. (2001) recently examined the nature of the nouns produced by children whose entire noun vocabulary was between 0- 25, 26- 50, or 51 or more. These children ranged from 17 to 21 months old. The children with the smallest vocabularies produced on average, 23% names for people, 33% names for artifacts, 21% names for animals, and only 7% names for parts-- and these were all body parts. Children with 26-50 nouns produced on average 20% names for people, 37% names for artifacts, 18% names for animals, and 5% names for body parts. In this age group, there was also a single mention of the word hole, a "negative" part term. Children with greater than 51 nouns produced on average 20% names for people, 39% names for artifacts, 14% names for animals, and still only 6% names for body parts. This group of children also produced one mention each of hole and pocket, both negative part terms. These numbers accord well with other estimates of the overwhelming prominence of names for objects in the early vocabulary, the relative paucity of object part terms, and within part terms, the prominence of body part names (Andersen, 1975; Bloom, 1973; Gentner, 1982; Gentner & Boroditsky, 2000; Nelson, 1974.)

These results reflect the natural prominence of the OBJECT as a unit in many aspects of cognition. Even past the early points of language learning, this prominence guides the acquisition of new names: During the preschool years, children assume that a novel count noun mentioned in the context of a novel object refers to the whole object, rather than one of its parts or properties. In order to derail this preference for the object interpretation, the novel name must be introduced in the context of a familiar object whose name the child already knows (Markman & Wachtel, 1988). Thus, one reason for the paucity of object part terms may be that whole objects regularly trump parts as natural units for naming.

Nonetheless, names for parts are acquired in the early vocabulary, and the acquisition of part names provides us with the opportunity to test how naturally we can fit data on the naming of parts -- by children and adults-- into existing theories of how the visual system parses objects into their main parts. Just as the case of objects has shown, the evidence on parts suggests some cases where visual theories provide a natural support for the language of parts. In other cases, the naming of object parts requires more than perceptual theories currently provide.

3.1 Evidence, Part A: Where perception supports language

Current theories consider object parts to be critical to the process of object recognition: Objects are assumed to be mentally organized in terms of parts and their spatial relationships, and processing of these is thought to be a mandatory part of the early-level mechanisms involved in object recognition (Biederman, 1987; Hoffman & Singh, 1997; see Singh & Hoffman, this volume). The perception of parts therefore plays a key role in understanding object perception, and this has led theorists to consider the mechanisms by which the visual system parses objects into their key parts. Some theorists have suggested that the mechanisms guiding object parsing may deliver up units appropriate to encoding by language (Hoffman & Richards, 1984).

It is interesting to observe that representation of object in terms of their **parts** already entails rich mental structure. This becomes evident as soon as one contrasts the notion of a **part** with that of a **piece** (Cruse, 1986). In order to generate *pieces* of an object, one need only divide it up such that topological stability and spatio-temporal continuity are preserved: The pieces must come from the same whole object and one must be capable of treating each piece as a spatial unit. However, the means for dividing the object into pieces are wholly arbitrary: I can use any scheme I wish and the result will still be a legitimate set of object pieces. Moreover, the relationship among resulting pieces is transitive: If I cut a hat into six pieces, then a piece of Piece A is still a piece of the hat, and piece of the piece of Piece A is still a piece of the hat, and so forth.

Contrast this with an object's **parts**. These must also possess topological stability and spatio-temporal continuity. However, unlike pieces, objects are divided into their *parts* according to motivated boundaries (Cruse, 1986)-- the hat may be divided into its crown, brim, band, and feather. Each of these parts can be sensibly pointed out-- either by merely pointing to the part, or -- importantly-- by naming it. This is quite unlike the pieces of the hat, which hold no conceptual priority and therefore are not given names. The conceptual organization of parts also interacts with relationships of transitivity: Although the spine of the feather is a part of the feather, and the feather is a part of the hat, the spine of the feather is not a part of the hat.

How are objects parsed into their parts in theories of visual perception? There have been two main approaches. One assumes that the visual system represents each object part as an individual generalized cone; during object recognition, these units are fitted to the image so as to achieve a match, which is the basis for recognition (Marr & Nishihara, 1978). In Marr and Nishihara's scheme, the parts are organized as a hierarchy, in which the endpoints of the central axis for each unit serve as the attachment points for the axis of the unit at the next level of the hierarchy (see Figure 8, adapted from Marr and Nishihara, 1978). Using this approach, names for object parts could be mapped naturally to each generalized cone. For example, the animal figures shown in Figure 8 decompose naturally into units that can be naturally labelled by the English lexicon, e.g. head, neck, tail, leg, etc. This approach to mapping names onto perceptual units is also consistent with Biederman's (1987) theory of recognition-by-components. In Biederman's theory, parts are fitted to a pre-determined set of volumetric units (geons), and part boundaries are set by the boundaries of these geons.

Figure 8. As discussed by Marr & Nishihara (1978), objects can be represented in terms of a hierarchically-structured set of geons, with units at each level attached to units at the next level (Figure from Marr & Nisihara, 1978, reproduced by permission of publisher).

A different approach to object parsing has been taken in a theory developed by Hoffman and colleagues (Hoffman & Richards, 1984; Hoffman & Singh, 1997; see Singh & Hoffman, this volume). Unlike the volumetric approach, Hoffman's theory does not make any assumptions about the pre-determined nature of parts, but rather, segments objects using a quite general computational scheme that can be applied to any 2D edge or 3D surface. In the general case, an object's part boundaries are delineated by using points of local minima on the edge or surface. As first pointed out by Hoffman & Richards, when this scheme is used, it is easy to see how familiar objects-- such as the profile of a face-- can be parsed into its main parts (see Figure 9, see also Hoffman & Singh, 1997). Moreover, these parts are appealingly linked to the names we use for familiar parts: In the case of the face, the scheme yields parts we call nose, forehead, lips, chin, etc. Hoffman and Richards further showed that the computational scheme can readily account for the new parsing that follows from figure-ground reversals. As shown in Figure 9, when this is done, the parts also change, since the minima that define the part boundaries now become maxima of curvature, and vice versa. Again, the names for the new parts following from these cuts map neatly onto our labels for the parts of the new object that is now the figure: The lip, bowl, stem, and base of the goblet.

Figure 9. The main units of the faces shown can be produced by the visual parsing algorithm described by Hoffman & Richards (1984). Hoffman points out that these units correspond to the main named parts of the face (e.g. lips, chin, nose, mouth, etc.), suggesting a natural mapping between the units produced by perception and those named by language. See text for discussion.

The delineation of parts by this analysis leaves open a number of important questions about the full structure of any given part, and in recent development of the theory, Hoffman and Singh (1997) explore how the minima rule interacts with other factors. For example, although we can determine the borders of a part by using the minima algorithm, this leaves open the nature of the part "cuts"-- those boundaries that do not lie directly along the external contour or surface of the object. Similarly, contour minima appear to interact with the relative size of a potential part; some parts that fit within the minima rule make more salient-- thus "better"-- parts than others. Singh and Hoffman (1994) discuss these issues, acknowledging that the complete theory of how we determine what constitutes a legitimate object part awaits exploration of these and many other factors.

How do the volumetric unit and minima-rule approaches fare, respectively, in mapping from the perception of parts to the naming of object parts? We consider two principal kinds of named parts: Parts that have specific names, and parts that refer to regions located along axes.

i. Parts that have specific names: Handles, knobs, fingers

Both approaches would appear to fare reasonably well in providing units appropriate to the names for many common object parts. However, there are also limitations. The volumetric approach provides a parsing of all components of many common objects, and any one of these could in principle be named using a part term. The mimima-rule approach is more flexible, by providing the means to parse any object, and is especially useful in cases of natural kind objects, which grow, become squashed, and move, and hence are much less likely to be appropriately characterized by combinations of geons (see, e.g. Leyton, 1992).

It should be noted, however, that many of the parts that are available to these visual parsing schemes do not ordinarily receive names, even if they are very central and salient parts. For example, we have names for the handle, spout, and lid of a teapot, but no name for the central "body" portion (Cruse, 1986). The use of the term "body" is an extension used to name the central "default" parts of many objects; it is not particular to the teapot. The pattern of naming various parts of an object that serve particular functions, but not the remaining central part, is common to many other common objects, e.g. cars, cups, etc.

As another example of the complexity of mapping part names onto the parts yielded by visual parsing schemes, a particular object might be visually parsed into a larger set of parts than ultimately get named, with several visual-parts being collapsed to yield a single named-part. One example of this is found in cross-linguistic differences in the assignment of body -part terms (Andersen, 1978). Some languages, like English, use a single term (nose) to refer to the region from the bridge of the nose to the tip; others (like Tarascan) use a single term to include the latter plus the forehead. Whereas English uses the word leg to refer to the region from the top of the thigh to the ankle (but not the foot), others include the region of the foot ending where the toes begin, and others include the toes as well.

Yet another kind of example comes from observations by Schyns and Murphy (1994), who show that an object such as the lamp in Figure 10 would be visually parsed into five parts, but would have only four named parts-- lamp-shade, switch, neck, and base. This is because the lamp-shade, though visually parsed into two units (e.g., by the Hoffman and Richards, 1984 algorithm), is named as a single unit. Schyns and Murphy argue that the units served up by visual parsing schemes do not always persist into higher-level representations (see Section 3.3 for more discussion).

There are two different ways to capture the relationship between visual parsing schemes and part naming. One possibility is that named parts are always **consistent** with the boundaries of visual parsing. This would encompass examples where legitimate visual parts are collapsed under a single name into a larger unit, and would also prohibit the formation of named parts that violate visually-parsed boundaries—such as the combination of two spatially disjunctive units (Singh & Landau, 1998). This rule is appealing, but probably still needs to

Figure 10. The lamp shown in this figure can be visually parsed into five main units, but only four are naturally named—the lampshade, switch, neck and base (after Schyns & Murphy, 1994). This shows that the units named by language do not necessarily map in one-to-one fashion onto those produced by perception.

be modified, because there are cases in which learning can produce unitizing of parts that do not correspond in any clear fashion to a visual parse (for example, the lamp in Figure 10; also see Section 3). A second possibility is to cast the rule in terms of a one-way relationship between visual parsing and naming of parts: A part name may be **licensed by** the existence of a visually parsed unit. That is, any visually parsed unit could serve as a natural unit for naming, as could any combination of visually parsed units. This possibility accounts for the support provided by the visual system, but does not limit naming to those units afforded by vision, and hence may most naturally account for the broadest range of naming phenomena.

ii. Parts that represent regions located at the ends of axes: Top and bottoms

A particularly interesting case of the relationship between visual representations of objects and naming concerns the small group of terms found in many languages and used to name spatial regions of objects: In English, these are terms such as top, bottom, front, back, and side. These terms do not necessarily name parts that result from visually parsing an object. Rather, they refer to **regions** that lie at the ends of the three major orthogonal axes of objects. The boundaries of these regions often have no obvious perceptual discontinuity; for example, the top and bottom of a fork are the regions corresponding to some portion of the tines and some portion of the handle (with assignment varying somewhat over individuals, see Figure 11 and Section 3.2.ii).

What aspect of object representation is engaged when people assign objects their top,

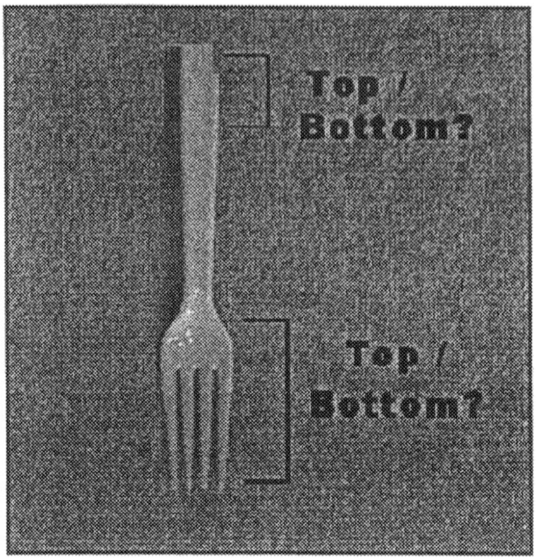

Figure 11. Some named object parts have indeterminate regions, and can be flexibly assigned to these regions. In the fork shown above, where is the end of the "top" and "bottom" of the fork? And which end should properly be called the "top" vs. the "bottom"?

bottom, front, back and side? Volumetric approaches to object parsing represent the main axis of each object part, since generalized cylinders are cross-sections swept along a central axis. For multi-part objects, one would further need to designate the single part-- or combination of parts-- that serves to orient the object more globally. This global axis is often the axis of symmetry. For example, in Figure 12, the axes of volumes representing the aligned torso and head symmetrically bifurcate the entire body and give us the main axis of the entire object, which could provide a partial foundation for the spatial part terms top and bottom.

However, as Landau and Jackendoff (1993) observed, use of spatial part terms requires several further distinctions. First, in order to apply the terms front/back, right/left and side, we would require assignment of secondary and tertiary axes to each object (and to each object part, if we want to assign these terms to the parts themselves, e.g. the front/back of the arm). Assigning the location of these additional "orienting" axes would require some algorithm to decide which dimension is secondary and which is tertiary, hence how one should assign the pairs front/back vs. side/right/left. Second, in order to distinguish between the opposite ends of any single axis, we would require assignment of direction, yielding "directed" axes (as in Figure 12). Terms that are applied asymmetrically to an axis' ends (such as front/back or right/left) would engage such directed axes, whereas terms that are applied symmetrically to an axis' ends (such as side) would require only orienting axes, but

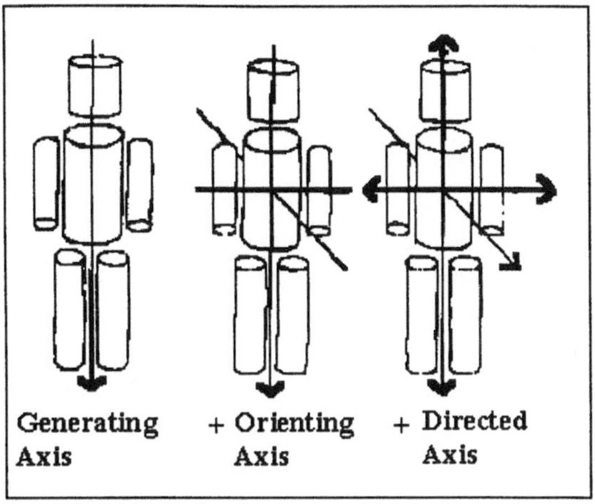

Figure 12. Three different kinds of axes are required to fully capture the differentiated set of spatial part terms—top, bottom, front, back, right, and left. See text for discussion. (Figure adapted from Landau & Jackendoff, 1993 by permission of publisher).

no direction.

The three orthogonal axes and their directional assignments thus serve as the representational basis for applying spatial region terms. This in turn implies that the geometric analysis of objects by our visual system that is linked to the use of linguistic part terms engages a geometric representation of objects. Although such geometric representations do not tell the whole story of how spatial part terms are applied (see Section 3.2.i), there is evidence that this aspect of object representation is foundational in the mapping between perception and language. First, the use of spatial part terms emerges in production between ages 2 and 3 (Clark, 1972). Terms that engage the object's main axis (i.e. top and bottom) appear to cause less difficulty for children than terms that engage the secondary or tertiary axes. Abundant literature attests to the difficulties children have in sorting out front and back (Kucjaz & Maratsos, 1975), and later, right and left. Children first sort out which axis is pertinent for which pairs of terms, and only later sort out which direction should be assigned to which term within the pair (E. Clark, 1972).

Second, the use of the geometric model for assignment of spatial part terms appears in languages world-wide, and most strikingly, in languages whose structure is quite different from English. Specifically, Levinson (1992) has described the nature of body-part terminology in Tzeltal, and argued that the use of these terms to designate spatial regions of objects stems from a strict algorithmic application of the principles embodied in visual object recognition. The Tzeltal system has a stock of terms -- like English-- that refer to human body parts, e.g. head, foot, back, belly, nose, etc. Also like English, these terms can be used to refer to parts of artifacts-- for example, we speak of the "head" of the table, the "foot" of the chair, etc. In Tzeltal, the use of body part terms to refer to artifact regions is more dense than in English; Levinson lists 14 different "core" body part terms that are regularly used to refer to spatial regions of artifacts. These terms can be applied in generative fashion-- to new as well as old objects-- but how?

Many authors have suggested that Tzeltal is a particularly "visual" language, and that the source body-parts are applied to artifact parts by a mechanism of metaphorical extension. That is, there is some loose connection between the source and destination, but it need not be highly regular nor systematic across users. Levinson argues that this view is wrong; and instead, that assignment is done by guidance from the visual system, which specifies which regions of objects should be named by which body part terms. Levinson's analysis draws on many of the same concepts in visual representation as we have already discussed. His analysis rests on Marr's view of object representation, and he especially links language to aspects of representation that may reside in lower levels of visual analysis, earlier than the final output of the visual system. For example, he points out that language engages aspects of visual representations -- such as axial structure-- which are not part of our everyday conscious awareness.

The application of Tzeltal body part terms in Levinson's analysis is a straightforward combination of axes and their directions, combined with more particular properties of an object's shape. For example, the main axis of an object, combined with direction, will generate the location of the "top" of an object-- which will receive the term "s-jol" (head-of) if it is not too pointed, and "s-ni" (nose-of) if it is pointed. The head of the secondary axis is usually called "s-pat" (back), and this is usually the surface with fewer features; the opposite end of this axis can be called "x-ch'ujt" (belly), and if it is flat, it is called "y-elaw" (face). As Levinson observes, there is some choice in the particular term that is applied to a given end of an axis, and this is usually determined by general shape characteristics of the region (e.g. pointedness, flatness, convexity, etc.).

The case of spatial parts terms, whether in English or Tzeltal provides a compelling example of how representations in the visual system must interface with the linguistic system, to provide the foundations for naming spatial regions. However, as we will see next, visual representations of objects do not completely account for the use of spatial part terms, raising again the possibility of a certain degree of independence between perceptual representations of objects and the language we use to talk about them.

3.2 Evidence, Part B: Where more than perception is required

i. Spatial regions depend on object function as well as geometry

The geometric approach to assigning spatial part terms is appealing in that the correspondence between vision and language appears to be fairly clear. Indeed, for novel objects that may be represented solely in terms of their geometric properties, the visual representations may provide both a necessary and sufficient means of naming regions. However, the assignment of spatial part terms to familiar objects appears to depend very much on the object's function, as well as other aspects of its category that are not clearly derivable from current theories of visual object representation. The importance of function in assignment of part terms has long been noted by linguists such as Fillmore (1975), who observed that the "front" of an animate object is typically that region having crucial functional features (such as eyes). These can be put into competition with other important properties (such as motion), and typically win, evidenced in the way we naturally express a crab's movement: It walks *sideways*.

Although observations such as these are well-known, there has been relatively little systematic work on the rules that people use in assigning spatial part terms to object regions (but see Carlson-Radvansky & Radvansky, 1996, for related work). Is the visual-geometric representation primary, or does it interact with functional knowledge? Does the primacy of geometric and functional information change over development? Our lab has begun to examine these issues by investigating how people apply spatial part terms to a wide range of common objects, including glasses, cameras, pieces of furniture, common writing and measuring utensils, etc. (see Figure 13 for some samples). In one experiment, the objects are presented to people in an plastic bag; they must retrieve them one at a time, and indicate the top, bottom, front, back, and side. People typically tend to retrieve objects and orient them as if in normal use, for example, retrieving the eyeglasses and holding them in front of the body oriented as if they were wearing them, retrieving a soda can and placing it upright in front of them, retrieving a toy dresser and placing it with the drawers facing their own body.

The patterns of labelling suggest that people construct "models" of different objects, with the models following from knowledge of the objects' functions as well as geometry. The parts are labelled in accord with these models. Because the functions of different objects

Figure 13. The assignment of spatial part terms to common everyday objects requires the construction of a mental model that includes both geometric and functional information. For example, considering the dresser, the camera, and the glasses, which parts should be called the top, bottom, front, back and side? For most people, the answer varies, depending on the particular object and its function. (Photographs courtesy of Nicole Kurz)

can vary so much, application of spatial part terms does not necessarily follow geometric principles across different objects. For example, for a camera and eyeglasses, spatial part terms are assigned such that top and bottom are consistent with gravitational up/down when holding the object as if it is to be used; back is assigned to the part through which the user looks, and front the part which faces the rest of the world. In contrast, pieces of furniture such as dressers have their front assigned as the part facing the user, i.e. the surface with drawerknobs is labelled front, and its spatial opposite the back. Other objects are labelled using top and bottom as their user-relevant regions: The tops of pencils are the region with the eraser, and the bottom the region with the point; the front is usually the surface with writing on it, and the back the region at the other end of the axis. In contrast, the tops of rulers are the surfaces with measurement indicators, the bottoms are the regions opposite to these (and blank); and the front and back are sometimes assigned by the same individual redundantly to these same regions (with top and front labelling the same region; bottom and back the same region.)

These observations clearly indicate that the assignment of spatial part terms relies not only on geometric considerations, but also world knowledge about the object and what it is used for. Geometric representations may interact with world knowledge from the earliest points in development, or one may precede the other. At present, it seems reasonable to conclude that the acquisition of spatial part terms may depend on both geometric and functional considerations; and that their relative use may depend on familarity with the object's category.

ii. The relationships among object parts in vision may be different from that in language

As described above, most vision theorists describe objects in terms of parts. In some theories, such as Marr and Nishihara (1978) additional parts can be added recursively, such that highly complex shapes can emerge from the constrained attachments of additional parts. For example, in Marr and Nishihara's model, the human body is composed of cylinders representing the torso and head; attached to the torso are cylinders representing arms and legs; the arms are further decomposed into upper and forearm; the forearm is attached to the hand, which is attached to the fingers.

How are the relationships among these parts specified in theories of vision? For the most part, the relationships only specify how individual parts are attached to each other, e.g. the knee-bone's connected to the leg-bone, the leg-bone's connected to the ankle-bone, etc. These attachment relationships can be expressed linguistically by spatial prepositions and verbs (attached to the top/ bottom/right/left, etc.). In fact, Biederman's theory specifies attachment relationships that could readily be translated into the set of spatial part terms, for example, attached END-TO-END, SIDE-TO-END, etc.

Yet our linguistic treatment of how parts are related reveals considerably more complexity than this limited set of attachment relationships. Transitivity relationships among parts adhere to certain rules that would seem to reside outside of our visual representations of objects, at least, in terms of currently available theories. For example, we might say that a house has a door, and that the door has a handle, but we would not claim that the house has a handle, even though these might be in sufficient spatial proximity that it could be merited on visual grounds. Cruse (1986) has suggested two causes of such transitivity failures. The first concerns what he calls "functional domain". Depending on context, superficially similar relationships might show transitivity in one case but not another. He gives the example of the door and handle (as above), in which transitivity fails, and contrasts it to the case in which we could say the jacket has sleeves, the sleeves have cuffs, and the jacket has cuffs. The difference, Cruse suggests, is that handles have functions that apply only to their immediately dominating node in some conceptual hierarchy-- in this case, the door, but not house. In contrast, cuffs have a decorative function that applies both to sleeves and jackets-- and so the function can be realized both locally (the sleeve) and more globally (the jacket). Whether Cruse is correct or not, it does seem striking that part-of relationships of this sort do not obey rules that could easily be applied from current visual theories.

Another kind of transitivity failure may be due to a conceptual (but not visual) distinction between parts that are integral parts of an object vs. parts that are "merely attached" to the rest of an object. As Cruse (1986) points out, one can describe parts that are merely attached using the predicate "attached", but one cannot do the same with integral parts. Thus, it is fine to describe a hand as being "attached"to the arm, but clearly the hand is not "part of" the arm. In contrast, the palm is "part of" the hand, but not "attached to" the hand. Cruse further notes that the contrast can be seen in the kinds of inferences that can be made. If I am touching the elbow (which is an integral part of the arm), I am also touching the arm; but if I am touching the hand (which is only an attachment, not a part of the arm), I am **not** touching the arm.

These diagnostics show that the relationship PART-OF is conceptually different from the kinds of relationships currently available in perceptual theories. In fact, Cruse concludes that, ultimately, "the question of whether a finger can be said to be part of an arm cannot be settled by examining human bodies-- it is a linguistic question." If he is correct, the relationship part-of will be captured most coherently by a level of representation that is distinct from our visual representation of objects.

3.3 Evidence, Part C: Learning affects how we form parts, and hence may affect how we come to name parts

Schyns and Murphy (1994) considered the relationship between the perceptual and conceptual representations of object parts, and proposed that these representations emerge from different constraints, and hence have quite different characteristics. They specifically considered the algorithm proposed by Hoffman and Richards (1984) and suggested that, although this scheme might be useful in explaining how the visual system extracts parts, it would not suffice to capture many important phenomena regarding human conceptualization of parts. Rather, Schyns and Murphy argued that the segmentation of objects into parts might also be driven by conceptual constraints, expressed specifically by their "functionality principle": "If a fragment of a stimulus categorizes objects (distinguishes members from nonmembers), the fragment is instantiated as a unit in the representational code of object concepts." (p. 310).

This principle predicts that our representation of objects parts can change radically as we undergo different learning experiences, especially those that require us to sort sets of objects into different categories. Thus, although the visual system might, in some cases, prefer to parse objects according to algorithms engaging either volumetric primitives (Biederman, 1987) or contour characteristics (Hoffman & Richards, 1984), these parsings will only be preserved as our representation of an object's parts to the extent that it serves to distinguish one set of objects from another. This view is consistent with E.J. Gibson's (1969) theory of perceptual learning, which emphasizes the flexibility of learning to pick up different properties, depending on the task. The implications of Schyns and Murphy's observations for part naming are enormous: It predicts that a single object's part structure will vary in accord with different learning experiences and that the development of part naming will rest importantly on higher-level conceptual processes and so may change over development. Schyns and Murphy also suggest that, contrary to many models of the relationship between perception and cognition, the importance of both factors in object parsing suggest that the two cannot be divided into "lower" or "early" processes vs. "higher" or "later" processes; rather, both kinds of mechanisms are tightly interrelated.

The evidence presented by Schyns and Murphy is compelling. In a preliminary experiment, they showed that people who observed simple pipe-like objects from multiple viewpoints (as in Figure 14) and were asked to circle the "parts" systematically violated parsing schemes that would obtain from existing visual parsing algorithms. For example, when asked to circle the "parts" of the tube, people tended to group together several distinguishable segments of the tube as a single part. Second, people actually created parts where there were no clearly distinguishable parts in the image. For example, because they observed two clear segments at the "tail" of the first figure, they later segmented the "tail" of the last figure into two parts corresponding to these segments-- even though there was no evidence from the pictured object for a boundary. Because people initially saw the tube with a two-part "tail", they later assumed that a similar object also had such a two-part tail. Schyns and Murphy liken this to our tendency to mentally parse the arm into an upper and lower arm, even when the entire arm is hidden by a sleeve.

The role of experience was more closely examined in a further series of elegant experiments which demonstrated that different learning experiences could lead to different parsing of the same objects. People were presented with complex random-looking "Martian

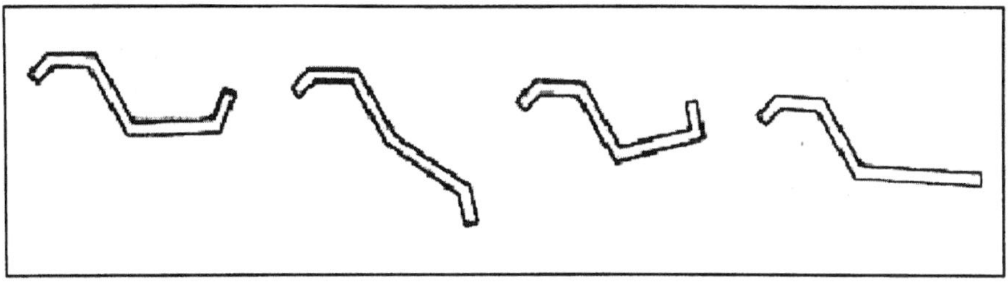

Figure 14. Pipe-like objects used by Schyns and Murphy (1994) to test the flexibility of perceived part-structure. Having parsed the tube-like object on the far left into five major parts, people often later parsed the object on the far right into five parts as well, even though no contour discontinuity marked the two parts in the "tail". Schyns and Murphy argued that our part-representations of objects are flexible, susceptible to experience and learning, and guided by high-level knowledge. (Figure reproduced from Schyns and Murphy by permission of publisher.)

rocks", which incorporated numerous bumps and protrusions. These bump-protrusion complexes were not salient as units prior to the learning experiences. For example, when naive subjects were asked to circle "parts" of the objects, they almost never circled the parts that they later learned.

However, people were then shown a set of Martian rocks and asked to study these so that they could learn what the rocks were like in general. One group of people saw five rocks for which one complex bump-protrusion chunk-- the target part-- was always present. People in a second group saw five rocks for which a different complex bump-protrusion chunk was present. Also contained in each study set was a single rock from the non-target group. After seeing each rock, people were asked to circle the target part. Over the learning trials, people came to correctly identify the target part, even though it was embedded in a highly complex configuration and was very complex itself. Learning was evident in the decreased number of non-target parts people circled as they moved through the learning trials.

Following this learning phase, people were exposed to a new group of objects in which the target parts from both rock groups were placed adjacent to each other within the new rocks. In addition to the people who had already been tested, a third group of subjects was included-- these people saw only the new rocks. After a set of learning trials with these new rocks, people from all three groups were asked to circle the "parts" of additional new rocks. The striking result was this: People who had originally seen target parts A now circled parts A and B as distinct parts. So did people who had originally seen target parts B. But people who had only seen the combination rocks (with parts A and B adjacent to each other), only circled the complex A-B part as a single unit. That is, the particular sets of objects people had seen during the learning phase led them to form qualitatively different part units, despite the fact that they were confronted during test with exactly the same novel rocks.

Schyns and Murphy argue that as people learned to identify parts critical to their target category, they also learned to reject units that were not important. They further argue that the process of learning can lead to the creation of novel parts, which come to have a status similar to existing familiar parts (such as wheel, handle, etc.). For Schyns and Murphy, these parts would then be a component of the representational battery that people use to categorize new objects.

3.4 Summary of Case 2

Just as with objects, the evidence on object parts suggests that the visual system has at its disposal the means to parse objects into coherent parts. However, the relationship between these visually parsed units and the linguistic assignment of terms to object parts is not directly determined by such parsing algorithms. Part terms may be consistent with visually parsed parts. However, they are not identical: Some visually parsed units never receive names, others may represent complex combinations of visually parsed units, parts may be formed through learning experiences, and the application of particular part terms to an object's region engages more than the object's geometry. Finally, as with objects names, part names appear to be governed by some principles that are not transparently available to the perceptual systems. The most obvious case of this concerns the relationships among object part terms, which often violate transitivity.

4.0 CONCLUSIONS

This chapter began with the observation that our capacity to talk about the spatial world is deceiving in its apparent simplicity: The remarkable ease with which we use language to talk about our perceived world might lead us to assume that a simple theory-- in which perception and language are exactly and perfectly redundant-- will explain how this is accomplished. The evidence reviewed, however, indicates that even some of the simplest cases of mapping between perceptual units and language can be quite complex. Some aspects of our representations of objects and their parts do not appear to be encoded in the representations we use to talk about objects and their parts. For example, the non-linguistic representation of an object's shape that we use for recognition is surely more detailed than our representation of the same object for the purposes of naming; our non-linguistic representation of object parts overdetermines what kinds of parts will be named. Symmetrically, some aspects of the language of objects and their parts do not appear to be encoded in the representations we use to perceive or understand objects and their parts. Examples include the encoding of object types and some conditions for tracing their identity, the encoding of object parts as they interact with functional knowledge, and the logic of how parts relate to each other.

How, then, are these different kinds of representations linked to each other? Forming a mapping across levels requires that different kinds of representations become bound together, presumably by connecting corresponding aspects of each representation-- aspects such as [OBJECT], or [PART-OF]. This binding would ensure that the other aspects of the representation -- which are not shared over levels-- are nevertheless systematically engaged as part of the representations of the word. Thus, underlying our capacity to talk about objects and parts are sets of highly complex representations, which are bound together by simple but fundamental commonalities. These rich representations emerge early in development, under widely diverse learning conditions, and with no formal tutoring. This, and our naive blindness to their complexity serves as a reminder of the ingenuity of the brain and mind in constructing for us a seamless world.

ACKNOWLEDGEMENTS

Preparation of this paper and results reported herein were supported in part by grants #12-0194 from the March of Dimes Foundation, 1 RO1 MH55240 from the NIMH, and 2 RO1 HD28675 from the NICHD. I thank Ray Jackendoff fcr helpful discussion of many of the issues treated in this chapter; and Andrea Zukowski, Nicole Kurz, and Swapnil Raman for assistance in preparing the chapter.

REFERENCES

Andersen, E. (1975). Cups and Glasses: Learning that boundaries are vague. *Journal of Child Language, 2*(1), 79-103.

Andersen, E. (1978) Lexical universals of body-part terminology. In J.H. Greenberg (Ed.), *Universals of human language*. Stanford, CA: Stanford University Press.

Baillargeon, R. (1995). Physical reasoning in infancy. In M.S. Gazzaniga (Ed.), *The cognitive neurosciences*, (pp. 181-204). Cambridge, Mass: MIT Press.

Baldwin, D. (1992). Clarifying the role of shape in children's taxonomic assumption. *Journal of Experimental Child Psychology, 54*, 392-416.

Behl-Chadha, G. (1996). Basic level and superordinate-like categorical representations in early infancy. *Cognition, 60*(2), 105-141.

Biederman, I. (1987). Recognition-by-components: A theory of human image understanding. *Psychological Review, 94*, 115-147.

Bloom, L. (1973) *One word at a time.* The Hague: Mouton.

Bloom, P. (1996). Intention, history, and artifact concepts. *Cognition, 60*, 1-29.

Bloom, P., Peterson, M., Nadel, L., and Garrett, M. (1996) *Language and space*. Cambridge, Mass: MIT Press.

Bowerman, M. (1996). Learning how to structure space for language: A cross linguistic perspective. In P. Bloom, M. A. Peterson, L. Nadel, & M. F. Garrett (Eds.), *Language and Space*. (pp. 385-436). Cambridge, MA: MIT Press.

Brown, A. (1990). Domain-specific principles affect learning and transfer in children. *Cognitive Science, 14*, 107-133.

Brown, R. (1958). *Words and things: An introduction to language*. New York: Free Press.

Carlson-Radvansky, L. & Radvansky, G. (1996) The influence of functional relations on spatial term selection. *Psychological Science, 7* (1), 56-60.

Clark, E. (1972). On the child's acquisition of antonyms in two semantic fields. *Journal of Verbal Learning and Verbal Behavior 11*, 750-758

Clark, E. (1973). What's in a word? On the child's acquisition of semantics in his first language. In T. E. Moore (Ed.), *Cognitive development and the acquisition of language* (pp. 65-110). New York: Academic Press.

Clark, H. (1973). Space, time semantics, and the child. In T. E. Moore (Ed.), *Cognitive Development and the acquisition of language*. New York: Academic Press.

Cruse, D. A. (1986). *Lexical semantics*. Cambridge: Cambridge University Press.

Davidoff, J., Davies, I., & Roberson, D. (1999). Colour categories in stone-age tribe. *Nature, 398*, 203-204.

Eimas, P., & Quinn, P. (1994). Studies on the formation of perceptually based basic-level categories in young infants. *Child Development, 65*(3), 903-917.

Fillmore, C. (1997). *Lectures on Deixis*. Stanford, CA: CSCI.

Fodor, J. A. (1998). *Concepts: Where Cognitive Science went wrong*. New York: Oxford University Press.

Gelman, S. & Taylor, M. (1984) How two-year-old children interpret proper and common names for unfamiliar objects. *Child Development, 55* (4): 1535-1540.

Gelman, S. A., & Wellman, H. M. (1991). Insides and Essences-Early understanding of the non-obvious. *Cognition, 38*(3), 213-244.

Gentner, D. (1978). What looks like a jiggy but acts like a zimbo? A study of early word meaning using artificial objects. *Papers and Reports on Child Language Development, 15*, 1-6.

Gentner, D. (1982). Why nouns are learned before verbs: Linguistic relative vs. natural partitioning. In S. Kuczaj (Ed.), *Language development: Language, culture, and cognition*. Hillsdale, NJ: Eribaum.

Gentner, D., & Boroditsky, L. (2000). Individuation, relativity and early word learning. In M. Bowerman & S. Levinson (Eds.), *Language acquisition and conceptual development*. Cambridge, England: Cambridge University Press, in press.

Gibson, E.J. (1969) *Principles of perceptual learning and development*. New York:

Appleton-Century Crofts.

Hall, D.G. (1994) Semantic constraints on word learning: Proper names and adjectives. *Child Development, 65*(5): 1299-1317.

Hall, D. G. (1998). Continuity and the persistence of objects: When the whole is greater than the sum of the parts. *Cognitive Psychology, 37*(1), 28-59.

Hayward, W., & Tarr, M. (1995). Spatial language and spatial representations. *Cognition, 55*, 39-84.

Heider, E. R., & Oliver, D. C. (1972). The structure of the color space in naming and memory for two languages. *Cognitve Psychology, 3*(2), 337-354.

Herskovits, A. (1986*). Language and spatial cognition: An interdisciplinary study of the prepositions in English.* Cambridge: Cambridge University Press.

Hobbes, T. (1672/1913). *Metaphysical system of Hobbes in twelve chapters.* Chicago, IL: Open Court Publishing. (Original work published 1672).

Hoffman, D., & Richards, W. (1984). Parts of recognition. *Cognition, 18*, 65-96.

Hoffman, D., & Singh, M. (1997). Salience of visual parts. *Cogntion, 63*(1), 29-78.

Imai, M., Gentner, D., & Uchida, N. (1994). Children's theories of word meaning: The role of shape similarity in early acquisition. *Cognitive Development, 9*(1), 45-75.

Jackendoff, R. (1983). *Semantics and cognition.* Cambridge, Mass: MIT Press.

Jackendoff, R. (1990) *Semantic structures.* Cambridge, Mass: MIT Press.

Jackendoff, R. (1996) The architecture of the linguistic-spatial interface. In P. Bloom, M.A. Peterson, L. Nadel, and M. F. Garrett (Eds.), *Language and space.* (pp.. 1-30). Cambridge, Mass: MIT Press.

Katz, N., Baker, E., & Macnamara, J. (1974). What's in a name? A study of how children learn common and proper names. *Child Development, 45*, 469-473.

Keil, F. (1989). *Concepts, Kinds, and Cognitive Development.* Cambridge, Mass: CambridgeUniversity Press.

Keil, F. (1994). Explanation, association, and the acquisition of word meaning. In L. Gleitman & B. Landau (Eds.), *The acquisition of the lexicon.* Cambridge, Mass: MIT Press.

Kellman, P. J., & Arterberry, M. E. (1998*). The cradle of knowledge: Development of perception in infancy*. Cambridge, MA: The MIT Press.

Kellman, P. J., & Spelke, E. S. (1983). Perception of partly occluded objects in infancy. *Cognitive Psychology, 15*(4), 483-524.

Kemmerer, D. (1999). "Near" and "far" in language and perception. *Cognition, 73(*1), 35-63.

Kuczaj, S. A., & Maratsos, M. P. (1975). On the acquisition of front, back, side. *Child Development, 46*, 202-210.

Landau, B. (2000). Linguistic and non-linguistic representations of space in children with Williams Syndrome: Evidence for reference systems. Manuscript in preparation.

Landau, B., & Jackendoff, R. (1993). "What" and "where" in spatial language and spatial cognition. *Behavioral and Brain Sciences, 16*, 217-265.

Landau, B., Jones, S., & Smith, L. (1992). Syntactic context and object properties in early lexical learning. *Journal of Memory and Language, 31*, 807-825.

Landau, B. and Leyton, M. (1999) Perception, object kind, and object naming. *Spatial Cognition and Computation,, 1* (1), 1-29.

Landau, B., & Shipley, E. (2000). Labelling patterns and object naming. *Developmental Science, 4* (1), 109-118.

Landau, B., Smith, L., & Jones, S. (1988). The importance of shape in early lexical learning. *Cognitive Development, 3*, 299-321.

Landau, B., Smith, L., & Jones, S. (1996) Object shape, object function, and object name. *Journal of Memory and Language, 36(*1): 1-27.

Landau, B., Smith, L., & Jones, S. (1998) Object perception and object naming in early development. *Trends in Cognitive Sciences, 2*(1), 19-24.

Leslie, A. M., Fei, X., Tremoulet, P. D., & Scholl, B. J. (1998). Indexing and the object concept: developing 'what' and 'where' systems. *Trends in Cognitive Science, 2*(1), 10-18.

Levinson, S. C. (1992). Vision, shape, and linguistic description: Tzeltal body-part terminology and object description. Working paper No. 12, Cognitive Anthropology Research Group, Max Planck Institute for Psycholinguistics.

Levinson, S. C. (1996). Frames of reference and Molyneux's question: Crosslinguistic evidence. In P. Bloom, M.A. Peterson, L. Nadel, & M. Garrett (Eds.), *Language and space*. Cambridge, Mass: MIT Press.

Leyton, N. (1992). *Symmetry, causality, mind.* Cambridge: MIT Press.

Macario, J. F. (1991). Young children's use of color in classification: Foods and canonically colored objects. *Cognitive Development, 6*(1), 17-46.

Malt, B. and Johnson, E.C. (1992) Do artifact concepts have cores? *Journal of Memory and Language, 31*, 195-217.

Malt, B. C., Sloman, S. A., Gennari, N. N. R., Shi, M. Y., & Wang, Y. (1999). Knowing versus naming: Similarity and the linguistic categorization of artifacts. *Journal of Memory and Language, 40*(2), 230-262.

Mandelbrot. (1982). *The fractal geometry of nature*. San Francisco, CA: Freeman.

Mandler, J.M. (1992) How to build a baby:II Conceptual primitives. *Psychological Review, 99* (4), 587-604.

Mandler, J.M. and Bauer, P.J. (1988) The cradle of categorization: Is the basic level basic? *Cognitive Development, 3* (3), 247-264.

Mandler, J.M. and McDonough, L. (1998) Studies of inductive inference in infancy. *Cognitive Psychology, 37* (1), 60-96.

Markman, E.M. (1989). *Categorization in children: Problems of induction.* Cambridge: Bradford/MIT Press.

Markman, E. M., & Wachtel, G. (1988). Children's use of mutual exclusivity to constrain the meanings of words. Cognitive Psychology, 20, 121-157.

Marr, D. (1982). *Vision. New York: Freeman.*

Marr, D., & Nishihara, H. (1978). Representation and recognition of the spatial organization of three-dimensional shapes. *Proceedings of the Royal Society of London B, 200*, 269-294.

Marr, D., & Vaina, L. (1982). Representation and recognition of the movement of shapes. *Proceedings of the Royal Society of London, 214*, 501-524.

Medin, D., & Ortony, A. (1989). Psychological essentialism. In S. Vosniadou & A. Ortony (Eds.), *Similarity and analogical reasoning*. New York: Cambridge University Press.

Miller, G., & Johnson-Laird, P. (1976). *Language and perception.* Cambridge,MA: Belknap Press.

Milner, A. D., & Goodale, M. A. (1995) *The visual brain in action.* Oxford: Oxford University Press.

Munnich, E., Landau, B., & Dosher, B. (2001) Spatial language and spatial representation: What is universal*? Cognition,*. in press.

Nelson, K. (1974). Concept, word, and sentence: Intercorrelations in acquisition and development. *Psychological Review, 81*, 267-285.

Putnam, H. (1977) Is semantics possible? In S. P. Schwartz (Ed.), *Naming, necessity, and natural kinds*. (pp. 66-101). Ithaca, N.Y.: Cornell University Press.

Quinn, P. C., & Eimas, P. D. (1996). Perceptual cues that permit categorical differentiation of animal species by infants. *Journal of Experimental Child Psychology, 63*(1), 189-211.

Regier, T. (1996). *The Human semantic potential: Spatial language and constrained connectionism*. Cambridge, MA: MIT Press.

Rosch, E., Mervis, C., Gray, W., Johnson, D., & Boyes-Braem, P. (1976). Basic objects in natural categories. *Cognitive Psychology, 8*, 382-439.

Scholl, B. J., & Pylyshyn, Z. W. (1999). Tracking multiple items through occlusion: Clues to visual objecthood. *Cognitive Psychology, 38*(2), 259-290.

Schyns, P. G., & Murphy, G. L. (1994). The ontogeny of part representation in object concepts. In D.L. Medin (Ed.), *The psychology of learning and motivation: Advances in research and theory, Vol. 31* (pp. 305-349). New York: Academic Press.

Singh, M., & Hoffman, D. D. (1997). Constructing and representing visual objects. *Trends in Cognitive Sciences, 1*(3), 98-102.

Singh, M., & Landau, B. (1998). Parts of visual shape as primitives for categorization. *Behavioral and Brain Sciences, 21*(1), 36.

Smith, L., & Heise, D. (2000) Infants' use of textural information to discriminate between artifacts and natural kinds. Manuscript submitted.

Smith, L., Jones, S., & Landau, B. (1992). Count nouns, adjectives, and perceptual properties in novel word interpretations. *Developmental Psychology, 28*(2), 273-286.

Smith, L., Jones, S., & Landau, B. (1996). Naming in young children: A dumb mechanism? *Cognition, 60*, 143-171.

Smith, L.B., Jones, S.S., Landau, B., Gershkoff-Stowe, L., and Samuelson, L. (2001) Object name learning provides on-the-job training for attention. *Psychological Science*, in press.

Soja, N. (1992). Inferences about the meaning of nouns: The relationship between perception and syntax. *Cognitive Development, 7*, 29-46.

Soja, N., Carey, S., & Spelke, E. (1991). Ontological categories guide young children's inductions of word meanings: Object terms and substance terms. *Cognition, 38*, 179-211.

Spelke, E., Gutheil, G., & Van de Walle, G. (1995). The Development of object perception. In S. M. Kosslyn & D. N. Osherson (Eds.), *Visual Cognition* (Vol. 2, pp. 297-330). Cambridge, MA: MIT Press.

Subrahmanyam, K., Landau, B., & Gelman, R. (1999). Shape, material and syntax: Interacting forces in child's learning in novel words for objects and substances. *Language and Cognitive Processes, 14*(3), 249-281.

Talmy, L. (1983). How language structures space. In H. Pick & L. Acredolo (Eds.), *Spatial orientation: Theory, research, and application*. New York: Plenum Press.

Tarr, M. J., & Bulthoff, H. H. (1995). Is human object recognition better described by geon structural descriptions or by multiple views- comment on Biederman and Gerhardstein (1993). *Journal of Experimental Psychology- Human Perception and Performance, 27*(6), 1494-1505.

Tarr, M. J., & Pinker, S. (1990). When does human object recognition use a viewer-centered reference frame? *Psychological Science, 1*(4), 253-256.

Waxman, S. R. (1990). Linguistic biases and the establishment of conceptual hierarchies: Evidence form preschool children. *Cognitive Development, 5*(2), 123-150.

Waxman, S., & Markow, D. (1995). Words as invitations to form categories: Evidence from 12 month-old infants. *Cognitive Psychology, 29*, 257-302.

Waxman, S.R.,& Senghas, A. (1992). Relations among word meanings in early lexical development. *Developmental Psychology, 28*(5), 862-873.

Willats, P. (1992) Seeing lumps, sticks, and slabs in silhouettes. *Perception, 21* (4), 481-496.

Woodward, A. L., Markman, E. M., & Fitzsimmons, C. M. (1994). Rapid word learning in 13- and 18-months olds. *Developmental Psychology, 30*(4), 553-566.

Woodward, A. L., & Markman, E. M. (1998). Early word learning. In D. K. Kuhn & R. S. Siegler (Eds.), *Handbook of Child Psychology: Cognition, Perception, and Language* (Fifth ed., Vol. 2, W. Damon, Ed.). New York: John Wiley & Sons, Inc.

III.

ATTENTION

Attention is hard to define, which is perhaps why William James began his definition by saying that "Everyone knows" what it is. While we might be hard pressed to provide a definition that is both brief and satisfactory, one might think of it as the interface at a given time between our knowledge of the world and the actual world. Yet this definition of 'attention' might also fit 'perception'. So what is the difference, or the relation, between perception and attention? Is the question complicated or merely confused? Lloyd Kaufman, in his 1974 book *Sight and Mind*, suggested that "One of the most fascinating anomalies in human thought is the prevalent notion that somehow perception and attention are distinct psychological processes." One way of distinguishing (and relating) perception and attention, suggested in early attention research, was that attention acts as a switch or filter among possible incoming sensory channels. Unfortunately, no simple version of this idea has prospered.

As researchers move beyond models in which attention acts as a filter selecting among competing sensory streams, and serving up its outputs for perception, the distinction between perception and attention becomes murky at best. The chapters in this section were written by some of the researchers who have begun to reveal the complex interactions between attention and perception in the domains of visual segmentation and grouping. The two chapters review basic findings showing that aspects of one domain influence the other, and present models of how that influence may arise. The chapter by James Enns and Vincent Di Lollo offers a novel approach to understanding how attention may influence the perception of a briefly glimpsed object. The chapter by Shaun Vecera and Marlene Behrmann provides an account for the observation that attending to a part of an object influences the way we process the rest of the object. They also review the research showing that perceptual grouping influences how we attend to the various parts of a scene.

From Fragments to Objects – Segmentation and Grouping in Vision
T.F. Shipley and P.J. Kellman (Editors)

5

AN OBJECT SUBSTITUTION THEORY OF VISUAL MASKING

James T. Enns and Vincent Di Lollo, Department of Psychology, University of British Columbia, Vancouver, Canada V6RT 1Z4

ABSTRACT

The brief presentation of a visual display, although clearly visible when shown by itself, can be rendered invisible by the subsequent presentation of a second visual display in the same location. Recent studies of *backward masking* of this kind have revealed several new effects that are not predicted by standard theories of masking. Among these are masking by four small dots that surround but that do not touch the target object, and masking by a surrounding object that remains on display after the target has been turned off. A critical ingredient in both these masking effects is the focus of spatial attention: almost no masking occurs if attention can be rapidly focused on the target, but powerful masking ensues if attention to the target is delayed. A new theoretical framework, inspired by recent developments in neuroscience, is described to explain both these and more traditional forms of masking. In addition to accounting for backward masking, this framework sheds light on several other active areas of vision research, including work on the attentional blink, inattentional blindness, and change blindness.

INTRODUCTION

Among the most widely used and powerful tools available to researchers of visual perception is that of masking. At the most general level, masking refers to a reduction in the visibility of a visual object (the target) that is caused by the presentation of a second object (the mask) close to the target in space or time. In the purely spatial domain, the visibility of a target is greatly reduced if nontarget items are also presented nearby, an effect aptly referred to as *crowding* (Bouma, 1970). Introducing a temporal interval between the target and mask objects leads to wonderfully complex interactions between spatial and temporal variables. For example, a target that is highly visible when presented briefly in isolation, can be made completely invisible by the later presentation of a nontarget object in the same spatial location, or even in nearby but nonoverlapping locations. *Backward masking* of this kind has its strongest influence, not when target and mask objects are presented simultaneously, as intuition might suggest, but rather when a brief interval of 50-100 milliseconds intervenes between the presentation of target and mask.

Spatial-temporal interactions such as these provide a unique glimpse into the workings of the visual system. They inform us of processes involved in the emergence of a percept that would otherwise remain hidden to the behavioral researcher. These include the amount of time required to form a percept that is immune from the influences of later presented objects (Averbach & Coriell, 1961), the spatial range of influence between multiple objects in the visual field (Brietmeyer, 1984), and the extent to which visual information is processed outside of conscious awareness (Debner & Jacoby, 1994).

In this chapter we summarize insights that have recently been gained through studies of visual masking. However, before setting out, it is important to point out that there are two rather distinct ways in which masking is used in modern studies of vision. On the one hand, masking is a tool of convenience in a large number of vision experiments. It is no secret among researchers that masking is a handy way to adjust the difficulty of a task so that accuracy falls into a measureable range (somewhere between chance levels of responding and perfection). An informal survey of a recent volume of *Perception & Psychophysics* (1999, Vol. 61) indicated that 14 of 93 (15%) articles on vision used some form of backward masking. A typical stated rationale for backward masking is that it limits visual access to the target for a controlled period of time; the mask is said to erase the target from the mind. A second and much smaller group of researchers use masking to investigate the fine-grained spatial and temporal aspects of perception. The same journal volume contained only 5 (5%) articles in which masking itself was under investigation. We therefore hasten to add that although the present chapter may at times seem written primarily for this smaller second audience, the new insights into visual masking have implications that are equally important for those using masking as a tool of convenience, as they are for those studying the perceptual mechanisms of masking.

THE STANDARD VIEW OF VISUAL MASKING

Visual masking that involves both spatial factors (patterns or forms) and temporal factors (pattern durations and interstimulus intervals) is typically divided into two types, based on the spatial relations that exist between the contours in the target and mask patterns. Masking that involves spatial superposition of contours (although these contours may be separated in time) is commonly refered to as *pattern masking*; when it involves closely adjacent but nonoverlapping contours it is called *metacontrast*. These two forms of masking are differentiated not only by these well-defined spatial relations between target and mask contours, but they are generally believed to depend on different underlying mechanisms.

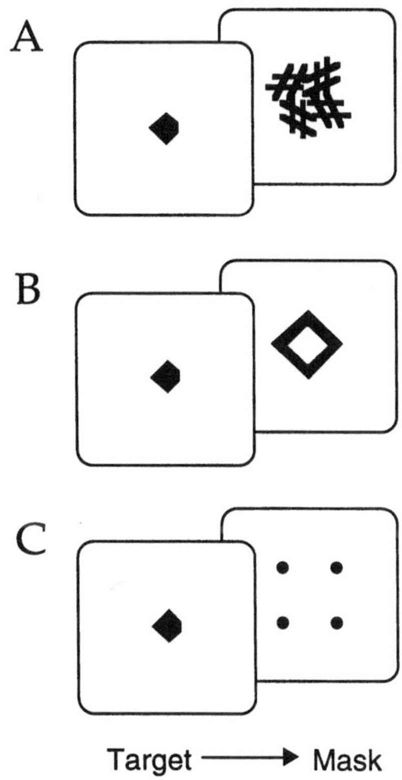

Figure 1. Three different potential masking stimuli in experiments in which observers attempt to identify a briefly presented target followed by the mask. The observer's task is to indicate which corner of the diamond has been removed. (A) Pattern mask: Contours of the mask are spatially superimposed on the contours of the target. (B) Metacontrast mask: Mask contours fit snugly around but do not overlap the target contours. (C) Four-dot mask: Four small dots surround the target. There are no standard theories which predict that masking will occur with the four-dot mask.

Typical examples of stimuli used in each of these kinds of masking experiments are shown in Figures 1a and 1b. In contrast to these masks, Figure 1c is a new type of masking display that we will have more to say about after reviewing the standard masking effects.

Pattern masking presents the visual system with two different kinds of spatio-temporal conflict. One conflict occurs when the target and mask are perceived as part of the same unitary pattern, a consequence of the imprecise temporal resolution of the visual system. In this case, masking is akin to the addition of spatial noise (the mask) to the signal (the target) at early levels of visual representation and so is referred to as masking by *integration* (Breitmeyer, 1984; Kahneman, 1968; Scheerer, 1973; Turvey, 1973). The temporal signature of this form of masking is approximate symmetry around a maximum level of masking at a stimulus onset asynchrony (SOA) of 0 ms, with a complete release from masking beyond an SOA of about 100 ms in each direction.

A second conflict arises when processing of a first pattern (the target) is interrupted by a second pattern (the mask) that appears in the same spatial location before the target pattern has been fully processed. This conflict does not involve the early stages of processing where contours are defined, but instead involves a competition for the higher-level mechanisms involved in object recognition. It is referred to as masking by *interruption* and is aptly described by an analogy in which targets and masks are "customers" coming before the "clerk" of the visual system (Kolers, 1968). The amount of time the clerk spends with the first customer (the target) is sharply curtailed if a second customer (the mask) enters the store. The temporal characteristics are also very different from masking by integration. Interruption masking can occur only when the mask follows the target in time. Therefore, the masking function is referred to as U- or J-shaped, because target accuracy is often lowest at SOAs that are greater than zero, before it begins to improve at even longer SOAs (Bachmann & Allik, 1976; Michaels & Turvey, 1979). An illustration of how perception varies with mask SOA is shown in Figure 2.

In addition to being distinguishable by their temporal signatures, pattern masking processes are dissociable by manipulations of stimulus properties (which influence integration masking) and informational attributes (which influence interruption masking). For example, increasing the luminance contrast of the target diminishes the integration masking effect, whereas increasing the contrast of the mask increases it. At the same time, manipulations of contrast have little if any effect on interruption masking (Breitmeyer, 1984; Spencer & Shuntich, 1973). Conversely, presenting a varying number of potential target items from trial to trial (i.e., a manipulation of set size) has very little effect on masking by integration, although it works powerfully to increase masking by interruption (Breitmeyer, 1984; Spencer & Shuntich, 1973; Turvey, 1973).

Metacontrast masking occurs when a target shape is displayed that fits closely around

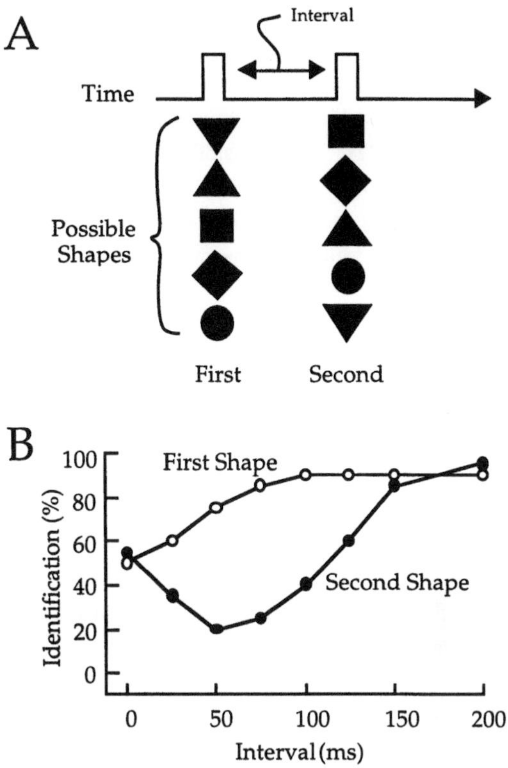

Figure 2. Backward pattern masking is often U- or J-shaped, referring to the finding that the largest influence of the mask occurs when the mask follows the target with a stimulus onset asychrony (SOA) of 100-150 milliseconds. (A). Two shapes are presented briefly in the same visual location, separated by a variable interval. (B). Identification accuracy for the first (open symbols) and second (closed symbols) as a function of interstimulus interval. Redrawn based on Bachmann & Allik, 1976.

the contours of one or more masking shapes (Alpern, 1953; Breitmeyer, 1984; Werner, 1953). Importantly, it only occurs within a narrow band of temporal intervals. When the interval between the brief presentations of target and mask is either very brief or very long, the target is clearly visible. At intermediate SOAs, however, perception of the target is impaired, leading to a U-shaped function of accuracy over SOA. The main mechanisms thought to be at work here involve inhibitory interactions between neurons representing the contours of the target and the mask (Breitmeyer & Ganz, 1976; Macknik & Livingstone, 1998; Weisstein, Ozog & Szoc, 1975). The main idea in these "two-channel" theories is that the onset of each shape initiates neural activity in two channels; one that is fast acting but short lived, the other slower acting but longer lasting. The faster channel signals stimulus onset; while the slower channel contains information about shape and color. Metacontrast masking occurs when the faster acting signals from the mask onset inhibit the activity of slower signals carrying information about the earlier target. In addition to the temporal aspects of metacontrast, a key piece of evidence consistent with this theory concerns the exquisite relationship between masking strength and contour proximity (Breitmeyer, 1984; Growney, Weisstein & Cox, 1977). Target visibility is sharply increased as the proximity between target and mask contours is increased, with little masking occuring beyond separations of 0.3 degrees near the fovea. The same contour proximity relations exist outside the fovea, although they appear scaled to the decreased spatial acuity that occurs with eccentricity.

FINDINGS THAT DO NOT FIT THE STANDARD VIEW

Although these standard views are able to account for a vast portion of the empirical data on visual masking, there are several persistent findings that complicate the picture. Consider first the perceptual fate of masked targets. In the standard view, backward masking by pattern is said to terminate the processing of the target at a precategorical level (Kolers, 1968; Turvey, 1973). However, a phenomenon known as *masked priming* indicates that, despite the masking, processing of the target continues to lexical and even semantic levels. In typical priming experiments, a target is identified more easily if it is preceded by a semantically-related prime word (Cheesman & Merikle, 1986; Meyer, Schvaneveldt, & Ruddy, 1975). In masked priming, the prime word is followed by a spatially superposed pattern so that observers cannot report it. Yet, the same facilitation is found in masked priming as in typical priming (Debner & Jacoby, 1994; Marcel, 1983a; 1983b; Cheesman & Merikle, 1986). Masked priming has also been obtained when primes and targets are inserted in a rapid visual stream of distractor items that act as masks (Shapiro, Driver, Ward & Sorensen, 1997). Clearly then, backward masking does not interrupt target processing at an early level, as claimed by extant theories. What appears to be disrupted is not the visual analysis of a masked target, but the access to this analysis by conscious processes. Despite being unavailable to consciousness, masked targets nonetheless influence events at advanced stages of processing.

A second finding that is difficult to reconcile with the standard view is that there is little evidence of suppression of the target signal by a backward mask when direct neurophysiological measures are taken. An example involving pattern masking comes from a study of event-related potentials (ERPs) in which observers tried to detect words embedded in a rapid visual stream of random letter strings (Luck, Vogel & Shapiro, 1996; Vogel, Luck & Shapiro, 1998). In this case, each subsequent letter string acts as a backward mask for the previous item, serving to sharply reduce accuracy for the target word in some conditions. Yet many of the ERP signals associated with the target word (e.g., P1, N1, N400) were indistinguishable for the conditions in which behavioral masking did and did not occur. The one ERP signal that did show evidence of target suppression was the P3 component, a signal widely believed to reflect the conscious contents of working memory.

A similar story applies to metacontrast masking. Single-unit microelectrode recordings from cat and monkey visual cortex show that masking is associated with a reduction in peak responses occurring only beyond 80 ms and as late as 400 ms after stimulus onset (Bridgeman, 1975; 1980; 1988; von der Heydt, Friedman, Zhou, Komatsu, Hanazawa & Murakami, 1997). Contrary to expectations from two-channel theories, early visual components are affected minimally, if at all. Homologous results have been obtained for ERP recordings in humans (Jeffreys & Musselwhite, 1986; Vaughn, 1969). At the same time, optical imaging techniques show that cells in area V1 in monkey that are positioned to signal a target shape are suppressed when closely surrounded by masking shapes that lead to perceptual masking (Macknik & Haglund, 1999). This leaves us with the paradox that while some measures indicate no suppression of the the early visual signal from a masked target, other suggest that the earliest stages of visual processing are indeed influenced by a masking stimulus. As we will see, this paradox is resolved by the idea of cortical 'multiplexing' (Bridgeman, 1980, Mumford, 1992), with the same neurons participating in different computations at various stages in the processing of a visual display.

Finally, current thinking is not easily accommodated to the notion that spatial attention plays an important role in visual masking. We mentioned earlier that one of the distinguishing characteristics of integration versus interruption mechanisms was their differential sensitivity to attentional manipulations such as set size (Spencer & Shuntich, 1970). Yet, there have been no theories of interruption masking in which increases in set size are predicted to result in larger masking effects. The same is true for metacontrast masking. It was reported as early as 1961 (Averbach & Coriel) that a ring used as a backward mask had no influence on the report of a single letter, while the same ring effectively masked the letter when it was accompanied by 3 other letters in the target display. However, this finding was not followed up by subsequent theoretical developments (Breitmeyer, 1984). Recently, it has also been demonstrated that metacontrast masking is modulated by the way in which the observer subjectively organizes an ambiguous display (Ramachandran & Cobb, 1995). Clearly, all forms of masking await an account in which spatial attention plays an integral role in the masking that occurs.

FORMS OF MASKING THAT DEFY THE STANDARD VIEW

In our lab we have been exploring two new forms of masking over the past several years that are particularly difficult to assimilate into the standard views. Here we give only a brief introduction to these forms of masking in order to give the reader a flavor of the phenomena that need to be explained. Interested readers can experience these masking effects first hand through demonstrations on the world wide web (http://www.interchange.ubc.ca/enzo/osdescr.htm) and can read about them in greater detail in other papers (Di Lollo, Bischof & Dixon, 1993; Di Lollo, Enns & Rensink, 2000; Enns & Di Lollo, 1997).

The first form of masking occurs when a briefly presented target is followed by four dots that surround, but that do not touch, a target shape (Enns & Di Lollo, 1997). Standard theories predict no masking in this case, since the four dots are neither a pattern that is superimposed on the target, nor do they contain contours that closely surround the target contours. Nonetheless, strong masking does occur. Furthermore, four dot masking is critically dependent on the target shape appearing in unpredictable locations, or on the presence of other nontargets in the display. When attention can be focused on the target location prior to target-mask sequence, no masking occurs. On the other hand, when attention cannot be focused prior to the arrival of the target, backward masking ensues. An illustration of stimuli from a four dot masking experiment is shown in Figure 1C.

The second form of masking occurs when a brief display of a metacontrast-like target shape plus mask is continued with the mask shape alone (Di Lollo, Bischof & Dixon, 1993). The temporal relations among stimuli in this form of masking are illustrated in Figure 3. We refer to this as masking by *common onset* because there is no longer a temporal interval between the onsets of the target and mask. Target and mask come into view simultaneously,

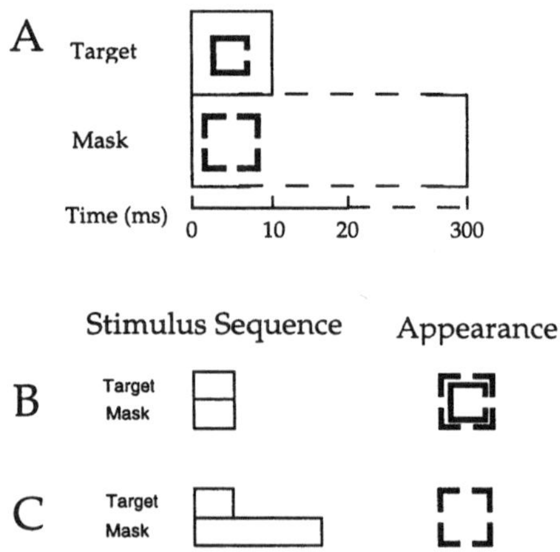

Figure 3. Schematic representation of the stimulus sequence in common-onset masking. (A) The sequence begins with a combined display of the target and the mask. After a brief period, the target is turned off, and the mask remains on view alone for various durations which can include a duration of zero. (B) When the duration of the trailing mask is equal to zero, the target and the mask both start and end together. In this case, both stimuli are seen clearly and distinctly. (C) When the duration of the trailing mask exceeds about 100-150 ms, the target is not seen, and the area within the mask appears empty.

followed by the termination of only those parts of the display that belong to the target. Notably, no masking occurs if the brief presentation of target and mask terminate simultaneously, indicating that the duration and contrast of the display items are sufficient to support perception. Yet, a small postponement in the termination of the mask begins to yield masking, with masking increasing in strength along with mask duration, until an asymptote is reached at a mask duration of 150 ms or so. This is clearly a form of masking that is not predicted by the previously described mechanisms of *integration* (which would incorrectly predict maximum masking at a mask duration of 0 ms), *interruption* (which depends on a second pattern to interrupt processing of the first), or *metacontrast* (which depends on a fast acting signal associated with the mask co-occuring with the slower signal of the target). Instead, the key ingredient for common onset masking appears to be that the mask remains on view following the termination of the target.

These two new forms of masking were recently combined in a series of experiments in which an initial brief display, consisting of several potential targets plus four small dots surrounding one of the items, was followed without interruption by a second display containing only the same four small dots. The observer's task was to report the item singled out by the four dots (Di Lollo, Enns & Rensink, in press). As shown in Figure 4, little or no

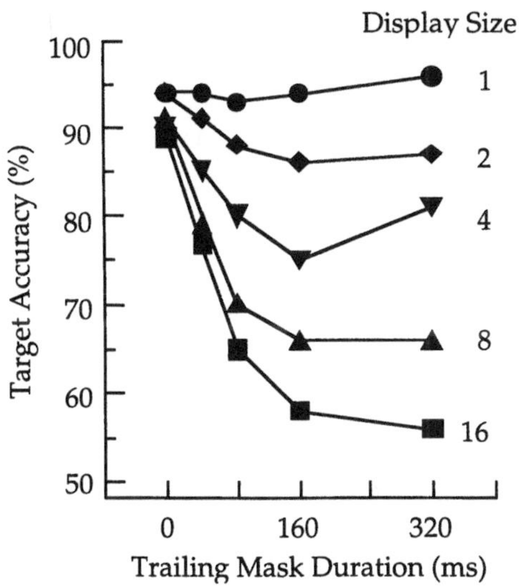

Figure 4. Target identification accuracy in a four-dot masking study (Di Lollo, Enns & Rensink, in press, Experiment 3). No masking occurs when attention can be rapidly deployed to the target location, as occurs for set size equals one. Accuracy is also affected little by increases in set size, provided that the four-dot mask terminates with the target display. However, pronounced masking occurs as both set size and mask duration are increased. According to the object substitution hypothesis, this occurs because the representation of the unattended target has been replaced by the mask representation before target identification could be completed.

masking occurred when the number of potential targets was one or when the mask terminated along with the target display. In contrast, pronounced masking occurred when several potential targets were displayed and when the mask remained on view following target display termination. Other experiments in the same study indicated that little masking occurred, even with a large display size, if the target differed from all other nontarget items by a very distinctive feature, or when the four dots preceded the target display by 90 ms. These findings indicate that common onset masking by four dots is critically dependent on the focus of spatial attention.

AN ACCOUNT OF MASKING BASED ON CORTICAL REENTRY

Our views on masking emerged from a desire to incorporate recent advances in neuroscience into thinking on the psychophysics of masking. Our starting point was the principle that communication between two brain areas is never one way. If a source area sends signals to a target area, then the target area sends signals back to the source area through reentrant pathways (Damasio, 1994; Felleman & Van Essen, 1991; Zeki, 1993). Two aspects of this connectivity are especially salient for masking. First, most visual centres have reentrant connections with area V1, which is where stimulation first enters the cortex. Thus, neurons in V1 can be activated by reentrant fibers from extrastriate cortex (Bullier, McCourt & Henry, 1988; Mignard & Malpeli, 1991). Second, it is a general rule that the size of the receptive fields is smallest in V1 and increases progressively in higher centres. Because a receptive field in V1 is small, any given unit has no way of "knowing" whether the external stimulus is an isolated edge or part of a more complex configuration. By the same token, a high-level unit might "know" the total configuration, but not its exact spatial location. However, an ongoing exchange of information between levels can be used to resolve this issue.

Numerous examples illustrating these principles have now been reported using single-unit recordings in visual cortex of cat and monkey (Hupe, James, Payne, Lomber, Girard & Bullier, 1998; Sillito, Jones, Gerstein & West, 1994; Lamme, Zipser & Spekreijse, 1997). They suggest that cortical reentrant signals are used to test for the presence of specific patterns in the incoming activity. It is as though the circuits actively search for a match between a descending code representing a perceptual hypothesis and the initial pattern of low-level activity. When such a match is found, the neural ensemble is "locked" onto the stimulus. For example, in one study, responses from V1 neurons were recorded in awake monkeys fitted with chronic microelectrode implants, viewing a textured figure on a background (Lamme et al., 1997). In the first part of the study, three stages of processing were revealed in the neural response. In the first 80 ms following stimulus onset, neurons responded only to local features presented within their receptive fields. Between 80-120 ms the same neurons began to respond to figure boundaries outside of their traditionally defined receptive fields. Finally, after about 120 ms the neurons responded to the surface of the figure. The authors concluded that the neurons in area V1 participate first in local feature detection, then in high-order boundary detection, and then in figure-ground assignment. In the second part of the study direct evidence of reentrant processing was obtained after the animals underwent extensive lesioning to extrastriate cortex ipsilateral to the recording site. After surgery, the V1 activity corresponding to the first two stages was still very much in evidence, but the V1 activity corresponding to figure-ground processing was missing. Behaviourally, the animals were no longer capable of distinguishing figure from ground. This indicates that reentrant processing is critical for establishing the sensitivity of V1 neurons to global attributes of a display.

We recently incorporated these neuroscience finding into a computational model of masking (Di Lollo, Enns & Rensink, in press). The central assumption is that perception is based on the activity of three-layer modules similar to that illustrated in Figure 5, arrayed over the visual field. Each module can be conceptualized as a circuit involving the connections between cortical area V1 and a topographically related region in an extrastriate visual area. The output of each module is a representation of the spatial pattern within its receptive field.

Although we do not describe the model in detail here, we summarize the behavior of the model in response to two different kinds of displays: a brief display in which the target and a four dot mask terminate together, and the identical display with the exception that the four dot mask remains on view after the target has been turned off. As shown in the data in

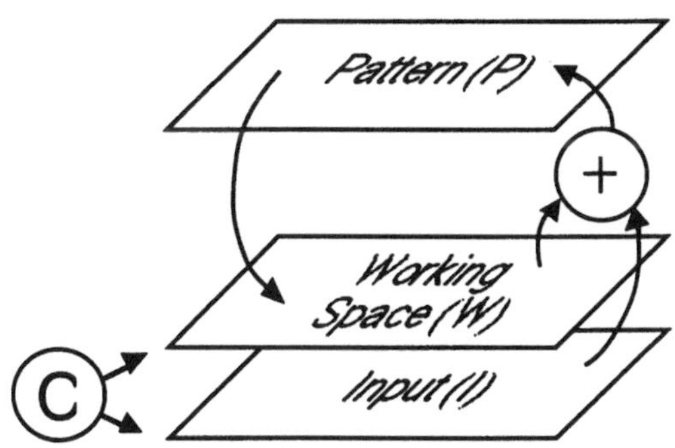

Figure 5. A computational model for object substitution (Di Lollo, Enns & Rensink, in press). A large number of three-layer modules, such as the one shown here, are arrayed over the visual field. Stimuli from the visual field arrive at the Input Layer, where the receptive fields are small, the features coded are simple, and activation decays rapidly unless maintained by continued visual input. The contents of the Input Layer are summed with the current contents of Working Space, and sent to the Pattern Layer, where the receptive fields are much larger and code for more complex patterns.

Figure 4 and in the demonstrations on the internet, only the latter display produces masking by four dots, which increases in strength as a function of mask duration.

The onset of a new visual event initiates activity in all layers on the first cycle. The activity in the Pattern Layer is then fed back to the Working Space by means of a simple overwriting operation. In this transfer, pattern information is translated back to the pixel-like codes of the Input Layer, permitting a direct comparison. This comparison is necessary because the initial wave sent to the Pattern Layer may have been unclear, it may activated more than one pattern, and because the spatial resolution of the Pattern Layer is inherently coarse. If the code in the Pattern Layer is to be successfully bound to its actual display location, it is necessary that the reentrant signals be placed in spatial registration with the active signals in the Input Layer.

Most important for masking is that the contents of the Input Layer change dynamically with new visual input. The contents of the Pattern Layer change more slowly because its input is a weighted sum of what is currently in the Input Layer and what was in the Working Space on the previous iteration. This produces a degree of inertia in response to changes in input that is an unavoidable consequence of reentrant processing. If the visual input changes during this critical period of inertia, masking will ensue. We refer to this process as *object substitution* because the emerging representation of a target in the Pattern Layer has been replaced by the emerging representation of the mask as the object occupying a given spatial location.

A Brief Display in Which all Items Terminate Together

The onset of the display triggers activity in the lower levels of the visual system, leading to the formation of a tentative shape hypothesis at higher levels. Such hypotheses require verification because the initial signal may have been unclear, it may even have activated more than one hypothesis, and because the larger receptive fields at the higher levels do not preserve precise location information. These ambiguities can be resolved by comparing the high-level codes with the ongoing low-level activity generated by the initial stimulus. Broadly conceived, these iterations of reentrant activity can be regarded as a binding process in which specific visual features are linked to the appropriate objects in space. When all items in the display terminate together, activity in the lower levels begins to subside, yielding the phenomal experience of rapidly fading visible persistence. As the common onset masking data show (see Figure 4), observers are able to identify a target very accurately when all briefly presented display items begin and terminate together.

A Brief Display in Which the Mask Continues as a Trailing Pattern

When the target items are turned off first, leaving only the four-dot mask in the target location, an ambiguity is created as to the identity of the target. The ongoing activity at low levels in the system now consist only of an image of the mask, despite the fact that earliest descending signals were generated by an hypothesis consistent with the target. Given this kind of a conflict, what is perceived will depend on the number of iterations required for target identification. If only a few iterations are required, the task may be completed before the signal from the target has faded completely and the four-dot percept has grown too strong. However, if more iterations are needed the probability that the "mask alone" percept will replace the "target plus mask" percept grows rapidly. At the longest mask durations, only the four dots of the mask are perceived, with the area between the dots appearing empty.

The object substitution model therefore accounts in a very natural way for the relation between masking and spatial attention. Because the main mechanism involves successive iterations of reentrant processing, any variable that increases the number of iterations required to identify a target will also increase the strength and the temporal course of backward masking. One of the best known ways to delay target identification is to distribute spatial attention widely over the visual field or even to explicitly misdirect attention to nontarget locations (Posner, 1980). This delay seems to reflect a fundamental limit on the number of items that can be consciously attended at any time (Pashler, 1994; Pylyshyn & Storm, 1988). Our model incorporated this aspect of perception by assuming that attention is deployed to the location of the target as a joint function of set size (Treisman & Gelade, 1980), the degree of similarity among items (Duncan & Humphreys, 1989; Wolfe, Cave & Franzel, 1989) and whether a spatial pre-cue had been presented before the onset of the search array (Eriksen, 1995).

In addition to providing a useful framework for masking by four dots and by common onset, the object substitution model can account for the standard masking effects. Indeed, seen from this perspective, there is no difference in principle between masking with common onset and the broad characteristics of metacontrast and pattern masking. All forms of backward masking will be subject to the consequences of having the representation of a temporally leading target being replaced by that of the mask if it follows closely in time and appears at the same location before target identification is complete. We fully expect that there will be minor differences unique to each form of masking, with for example, metacontrast masking having specific types of local contour interactions that are not shared by pattern masking or masking by four dots. However, the critical requisite for *object substitution* that all forms of backward masking share, is that the mask continue to be visible during the period in which the iterations between higher level pattern representations and lower level contour representations are likely to occur.

Finally, the object substitution model makes sense of a number of findings in the masking literature that until now have posed genuine puzzles for the standard view. For instance, it is now easier to understand why both pattern masking (Spencer & Shuntich, 1970) and metacontrast (Averbach & Coriel, 1961), which ostensibly have such different mechanisms, are similar when set size is varied: very little masking when the target is the only item on the display, along with pronounced masking of the same item when the target is one of several display items. As was the case for the masking by four dots (see Figure 4), by the time spatial attention has been deployed to the target location in the larger displays, only the mask item is available for conscious report.

A second result that is easily explained by the object substitution model is the somewhat curious finding that the effectiveness of a backward mask increases with mask duration (Dixon & Di Lollo, 1994). Neither the standard views of interruption masking (based on the termination of target processing) nor those of metacontrast (based on channel inhibition) predict that a mask's influence will increase with its duration. The object substitution model, however, makes precisely this prediction, since a mask of longer duration will be more likely to complete and reinforce the iterative pattern confirmation process. As the common onset masking experiments show, this prediction is borne out in the data (Di Lollo, Enns & Rensink, in press).

Third, the object substitution model predicts that a mask will do more than simply terminate target processing; the mask will itself become the new focus of object identification mechanisms. This predicted substitution has been observed quite directly in studies conducted on visual masking in rapid serial visual presentations (Chun, 1997; Martin, Isaak & Shapiro, 1995). When observers fail to correctly report the identity of a masked target, their false reports are usually for the item that follows, and therefore has masked, the target. Of course, this effect is much more difficult to observe in traditional studies of pattern and metacontrast masking because the observer is almost never asked to report directly on their perception of the mask.

Fourth, the object substitution model has a ready explanation for the large imbalance that it known to exist between forward and backward masking effects. As reviewed earlier, forward masking, when it is even observed, has a very narrow temporal window and is fully accounted for by the inherent temporal smearing of the visual system, which reduces it to the mechanisms of masking by spatial crowding and noise integration. Backward masking, on the other hand, has a much wider temporal window and is often much larger in magnitude. As we have also discussed, both of these characteristics can be easily exaggerated through manipulations of set size (Spencer & Shuntich, 1970) and target-mask similarity (Breitmeyer, 1984). This large bias favoring the effectiveness of backward masking is exactly what is predicted if the primary mechanism involves the replacement of an emerging object representation with another because the initial representation has been contradicted by subsequent input.

Fifth, it is important to note that object substitution is agnostic with respect to how conscious perceptual processes differ from non-conscious ones. Previous theories of masking made the prediction that non-conscious priming should not occur, because the mechanisms of masking are at a level prior to complete target identification. Object substitution is not burdened by such constraints, as it merely assumes that attention is space- and time-limited. If the sensory input has changed before attention can be devoted to the target item, then masking will occur, meaning that the identity of the target will not be consciously accessible. However, this in no sense rules out the possibility that mechanisms not available to consciousness may have processed the target to the extent that it influences other processes.

Object Substitution and Visual Attention

One of the most important practical implications to arise from our understanding of object substitution is that backward visual masking does not merely terminate the processing of a target display. Rather the perceptual processes associated with conscious perception will now be actively engaged in perception of the mask. In addition to helping us understand why masks that are visually similar to the target are generally the most effective (Breitmeyer, 1984), this observation makes it clear that the characteristics of the mask chosen in a given experiment will themselves play an important role in the determination of task performance. As such, if a mask is being used to control task difficulty, one should always consider how the mask itself may be influencing performance.

An example of this cautionary principle can be seen in recent research on the *attentional blink,* in which perception of the second of two briefly presented targets is impaired if it is presented with a temporal lag of up to 500 ms after the first target (Shapiro, 1994). For example, observers may be asked to report the identity of two letters inserted into a visual stream of digits. Although accuracy of report for the first letter is nearly perfect, accuracy in identifying the second letter is reduced substantially. This deficit has been attributed to the second target being unattended while processing resources are devoted to the first target. However, it has long been recognized that the second target must be masked in order for the attentional blink to occur. Ostensibly, the purpose of masking is to increase the difficulty of processing the second target, thereby bringing accuracy within a measurable range. But if this were the principal function served by masking, then either simultaneous (integration) or backward (interruption) masking should produce the same effect, and the second target deficit should be found using either procedure.

In fact, the accuracy deficit occurs in this task only if backward masking is used (Brehaut, Enns & Di Lollo, 1999; Giesbrecht & Di Lollo, 1998). If a simultaneous mask is used, identification of the second target is impaired equally across all lags, but the lag-dependent deficit that is the hallmark of the attentional blink is missing. This points to object substitution as the mechanism of masking. That is, while unattended, the second target is vulnerable to replacement by the trailing mask. As a consequence of this replacement, the mask is substituted for the second target as the object for eventual conscious registration. On the basis of these results, it is clear that backward masking of the second target is more than a methodological convenience: it reveals the workings of mechanism that would have gone undetected had masking been used merely as a tool of convenience.

We believe that masking by object substitution also has direct relevance to the recently popularized phenomena of 'inattentional blindness' and 'change blindness.' Consider first *inattentional blindness*, which refers to objects that are presented to the visual system but not seen because the observer is attending to something else (Mack & Rock, 1998). A typical way of studying this involves a procedure in which observers are asked to report which of two intersecting lines is longer in a brief display. These lines can be presented either at the fovea or in the periphery, and the task can be made arbitrarily difficult by varying the difference in length between the horizontal and vertical lines. After 3 or 4 trials of this task have been completed, a critical stimulus is presented unexpectedly in one quadrant of the crossed lines, about 2 degrees from the center. The observer is then asked whether they have seen anything on the screen other than the cross figure, that is, anything that has not been present on previous trials. A large variety of stimuli presented in this way go undetected by observers. Not only do observers deny seeing anything new, but they are unable to describe what it looks like when asked to guess, nor are they able to select the correct item when it is shown to them again in a recognition test.

One of the details of the inattentional blindness procedure that has not been given much consideration is the role played by a pattern mask, which is presented immediately following the display of the intersecting lines and remains on view for 1.5 s. The authors use the mask for the conventional purpose of preventing any additional processing of the display after it is removed from the screen. However, the object substitution hypothesis predicts that it is perception of the mask that interferes directly with access to the briefly presented and undetected targets. More specifically, it predicts that inattentional blindness will increase directly with the duration of the mask.

Change blindness refers to a phenomenon in which large changes to the visual world go undetected if attention is not already focused on the objects or area in which the change occurs. Some of the earliest reports involved observers who did not notice changes made during an eye movement while inspecting a photograph (e.g., a switch in the hats worn by two gentlemen), although these same changes were easily detected when they occurred during a fixation (Grimes, 1996; McConkie & Currie, 1996). Subsequent reports indicated that similar results could be obtained if the changes occurred during a brief visual interruption in the scene (Rensink, 2000; Rensink, O'Regan & Clark, 1997), if the changes occurred during a 'cut' in a movie (Levin & Simons, 1997; Simons, 1996), and even if they occurred during a real-world conversation between an unwitting participant and an actor. In this case it was the actor who exchanged places with another actor when a door being carried by other actors briefly interrupted the conversation (Simons & Levin, 1998).

In each of these cases of change blindness, it is clear that the focus of attention is an important predictor. Changes are detected more readily when they occur to objects that are of interest to the observer (Rensink, O'Regan & Clark, 1997; Rensink, 2000), and when they occur in locations that have had attention drawn to them by a salient cue such as local visual transient or a unique color (Rensink, O'Regan & Clark, 1997; Scholl, 2000). However, there has been less systematic study so far on the role played by the visual image that replaces the retinal (or environmental) location of the original image. From the perspective of object substitution, the important role played by this new image is that it prevents access to the fading representation of the original image. Instead, ongoing iterative perceptual processes are now busy confirming that the newly presented image does indeed contain the patterns and colors hypothesized by recent input into the system. Only when attention is focused on an object prior to the changed image are conscious visual processes able to detect the difference.

Finally, a word of caution. Although in the foregoing examples of attentional blink, inattentional blindness, and change blindness, a backward visual mask is a critical factor in causing a failure to 'see' objects that are clearly registered on the retina, it is important to be clear that the mechanism being proposed is not inherently tied to masking. Instead, backward masking is a methodological window that gives a glimpse into the mechanisms of iterative reentrant processing and the limited ability of conscious perception to monitor the perceptual products of these processes (Di Lollo, Enns & Rensink, in press). In support of this view, there have been recent reports in each of these areas of research, showing that failures of perception can be induced even in the absence of a mask. For instance, an attentional blink is observed without masking if the nature of the perceptual task is sufficiently different for the first and second targets (Enns, Visser, Kawahara & Di Lollo, in press), inattentional blindness has been reported when the unexpected and unattended stimulus is not followed by a mask (Mack & Rock, 1998); and change blindness can be induced by simply splashing 'mud' unexpectedly onto parts of a picture other than the target (O'Regan, Rensink & Clark, 1999). Importantly for the object substitution hypothesis, each of these manipulations involves a misdirection of attention, away from the visual target that goes undetected. While attention is focused on the task of identifying the first target in a visual stream, or has been 'captured' by mudsplashes while viewing a scene, and before attention can be redeployed to the critical visual target, the iterative processes involving the critical target have lost all trace of second target or the change that occurred to the target object.

BROADER IMPLICATIONS FOR VISUAL PERCEPTION

It is possible that what we have learned about masking from the study of object substitution may have wider currency in helping us to understand other aspects of visual perception. For example, a number of researchers studying the relations between visual imagery and perception have made the intriguing observation that sensory input seems to compete directly with the contents of imagination for the control of consciousness (Kosslyn &

Rabin, 1999; Farah, 1989). In one study observers were asked to recall from memory whether President Lincoln, who is depicted on the American penny, faces to the right or left (Kosslyn & Rabin, 1999). Although accuracy in this task was significantly above chance levels when this task was performed from memory alone, it did not differ from chance when observers were asked to choose from two outline drawings, one facing left, the other right. The authors interpreted this to mean that the image-based memory necessary to perform this task requires the same neural machinery as the perception of the two outlines in the recognition task. As in the case of masking by object substitution, the conscious brain has a tendency to resolve conflicts between top-down (reentrant) and bottom-up (sensory input) signals in favor of the immediate sensory input. Although such a bias is probably highly advantageous for most aspects of perception, since it permits one to see what is actually on view, it can lead to failures in being able to access visual memories; both very short-term ones in the case of backward masking, as well as longer term ones in the case of visual imagery.

We should also be humbled by the realization that what may appear to be newly uncovered principles of object substitution have been known to magicians and tricksters for thousands of years. At least they have been known in the sense that an audience can be reliably fooled if certain rules are followed. An especially good example based on object substitution involves an old card trick that has recently gained a new life on the internet. In this trick, the audience is shown six face cards and asked to choose one, but not to tell any other audience member, or the trickster, which card has been chosen. With each member of the audience having their card firmly and privately in mind, the trickster removes all six cards and says, with a flourish "I have the power to read your mind. Your chosen card will now be removed from the set." Five cards are returned to view, and invariably the chosen card is not among them. The trick works very well, as evidenced by the large amount of speculation that it has generated on the internet. Much of this speculation concerns how a large audience (in this case world wide) can be coerced into chosing the same card, which appears to many to be the basis of the trick. But, as with all good tricks, the apparent basis is not the actual basis of the trick. The simple trick is that the cards in the second display are five entirely new face cards.

Why does this trick fool people? Very simply, for two reasons that are at the heart of the object substitution hypothesis. First, observers do not detect changes to objects that they have not attended. All attention in the first display is focused on the card selected for memory by the observer. Secondly, observers assume that unless otherwise informed, the visual world consists of the objects that are currently on view. It does not occur to them to doubt that the second five cards are different from the first five that were not selected. While this may be a generally useful assumption, perhaps even an evolutionary adaptation in the service of visually guided action, it does leave us vulnerable to events that violate this belief in a 'stable world'. Such events include the fun of magic, but they also include the more serious everyday realities of traffic accidents, human-computer interaction, and eye witness testimony.

AKNOWLEDGEMENTS

The research described in this chapter was supported by grants from the Natural Sciences and Engineering Research Council of Canada to both authors. Correspondence may be addressed to either J. T. Enns (jenns@psych.ubc.ca) or V. Di Lollo (vince.dilollo@ubc.ca), Department of Psychology, University of British Columbia, 2136 West Mall, Vancouver, B. C., Canada V6T 1Z4.

REFERENCES

Alpern, M. (1953). Metacontrast. *Journal of the Optical Society of America, 43*, 648-657.

Averbach, E., & Coriel, A. S. (1961). Short-term memory in vision. *Bell Systems Technical Journal, 40,* 309-328.

Bachmann, T., & Allik, J. (1976). Integration and interruption in the masking of form by form. *Perception, 5*, 79-97.

Bouma, H. (1970). Interaction effects in parafoveal letter recognition. *Nature, 226,* 177-178.

Brehaut, J.C., Enns, J.T., & Di Lollo, V. (1999). Visual masking plays two roles in the attentional blink. *Perception & Psychophysics, 61*, 1436-1448.

Breitmeyer, B. G. (1984). *Visual masking: An integrative approach.* New York: Oxford University Press.

Breitmeyer, B. G., & Ganz, L. (1976). Implications of sustained and transient channels for theories of visual pattern masking, saccadic suppression, and information processing. *Psychological Review, 83,* 1-36.

Bridgeman, B. (1975). Correlates of metacontrast in single cells of the cat visual system. *Vision Research, 15,* 91-99.

Bridgeman, B. (1980). Temporal response characteristics of cells in monkey striate cortex measured with metacontrast masking and brightness discrimination. *Brain Research, 196*, 347-364.

Bridgeman, B. (1988). Visual evoked potentials: Concomitants of metacontrast in late components. *Perception & Psychophysics, 43,* 401-403.

Bullier, J., McCourt, M. E., & Henry, G. H. (1988). Physiological studies on the feedback connection to the striate cortex from cortical areas 18 and 19 of the cat. *Experimental Brain Research, 70*, 90-98.

Cheesman, J., & Merikle, P. M. (1986). Distinguishing conscious from unconscious perceptual processes. *Canadian Journal of Psychology, 40,* 343-367.

Chun, M. M. (1997). Temporal binding errors are redistributed in the attentional blink.

Perception & Psychophysics, 59, 1191-1199.

Damasio, A. R. (1994). *Descartes' error.* New York: Putnam's.

Debner, J. A., & Jacoby, L. L. (1994). Unconscious perception: Attention, awareness, and control. *Journal of Experimental Psychology: Learning, Memory, and Cognition, 20,* 304-317.

Di Lollo, V., Bischof, W. F., & Dixon, P. (1993). Stimulus-onset asynchrony is not necessary for motion perception or metacontrast masking. *Psychological Science, 4,* 260-263.

Di Lollo, V., Enns, J. T., & Rensink, R. A. (in press). Competition for consciousness among visual events: The psychophsyics of reentrant visual processes. *Journal of Experiental Psychology: General, 129,* 481-507.

Dixon, P., & Di Lollo, V. (1994). Beyond visible persistence: An alternative account of temporal integration and segregation in visual processing. *Cognitive Psychology, 26,* 33-63.

Duncan, J. & Humphreys, G. (1989). Visual search and stimulus similarity. *Psychological Review, 96,* 433-458.

Enns, J. T., & Di Lollo, V. (1997). Object substitution: A new form of masking in unattended visual locations. *Psychological Science, 8,* 135-139.

Enns, J. T., Visser, T. A. B., Kawahara, J., & Di Lollo, V. (in press). Visual masking and task switching in the attentional blink. Chapter to appear in Shapiro, K. (Ed.), *The limits of attention: Temporal constraints on human information processing.* Oxford University Press.

Eriksen, C. W. (1995). The flankers task and response competition: A useful tool for investigating a variety of cognitive problems. *Visual Cognition, 2,* 101-118.

Farah, M.J. (1989). The neural basis of imagery. *Trends in Neurosciences, 12,* 395-399.

Felleman, D. J., & Van Essen, D. C. (1991). Distributed hierarchical processing in primate visual cortex. *Cerebral Cortex, 1,* 1-47.

Ganz, L. (1975). Temporal factors in visual perception. In E. C. Carterette & M. P. Friedman (Eds.) *Handbook of Perception, Vol. 5,* (pp. 169-231). New York: Academic Press.

Giesbrecht, B. L., & Di Lollo, V. (1998). Beyond the attentional blink: Visual masking by object substitution. *Journal of Experimental Psychology: Human Perception and Performance, 24,* 1454-1466.

Grimes, J. (1996). On the failure to detect changes in scenes across saccades. In K. Akins (Ed.). *Perception* (pp. 89-110). New York: Oxford University Press.

Growney, R., Weisstein, N., & Cox, S. I. (1977). Metacontrast as a function of spatial separation with narrow line targets and masks. *Vision Research, 17,* 1205-1210.

Hupe, J. M., James, A. C., Payne, B. R., Lomber, S. G., Girard, P., & Bullier, J. (1998). Cortical feedback improves discrimination between figure and ground by V1, V2, and V3 neurons. *Nature, 394,* 784-787.

Jeffreys, D. A., & Musselwhite, M. J. (1986). A visual evoked potential study of metacontrast masking. *Vision Research, 26,* 631-642.

Kahneman, D. (1968). Method, findings, and theory in studies of visual masking. *Psychological Bulletin, 70,* 404-425.

Kolers, P. A. (1968). Some psychological aspects of pattern recognition. In P. A. Kolers & M. Eden (Eds.), *Recognizing Patterns.* Boston, MIT Press.

Kosslyn, S. M., & Rabin, C. (1999). The representation of left-right orientation: A dissociation between imagery and perceptual recognition. *Visual Cognition, 6,* 497-508.

Lamme, V. A. F., Zipser, K., & Spekreijse, H. (1997). Figure-ground signals in V1 depend on extrastriate feedback. *Investigative Ophthalmology & Visual Science, 38,* S969 (abstract).

Levin, D.T., & Simons, D.J. (1997). Failure to detect changes to attended objects in motion pictures. *Psychonomic Bulletin and Review, 4,* 501-506.

Luck, SJ, Vogel, E.K., & Shapiro, KL (1996). Word meanings can be accessed but not reported during the attentional blink. *Nature, 383,* 616-383.

Mack, A., & Rock, I. (1998). *Inattentional Blindness.* The MIT Press, Cambridge, MA.

Macknik, S.L., & Haglund, M.M. (1999). Optical images of visible and invisible percepts in the primary visual cortex of primates. *Proc. National Acad. Sciences, 96,* 15208-15210.

Macknik, SL & Livingstone, MS (1998) Neuronal correlates of visibility and invisibility in the primate visual system. *Nature Neuroscience, 1,*144-149.

Marcel, A. J. (1983a). Conscious and unconscious perception: Experiments on visual masking and word recognition. *Cognitive Psychology, 15,* 197-237.

Marcel, A. J. (1983b). Conscious and unconscious perception: An approach to the relations between phenomenal experience and perceptual processes. *Cognitive Psychology, 15,* 238-300.

Martin, J., Isaak, M. I., & Shapiro, K. L. (1995). *Probe identification errors support an interference model of the attentional blink in rapid serial visual presentation.* Poster presented at the Annual Meeting of the American Psychological Society, New York, NY.

McConkie, G.W., & Currie, C.B. (1996). Visual stability across saccades while viewing complex pictures. *Journal of Experimental Psychology: Human Perception and Performance, 22,* 563-581.

Meyer, D. E., Schveneveldt, R. W., & Ruddy, M. G. (1975). Loci of contextual effects on visual word recognition. In P. M. A. Rabbitt & S. Dornic (Eds.), *Attention and performance V* (pp. 98-118). New York: Academic Press.

Michaels, C. F., & Turvey, M. T. (1979). Central sources of visual masking: Indexing structures supporting seeing at a single, brief glance. *Psychological Research, 41,* 1-61.

Mignard, M., & Malpeli, J. G. (1991). Paths of information flow through visual cortex.

Science, 251, 1249-1251.

Mumford, D. (1992). On the computational architecture of the neocortex II. The role of cortico-cortical loops. *Biological Cybernetics, 66,* 241-251.

O'Regan J.K., Rensink R.A., Clark J.J. (1999). Change-blindness as a result of 'mudsplashes'. *Nature, 398,* 34.

Pashler, H. (1994). Dual-task interference in simple tasks: Data and theory. *Psychological Bulletin, 16,* 220-224.

Posner, M. I. (1980). Orienting of attention. *Quarterly Journal of Experimental Psychology, 32,* 3-25.

Pylyshyn, Z., & Storm, R.W. (1988). Tracking multiple independent targets: Evidence for a parallel tracking mechanism. *Spatial Vision, 3,* 179-197.

Ramachandran, V. I., & Cobb, S. (1995). Visual attention modulates metacontrast masking. *Nature, 373,* 66-68.

Rensink, R. A. (2000). Visual search for change: A probe into the nature of attentional processing. *Visual Cognition, 7,* 345-376.

Rensink, R.A., O'Regan, J.K., & Clark, J.J. (1997). To see or not to see: The need for attention to perceive changes in scenes. *Psychological Science, 8,* 368-373.

Scheerer, E. (1973). Integration, interruption and processing rate in visual backward masking. *Psychologische Forschung, 36,* 71-93.

Scholl, B.J. (2000). Attenuated change blindness for exogenously attended items in a flicker paradigm. *Visual Cognition, 7,* 377-396.

Shapiro, K. L., Driver, J., Ward, R., & Sorensen, R. E. (1997). Priming from the attentional blink: A failure to extract visual tokens but not visual types. *Psychological Science, 8,* 95-100.

Shapiro, K.L. (1994). The attentional blink: The Brain's eyeblink. *Current Directions in Psychology, 3,* 86-89.

Sillito, A. M., Jones, H. E., Gerstein, G. L., & West, D. C. (1994). Feature-linked synchronization of thalamic relay cell firing induced by feedback from the visual cortex. *Nature, 369,* 479-482.

Simons, D.J. (1996). In sight, out of mind: When object representations fail. *Psychological Science, 7,* 301-305.

Simons, D.J., & Levin, D.T. (1998). Failure to detect changes to people during a real-world interaction. *Psychonomic Bulletin and Review, 5,* 644-649.

Spencer, T. J., & Shuntich, R. (1970). Evidence for an interruption theory of backward masking. *Journal of Experimental Psychology, 85,* 198-203.

Treisman, A., & Gelade, G. (1980). A feature integration theory of attention. *Cognitive Psychology, 12,* 97-136.

Turvey, M. T. (1973). On peripheral and central processes in vision: Inferences from an information-processing analysis of masking with patterned stimuli. *Psychological*

Review, 81, 1-52.

Vaughn, H. H., Jr. (1969). The relationship of brain activity to scalp recordings of event-related potentials. In E. Donchin and D. Lindsley (Eds.), *Average evoked potentials,* (pp. 45-94), NASA: Washington, D. C.

Vogel, E.K., Luck, SJ, & Shapiro, KL (1998). Electrophysiological evidence for a postperceptual locus of suppression during the attentional blink. *Journal of Experimental Psychology: Human Perception and Performance, 24,* 1656-1674.

von der Heydt, R., Friedman, H. S., Zhou, H., Komatsu, H., Hanazawa, A., & Murakami, I. (1997). Neuronal responses in monkey V1 and V2 unaffected by metacontrast. *Investigative Ophthalmology & Visual Science, 38*, S459.

Weisstein, N., Ozog, G., & Szoc, R. (1975). A comparison and elaboration of two models of metacontrast. *Psychological Review, 82,* 325-343.

Werner, H. (1935). Studies on contour: I. Qualitative analysis. *American Journal of Psychology, 47*, 40-64.

Wolfe, J. M., Cave, K. R., & Franzel, S. L. (1989). Guided search: An alternative to the feature-integration model for visual search. *Journal of Experimental Psychology: Human Perception and Performance, 15*, 419-433.

Zeki, S. (1993). *A Vision of the Brain.* Oxford: Blackwell.

From Fragments to Objects – Segmentation and Grouping in Vision
T.F. Shipley and P.J. Kellman (Editors)

6

ATTENTION AND UNIT FORMATION: A BIASED COMPETITION ACCOUNT OF OBJECT-BASED ATTENTION

Shaun P. Vecera[†] *and Marlene Behrmann*[‡]
† Department of Psychology, University of Iowa, Iowa City, IA 52242-1407 USA
‡ Department of Psychology, Carnegie Mellon University, Pittsburgh, PA 15213 USA

ABSTRACT

Because the visual system cannot process all of the items present in a visual scene, some stimuli must be selected over others to prevent the visual system from becoming overloaded. Visual attention allows some stimuli or events to be processed instead of others. Most research on attentional selection has focused on spatial or location-based attention, in which the locations occupied by stimuli are selected for further processing. Recent research, however, has demonstrated the importance of objects in guiding attentional selection. Because of the long history of spatial attention research, theories of spatial attention are more mature than theories of other visual processes, such as object segregation and object attention. In the present chapter, we outline a biased competition account of object segregation and attention, following similar accounts that have been developed for visual search (Desimone & Duncan, 1995). In the biased competition account, there are two sources of visual information that allow an object to be processed over other objects: bottom-up information carried by the physical stimulus and top-down information based on an observer's goals. We use the biased competition account to combine many diverse findings from both behavioral and neurobiological studies of object attention.

Until the mid-1980s, the majority of research on selective visual attention studied spatial attention and the processes by which stimuli were selected on the basis of their location. Distinctions on topics such as the movement of the spatial focus (does it move smoothly through space or does it jump from place to place?) and the shape of the spatial window (is it a spotlight, a zoom lens, or a gradient?) were important to the theoretical perspectives that dominated the literature. However, the tide began to change with increasing demonstrations that objects may be the recipients of visual attention. With increasing demonstrations of so-called "object-based" attention, the strong spatial (or location-based) account fell from favor. Although there was initial debate over whether attention selects objects or locations, many researchers studying visual attention would agree that both forms of selection are possible because it is unlikely that there is a single attentional "bottleneck" or limitation (e.g., Allport, 1993; Haimson & Behrmann, in preparation; Luck & Vecera, 2000; Vecera & Luck, 2000).

Once the object-based versus location-based debate has been put aside, other interesting questions regarding the nature of attentional selection arise. For example, what processes form the objects that are selected? How are object-based selection and location-based selection combined to produce coordinated behavior? What are the neural mechanisms that underlie these forms of attentional selection? In this chapter we attempt to answer these questions by reviewing the recent object-based attention literature, including behavioral and neurobiological studies. Because space-based selective attention has been studied longer and more intensively than object-based selection, theoretical accounts of spatial attention are more mature than those of object attention (for theories of spatial attention see Desimone & Duncan, 1995; Mozer & Sitton, 1998; Sperling & Weichselgartner, 1995; Treisman, 1988; Wolfe, 1994). Because there are few theoretical account of object attention, our goal here is to illustrate the types of attentional phenomena that theories of object-based attention must explain and to outline a "biased competition" account of object-based attentional selection. Following previous work (Vecera, in press), we extend the biased competition account of visual search (Desimone & Duncan, 1995) to the selection of objects by attentional processes (also see Behrmann & Haimson, 1999; Haimson & Behrmann, in preparation; O'Craven, Downing, & Kanwisher, 1999). Our account is intended to provide a framework for organizing the object-based attention literature and, hopefully, generating questions for future research (Vecera, in press).

In what follows, we first discuss the visual processes relevant for object attention. We next outline generally the biased competition account of visual search presented by Desimone and Duncan (1995), and then apply the principles of biased competition to behavioral results that support object-based selection. We then discuss the cognitive neuroscience of object-based attention, focusing primarily on neuropsychological patients and neurophysiological studies. We summarize these results and discuss their relation to the biased competition account that we outline for the behavioral studies of object attention.

WHAT IS AN OBJECT?

Before reviewing findings and accounts of object-based attention, we must be clear what the term "object" means. In the context of attentional selection, "objects" refer to perceptual groups or units (see Logan, 1996, for example). These perceptual groups are formed through the application of the well-known gestalt principles of organization, principles such as proximity, similarity, good continuation, closure, connectedness, and so forth. Multiple theoretical accounts and many empirical results suggest that gestalt principles operate early in visual processing at a preattentive level (e.g., Julesz, 1984; Neisser, 1967; Treisman & Gelade, 1980). Further, a single perceptual group may have a hierarchical organization. A perceptual group may contain parts, and there are perceptual principles that can be used to define the parts of a perceptual group (e.g., Hoffman & Richards, 1984; Hoffman & Singh, 1997; Vecera, Behrmann, & Filapek, in press; Vecera, Behrmann, & McGoldrick., 2000). These perceptual grouping principles allow visual space or spatiotopic features to be organized. We refer to this perceptual grouping definition of "object" as a "grouped array" representation. The grouped array is an array-format, or spatiotopic, representation that codes features in specific retinal locations, similar to Treisman's (1988) feature maps. Various gestalt grouping principles organize this array into coherent chunks of visual information that correspond to objects or shapes. (Also see the next section of this volume for computational models of unit formation and grouping.) The spatial representations that underlie object-based attention may be shared with spatial attention (see Valdes-Sosa et al., 1997, for relevant results, which we discuss below).

Our definition of "object" points out a close connection between object segregation processes and object-based attention processes. Object segregation refers to the visual processes that determine which visual features combine to form a single shape and which features combine to form other shapes. Object segregation is synonymous with perceptual organization, the term used in conjunction with the gestalt principles of visual organization (e.g., Wertheimer, 1923/1958). The ability to perform figure-ground segregation and distinguish foreground shapes ('figures') from background regions also involves segregation processes (e.g., Rubin, 1915/1958), although figure-ground segregation may follow earlier image segregation processes (Vecera & O'Reilly, 1998). An example of object segregation appears in Figure 1, which contains two perceptual groups that are formed by the gestalt principles of proximity and good continuation.

The features are individual line segments that are organized into two distinct shapes—two lines, a straight line and a squiggly line. Note that these two "objects" (lines) are approximately equal in their salience. Neither object appears to grab attention more effectively than the other object. However, in such a display, empirical evidence indicates that one of these objects could be selectively attended.

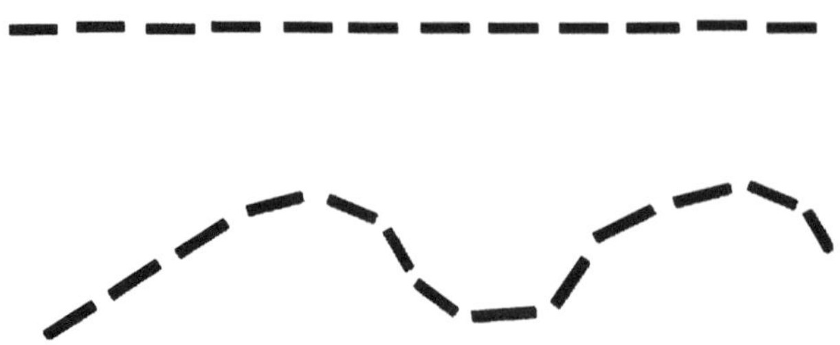

Figure 1. An example of object segregation in which gestalt proximity and good continuation form two perceptual groups (two lines). The small straight lines of line the top group together because they are closer to one another than the small lines of the bottom line.

The fact that the two objects in Figure 1 have approximately equal salience indicates that the human visual system must be capable of somehow creating a processing bias favoring one of theseobjects over the other. Object-based attention (that is, directing attention to one of these objects) may provide a mechanism for favoring either the straight line or squiggly line in Figure 1. Object-based attention refers to the visual processes that select a segregated shape from among several segregated shapes. As we noted above, object segregation and object-based attention likely are interrelated—before a shape can be selected, the features of the shape first must be segregated from features of other shapes to some extent. In Figure 1, before an observer could attend to the squiggly line, the features of that line must be grouped together (and grouped separately from the features of the straight line). Further, object-based attention is more efficient when it is directed to a single object; that is, observers can select either the straight line or the squiggly line with relatively little effort. In contrast, it is more difficult to divide object-based attention across multiple objects; if an observer needed to attend to both lines, object-based selection would be more effortful. Object-based attention either would have to shift between the two lines or would need to be divided between the two lines. Either shifting or division of attention cause performance to decline; this declining performance is the basis of many object-based attentional effects reported in the literature (e.g., Baylis & Driver, 1993; Behrmann, Zemel, & Mozer, 1998; Duncan, 1984, 1993a, 1993b; Egly, Driver, & Rafal, 1994; Vecera, 1994; Vecera & Farah, 1994). Many of these object-based attentional effects are influenced by the spatial position of objects, indicating that object-based attention may involve the selection of grouped locations (Vecera, 1994; Vecera & Farah, 1994). However, the coordinate system of these grouped locations is poorly understood, and not all forms of object selection may involve attending to grouped locations (Vecera & Farah, 1994; Lee & Chun, in press).

In sum, any account of object-based attention needs to explain (1) the segregation processes that provide the input to object attention and (2) the object selection effect, in which one object and all of its features are more readily attended than multiple objects (or multiple features on different objects). We now turn to the key ideas behind the biased competition account that we will discuss in conjunction with behavioral studies of object attention. Because visual scenes contain many objects that compete with one another for attention, the visual system must allocate processing to one object over others. This allocation is achieved by biasing processing toward one object. This bias provides a resolution for the competition between objects. For example, the two objects in Figure 1 compete with one another for attention, yet observers can selectively process either of the lines, even though neither line has an 'inherent' processing advantage. The biased competition account attempts to explain how some objects are selected over others (also see Vecera, in press).

BIASED COMPETITION AND VISUAL SEARCH

The biased competition account we discuss relies heavily on the biased competition account of visual search outlined by Desimone and Duncan (1995; also see Cohen & Huston, 1994; Harter & Aine, 1984, for similar accounts). Visual search refers to the collection of visual processes that allow us to "find what we are looking for" (Wolfe, 1998) by using spatial attention to combine the features of objects (e.g., Treisman, 1988; Treisman & Gelade, 1980). Thus, visual search involves spatial selective attention. In a typical visual search task, several visual stimuli are present and an observer searches for a target among the distracting stimuli (e.g., find the black vertical bar among black horizontal bars and white vertical bars). Searching for a friend's face (the target) in a restaurant containing many people (the distractors) would be an example of real world visual search. Note that we are using the visual search paradigm to introduce the principles of biased competition. We are not endorsing any particular theoretical view or model of visual search. Similar biased competition ideas can be applied to other experimental paradigms (e.g., simple spatial cuing with peripheral and central precues), and we focus on visual search to illustrate the biased competition account discussed by Desimone and Duncan (1995).

There are two important results from the visual search paradigm. First, targets that are highly salient (i.e., quite different from the background distractors) "pop out" and grab attention immediately and effectively (Figure 2A). These "feature searches" are performed efficiently in that the number of irrelevant distractors does not influence the time to search. Second, targets that are formed by a conjunction of features that are shared with the distractors require effortful search (Figure 2B). These inefficient conjunction searches are highly dependent upon the number of distractors present in a display; as the number of distractors increases, response times also increase (see Wolfe, 1998, for a comprehensive review of visual search).

How can these two results, which appear to be quite different, be explained? Desimone and Duncan's (1995) biased competition model provides an answer. There are two general principles of their account. First, multiple visual stimuli compete for attention.

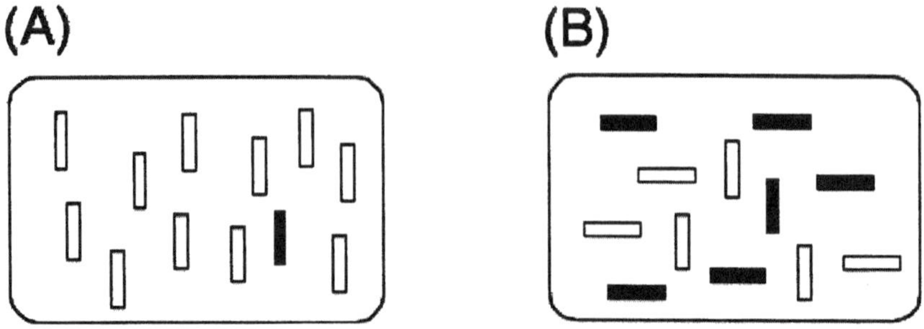

Figure 2. Sample visual search displays in which subjects search for a black vertical line. (A) An efficient feature search in which the target pops out from a homogeneous background. (B) An inefficient conjunction search in which the target does not pop out because the distractors share both black and vertical features with the target.

Second, the competition for attention is biased toward some stimuli over others. This biasing comes from two sources of information: bottom-up sources that arise from sensory stimuli present in a scene and top-down sources that arise from the current behavioral goals. Visual search performance requires both bottom-up stimulus sources and top-down control sources to be considered and balanced against one another, each source of information providing constraints on visual processing.

In the biased competition account of visual search, the display presented in a visual search task provides the bottom-up information that is searched through; this information indicates where objects are located and which features are present at each location. In efficient visual search (Figure 2A), the target may pop out from the distractors because of a possible bottom-up bias to orient attention to local inhomogeneities (e.g., Sagi & Julesz, 1985), which may involve a preference for orienting to novel items in a display. The abrupt appearance of a new object or shape also captures attention in an efficient manner (Yantis & Jonides, 1984; see Yantis, 1998, for a review), suggesting that abrupt onsets bias bottom-up attentional orienting. Thus, efficient visual search is almost exclusively driven by bottom-up input to the visual system, allowing salient targets to pop out and control spatial attention. In some search tasks, however, bottom-up pop out may involve top-down parameters: Some search targets only pop out if they are task-relevant and are the target of a visual search (Yantis & Egeth, 1999).

Under Desimone and Duncan's (1995) account of visual search, inefficient visual search may arise when there is no unique bottom-up stimulus characteristic to influence attentional allocation. Such a conjunction search (Figure 2B) may depend heavily on the top-down control of spatial attention in which items in a scene are examined in a sequential or sequential-looking manner. The primary source of top-down control in Desimone and Duncan's (1995) account is the target's description or identity—what is referred to as a "target template" (also see Duncan & Humphreys, 1989). Visual search must be sensitive to the goals of an observer; that is, an observer must be able to search for targets that may not be biased by the bottom-up input to the visual system. The target template is based on the visual features of the target (e.g., "black and vertical" in Figure 2). In visual search experiments, the target template typically is based on an experimenter's instructions ("search for a black, vertical bar") that is stored in visual working memory for the duration of the task or trial (e.g., Duncan & Humphreys, 1989; but see Woodman, Vogel, & Luck, in press). The target template acts to weight the incoming bottom-up stimulus information to allow attention to be biased toward one bottom-up input over another. In a less efficient conjunction search (Figure 2B), no single piece of bottom-up information is unique to the target item, so the bottom-up biases are less effective in guiding attention to the target. Top-down constraints are required to resolve the competition among the bottom-up inputs and bias attention toward the black, vertical line.

This brief overview of Desimone and Duncan's (1995) account highlights the two primary sources of attentional control in visual search—bottom-up and top-down sources. The biased competition model has proven useful in describing a range of behavioral, neurobiological, and neuroimaging data from experiments that rely on spatial attention, which suggests that the general approach of combining stimulus information and goal-related information may provide an accurate description of many attentional phenomena. How well could a biased competition approach explain the results from the emerging literature on object-based visual attention? We address this question in the subsequent sections by outlining a biased competition framework for object-based attentional control.

BIASED COMPETITION AND OBJECT-BASED ATTENTION

Bottom-Up Biases in Object Attention

In multi-object scenes, objects or regions compete with one another in two respects. The first type of competition occurs within object segregation processes and the perceptual regions formed by these processes. The outcome of this competition is a perceptual group that is more salient than other groups. Figure-ground segregation provides an ideal example: Symmetric figures, which are perceived as lying in the foreground, are more salient and shape-like than asymmetric backgrounds. In some displays, however, there may not be a salient group that "wins out" over other groups. This could occur, for example, in scenes that contain two asymmetric regions; because neither region has the bottom-up cue of symmetry, neither has a processing advantage over the other. The second type of competition occurs within object-based attentional processes; the outcome of this competition is the selection of one perceptual group or figure over another. Object attention is likely to be necessary when there are no salient regions defined by object segregation cues, as when two asymmetric regions abut in a figure-ground display. Directing object-based attention to one of these regions would allow that region to be selected and become attentionally more salient than the unattended region. Although these two sources of competition are highly interrelated, they tend to be discussed as separate in the visual cognition literature. Our main focus here will be on object-based attention and the sources of bottom-up information that bias the allocation of object attention.

Most of the object-based attention literature can be characterized as a search for the image grouping cues that influence attentional allocation in a bottom-up manner. Several studies, for example, have used Eriksen's flanker task to determine the stimulus cues that guide attentional selection of objects. The flanker task was one of the earliest paradigms developed to study spatial selective attention (e.g., Eriksen & Eriksen, 1974; Eriksen & Hoffman, 1973). Observers are instructed to report a target letter appearing at a location (e.g., at the fixation point); the target letter is surrounded, or flanked, by non-target letters which are either compatible with or incompatible with the response to the target. For example, observers are instructed to determine if a target letter is an H or a T; the target letter is either flanked by compatible letters (e.g., H flanked by other Hs) or by incompatible letters (e.g., H flanked by Ts). The flankers influence how the target is processed: Flankers compatible with the target letter speed target identification and flankers incompatible with the target slow target identification.

The attentional selection involved in the flanker task can be biased by several object-grouping effects. Perhaps the earliest demonstration of object-grouping in the flanker task came from Driver and Baylis (1989), who reported that targets and flankers that moved together were processed as a single perceptual group (but see Kramer et al., 1991, for a failure to replicate). Driver and Baylis' (1989) results suggest that attention is biased to process simultaneously items moving in a common direction. These observations were extended to other bottom-up cues by Baylis and Driver (1992), who demonstrated that targets and flankers that were the same color were processed as a single group and that targets and flankers that were grouped through good continuation were processed simultaneously. In a similar manner, Kramer and Jacobson (1991) showed that connectedness biased attentional selection in a flanker task. A target that was physically connected to the flankers was attended as a single unit or group; a target that was not connected to the flankers could be selectively attended with little influence from the surrounding flankers. As with other gestalt cues, connectedness cues bias attention to select items that are physically connected to one another (see Palmer, 1992, 1999, for a discussion of the connectedness grouping cue).

A bottom-up bias over object selection also has been observed in spatial cuing tasks. Observers are given advance information about a target's location by a spatial precue, and responses to targets are typically more accurate and faster when the cue and target appear at the same location (validly cued target) than at different locations (invalidly cued targets; see Posner, 1980; Posner et al., 1980). Egly and colleagues used a spatial cuing task to study object-based attention (Egly et al., 1994; also see Vecera, 1994). In this task, depicted in Figure 3, observers viewed two rectangles. The rectangles were perceptual groups formed by closure and common region. One end of one of these shapes was cued, and a target appeared after the cue. Observers were instructed to detect the onset of the targets, and the targets could appear in one of three locations: at the spatially cued location (Figure 3A), in the opposite end of the cued object (Figure 3B), or in the uncued object (Figure 3C). The targets that appear at the uncued location in the cued object are the same spatial distance from the cued region as the targets that appear in the uncued object. Using this task, Egly et al.

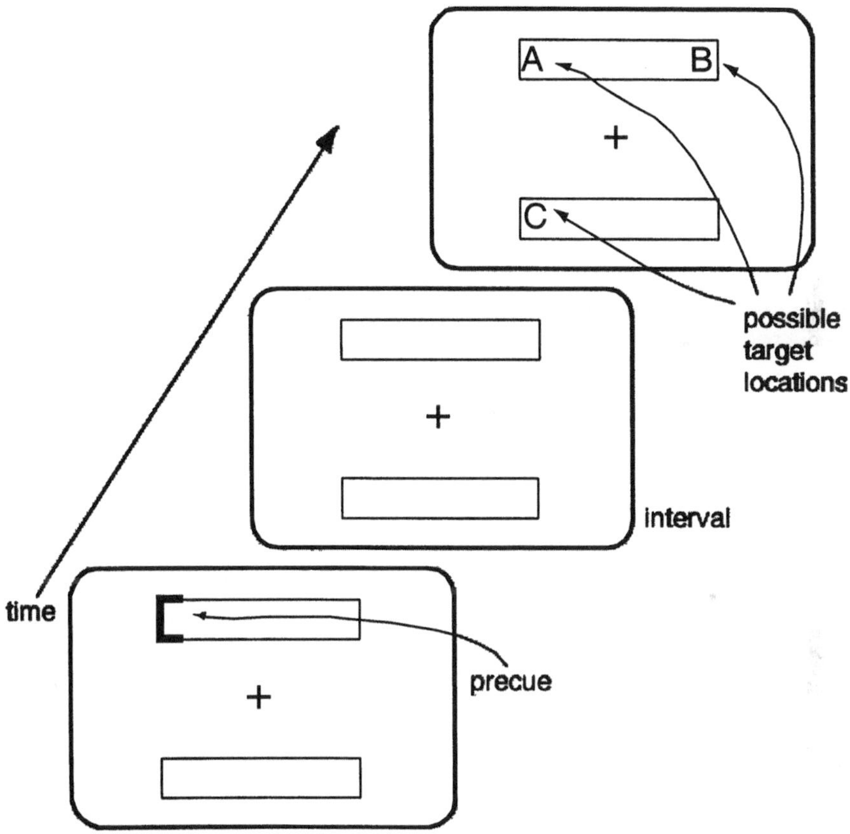

Figure 3. Egly et al.'s (1994) cuing task which was developed to study object-based attention. Two rectangles appear, and the end of one is precued with a peripheral precue. After a delay, a target appears at one of three locations: (A) a validly cued target; (B) an invalidly cued target that appears in the cued object; (C) an invalidly cued object that appears in the uncued object. Subjects are faster to detect invalidly cued targets appearing in the cued rectangle faster than those appearing in the uncued rectangle.

reported that observers showed a spatial cuing effect; observers were faster to detect targets at the spatially cued location than at either of the uncued locations. More important, observers exhibited an object effect by detecting targets appearing in the cued object faster than targets appearing in the uncued object. These results indicate that closure and connectedness bias the allocation of spatial attention. When spatial attention is summoned to a cued location, attention can spread or move more easily within a closed region than between closed regions. We should note the possibility that this task also may involve top-down information under a biased competition account; we discuss this possible top-down effect later.

Finally, bottom-up biases in attention exist for the segregation of an object into parts. Bottom-up image cues that allow an object to be decomposed into its parts, such as minima of curvature cues (Hoffman & Richards, 1984; Hoffman & Singh, 1997; Singh & Hoffman, this volume), influence attentional selection. Some of our recent research demonstrates that observers are more accurate reporting features from a single part of an object than from multiple parts of an object (Vecera, Behrmann, & Filapek, in press; Vecera, Behrmann, & McGoldrick, 2000). These part-based attentional costs do not appear to be caused by selection with a simple spatially-based attention mechanism such as a "spotlight" because changing the physical separation between the parts of an object influences attention very little, if at all (Vecera, Behrmann, & Filapek, in press). The cost of dividing attention between two parts did not increase as the spatial separation of the parts increased. In some experimental paradigms, attention appears to select the parts themselves, and not the visual space occupied by the parts.

Information contained in a visual scene—bottom-up information—appears to both define perceptual groups and bias some groups to be more easily perceived than others. Once these segregation processes have operated, perceptual groups then bias the allocation of visual attention. In general, features or stimuli that group together based on the gestalt principles bias attentional selection. Attention must obey those perceptual units formed by gestalt grouping processes, allowing attention to shift more easily within a group than between groups, for example.

Although object attention obeys the boundaries and groups formed by grouping processes, object attention is not guided entirely by these bottom-up biases. Visuomotor behavior would be severely limited if humans only recognized, attended, and acted upon objects defined by bottom-up criteria. Visual attention must be modulated by information that is relevant to current behavior or goals. This modulation of attention comes in the form of top-down inputs that can bias the competition among perceptual groups or objects. In the next section, we review some of the sources of top-down information that may influence or guide object attention.

Top-Down Biases in Object Attention

In many cases, visual scenes do not contain an isolated, perceptually salient region that is uniquely relevant to the current behavior, such as searching for a coffee cup on a cluttered desk. Instead, there may be multiple regions or objects that have equal salience or, in the worst case, there may be an irrelevant object that is more salient than the object relevant to a current goal. For example, if an observer's current goal is to drink from the coffee cup, an error message abruptly appearing on the computer monitor would conflict with the goal-relevant object (the coffee cup). Top-down sources of information are needed either to bias attention to one of many equally salient objects or groups or to overcome a salient but behaviorally-irrelevant object or group. What sources of top-down information influence object attention, and what evidence is there for these top-down influences? There are at least three sources of top-down information in object attention tasks: (1) object recognition processes, (2) perceptual "set" processes, and (3) endogenous spatial attention processes. We discuss these sources in turn (see Vecera, in press, for a more detailed discussion).

Top-down biases from object recognition processes. Object representations stored in long-term visual memory represent familiar objects, such as a familiar face or a word. Behavioral studies have shown that familiar objects can provide top-down feedback to object attention processes. For example, Vecera & Farah (1997) demonstrated that familiar objects (upright letters) are selected by object attention more rapidly than less-familiar objects (rotated letters).

Observers viewed displays that contained two overlapping transparent letters, such as those shown in Figure 4A and were asked to determine if two small Xs were on the same shape or on different shapes. This task requires observers to first segregate the two regions from one another and then to orient attention to the Xs in order to determine if the Xs are either on the same shape or on different shapes. Vecera and Farah's (1997) results suggested an object-based attention effect in this task: Observers were faster to respond when the Xs were on the same object than when they were on different objects. There also was an effect of object familiarity; reaction times were faster to the familiar upright letters than to the less-familiar, rotated letters (also see Kimchi & Hadad, submitted, for similar results). Further, in their final experiment, Vecera and Farah (1997) showed that object familiarity can override bottom-up stimulus cues such as connectedness and common region. Two unconnected regions could be grouped together and attended if those unconnected regions formed a familiar, upright letter. Thus, object attention appears to be influenced by shape familiarity in a top-down manner, and top-down familiarity cues can, in some cases, override bottom-up cues.

The influence of shape familiarity on object attention also was demonstrated by Zemel and colleagues (Zemel, Behrmann, Bavelier, & Mozer, submitted). In a series of studies,

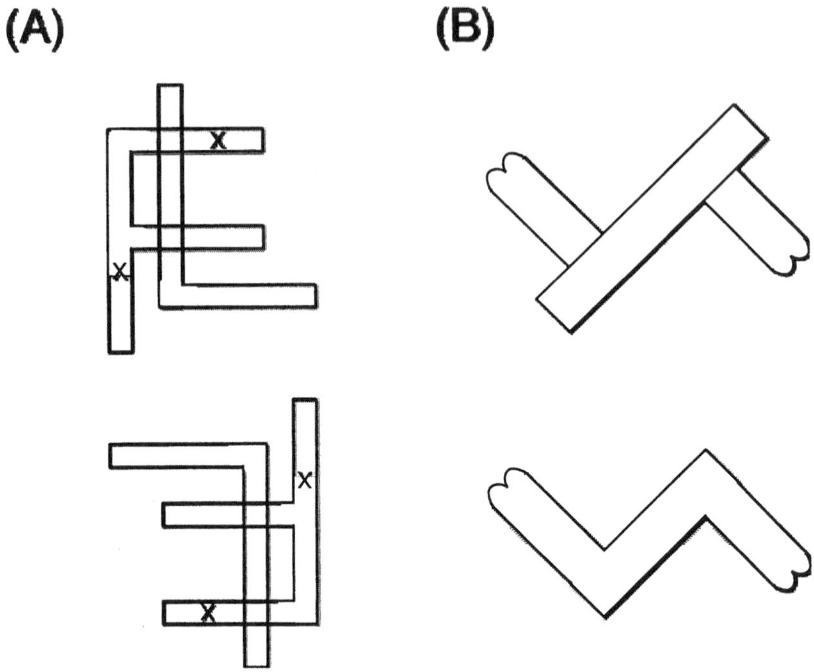

Figure 4. (A) Stimuli used by Vecera and Farah (1997) to study familiarity effects in object segregation and object-based attention. Familiar objects, such as upright letters, are selected and processed faster than less-familiar objects, such as upside down letters. (B) The Z-shaped displays used by Zemel et al. (submitted) to study the effects of learning on object attention. In the top panel, bottom-up cues typically lead to the perception of mis-aligned ends as being on different objects. However, if subjects see Z-shaped stimuli in the course of the experiment, as shown in the bottom panel, they interpret mis-aligned object ends (top) as being on a single object.

observers were shown an initially ambiguous display such as that shown in the top panel of Figure 4B. Naive observers who were required to decide whether the bumps at the end of the Z-shaped display were the same or different were slow at making this decision compared with the situation in which the bumps appeared at the end of a single, continuous bar (bottom panel of Figure 4B), suggesting that the Z-shaped displays were processed as two objects. Half the observers were then exposed to a stimulus display which is consistent with a single-object interpretation of the Z-display whereas the other half were only exposed to the fragments and no linking stimulus. When the observers were tested on the ambiguous displays again, only those subjects who had seen the linking Z displays, and not those who saw the fragments, showed reaction times to make the bump judgements as quickly on the unusual novel displays as on the single continuous bar. These data provide further support for the idea that experience with or familiarity of visual input can influence the segregation and perceptual organization of displays.

Perceptual set. Another mechanism for top-down bias signals in object attention comes from "perceptual set." Perceptual set loosely refers to the expectancies or goals held by an observer, which typically is established by the task-relevant instructions provided by an experimenter in a laboratory setting. For example, an observer could be instructed to report the shape of a red object that could appear anywhere in the display or report the identity of the object that appears at the 3 o'clock position in a cluttered array. In general, any type of task instruction provided by an experimenter may establish a specific perceptual set. Of course, in everyday behavior, there is no experimenter to establish perceptual set, and set must be established by the individual's current goals. In visual search tasks, for example, the target template may be akin to perceptual set. In object attention tasks, perceptual set may be a more general form of a "target template" because perceptual set refers to several possible types of information that observers can use to guide their behavior. Admittedly, the notion of perceptual set is vague and, therefore, the mechanisms that underlie perceptual set may be difficult to study. Nevertheless, several studies have shown that instructions provided by an experimenter can influence the manner in which objects are attended, supporting the notion that top-down information can bias bottom-up object selection.

A now-classic example of the influence of perceptual set on object selection comes from Neisser and Becklen (1975), who had observers view two spatially overlapping films that were played simultaneously. One film contained two sets of hands playing a "hand game" and the other film contained a basketball game. Because the films were spatially overlapped and because both films were approximately equally salient, there were few, if any, bottom-up cues to favor one film clip over the other. However, Neisser and Becklen (1975) instructed observers to attend to one film or both films. Not only could observers use this instruction to monitor the films, observers also showed an object-based (or film-based) attentional effect; observers were better able to monitor a single film (e.g., the basketball game only) than to divide their attention across both film clips. The experimenter's instructions allowed observers to selectively attend one of the two films, and attention was directed more effectively to a single event (i.e., film clip) than to multiple events.

Duncan's (1984) study of object-based attention also may demonstrate an influence of perceptual set. Observers viewed two overlapping objects, a box and a line, and each of these objects varied on two attributes. Observers reported pairs of attributes, which were located on either the same object (e.g., report the two attributes of the box) or on different objects (e.g., report one attribute of the box and one attribute of the line). The specific attributes to be reported were told to the observers at the beginning of the experiment (or at the beginning of a block of trials in Vecera and Farah, 1994, who used a similar procedure). The instructions provided to the observer biased attention toward the relevant attributes; thus, the observers' perceptual set influenced the allocation of attention to either one object or two. Using this paradigm, Duncan (1984) found that observers were more accurate reporting attributes from the same object than from different objects, thereby showing an object-based effect on attentional selection (also see Vecera & Farah, 1994).

Recent results reported by Baylis and Driver (Baylis, 1994; Baylis & Driver, 1993) also show the effects of perceptual set on object attention. Observers viewed figure-ground stimuli that contained three regions (Figure 5A) in which the central region was one color (e.g., red) and the two flanking regions were another color (e.g., green). Observers were asked to attend to two of the bent edges in the display and to report which apex was above the other. To manipulate whether observers attended one or two objects, Baylis and Driver (1993; Baylis, 1994) manipulated perceptual set by instructing each observer to pay attention to either the color red or the color green. On some trials, the central region was red, and observers attended to a single object; on other trials, the two flanking regions were red and observers attended to two objects. Observers were faster to compare the apices when one object was attended than when two objects were attended. This object-based effect occurred even though the apices were identical between the central and flanking regions in a subset of the trials. Thus, object-based attention can be influenced by perceptual set: Observers responded faster and more accurately if perceptual set, based on the experimenter's instructions, biased selection of a single region than multiple regions.

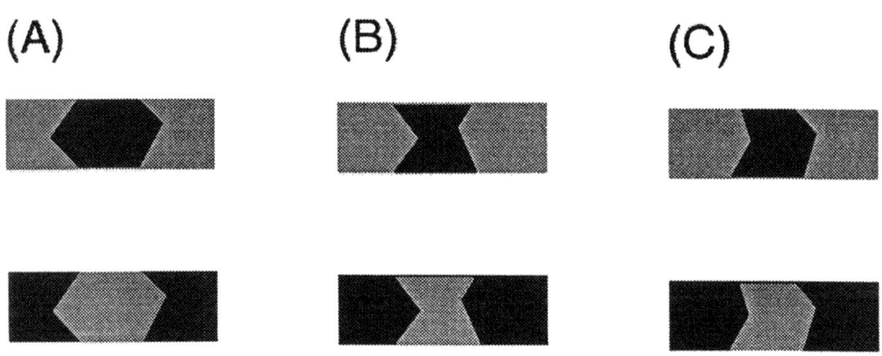

Figure 5. Stimuli in which perceptual set can create top-down effects in object-based attention tasks. (A) Stimuli used by Baylis and Driver (1993). If observers are instructed to perceive the black region, then the top panel involves attending to one object (the central black region) and the bottom panel involves attending to two objects (the flanking black regions). (B) Stimuli used by Gibson (1994) to show that a reversal of convexity reverses the object attention effects observed by Baylis and Driver (1993). (C) Ambiguous stimuli that do not contain convexity cues from Baylis (1994). See text for additional details.

Although Baylis and Driver's (1993) results appear consistent with a top-down biasing influence from perceptual set, there is a potential difficulty with their findings. This difficulty, pointed out by Gibson (1994), resulted in a theoretical exchange in the literature regarding the nature of perceptual set, bottom-up cues, and object-based attention (see Baylis, 1994; Gibson, 1994). This theoretical exchange can be understood better when viewed from the perspective of the biased competition that we have been outlining. The confound in the Baylis and Driver stimuli is visible in Figure 5A: The stimuli in Figure 5A contain a bottom-up cue to segregation—the central region was always convex and the two adjacent regions were always concave. Gibson (1994) correctly noted that convexity is a salient determinant of figure-ground segregation and, therefore, Baylis and Driver's (1993) results could have been caused by easier segregation of the central region, not object-based attention to a single region. That is, the convex region may have "popped out" to observers, allowing the apices of the central, convex region to be reported faster than the apices of the flanking, concave regions.

Gibson (1994) conducted a study in which he reversed the convexity in the stimuli by making the two flanking regions convex and the central region concave (Figure 5B). Interestingly, Gibson (1994) found that reversing the convexity also reversed the so-called object attention effect: Observers who viewed the stimuli in Figure 5B were faster to compare the apices when the two flanking regions were perceived as figure than when the central region was perceived as figure, a reversal of Baylis and Driver's (1993) results. Gibson's (1994) results suggest that salient bottom-up information, such as convex regions, may capture attention more effectively than less salient bottom-up information (concave regions). Object-based attention can be applied to multiple regions more effectively than to a single region, provided there is stimulus information (e.g., convexity) that favors the multiple-region interpretation of the scene over the single-region interpretation. In subsequent research, however, Baylis (1994) demonstrated an object-based effect in displays that had equal convexity between the central region and adjacent regions (Figure 5C). It is easier to select a single region than multiple regions when bottom-up cues are equated with one another and the only influence on object-based attention is perceptual set.

This exchange on the role of perceptual set in object attention is more than a minor disagreement about a stimulus confound when viewed from a biased competition account. The Baylis/Gibson exchange clearly shows that both bottom-up information and top-down perceptual set information can influence object attention. If bottom-up information, such as convexity, favors a two-object interpretation of a scene, attention may more easily select two objects than one object (Gibson's, 1994, results). However, bottom-up information alone does not guide object attention because equating all bottom-up cues allows perceptual set to have a continuing influence on object attention, which selects a single region more easily than two regions (Baylis', 1994, results).

Finally, Chen (1998) recently reported that object-based attentional effects were influenced by subjects' organization of a stimulus. Subjects viewed stimuli that could be perceived as either two objects (two V-shaped objects) or as one object (a single X-shaped object). Chen (1998) found that the instructions given to the subjects influenced object-based effects. Specifically, the subjects who were told they would see two V-shaped objects showed object-based effects; these subjects were faster to discriminate stimuli presented on a precued V shape than those stimuli presented on an uncued V shape. However, the subjects who were told to perceive the display as containing a single X showed no differences in discriminating stimuli on one region of the X shape or another region of the X shape. Subjects' perceptual set—the instructions provided by the experimenter—influenced how subjects organized and attended the displays.

Top-down biases from spatial attention. The studies that have used perceptual set to bias observers raise the issue of the mechanism that underlies perceptual set. Perceptual set can be viewed as an expectancy effect or a task demand imposed by the experimenter, but what are the visual processes involved in expectation or task demand? One possibility is that perceptual set involves the voluntary (or endogenous) control of spatial attention (e.g., Shulman, 1992; Tsal, 1994). Observers may voluntarily allocate their spatial attention to the region in the scene that is consistent with the instructions provided by the experimenter. For example, in Baylis and Driver's (1993) studies discussed above, observers who were instructed to attend to the red region may have shifted spatial attention to the red region, biasing this region to be perceived as figure. This account of perceptual set does find some empirical support in studies that show that overt attention—that is, eye fixation location—can influence the interpretation of a scene (e.g., Peterson & Gibson, 1994; Peterson & Hochberg, 1983). A voluntary spatial attention view of perceptual set suggests that spatial attention more generally may provide another top-down biasing signal in the biased competition account. There are a handful of studies that can be interpreted as demonstrating a top-down bias from spatial attention to object attention.

Perhaps one of the most straightforward tasks that shows how a spatial precue (and spatial attention) can influence object selection is the cued detection task developed by Egly et al. (1994) that was discussed earlier (see Figure 3). Recall that the target usually appears at the cued location (Figure 3A); when the target appears at an uncued location it may appear within the cued object (Figure 3B) or in the other, uncued object (Figure 3C). The important result is that observers are faster to respond to targets appearing in the uncued end of the cued rectangle than at either end of the uncued rectangle. The object selection demonstrated in this paradigm may involve a top-down component in addition to the bottom-up cues of closure and common region that define the two rectangles as separate objects. The spatial precue likely allows spatial attention to bias attention in a top-down manner: Because the two rectangles are identical, there is no bottom-up bias to favor attention to one object over the other (as in the two lines in Figure 1). Therefore, if there was no spatial precue, each object should have an equal chance of being attended, and presumably object attention would select one of the two objects randomly. The spatial precue acts to bias processing toward the cued object, allowing observers to respond faster to targets appearing in the cued object than in the uncued object. The processing bias for the cued object remains even when the object moves its position (e.g., Lamy & Tsal, 2000).

The top-down role of spatial attention on object selection has been demonstrated more recently in a series of studies reported by Lavie and Driver (1996), who investigated the combined roles of spatial attention and object attention by using spatial precues with an object-based attention task. Observers viewed two overlapping lines (objects) and discriminated features that appeared on the same line (same object) or different lines (different objects). In their final study, Lavie and Driver (1996) precued the adjacent ends of the different objects, as shown in Figure 6. The spatial precue summoned attention to a subregion of the display that contained features from the different objects. This spatial precue abolished object-based attention; that is, observers were just as fast to report features on the same object as features on different objects. Because spatial attention was restricted to a subregion of the display, the entirety of both objects was no longer in a spatially attended

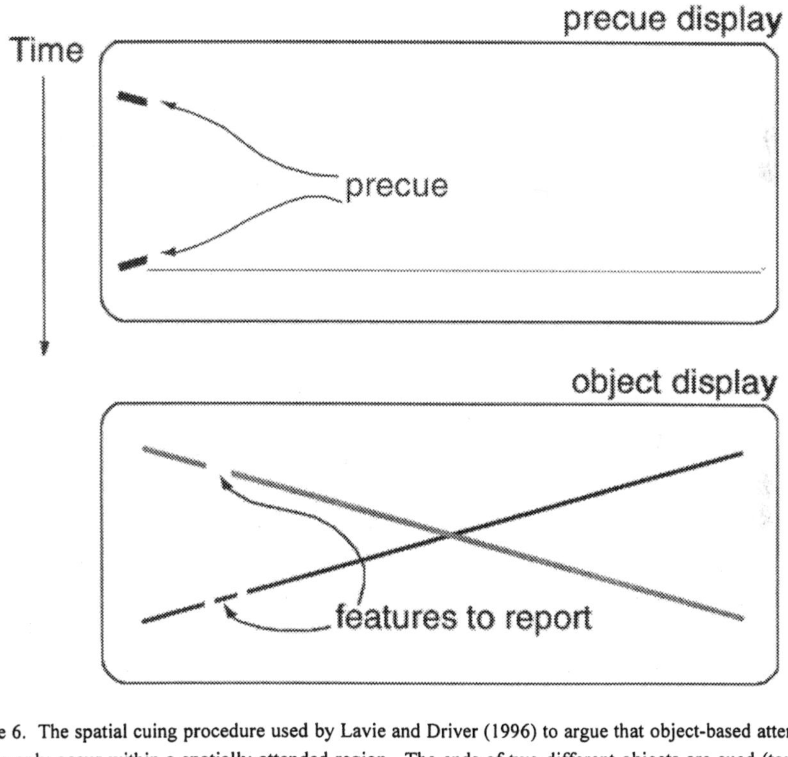

Figure 6. The spatial cuing procedure used by Lavie and Driver (1996) to argue that object-based attentional effects only occur within a spatially attended region. The ends of two different objects are cued (top), and subjects are asked to determine if two features are the same or different. The features most frequently appear near the cued regions; that is, the features are usually on different objects. When different objects are consistently precued, object-based attention effects disappear in this task.

region. Lavie and Driver (1996) concluded that object attention only occurs within a spatially attended region.

Although Lavie and Driver's (1996) results suggest a top-down influence from spatial attention to object attention processes, their explanation does not necessarily appeal to the mechanisms of biased competition. However, a biased competition account can readily explain the results from Lavie and Driver's (1996) final study without the need to suggest that object attention only occurs within a spatially attended region. An additional piece of procedural information is needed to explain Lavie and Driver's (1996) results with a biased competition account: The spatial precues used in their study were highly predictive. On 70% of the trials, observers were precued to attend to different objects. The top-down inputs from spatial attention were highly predictive and may have biased observers to adopt a spatial orienting strategy in which the objects were effectively ignored. The perceptual set established by a frequent spatial precue was to attend to different objects.

It follows from a biased-competition account that less-predictive spatial precues, in which the top-down inputs are weaker than those used by Lavie and Driver (1996), may not abolish object-based attention. Gilds & Vecera (submitted) tested this possibility by allowing the bottom-up object segregation cues to compete against non-predictive spatial precues. When the spatial precue was valid on 50% of trials (compared to 70% of the trials in Lavie & Driver, 1996), observers were faster to respond to features on the same object than on different objects. The spatial precue did not abolish the object-based effect, unlike what Lavie and Driver (1996) found using highly predictive spatial precues. Thus, object attention may no occur only within a spatially attended region; instead, both bottom-up and top-down factors influence object attention and the <u>strengths</u> of the top-down inputs also must be considered. Highly predictive (i.e., strong) spatial precues may allow observers to favor a spatial-selection strategy over an object-selection strategy, as in Lavie and Driver's (1996) results. These strategies may be established by observers' perceptual set, and perceptual set may be established through the statistical regularities of a task.

Summary

Both bottom-up, stimulus-driven cues and top-down, goal-driven cues can influence object attention. The allocation of object-based attention within a scene is dependent upon the cooperation and competition of bottom-up and top-down cues. Presumably, both sources of information influence behavior in important ways. For example, our visual systems need to be sensitive to bottom-up cues because these cues contain information regarding salient information in the external world. However, to maintain flexible behavior that is not entirely stimulus driven, visual processing must be modified by an observer's goals.

In the foregoing review, we have interpreted only behavioral results within the biased competition framework. In addition to the behavioral results, there are many recent results from cognitive neuroscience that also appear to support a biased competition account of object attention, such as findings that demonstrate neurons in primary visual cortex are sensitive to both figure-ground relations (e.g., Lamme, 1995; Zipser et al., 1996) and object-based attention (e.g., Roelfsema et al., 1998). In the next section, we discuss the cognitive neuroscience of object-based attention, including neuropsychological and neurophysiological approaches. Our goal in the next section is to show that the biased competition account of object attention provides a framework for results from different methodologies.

COGNITIVE NEUROSCIENCE OF OBJECT-BASED ATTENTION

Two important avenues of research in cognitive neuroscience have contributed to our understanding of object-based attention. The first avenue involves studies of humans with damage to the visual system, usually acquired in adulthood as a consequence of stroke, tumor, or trauma. The second avenue involves the study of nonhuman primates and includes behavioral studies as well as single neuron recording studies of awake, behaving animals.

Neuropsychology of Object-Based Attention

Data obtained from individuals with deficits following brain damage traditionally have provided an important source of evidence for theories of visual processing and, more recently, for theories of object-based attention. Two patient populations are of particular interest for the current purpose: patients with agnosia following lesions to the ventral or occipito-temporal cortical visual pathway and patients with hemispatial neglect following lesions to the dorsal or occipito-parietal pathway. We consider each neuropsychological deficit in turn.

Visual agnosia. The data from patients with visual agnosia is particularly relevant for understanding the processes involved in object segregation or the derivation of perceptual groups. Visual agnosia refers to an inability to identify or recognize even common objects presented in the visual modality, with intact semantics and recognition of objects through other sensory modalities. This disorder includes, at one end of the spectrum, a fairly low-level deficit such as the inability to extract featural elements from a display and, at the other end of the spectrum, a rather higher-level deficit such as the failure to assign meaning to an object despite the derivation of an intact percept (see Farah, 1990; Humphreys & Riddoch, 2000a, for reviews of this literature). Of particular relevance for the present discussion are a group of agnosic patients who mostly have available to them the features or elements in the display but who are unable to group these features into a meaningful and rich percept. These patients have problems with processes involved in perceptual organization, including figure-ground segregation, binding shapes from featural forms and binding surface properties to shapes. The consequence of the failure to individuate an object, part of an object or even a group of objects is that attention can not be biased to select specific object/s for further processing as no candidates are available. The standard behavioral effects associated with object-based attention, such as the facilitation of features of a single object, are consequently not obtained with these patients.

The absence of these object-based attention effects is exemplified in the performance of patient, JW, whom we have studied in some depth over the past few years (Vecera & Behrmann, 2000; Vecera & Behrmann, 1997). JW was in his late thirties when he suffered a severe cardiac event, the result of which was an anoxic encephalopathy (deprivation of oxygen from the brain). Although no focal masses or obvious infarcts are visible on neuroimaging, multiple hypodensities are seen in both occipital lobes on CT scan as well as more minor hypodensities in the right parietal lobe. A mild upper left visual field cut is present although this has no adverse effect on his performance in the tasks we conducted. JW appears to be unable to integrate contours as manifest in his inability to trace around the edges of two overlapping rectangles. He also performs at chance on the Efron (1968) shape matching task in which the subject is required to match two rectangles which vary in shape but are equal in area. Although JW is able to group elements in an image to some extent, based on Gestalt properties such as similarity or proximity, his ability to organize an image based on good continuation, closure or symmetry is poor. JW's visual disorder impairs his ability to recognize objects, even those that are encountered frequently, as well as faces and letters (for review of similar patients, see (Heider, 2000).

Most relevant for the current purpose is that JW does not benefit from within-object cueing, as evident in his performance on an Egly et al. (1994) object-based attention cuing task (Vecera & Behrmann, 1997). As mentioned previously, this task involves a precue followed by a target which appears either in the cued location (valid condition), in a location on the cued object but at the opposite end of the cued location (invalid, within-object condition) or in a location on the noncued object that is equidistant to the within-object location (invalid, between-object location). Normal subjects matched to JW (as well as the controls in the original experiment; Egly, Driver, & Rafal, 1994) detect the presence of the target most rapidly in the valid condition. The more important result is that they also detect the target faster in the within-object than in the between-object condition, reflecting the benefit accrued from sharing a location on the same object as the cue. This is the facilitation afforded by object-based attention. JW also shows fastest performance in the valid condition, reflecting normal spatial orienting. Unlike the control subjects, however, he showed no difference between the within- and between-object conditions. The absence of the object-based attention advantage likely reflects the failure on JW's part to establish the two objects as separate perceptual groups and to benefit from this segregation. JW's failure to organize the image perceptually precludes any benefit from the cued object. The finding that JW was still able to orient to spatial locations (fastest performance in the valid condition) reflects the separation of spatial- and object-based attentional processing. That JW had preserved the ability to deploy spatial attention is verified in another experiment using the same paradigm but in which the distance between the two objects is manipulated. JW again showed fastest performance on the valid condition. Consistent with characteristics of spatial-based attention, when the distance between the rectangles was reduced, JW detected the target faster in the invalid, between object condition than in the invalid, within-object condition as the former is spatially closer to the cue than the latter. Taken together, these findings illustrate how a deficit in the analysis and assembly of features can impair the subsequent operation of object-based attention when the image is not fully or correctly segmented. Spatial attention, however, is not dependent on perceptual grouping and operates independently and apparently normally.

The inability to organize an image perceptually is also the hallmark feature of integrative agnosia. This label was coined by Riddoch and Humphreys (1987) specifically to distinguish between patients who can perform feature analysis but who fail to integrate the features from other patients who are agnosic but with different underlying problems. As with JW, these patients also do not show object-based attention effects because they fail to organize the incoming image perceptually. Their perceptual performance however, is slightly better than that of JW who does not always have the elemental features in a display available to him. This is reflected in his less-than-normal performance on search tasks for some elementary features. In some cases, for example, searching for a target line feature which is less than 45 degrees different from the background distractor, JW does not show popout or normal target detection as the number of distractors increase (Mapelli and Behrmann, unpublished observations). In contrast, integrative agnosic patient, HJA, described in detail by Riddoch and Humphreys (Humphreys & Riddoch, 1987; Riddoch & Humphreys, 1987) is able to perform popout visual search for a feature that differs from the distractors in orientation. It is only when the target requires a conjunction of features or when the distractors differ from each other and require some form of grouping that performance is most obviously impaired (Humphreys & Riddoch, 2000b; Humphreys et al., 1994).

CK, a patient whom we have studied, exhibits performance similar to HJA. Like HJA, he fails to recognize common objects and is severely alexic. CK fails at figure-ground segregation tasks and his performance is poor when objects overlap compared with when they are depicted in isolation (Behrmann, Moscovitch, & Winocur, 1994). Critically, CK does not show a single-object advantage, namely, the ability to process the features of a single object in parallel. For example, we tested him on a paradigm in which subjects are required to decide, as quickly as possible, whether the number of bumps appearing at two of the four possible ends of overlapping rectangle are the same or not (Behrmann, Zemel, & Mozer, 1998; Behrmann, Zemel, & Mozer, 2000). As shown in Figure 7A, there are three conditions in this task, shown in the three rows, all of which are crossed with same/different judgements, as reflected in the columns. In the first, the single object condition, the bumps appear at the ends of a single, unoccluded objects. In the second condition, the bumps appear at the end of

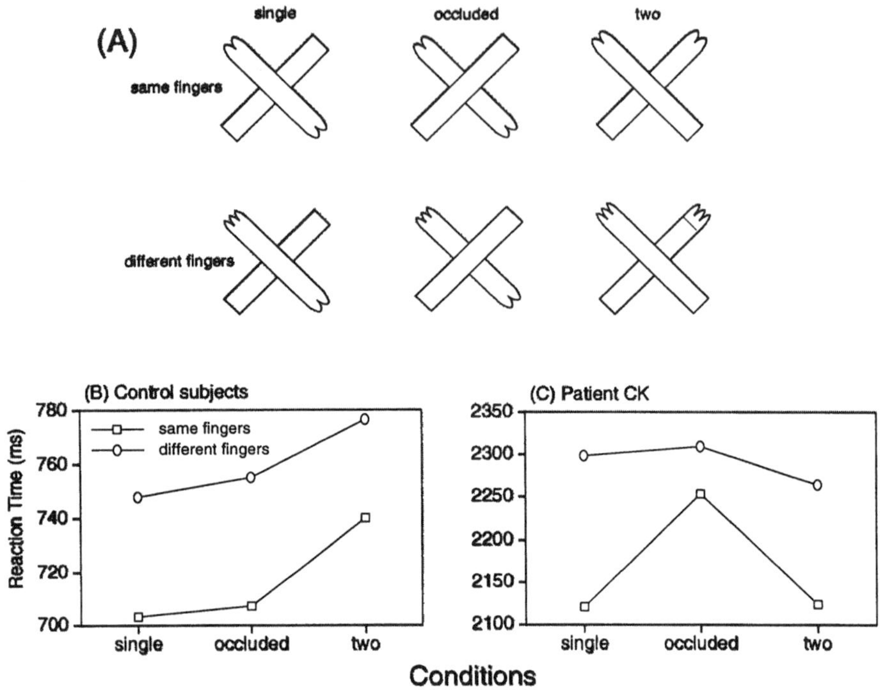

Figure 7. (A) Examples of displays from Behrmann et al.'s (1998) object attention task. Same and different judgements, shown in columns, are made to bumps appearing at ends of a single, unoccluded object, of two different objects or of a single, occluded object. (B) Reaction time data obtained from normal subjects (left panel; data from Behrmann et al., 1998) and patient CK (right panel) on the single, occluded and two object conditions for same and different trials.

two different objects and, in the third condition, the bumps appear at the ends of an occluded object. Whereas the normal subjects are equivalently fast to make the bumps decision on the single and occluded object, and both of these conditions are faster than the two-object condition, especially for 'same' judgements, this was not so for CK. Aside from the enormous intercept differences between the controls and patient CK, CK shows no difference between the single and the two object condition, reflecting the absence of the single-object benefit (Figure 7B). Interestingly, his performance for 'same' occluded objects is disproportionately slow, suggesting that he has difficulty integrating or processing in parallel the spatially discontinuous component parts. Taken together, the data from the agnosic patients reveals the failure of perceptual organization or object derivation. In the absence of candidate objects or groups of objects, attention cannot be biased preferentially to enhance the features of the possible objects and, thus, object-based attention no longer operates normally.

Visual hemispatial neglect. Hemispatial neglect refers to a deficit in which patients do not orient to or report information appearing on the side of space opposite the side of the brain lesion. Thus, following a lesion to the right hemisphere, patients may only draw information on the right, ignoring corresponding information on the left, may only eat from the right side of the plate and may only dress or apply make-up to the right side of the body (see Bisiach & Vallar, 2000; Vallar, 1998, for review of the phenomena). These patients, like those with agnosia as reviewed above, have a problem in deriving a coherent percept and, consequently, have disorders of object-based attention. In the case of hemispatial neglect, the problem arises specifically because these patients do not process or represent adequately the information occurring on the contralesional side. The question is what consequences this spatial deficit has for object-based attention.

The failure to represent contralesional information has recently been thought of as a failure to select information on the contralesional side as a consequence of a biased spatial competition mechanism. Neglect is thought to arise from a gradient of spatial attention or bias such that, following brain damage, fewer neurons are available to represent information on the contralesional than on the ipsilesional side. The consequence of this is that information on the ipsilesional side is activated so much more strongly than contralesional information that it invariably wins in a winner-take-all outcome. This imbalance as a function of neuronal distribution occurs not only between the two hemifields but also within a single hemifield, giving rise to better performance even for stimuli on the relative left of the right visual field. This theoretical interpretation of neglect has received much support not only from studies which describe the distribution of neurons in parietal cortex (Duhamel & Hamed, personal communication; Rizzolatti, Berti, & Gallese, 2000) and from neuropsychological studies of patients (Cate & Behrmann, 2000; di Pellegrino, Basso, & Frasinetti, 1998; di Pellegrino, Basso, & Frassinetti, 1997), but also from studies which explore the nature of the competition which manifests after parietal damage (Cohen, Romero, Servan-Schreiber, & Farah, 1994; Mozer, 1999; Pouget & Driver, 2000).

Of most interest to the present issue is that contralesional information can be detected under some circumstances. For example, in those cases where contralesional information can be grouped with the corresponding ipsilesional information, selection of information on the left is possible and extinction of the contralesional information can be overridden. It is the knowledge about objects and their structure that offsets the negative bias associated with the contralesional information. For example, Ward, Goodrich, and Driver (1994) showed that when the contralesional item could be grouped with the ipsilesional information on the basis of Gestalt factors such as similarity (for example, a bracket on the left and a bracket on the right) or symmetry, report of the left-sided stimulus improved by roughly 50% compared to when the left sided information could not be grouped with a simultaneous right sided stimulus. The same pattern was obtained when the two items formed a familiar configuration (for example, an arrow made of a left arrowhead and a right horizontal bar). This modulation of extinction of the contralesional information has suggested that, in the context of a competitive mechanism, the negative bias for the contralesional information is reduced such that contralesional and ipsilesional information form a single group and cooperate rather than compete.

The reduction of extinction through grouping has now been replicated in several studies with parietal patients and better processing of the contralesional information has been shown when the left-sided information can be grouped by bottom-up factors such as color and proximity field (Driver & Halligan, 1991) or brightness or collinear edges (Gilchrist, Humphreys, & Riddoch, 1996; Rorden, Mattingley, Karnath, & Driver, 1997). A reduction in contralesional extinction is also seen when the left information is grouped with the right information by a global outline (Farah, Wallace, & Vecera, 1993). We also see modulation of poor left-sided processing when the contralesional information forms the left side of an illusory contour (Kanizsa-type figure), of a partially occluded figure (Mattingley, David, & Driver, 1997; see also Driver, Baylis, & Rafal, 1992) or of any well-configured object or whole (Gilchrist et al., 1996; Humphreys & Riddoch, 1994).

Low-level mechanisms of edge assignment may also influence the neglect outcome, with attention being allocated exclusively to those shaped regions to which an edge has been assigned. When viewing ambiguous 2D displays comprising adjacent regions separated by a common vertically oriented articulated contour, the region on the left is perceived as being figure and is matched or copied better than the region to the right (Driver, Baylis, & Rafal, 1992; Marshall & Halligan, 1994; Mattingley, Price, & Driver, 2000; Peterson, Gerhardstein, Mennemeier, & Rapcsak, 1998). Performance, however, was also influenced by the familiarity of the object in that the region on the left was picked as figure with even greater frequency when the contralesional information corresponded to a high denotative (familiar) object (Peterson et al., 1998). Interestingly, even when the dividing contour depicted a high denotative object, the low denotative region on the left was still identified as figure despite the fact that the patient could identify the high denotative shapes when they appeared to the right (Mattingley et al., 2000). This finding attests to the robust and powerful influence of edge assignment in modulating what is neglected and what is perceived.

Temporal processes can also influence extinction. Recent data from the study of patient GK, who has bilateral parietal lesions, suggests that extinction may arise from the temporary binding of the information (Riddoch, Humphreys, & Nys, 2000). In their study, they demonstrated that GK could report two stimuli when the onset of the stimuli was common (but not the offset) and the display duration was short (300 ms and less) but not when it was above 500 ms. The term 'anti-extinction' was adopted by the authors to indicate the recovery of the extinguished contralesional information. In this case, the temporal similarity between the contralesional and ipsilesional stimuli, rather than their common form characteristics, was sufficient for them to be equally activated and reported. Although common onset suffices for anti-extinction effects, when it is pitted against other object-segmentation cues such that the contralesional and ipsilesional information appear to belong to different objects, the advantage of common onset is overridden and extinction is, once again, observed.

Top down lexical effects also play a role with less extinction for known, familiar objects than for unknown objects (Ward & Goodrich, 1996; Ward et al., 1994) and for left-sided stimuli that form a unified lexical representation with the right-sided item (for example, COW BOY as opposed to COW SUN; Behrmann, Moscovitch, Black, & Mozer, 1990; Brunn & Farah, 1991).

Taken together, these findings suggest that visual elements may enter into grouping prior to or simultaneous with the distribution of spatial attention. The extent to which the elements cohere and form a robust perceptual group may determine whether neglect is observed or not.

Physiology of Object-Based Attention

In contrast to the focus on parietal lobe involvement in neuropsychological studies of object selection, physiological studies have implicated several other cortical areas in object attention. Neurophysiological studies from behaving monkeys have implicated primary visual cortex (V1) and the supplementary eye fields (SEF) in coding objects for attentional orienting. Human electrophysiological studies have suggested shared mechanisms between object-based and space-based selection, consistent with attentional selection from a grouped spatial array (Vecera, 1994; Vecera & Farah, 1994) that involves both object segregation processes and object attention processes.

Over the past few years, a potential conundrum has arisen in neurophysiological studies of visual attention (Posner & Gilbert, 1999): Does visual attention operate at the level of primary visual cortex, or V1? Many earlier studies failed to find V1 attention effects in this area (e.g., Luck et al., 1997; Moran & Desimone, 1985), but more recent studies of appear to show attention effects in this visual area (Gandhi et al., 1999; Motter, 1993; Roelfsema et al., 1998). Object-based attentional orienting may provide an explanation for when V1 attentional effects will be observed—attention may operate at the level of V1 when objects are selected. V1 may provide a neural substrate for a grouped-array representation.

In an important study, Roelfsema and colleagues demonstrated object-based attentional effects in area V1. Specifically, Roelfsema et al. (1998) demonstrated that attending to one of two objects in a display results in enhanced firing for neurons whose receptive fields contain features of the attended object. Monkeys viewed scenes containing two objects (simple curves); one of the objects was connected to the fixation point, and monkeys were trained to attend to this object. The monkeys' task was to make an eye movement from the fixation point to the opposite end of the attended curve. Segments of the curves fell within receptive fields of V1 neurons. The neuronal responses were larger when a receptive field contained a segment of the attended curve than a segment of the unattended curve. This object-based attentional modulation in area V1 is important because previous studies of spatial attention were equivocal in finding V1 attentional modulation. Neurons in V1 may exhibit attentional modulation when an object can act as the recipient or focus of attention; neurons in V1 may not appear to exhibit attentional modulation with blank displays or nonorganized cluttered displays. Objects may need to be present to receive the top-down feedback from spatial attention processes.

Beyond the object-based effects observed in primary visual cortex, neurophysiological studies also have suggested that object-based effects can occur in the oculomotor system. Olson and Gettner (1995, 1999) showed that neurons in the supplementary eye fields (SEF), located on the dorsomedial surface of the frontal lobes, represent object-centered spatial selectivity for the direction of eye movements. SEF neurons seem to code for spatial positions within an object, such as the left side of the object. Olson and Gettner trained monkeys to make eye movements to the onset of a visual target. The target appeared in one of three conditions: alone in an otherwise blank display, at the left end of an object (a rectangle), or at the right end of an object. The absolute direction of the eye movement was identical in all three conditions; that is, the monkeys' eyes moved in exactly the same direction and same distance across these conditions. Although the eyes moved identically, a subset of SEF neurons fired at higher rates when eye movements were executed to a specific region of the object, regardless of object's absolute spatial location. For example, some neurons responded vigorously to eye movements to the right side of the object; the same eye movement that landed on the left side of the object resulted in a smaller neuronal response. Thus, SEF neurons code for locations within an object; how these locations are coded (e.g., in a grouped array or in another representation) is unknown.

Finally, several recent studies have investigated object selection by using event-related potential (ERP) studies with humans. Kramer and colleagues (Weber, Kramer, & Miller, 1997) took issue with the late, object-based visual working memory selection explanation of Duncan's (1984) results offered by Vecera and Farah (1994). Instead, Weber et al. hypothesized that selection in this task may occur at the perceptual level from a grouped array representation. To determine if object selection in Duncan's task occurred from a spatiotopic array, Weber et al. had subjects perform a version of this task while ERPs were recorded from scalp electrodes. Two overlapping objects were presented to the left or right of fixation, and subjects reported pairs of attributes from these objects. The attributes appeared either on the same object or on different objects. On two-thirds of the trials, a task-irrelevant probe stimulus followed the presentation of the object stimuli. Task irrelevant probes have been used extensively to study spatial attention (see Hillyard et al., 1998; Luck, 1998; Luck & Vecera, in press; Vecera & Luck, in press, for reviews). Early ERP components, specifically the P1 and N1 components, are generated by task irrelevant probes, and the voltage amplitudes of these components are larger when the probes appear at attended locations than at unattended locations (Luck, 1998).

Weber and colleagues reasoned that if attention was selecting from a grouped spatial array, then probes that appeared at the location of the two overlapping stimuli should evoke larger responses when subjects report attributes from the same object than from different objects. The results appeared to support this predicted outcome. Behaviorally, subjects were more accurate reporting attributes from the same object than from different objects. The irrelevant-probe evoked P1 components had larger amplitudes in the same-object condition than in the different-object conditions. However, this P1 effect is correlational with the object effect observed in the behavioral data, and, therefore, the P1 effect could be due to other variables. For example, the P1 effect could have been caused by the abrupt onset of the objects; abrupt onsets are known to capture spatial attention (Yantis, 1998; Yantis & Jonides, 1984). The capture of spatial attention by the abrupt appearance of the objects may have been modulated indirectly by the same-object and different-objects conditions. Specifically, in the same-object condition, spatial attention could have been captured and allocated to a smaller region in the object display; in the different-objects condition, spatial attention could have been captured and allocated to a larger region of the object display. The size of the spatial focus may not cause the object effect observed in the behavioral data but may produce differences in the amplitude of the P1 component.

Although some aspects of Weber et al.'s data may not support grouped-array selection, results presented by Valdes-Sosa et al. (1997) are very compelling. Valdes-Sosa et al. had subjects view displays containing two superimposed surfaces that occupied the same spatial location and rotated in opposite directions; subjects' subjective impressions were to see two separate moving surfaces, or objects. Subjects were asked to selectively attend to one of the two surfaces. Either the attended surface and the unattended surface moved in a linear (i.e., non-rotational) motion. These motion onsets were used to generate ERPs. Motion changes to the attended surface produced early ERP components with larger amplitudes than stimuli presented on the unattended surface. Specifically, changes on the attended surface generate larger P1, N1, and N2 components compared to changes on the unattended surface. The P1 and N1 components typically are modulated by spatial attention (see Hillyard et al., 1998; Luck, 1998), suggesting a spatial component in Valdes-Sosa et al.'s data that occurred despite the spatial overlap between the two objects. The similarity of these effects to the spatial attention effects described above suggest that some object-based effects may be generated by neural processes shared with spatial attention. Attentional selection may be occurring from a grouped spatial array in which motion segregation cues allow the two dot surfaces to be separated from one another on the basis of a bottom-up image cue—common motion. This stimulus cue may have allowed the two dot surfaces to be segregated in depth, which then permitted object-based attention to select one surface over the other.

Connections to Biased Competition

The biased competition framework we outlined earlier may lend some conceptual organization to the results from neuropsychological patients and single-unit recordings just reviewed. Different populations of neuropsychological patients appear to have become insensitive to particular object attention cues. For example, patient JW (Vecera & Behrmann, 1997), who had visual form agnosia, was unable to make use of bottom-up image cues for segregating the visual field and attending to objects. In contrast, patients with hemineglect may be able to make use of bottom-up information, but attentional processes, which may influence object segregation in a top-down manner, appear to be disrupted in these patients.

The neurophysiological results we reviewed also can be interpreted within the biased competition framework we have outlined. Most of the studies conducted to date have investigated the bottom-up control of object-based attention. Olson and Gettner's (1995, 1999) research demonstrates that oculomotor control is influenced by shapes in the visual environment. Roelfsema et al.'s (1998) curve tracing results suggest that attentional processes are influenced by the structure of the images that are being searched. But, the curve that is selected in the curve-tracing task is due to behavioral goals (i.e., where the monkey must move its eyes), a top-down factor, pointing to both bottom-up and top-down influences in Roelfsema et al.'s (1998) task. A similar conclusion comes from Landman et al. (2000, cited in Lamme et al., 2000), who discussed recent results from their lab demonstrating different time courses for bottom-up and top-down processing components. Landman et al. (2000) discuss the results of research in progress that presented monkeys with a multi-object scene while multiunit recordings were made from area V1. Based on previous research (e.g., Lamme, 1995), V1 appears to play a role in segregating an object from the background (figure-ground segregation). In the multi-object displays, object segregation occurred temporally early and did not depend upon the number of objects in the display. However, a temporally later component of the physiological response did depend on the number of objects in the display, indicating an object-based attentional component. Image-based bottom-up cues to object segregation appear to influence processing early, followed by top-down attentional factors. Finally, Valdes-Sosa et al.'s (1997) electrophysiological results suggest that stimulus cues, namely common motion, can establish perceptual groups that are then selected by attention; the attentional selection observed in this task bears a striking similarity to spatial selection. Thus, Valdes-Sosa et al.'s findings may be interpreted as an early object segregation process influencing later attentional processes in a bottom-up manner.

Summary and Conclusions

Visual scenes typically contain many objects that compete for attention. Some of these objects may be more salient than others, and some of these objects may be more relevant for a current behavioral goal than others. Object salience and goal or task relevance characterize the two main influences on object attention under the biased competition framework we have proposed here. In this chapter, we outlined a biased competition framework for object-based attentional selection. The strength of this framework is that it provides a conceptual structure for interpreting the many behavioral results regarding object-based attentional selection. We admit that the framework may ultimately be unfalsifiable, but the framework is useful to the extent that it (1) organizes previous research, (2) suggests directions for future research (e.g., studying the control parameters that influence top-down and bottom-up aspects of object attention), and (3) generates more specific, falsifiable theories of object selection. We also reviewed several recent findings on the neural mechanisms that may be involved in object-based attention, and these results also may be accommodated within the biased competition framework.

We would like to conclude by pointing out that the general principles of our biased competition framework are consistent with the principles of parallel distributed processing (PDP) models and that the biased competition view could be instantiated concretely in a PDP models. Our own efforts at computational modeling (e.g., Mozer, Zemel, Behrmann, & Williams, 1992; Vecera & O'Reilly, 1998, 2000) are consistent with the idea that there are multiple cues to object segregation and attention. The theoretical usefulness of the biased competition account we have presented will be determined by this account's ability to guide the development of future computational models as well as future experimental studies.

AKNOWLEDGEMENTS

The authors thank Steve Luck, Mike Mozer, Kendra Gilds, Ed Vogel, and Geoff Woodman, for discussing several of the empirical results that we reviewed. Correspondence can be addressed to Shaun P. Vecera, Department of Psychology, E11 Seashore Hall, University of Iowa, Iowa City, IA 52242-1407. Electronic mail can be sent to: shaun-vecera@uiowa.edu.

REFERENCES

Allport, A. (1993). Attention and control: Have we been asking the wrong questions? A critical review of twenty-five years. In D. E. Meyer & S. Kornblum (Eds.), *Attention and Performance XIV* (pp. 183-218). Cambridge, MA: MIT Press.

Baylis, G. C. (1994). Visual attention and objects: Two-object cost with equal convexity. *Journal of Experimental Psychology: Human Perception and Performance*, *20*, 208-212.

Baylis, G. C., & Driver, J. (1992). Visual parsing and response competition: The effect of grouping factors. *Perception & Psychophysics*, *51*, 145-162.

Baylis, G. C., & Driver, J. (1993). Visual attention and objects: Evidence for hierarchical coding of location. *Journal of Experimental Psychology: Human Perception and Performance*, *19*, 451-470.

Behrmann, M., & Haimson, C. (1999). The cognitive neuroscience of visual attention. *Current Opinion in Neurobiology*, *9*, 158-163.

Behrmann, M., Moscovitch, M., Black, S. E., & Mozer, M. C. (1990). Perceptual and conceptual factors in neglect dyslexia: Two contrasting case studies. *Brain*, *113*, 1163-1183.

Behrmann, M., Moscovitch, M., & Winocur, G. (1994). Intact visual imagery and impaired visual perception in a patient with visual agnosia. *Journal of Experimental Psychology: Human Perception and Performance*, *20*, 1068-1087.

Behrmann, M., Zemel, R., & Mozer, M. C. (1998). Object-based attention and occlusion: Evidence from normal subjects and a computational model. *Journal of Experimental Psychology: Human Perception and Performance*, *24*, 1011-1036.

Behrmann, M., Zemel, R., & Mozer, M. C. (2000). Occlusion, symmetry, and object-based attention: Reply to Saiki (2000). *Journal of Experimental Psychology: Human Perception and Performance*, *26*, 1497-1505.

Bisiach, E., & Vallar, G. (2000). Unilateral neglect in humans. In F. Boller & J. Grafman (Eds.), *Handbook of neuropsychology*. North-Holland, Amsterdam: Elsevier Science.

Brunn, J. L., & Farah, M. J. (1991). The relation between spatial attention and reading: Evidence from the neglect syndrome. *Cognitive Neuropsychology*, *8*, 59-75.

Cate, A., & Behrmann, M. (2000). *Hemispatial neglect: Spatial and temporal influences.* Manuscript submitted for publication.

Chen, Z. (1998). Switching attention within and between objects: The role of subjective organization. *Canadian Journal of Experimental Psychology*, *52*, 7-16.

Cohen, J., Romero, R., Servan-Schreiber, D., & Farah, M. J. (1994). Mechanisms of spatial attention: The relation of macrostructure to microstructure in parietal neglect. *Journal of Cognitive Neuroscience*, *6*, 377-387.

Cohen, J. D., & Huston, T. A. (1994). Progress in the use of interactive models for understanding attention and performance. In C. Umiltá & M. Moscovitch (Eds.), *Attention and Performance XV* (pp. 453-476). Cambridge, MA: MIT Press.

Desimone, R., & Duncan, J. (1995). Neural mechanisms of selective visual attention. *Annual Review of Neuroscience*, *18*, 193-222.

di Pellegrino, G., Basso, G., & Frasinetti, F. (1998). Visual extinction as a spatio-temporal disorder of selective attention. *NeuroReport*, *9*, 835-839.

di Pellegrino, G., Basso, G., & Frassinetti, F. (1997). Spatial extinction on double asynchronous stimulation. *Neuropsychologia*, *35*, 1215-1223.

Driver, J., Baylis, G. C., & Rafal, R. D. (1992). Preserved figure-ground segregation and symmetry perception in visual neglect. *Nature, 360*, 73-75.

Driver, J., & Halligan, P. W. (1991). Can visual neglect operate in object-centered coordinates: An affirmative study. *Cognitive Neuropsychology, 8*, 475-496.

Duncan, J. (1984). Selective attention and the organization of visual information. *Journal of Experimental Psychology: General, 113*, 501-517.

Duncan, J. (1993a). Similarity between concurrent visual discriminations: Dimensions and objects. *Perception & Psychophysics, 54*, 425-430.

Duncan, J. (1993b). Coordination of what and where in visual attention. *Perception, 22*, 1261-1270.

Duncan, J., & Humphreys, G. W. (1989). Visual search and stimulus similarity. *Psychological Review, 96*, 433-458.

Efron, R. (1968). What is perception? *Boston Studies in Philosophy of Science, 4*, 137-173.

Egly, R., Driver, J., & Rafal, R. D. (1994). Shifting visual attention between objects and locations: Evidence from normal and parietal lesion subjects. *Journal of Experimental Psychology: General, 123*, 161-177.

Eriksen, B. A., & Eriksen, C. W. (1974). Effects of noise letters upon the identification of a target letter in a nonsearch task. *Perception & Psychophysics, 16*, 143-149.

Eriksen, C. W., & Hoffman, J. (1973). The extent of processing of noise elements during selective encoding from visual displays. *Perception & Psychophysics, 14*, 155-160.

Farah, M. J. (1990). *Visual Agnosia.* Cambridge, MA: MIT Press.

Farah, M. J., Wallace, M., & Vecera, S. P. (1993). "What" and "where" in visual attention: Evidence from the neglect syndrome. In I. H. Robertson & J. C. Marshall (Eds.), *Unilateral neglect: Clinical and Experimental Studies* (pp. 123-138). Hove, UK: Erlbaum.

Gandhi, S. P., Heeger, D. J., & Boynton, G. M. (1999). Spatial attention affects brain activity in human primary visual cortex. *Proceedings of the National Academy of Sciences, 96*, 3314-3319.

Gibson, B. S. (1994). Visual attention and objects: One versus two or convex versus concave? *Journal of Experimental Psychology: Human Perception and Performance, 20*, 203-207.

Gilchrist, I. D., Humphreys, G. W., & Riddoch, M. J. (1996). Grouping and extinction: Evidence for low-level modulation of visual selection. *Cognitive Neuropsychology, 13*, 1223-1249.

Gilds, K. S., & Vecera, S. P. (submitted). *The influence of spatial attention on object-based selection.* Manuscript submitted for publication.

Goldsmith, M. (1998). What's in a location? Comparing object-based and space-based models of feature integration in visual search. *Journal of Experimental Psychology: General, 127*, 189-219.

Haimson, C., & Behrmann, M. (in preparation). *Objects in attention: The many faces of object-based selection.*

Harter, M. R., & Aine, C. J. (1984). Brain mechanisms of visual selective attention. In R. Parasuraman & D. R. Davies (Eds.), *Varieties of Attention* (pp. 293-321). Orlando, FL: Academic Press.

Heider, B. (2000). Visual form agnosia: Neural mechanisms and anatomical foundations. *Neurocase, 6*, 1-12.

Hillyard, S. A., Vogel, E. K., & Luck, S. J. (1998). Sensory gain control (amplification) as a mechanism of selective attention: Electrophysiological and neuroimaging evidence. *Philosophical Transactions of the Royal Society of London, 353B*, 1257-1270.

Hoffman, D. D., & Richards, W. (1984). The parts of recognition. *Cognition, 18*, 65-96.

Hoffman, D. D., & Singh, M. (1997). Salience of visual parts. *Cognition, 63*, 29-78.

Humphreys, G. W., & Riddoch, M. J. (1987). *To See but not to See: A Case-Study of Visual Agnosia.* Hillsdale, NJ: Erlbaum.

Humphreys, G. W., & Riddoch, M. J. (1994). Attention to within-object and between-object spatial representations: Multiple sites for visual selection. *Cognitive Neuropsychology, 11*, 207-241.

Humphreys, G. W., & Riddoch, M. J. (2000a). Knowing what you need but not what you want: Affordance and action-defined templates in neglect. *Behavioral Neurology.*

Humphreys, G. W., & Riddoch, M. J. (2000b). Neuropsychological disorders of visual object recognition and naming. In F. Boller & J. Grafman (Eds.), *Handbook of Neuropsychology* (Vol. 4). North-Holland: Elsevier Science.

Humphreys, G. W., Riddoch, M. J., Donnelly, N., Freeman, T., Boucart, M., & Muller, H. M. (1994). Intermediate visual processing and visual agnosia. In M. J. Farah & G. Ratcliff (Eds.), *The Neuropsychology of High-Level Vision* (pp. 63-101). Hillsdale, New Jersey: Lawrence Erlbaum.

Julesz, B. (1984). A brief outline of the texton theory of human vision. *Trends in Neurosciences, 6*, 41-45.

Kimchi, R., & Hadad, B. (2000). *Influence of past experience on perceptual grouping.* Manuscript submitted for publication.

Kramer, A. F., & Jacobson, A. (1991). Perceptual organization and focussed attention: The role of objects and proximity in visual processing. *Perception & Psychophysics, 50*, 267-284.

Kramer, A. F., Tham, M.-P., & Yeh, Y.-Y. (1991). Movement and focused attention: A failure to replicate. *Perception & Psychophysics, 50*, 537-546.

Lamme, V. A. F. (1995). The neurophysiology of figure-ground segregation in primary visual cortex. *Journal of Neuroscience, 15*, 1605-1615.

Lamme, V. A. F., Supér, H., Landman, R., Roelfsema, P. R., & Spekreijse, H. (2000). The role of primary visual cortex (V1) in visual awareness. *Vision Research, 40*, 1507-

1521.

Lamy, D., & Tsal, Y. (2000). Object features, object locations, and object files: Which does selective attention activate and when? *Journal of Experimental Psychology: Human Perception and Performance*, *26*, 1387-1400.

Landman, R., Lamme, V. A. F., & Spekreijse, H. (2000). Gradual transition from preattentive to attentive components in a neural correlate of figure-ground segregation in monkey V1. *Investigative Ophthalmology and Visual Science*, *40* (Suppl. S200).

Lavie, N., & Driver, J. (1996). On the spatial extent of attention in object-based visual selection. *Perception & Psychophysics*, *58*, 1238-1251.

Logan, G. D. (1996). The CODE theory of visual attention: An integration of space-based and object-based attention. *Psychological Review*, *103*, 603-649.

Luck, S. J. (1998). Neurophysiology of selective attention. In H. Pashler (Ed.), *Attention* (pp. 257-295). East Sussex, UK: Psychology Press.

Luck, S. J., Chelazzi, L., Hillyard, S. A., & Desimone, R. (1997). Neural mechanisms of spatial selective attention in areas V1, V2, and V4 of macaque visual cortex. *Journal of Neurophysiology*, *77*, 24-42.

Luck, S. J. & Vecera, S. P. (2000). Attention: From tasks to mechanisms. To appear in H. Pashler & S. Yantis (Eds.), *Steven's Handbook of Experimental Psychology*.

Marshall, J. C., & Halligan, P. W. (1994). The yin and yang of visuo-spatial neglect: A case study. *Neuropsychologia*, *32*, 1036-1057.

Mattingley, J. B., David, G., & Driver, J. (1997). Pre-attentive filling in of visual surfaces in parietal extinction. *Science*, *275*, 671-674.

Mattingley, J. B., Price, M. C., & Driver, J. (2000). *Figure-ground segmentation of ambiguous 2D displays: Clues to object-based visual neglect*. Paper presented at the Cognitive and Neural Bases of Spatial neglect, Como, Italy.

Moran, J., & Desimone, R. (1985). Selective attention gates visual processing in the extrastriate cortex. *Science*, *229*, 782-784.

Motter, B. C. (1993). Focal attention produces spatially selective processing in visual cortical areas V1, V2 and V4 in the presence of competing stimuli. *Journal of Neurophysiology*, *70*, 909-919.

Mozer, M. C. (1999). Explaining object-based deficits in unilateral neglect without object-based frames of reference. In J. A. Reggia, E. Ruppin, & D. Glanzman (Eds.), *Disorders of Brain, Behavior, and Cognition: The Neurocomputational Perspective* (pp. 99-119). Amsterdam: Elsevier.

Mozer, M. C., & Sitton, M. (1998). Computational modeling of spatial attention. In H. Pashler (Ed.), *Attention* (pp. 341-393). Hove, UK: Psychology Press.

Mozer, M. C., Zemel, R. S., Behrmann, M., & Williams, C. K. I. (1992). Learning to segment images using dynamic feature binding. *Neural Computation*, *4*, 650-665.

Neisser, U. (1967). *Cognitive Psychology*. New York: Appleton-Century-Crofts.

Neisser, U., & Becklen, R. (1975). Selective looking: Attending to visually specified events. *Cognitive Psychology, 7*, 480-494.

O'Craven, K. M., Downing, P. E., & Kanwisher, N. (1999). fMRI evidence for objects as the units of attentional selection. *Nature, 401*, 584-587.

Olson C. R., & Gettner, S. N. (1995). Object-centered direction selectivity in the macaque supplementary eye field. *Science, 269*, 985-988.

Olson C. R., & Gettner, S. N. (1999). Macaque SEF neurons encode object-centered directions of eye movements regardless of the visual attributes of instructional cues. *Journal of Neurophysiology, 81*, 2340-2346.

Palmer, S. E. (1992). Common region: A new principle of perceptual grouping. *Cognitive Psychology, 24*, 436-447.

Palmer, S. E. (1999). *Vision Science: From Photons to Phenomenology*. Cambridge, MA: MIT Press.

Peterson, M. A., Gerhardstein, P. C., Mennemeier, M., & Rapcsak, S. Z. (1998). Object-centered attentional biases and object recognition contributions to scene segmentation in left and right hemisphere patients. *Psychobiology, 26*, 557-570.

Peterson, M. A., & Gibson, B. S. (1994). Object recognition contributions to figure-ground organization: Operations on outlines and subjective contours. *Perception & Psychophysics, 56*, 551-564.

Peterson, M. A., & Hochberg, J. (1983). Opposed-set measurement procedure: A quantitative analysis of the role of local cues and intention in form perception. *Journal of Experimental Psychology: Human Perception and Performance, 9*, 183-193.

Posner, M. I. (1980). Orienting of attention. *Quarterly Journal of Experimental Psychology, 32A*, 3-25.

Posner, M. I., Snyder, C. R. R., & Davidson, B. J. (1980). Attention and the detection of signals. *Journal of Experimental Psychology: General, 109*, 160-174.

Posner, M. I., & Gilbert, C. D. (1999). Attention and primary visual cortex. *Proceedings of the National Academy of Sciences, 96*, 2585-2587.

Pouget, A., & Driver, J. (2000). Relating unilateral neglect to the neural coding of space. *Current Opinion in Neurobiology, 10*, 242-249.

Riddoch, M. J., & Humphreys, G. W. (1987). A case of integrative visual agnosia. *Brain, 110*, 1431-1462.

Riddoch, M. J., Humphreys, G. W., & Nys, G. (2000). *Characteristics of anti-extinction and extinction effects*. Paper presented at the Cognitive and Neural Bases of Spatial neglect, Como, Italy.

Rizzolatti, G., Berti, A., & Gallese, V. (2000). Spatial neglect: Neurophysiological bases, cortical circuits and theories. In F. Boller & J. Grafman (Eds.), *Handbook of Neuropsychology*. North-Holland, Amsterdam: Elsevier Science.

Roelfsema, P. R, Lamme, V. A. F, & Spekreijse, H. (1998). Object-based attention in the primary visual cortex of the macaque monkey. *Nature, 395*, 376-381.

Rorden, C., Mattingley, J. B., Karnath, H.-O., & Driver, J. (1997). Visual extinction and prior entry: Impaired perception of temporal order with intact motion perception after unilateral parietal damage. *Neuropsychologia, 35*, 421-433.

Rubin, E. (1915/1958). Figure and ground. In D. C. Beardslee & M. Wertheimer (Eds.), *Readings in Perception* (pp. 194-203). Princeton, NJ: Van Nostrand. (Original work published 1915.)

Sagi, D., & Julesz, B. (1984). Detection versus discrimination of visual orientation. *Perception, 13*, 619-628.

Shulman, G. L. (1992). Attentional modulation of a figural aftereffect. *Perception, 21*, 7-19.

Sperling, G., & Weichselgartner, E. (1995). Episodic theory of the dynamics of spatial attention. *Psychological Review, 102*, 503-532.

Treisman, A. (1988). Features and objects. The fourteenth Bartlett memorial lecture. *Quarterly Journal of Experimental Psychology, 40A*, 201-237.

Treisman, A., & Gelade, G. A. (1980). A feature-integration theory of attention. *Cognitive Psychology, 12*, 96-136.

Tsal, Y. (1994). Effects of attention on perception of features and figural organisation. *Perception, 23*, 441-452.

Valdes-Sosa, M., Bobes, M. A., Rodriguez, V., & Pinilla, T. (1998). Switching attention without shifting the spotlight: Object-based attentional modulation of brain potentials. *Journal of Cognitive Neuroscience, 10*, 137-151.

Vallar, G. (1998). Spatial hemineglect in humans. *Trends in Cognitive Sciences, 2*, 87-96.

Vecera, S. P. (1994). Grouped locations and object-based attention: Comment on Egly, Driver, & Rafal (1994). *Journal of Experimental Psychology: General, 123*, 316-320.

Vecera, S. P. (in press). Toward a biased competition account of object-based segregation and attention. *Brain and Mind.*

Vecera, S. P., & Behrmann, M. (1997). Spatial attention does not require preattentive grouping. *Neuropsychology, 11*, 30-43.

Vecera, S., & Behrmann, M. (2000). *What are the inputs to object recognition processes? Considerations from apperceptive agnosia.* Manuscript submitted for publication.

Vecera, S. P., Behrmann, M., & Filapek, J. C. (in press). Attending to the parts of a single object: Part-based selection limitations. *Perception & Psychophysics.*

Vecera, S. P., Behrmann, M., & McGoldrick, J. (2000). Selective attention to the parts of an object. *Psychonomic Bulletin & Review, 7*, 301-308.

Vecera, S. P., & Farah, M. J. (1994). Does visual attention select objects or locations? *Journal of Experimental Psychology: General, 123*, 146-160.

Vecera, S. P., & Farah, M. J. (1997). Is visual image segmentation a bottom-up or an interactive process? *Perception & Psychophysics, 59*, 1280-1296.

Vecera, S. P., & Luck, S. J. (2000). Attention. To appear in V. S. Ramachandran (Ed.),

Encyclopedia of the Human Brain. San Diego: Academic Press.

Ward, R., & Goodrich, S. (1996). Differences between objects and nonobjects in visual extinction. *Psychological Science*, *7*, 177-180.

Ward, R., Goodrich, S., & Driver, J. (1994). Grouping reduces visual extinction: Neuropsychological evidence for weight-linkage in visual selection. *Visual Cognition*, *1*, 101-129.

Weber, T. A., Kramer, A. F., & Miller, G. A. (1997). Selective processing of superimposed objects: An electrophysiological analysis of object-based attentional selection. *Biological Psychology*, *45*, 159-182.

Wertheimer, M. (1923/1958). Principles of perceptual organization. Translated in D. C. Beardslee & M. Wertheimer (Eds.), *Readings in Perception* (pp. 115-135). Princeton, NJ: Van Nostrand. (Original work published in 1923.)

Wolfe, J. M. (1998). Visual search. In H. Pashler (Ed.), *Attention* (pp. 13-73). East Sussex, UK: Psychology Press.

Woodman, G. F., Vogel, E. K., & Luck, S. J. (in press). Visual search remains efficient when working memory is full. *Psychological Science*.

Yantis, S. (1998). Control of visual attention. In H. Pashler (Ed.), *Attention* (pp. 223-256). Hove, UK: Psychology Press.

Yantis, S., & Egeth, H. E. (1999). On the distinction between visual salience and stimulus-driven attentional capture. *Journal of Experimental Psychology: Human Perception & Performance*, *25*, 661-676.

Yantis, S., & Jonides, J. (1984). Abrupt visual onsets and selective attention: Evidence from visual search. *Journal of Experimental Psychology: Human Perception and Performance*, *10*, 601-621.

Zemel, R. S., Behrmann, M., Bavelier, D., & Mozer, M. C. (submitted). *Experience-dependent perceptual grouping and object-based attention*. Manuscript submitted for publication.

Zipser, K., Lamme, V. A. F., & Schiller, P. H. (1996). Contextual modulation in primary visual cortex. *Journal of Neuroscience*, *16*, 7376-7389.

IV.

MODELS OF SEGMENTATION AND GROUPING

The progression of scientific work in most fields follows a consistent trend. Everyday observations are followed by interesting or curious phenomena, sometimes named for their discoverers; in perception, examples are the "Fröhlich," "Pulfrich" or "McCullough" effects (it is not clear why the discovers' names so often end in "h"). Over time, researchers turn up some unifying principles that connect the loose collection of effects and phenomena. Later come precise models and explanatory theories.

In this progression, object perception seems to be somewhere in the middle. One reason for producing this book is the editors' and authors' belief that there are now substantial unifying principles and the beginnings of precise models and explanations to write about. The chapters in this section convey recent attempts to systematize, model, and theorize about object perception.

As Marr (1982) told us, adequate explanations of vision, and of information processing phenomena generally, must include accounts at multiple levels. The chapters in this section reflect this requirement in their diversity. Philip Kellman, Sharon Guttman, & Thomas Wickens propose a general framework for considering the information processing tasks in object perception, and consider these tasks from the standpoint of formal models, neural-style models and relations between the two. Barbara Gillam systematically examines the notion of grouping in perception, starting with its (sometimes forgotten) historical roots and exploring the varied phenomena of grouping, their possible connections and their particular role in occlusion phenomena. David Jacobs approaches perceptual organization using the Bayesian and generic view concepts that typify computational vision approaches to object recognition. Perceptual organization can be looked at as a process of fitting models to data, of which an important component is knowledge of prior odds about what kinds of shapes exist in the world. Rob Van Lier presents a comprehensive and up-to-date view of structural information theory (SIT), embodying classic and recent versions of the idea that perception and recognition of objects follows principles of simplicity or least information. Heiko Neumann & Ennio Mingolla delve comprehensively into neural-style models, providing an accessible yet sophisticated and detailed view of current models and issues. Manish Singh & Donald Hoffman grapple with the ways in which human vision organizes shapes into parts. After considering the geometric information for parsing shapes into parts, they show the importance of parts for a number of phenomena in perceptual organization and visual cognition.

From Fragments to Objects – Segmentation and Grouping in Vision
T.F. Shipley and P.J. Kellman (Editors)

7

GEOMETRIC AND NEURAL MODELS OF OBJECT PERCEPTION

Philip J. Kellman, Sharon E. Guttman, and Thomas D. Wickens
Department of Psychology, University of California, Los Angeles, CA 90095-1563 USA

INTRODUCTION

It is an exciting time to study visual object perception. Although object perception research has a long tradition, lately its visibility in cognitive science and neuroscience has greatly increased. One reason for heightened interest is that diverse areas of research now suggest a central role for objects in many aspects of human cognition, including the organization of attention, perception, knowledge representation, and language.

Meanwhile, approaches to studying object perception have expanded and matured. Since the Gestalt psychologists first framed basic questions, significant progress has been made in identifying key principles and describing important phenomena. For the most part, however, these ideas have not coalesced into a coherent structure. A textbook in perception is more likely to offer a catalog of phenomena on "perceptual organization" than a systematic account of how objects are perceived.

The situation is changing. We can glimpse, if only schematically, an interrelated set of information processing tasks that enable us to perceive objects. Moreover, we are beginning to understand both the computations and the neural mechanisms that accomplish these tasks. We owe this current good fortune to several developments, not least of which is an expanding body of research on contour, surface, and object perception. More formal computational analyses of these problems have also progressed substantially. Accompanying these recent developments are comparatively mature psychophysical and neurophysiological accounts of the earliest stages of visual cortical processing. Together, these converging areas of research provide a strong foundation for understanding functions of the visual system that depend on, but go far beyond, basic sensitivity to contrast and orientation.

In this chapter, we have several goals. One is to present an overall theoretical picture of the processes of object perception, extending from the early extraction of edges and junctions to the higher-order tasks of unit formation and shape perception. This framework sets the stage for our second goal: to emphasize several issues that confront object perception researchers and indicate specific questions for continuing research. As we will see, some tasks of object perception are relatively well understood, whereas others remain vague. Much of the value of any overall framework lies in highlighting areas where more work is needed.

Our final goal in this chapter is to enlarge the domain. The study of visual object perception has tended to focus on static, two-dimensional (2-D) images. In the natural environment, human perception both grapples with and benefits from information in three dimensions and information given over time through object and observer motion. The research that we will consider on three-dimensional (3-D) and kinematic object perception falls well outside the scope of existing models. Nonetheless, we will indicate points of continuity in the constraints and processes that may, in time, lead toward a unified account of two-dimensional, three-dimensional, and dynamic processing in object perception.

Geometric, Process, and Neural Models

Efforts at modeling the processes of object perception have evolved in two different directions. Investigations of one kind have addressed the stimulus relationships that govern the perception of objects. The aim of these efforts is to specify precisely the spatial and temporal relations of contours and surfaces that determine perception of an object's unity and shape. We will label the theoretical accounts derived from these investigations as *geometric models*. One such approach — Kellman and Shipley's (1991) model and its extensions — will be considered in detail.

Other efforts, somewhat independent from the first type, have focused on devising *neural models* that perform the kinds of computations necessary for various aspects of object perception. In the section of this chapter on neural models, we will examine some of the psychophysical and neurophysiological research on which these models are based, and spotlight three models of object perception processes: the model of Heitger, Rosenthaler, von der Heydt, Peterhans, and Kübler (1992) for edge and junction detection; the model of Yen and Finkel (1998) for contour integration; and a later elaboration of the Heitger et al. model (Heitger, von der Heydt, Peterhans, Rosenthaler, & Kübler, 1998) as an example of a neural-style model of contour interpolation. These computational models have been chosen both for the success of their simulations and, more importantly, their use of biologically plausible mechanisms in their implementation.

One might think that detailed proposals concerning the neural interactions subserving object perception would await a precise understanding of relevant stimulus relationships. That is, neural models might presuppose complete geometric models. In practice, this has not been the case. Rather, concepts for implementing contour, surface, and object processes via neural circuitry have co-evolved with experimental and theoretical work on the stimulus relationships that govern object perception.

This co-evolution has important implications. On the positive side, work on issues of implementation in neural circuitry need not await a finished geometry and psychophysics of object perception. On the negative side, existing neural models do not implement all that is known even now about the geometry of object formation, nor, obviously, can they encompass factors that are not yet determined. Our task, then, after describing the different types of models, will be to assess their relationships: how geometric and neural models can each advance the other type, and, indeed, how they can merge into a complete picture of object perception. As this complete picture is still beyond reach, we use the opportunity to highlight issues for future research.

A Framework for Object Perception: Tasks, Geometry, and Processes

Much of what we know about object perception can be captured in the framework displayed in Figure 1. This process model combines established findings with several hypotheses about the representations and information processing tasks involved with visual object perception.

In the model, rectangular boxes indicate functions or processes, and octagonal ones indicate representations. Note that the model is rather conservative regarding representations. Aside from output representations of shape and unity (the specification of which regions belong to a single form), there is only one intermediate representation: the *visible regions representation*. The nature and evidence supporting the existence of these representations will be discussed below.

Overview of the Model

The processing scheme described by Figure 1 begins with the input to the model: the optic array itself. Although much of our discussion will focus on a single static image as the input, a complete model should utilize the time-varying optic array, sampled by two eyes of an observer. Both depth and motion play important roles in segmentation and grouping, as we will consider later.

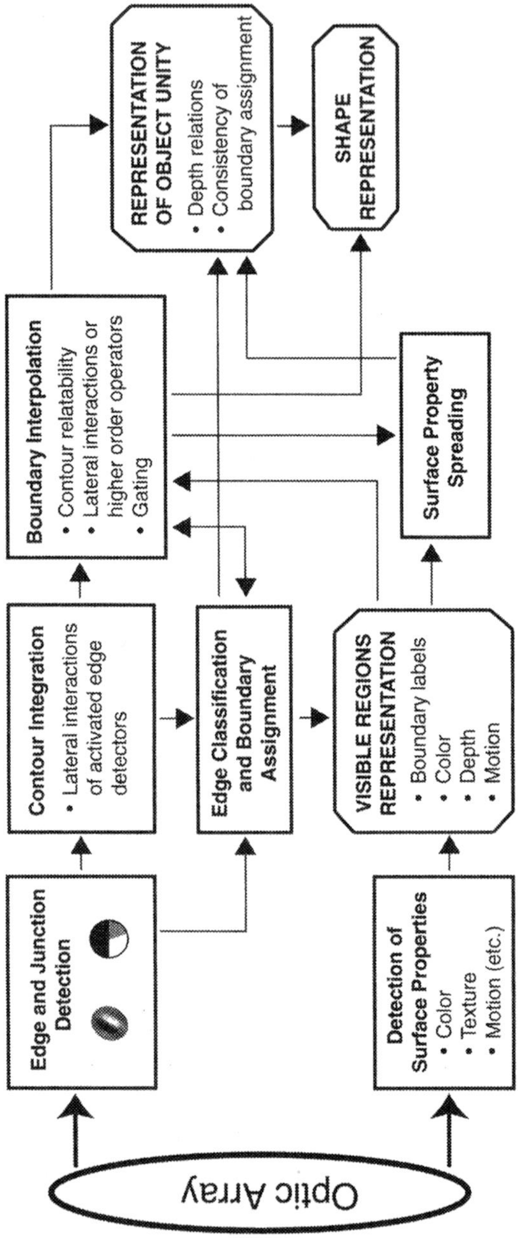

Figure 1. A Framework for Object Perception. Rectangles indicate functions or processes and octagons indicate representations. See text for details.

The visual system extracts two types of information from the optical input. Characteristics of luminance, color, texture, depth, and motion enter a surface processing stream, which represents these properties in relation to their surface locations; this information later will be used to help determine connections among spatially-distinct visible regions. *Discontinuities* in luminance, color, texture, depth, and motion enter a separate stream concerned with the detection of edges and junctions, and, later, the processing of meaningful contours.

In the contour stream, local activations of orientation-sensitive units are integrated according to their spatial relations to form visible contours. Some of these contours are classified as occluding edges, based in part on junction information. At occluding edges, the direction of boundary assignment is determined, thus indicating which of two adjacent surfaces "owns" the contour.

In the surface stream, spatially contiguous locations possessing homogeneous or smoothly varying surface attributes, including depth, become grouped together. The grouping in this stream complements the edge process, in that it depends on the *absence* of the surface discontinuities extracted by the edge stream. Together, the contour and surface streams define tokens in the visible regions representation. This representation labels relatively homogeneous regions as connected surface areas, encodes the locations and orientations of edges and corners of these regions, and specifies for each edge whether it is owned by that region or by another region.

Because of occlusion, visible regions are not objects. In fact, they bear a complex relationship to the objects in the physical world. For the objects of perception to correspond to meaningful objects in the world, interpolation processes must operate to connect visible regions under occlusion.

Evidence suggests the existence of two such interpolation processes (Kellman & Shipley, 1991; Yin, Kellman, & Shipley, 1997). The *boundary interpolation process* connects oriented edges across gaps, according to the geometry of contour relatability. These interpolated boundaries most often appear as occluded contours, but given certain depth relationships, may also be perceived as illusory contours. The *surface interpolation process* complements the boundary process, in that it can lead to perceived connections among visible regions even when the object's boundaries are not well specified. Unlike the boundary interpolation process, however, operation of the surface interpolation process requires that two visible surfaces match or fall along a smooth gradient. When one of these criteria is satisfied, surface qualities spread under occlusion within real and interpolated boundaries.

Regions connected by the interpolation processes feed into two output representations. The *units representation* encodes explicitly the connectedness of visible regions under occlusion. When the surface interpolation process alone has given all or some of these connections, overall shape may be vague. More often, boundary interpolation accompanies surface interpolation, and a determinate shape is encoded in the *shape representation*. This representation serves as the primary input to object recognition.

The framework described operates "bottom-up." That is, the basic process model does not incorporate any feedback from higher levels to earlier ones. Object perception undoubtedly can proceed without such feedback, and likely does so in cases where there is no obvious involvement of familiarity or symmetry. Whether there really are top-down influences in basic segmentation and grouping processes, as opposed to recognition from partial input, remains controversial (e.g., Kellman, 2000; van Lier, 1999), as we will see below. One valuable aspect of the current framework is that it allows us to consider explicitly the loci and nature of putative top-down effects.

As an example, Peterson and her colleagues (e.g., Peterson, 1994; Peterson & Gibson, 1991, 1994) have argued that figure-ground segregation in otherwise ambiguous stimuli can be influenced by the familiarity of a shaped region; the familiar shape is more likely to be seen as figure. Such an effect could be incorporated into the model as shown in Figure 2. Figure-ground determination corresponds to boundary assignment in the model. For familiar shape to influence boundary assignment, the shape of some contour or region must be encoded and recognized — matched to a representation stored in memory. As a result of the match, the boundary assignment of the stored representation feeds back via the current shape representation to determine the boundary assignment of the stimulus.

We present this example only to illustrate how top-down effects could, in principle, be incorporated into the model. Other, perhaps more controversial, ideas about top-down processing are considered later in this chapter.

Having completed our overview of the model, we now look more closely at the constituent processes and representations, beginning with the extraction of edges and junctions.

Edge and Junction Detection

For our purposes, stimulus encoding in the earliest cortical visual areas — V1 and V2 — represents the starting point for the computations leading to edges, contours, surfaces, and objects. Individual cells in these areas respond to luminance contrast in particular areas of the visual field, with selectivity for specific orientations and spatial frequencies (e.g., Campbell, Cooper, & Enroth-Cugell, 1969; Hubel & Wiesel, 1968). By area V2, and perhaps earlier, many cells respond selectively to particular binocular disparities, providing the basis for stereoscopic depth perception (Fischer & Poggio, 1979). Some cells in the early cortical areas also respond preferentially to motion, although areas upstream, particularly area V5 (the human homologue to macaque area MT), appear to be specialized for motion processing.

The framework in Figure 1 assumes that these early cortical responses form the inputs into processes that detect meaningful edges and contour junctions in the optical

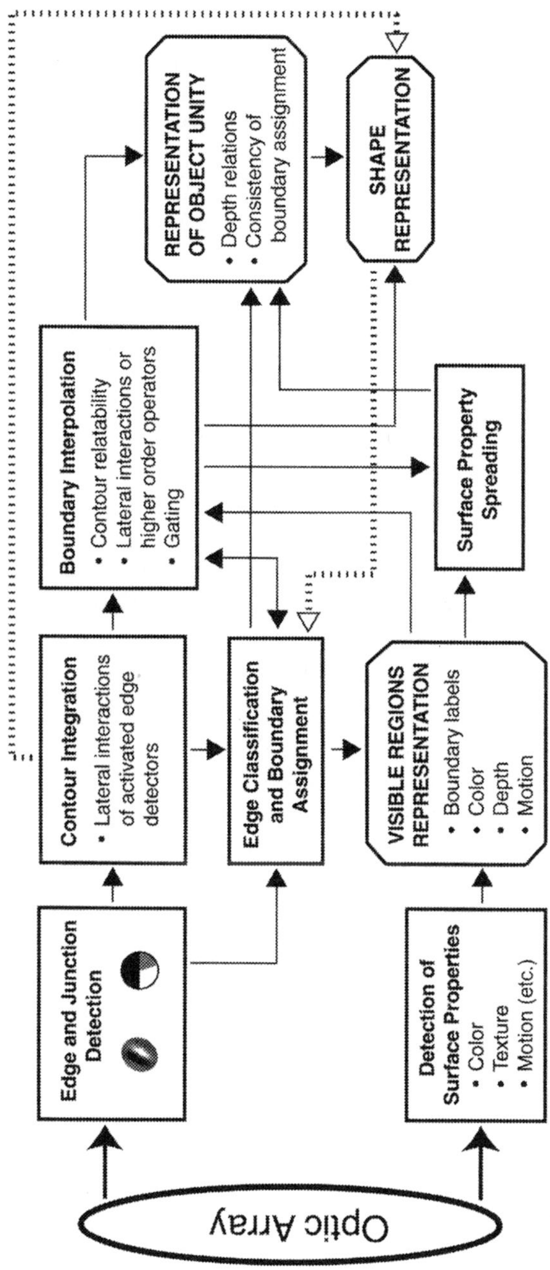

Figure 2. Illustration of a possible top-down effect of contour shape on boundary assignment. See text for details.

projection (Heitger et al., 1992; Marr & Hildreth, 1980; Morrone & Burr, 1988; but see Watt, 1994, for an alternative approach). Although it appears as a simple box in the model, there actually are several complexities even at this stage.

Multiple Edge Inputs. Object perception utilizes several types of edge inputs, including luminance and chromatic changes, but also discontinuities in texture, stereoscopic depth, and motion (Gibson, Kaplan, Reynolds, & Wheeler, 1969; Julesz, 1971; Shipley & Kellman, 1994). To complicate matters further, both object motions and image displacements given by observer motion contribute to edge processing.

Though luminance discontinuities receive the most attention in discussions of edge detection, some of these other edge inputs actually may be more important. The usefulness of luminance discontinuities for edge detection rests on certain ecological facts — facts about the physical world and the information it makes available for perception. Luminance and chromatic edges provide meaningful information because separate objects and surfaces in the world tend to be made of different materials that interact with light differently. Thus, significant boundaries in the world often correspond to locations at which the amount or spectral composition of light changes abruptly.

The same logic applies to edges detected from discontinuities in texture, depth, and motion. Adjacent surfaces in the optic array often project from different objects, but these will, in general, be at different depths. Thus, a stereoscopic depth map will have discontinuities at surface boundaries. The same is true of the velocity field, in which optical change is registered at each visible feature: velocity discontinuities will appear at boundaries during object or observer motion.

Whereas luminance, color, and texture edges may correspond to markings on a surface, motion and depth discontinuities rarely arise in the absence of a boundary between two objects. The high ecological validity of motion and depth edges suggests that they play a primary role in the detection of meaningful edges in the world. More research is needed to determine how the visual system integrates these various sources of edge information.

Junctions. Contour junctions can be defined as points along a contour that have no unique orientation. More intuitively, a junction is an intersection of two or more contours in the optical projection. Contour junctions include the sharp corners of objects, as well as the points where contours of separate objects intersect.

Contour junctions of all types play an important role in the segmentation and grouping of objects. Kellman and Shipley (1991) observed that the contours interpolated between two visible regions invariably begin and end at junctions, which they labeled "tangent discontinuities" (TDs). In fact, Kellman and Shipley presented a proof that *all* instances of occlusion produce TDs in the optical projection. This ecological invariant may be the reason that junctions figure prominently in initiating contour interpolation processes: TDs are a

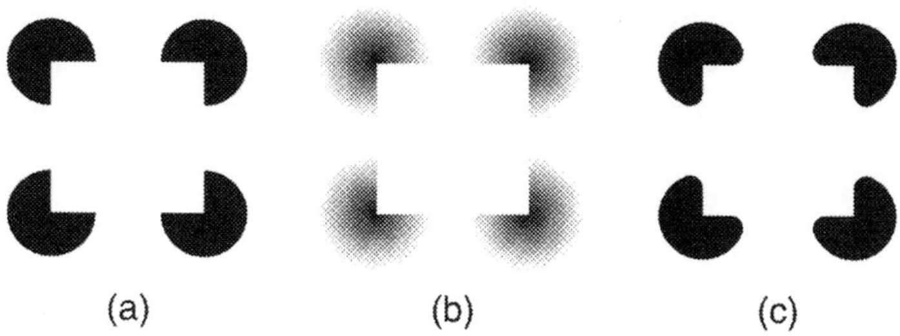

Figure 3. Three variations of the Kanizsa square. (a) Illusory contours clearly are visible in the classical display, which contains uniformly colored inducers and sharp tangent discontinuities. The illusory contours remain visible in (b), despite the elimination of luminance discontinuities from the inducers. The illusory contours become weak or absent with the rounding of tangent discontinuities (c). Figure B redrawn from *Vision Research, 33*, Lesher, G. W., & Mingolla, E., The role of edges and line-ends in illusory contour formation, pp. 2253-2270, Copyright 1993, with permission from Elsevier Science. Figure C redrawn from *Perception, 27*, Tse, P. U., & Albert, M. K., Amodal completion in the absence of image tangent discontinuities, pp. 455-464 (Fig 8, p. 460), Copyright 1988, with the permission of Pion Ltd., London.

potentially rich source of information about the loci of occlusion. In illusory contour displays, for which tangent discontinuities *can* be eliminated, the rounding of TDs eliminates or vastly reduces the perception of interpolated contours (Shipley & Kellman, 1990).

Some researchers have questioned the generalization that interpolated contours must begin and end at TDs. Lesher and Mingolla (1993) presented a Kanizsa-style illusory contour display in which the inducers changed gradually in luminance, thus blending into the background (Figure 3b). Phenomenologically, this display supports the formation of illusory contours, even though, formally speaking, the inducers contain no bounding edges and thus cannot have any discontinuities in edge direction.

Although this display raises interesting issues, it does not bear directly on the role of TDs. Close inspection suggests that removing the luminance discontinuities that normally define edges, as in Lesher and Mingolla's display, does not entail the removal of tangent discontinuities — sudden changes in the slope of an edge. Despite the luminance gradient, the edges remain reasonably clear and well-localized. In all likelihood, contrast-sensitive neurons selective for low spatial frequencies respond to the gradients much as they do to "real" edges, giving rise to perceived contours. The relevant tangent discontinuities are defined by the perceived edges.

Other researchers have pointed out that weak illusory contours sometimes arise from inducers with slightly rounded corners (Figure 3c; Hoffman, 1998; Shipley & Kellman, 1990; Tse & Albert, 1998). Neurons selective for low spatial frequencies may, once again, be responsible for this phenomenon. Low spatial-frequency operators cannot discriminate between regions of high curvature and sharp junctions. In essence, rounded corners *are* tangent discontinuities to neurons that encode information at larger spatial scales. The conflict between these coarse-coding neurons, which register TDs, and cells that respond to higher spatial frequencies, which detect the rounded corners, likely explains why the illusory contours in these displays appear quite weak. When high spatial frequencies — and this conflict — are eliminated by squinting or by increasing viewing distance, the perceived strength of the illusory contours increases substantially.

Available evidence supports the crucial role of contour junctions in boundary interpolation (e.g., Shipley & Kellman, 1990), which in turn is crucial for unit formation and shape perception, as we consider shortly. To support these and other perceptual tasks, both edge and junction information may be extracted early in cortical processing and at multiple spatial scales. Although the mechanisms of junction detection have, as yet, received little attention, a promising approach may be found in the model of Heitger et al. (1992). This model proposes a specific operator that extracts "key points," which includes both contour ends and junctions. We examine this model in more detail below.

Contour Integration

The problem of contour integration involves representing a visible contour as continuous. Meaningful contours extend well beyond the receptive fields of oriented neurons in early cortical visual areas. Therefore, representation of a contour as a connected unit requires the integration of information from neurons with receptive fields tuned to different regions of space. Several recent studies address possible mechanisms for linking the separate responses of orientation-sensitive units (e.g., Moulden, 1994; Pettet, McKee, & Grzywacz, 1998; Yen & Finkel, 1998).

These investigations of contour integration ultimately may help to answer another important question: whether a similar mechanism governs *boundary interpolation* — the connection of edges across gaps in the input. Field, Hayes, and Hess (1993) investigated the spatial relations necessary for contour integration in a series of elegant empirical studies. The relations they uncovered mirror the formal requirements of Kellman and Shipley's (1991) model of contour interpolation across gaps. This finding suggests a close relationship between contour integration and contour interpolation, an idea that will be further explored later in this chapter.

Other important issues about contour integration involve the nature of the representation and underlying neural mechanisms. Explicit contour representations presumably are important for assigning contours to objects and for encoding shape. Whereas earlier stages of visual processing may be viewed as more or less direct responses to energy variables in the input, contour integration entails a symbolic representation (i.e., an explicit description about a specific aspect of an object or surface). Reversible figure-ground displays are among the many visual phenomena implying that contours are, indeed, explicitly represented as unitary entities. In these displays, a contour separating two regions switches its boundary assignment (which region it "belongs to") as a unit; we do not experience switching of parts of contours. Thus, it appears that by this stage of visual processing, contours, and not smaller fragments, are the units to which boundary assignment applies.

Edge Classification and Boundary Assignment

To perceive objects, it is not sufficient merely to detect edges. Some edges in the visual array delimit the boundaries of objects, whereas others represent shadows or textural markings on a surface. The process of distinguishing these possibilities is termed *edge classification*. Edge classification, most importantly, results in the identification of *occluding edges*: locations where an object or surface comes to an end. As the name suggests, these edges also mark places at which one surface continues behind another.

A critical piece of information for edge classification may be the convergence of different kinds of evidence. Shadows and textural markings typically produce only one or two types of discontinuity in the visual input (luminance and color for textural markings; luminance and perhaps motion for shadows). By contrast, occluding edges often involve discontinuities in multiple perceptual properties, including luminance, color, texture, motion, and stereoscopic depth. Therefore, the visual system may, in part, define occluding edges by the convergence of several discontinuities in the same spatial location.

Closely related to edge classification is *boundary assignment*, or figure-ground perception. Many visible edges are occluding edges, which, as the Gestalt psychologist Kurt Koffka put it, have a "one-sided function." A contour appearing in the optical projection represents the boundary of the surface on one side, whereas the surface on the other side continues behind. Each such edge poses a problem to the visual system insofar as it defines the shape only of the surface in front; no local sensory information is received about the location, shape, or other characteristics of the surface continuing behind. Interpolation processes, described below, pursue the task of recovering object unity and shape despite occlusion.

Several kinds of information contribute to boundary assignment. In ordinary perception, stereoscopic and kinematic cues to depth (including motion parallax and accretion-deletion of texture) probably play the most important role. Occluding edges signaled by kinematic and stereoscopic discontinuities carry with them depth-order information that reveals, unambiguously, the appropriate boundary assignment: the nearer surface owns the boundary.

Another source of information comes from contour junctions. In particular, "T" junctions, which underlie the depth cue of interposition, may be helpful in determining boundary assignment. As shown in Figure 4, contour junctions can be classified into different categories (e.g., Barrow & Tenenbaum, 1986), depending on their configurations. The defining feature of a T-junction is a smooth, continuous contour on which another contour

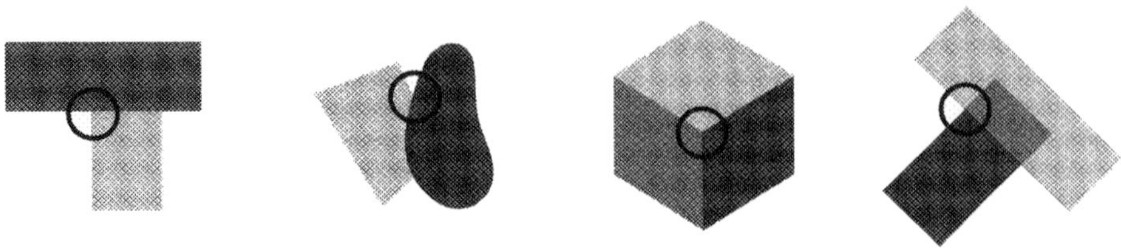

Figure 4. Types of contour junctions. In a classic T-junction (a), the "roof" is seen as passing in front of the "stem." The junction in (b) also is a "T," as a terminating contour meets a continuing contour; the relative orientation of the two contours is irrelevant. Other types of junctions assist with image segmentation, but are not immediately relevant to boundary assignment. The Y-junction (c) depicts an object corner, whereas the X-junction (d) indicates transparency.

terminates (Figure 4a); the absolute and relative orientations of the two contours are incidental (Figure 4b). Once the visual system has encoded a T-junction, the depth relation of the two constituent contours follows: the one forming the "roof" of the T appears to be in front of the one forming the "stem." Therefore, the surface that is uninterrupted by the "stem" owns the contour in question.

In his classic discussion of figure-ground organization, Rubin (1915) emphasized a third class of boundary assignment cues: the relations among visible areas. Rubin noted, for example, that an enclosed area tends to be seen as figure, whereas the enclosing area is perceived as ground. Other factors discussed by Rubin involve orientation, convexity, and symmetry. These relational cues to boundary assignment may be considered relatively weak, as they will readily be overridden by depth information given by stereopsis, kinematic cues, or T-junctions. Finally, as mentioned earlier, the familiarity of a contour shape may influence boundary assignment (Peterson & Gibson, 1991; Rubin, 1915).

The Visible Regions Representation

Apart from the final outputs of unity and form, the process model presented in Figure 1 contains one intermediate representation: *the visible regions representation.* This representation makes explicit the unity of a continuous visible area; that is, it encodes the visible points in certain regions as belonging to a single, uninterrupted surface.

The visible regions representation captures several important properties of earlier proposals. Like the intended results of image segmentation algorithms (e.g., Wang & Terman, 1997), it partitions the optic projection into distinct, non-overlapping regions. Like Marr's (1982) 2.5-dimensional sketch, it assigns observer-relative depth to these regions. The visible regions representation also resembles the *uniform connectedness* idea of Palmer and Rock (1994): the visual system encodes closed regions with homogeneous surface properties as a single unit. However, Palmer and Rock treated common surface lightness, color, and texture as the primary determinants of uniform connectedness; motion and depth were attributed secondary roles. By contrast, our visible regions representation assumes that depth relations, given by stereoscopic and motion parallax cues, take precedence over the commonality of lightness and color. A surface that is continuous in depth but contains various discontinuities in surface coloration would be encoded as a single unit in the visible regions representation. Conversely, the visible regions representation would tag as separate two adjacent, homogeneously textured regions with an abrupt change of binocular disparity between them.

A number of facts support the idea that human perception incorporates an intermediate representation of visible regions. For example, although complete object representations are one result of perceptual processes, we have little trouble seeing which areas of objects are partly occluded. Moreover, artists can paint or draw the visible regions of objects. Although this ability may take some practice, it might not be possible at all without some explicit representation of visible regions.

The visible regions representation probably should *not* be understood as a set of frontoparallel image fragments (unlike the results of region segmentation processes in machine vision). One of the major problems facing art students is foreshortening — drawing the correct projected size of an object slanted in depth, relative to other objects. For example, if one's hand is rotated away from the vertical (around a horizontal axis), it projects a very small vertical extent to the eye. Novice art students tend to draw the hand's projection as much too tall. This error suggests that the visible regions representation is not a canvas-like or image-like sheet, but a representation that includes depth. The art student can see which parts of the hand are visible, but these are seen at true size, oriented in depth; depicting them as frontoparallel fragments on a canvas presents difficulties.

Boundary Interpolation

As a consequence of occlusion, many objects in ordinary environments project to the eyes as multiple, spatially distinct fragments. As a result, a single object may be represented, at an intermediate stage, as several visible regions. Interpolation processes allow the visual system to assign these spatially distinct visible regions to a unitary object. Ultimately, these processes lead to more complete object representations, crucial for extracting meaningful information about an object's shape.

By definition, interpolation processes connect parts across gaps in the input. There appear to be two types: *boundary interpolation*, which we consider in this section, and *surface interpolation*, which we consider in the next.

Geometric Model of Boundary Interpolation: Kellman and Shipley (1991). In the Kellman and Shipley model, tangent discontinuities (TDs) mark the possible starting points for boundary interpolation. However, not all TDs lead to boundary interpolation. Some types of contour junctions indicate that the boundary has come to an end and should not be continued (e.g., a Y-junction; see Figure 4c). In other cases, a contour may be seen as passing behind an occluder, but does not link up perceptually with any other visible contour. Evidence suggests that these boundaries are, nonetheless, represented as continuing behind the junction point, perhaps for some fraction of the visible edge's length (He & Nakayama, 1994; Kanizsa, 1979; Yin, Kellman, & Shipley, 1997). We call this phenomenon amodal *continuation* to distinguish it from interpolation or completion. Yin et al.'s data suggest that amodally continued contours follow the direction of the visible edge's tangent at its point of occlusion.

Boundary *interpolation* occurs when a contour that disappears behind a surface, thus creating a TD, connects to a spatially separated contour on the other side of an occluding object. This interpolation process proceeds only when the visible contours, and their TDs, satisfy certain geometric relationships. These relationships, first suggested by the Gestalt idea of good continuation, have been formalized in the construct of contour *relatability* (Kellman & Shipley, 1991, 1992).

The notion of relatability expresses the conditions necessary for interpolation between two visible edges. Intuitively, two edges separated by a gap or occluder are relatable if they can be connected with a continuous, monotonic (singly inflected) curve. The relatability criterion embodies the constraint that the boundaries of objects tend to be smooth.

Mathematically, relatability can be defined with reference to the construction shown in Figure 5. In this diagram, E_1 and E_2 represent the edges of surfaces. R and r depict the perpendiculars to these edges at the point where they lead into a tangent discontinuity; R is defined as the longer of the two perpendiculars. The angle of intersection between R and r is termed φ. Relatability holds whenever a smooth, monotonic curve can be constructed starting from the endpoint of E_1 (and matching the slope of E_1 at that point) and proceeding through a bend of not more than a 90° to the endpoint of E_2 (and matching the slope of E_2 at that point).

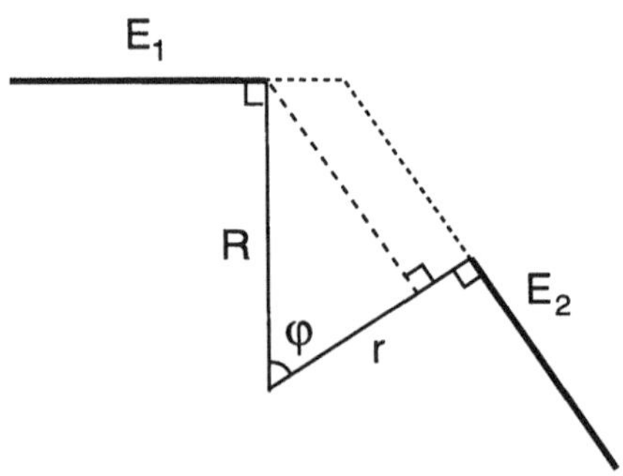

Figure 5. Geometric relationship for defining whether two edges (E_1, E_2) are relatable. See text for details. After Kellman and Shipley (1991).

More formally, E_1 and E_2 are relatable if and only if:

$$0 \leq R\cos\varphi < r.$$

This equation can be unpacked in two steps. The left-hand side of the inequality expresses the limitation that the curve constructed to connect E_1 and E_2 cannot bend through more than 90°; if φ is greater than 90°, then cos φ is negative. The right-hand side of the inequality states that the projection of R onto r (i.e., R cos φ) must fall within the extent of r. If this inequality is violated (i.e., $R \cos \varphi \geq r$), then any connection between E_1 and E_2 would have to be doubly inflected to match the slopes at the TDs, or would have to introduce sharp corners where the interpolated edge meets the physically specified edge. According to this model, boundary interpolation does not occur in such cases.

Although the definition gives the limits of relatability, it is not intended as an all-or-none concept. Kellman and Shipley (1992) described contour relatability as decreasing monotonically with deviations from collinearity, falling to zero at a relative angle of 90°. Singh and Hoffman (1999) proposed a specific measure for this graded decrease.

The basic notion of relatability may be extended in several ways. First, the relatability criterion, as originally formulated, considers only the tangents at the points of discontinuity. It is possible that the boundary interpolation mechanism also utilizes the curvature of the visible contours (e.g., Guttman & Sekuler, 2001; Takeichi, Nakazawa, Murakami, & Shimojo, 1995). This is not entirely clear, however, as the issue of curvature may be confounded with the issue of how much of a contour is used to determine its slope at the point of tangent discontinuity. Second, it now appears that straightforward extensions of the static, 2-D relatability construct govern both 3-D contour interpolation (Kellman, Yin, Shipley, Machado, & Li, 2001) and dynamic visual interpolation, when visible contours appear sequentially in time (Palmer, Kellman, & Shipley, 1997). We discuss these developments briefly at the end of the chapter.

Relatability and Good Continuation. The notion of contour relatability descends from the Gestalt idea of good continuation. Specifically, it formalizes the original Gestalt principle in some respects and extends it in others.

Max Wertheimer, in his classic (1923/1958) paper *Untersuchungen zur Lehre von der Gestalt* ("Laws of organization in perceptual forms"), presented a number of figures illustrating the principle of good continuation. The displays, which involved the segmentation of line drawings with fully visible contours, were accompanied by this advice:

> On the whole, the reader should find no difficulty in seeing what is meant here. In designing a pattern, for example, one has a feeling how successive parts should follow one another; one knows what a "good" continuation is, how "inner coherence" is to be achieved, etc.; one recognizes a "good Gestalt" simply by its own "inner necessity."

Though the demonstrations were compelling, neither Wertheimer nor his successors offered a real definition of "good continuation." Michotte, Thinès, and Crabbé (1964) extended the idea of good continuation to the problem of partly occluded objects; again, the notion remained intuitive, illustrated by compelling displays, rather than formally characterized.

So just what is the "good" in good continuation? An obvious candidate involves mathematical notions of smoothness. But which notion of smoothness? A number of possibilities exist (e.g., Prenter, 1989). Kellman and Shipley's (1991) model defines smoothness in reference to the first derivatives, or slopes, of contours. Formally, a contour is smooth if there are no discontinuities in its first derivative; both sharp corners and contour intersections violate this description of smoothness. As Kellman and Shipley pointed out, this definition has the benefit of producing a complementary relationship between first-order contour continuity as the basis for interpolation and first-order discontinuities (i.e., TDs) as the basis for image segmentation. As previously discussed, the latter indicate possible loci of occlusion and mark the beginning and end points of interpolated edges.

In addition to specifying the relevant smoothness notion, relatability imposes additional constraints not embodied in earlier notions of good continuation. One such constraint is monotonicity: interpolated contours bend in one direction only. A general notion of smoothness permits double inflections, whereas relatability excludes them (apart from a small threshold tolerance for misalignment of relatable edges; see Shipley & Kellman, 1992a). This limitation has not been universally accepted; a number of investigators suggest that doubly-inflected interpolations may occur in object completion (Liu, Jacobs, & Basri, 1999; Takeichi et al., 1995). Another constraint expressed in the notion of relatability is the limitation that interpolated contours cannot bend through more than 90°, an idea that has received substantial empirical support (Field et al., 1993; Polat & Sagi, 1993, 1994).

In sum, by formalizing and adding constraints to the original notion of good continuation, relatability produces clear predictions that can be empirically assessed. Although some aspects of the model may require elaboration, available evidence, as we will see shortly, supports relatability as a formal account of the basic geometry of human boundary interpolation.

<u>The Identity Hypothesis in Contour Interpolation</u>. The geometry and processes of contour interpolation in the Kellman and Shipley (1991) model apply equally to several interpolation phenomena that, traditionally, have been considered separately. In particular, the *identity hypothesis* suggests that the same contour interpolation process connects contours under occlusion (amodal completion), creates illusory contours (modal completion), and plays a role in other contour-connection phenomena including certain transparency displays.

Figure 6 depicts partly-occluded, illusory, and transparent shapes having equivalent physically-specified contours and gaps. Phenomenally, the shape of the interpolated contours is the same in the three images. More importantly, however, we believe that the same interpolation process gives rise to the interpolated contours in all cases. The perceptual differences among these phenomena reside only in the depth ordering of the interpolated

(a) (b) (c)

Figure 6. An illustration of the identity hypothesis: (a) partly occluded square; (b) illusory square; (c) transparent square. Although they appear quite different, these three images formally are similar in that the same physically-specified edges define the central figure in each case. According to the identity hypothesis, the process that interpolates edges across gaps also is the same in these cases.

contours and other surfaces; the processing of relative depth may *interact* with the boundary interpolation process, but relies on a different mechanism.

A large body of evidence supports the idea that a common boundary interpolation process serves modal and amodal completion (Kellman, Yin, & Shipley, 1998; Ringach & Shapley, 1996; Shipley & Kellman, 1992a). For example, Kellman et al. found that partly occluded contours can join illusory contours to produce a shape with clearly defined boundaries. (An example appears below in Figure 15.) This merging suggests that illusory and occluded contours arise from a common mechanism.

Several other theoretical arguments support the identity hypothesis. A compelling one relates to some interesting phenomena that we have termed *self-splitting objects*; examples appear in Figure 7. Remarkably, in these cases, homogenous areas split into two perceived objects. The Kellman and Shipley (1991) model explains this effect as follows. The display in

(a) (b) (c)

Figure 7. Self-splitting objects. (a) This shape typically is seen as two elongated black forms, even though the entire figure possesses identical surface properties. (b) Arrows indicate tangent discontinuities and dotted lines mark the resulting interpolated contours of the same self-splitting object. (c) Despite uniform surface qualities, most observers describe this image as two interlocking rings.

Figure 7a contains four TDs (marked with arrows in Figure 7b), each of which can initiate contour interpolation processes. Four pairs of edges lead into the TDs; as each pair satisfies the relatability criteria, contour interpolation connects all four edges (indicated in Figure 7b by dotted lines). Closed contours, comprised of physically-specified and interpolated contour segments, define each of the two perceived objects.

For our present purpose, the relevant question is: How do we interpret these objects' interpolated boundaries? That is, do they appear as illusory contours or as partly occluded contours? At any time, one of the two objects in Figure 7a appears to cross in front of the other. The boundaries of the object in front appear as illusory contours, whereas those of the object in back appear as occluded contours. However, the depth ordering of the two objects is unstable over time; which object appears in front may fluctuate. When one object switches from being in front to being in back (or vice versa), its contours switch from being illusory to being occluded (or vice versa).

Self-splitting objects do not always possess this instability of depth order. The display in Figure 7c appears to be more stable. Most observers describe the figure as containing two interlocking rings. However, the "two rings" possess identical surface qualities; therefore, the boundaries that separate the objects must be attributed to the contour interpolation processes described above.

Implicit in the idea of "interlocking," the perceived depth ordering of the two rings varies across the image; the ring at the top appears to pass in front of its counterpart on the right side of the display, but beneath it on the left. Petter (1956) studied displays of this sort and discovered that this perceptual outcome follows a rule, which we can state as follows: *Where interpolated boundaries cross, the boundary that traverses the smaller gap appears to be in front*. Thus, the thicker parts of the rings appear to lay on top of the thinner parts, as the former have smaller gaps in the physically-specified contour.[1]

The relevance of Petter's effect to the identity hypothesis becomes apparent when one considers the nature of the rings' perceived boundaries. As in the case we considered above, we perceive illusory contours where the rings pass in front, but partly occluded contours where they connect behind. However, according to Petter's rule, the perception of each interpolated contour as in front or behind — and, in turn, as "illusory" or "occluded" — depends on its length relative to the interpolated contours that cross it. Logically, this statement implies some sort of comparison or competition involving the crossing interpolations. To accomplish this comparison, the visual system must first register the various sites of interpolation. As stated above, comparing the lengths of the interpolations precedes the determination of whether an interpolated contour ultimately will appear as in front of or as

[1] Looking back at Figure 7a, we can now see that Petter's rule can explain the instability of perceived depth order in Figure 7a: the two overlapping objects have interpolated contours of very similar length.

behind other contours (and, thus, as illusory or occluded); therefore, the registration of interpolation sites also precedes the determination of depth ordering. That is, at least in some cases, *contour interpolation processes must operate prior to the processes that determine the final depth ordering of the constructed contours.* This, in turn, implies that there cannot be separate mechanisms for the interpolation of contours in front of versus behind other surfaces; illusory (i.e., in front) and occluded (i.e., behind) contours arise from the same contour interpolation process.

In sum, both empirical studies and logical arguments indicate that contour interpolation relies on a common mechanism that operates without regard to the final determination of illusory or occluded appearance. The subjective appearance of interpolated contours depends on mechanisms responsible for assigning relative depth, which lie outside and sometimes operate subsequent to the interpolation process itself. In the discussion that follows, we use studies of occlusion, illusory contours, and other contour-connection phenomena interchangeably in examining the nature of the boundary interpolation process.

Empirical Studies of Boundary Interpolation. A variety of experimental studies support relatability as a formal description of the boundaries interpolated by the visual system (Kellman & Shipley, 1991; Shipley & Kellman, 1992a). Some of the best evidence comes from an elegant paradigm introduced by Field et al. (1993) for the study of contour integration. The stimuli in these experiments consisted of arrays of spatially separated, oriented Gabor patches, which are small elements consisting of a sinusoidal luminance pattern multiplied by a Gaussian window; a Gabor patch closely approximates the ideal stimulus for the oriented receptive fields of V1 simple cells. In some arrays, twelve elements were aligned along a straight or curved "path," constructed by having each element in the sequence differ by a constant angle from its neighbors (0° for a straight, collinear path; ±15°, for example, to create a curved path). The remainder of the array consisted of elements oriented randomly with respect to one another and the path, creating a noisy background. In the experiments, observers judged which of two successively and briefly presented arrays contained a path.

The results of Field et al.'s (1993) experiments strongly support the notion of relatability. When the positional and angular relations of successive path elements satisfied the relatability criterion, observers detected the stimulus efficiently. Contour detection performance declined gradually as the orientation difference between elements increased, falling to chance at around 90°. Moreover, complete violations of relatability, accomplished by orienting the elements perpendicular to the path rather than end-to-end along it, resulted in drastically reduced task performance. Together, these data suggest that interpolated contour connections require specific edge relationships, the mathematics of which are captured quite well by the notion of relatability. Moreover, interpolated contours become salient, allowing them to play a meaningful role in higher-level object perception processes.

In addition to degree of curvature, the strength of boundary interpolation depends on the relative extents of the physically-specified edges and gaps in a scene. Interpolation strength appears to be a linear function of the *support ratio*, the proportion of total edge length that is physically-specified, as opposed to interpolated. This relationship holds over a wide range of display sizes (Lesher & Mingolla, 1993; Ringach & Shapley, 1996; Shipley & Kellman, 1992b). In essence, the support ratio idea makes precise a version of the Gestalt law of *proximity*: nearer elements are more likely to be grouped together.

Recent work by Geisler, Perry, Super, and Gallogly (2001) further suggests that relatability may capture certain spatial relationships between visible contours that have a high probability of belonging to the same object. Through an analysis of contour relationships in natural images, Geisler et al. found that the statistical regularities governing the probability of two edge elements co-occurring correlate highly with the geometry of relatability. In other words, two visible edge segments associated with the same contour meet the mathematical relatability criterion far more often than not. In sum, the success of relatability in describing perceptual interpolation processes may derive from ecological regularities that characterize the natural environment.

Surface Interpolation

The boundary interpolation process appears to operate without sensitivity to the similarity of surface properties (Kellman & Loukides, 1987; Kellman & Shipley, 1991; Shapley & Gordon, 1987; Shipley & Kellman, 1992a). Using a large sample of randomly generated figures, Shipley and Kellman found evidence that object completion under occlusion proceeds similarly whether relatable pieces are of the same or different luminance and color. These data indicate that contour interpolation does not depend on the Gestalt principle of *similarity*; relatability governs edge completions regardless of whether the connecting regions are similar in luminance, spectral characteristics, or texture.[2]

This characteristic of boundary interpolation does *not* imply that surface similarity cannot influence object completion. Kellman and Shipley (1991) described a surface spreading process that complements boundary interpolation in the completion of partly occluded objects. The process may be related to phenomena described some time ago in retinal stabilization experiments (Yarbus, 1967; cf., Grossberg & Mingolla, 1985). Yarbus presented displays containing a circle of one color surrounded by an annulus of a different color. The boundary between the inner circle and outer ring was stabilized on the retina, which

---

[2] A few phenomena in the literature, especially an intriguing demonstration by He and Ooi (1998), suggest that this conclusion may need to be qualified. Although the contour interpolation process tolerates wide variation in the surface characteristics of the regions being connected, there may be some constraints involving contrast polarity that we do not, as yet, fully understand.

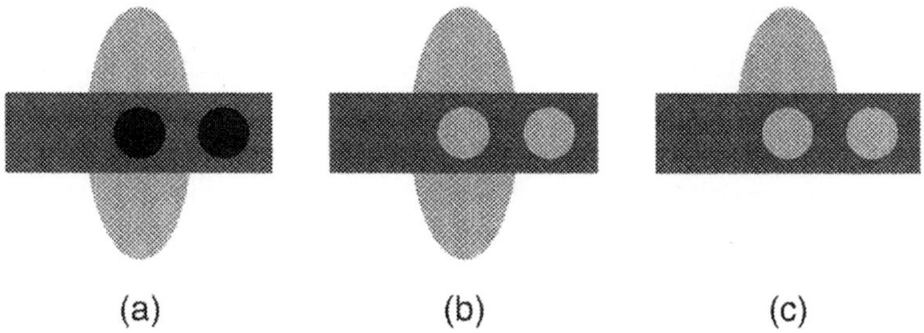

Figure 8. Some effects of the surface interpolation process: (a) no surface spreading; (b) surface spreading within interpolated boundaries; (c) surface spreading within amodally continued boundaries. See text for details.

caused it to disappear after several seconds. Following the disappearance of this boundary, the color of the annulus (whose outer boundary was not stabilized) spread throughout the entire circle.

A similar surface spreading process may operate under occlusion (Kellman & Shipley, 1991). Surface qualities spread behind occluding edges; however, interpolated boundaries confine the spread in much the same way as physically-specified boundaries. Figure 8 illustrates some effects of this surface spreading process.

In Figure 8a, both circles appear as spots on a background because their surface qualities differ from other regions in the image. In Figure 8b, the right-hand circle still looks much like a spot, but the left-hand circle is seen as a hole in the occluding surface. This percept depends on the similarity between the surface lightness of the circle and the partly occluded ellipse. Because the circle lacks TDs, its link to the ellipse cannot be attributed to the boundary interpolation process. Surface spreading alone governs the perceived connection. The fact that the right-hand circle retains its appearance as a spot indicates that the interpolated boundaries of the partly occluded figure confine the surface spreading process. Figure 8c illustrates that, in the absence of relatable edges, surface completion can still occur; the left-hand circle appears as a hole, with its visible area linked to the visible half-ellipse. For such cases, Kellman and Shipley (1991) proposed that the surface spreading process is confined within an area partially bounded by the tangent extensions of the partly occluded object (i.e., lines tangent to the visible contours at the points of occlusion). This idea draws on the notion that, even in the absence of connection to other visible edges, contours continue amodally for some distance behind occluders (He & Nakayama, 1994; Kanizsa, 1979). The right-hand circle of Figure 8c appears as a spot, rather than a hole, because it falls outside the tangent extensions of the half-ellipse.

These observations and hypotheses have been confirmed in a series of experiments. Using displays resembling those in Figure 8, Yin, Kellman, and Shipley (1997) tested whether surface qualities spread within relatable edges and also within extended tangents of non-relatable edges that continue behind occluders. For a number of displays with varying edge and surface similarity relations, observers made a forced-choice judgment of whether a circular area appeared to be a hole in a surface or a spot on top of the surface. If the data suggested a "hole" rather than a "spot" percept, then Yin et al. (1997) assumed that the surface properties of the partly occluded shape spread to the location of the test circle. The results indicated that observers tend to perceive the circle as a hole if and only if its surface properties match those of the partly-occluded shape, and it resides either within relatable edges (left-hand circle in Figure 8b) or within the tangent extensions of non-relatable edges (left-hand circle in Figure 8c); a "spot" percept resulted if the circle's surface properties differed from that of the partly-occluded shape (Figure 8a) and/or if it fell outside of the relatable edges (or non-relatable tangent extensions; right-hand circles in Figures 8b and 8c, respectively). In a subsequent pair of experiments, Yin, Kellman, and Shipley (2000) studied surface completion using an objective performance paradigm that pitted the effects of surface completion against small amounts of binocular disparity in making a circle look like a hole versus a spot. Results indicated that surface spreading inside of relatable edges reduced sensitivity to contradictory disparity information; judgments of depth were not affected by surface similarity in displays lacking relatable edges. Together, these findings strongly suggest that surface spreading alone can lead to perceived connections under occlusion. The surface interpolation process operates within relatable edges and also within the tangent extensions of contours without relatable edges.

The characteristics of the surface spreading process may help to clarify some apparent confusions regarding object completion phenomena. Tse (1999a, 1999b) created a number of pictorial displays in which distinct regions appear to be connected despite a lack of relatable edges. Tse argued that these displays disconfirmed contour relatability as an explanation of interpolation and that a new notion of "volume completion" may be required. However, this argument neglects the surface completion process, which operates separately from and complements contour relatability (Kellman & Shipley, 1991). The rules of the surface completion process, which previously have been experimentally supported (Yin, Kellman, & Shipley, 1997, 2000), predict virtually all of the results reported by Tse (e.g., Experiments 1-5 in Tse, 1999a). Although Tse's data do not adequately separate a volume completion hypothesis from the known effects of the surface spreading process, his question of whether volumes per se (or 3-D contour and surface relations) play important roles in object formation is an important one. We consider some experimental evidence on three-dimensional boundary and surface interpolation (Kellman, Machado, Shipley, & Li, 1996; Kellman, Yin, Shipley, Machado, & Li, 2001) in a later section.

In sum, surface spreading and edge relatability appear to play complementary roles in object perception. Both the edge and the surface interpolation processes can, themselves, specify connections under occlusion. Whereas contour interpolation establishes the shape of an object's boundaries, surface qualities (lightness, color, and texture) spread within real and interpolated boundaries, and along their tangent extensions, to further specify other aspects of the object's appearance.

The Units Representation

One output of object perception processes may be a representation describing which visible regions belong to the same object or surface. This output, the *units representation*, is depicted in Figure 1. The motivation for a distinct units representation, independent of a description of shape, comes from situations in which an object's shape is wholly or partly indeterminate. In Figure 9a, several fragmented regions of a surface are visible, but all of their visible edges belong to occluding regions. The surface appears to have continuity, yet it is shapeless. In the natural environment, the sky seen through trees mirrors this example. Figure 9b shows a case in which there is some visibility of object contours, but poor specification of the overall shape. Nevertheless, the surface interpolation process reveals the unity of the various dark areas.

When the visual system receives adequate shape information, unity and shape may be encoded together. However, we suggest that shape descriptions ordinarily presuppose a representation of unity.

(a)

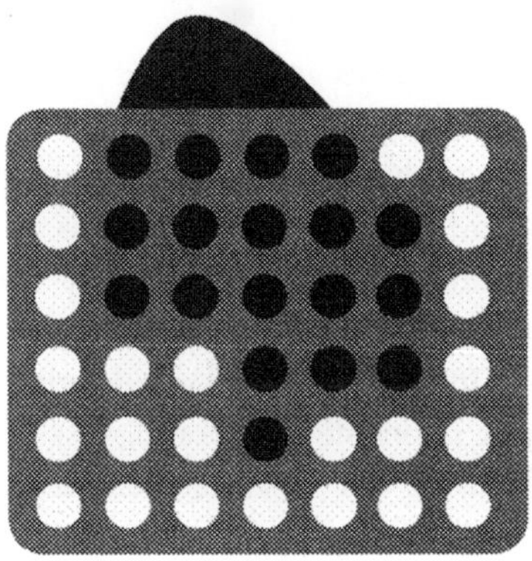

(b)

Figure 9. In (a), we perceive a unitary black surface despite a complete absence of shape information. In (b), surface spreading gives the unity of the partly occluded surface.

The Shape Representation

Description of object shape is one of the most important results of object perception processes. The exact nature of shape descriptions in the brain remains an unsolved problem. It appears that shape descriptions are true 3-D representations, or at least incorporate viewer-relative variations in depth, as in Marr's 2.5-D sketch (Liu, Kersten, & Knill, 1999; Marr, 1982).

A stronger commitment can be made, we believe, regarding *what* receives a shape description: In ordinary perception, the visual system assigns shape descriptions to unitary objects. A connected surface whose overall boundaries are indeterminate may also receive a limited shape description, as may the natural parts of objects. However, the visual system does *not* naturally assign shape descriptions to regions that encompass parts of separate objects. Moreover, visible regions, as opposed to natural parts of objects, do not automatically receive shape descriptions, although they can be recovered, with effort, from the visible regions representation. These claims — that shape descriptions are automatically given to objects but not to arbitrary arrays — have interesting and testable empirical consequences regarding object recognition and perceptual classification.

Having considered the various processes and representations involved in object perception, we turn now to neural models of three specific processes: contour and junction detection, contour integration, and contour interpolation.

NEURAL MODELS

Whereas geometric and process models aim to capture the stimulus relationships and information processing operations that determine contour and object perception, neural models emphasize how these computations can be carried out by neural circuitry. To date, no comprehensive neural model exists to perform the multitude of tasks involved with object perception, diagrammed in Figure 1 and discussed in relation to geometric and process models. Existing neural models differ in which subset of object perception tasks they address.

In this section, we will describe three neural-style, computational models that perform specific information processing tasks necessary for object perception. The first, by Heitger, Rosenthaler, von der Heydt, Peterhans, and Kübler (1992), extracts edge segments, lines, and junctions from a two-dimensional scene. This model builds upon the one-dimensional feature detection model of Morrone and Burr (1988), extending the edge- and line-detection algorithms into the second dimension, and adding operators that detect discontinuities (junctions) explicitly.

The other two models describe the integration of elements across space to form meaningful edges and contours. The model of Yen and Finkel (1998) implements a contour integration algorithm, by which spatially distinct contrast elements (Gabor patches) are bound together to form an extended contour. The model of Heitger, von der Heydt, Peterhans, Rosenthaler, and Kübler (1998) performs boundary interpolation, constructing a contour across gaps in the physical stimulus. Although these models differ substantially in their structure and architecture, a deeper examination shows that they share many common characteristics, albeit differently implemented.

All of these models employ the functional architecture of the earliest visual cortical areas; their building blocks resemble known neural units. As its starting point, each model postulates a set of linear filters with responses similar to those of the simple cells of primary visual cortex (V1). These units each respond to local stimulus contrast of a particular orientation and spatial frequency. The filters come in pairs, one member of which has an even-symmetric receptive field, and the other an odd-symmetric receptive field. Although slightly different representations of the filters are used by the different authors, they extract essentially equivalent information from the stimulus. At this point the models diverge, combining filter responses in different ways to extract the desired information.

Edge and Junction Detection: Heitger et al. (1992)

The detection and location of contour terminations and junctions represents an important early step in identifying objects in the scene. Although numerous models exist for edge detection, relatively little computational work has addressed the neurophysiological mechanisms involved in the detection and classification of junctions. One promising approach to this problem emphasizes the importance of *end-stopped cells* — neurons triggered by the termination of an edge in their receptive fields (Heitger et al., 1992; Peterhans & von der Heydt, 1991, 1993; Peterhans, von der Heydt, & Baumgartner, 1986). Heitger et al. (1992) constructed their edge and junction detection model to be roughly concordant with physiological evidence from areas V1 and V2 in the monkey. Figure 10 shows the basic architecture of the model, along with its extensions in Heitger et al. (1998).

The model's implementation begins with filters known as *S-operators*, the functional organization of which closely resembles the simple cells of primary visual cortex (Hubel & Wiesel, 1968). The model postulates six pairs of S-operators at each location, oriented 30° apart. These filters approximate odd-symmetric and even-symmetric Gabor functions, but are adjusted to eliminate any response to homogenous fields. These odd- and even-symmetric operators commonly are conceptualized as bar and edge detectors, respectively, but this characterization is oversimplified because they do not give unambiguous responses to lines and edges (Morrone & Burr, 1988). Thus, determining the nature of the detected feature requires an explicit comparison of the S-operator outputs.

In the second stage of the model, *C-operators*, analogous to complex cells, collect the responses of the even and odd S-operators. The C-operators determine the "local energy" within an orientation channel (Morrone & Burr, 1988), calculated as the root-mean-square average of the responses of the S-operators:

$$C = \sqrt{S_{odd}^2 + S_{even}^2}$$

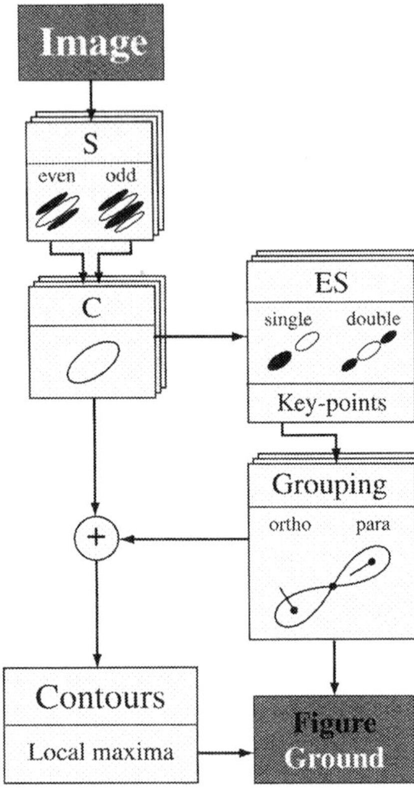

Figure 10. Architecture of the Heitger et al. (1992) and Heitger et al. (1998) models. The early model implements the stages through the end-stopped (ES) operators and the extraction of the key points; the later model describes the grouping of points and the extraction of contours. Redrawn from *Image and Vision Computing*, *16*, Heitger, F., von der Heydt, R., Peterhans, E., Rosenthaler, L., & Kübler, O., Simulation of neural contour mechanisms: Representing anomalous contours, pp. 407-421, Copyright 1988, with permission from Elsevier Science.

C-operators, like complex cells, respond to any appropriately oriented edge or line within their receptive fields, and do not differentiate bright lines from dark ones. In essence, C-operators localize oriented luminance discontinuities, without regard to their nature. Information about whether a detected feature is a line or an edge can be recovered by comparing the relative responses of the even- and odd-symmetric S-operators that served as inputs.

The third stage in the model combines the output of the C-operators to form *end-stopped operators*. These operators, analogous to V1 and V2 end-stopped cells, provide an explicit representation of edge and line terminations, corners, and strongly curved contours. End-stopped operators are constructed by taking differences in output between two or three

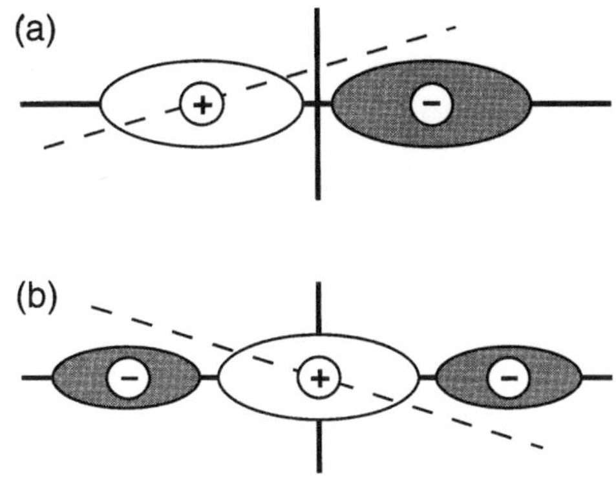

Figure 11. End-stopped operators constructed by taking differences in the responses of identically-oriented C-operators: (a) single-stopped operator; (b) double-stopped operator. Positive input is indicated by "+", and negative input is indicated by "–"; these inputs have balanced weights. Dotted lines depict an off-oriented stimulus that could stimulate the central receptive field without stimulating the inhibitory zones, thus causing the operator to respond to a long line or edge. Redrawn from *Vision Research, 32,* Heitger, F., Rosenthaler, L., von der Heydt, R., Peterhans, E., & Kübler, O., Simulation of neural contour mechanisms: From simple to end-stopped cells, pp. 963-981, Copyright 1992, with permission from Elsevier Science.

identically oriented C-operators, displaced along the axis of orientation (Figure 11).

There are two types of end-stopped operators. The *single-stopped operators* have one excitatory and one inhibitory zone, constructed by taking the difference in the responses of two identical C-operators, positioned end to end (Figure 11a). These operators respond maximally to a line along the orientation of the operator that terminates between the two zones. The *double-stopped operators* have inhibitory zones on either side of a central excitatory zone; the inputs are weighted so that the flanking C-operators, when summed together, precisely match the central C-operator (Figure 11b). Double-stopped operators respond best to a small disk. As with the S- and C-operators, the model includes end-stopped operators oriented every 30°.

The usefulness of the end-stopped operators for highlighting 2-D image features is limited by their responses to extended lines that pass obliquely through their receptive fields (dashed lines in Figure 11). To minimize these responses, Heitger et al. (1992) proposed a system of horizontal inhibition that suppresses signals to such off-axis stimuli. The end result is a system of operators that respond specifically, with very few false alarms, to endpoints of lines, corners of objects, and regions of strong curvature.

As its final step, Heitger et al.'s (1992) model identifies *key points*, defined as locations where the summed response of the single- and double-stopped operators reaches a local maximum. In simulations, these key points corresponded well to the endpoints and junctions of lines and edges. Heitger et al. hypothesize that the key points, many of which arise from the occlusion of one edge by another, play a critical role in initiating edge interpolation processes (see also Kellman & Loukides, 1987; Shipley & Kellman, 1990).

Once the key points are located, their characteristics are defined by the relative responses of the two types of end-stopped operators. That is, different types of features (end-points, corners, curves) produce different characteristic response patterns across the single- and double-stopped operators. In general, the double-stopped operators identify the tangents to sharply curved edge segments. By contrast, the single-stopped operators indicate the direction of a terminating edge. Thus, at a T-junction, the single-stopped operators pointing in the direction of the T's "stem" would respond, but those oriented along the "roof" would be silent. At a corner, however, the single-stopped operators would signal the orientations of *both* edges converging at that point. Therefore, the relative responses of the various end-stopped operators provide useful information, not just for locating junctions, but also for their classification.

Heitger et al.'s model has several strengths that make it a plausible depiction of contour and junction detection. First, all of the hypothesized operators have clear correlates in the human visual system: S-operators correspond to simple cells, C-operators to complex cells, and end-stopped operators to end-stopped cells. Second, the responses of these operators build upon one another in ways that are similar to hypothesized interactions in early human vision (Gilbert, 1994; Hubel & Wiesel, 1968). Third, casual inspection of simulation output suggests a strong correspondence between perceived features and activity in the various operators. It should be noted, however, that Heitger et al. did not compare the model's output to any psychophysical data, although they presented results for two test images. Further study is needed to assess the model's performance on real-world, noisy images and its agreement with human perceptual processing.

A second limitation of the Heitger et al. (1992) model involves what happens after the filtering described. The model yields maps of local image features: an edge map, comprised of the locations of significant activity in the C-operators, and a map of key points. In effect, it implements the edge and junction detection box depicted in Figure 1. However, it does not describe how this information is combined or integrated into the perception of contours. This issue is addressed in the other models we discuss: that of Yen and Finkel (1998) and Heitger et al. (1998).

Contour Integration: Yen and Finkel (1998)

Perceiving objects requires that, at some level of visual processing, each object's boundary is represented explicitly as a connected, unified entity. Several familiar phenomena support this claim. For example, in reversible figure-ground displays, the contour between two regions tends to switch its boundary assignment as a unit, not piecemeal. The construction of higher-level contour units — beyond local orientation responses — requires linking together the products of many of the kinds of operators we have already considered.

We do not yet fully understand how a contour token (or a unitary object, for that matter) is realized by neural activity. In recent years, however, both neurophysiological and psychophysical studies have provided suggestive clues. Specifically, evidence suggests the existence of extensive horizontal connections among neurons at early stages of visual processing (e.g., Kapadia, Ito, Gilbert, & Westheimer, 1995; Polat & Sagi, 1993, 1994; Ts'o, Gilbert, & Wiesel, 1986). Importantly, a majority of these interactions occur between neurons with similar orientation preferences; this means that neurons responding to different regions of a smooth, continuous contour may "speak" to one another, and thus process the contour as a whole. Neurophysiological research further suggests that the association among like-oriented neurons may be achieved via correlated firing patterns, or neural synchrony, in addition to a simple facilitation of activity (Livingstone, 1996; Ts'o et al., 1986).

Yen and Finkel (1998) proposed a model that accounts for contour integration and perceived contour salience by temporal synchronization of responses in a network of interconnected units akin to oriented cortical cells. The basic processing units of the model, which represent the output of oriented V1 cells, are pairs of linear steerable filters, one with an even-symmetric receptive field and the other with an odd-symmetric receptive field. Although the implementation differs, the combined responses of these units bear a strong similarity to the responses of the C-operators in Heitger et al.'s (1992) model.[3]

The responses of the basic processing units are modified by long-range horizontal connections; the sign and strength of the neural interactions depend jointly on the relative location and orientations of the two interconnected cells. The model's processing utilizes three sets of horizontal connections. The primary facilitatory connections, termed *co-axial*, closely resemble the association field hypothesized by Field et al. (1993), with linkages spreading out in circular arcs from the orientation axis of the neuron (Figure 12). For these connections, association strength decreases rapidly with increasing distance, curvature, and as local orientation deviates from the relevant circular arc. A second set of facilitatory connections entails interaction between cells with parallel receptive fields (see Figure 12); the strengths of these *trans-axial* connections also fall off rapidly with distance and deviation from the preferred orientation. In the model, the co-axial and trans-axial connections compete, so that only one set can be active in a given unit at a given time.

The third set of horizontal interactions operates during a second stage of processing, becoming influential only after the facilitative activity has stabilized. The inhibitory connections suppress the responses of all units whose total facilitation from other active units falls below some threshold. This inhibition helps to distinguish the contour signal from

---

[3] One difference might be the fact that, due to the nature of the steerability computation, only the "preferred" edge orientation for a given location survives in the output representation of Yen and Finkel's (1998) model; in Heitger et al.'s (1992) model, activations in the various orientation channels all contribute to the derived edge map. Freeman and Adelson (1989) offer useful insight into the computational advantages of steerable filters.

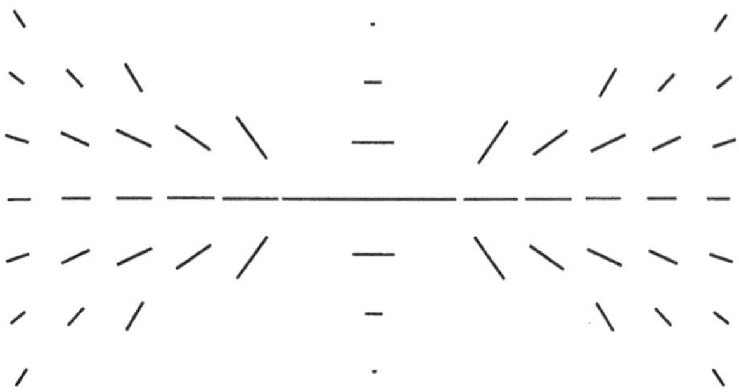

Figure 12. Connectivity pattern of a horizontally-oriented cell, located at the center of the image. At each given location, the "preferred" orientation of the connection is represented by the orientation of the line, while the length of the line is proportional to connection strength. Reprinted from *Vision Research, 38,* Yen, S. C., & Finkel, L. H., Extraction of perceptually salient contours by striate cortical networks, pp. 719-741, Copyright 1998, with permission from Elsevier Science.

background noise by minimizing the responses of cells that are facilitated by accidental alignment of unrelated contour elements.

In Yen and Finkel's (1998) model, contour integration depends on synchronization of neural units responding to interrelated contour segments. According to the model, the activity of strongly facilitated neurons begins oscillating over time, which allows them to synchronize with other similarly oscillating cells. Initially, these "bursting" cells oscillate with a common temporal frequency but different phases. Over time, the phase of each oscillating neuron is modulated by the phase of the oscillators with which they are associated; the strengths of these phase modulations mirror the strengths of the facilitatory connections between the two cells. The oscillations between bursting cells with strong, reciprocal, facilitatory connections rapidly come into phase, and neural synchrony is achieved. The model assumes that a set of commonly oscillating cells leads to the perception of a meaningful contour (although no particular mechanism is provided to extract this information), and that different contours synchronize independently so that they are perceived as separate entities. Yen and Finkel further proposed that the perceptual salience of a contour equals the sum of the activity of all synchronized cells, such that long contours (which activate more units) become more salient than shorter contours.

Yen and Finkel (1998) compared the simulations of their model against a range of psychophysical data, with generally positive results. Importantly, the model achieved all of its successes using a single set of parameters. Among the observations for which the model can account are the findings that closure enhances the visibility of smooth contours (Kovács & Julesz, 1993; Pettet, McKee, & Grzywacz, 1998), and that contrast sensitivity to an oriented target is enhanced by the appropriate placement of like-oriented flanking stimuli (Kapadia et al., 1995; Polat & Sagi, 1993, 1994).

Even more importantly, Yen and Finkel's model can simulate effectively the contour integration data provided by the experiments of Field et al. (1993). Specifically, the results suggested that the ability to detect a contour consisting of spatially distinct Gabor patches decreases with increasing path curvature, increasing distance between successive elements, and increasing deviation of local orientation from the overall contour path. The model's performance correlated highly with human data across all of these stimulus manipulations.

Yen and Finkel's model is distinguished from other contour integration models in its use of temporal synchronization to determine contour salience. An alternative approach, in which salience depends solely on facilitation of neural activity (Pettet et al., 1998), also can explain several psychophysical effects. However, whereas a synchronization model might represent separate contours by synchronizing each neural population independently, activity-based models may experience some difficulty in representing multiple contours as independent entities, especially when the contours in question occupy neighboring regions of space.

In sum, Yen and Finkel's (1998) model provides a dynamic binding scheme for contour integration — combining information across receptive fields sensitive to different regions of space. This model complements nicely the junction detection algorithms proposed by Heitger et al. (1992). Both models begin with the same type of information: activity in units akin to V1 complex cells. However, whereas Yen and Finkel focus on representing connected contours explicitly, Heitger et al. concentrate on the detection of object-relevant junctions (key points). As both of these tasks play important roles in the object perception process, an integration of the two approaches into a single processing scheme would represent a clear advance in the development of a thorough model of early human vision.

It should be noted, however, that this general approach to contour and junction processing limits its focus to *luminance* edges. As discussed earlier, edge detection, in reality, depends on multiple inputs; discontinuities in color, texture, stereoscopic depth, and motion all can lead to the perception of an occluding edge. Our understanding of both junction detection and contour integration may benefit from an attempt to extend existing algorithms to non-luminance edge inputs.

Another limitation of Yen and Finkel's (1998) model is that it is set up to work at one level of spatial scale. In fact, the model not only filters at a single level of scale, but also restricts the stimuli for its simulations to Gabor patches of one size. We consider the issue of single versus multiple-scale filtering in relation to this and other models below.

An additional avenue for future research involves applying the contour integration mechanisms proposed by Yen and Finkel (1998) to the problem of contour *interpolation*. Considerable behavioral and neurophysiological evidence suggests a common representation of physically-defined and illusory contours at some levels of visual processing (e.g., Dresp & Bonnet, 1995; Dresp & Grossberg, 1997; Greene & Brown, 1997; Peterhans & von der Heydt, 1989; von der Heydt & Peterhans, 1989). Moreover, the co-axial facilitatory connections used in the contour integration model correspond nicely to the geometric requirements for edge interpolation proposed by Kellman and Shipley (1991).

In its current state, Yen and Finkel's (1998) model cannot account for the perception of interpolated contours. In short, the model assumes that the facilitatory connections are modulatory in nature, meaning that a neuron cannot become active through lateral interactions alone. Because the facilitatory interactions are effective only for neurons with luminance contrast within their receptive field, the units in Yen and Finkel's model could not respond to an illusory or occluded contour. This assumption is appropriate to a model of V1 interactions, as neurons responsive to illusory contours probably do not exist at this cortical level (Peterhans & von der Heydt, 1989; von der Heydt & Peterhans, 1989). However, similar neurons exist in V2, where neurons do respond to interpolated contours. Therefore, it would be interesting to determine whether lateral interactions similar to those envisioned by Yen and Finkel, without the "modulation only" assumption, could explain the perception of illusory and occluded contours.

Boundary Interpolation: Heitger et al. (1998)

As we noted, the Heitger et al. (1992) model extracts edge maps and key points from a scene, but does not address how these outputs could be used to extract meaningful contours. The boundary interpolation model of Heitger et al. (1998) builds upon these researchers' earlier ideas about the detection of contours and key points (Heitger et al., 1992). Figure 10 depicts the basic architecture of the model, including the processing stages originally described by Heitger et al. (1992).

The goal of the interpolation model is to group together key points to establish contours that are not specified by luminance contrast. The grouping algorithm is based on the well-established idea that interpolated boundaries tend to begin and end at contour discontinuities (e.g., Kellman & Shipley, 1991; Shipley & Kellman, 1990). In general, grouping occurs when two single-stopped operators at key points fall in a specific spatial arrangement.[4]

One form of grouping, referred to as *para* grouping, generates illusory contours such as those seen in Figure 13a. When applied to the notched circles, the early stages of the model detect all of the luminance-defined edges and generate key points at the discontinuities. The lines extending from these points indicate the open-ended direction of the single-stopped responses that generated the points. For two key points to become grouped together, the active single-stopped operators must possess characteristics that match a particular *grouping field.*

[4] The Heitger et al. (1998) model is elaborated in considerable formal and quantitative detail, which makes its predictions explicit for particular stimulus inputs. In our discussion, we have omitted much of this detail.

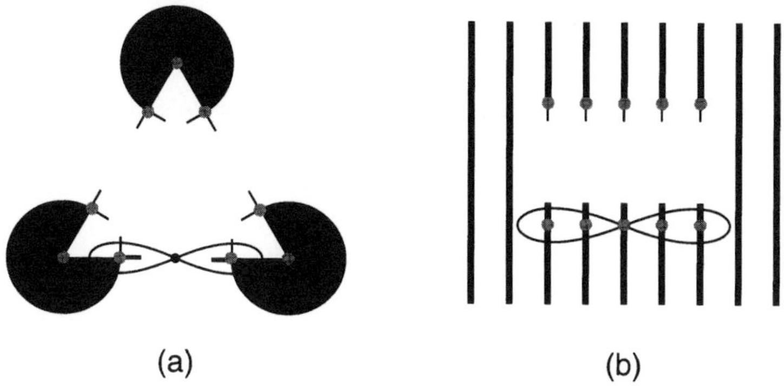

Figure 13. Two examples of the grouping of key points in the Heitger et al. (1998) model: (a) *para* grouping; (b) *ortho* grouping. Gray dots indicate key points, and the short lines extending from the key points indicate the orientation of the associated single-stopped operator. The key points falling within the lobular field produce strong responses along the illusory contour. Redrawn from *Image and Vision Computing, 16,* Heitger, F., von der Heydt, R., Peterhans, E., Rosenthaler, L., & Kübler, O., Simulation of neural contour mechanisms: Representing anomalous contours, pp. 407-421, Copyright 1988, with permission from Elsevier Science.

For *para* grouping, the grouping field (depicted in Figure 13a along the lower contour of the illusory figure) decreases in strength with distance from the origin and as orientation deviates from the axis of the field; the lobular shape prevents the grouping of nearby, but unrelated, key points. The grouping algorithm convolves this field with the responses of single-stopped operators at the key points; if a sizeable response emerges, indicating that the single-stopped outputs fell in the appropriate spatial relationship, then the key points become grouped. The numerical value of this computation is assigned to the image point corresponding to the center of the grouping operator. In the example in Figure 13a, each lobe of the *para* grouping field contains a key point with a single-stopped response aligned along its axis, and a second single-stopped response pointing orthogonal to it. The two aligned responses, when convolved with the field, produce a significant output and thus a high value at the central location of that grouping operator. According to Heitger et al. (1998), this output forms the basis of illusory contour perception.

The second form of grouping, referred to as *ortho* grouping, generates illusory contours that run orthogonal to the inducing line-ends, as illustrated in Figure 13b. The grouping algorithm parallels that described above, except that the *ortho* grouping field prefers end-stopped responses oriented orthogonally to its axis. The key points in Figure 13b become grouped via convolution with the *ortho* grouping field.

In the model, the grouping operators occupy the points of a grid, and at each point are available at 30° orientation steps. Once the *para* and *ortho* grouping responses have been determined, they are combined with the responses of the C-operators to luminance edges. The final, perceived contours correspond to the maxima in the combined representation of the

C-operator and grouping output. For the displays in Figure 13, this combination generates an output image that includes both the real contours and the illusory contours typically perceived by human observers.

In addition to contour interpolation, the grouping mechanisms contribute to the process of boundary assignment. Figure-ground determination arises from the assumption that most key points with end-stopped responses approximately orthogonal to a contour result from occlusion; therefore, the terminating contours that give rise to these key points are assumed to fall on a background surface. Thus, the model compares the responses of end-stopped operators sensitive to one direction of termination with the responses of like operators sensitive to the opposite direction; the side of the contour with the line-ends producing the greater end-stopped response is assigned as "background," and the other side of the contour is deemed "foreground."

To summarize, Heitger et al.'s (1998) model builds from simple units a relatively complex processing scheme that can interpolate contours and determine boundary assignment. When applied to scenes, the model shows some ability to connect the contours of objects that have been occluded by other objects and to distinguish the occluding objects by enhancing contours of low contrast.

The Heitger et al. (1998) model successfully performs contour interpolation using a reasonable architecture for neural processing. The model's basic processing units correspond to neurons known to exist at early stages of cortical visual processing: simple, complex, and end-stopped cells. To accomplish the higher-level tasks (boundary assignment and contour interpolation), the model combines the responses of these basic units in neurally plausible ways. For example, the grouping response depends on a multiplicative "AND" operator. Evidence for such an operator has been found in electrophysiological studies, in which contour-sensitive neurons in area V2 responded when two luminance-defined edge elements flanked its receptive field, but not when either element appeared alone (Peterhans & von der Heydt, 1989).

Interestingly, there is a high degree of similarity between the shape of the grouping fields in Heitger et al.'s (1998) model and the geometry of horizontal interactions proposed by Yen and Finkel (1998) for contour integration. The shape of the *para* grouping field closely mirrors the co-axial connections for integration, whereas the shape of the *ortho* grouping field resembles the trans-axial connections. As previously discussed, several lines of evidence converge on the possibility of a common mechanism for the perception of physically-specified and interpolated contours (e.g., Dresp & Bonnet, 1995; Dresp & Grossberg, 1997; Greene & Brown, 1997; Peterhans & von der Heydt, 1989; von der Heydt & Peterhans, 1989). Therefore, although very different implementations characterize the two models, the similarity in shape of the grouping fields for contour interpolation (Heitger et al., 1998) to the horizontal connections for contour integration (Yen & Finkel, 1998) fits well with our geometric understanding of these perceptual processes.

Heitger et al.'s (1998) model, however, is not without its limitations. For one, some of the operators appear to have been designed to produce a particular result, with little theoretical or empirical justification for either their existence or their nature. Second, the grouping process depends on some complex weighting structures for cross-orientation inhibition (not discussed above), necessary to suppress grouping when signals of multiple orientations exist in a single location. Despite the overall neural plausibility of the model, the proposed weightings may be difficult to implement in simple neural circuitry. Some other issues of more general significance, such as the relation of the Heitger et al. (1998) model to the perception of partly occluded contours, are taken up in the next two sections.

ISSUES FOR GEOMETRIC AND NEURAL MODELS

As we have seen, recent work has led to an understanding and quantification of the spatial relations crucial for object perception, as well as the development of neural-style models of some underlying processes. This progress raises a number of important issues for future work. Some involve unsolved problems within the domains addressed individually by geometric or neural models. A number of other issues involve connecting these two types of models. We consider some important examples of each type below. First, we address problems intrinsic to neural models, in their current instantiation. Next, we consider connections between geometric and neural models, emphasizing knowledge about geometry and processes that could be, but have not yet been, implemented in neural-style computational models. In a final section, we examine the frontier in research on geometric models: phenomena that suggest the need for major changes or additions to all current models in order to capture key aspects of object perception.

Neural Models of Contour Processes: Issues and Challenges

Contour Interpolation: Higher-Order Operators vs. Network Models. How does the nervous system carry out contour interpolation across gaps in the input? The model of Heitger et al. (1998), considered above, addresses this question directly. In this model, real edge inputs on either side of a gap feed into nonlinear, higher-order grouping operators. The activation of these operators, centered over a discontinuity in edge input, may be used to define an illusory contour existing across the gap.

Alternatively, interpolation may be carried out by an interactive network of orientation-signaling units (e.g., Field et al., 1993). According to this idea, luminance-defined edges activate some oriented units, leading to facilitative interactions with other units that do not receive direct stimulus input. Interpolation occurs when a path of units, defined on either end by directly-stimulated units, becomes active as the result of these interactions. Although the model of Yen and Finkel (1998) prohibits the activation of units that receive no direct stimulus input and thus cannot perform contour interpolation in its current state, its network architecture is highly compatible with this general concept of interpolation.

Can existing data determine which approach to interpolation — or perhaps what combination of network interactions and higher-order operators — is correct? We doubt that this issue can be decided from present knowledge. Each approach presents some clear advantages along with some equally obvious difficulties.

One advantage of the higher-order operator approach involves its apparent consistency with certain perceptual and neurophysiological findings. Heitger et al. (1998) note that single-cell recording data from area V2 of the macaque indicate that cells responding to illusory contours combine the inputs of two adjacent areas multiplicatively (Peterhans & von der Heydt, 1989). In other words, neurons signaling illusory contours cannot be activated without real contour activation on both sides of the gap. This finding fits nicely with the perceptual fact that noticeable illusory contours do not arise from a single inducing element. Moreover, psychophysical work suggests that thresholds for detecting low-contrast, oriented stimuli decrease when co-axial stimuli appear on both sides, but not when a single flanking stimulus is presented (Polat & Sagi, 1993).

All of these findings may be explained by the existence of higher-order operators that group like-oriented stimuli and facilitate interpolation. Alternatively, the results could be captured by a network model that requires facilitation from units on both sides to produce an above-threshold response in intermediate neurons. Indeed, in suggesting that the thresholds of intermediate units can be affected by flanking stimuli (Polat & Sagi, 1993), the work on lateral interactions seems more consistent with a network-style model than with a higher-order operator model. Nonetheless, further research is needed to distinguish the approaches.

A potential drawback of higher-order operators involves curved interpolations, which occur readily in perception. In the Heitger et al. (1998) model, interpolation of collinear edges depends on the *para* grouping process. Para grouping utilizes collinear grouping fields to specify whether an interpolation should occur at each image point; non-collinear grouping fields are not envisioned within the Heitger et al. model. As a result, points along mildly curving illusory contours can produce non-zero interpolation responses only if both inducing edges fall at least partially within the grouping fields of a collinear operator. Thus, this scheme could interpolate between two input edges whose relative orientations are approximately 150° to 180°. By contrast, psychophysical research suggests that interpolated contours may be induced by edges whose relative orientations fall between 180° (collinear) and 90° (Field, Hayes, & Hess, 1993; Kellman & Shipley, 1991). The para grouping mechanism of Heitger et al. cannot easily account for curved interpolations in illusory and occluded contour perception.

The Heitger et al. (1998) model does allow for non-collinearity in the *ortho* grouping process. For this process, recall that illusory contours arise from appropriately oriented line ends, and that interpolation orthogonally to the line ends specifies an occluding contour. At line ends, the authors argue, the exact orientation of the occluding contour may be poorly specified; hence, the model's operators allow 30 degrees of orientation change between adjacent inducers. Though these operators could produce appropriately curved interpolated contours, they seem somewhat *ad hoc* when one considers the context in which they are introduced. Even more problematic, the introduction of similar units into the para grouping process likely would cause an unrealistic proliferation of the number of higher-order operators necessary to account for the varied, possible curvatures of perceptible interpolated contours.

This limitation in accounting for curved interpolations can be overcome by appealing to network-style models. By recruiting intermediate units along various curved paths, network-style models can interpolate curves without necessitating the introduction of an unwieldy number of operators. As previously suggested, Yen and Finkel's (1998) model for the integration of visible contours may be extended to contour interpolation simply by allowing facilitative interactions among intermediate units in the absence of direct stimulus-driven activation.

Nevertheless, network-style models also have drawbacks. Whereas contour integration conceivably could depend solely on facilitative interactions among V1 neurons, the network interactions responsible for illusory and occluded contours arguably must require an additional layer or network. Simply put, interpolated contours can be distinguished easily from visible edges, despite their perceptual status as real contours that connect under occlusion. If real and interpolated contours depended on identical network computations, with neural units activated either by direct stimulus inputs or lateral interactions, then it becomes difficult to see how occluded and "visible" contours could be distinguished. An arrangement in which V1 inputs feed into a separate network layer could handle this problem; information about stimulus-driven activations could be preserved in the earliest layer, whereas interpolated contours could be computed in the next.

Another computational task that may be harder for network models than for higher-order operators involves enforcing monotonicity. Research indicates that interpolated contours bend in one direction only (Kellman & Shipley, 1991); this monotonicity constraint effectively rules out, beyond a very small threshold tolerance, doubly inflected contour interpolations. Evidence suggests that interpolation breaks down when initially collinear edges are misaligned by more than about 10 or 15 minutes of visual angle (Shipley & Kellman, 1992a).

The difficulty with enforcing monotonicity in a simple network of interactions, illustrated in Figure 14, arises from the fact that an intermediate neuron could be facilitated by two flanking neurons that would not facilitate one another. Figure 14a shows a luminance edge with excitatory connections branching outward to approximately ±45°. Two such edges, displaced horizontally and vertically, are shown in Figure 14b. Note that an intermediate unit (shown as a dotted gray segment) between the two stimulus-driven units should, according to a simple network model, be facilitated by both. Nonetheless, such misaligned inputs do not

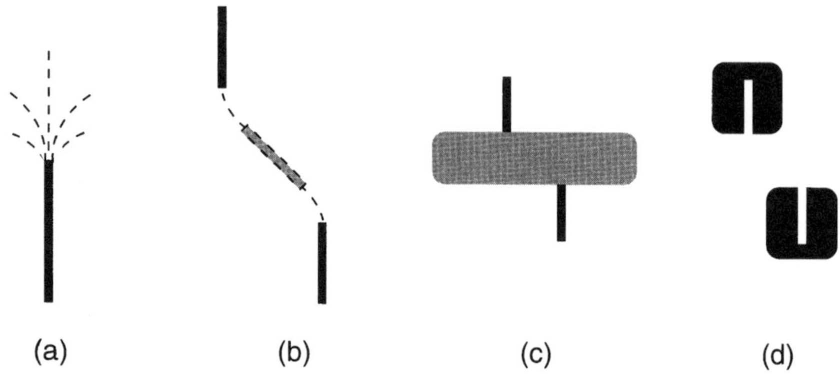

Figure 14. An illustration of the monotonicity problem. A simple network scheme (a and b) cannot easily enforce the monotonicity constraint: the notion that interpolated contours cannot be doubly-inflected (c and d). See text for details.

support interpolation (Figures 14c and 14d). Therefore, network models must use some scheme to exclude formation of an interpolated edge between two such inputs.

The point to be distilled from much of the foregoing discussion is that there are computational tradeoffs between models that use higher-order operators and models that perform interpolation in a network of interacting, oriented units. The ability of units in a network to link up in different ways is a strength: it provides the model with flexibility. On the other hand, the fact that contours are encoded over a number of neurons, each of which "knows" only about its own activity, raises a problem of labeling or identifying the emergent structure. (There is, after all, no homunculus looking at the network's output.) In higher-order operator models, an operator's output can be easily labeled for further processing based on its nature and location. At the same time, the flexibility needed for finding varied image properties, such as contours of various curvatures, may require unreasonable proliferation of operator types. Further research may reveal that both processing strategies, operating at different levels, combine to perform basic computations in object perception.

Multi-Scale Filtering. In the natural environment, images contain significant contrast variations at different spatial scales. Consequently, numerous researchers have suggested that visual processing requires the integration of information across multiple spatial frequency channels (e.g., Marr & Hildreth, 1980; Morrone & Burr, 1988).

The neural-style models we have considered all utilize a single level of scale. By contrast, a number of tasks in object perception appear to require multiscale modeling. For example, consider the problem of distinguishing meaningful edges from noise. Because many occluding edges involve abrupt changes between regions with different properties (e.g., luminance, color, texture, motion and/or depth), they will produce activation at the same location in channels at different spatial scales. Similarly, edge classification (e.g., distinguishing between an occluding edge and a shadow) often may be accomplished using multiscale information. A shadow's penumbra, for example, involves a gradual luminance change over space; this might activate a low spatial frequency detector strongly, but a high frequency detector only minimally.

Similar considerations may apply to the detection and classification of junctions. For example, low spatial frequency filters may explain our ability to recognize a square with rounded edges as a square; by contrast, our ability to distinguish squares with rounded corners from those with sharp corners might depend on high spatial frequency operators. Low spatial frequency filters may miss important details, whereas high spatial frequency filters often cannot distinguish meaningful information from noise.

As discussed earlier, tangent discontinuities play a crucial role in initiating the contour interpolation process. For effective interpolation, filtering on a fine scale seemingly would be crucial for distinguishing actual TDs from regions of high curvature; however, filtering at a coarse scale also is important for excluding the responses of fine junction filters to local noise. By integrating over multiple spatial scales, true junctions may be accurately disambiguated from other possibilities (Marr & Hildreth, 1980; Watt & Morgan, 1985; Witkin, 1983). Incorporating edge and key point detection at multiple levels of scale, as well as elaborating algorithms for integrating information across different spatial frequency channels, are important goals for future work.

<u>Output Representations</u>. Figure 1 set out an overall framework of tasks and processes required for object perception. In this context, it is important to review what actually has been accomplished by the neural models we have considered. Heitger et al.'s (1992, 1998) models seek to locate edges and junctions (key points), and to interpolate illusory contours between visible edges. The models' outputs, which come from convolution operations, consist of numerical values assigned to two-dimensional image coordinates. These output maps may be viewed as images themselves. Upon inspection, one can see the locations of edges, junctions, or illusory contours.

With these sorts of outputs, it is easy to become confused about what a model has and has not accomplished. When viewing an output "image," we bring along our own grouping and segmentation routines, and we may suppose that the image contains bounded objects. Crucially, however, the final representations in the Heitger et al. models (1992, 1998) do not represent explicitly any linked contours, any units, or any shapes in the scene.

How are the maps produced by Heitger et al.'s (1992, 1998) filters used to segment and group contours and objects? These issues remain to be modeled. Yen and Finkel's (1998) work suggests a useful algorithm for one necessary task — that of integrating local edge responses into a meaningful contour. Further research is needed to determine how the visual system might develop the other symbolic representations required for object perception. Besides visible contour tokens, these include representations of visible regions, interpolated edges, units, and shapes.

Connecting Geometric and Neural Models

The Common Interpolation Mechanism for Occluded and Illusory Contours. In discussing a geometric model of contour interpolation, we described findings and phenomena indicating that a common contour interpolation process governs illusory and occluded contours. Most importantly, we presented the argument that, in at least some cases (e.g., self-splitting objects), contour interpolation logically must occur prior to the determination of modal (illusory) or amodal (occluded) appearance. This need not always be the case; clear depth order information is often available prior to interpolation. Cases in which interpolation occurs prior to final depth ordering, however, unmask the fact that there cannot be separate interpolation processes for contours that ultimately appear in front of, or behind, other surfaces. Rather, the differing phenomenology of illusory and occluded contours derives from depth ordering information that arises at various processing stages.

Most neural-style models have addressed either illusory or occluded contours, but not both. For example, the model of Grossberg and Mingolla (1985) described the gap-filling process as a means of surmounting occlusion by retinal veins, but not occlusion by nearer objects. Accordingly, only modal contours could be interpolated by that model. (More recent proposals by Grossberg and colleagues (e.g., Grossberg, 1994), however, may be more compatible with the identity hypothesis.)

The interpolation model we have considered in some detail — that of Heitger et al. (1998) — is interesting in this regard. This model is motivated, in part, by single-cell recordings indicating that some V2 cells respond to illusory contours but not to comparable occlusion displays (Peterhans & von der Heydt, 1989). Thus, the model is designed to account for illusory, but not occluded, contours. For most occluded contours, the *para* grouping process, which connects edge inputs of like orientation, would be blocked by contour junction information on the occluding surface, which contradicts the existence of an illusory edge in the foreground. Nevertheless, Heitger et al.'s simulations do produce interpolation responses for some occluded contours, such as the partly occluded circles in the standard Kanizsa triangle display. The authors consider the latter result to be something of an embarrassment; it is described as "a limitation of the present model" (p. 414).

We believe that the model's responses need not be a source of embarrassment. As described above, evidence implicates a common interpolation process for illusory and occluded contours. Moreover, the process seems to be somewhat promiscuous. As we will suggest below, the edge interpolation mechanism appears to create some contour connections that never reach conscious perception; they are deleted based on contour junction and boundary assignment information, as well as processes that require consistent depth order of surfaces in a scene. Accordingly, a better fit to existing data is a relatively unconstrained

Figure 15. Example of a quasimodal object. The central white ellipse has interpolated contours at four locations. Each connection links an occluded contour with an illusory contour. The effect is visible in each image, but it is more vivid when stereoscopic disparity gives the appropriate depth relations. To obtain the stereoscopic effect by free fusion, either cross-fuse the left and middle images, or diverge the eyes to fuse the middle and right images. After Kellman, Yin, and Shipley (1998).

interpolation process, followed by both "gating" effects (that delete some contours) and depth ordering effects (that lead to the differing illusory or occluded appearance). The model of Figure 1 indicates this idea with an interactive connection between boundary assignment and edge classification processes and the outputs of contour interpolation.

Do any single-cell recording data rule out such a scheme? It is worth noting that Peterhans and von der Heydt (1989) did find cells in V1 that responded to both their illusory contour and the related occlusion displays, although they ventured that these results may have been artifactual. Another possibility is that the equivalent responses of V1 cells to illusory and occluded contours indicate a common contour interpolation step, whereas the nonequivalent responses of V2 cells indicate that depth information relevant to the final contour appearance has come into play. At this point, we lack any sufficiently detailed mapping of computations onto cortical layers to determine the probable location of cells carrying out the common interpolation step.

Hopefully, it is clear why we have argued for a common interpolation step in object formation. One other phenomenon underscores the difficulties of approaching interpolation separately for illusory and occluded contours. Figure 15 illustrates interpolation in a situation that fulfills the requirements for neither illusory nor occluded contours — the case of so-called *quasimodal* objects.[5] At each of four gaps in the figure, interpolation creates an edge that is

---

[5]The term *quasimodal* is used to describe cases that fall in between amodal and modal completion (the latter terms used by Michotte, Thines, & Crabbe, 1964, to describe interpolation of occluded and illusory objects respectively). The displays were initially described as "hybrids," with the alternative term quasimodal mentioned with tongue (pen) in cheek. However, a unanimous vote of the reviewers of Yin et al. (1998) established quasimodal as the preferred technical term.

occluded on one end and illusory on the other. Kellman, Yin, and Shipley (1998) studied quasimodal displays using an objective performance paradigm (the "fat-thin" method of Ringach & Shapley, 1996) known to be sensitive to contour interpolation and found that they provided virtually identical facilitative effects on classification performance as the equivalent displays containing only illusory or occluded contours.

The model of Heitger et al. (1998) would not interpolate contours in quasimodal displays. However, quasimodal contours present no special problem in our model. An interpolated contour initially is constructed depending on the spatial relations of two visible contours. However, the initial interpolation step does not determine the constructed contour's relation to other contours or surfaces in the scene. Thus, depth ordering processes subsequently can place an interpolated contour either in front of or behind other surfaces, depending on depth information about other objects in the scene and other interpolations (as in Petter's Effect). A quasimodal contour simply is an interpolated contour that, based on these depth ordering influences, finds itself in front of some surfaces and behind others.

In sum, our analysis suggests that neural models must be elaborated in a way that provides a common interpolation step whose outputs are subject to gating and depth ordering effects that lead to a number of different perceptual outcomes. A model of illusory contour formation alone, as proposed by Heitger et al. (1998) would leave open how unit formation under occlusion — arguably the most important function of interpolation — could occur. More importantly, however, our framework is most consistent with known phenomena, and may offer some useful hints in the search for the neural substrates of interpolation.

Support Ratio. One well-established quantitative finding from research on contour interpolation is the notion of *support ratio* (Banton & Levi, 1992; Shipley & Kellman, 1992b). Consider an interpolated edge to consist of two physically-specified segments (e.g., given by luminance contrast) and an intervening gap. Over a wide range of display sizes, up to and perhaps beyond 10 degrees of visual angle, interpolation strength increases linearly with support ratio — the ratio of physically-specified segments to total edge length (physically-specified segments plus gap). Support ratio makes ecological sense as a property influencing object perception in that it is scale invariant. For partly occluded objects, changes in viewing distance leave support ratio unchanged, so long as viewing distance is large relative to the depth separation of the occluding and occluded objects.

Support ratio is an example of a robust finding about the geometry of object perception that is not implemented in current neural models of interpolation. For example, in the Heitger et al. (1998) interpolation model, grouping operators have fixed retinal size, and therefore are not scale invariant. Due to the size and configuration of the operators, grouping does produce similar shapes over a limited range of scales. However, it appears that some changes in the operator would be needed to obtain results fully consistent with human psychophysical data on support ratio.

Surface Interpolation. Earlier we described and illustrated the surface interpolation process that operates under occlusion (e.g., Yin et al., 2000). No current neural-style models incorporate this aspect of processing, which influences unit formation and object perception more generally. Grossberg and Mingolla (1985) described complementary processes involving contours and surface features, including a notion of surface spreading in modal displays (e.g., in "neon" color spreading). The surface spreading process under occlusion may be closely related to modal spreading phenomena, but the specifics remain unclear. Likewise, the specific interactions of contour and surface processes found by Yin et al. (1997, 2000) have not been implemented in terms of underlying neural units.

Geometric Models: Issues and Challenges

In the previous section, we considered discrepancies between the known geometry of interpolation and current neural-style models. To conclude, we raise several challenges for advancing geometric and process models of object perception themselves. These challenges are of several different types. First, we consider one part of the geometry of contour interpolation that is not fully understood: the misalignment of parallel contours. Next, we consider issues regarding the relation of a contour interpolation processing stage to the final appearance of contours. Then, we ask whether the relatively local, bottom-up model we have suggested is adequate to accomplish object perception; in particular, we address the question of top-down influences. Finally, in the last two sections, we consider findings indicating that the domain of object perception models must be radically enlarged; specifically, models must be broadened from the consideration of static, 2-D images to encompass 3-D and spatiotemporal (motion-carried) information for object formation.

Contour Misalignment and Interpolation. An example of an unresolved problem in geometric models is the problem of contour misalignment. Strictly speaking, the geometry of relatability should not tolerate any misalignment of parallel (or co-circular) edges. As with the application of any mathematical concept to perceptual processing, we would expect that the notion of alignment is not absolute; that is, there should be some small tolerance for misalignment. This expectation follows from several factors, including the spatial scale and resolution of the neurons encoding the relevant visual properties, and internal noise in perceptual systems. Indeed, evidence from both perceptual report (Shipley & Kellman, 1992a) and objective performance paradigms (Yin, Kellman, & Shipley, 1998) suggests a small tolerance for misalignment: contour interpolation appears to break down when misalignment exceeds about 10 to 15 minutes of visual angle. This value is much larger than Vernier acuity thresholds, but interestingly, it is about the magnitude of misalignment found in the Poggendorf illusion (Robinson, 1972). The Poggendorf and related illusions produce significant distortions in the perceived alignment and relative orientations of visible contours. Tolerance for an amount of

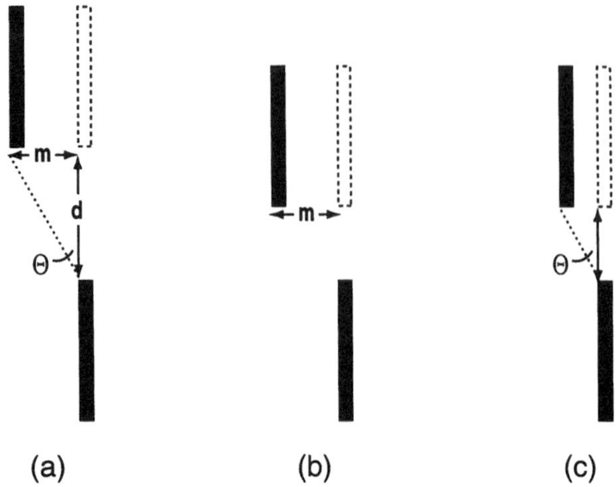

Figure 16. Possible determinants of the threshold for misalignment in contour interpolation. (a) Horizontal misalignment, *m*, and vertical separation, *d*, determine angle Θ. In (b), the edges have the same horizontal misalignment, *m*, as in Figure (a), but with the vertical separation, *d*, reduced. If tolerance depends only on *m*, then the effect of misalignment on this display should be similar to that in Figure (a). In (c), both the horizontal misalignment, *m*, and vertical separation, *d*, have been reduced proportionately from Figure (a), thus preserving angle Θ. If misalignment tolerance depends on *m*, then the effect of misalignment on this display should be smaller than in Figure (a); if misalignment tolerance depends on Θ, then the effect of misalignment on this display should be similar to that in Figure (a).

misalignment of the same order of magnitude as in these illusions may allow the visual system to connect appropriate contours despite distortions that occur in spatial vision.

The value of 10 to 15 minutes of misalignment may not be a constant of nature, however. Instead, it may be an artifact of the display sizes used in the few studies that have examined this issue. If a constant value of misalignment determines whether or not contours get interpolated, then interpolation would not be invariant with viewing distance; in other words, some contours that appear connected from far away would appear disconnected when the viewer moves closer. A scale-invariant relationship, such as that depicted in Figure 16, more likely determines tolerable misalignment. The relevant geometry may be the ratio of contour misalignment to contour separation (or, equivalently, the angle Θ; see Figure 16). We currently are carrying out studies to disentangle whether this scale-invariant, angular notion or an absolute retinal misalignment value governs contour interpolation.

Contour Interpolation and Perceived Contours. Our earlier discussion suggested that contour interpolation mechanisms operate between oriented edges whenever they satisfy the geometric constraints of relatability. This idea raises an interesting question: Is relatability a sufficient condition for perceiving interpolated contours (illusory or occluded)? Some exceptions seem

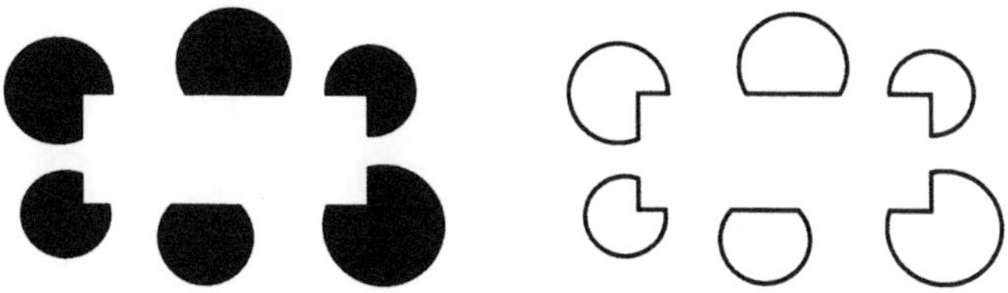

Figure 17. Filled inducers lead to the perception of strong illusory contours, whereas identical figures composed of outlines fail to elicit illusory contour perception. After Guttman and Kellman (2001).

readily apparent. For example, it is well known that unfilled, outline figures do not effectively evoke illusory contours, even when these outlined inducers have identical edge relationships to filled inducers that do produce robust interpolated contours (Figure 17). If contour interpolation depends on the relative orientation and position of physically-defined edges, then what explains the different appearances of these two displays?

Guttman and Kellman (2000) recently addressed this question in a series of experiments. In each experiment, observers viewed shapes with edges defined by either filled or outline notched-circle inducers. For each image, observers performed a classification task that could be carried out either by judging the overall shape depicted by the real and interpolated edges, or by examining the edge orientations of individual elements (Figure 18). In some studies, we measured reaction time for making a speeded classification judgment; in other experiments, stimuli were masked after a brief exposure, and sensitivity (d') for discrimination was measured.

The results of these experiments suggested that a low-level contour linking mechanism operates between outline inducers, even though no interpolated contours are perceived (Guttman & Kellman, 2000). As in previous studies, the classification tasks appeared to be sensitive to the process of contour interpolation; manipulations that disrupted the geometry of edge relatability, such as turning the inducers outward, rounding tangent discontinuities, or misaligning the contours (as in Figure 18), dramatically reduced classification performance. However, in all experiments, performance was both accurate and rapid for shapes defined by outline inducers as well as shapes defined by filled inducers. This proficiency would not be expected in the absence of interpolation. Results from a priming experiment provided converging evidence for contour interpolation between appropriately oriented outline inducers (Guttman & Kellman, 2000).

These data are consistent with an interesting theoretical proposal: *Contour interpolation occurs at an early processing stage whenever visible edges satisfy the relatability criteria, but not all interpolated contours ultimately are manifest in perception.* To progress to later stages of representation, interpolated contours must pass certain gating criteria, such as requirements about consistency of boundary assignment. The outline figures in our experiments are not recruited into the final perceptual representations of unity and

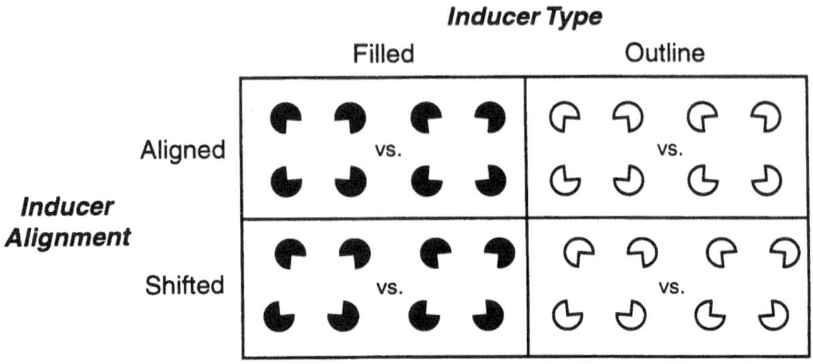

Figure 18. An example of one of the tasks used by Guttman and Kellman (2000) to investigate the operation of interpolation mechanisms on "illusory" figures composed of outline inducers. For these stimuli, observers made a fat-thin judgement based on the rotation of the corner elements — or on the overall appearance of the illusory figure. Control stimuli consisted of misaligned inducers, which contain disrupted edge relationships.

shape that are available to consciousness. Nonetheless, outlines, like filled inducers, appear to trigger contour interpolation responses at an early stage that influence performance on classification tasks.

If true, the idea that all relatable contours are interpolated at an early stage, then subjected to gating mechanisms, may clarify several issues in object perception. Consider the outline displays depicted in Figures 17 and 18. *Why* do these stimuli fail to support illusory contours? Clearly, both filled and outline inducing patterns will produce edge and junction responses in the models we have considered. These outputs may, in turn, produce interpolation responses linking contours across gaps. Only some of these interpolation responses, however, may be recruited into the final perceptual representation, depending on criteria imposed subsequently. One such criterion may be consistency of boundary assignment (Nakayama, Shimojo, & Silverman, 1989). If interpolated contours are constructed at an early stage but lead to contradictory results in assigning boundary ownership to the objects in the scene, the perception of interpolated boundaries may not occur. In outline displays, boundary assignment considerations likely are the factor preventing illusory contour perception. Thin lines may always be encoded as "owning" their boundaries (see Kellman & Shipley, 1991, for discussion). Moreover, a closed outline form may have an even stronger tendency for its boundary to be intrinsic (i.e., owned by the outline shape). An assignment of boundary ownership to an outline inducer is incompatible with perception of an illusory form, because perception of the form would require a reversal of boundary assignment, such that the illusory figure owns the boundary.

The idea that interpolation mechanisms operate on all relatable contours at some stage is consistent with suggestions that contour interpolation occurs relatively early in cortical visual processing. Although imaginable, it seems unlikely that information regarding boundary assignment is present early enough to prevent "inappropriate" interpolation. Feedback from higher levels to V1 and V2 could, theoretically, provide the necessary boundary assignment information to allow interpolation between some appropriately oriented contours but not others. However, this explanation cannot account for the proficient classification of shapes delineated by outline inducers (Guttman & Kellman, 2000).

More likely, the lateral interactions necessary for contour interpolation are engaged by any appropriately oriented edges, regardless of junction type and whether they ultimately lead to the perception of interpolated contours. By this interpretation, boundary assignment processes subsequently delete any inappropriately interpolated contours at later stages of processing (or through feedback to the early interpolation mechanism), thus preventing their conscious perception. Alternatively, it is also possible that all interpolated contours continue to reside in the visual system, but cannot be seen unless the visual system also constructs a bounded *surface*. Boundary assignment processes may facilitate the perception of a central illusory surface in figures consisting of filled inducers, but prevent this perception in the case of figures consisting of outline inducers. Accordingly, the absence of a surface in the latter case would render any interpolated contours "invisible" to conscious visual perception. The way in which boundary assignment processes interact with interpolation mechanisms is an important question for future research.

Symmetry, Regularity, and Familiarity in Object Perception. The Gestalt notion of Prägnanz describes the tendency of perceptual processing to maximize the simplicity and/or regularity of perceived forms. In Bayesian approaches to computational vision, perceptual outcomes might include information about the prior likelihood of particular objects existing in the environment. What these perspectives have in common is the idea that object perception may not be accomplished through purely feed-forward, relatively local processes. Instead, global and/or top-down influences may affect one or more stages of processing in object perception. Although suggestions about such influences have been perennial (e.g., Kanizsa, 1979), it remains controversial whether and how notions such as object symmetry, regularity, familiarity, and likelihood actually affect the processes of object perception.

As the claims and phenomena in this domain have been diverse (not to mention confusing), we think it is important to distinguish three ways in which such effects might arise, with reference to the model presented in Figure 1. As given, the model is primarily "bottom up," in that representations of unified objects derive from stimulus information and computations on that input.

One way that object familiarity or regularity might affect object perception processes would be through some feedback loop or "top-down" influence. Top-down processing encompasses any effects in which the possible *outcomes* of processing directly affect the processing itself. That is, some relatively early stage of processing activates a late representation, probably the shape representation; the activated shape representation then feeds back to and influences the outcome of some earlier processing stage(s). We will call this sort of top-down processing a *Type I effect*. As an example of a Type I effect, recall the suggestion given in Figure 2 about how familiar shape might affect boundary assignment (Peterson, 1994; Peterson & Gibson, 1991, 1994). The results from contour integration might activate a shape representation, which then feeds back to influence boundary assignment; this top-down influence makes it more likely that the familiar shape will "own" the contour.

A second kind of effect — let us call it a *Type II effect* — occurs when the products of some fairly early stage of processing take a direct shortcut to a late representation, which can then be used in some cognitive task. Type II effects differ from Type I effects in that activation of the late representation does not influence earlier processing in any way. For example, suppose that one owns a pair of athletic shoes of a unique purple color. Suppose that one such shoe resides on a bed, mostly covered by a blanket, so that only one small purple patch is visible. Viewing this scene, only a small purple patch becomes available in the visible regions representation, and this patch does not own its boundaries; in this case, the visual system lacks sufficient information to perform boundary interpolation and recover shape through the processes given in the model. However, the purple color alone may activate a memory representation of the uniquely colored shoes. Therefore, the observer can "recognize" the shoes, in the sense that some representation of the shoes becomes active. This can be modeled in terms of Bayesian priors — the patch of purple may be highly correlated with the presence of these shoes.

The shoe scenario exemplifies a Type II effect because recognition (a cognitive task) has been accomplished while bypassing several processing stages; in fact, Type II effects may best be described as shortcuts that result in "recognition from partial information" (Kellman, 2000). The example cannot be described as a Type I effect, as activation of the shoe representation need not have any effect on earlier stages of processing, like contour integration or boundary interpolation; these processes may continue to produce indeterminate outputs. We should note, however, that the detailed contour and surface processes of the model can proceed in parallel with these sorts of recognition shortcuts. That is, multiple representations may emerge from processing (van Lier, van der Helm, & Leeuwenberg, 1995), one from the full array of contour and surface processes (integration, interpolation, unit formation, etc.), and the other from a processing "shortcut" whereby some early representation activates a shape representation directly.

Finally, symmetry or regularity information may affect a particular component process in object perception without any feedback from later representations. That is, some functions in the model in Figure 1 may take into account stimulus information from outside the immediate processing area, thus allowing global symmetry or regularity to affect the perceptual outcome. We will refer to these sorts of global influences, which occur without any top-down processing, as *Type III effects*.

Sekuler, Palmer, and Flynn (1994) reported evidence suggesting that symmetry influences object completion in displays like the one shown in Figure 19. In this example, the presence of symmetry, which resulted in "global" completion, could have influenced perceptual processing via any of the three kinds of effects. That is, the three visible lobes (Figure 19a) may have activated a later representation of a fully symmetric object, which then fed back to influence the interpolation process; in this case, the role of symmetry would be a Type I effect. However, symmetry may influence perception without any feedback from a higher-level representation, as a Type I effect requires. If symmetry influences visual interpolation in general, whether the resulting figure is familiar or unfamiliar (and thus whether or not a later shape representation exists), then the effect may be better understood as a Type III effect. That is, the process of contour interpolation itself may take symmetry into account; whereas we have stressed local edge relationships in guiding the boundary interpolation process, the visual system might instead use some algorithm whereby the three visible lobes in Figure 19a trigger the generation of a fourth lobe. Finally, symmetry's influence could be a Type II effect — symmetry may not affect contour interpolation per se, but instead might simply activate some representation of a symmetric object through recognition from partial information. Sekuler et al.'s data were derived from a priming

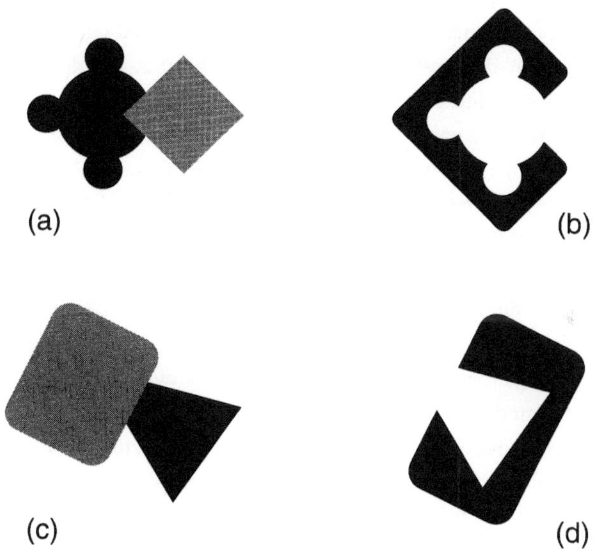

Figure 19. Global completion and the identity hypothesis: (a) Partial occlusion display in which symmetric completion (i.e., interpolation of a fourth rounded lobe behind the occluder) may, theoretically, occur. (b) Illusory contour display in which the central figure has equivalent visible edges to Figure (a); a locally smooth completion, rather than a globally symmetric completion, is seen. (c) Partial occlusion display with non-relatable edges in which interpolation of a triangle has been claimed. (d) Illusory contour display with visible contours equivalent to Figure (c). Observers do not perceive a triangular or other contour completion.

paradigm; during priming experiments, observers view both occluded and unoccluded versions of the stimuli over a large number of trials. After a few exposures, a partly occluded, potentially symmetric form might activate directly the stored representation of the symmetric counterpart.

How might we determine the actual locus of the symmetry effect? We have already mentioned one consideration suggesting that symmetry might involve a Type II effect — recognition from partial information. Recall the *identity hypothesis*, the idea that a common contour interpolation process underlies partly occluded and illusory contours. If true, the identity hypothesis sheds light on the nature of the symmetry effect because symmetry-based or global completion phenomena *never* are experienced in illusory figures. As an example, Figure 19b shows an illusory object with physically-defined edges equivalent to those in Figure 19a. The reader may notice that there is no appearance of a fourth lobe in the illusory figure display. In fact, most observers perceive a smooth illusory contour connecting relatable edges. Thus, given the logical arguments and empirical findings supporting the identity hypothesis (Kellman & Shipley, 1991; Kellman, Yin, & Shipley, 1998; Ringach & Shapley, 1996; Shipley & Kellman, 1992a), we would argue that the contour interpolation process underlying both illusory and occluded contour completion is not influenced by symmetry.

If the identity hypothesis is true, then why should global completion occur in occluded but not illusory object displays? The answer may be that the displays trigger the same perceptual processes of contour and surface interpolation, but only occluded figures activate a shape representation from partial information. But why doesn't recognition from partial information occur with illusory figures? In one sense it may. With an illusory figure, an observer certainly could report that the visible lobes "suggest" or "remind them of" the appropriate symmetric figure; however, the observer would not *see* any illusory contours along the figure's boundaries (i.e., the contours have no modal presence). Thus, there exists an obvious discrepancy between what is suggested by partial information and the contours actually interpolated; as a result, the perceptual system rejects the symmetric figure as actually existing in the image. With occluded figures, however, the difference between the representation activated via recognition from partial information and the representation activated through contour interpolation may not be so obvious. By definition, part of an occluded object is hidden from view, and the hidden parts have no sensory presence. Thus, both interpretations — the local representation developed through contour interpolation and the global representation induced by a Type II effect — are possible. Thus, an observer may perceive a partly occluded object as a globally symmetric form, due to a recognition from partial information, whereas this representation is rejected in the case of illusory figures because nothing is hidden.

The idea that Type II effects — recognition from partial information — are responsible for certain "global effects" in contour interpolation may clarify certain issues. First, pointing to an occlusion display similar to the one shown in Figure 19c, Boselie and Wouterlood

(1992) argued against Kellman and Shipley's (1991) relatability geometry, presumably because they found the presence of a triangle in the display to be obvious. (The visible edges of the black figure are not relatable, because they violate the 90 degree bending limit for interpolated contours.) However, it is doubtful that contour interpolation occurs in this display, even though the image clearly makes us think of triangles. Consider the illusory contour version, which contains the same visible edges, shown in Figure 19d. No third point of a triangle is visible.

Second, the research literature on the completion of partly occluded objects contains several conflicting reports about global and local processing (e.g., Boselie, 1988, 1994; Sekuler, Palmer, & Flynn, 1994). We suggest that "local" effects derive from actual contour interpolation processes, whereas "global" effects depend on recognition from partial information. Importantly, the only objective data supporting global percepts come from priming studies. Priming occurs at many levels (e.g., Kawaguchi, 1988), from the most basic representation of the stimulus to conceptual interpretations (e.g., a picture of a fork would probably prime the word "knife"). Unfortunately, there have been no attempts to determine the level at which priming occurs for partly occluded objects.

How might we differentiate Type I, II, and III effects experimentally? Type II effects differ from the others in that recognition from partial information may occur without any influence on local contour perception. That is, when shape representations become activated through a "shortcut," there is no need for earlier stages of processing to include specification of precise boundaries in particular locations. When we see the tail rotor of a helicopter protruding from behind a building, we may activate an overall shape representation for "helicopter," but the boundaries of the hidden parts remain poorly specified. By contrast, contour interpolation processes (whether or not influenced by feedback from higher levels), *do* produce well-localized boundaries. Accordingly, it may be possible to distinguish Type II effects from Type I or Type III effects based on the precision of contour representations in partly-occluded or illusory contour displays.

Kellman and colleagues (Kellman, Shipley, & Kim, 1996; Kellman, Temesvary, Palmer, & Shipley, 2000) developed an objective paradigm to measure the precision of boundary localization. In these studies, observers viewed short presentations of partly occluded stimuli during which a small, briefly presented dot was superimposed somewhere on the occluder. On each trial, observers judged whether the probe dot fell inside or outside the occluded object's perceived boundaries. The position of the dot was adjusted on the basis of these responses; two interleaved staircase procedures gave certain threshold points for seeing the dot inside versus outside of the boundary. From these data, Kellman et al. derived estimates of perceived boundary position and precision of localization.

To minimize performance differences based on competing perceptual and recognition processes, Kellman et al. (1996, 2000) provided subjects with explicit strategy instructions. In the *global instruction condition*, subjects were told (with specific examples) that they should see the display as symmetric; in the *local instruction condition*, subjects were told that they should see the display as containing a simple curve connecting the two visible edges. In this manner, Kellman et al. sought to determine our best ability to localize boundaries under a global or local interpretation.

When subjects produced "local" completions, as predicted by relatability, their localization of boundaries was extremely precise (i.e., inside and outside thresholds differed very little). This finding held for both straight (collinear) and curved interpolations in a large range of displays. In contrast, "global" completions resulted in boundary localizations that were nearly an order of magnitude less precise for all displays; moreover, the estimated positions of the contour usually differed markedly from the predicted positions based on symmetry. These results held even when the predicted positions of the relatable (local) and symmetry-predicted (global) contours were equidistant from the nearest visible contours.

For a "triangle" display such as Figure 19d, Kellman et al. (1996) found that observers exhibited a large uncertainty about the location of the triangle's occluded vertex. Most subjects' best estimate of its position differed from the actual position (determined by extending the visible contours as straight lines) by at least 15% of the height of the triangle.

In sum, global influences like symmetry and familiarity apparently do not produce local contour interpolation. Contrary to Type III models, symmetry does not appear to work within the interpolation process to create precisely localized contours. Contrary to Type I models, although shape representations become active, they do not establish local contours via feedback to interpolation mechanisms. Thus, it appears that effects suggesting global perceptual completion may actually depend on recognition from partial information — Type II effects. Operating in parallel with the object perception processes we have outlined, partial information may activate later cognitive representations directly. Both processing routes play important roles in human object recognition; distinguishing them, however, may clarify the theoretical situation considerably.

Interpolation in Three-Dimensional Object Perception. Until now, most of our discussion of object perception has emphasized information in static, 2-D luminance images. This focus mirrors the research literature: although geometric studies using more complex stimuli have started to emerge, all existing neural-style models possess tight constraints on the kinds of inputs they can accept. Detailed models of the processes that extract information from such 2-D, static images represent an important advance, but even with further elaboration and new data, they cannot be complete.

Object perception is at least a four-dimensional process. It involves information derived not only from spatial variations across a frontoparallel plane, but from depth differences and changes over time given by motion. In fact, more modern views of perception suggest that the basic structure of the visual system includes mechanisms for extracting depth and spatiotemporal relationships (Gibson, 1966, 1979; Johansson, 1970; Marr, 1982). These accounts emphasize that perceptual systems adapted to serve mobile organisms in a 3-D world.

At a few junctures, we have already noted some relevant details. For example, perceived edges may depend on motion and stereoscopic depth discontinuities, as well as luminance contrast. Here we comment more generally on the role of depth and motion in object perception.

Consider the problem of perceiving object unity and boundaries in the 3-D world. Acquiring accurate representations of contour and surface orientations in three dimensions would seem to be of high priority for comprehension of and action within the environment. In terms of the processes of visual segmentation and grouping, it would seem that sensitivity to 3-D relationships among visible parts of contours and surfaces would be important in discovering the connected objects that exist in the world. Research suggests that contour and surface interpolation processes do, indeed, take edge and surface orientations in 3-D space as their inputs and produce interpolated contours and surfaces that extend through depth (Kellman, Machado, Shipley, & Li, 1996; Kellman, Yin, Shipley, Machado, & Li, 2001). Figures 20a and 20c illustrate 3-D interpolations, where the contour positions depend on stereoscopic depth information. Observers tend to perceive smooth contours and surfaces connecting the top and bottom white tabs across the intervening gaps. Figures 20b and 20d illustrate that misalignment in depth *disrupts* the interpolation processes. Although the monocular images fall within the tolerable misalignment for 2-D interpolation, the top and bottom white surface pieces do not appear to connect when the display is seen in depth.

Kellman et al. (1996) proposed that 3-D interpolation is governed by an elaboration of the notion of contour relatability to three dimensions. Informally speaking, two contours extending through depth are relatable if, in 3-D space, there is a smooth, monotonic connection between them. As with the original construct, two contours will be connected by the boundary interpolation process if and only if they are relatable.

For a more intuitive idea of 3-D relatability, the white surface patches given in the stereoscopic displays are shown below in side view (Figure 20). When the surfaces meet the 3-D relatability criteria, the contours in the side view also are relatable in two dimensions. Thus, the examples in Figures 20a and 20c meet the conditions of 3-D relatability, whereas Figures 20b and 20d contain misalignments in depth that disrupt relatability.

To study 3-D interpolation experimentally, Kellman et al. (1996) developed an objective task using the kinds of stimuli displayed in Figure 20. On each trial, observers viewed two surface patches, presented stereoscopically, that could be classified as lying in parallel planes (including the case of coplanarity) or intersecting planes. Observers made a speeded classification judgment by pressing one key for "intersecting" (as in Figures 20a and 20b), and another key for "parallel" (as in Figures 20c and 20d); note that the response did not depend on impressions of interpolation or the notion of 3-D relatability. Kellman et al. predicted that: (1) analogous to certain tasks using 2-D shapes, perception of a unified object

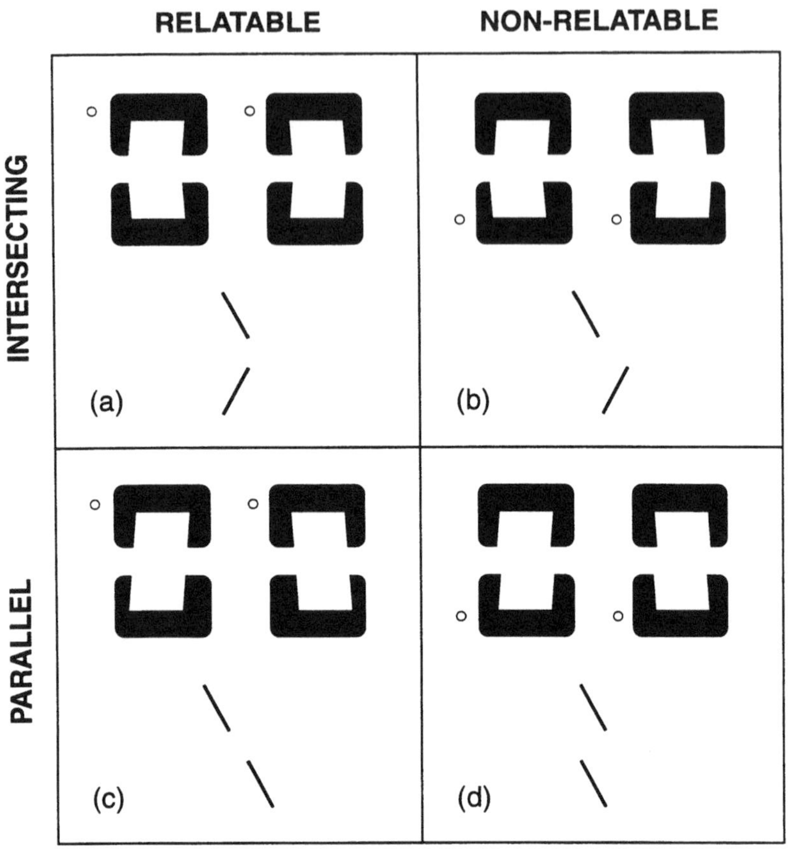

Figure 20. Displays used by Kellman et al. (1996) to test 3-D interpolation: (a) relatable, intersecting surfaces; (b) non-relatable, intersecting surfaces; (c) relatable, parallel (coplanar) surfaces; (d) non-relatable, parallel surfaces. To experience the stereoscopic effect, cross fuse the two images in each pair, using the small circles to focus. A side view of the two white surfaces appears below each stereoscopic pair.

would facilitate classification performance; and (2) perceived unity, as indexed by superior speed and/or accuracy, would depend on the relatability criteria.

The results of this study, which included a number of control groups to ensure that the results truly depended on depth relationships and interpolation, will be reported in detail elsewhere (Kellman et al., 2001). To summarize, all of the results supported the predictions: observers classified relatable displays more accurately and rapidly than non-relatable displays. These data suggest that relatability describes the conditions necessary for contour interpolation in depth.

The study of three-dimensional interpolation processes using objective tasks is in its infancy. Nonetheless, the results already indicate that models of object perception will need to be broadened to accept as inputs the 3-D positions and orientations of edges, and to produce interpolated contours and surfaces that extend through all three spatial dimensions.

Spatiotemporal Interpolation in Object Perception. When looking through dense foliage, an observer may see bits of light and color from the scene behind but may be unable to detect specific objects or spatial layout. However, if the observer moves parallel to the occluding foliage, the scene behind may suddenly be revealed. This ordinary experience suggests that humans have robust abilities to perceive the objects in a scene from information that arrives fragmented in both space and time.

Experimental work has begun to address our spatiotemporal integration abilities. For example, we have known for some time that illusory figures may arise from inducing elements that appear sequentially (e.g., Bruno & Bertamini, 1988; Kellman & Cohen, 1984; Kojo, Liinasuo, & Rovamo, 1993). Perception of these figures requires not only that the visual system integrate information over time, but also interpolate, as some parts of the object never project to the eyes. Similar situations often are encountered in everyday perception involving ordinary environments and moving objects or observers.

Current models of visual interpolation, such as the ones we have considered, are not configured to handle inputs that arrive fragmented over time. One obstacle to broadening our theories and models is the open-ended nature of the question: What stimulus relationships in both space and time lead to the perception of complete, unified objects? With the extra degree of freedom given by motion, the question seems daunting.

To simplify the problem, Palmer, Kellman, and Shipley (1997, 2000) proposed two simple hypotheses that would allow the geometry of spatial relatability to be generalized to the problem of spatiotemporal interpolation. Figure 21 illustrates these ideas. The *persistence hypothesis* (Figure 21a) suggests that the position and edge orientations of a briefly-viewed fragment are encoded in a buffer, such that they can be integrated with later-appearing fragments. In Figure 21a, an opaque panel containing two apertures moves in front of an object, revealing one part of an occluded object at time t_1 and another part at time t_2. If information concerning the part seen at t_1 persists in the buffer until the part at t_2 appears, then the standard relatability computation can be performed to integrate the currently visible part with the part encoded earlier.

In Figure 21b, the object moves behind a stationary occluder, again revealing one part through the bottom aperture at t_1 and a second part through the top aperture at t_2. This figure illustrates the *spatial updating hypothesis*. According to this idea, the visual system encodes a velocity signal of any moving objects or surfaces, in addition to their positions and edge orientations; once these surfaces become occluded, the visual system uses the velocity signal to update their spatial position over time. Thus, when a later-appearing object part (upper aperture at t_2) becomes visible, it can be combined with the updated position of the earlier-

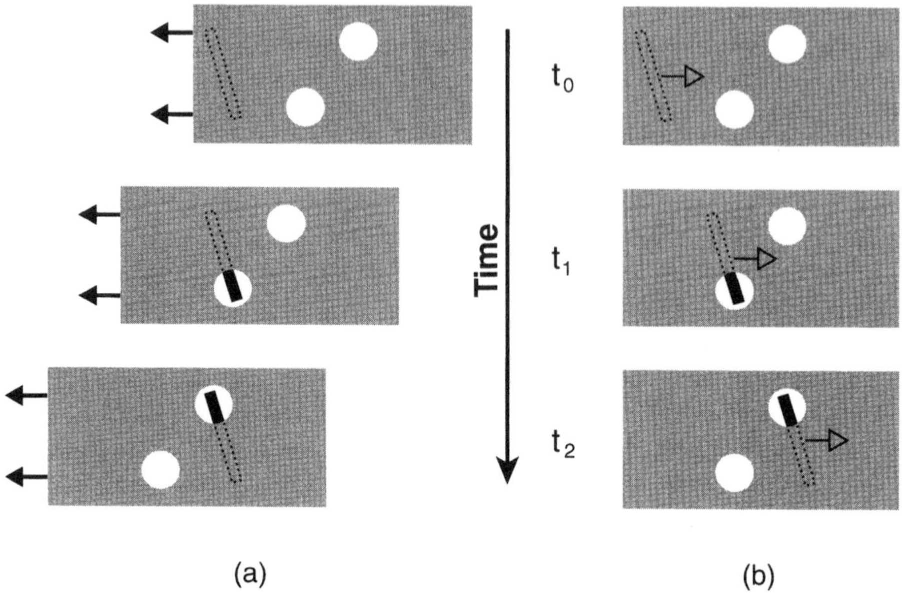

Figure 21. Illustrations of spatiotemporal relatability. (a) The moving occluder reveals relatable parts of the rod sequentially in time (t_1 and t_2). Perceptual connection of parts requires that the initially visible part persists over time in some way. (b) Parts of the moving rod become visible through apertures sequentially in time. Perceptual connection of the parts requires not only persistence of the initially visible part but positional updating based on velocity information. After Palmer, Kellman, and Shipley (1997).

appearing part (lower aperture at t_1) using the standard spatial relatability computation.

Ongoing investigations suggest that this notion of spatiotemporal relatability, based on the persistence and spatial updating hypotheses, may account for a number of phenomena in which observers accurately perceive moving objects that are exposed piecemeal and only partially from behind apertures (Palmer et al., 1997, 2000). Whether or not the current notion of spatiotemporal relatability proves to be an adequate account of dynamic object perception, it is clear that both geometric and neural-style models must be broadened to accept inputs over time, and also to assemble such sequentially available fragments into meaningful units and forms.

CONCLUSION

Research on object perception is a multifaceted enterprise. In this chapter, we have attempted to set out some of the information processing tasks that must be accomplished in the visual perception of objects, as well as our current state of knowledge regarding the underlying processing. One of the clearest themes in our discussion may be that multiple levels of analysis must be undertaken to understand the information, computations, and neural machinery involved in object perception. In particular, geometric models describe the tasks, information, and stimulus relationships necessary to accomplish visual segmentation and grouping, while neural-style models address how the processing might actually be carried out in neural circuitry. These two modeling efforts serve complementary functions, and neither can be fully appreciated without a thorough examination of the other. Although our knowledge about the different component tasks varies widely, today we are closer to a coherent view of object perception than ever before. Our understanding may be expected to advance even further as geometric, process, and neural models co-evolve.

ACKNOWLEDGMENTS

Preparation of this chapter was supported in part by research grants from the National Science Foundation (SBR 9496112) and the National Eye Institute (R01 EY13518) to PJK. We thank Patrick Garrigan and Evan Palmer for helpful discussions, Tim Shipley for useful comments on an earlier draft, and Stephanie Lau for general assistance. Correspondence should be addressed to Philip J. Kellman, UCLA Department of Psychology, 405 Hilgard Avenue, Los Angeles, CA 90095-1563 or via email (Kellman@cognet.ucla.edu).

REFERENCES

Banton, T., & Levi, D. M. (1992). The perceived strength of illusory contours. *Perception & Psychophysics, 52,* 676-684.

Barrow, H. G., & Tenenbaum, J. M. (1986). Computational approaches to vision. In K. R. Boff, L. Kaufman, & J. P. Thomas (Eds.), *Handbook of perception and human performance: Vol. 2. Cognitive processes and performance* (pp. 38.1-38.70). New York: John Wiley & Sons.

Boselie, F. (1988). Local versus global minima in visual pattern completion. *Perception & Psychophysics, 43,* 431-445.

Boselie, F. (1994). Local and global factors in visual occlusion. *Perception, 23,* 517-528.

Boselie, F., & Wouterlood, D. (1992). A critical discussion of Kellman and Shipley's (1991) theory of occlusion phenomena. *Psychological Research, 54,* 278-285.

Bruno, N., & Bertamini, M. (1990). Identifying contours from occlusion events. *Perception & Psychophysics, 48,* 331-342.

Campbell, F. W., Cooper, G. F., & Enroth-Cugell, C. (1969). The spatial selectivity of the visual cells of the cat. *Journal of Physiology, 203,* 223-235.

Dresp, B., & Bonnet, C. (1995). Subthreshold summation with illusory contours. *Vision Research, 35,* 1071-1078.

Dresp, B., & Grossberg, S. (1997). Contour integration across polarities and spatial gaps: From local contrast filtering to global grouping. *Vision Research, 37,* 913-924.

Field, D., Hayes, A., & Hess, R. F. (1993). Contour integration by the human visual system: Evidence for a local "association field." *Vision Research, 33,* 173-193.

Fischer, B., & Poggio, G. F. (1979). Depth sensitivity of binocular cortical neurons of behaving monkeys. *Proceedings of the Royal Society of London B, 1157,* 409-414.

Freeman, W. T., & Adelson, E. H. (1989). Steerable filters. *Image Understanding and Machine Vision, 14,* 114-117.

Geisler, W. S., Perry, J. S., Super, B. J., & Gallogly, D. P. (2001). Edge co-occurrence in natural images predicts contour grouping performance. *Vision Research, 41,* 711-724.

Gibson, J. J. (1966). *The senses considered as perceptual systems.* Boston: Houghton-Mifflin.

Gibson, J. J. (1979). *The ecological approach to visual perception.* Boston: Houghton-Mifflin.

Gibson, J. J., Kaplan, G. A., Reynolds, H. N., & Wheeler, K. (1969). The change from visible to invisible: A study of optical transitions. *Perception & Psychophysics, 5,* 113-116.

Gilbert, C. D. (1994). Circuitry, architecture and functional dynamics of visual cortex. In G. R. Rock & J. A. Goode (Eds.), *Higher-order processing in the visual system* (pp. 35-62). Chichester, England: John Wiley & Sons.

Greene, H. H., & Brown, J. M. (1997). Spatial interactions with real and gap-induced illusory lines in Vernier acuity. *Vision Research, 37,* 597-604.

Grossberg, S. (1994). 3-D vision and figure-ground separation by visual cortex. *Perception & Psychophysics, 55,* 48-120.

Grossberg, S., & Mingolla, E. (1985). Neural dynamics of form perception: Boundary completion, illusory figures, and neon color spreading. *Psychological Review, 92,* 173-211.

Guttman, S. E., & Kellman, P. J. (2000). Seeing between the lines: Contour interpolation without perception of interpolated contours. *Investigative Ophthalmology & Visual Science, 41*(4), S439.

Guttman, S. E., & Kellman, P. J. (2001). *Contour interpolation: Necessary but not sufficient for the perception of interpolated contours.* Manuscript in preparation.

Guttman, S. E., & Sekuler, A. B. (2001). *Visual completion of partly occluded objects: An exploration of spatial and temporal limits.* Manuscript submitted for publication.

He, Z. J., & Nakayama, K. (1994). Perceived surface shape not features determines correspondence strength in apparent motion. *Vision Research, 34,* 2125-2135.

He, Z. J., & Ooi, T. L. (1998). Illusory-contour formation affected by luminance contrast polarity. *Perception, 27,* 313-335.

Heitger, F., Rosenthaler, L., von der Heydt, R., Peterhans, E., & Kübler, O. (1992). Simulation of neural contour mechanisms: From simple to end-stopped cells. *Vision Research, 32,* 963-981.

Heitger, F., von der Heydt, R., Peterhans, E., Rosenthaler, L., & Kübler, O. (1998). Simulation of neural contour mechanisms: Representing anomalous contours. *Image and Vision Computing, 16,* 407-421.

Hoffman, D. D. (1998). *Visual intelligence: How we create what we see.* New York: W. W. Norton & Company.

Hubel, D. H., & Wiesel, T. N. (1968). Receptive fields and functional architecture of monkey striate cortex. *Journal of Physiology, 195,* 215-243.

Johansson, G. (1970). On theories for visual space perception: A letter to Gibson. *Scandinavian Journal of Psychology, 11*(2), 67-74.

Julesz, B. (1971). *Foundations of cyclopean perception.* Chicago: University of Chicago Press.

Kanizsa, G. (1979). *Organization in vision.* New York: Praeger.

Kapadia, M. K., Ito, M., Gilbert, C. D., & Westheimer, G. (1995). Improvement in visual sensitivity by changes in local context: Parallel studies in human observers and in V1 of alert monkeys. *Neuron, 15,* 843-856.

Kawaguchi, J. (1988). Priming effect as expectation. *Japanese Psychological Review, 31,* 290-304.

Kellman, P. J. (2000). An update on Gestalt Psychology. In B. Landau, J. Jonides, E. Newport, & J. Sabini (Eds.), *Essays in Honor of Henry and Lila Gleitman* (pp. 157-190). Cambridge, MA: MIT Press.

Kellman, P. J., & Cohen, M. H. (1984). Kinetic subjective contours. *Perception & Psychophysics, 35,* 237-244.

Kellman, P. J., & Loukides, M. G. (1987). An object perception approach to static and kinetic subjective contours. In S. Petry & G. E. Meyer (Eds.), *The perception of illusory contours* (pp. 151-164). New York: Springer-Verlag.

Kellman, P. J., Machado, L. J., Shipley, T. F., & Li, C. C. (1996). 3-D determinants of object completion. *Investigative Ophthalmology & Visual Science, 37,* S685.

Kellman, P. J., & Shipley, T. F. (1991). A theory of visual interpolation in object perception. *Cognitive Psychology, 23,* 141-221.

Kellman, P. J., & Shipley, T. F. (1992). Visual interpolation in object perception. *Current Directions in Psychological Science, 1*(6), 193-199.

Kellman, P. J., Shipley, T. F., & Kim, J. (1996, November). *Global and local effects in object completion: Evidence from a boundary localization paradigm.* Paper presented at the 37th Annual Meeting of the Psychonomic Society, Chicago, IL.

Kellman, P. J., Temesvary, A., Palmer, E. M., & Shipley, T. F. (2000). Separating local and global processes in object perception: Evidence from an edge localization paradigm. *Investigative Ophthalmology & Visual Science, 41*(4), S741.

Kellman, P. J., Yin, C., & Shipley, T. F. (1998). A common mechanism for illusory and occluded object completion. *Journal of Experimental Psychology: Human Perception and Performance, 24,* 859-869.

Kellman, P. J., Yin, C., Shipley, T. F., Machado, L. J., & Li, C. C. (2001). Visual interpolation of contours and surfaces in depth: A 3-D extension of spatial relatability. Manuscript in preparation.

Kojo, I., Liinasuo, M., & Rovamo, J. (1993). Spatial and temporal properties of illusory figures. *Vision Research, 33,* 897-901.

Kovács, I., & Julesz, B. (1993). A closed curve is much more than an incomplete one: Effect of closure in figure-ground segmentation. *Proceedings of the National Academy of Sciences of the United States of America, 90,* 7495-7497.

Lesher, G. W., & Mingolla, E. (1993). The role of edges and line-ends in illusory contour formation. *Vision Research, 33,* 2253-2270.

Liu, Z., Jacobs, D. W., & Basri, R. (1999). The role of convexity in perceptual completion: Beyond good continuation. *Vision Research, 39,* 4244-4257.

Liu, Z., Kersten, D., & Knill, D. C. (1999). Dissociating stimulus information from internal representation — a case study in object recognition. *Vision Research, 39,* 603-612.

Livingstone, M. S. (1996). Oscillatory firing and interneuronal correlations in squirrel monkey striate cortex. *Journal of Neurophysiology, 75,* 2467-2485.

Marr, D. (1982). *Vision.* San Francisco: W. H. Freeman and Company.

Marr, D., & Hildreth, E. (1980). Theory of edge detection. *Proceedings of the Royal Society of London B, 207,* 187-217.

Michotte, A., Thinès, G., & Crabbé, G. (1964). *Les complements amodaux des structures perceptives.* Louvain, Belgium: Publications Universitaires de Louvain.

Morrone, M. C., & Burr, D. C. (1988). Feature detection in human vision: A phase-dependent energy model. *Proceedings of the Royal Society of London B, 235,* 221-245.

Moulden, B. (1994). Collator units: Second-stage orientational filters. In G. R. Rock & J. A. Goode (Eds.), *Higher-order processing in the visual system* (pp. 170-184). Chichester, England: John Wiley & Sons.

Nakayama, K., Shimojo, S., & Silverman, G. (1989). Stereoscopic depth: Its relation to image segmentation, grouping, and the recognition of occluded objects. *Perception, 18,* 55-68.

Palmer, E. M., Kellman, P. J., & Shipley, T. F. (1997). Spatiotemporal relatability in dynamic object completion. *Investigative Ophthalmology & Visual Science, 38*(4), S256.

Palmer, E. M., Kellman, P. J., & Shipley, T.F. (2000). Modal and amodal perception of dynamically occluded objects. *Investigative Ophthalmology & Visual Science, 41*(4), S439.

Palmer, S., & Rock, I. (1994). Rethinking perceptual organization: The role of uniform connectedness. *Psychonomic Bulletin & Review, 1,* 29-55.

Peterhans, E., & von der Heydt, R. (1989). Mechanisms of contour perception in monkey visual cortex. II. Contours bridging gaps. *Journal of Neuroscience, 9,* 1749-1763.

Peterhans, E., & von der Heydt, R. (1991). Subjective contours: Bridging the gap between psychophysics and physiology. *Trends in Neurosciences, 14,* 112-119.

Peterhans, E., & von der Heydt, R. (1993). Functional organization of area V2 in alert macaque. *European Journal of Neuroscience, 5,* 509-524.

Peterhans, E., von der Heydt, R., & Baumgartner, G. (1986). Neuronal responses to illusory contour stimuli reveal stages of visual cortical processing. In J. D. Pettigrew, K. J. Sanderson, & W. R. Levick (Eds.), *Visual Neuroscience* (pp. 343-351). Cambridge, UK: Cambridge University Press.

Peterson, M. A. (1994). Object recognition processes can and do operate before figure-ground organization. *Current Directions in Psychological Science, 3(*4), 105-111.

Peterson, M. A., & Gibson, B. S. (1991). The initial identification of figure-ground relationships: Contributions from shape recognition processes. *Bulletin of the Psychonomic Society, 29,* 199-202.

Peterson, M. A., & Gibson, B. S. (1994). Must figure-ground organization precede object recognition? An assumption in peril. *Psychological Science, 5,* 253-259.

Petter, G. (1956). Nuove ricerche sperimentali sulla totalizzazione percettiva. *Rivista di Psicologia, 50,* 213-227.

Pettet, M. W., McKee, S. P., & Grzywacz, N. M. (1998). Constraints on long range interactions mediating contour detection. *Vision Research, 38,* 865-879.

Polat, U., & Sagi, D. (1993). Lateral interactions between spatial channels: Suppression and facilitation revealed by lateral masking experiments. *Vision Research, 33,* 993-999.

Polat, U., & Sagi, D. (1994). The architecture of perceptual spatial interactions. *Vision Research, 34,* 73-78.

Prenter, P. M. (1989). *Splines and variational methods.* New York: John Wiley & Sons.

Ringach, D. L., & Shapley, R. (1996). Spatial and temporal properties of illusory contours and amodal boundary completion. *Vision Research, 36,* 3037-3050.

Robinson, J. O. (1972). *The psychology of visual illusion.* London, UK: Hutchinson.

Rubin, E. (1915). *Synsoplevede figurer.* Copenhagen: Gyldendal.

Sekuler, A. B., Palmer, S. E., & Flynn, C. (1994). Local and global processes in visual completion. *Psychological Science, 5,* 260-267.

Shapley, R., & Gordon, J. (1987). The existence of interpolated illusory contours depends on contrast and spatial separation. In S. Petry & G. E. Meyer (Eds.), *The perception of illusory contours* (pp. 109-115). New York: Springer-Verlag.

Shipley, T. F., & Kellman, P. J. (1990). The role of discontinuities in the perception of subjective figures. *Perception & Psychophysics, 48,* 259-270.

Shipley, T. F., & Kellman, P. J. (1992a). Perception of partly occluded objects and illusory figures: Evidence for an identity hypothesis. *Journal of Experimental Psychology:*

Human Perception and Performance, 18, 106-120.

Shipley, T. F., & Kellman, P. J. (1992b). Strength of visual interpolation depends on the ratio of physically-specified to total edge length. *Perception & Psychophysics, 52,* 97-106.

Shipley, T. F., & Kellman, P. J. (1994). Spatiotemporal boundary formation. *Journal of Experimental Psychology: General, 123,* 3-20.

Singh, M., & Hoffman, D. D. (1999). Completing visual contours: The relationship between relatability and minimizing inflections. *Perception & Psychophysics, 61,* 943-951.

Takeichi, H., Nakazawa, H., Murakami, I., & Shimojo, S. (1995). The theory of the curvature-constraint line for amodal completion. *Perception, 24,* 373-389.

Tse, P. U. (1999a). Complete mergeability and amodal completion. *Acta Psychologica, 102,* 165-201.

Tse, P. U. (1999b). Volume completion. *Cognitive Psychology, 39,* 37-68.

Tse, P. U., & Albert, M. K. (1998). Amodal completion in the absence of image tangent discontinuities. *Perception, 27,* 455-464.

Ts'o, D. Y., Gilbert, C. D., & Wiesel, T. N. (1986). Relationships between horizontal interactions and functional architecture in cat striate cortex as revealed by cross-correlation analysis. *Journal of Neuroscience, 6,* 1160-1170.

van Lier, R. (1999). Investigating global effects in visual occlusion: From a partly occluded square to the back of a tree-trunk. *Acta Psychologica, 102,* 203-220.

van Lier, R. J., van der Helm, P. A., & Leeuwenberg, E. L. J. (1995). Competing global and local completions in visual occlusion. *Journal of Experimental Psychology: Human Perception and Performance, 21,* 571-583.

von der Heydt, R., & Peterhans, E. (1989). Mechanisms of contour perception in monkey visual cortex. I. Lines of pattern discontinuity. *Journal of Neuroscience, 9,* 1731-1748.

Wang, D., & Terman, D. (1997). Image segmentation based on oscillatory correlation. *Neural Computation, 9,* 805-836.

Watt, R. J. (1994). A computational examination of image segmentation and the initial stages of human vision. *Perception, 23,* 383-398.

Watt, R. J., & Morgan, M. J. (1985). A theory of the primitive spatial code in human vision. *Vision Research, 25,* 1661-1674.

Wertheimer, M. (1958). Principles of perceptual organization. In D. C. Beardslee & M. Wertheimer (Eds.), *Readings in perception.* Princeton, NJ: Van Nostrand. (Original work published 1923)

Witkin, A. P. (1983). Scale-space filtering. *Proceedings of the International Joint Conference on Artificial Intelligence, 8,* 1019-1022.

Yarbus, A. L. (1967). *Eye movements and vision.* New York: Plenum Press.

Yen, S. C., & Finkel, L. H. (1998). Extraction of perceptually salient contours by striate cortical networks. *Vision Research, 38,* 719-741.

Yin, C., Kellman, P. J., & Shipley, T. F. (1997). Surface completion complements boundary interpolation in the visual integration of partly occluded objects. *Perception, 26,* 1459-1479.

Yin, C., Kellman, P. J., & Shipley, T. F. (2000). Surface integration influences depth discrimination. *Vision Research, 40,* 1969-1978.

From Fragments to Objects – Segmentation and Grouping in Vision
T.F. Shipley and P.J. Kellman (Editors)

8

Varieties Of Grouping And Its Role In Determining Surface Layout

Barbara Gillam, University of New South Wales, School of Psychology, Sydney 2052, Australia

Grouping appears to have been first described in the early years of this century in Germany by Schumann (Ash, 1995) and developed as a concept by the Gestalt Psychologists. The Gestalt grouping principles to this day constitutes the basis of discussions of form perception in textbooks just as depth cues constitute the basis of depth perception. Unlike depth perception however, form perception does not appear to have triggered the curiosity of Ptolemy, Galen, Alhazen, Descartes, Locke, Helmholtz or even William James. Once introduced however grouping continued throughout most of last century to be an actively used concept in vision research with an escalation in popularity in the past ten years. Despite the wide usage, the concept of grouping remains vague and the term is rarely defined. In the first part of this paper I shall try and tease apart several of its meanings which are not usually distinguished in the literature. In the second part I shall extend the scope of influence normally attributed to grouping by showing how the presence or absence of element similarity is significant information for the perception of occlusion and spatial layout.

Segregation and Cohesion

Koffka (1935) makes several useful distinctions between the processes incorporated under the term *grouping* which tend to be ignored now, probably because they were not well-developed by him or else were developed in terms of now - discredited brain theory. The first such distinction is between "the forces of cohesion" determined by "equality of stimulation" and the "forces of segregation" determined by inequality "provided the inequality entails an abrupt change" (p 126).

Grouping measured by segregation. A number of methods designed to measure grouping use the ease of segregation of a set of elements from a context as the criterion. It is not clear even now to what degree perceived segregation of one set of elements from another is a manifestation of a failure of cohesive or associative processes between the two sets and to what extent it entails responding to their difference and/or a specific effect of the discontinuity (abrupt change) as Koffka claims (dissociative processes). The very large literature on texture segregation has overwhelmingly emphasised the dissociative aspect, the nature of the differences or discontinuities between textures which allow for effortless detection of the presence of difference. This has typically involved modelling the way texture is filtered so that the elements of the texture become unimportant and their grouping becomes an irrelevant concept. Because of its emphasis on dissociation this literature will not be reviewed here. When the elements are clearly separated however as in Beck's (1982) classical demonstration (Figure 1), similarity grouping in an associative sense may play a considerable role in what is perceived in that similarly oriented elements may be associated with each other and not with dissimilar ones. This appears likely in that orientation pop-out

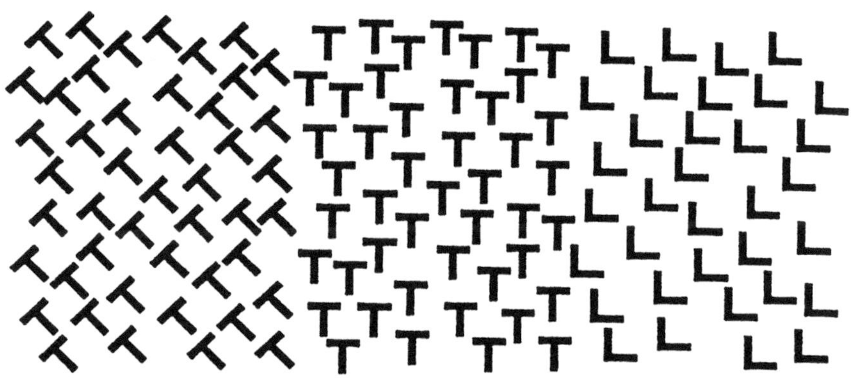

Figure 1. Segmentation after Beck (1982). The tilted Ts are segmented from the upright Ts whereas the Ls (a difference in line arrangement) are not.

depends on the similarity of the distracters to each other and not only on their dissimilarity to the target (Duncan & Humphries, 1989).

It is not possible to demonstrate purely associative processes using segregation criteria. For example all the Gestalt principles of grouping illustrated in a *Scientific American* article by Rock and Palmer (1990) (see Figure 2) including two new ones proposed by them,

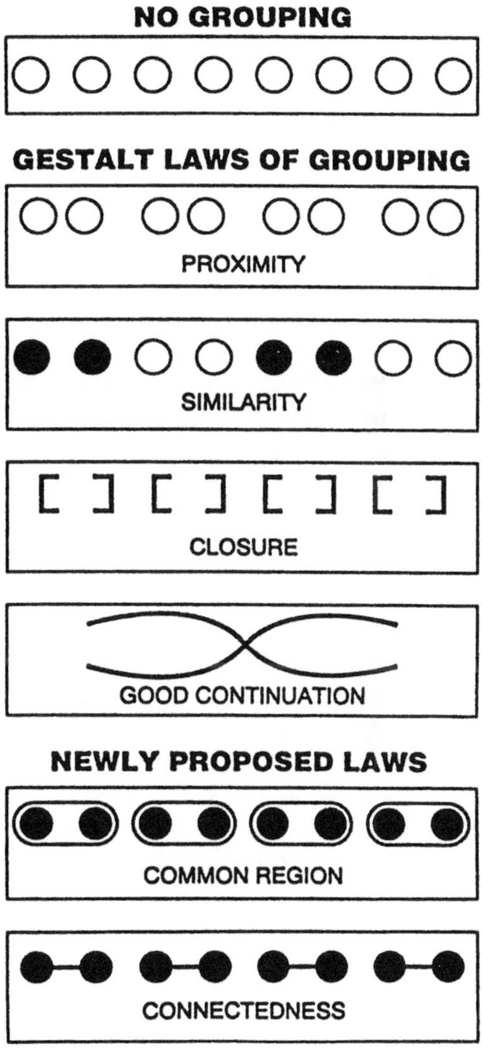

Figure 2. The Gestalt grouping principles (From Rock and Palmer, 1990)

"connection" and "common region", involve *relative* grouping; that is the greater apparent belonging of an element to one set of possible contexts rather than another. This criterion infers cohesive processes from segregative ones. Note in Figure 2 that the first row is labelled "no grouping". Presumably this would also apply to any of the pairs of dots in the third row if they were presented alone, yet each of these pairs is considered a group because it is seen as separate from the pair next to it. This illustrates the relative nature of many of the Gestalt grouping principles. To demonstrate associative or cohesive processes *per se* more direct criteria are required. Criteria which have this property will be introduced later.

Like texture segregation and the phenomenology of the Gestalt grouping principles visual search methods infer grouping from the segregation of a group from a context. In recent years a great deal of interesting research and physiological modelling has focussed on the parameters controlling the detectability of gabor patches arranged in smoothly curving paths among sets of randomly arranged gabor patches (Field, Hayes, and Hess, 1993; Hess and Field, 1999). This research could be regarded as a sophisticated exploration of the Gestalt principle of good continuation. The orientation of patches to the path and closure of the path (Kovaks and Julesz, 1993) are among the factors which have a powerful effect on the detectability of the path. Other recent authors who have used the search criterion for grouping include Elder and Zucker (1992) who measured the speed with which shapes popped out from a context to investigate the parameters determining their closure. In all the examples considered to date the more segregable a set of elements is from a context the stronger their grouping is considered to be. Pomerantz and colleagues (Pomerantz and Garner, 1973; Pomerantz, Sager and Stoever, 1977) on the other hand inferred grouping from the *inability* to selectively attend to elements related to contexts by similarity and closure thus basing conclusions about cohesion of element and context on an inability to segregate them when required.

In summary, the most common methods used in measuring grouping, including Gestalt phenomenology, texture segregation and search confound associative and dissociative processes.

<u>Grouping measured by pure cohesion criteria</u>. Techniques which measure cohesion directly are generally based on the ambiguity of contours with respect to a perceptual outcome, usually motion, although other outcomes such as depth could also be used. The resolution of ambiguity can be used to infer grouping in two different ways. (1) Given two or more possible states for each element, grouping can be inferred from a yoking of the elements with respect to alternation between the states. The Attneave triangles (Attneave, 1968) provide a good example (see Figure 3). Each triangle appears to be organised around one of three possible axis which causes it to appear to point in a particular direction. The important observation is that all the triangles appear to take on a common axis and to reverse their axes together; hence they can be regarded as a group in the sense that they are clearly not

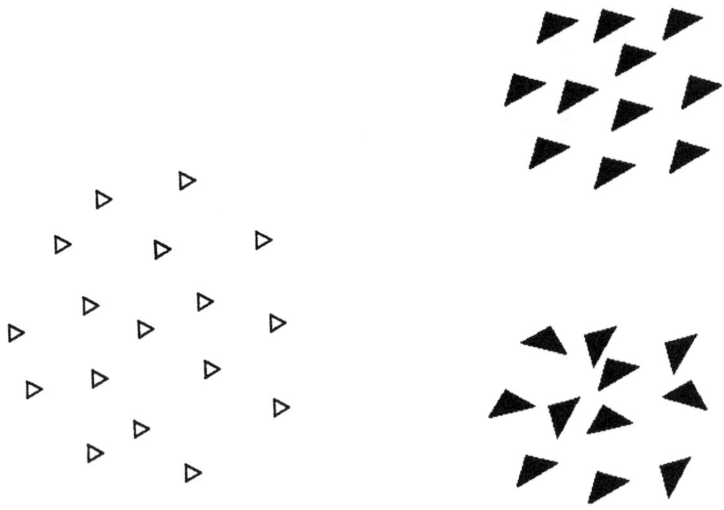

Figure 3. (a) The Attneave triangles (Attneave, 1968). The triangles appear to point in one direction then change and point in another. All triangles change direction together and are said to be aggregated (b) Triangles as an aggregate and as a cluster.

processed independently with respect to pointing direction. (2) A related but somewhat different criterion is the following: Individual elements can be perceived in one way when alone and in a quite different way when participating with other elements in an organised group. For example in the experiments of Shiffrar and Pavel (1991), separate contours that are actually parts of the four sides of a square rotating in the frontal plane appear to slip in a wobbly motion rather than rigidly rotating. The common axis of rotation is not perceived and motion is perceived locally relative to the aperture through which it is viewed. (see chapter 15 of this volume by Shiffrar). Changing certain stimulus parameters however, especially those which make the terminators of the contours less salient, may cause the four contours to be seen in relation to each other such that they appear to rotate rigidly around a common central axis in a coherent fashion forming a group (Shiffrar and Lorenceau, 1996).

Direct measures of coherence invariably use moving stimuli since these provide the most salient alternative states from which associative grouping can be evaluated. This approach appears to have been first used by Gillam, (1972). She used pairs or sets of (mainly) oblique contours under conditions of ambiguous rotary motion in depth. (A parallel projection of rotation was used and the contours moved in phase with one another. See Figure 4.) The measure of grouping was the apparent "rotational linkage" or the degree to which the contours appeared to rotate in the same direction and reverse together as a function of various stimulus parameters. The greater the proportion of time that contours appeared to

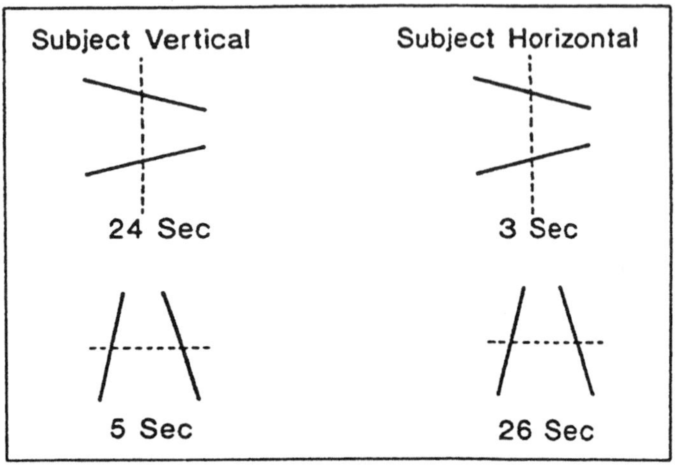

Figure 4. Column 1 shows the time in secs during a 60 sec exposure that a pair of oblique lines appears to "fragment" (lines rotate in opposite directions) for vertical and horizontal axis of rotation. Column 2 show that this pattern of results reverses when the head is tilted 90 degrees showing that the effect of orientation is entirely retinal.

be rotationally linked the stronger the cohesion or grouping was considered to be. Using this method Gillam and colleagues have shown for example that the grouping of a pair or set of contours is a function of relative orientation, with parallel lines grouped the most (Gillam, 1972), of the ratio of contour separation to their length (support ratio) (Gillam, 1981) and for a set of contours, the presence of end point alignment and vanishing point (Gillam, 1976). Collinearity or near collinearity was also shown to facilitate rotational linkage across a wide range of separations but with an influence of support ratio (Gillam and Grant, 1984). Interestingly changing the orientation of the entire stimulus (both contours and axis of rotation) by 90 deg was found to have a major effect on rotational linkage with grouping much greater for horizontal axis rotation. This orientation effect was entirely retinally determined, indicating that rotational linkage is tapping into early processes (see Figure 4).

Gillam has persistently considered this criterion, although it uses motion, to be tapping processes of form rather than processes unique to motion. In principle the same idea could be applied to static figures which are ambiguous with respect to orientation in depth, such as the lines of a Necker cube. In the static case one could ask under what conditions do all the lines in a configuration reverse orientation in depth at the same time? However, a reversal in orientation is much more salient for rotating lines since it then also entails a reversal in direction of rotation. Thus it is advantageous to use rotating contours to assess grouping by the common reversal criterion. Motion also has the advantage of creating an event – continuous rotary motion of sets of lines, which makes it easy to measure grouping quantitatively by cumulating the time periods during the event in which subjects report that the lines are rotating together. The rotational linkage criterion was also used by Eby and Loomis (1989) who actually coined the term. Ramachandran and Anstis (1983) introduced ambiguity in apparent motion using quadrants of points with alternating diagonal motion. Under these conditions apparent motion is ambiguous with respect to horizontal or vertical direction. Presenting multiple quadrants at the same time they showed that when one quadrant of points appeared to move horizontally the entire field of similar quadrants took on the same direction of apparent motion and when one quadrant reversed all did so. Similarly Shiffrar and colleagues as already described measured the coherence among the different local views of squares rotating on the frontal plane. Alais et al (1998) used the ambiguity of the motion of drifting oblique gratings (barber pole effect; Wallach, 1935) to measure the parameters controlling coherence of multiple views of such gratings with respect to direction of motion. The degree to which the motion of moving elements is determined locally or globally (for the group) has been shown to be influenced by a number of stimulus parameters such as relative spatial frequency, relative orientation and synchrony in temporal variations in element properties such as luminance. It is interesting that Alais et al make the same arguments as Gillam and her colleagues, that the grouping processes tapped by measuring the organisation of motion are not necessarily specifically motion processes but general processes of form.

A more indirect way of inferring grouping among separate components but one which is not based on segregation, has been proposed by Kellman and Shipley (1991). They found strong similarity in the parameters determining amodal completion, subjective contours and spontaneously splitting figures which they ascribe to an underlying grouping process which determines contour "relatability". Relatability could be regarded as a less Gestalt-theoretic term for good continuation. Kellman and Shipley's analysis has greatly sharpened our understanding of the process by which contours group end-to end.

Although amodal completion is an indirect criterion of grouping it has become widely used, especially in physiological studies/models of "grouping" eg. Grossberg, Mingolla and Ross (1997) and Sugita (1999).

In summary, methods which infer grouping from the elements taking on common states of depth or motion under conditions of ambiguity constitute a purer measure of associative grouping than either Gestalt phenomenology or methods involving search or segregation.

Pragnantz violated. In all the grouping research using motion criteria it is worth noting that the Gestalt principle of Pragnantz is violated as well as the rigidity principle, in that neither the simplest motion solution nor the most rigid of the possible motions is seen unless supported by context or by other forms of similarity.

To what extent do different measures agree? My earlier argument with respect to grouping criteria based on segregation was not that cohesive/associative processes are absent - but that more than associative processes may be involved. What we have called direct measures are based on associative processes alone. Nevertheless it is an empirical question whether the different criteria are in fact tapping into the same processes. The results are in general encouraging with respect to agreement among very different grouping criteria. Without being exhaustive, some comparisons are discussed below. Kellman and Shipley's (1991) criteria for relatability are strikingly confirmed by the findings of Field and colleagues (1993, 1999) using search for paths of gabor patches, namely that elements are linked when they can be joined by a smooth monotonic curve whereas elements which have equal proximity and similarity in orientation but cannot be joined by such a curve are not linked. Furthermore, in accordance with these findings, Gillam (1992) reported much greater rotational linkage between contours satisfying the monotonic curve criterion than between control contours which did not.

The dependence of grouping on the ratio of element separation to element size, essential if grouping is to be distance invariant, was reported by Gillam (1981) for rotational linkage and by Kellman and Shipley (1991) with respect to the various indices of perceptual completion.

Gillam (1981), using the rotational linkage criterion, found that closure is a monotonic function of the gap in a figure. This was also found by Elder and Zucker (1992) using a segregation (search) method. However Elder and Zucker's finding that contours of opposite motion polarity do not link by closure is not found using the rotational linkage method (Ebel, Spehar and Gillam, 1998). Rock and Palmer's (1990) proposed new grouping principle of element connectedness, based on phenomenological observations of line drawings, is not well-supported in a three–dimensional context. Using rotational linkage Gillam (1972) found no grouping of contours differing in orientation by 30 degrees (common rotation was for the duration expected by chance) despite their being joined along the axis of rotation. The other new "Gestalt" grouping principle introduced recently; common region (Palmer, 1992) has been shown to depend on the coplanarity of elements and region. Palmer showed this using stereopsis to determine coplanarity. Earlier Gillam and Broughton (1990), using the rotational linkage criterion, showed that adding a surrounding frame to two poorly grouped contours of different orientation greatly increased their coherence but only if frame and contours (which moved in phase with each other) were also perspectively consistent with a planar surface. Common region is only ecologically useful if it is consistent with coplanarity in the scene.

In summary, there is considerable although not complete agreement among different criteria concerning the factors influencing grouping.

AGGREGATION, UNIT FORMATION, AND CLUSTERING

Even considering only associative processes, at least two and possibly more meanings of the term grouping may need to be distinguished. Gillam and Grant (1984) distinguished between *aggregation* and *unit formation*[1]. Essentially aggregation implies some form of joint processing of separate elements but without the implication that they are organised into a form. Gillam and Grant propose as a criterion for aggregation that resolutions such as depth and motion are resolved in common for the group rather than being resolved for each member independently. Grouping in this sense is essentially the reduction of redundancy resulting from the similarity of a set of elements which (in common with proximity) allows common resolutions to be imposed. Again the Attneave triangles (Attneave, 1968) (Figure 1a) constitute a good example. When one triangle changes its direction of pointing so do all the others. They clearly are not processed independently. *But there is no emergent property.* A set of Attneave triangles does not have a spontaneously visible shape and the whole is not different from the sum of the parts except in the limited sense that the behaviour of the parts is linked with respect to phase of alternation. Another good example of aggregation is Ramachandran and Anstis's (1983) finding of a yoking of the motion resolutions of multiple bistable displays. Metelli's criterion of aggregation, that removing one of the grouped elements does not alter the appearance of the rest (Metelli, 1982) applies to both these examples (but see below).

Aggregation may appear superficially to be the same as what Trick and Enns, (1997) have called "clustering" - a precursor to the organisation of shape. They identify the term clustering with Koffka's term "unit formation" which means an assembly of variegated elements – a collection; a blob. Metelli (1982) uses the term "aggregation" similarly – referring to an aggregate as like a pile of garbage - an assembly of unconnected things. Although his criterion to distinguish an aggregate from a unit, namely that removing one element does not change the appearance of the rest, applies well to our definition of aggregation, this term as used by Gillam and Grant has a distinctly different meaning from clustering in Trick and Enns' sense or aggregation in Metelli's sense. Aggregation in the sense used by us does not involve treating the aggregate as a shape or object and certainly does not involve ignoring the properties of the components. The orientations of the Attneave triangles are critical to their aggregation. Clustering may be regarded as a crude form of grouping based on relative proximity alone whereas *similarity* as well as proximity is critical to aggregation. Figure 3(b) shows a set of triangles forming a cluster as opposed to those in Figure 3(a) which form what we call an aggregate.

On the other hand in *unit formation* as we have defined it, the combination of the parts results in emergent properties not present in the individual parts; properties such as a shape or

---

[1] In his textbook Palmer (1999) makes the same distinction using the same terms.

a novel motion in which the parts are subsumed. Unit formation tends to occur when grouping is by good continuation or closure for example. The coherence methods used by Shiffrar, Lorenceau and colleagues and by Alais et al (1998) measure unit formation by definition since their criterion for grouping *is* an emergent organisation – a motion pattern quite different from the local motions; not just a phase linking of the local motions as occurs with aggregation.

Rotational linkage can reveal both aggregation and organisation depending on what kind of linkage is measured. For example Gillam and Grant (1984) showed that collinear contours, which were perceived as a single rigid longer contour when the gap between them was small, ceased to form a rigid unit at greater separations, appearing to slip in opposite directions across the screen. They no longer appeared to have a common *axis* of rotary motion in depth. Unit formation clearly breaks down at greater contour separations. The critical observation is however that despite the failure of unit formation, contours at these separations showed strong aggregation for *direction* of rotary motion and always reversed together, presumably on the basis of their similarity in orientation. This illustrates the fact that unit formation and aggregation have different dependences on stimulus parameters. (The failure of unit formation at greater separations is a less spectacular form of the failure of unit formation shown in the work of Schiffrar and Lorenceau – the axis of rotation is not perceived correctly for the individual elements).

Some years ago Pomerantz and Pristach (1989) asserted that all the grouping effects obtained using the selective attention method could be attributed to the presence of emergent features and not to "perceptual glue". Perceptual glue insofar as it refers to grouping without emergent features appears to be similar to what we have called "aggregation". On the other hand grouping by the segregation criterion of Beck (1982) and others on the basis of similarity may be based on some combination of aggregation and dissociative processes without any implication or necessity that the segregated elements form a perceptual unit with emergent features.

Unit formation is generally regarded as impairing selective attention to the components. However this is not necessarily the case for aggregation. For example Rich and Gillam (2000) found that detection of a change in colour among a set of contours rotating in depth in phase and grouped by orientation and length was easier than for a control set of lines also rotating in phase whose orientations and lengths differed and were shown by the rotational linkage criterion to be less grouped. (The transient of the change was not visible because it occurred behind a narrow static bar as the set of contours passed through the median plane; their point of minimum extension). Rich and Gillam interpreted their results to mean that aggregation for some properties, such as orientation and length, allowed attention to be spread more efficiently across the group thus allowing easier detection of other properties such as colour change.

In summary, associative grouping may not necessarily involve an emergent feature (unit formation). An important but overlooked form of grouping is a yoking together of elements together in the processing of properties such as depth and motion, with the visual system taking advantage of redundancy but without generating emergent features. We call this process "aggregation".

Is aggregation a precursor to unit formation? The finding that synchronous luminance variations or similarities in spatial frequency among elements enhances the tendency for global organisation of motion (Alais et al, 1998) shows that *similarity* with respect to some properties can facilitate unit formation among other properties such as form and pattern of motion. However if we use as the criterion of aggregation that the members of the group, because of their redundancy, take on a *common state* with respect to some ambiguous property, aggregation has not been demonstrated here. The motions of the components when organised together are not common. Each part moves differently as part of a global motion pattern.

FUNCTIONS OF GROUPING – SOME CONSEQUENCES FOR SPATIAL LAYOUT

Grouping has traditionally been considered to have the function of forming objects for recognition or for directing selective attention. In this paper attention has been drawn to another grouping function; that is increasing efficiencies in processing by the aggregation of redundant elements but without forming objects. This section will outline some findings about another important role of grouping; the role it plays in the perception of occlusion and thus surface orderings in depth. Kellman and Shipley (1991) have already shown that grouping, in the form of "good continuation" or more specifically "relatability" may underlie perception of amodal completion or subjective contours across a gap between two shapes. Our argument is quite different. First in that we are concerned with grouping based on similarity rather than good continuation and second in that we show that such grouping among elements tends to reduce rather than increase the perception of occlusion and subjective contours at their edges or endpoints.

Occlusion entails seeing the terminators of a set of contours or the edges of shapes as *extrinsic* to the contours or the shapes themselves. The concept of extrinsic goes back to the figure/ground distinction (Rubin, 1915) in which a contour belongs (is intrinsic to) only the shape on one side (the figure) and does not belong (is extrinsic to) the shape on the other side (the ground). The figure is always seen as in front and occluding the ground. We argue here that a given set of contour terminators or shape edges can be seen as either intrinsic or extrinsic to the contours or shapes themselves depending on the relative grouping of the contours and their terminators. When for example a set of line terminators are collinear they (the terminators) are strongly grouped by good continuation. When however these strongly grouped terminators bound a set of contours which are not strongly grouped, for example contours which vary in orientation length and spacing, the strong grouping of the terminators is anomalous; it is relatively much greater than the grouping of the contours themselves. In this case the visual system may not group the contours and their terminators (odd as this may seem). The terminators may appear to be extrinsic to the contours they terminate and to come from a separate source; an occluding surface. This perceived extrinsicity of the terminators when the contours are poorly grouped is shown by the presence of a subjective contour along them, even when no luminance gradient is present to indicate such a contour. Subjective contours are generally seen as the edges of perceived occluding surfaces.

Gillam and Goodenough (1994) experimentally investigated the inverse relationship between the grouping of a set of contours and the strength of the perceived subjective contour along their aligned terminators (see Figure 5). They introduced computer generated randomness in length, orientation and width to a set of contours keeping the average value of these properties constant for each stimulus. (The particular set of random contours were different on every trial). Gillam and Goodenough compared the strength of subjective contour seen along the collinear terminators of these random contours with the strength of subjective contours along the terminators of sets of contours with the same orientation, length and separation as each other (see Figure 5). Subjective contours were much stronger at the terminators of the random contours. In another experiment Gillam and Goodenough found that even when all contours were oriented at right angles to the implicit line joining their terminations, the effect of random lengths and spacings of the lines was sufficient to produce a much stronger subjective contour than for similar contours with identical lengths and spacing. This is important in that the determinants of poor grouping in this case are remote

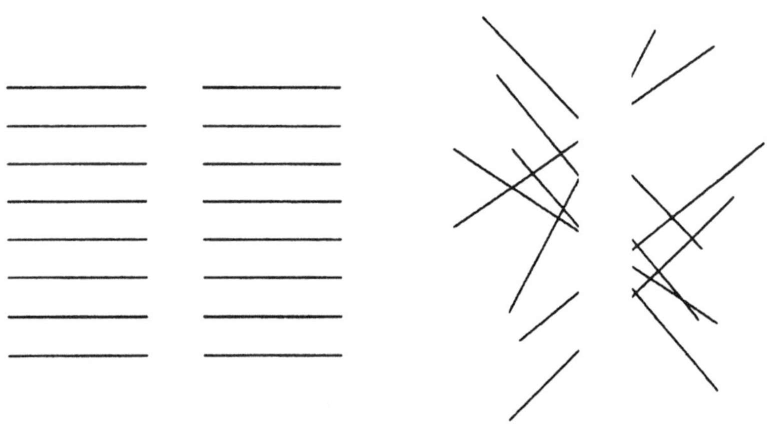

Figure 5. Sample figures from Gillam and Goodenough's experiment. Subjects reported much stronger contours for the random lines than for the regular lines (see text).

from the terminators and the finding thus reinforces the view that it is the degree of grouping of the contours rather than any local events at the terminators which is the determining factor in whether a subjective contour is seen along their alignment.

The subjective contours in Gillam and Goodenough's experiments which all used thin lines, were found to be much stronger when there were two sets of contours facing each other. The reason for this seems to be that two sets of contour terminators reinforce the perception of an occluding surface by delineating it on both sides. This does not seem to be necessary however when solid shapes are used instead of thin lines as illustrated in Gillam's (1997) figure *New York Titanic* (see Figure 6).

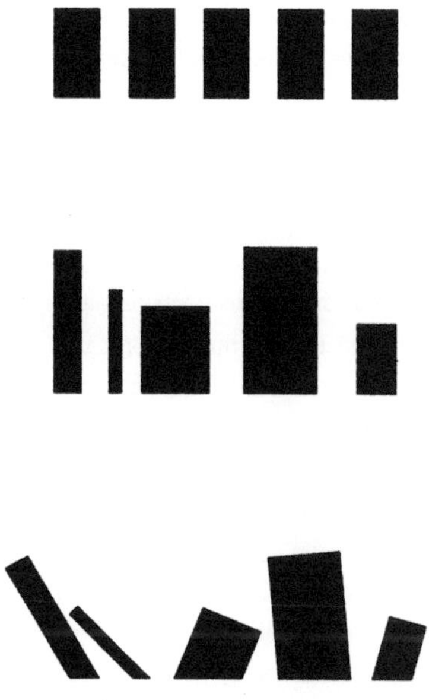

new york titanic 1997, inkjet on paper, 24 x 16 5 inches

Figure 6. "New York Titanic." All three sets of figures have equal total contact extent with the alignment at the bottom. Subjective contours at the alignment are weakest for the regular set at the top, strongest for the most irregular set at the bottom with the middle set in between in subjective contour strength.

There is a striking difference between the complete lack of a subjective contour along the bottom of the top set of shapes and the very strong subjective contour among the bottom set. The middle set gives an intermediate impression of subjective contour strength. Both the width of the combined aligned edges and the proportion of that width supported by a physical edge is the same in all three cases. There are two factors, both related to grouping, responsible for the strong effect in Figure 6. Firstly, the upper set of shapes are all identical in shape size and orientation and their alignment is another aspect of and precictable from that similarity. In the lower set the shapes vary in all three respects and their alignment is thus not predictable from their other properties and relationships. In this case edge alignment is aberrantly regular; an indicator of its extrinsic origin. The second contributing factor is a within figure rather than a between figure effect. In the upper set of shapes each bottom edge is predictable from the rest of the figure; grouped with it by parallelism to the opposite edge and orthogonality to the neighbouring edges. In the lower set on the other hand the bottom edge of each shape is neither parallel to the top edge nor orthogonal to the other edges. Thus it has the potential to be of extrinsic origin. Thus both between figure factors and within figure factors indicate an intrinsic origin of the alignment of the bottom edges in the upper set of shapes and an extrinsic origin in the lower set. These two factors presumably cooperate and reinforce each other to produce the strong effect. It is probably the reinforcing effect of the within figure factor which is responsible for the fact that a single set of edges is sufficient to produce a strong subjective contour in this case. This factor is not present in the thin line examples illustrated by Gillam (1987) and investigated by Gillam and Goodenough.

Gillam and Chan (in press) conducted an experiment using the method of paired comparison in which they measured subjective contour strength at alignments of sets of shapes like those in Figure 6 but with similarity varying along a greater variety of dimensions. There were 8 sets of five shapes all collinear along one edge but varying in similarity. Results for all 6 subjects showed that subjective contour strength was very closely related to the degree of dissimilarity of the shapes. In the same experiment with different subjects Gillam and Chan measured perceived occlusion directly. They used the same 8 figures but with a luminance contour drawn along the aligned edges of the shapes. Subjects were asked to compare for each pair of figures the impression that the shapes passed behind an occluder at the luminance contour. The order of the 8 figures with respect to perceived occlusion was almost identical (with only one reversal of order) with the order of subjective contour strength in the subjective contour task, and this held with a few reversals for each individual subject. This experiment shows directly that grouping influences perceived occlusion at aligned edges. It also supports the view that subjective contours arise directly from the processes involved in perceiving occlusion.

The processes we have described in which the grouping of contours or shapes with each other is taken into account in the visual system's determination of the presence or absence of occlusion at their aligned edges are very likely to have arisen as an implementation by the visual system of ecological constraints on visual stimuli. Occlusion by a nearer surface is the only ecologically common condition in which completely unrelated objects are aligned in the image. Thus alignment among otherwise unrelated surfaces is a very good indicator of occlusion. Our observations demonstrate that the visual system indeed implements this ecology. Thus irregularity/regularity may be registered at a low level through grouping processes or their absence in order to serve ecological constraints.

To summarise, we have shown that whether or not grouping among a set of contours is present or absent may be a significant determinant of occlusion perception.

General Summary and Conclusions

In this paper I have tried to tease apart some of the many meanings of the term "grouping" in the literature, which are not in general distinguished or analysed. The first distinction made was between cohesive and dissociative processes. It is argued that the best established methods of measuring grouping such as texture segregation, search and Gestalt phenomenology confound these processes. Methods which measure purely associative or cohesive processes among elements are generally based on measuring common resolutions of ambiguous states. It is generally found however that there is quite strong agreement between the different grouping criteria with respect to what the important determinants are.

I have argued that a further distinction needs to be made between *unit formation*, identified with the traditional Gestalt idea of the formation of a whole which is different from the sum of its parts, and *aggregation*, in which there is common processing of elements with respect to resolving properties such as depth or motion but without an emergent shape or feature resulting from the grouping.

Finally I show that similarity grouping influences the perception of occlusion in a negative way. When elements are similar and form a group on the basis of their other characteristics, alignment of their edges is consistent with this grouping and is not attributed to extrinsic causes; specifically an occluding surface. On the other hand when grouping is poor, edge alignment is aberrant and tends to be seen as extrinsic and attributed to the presence of an occluder. This results in the perception of a subjective contour.

The paper has merely scratched the surface in trying to bring some order into what is a very complex field and does not claim to have been exhaustive in its treatment of issues and approaches.

References

Alais, D., Blake, R. & Lee, S. (1998). Visual features that vary together over time group together over space. *Nature Neuroscience*, *1*, 160-164.

Ash, M.G. (1995). *Gestalt psychology in German culture 1890-1967.* Cambridge University Press.

Attneave, F. (1968). Triangles as ambiguous figures. *American Journal of Psychology, 81,* 447-453.

Beck, J. (1982). *Textural segmentation: Organization and representation in perception* (pp. 285-315). London: Lawrence Erlbaum.

Duncan, J. & Humphreys, G.W. (1989). Visual search and stimulus similarity. *Psychological Review, 96,* 433-458

Ebel, B., Spehar, B. and Gillam, B. (1999). Perceptual reversals as a measure of perceptual unit formation. *Investigative Ophthalmology and Vision Science Supplement.*

Eby, D.W., Loomis, J.M. & Solomon, E.M. (1989). Perceptual linkage of multiple objects rotating in depth. *Perception, 18,* 427-444.

Elder, J. & Zucker, S. (1992). The effect of contour closure on the rapid discrimination of two-dimensional shapes. *Vision Research, 33,* 981-991.

Field, D.J. Hayes, A. & Hess, R.F. (1993). Contour integration by the human visual system: Evidence for a local association fields. *Vision Research, 33,* 173-193.

Field, D.J., Hayes, A. & Hess, R.F. (2000). The roles of polarity and symmetry in the perceptual grouping of contour fragments. *Spatial Vision, 13,* 51-66.

Hess, R.F and Field, D.J (1999). Integration of contours: new insights. *Trends in Cognitive Science, 3,* 480-486

Gillam, B.J. (1972). Perceived common rotary motion of ambiguous stimuli as a criterion of perceptual grouping. *Perception and Psychophysics, 11,* 99-101.

Gillam, B.J. (1975). New evidence for 'closure' in perception. *Perception and Psychophysics, 17,* 521-524.

Gillam, B.J. (1976). Grouping of multiple ambiguous contours: Towards an understanding of surface perception. *Perception, 5,* 203-209.

Gillam, B.J. (1981). Separation relative to length determines the organization of two lines into a unit. *Journal of Experimental Psychology, 7,* 884-889.

Gillam, B.J. (1987). Perceptual grouping and subjective contours. In S. Petry and G. Meyer (Eds.), *The perception of illusory contours* (pp. 268-273). New York: Springer.

Gillam, B.J. (1992). The status of perceptual grouping 70 years after Wertheimer. *Australian Journal of Psychology, 44,* 157-162.

Gillam, B.J. (1997). "New York Titanic" in Catalogue *Thresholds: Limits of Perception.* New York: NY Arts Biennial

Gillam, B.J., & Broughton, R. (1990). Motion capture by a frame. *Perception and Psychophysics, 49,* 547-550.

Gillam, B.J. & Chan, E. Showing similar processes underlying the perception of occlusion at explicit T junctions and subjective contours at implicit T junctions: the negative role of grouping in both cases. (submitted)

Gillam, B.J. & Grant, T. Jnr. (1984). Aggregation and unit formation in the perception of moving collinear lines. *Perception, 13,* 659-664.

Gillam, B.J. & Goodenough, B. (1994). Subjective contours at line terminators. *Investigative Opthamology and Vision Science, 35,* 1627.

Gillam, B.J. & McGrath, D. (1979). Orientation relative to the retina determines perceptual organisation. *Perception and Psychophysics, 26,* 177-181

Gottschaldt, K. (1929). Uber den Einfluss der Erfahrung auf die Wahremung von Figuren. II. *Psychologische Forschung, 12,* 1-87.

Grossberg, S. Mingolla E. & Ross, W.D. (1997) Visual brain and visual perception: how does the cortex do perceptual grouping? *Trends in Neuroscience, 20,* 106-111.

Kellman, P.J. & Shipley, T.F. (1991). A theory of visual interpolation in object perception. *Cognitive Psychology, 23,* 141-221.

Koffka, K. (1935). *Principles of gestalt psychology.* New York: Harcourt, Brace & World.

Kovacs, I. & Julesz, B. (1993). A closed curve is much more than an incomplete one: Effect of closure in figure-ground segmentation. *Proceedings of the National Academy of Sciences, 90,* 7495-7497.

Metelli, F. (1982). Some characteristics of gestalt-oriented research in perception. *Organization and representation in perception* (pp. 219-233). London: Lawrence Erlbaum.

Palmer, S. E. (1999). *Vision science - photons to phenomenology.* Cambridge. MIT Press.

Palmer, S.E. (1992). Common region: A new principle of perceptual grouping. *Cognitive Psychology, 24,* 436-447.

Pomerantz, J.R. & Garner, W.R. (1973). Stimulus configuration in selective attention tasks. *Perception and Psychophysics, 14,* 565-569.

Pomerantz, J. R. & Pristach, E.A. (1989). Emergent features, attention and perceptual glue in visual form perception. *Journal of Experimental Psychology: Human Perception and Performance, 15,* 635-649.

Pomerantz, J.R. Sager, L. C. & Stoever, R.G. (1977). Perception of wholes and their component parts: Some configural superiority effects. *Journal of Experimental Psychology: Human Performance and Perception, 3,* 422-435.

Ramachandran, V.S. & Anstis, S.M. (1983). Perceptual organisation in moving patterns. *Nature, 304,* 529-531.

Rich, A. & Gillam, B. (2000). Failure to detect changes in colour for lines rotating in depth: the effects of grouping and type of colour change. *Vision Research, 40,* 1377-1384.

Rock, I. & Palmer, S.E. (1990). The legacy of Gestalt Psychology. *Scientific American, 262,* 84-90.

Rubin,E.(1915) *Synsoplevede Figurer.* Kobenhavn

Shiffrar, M. & Lorenceau, J. (1996). Improved motion linking across edges at decreased luminance contrast, edge width and duration. *Vision Research, 36,* 2061-2067.

Shiffrar, M. & Pavel, M. (1991). Percepts of rigid motion within and across apertures. *Journal of Experimental Psychology: Human Perception and Performance, 17,* 749-761.

Sugita, Y. (1999). Grouping image fragments in primary visual cortex. *Nature, 401,* 269-272.

Trick, L.M.& Enns, J.T. (1997) Clusters precede shapes in perceptual organisation. *Psychological Science, 8,* 124-129

Wallach, H. (1935). Uber visuell wahrgenommene Bewegungsrichtung. *Psychologische Forschung, 20,* 325-380.

From Fragments to Objects – Segmentation and Grouping in Vision
T.F. Shipley and P.J. Kellman (Editors)

9

AMODAL COMPLETION: A CASE STUDY IN GROUPING

Allison B. Sekuler[†] *and Richard F. Murray*[‡]
† *Department of Psychology, McMaster University, Hamilton, Ontario, L8S 4K1 Canada*
‡ *Department of Psychology, University of Toronto, Toronto, Ontario, M5S 3G3 Canada*

INTRODUCTION

Object perception is amazingly robust. We have little difficulty recognizing objects, despite the fact that retinal information about those objects varies dramatically from one moment to the next, and is often incomplete. One of the most common obstacles the visual system must overcome in order to recognize objects accurately is the partial occlusion of object contours and surfaces: Because most objects are opaque, they frequently occlude parts of themselves and parts of neighboring objects. Somehow, though, the visual systems seems to fill in missing information, so that we can interact appropriately with complete, meaningful objects.

In recent years, much research has focused on how the brain reconstructs this missing information, a process known as *amodal completion.* In some cases, researchers have been interested in the problem of amodal completion *per se.* However, we view amodal completion as a case study of the grouping and perceptual organization processes that are critical for object recognition more generally. First, as already mentioned, occlusion is ubiquitous, yet phenomenologically we seem to complete objects immediately and effortlessly. The completion of partly occluded objects is fundamental to object recognition, and because objects are so often occluded, the visual system has presumably developed efficient strategies to deal with the grouping of partly occluded contours. These same strategies may apply to other types of grouping as well. Second, partly occluded objects are structurally ambiguous: There are an infinite number of possible completions for any partly occluded object. By understanding how observers resolve the structural ambiguity of partly occluded objects, we can determine the relative importance of various perceptual organization factors for object perception. Third, as will be discussed shortly, partly occluded objects have a long microgenetic time course relative to unoccluded objects. In other words, the visual system takes a relatively long time to arrive at a final visual representation for partly occluded objects. This elongated time course allows us to look more closely at the representational evolution of objects, and at the factors that influence that evolution.

During the past decade, there has been an explosion of research on visual completion, and this chapter is not intended to be a comprehensive review of all the research in the field. We focus primarily on the completion of two-dimensional static contours and surfaces, rather than on volumetric completion, completion of kinetic contours, or the relationships between amodal and modal completion. Other chapters in this volume speak more directly to some of those issues (e.g., Bruno; Kellman, Guttman & Wickens; Shipley & Cunningham; Shiffrar; van Lier). The goal of this chapter is to provide a selective overview of some empirical results concerning the visual completion of partly occluded objects, providing a summary of the current state of research and pointing out areas where more research is needed. Furthermore, the chapter is written with an eye toward providing strong constraints on the development of biologically plausible models of visual completion in particular, and of grouping more generally. The basic outline of the chapter is as follows. First, we give a brief historical overview of the empirical methods used in the study of visual completion, and we summarize the attempts researchers have made to establish the reality and importance of visual completion. We then describe some recent work that has begun to determine the physiological and psychological levels at which completion occurs, and we discuss the effects of spatiotemporal context, defined in a broad sense, on the time course, strength, and form of completion. Finally, we discuss the effects of amodal completion on processing efficiency and on observers' strategies in discriminating the shapes of unoccluded and occluded stimuli, and the implications of these results for developing biologically plausible, computational models of visual completion and grouping.

EMPIRICAL APPROACHES

Gibson (1966, p. 203) noted that the everyday phenomena of occlusion are so familiar to us that we do not realize the need for an explanation. Indeed, the phenomenology of amodal completion is so compelling that many psychologists initially seemed to be satisfied with demonstrations based purely on appeals to subjective evidence (e.g., Kanizsa, 1979; Kanizsa & Gerbino, 1982). For example, experimenters might show observers a scene like Figure 1a and ask them to either draw or describe what completion they perceive, if any. A typical descriptive response is illustrated in Figure 1b ("A square behind a circle"), and a typical drawn response is illustrated in Figure 1c. Although the draw/describe approach dominated the study of amodal completion for quite some time, the information one can obtain from such studies is clearly limited by the nature of the task. First, the task is doubly subjective: It is subjective in that the observer must decide what response to make, based only on introspections that are accessible to no one else, and also in that the experimenter must interpret the response. For example, in the drawing illustrated in Figure 1c, one experimenter might interpret the lack of a sharp corner in the completed square as theoretically important, whereas another might interpret the same feature as a sign of laziness on the part of the subject. Second, in draw/describe tasks it is difficult to limit the time for which the observer processes the stimuli. This in turn makes it impossible to explore whether the internal representation of an occluded object changes over time – an issue that is critical for visual completion, as we discuss below.

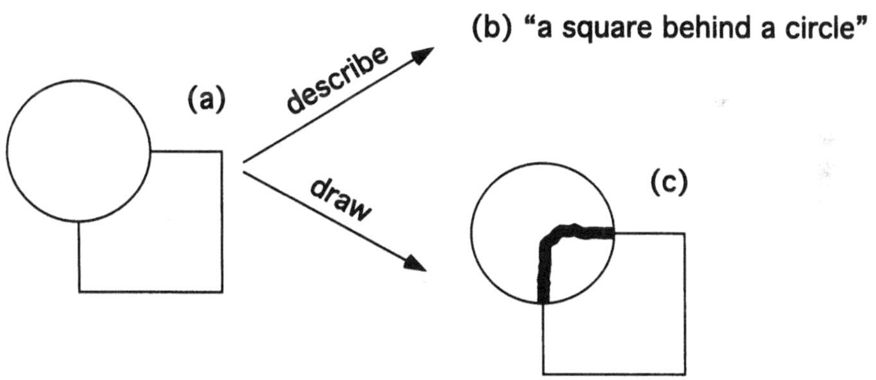

Figure 1. Illustration of the "describe" and "draw" paradigms. The observer views a stimulus as in (a), and either (b) describes or (c) draws the completion that he or she perceives.

These limitations of the draw/describe paradigm do not mean that phenomenology has no role in vision science. On the contrary, phenomenology serves a critical function in helping us frame important questions. Indeed, the modern study of completion began with the keen observational skills of Kanizsa and his colleagues. However, there are clear limitations to what phenomenology can reveal about the mechanisms underlying completion. Fortunately, over the past few decades, converging evidence from behavioral, physiological, and computational approaches has enabled us to begin to answer some important questions: In what objective sense does completion occur? What processes guide completion? How do those processes unfold over time? What neural systems control those processes?

A wide range of behavioral techniques and tasks have proved useful in recent years, including speeded matching tasks (Gerbino & Salmaso, 1985; Shore & Enns, 1997), adaptation (Brown & Weisstein, 1991), visual search (Davis & Driver, 1997; He & Nakayama, 1992; Rauschenberger & Yantis, 2001; Rensink & Enns, 1998), texture segregation (He & Nakayama, 1994c), primed matching (Bruno, Bertamini, & Domini, 1997; Guttman & Sekuler, submitted; Sekuler, 1994; Sekuler & Palmer, 1992; Sekuler, Palmer, & Flynn, 1994; van Lier & Wagemans, 1999), pattern discrimination (Gold, Murray, Bennett, & Sekuler, 2000; Murray, Sekuler, & Bennett, in press; Nakayama, Shimojo, & Silverman, 1989; Ringach & Shapley, 1996), dot localization (Kellman, Temesvary, Palmer, & Shipley, 2000; Takeichi, Nakazawa, Murakami, & Shimojo, 1995), object-based attentional cueing (Behrmann, Zemel, & Mozer, 1998; Moore, Yantis, & Vaughan, 1998; Pratt & Sekuler, in press), motion discrimination (He & Nakayama, 1994a; He & Nakayama, 1994b; Joseph & Nakayama, 1999; Sekuler & Sekuler, 1993; Sekuler & Sekuler, 1999; Yantis, 1995), and visual pursuit (Stone, Beutter, & Lorenceau, 2000). Variants of these tasks have also been adapted for the study of completion at the physiological level (Corballis, Fendrich, Shapley, & Gazzaniga, 1999; Giersch, Humphreys, Boucart, & Kovacs, 2000; Kersten, Shen, Ugurbil, & Schrater, 1999; Sugita, 1999).

Results from studies using these approaches support and extend results from phenomenological studies. For example, in the *primed matching paradigm* (Figure 2), observers view a priming stimulus and then judge whether a pair of test stimuli have the same shape or different shapes. The time taken to correctly identify "same" pairs depends on the representational similarity of the test shapes to the prime (Beller, 1971; Rosch, 1975a; Rosch, 1975b). For example, if observers are primed with a circle, they will be faster to respond "same" to a test pair of circles than to a test pair of 3/4-notched circles (Figure 2a). Conversely, if the prime is a 3/4-notched circle, observers will be faster to respond "same" to a pair of 3/4-notched circles than to a pair of circles (Figure 2b). This pattern of results is referred to as *basic shape priming*. With regard to occlusion, one interesting question is what happens when the priming stimulus is partly occluded, as in Figure 2c. Here, the prime we

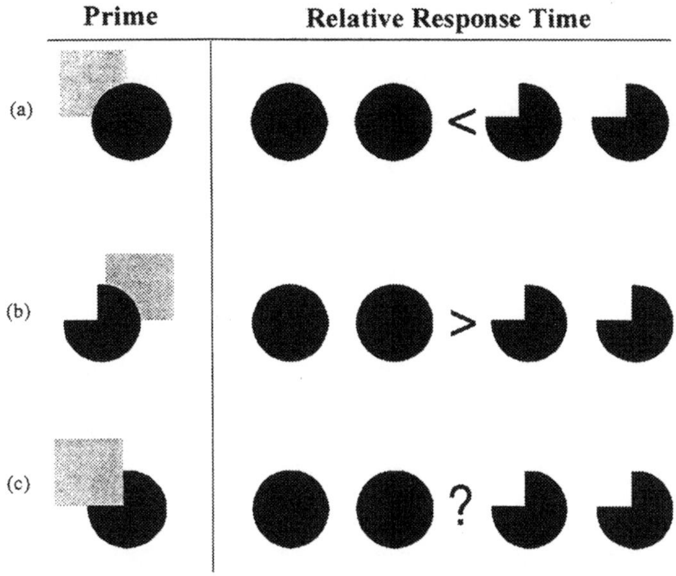

Figure 2. Priming stimuli (left) and expected patterns of responses (right) in the primed-matching paradigm. In this example, observers are told to attend to the lower of the two shapes in the priming stimulus. The relative response times for different test stimiuli are taken as a measure of how similar the internal representations of priming and test stimuli are. In this example, after viewing a circle prime, observers are faster to respond "same" to a pair of circles than to a pair of notched circles. After viewing a notched circle prime, observers are faster to respond "same" to a pair of notched circles than to a pair of circles. As described in the text, the difference in response times after viewing an occluded prime depends on the duration of the prime.

are interested in is the lower of the two shapes. Phenomenologically, observers describe the prime as a circle partly hidden behind a square (a complete representation). However, the pattern of information that reaches the eye is also consistent with the interpretation that a 3/4-notched circle is nudged up against the square (the mosaic representation). Sekuler and Palmer (1992) found that under some conditions the pattern of priming for occluded objects is similar to that of complete objects, and quite different from that of mosaic objects. This result may be taken as objective, albeit indirect evidence that the visual system treats occluded objects as if they were complete. We call this approach objective, in contrast to the draw/describe paradigm, because in the primed matching paradigm we do not ask observers about their subjective, introspective impressions of an occluded object: The inference that the visual system treats a partly occluded object as complete is based entirely on the effects of priming on observers' "same" and "different" responses to pairs of test shapes. This paradigm also has the advantage that it can be used to explore the developmental time course, or *microgenesis*, of visual completion. By presenting the prime for varying amounts of time while holding the interstimulus interval fixed, we can take snapshots of the stimulus representation at different times in its development. Using this technique, Sekuler and Palmer showed that completion requires a measurable amount of time. With long prime durations (100-200 ms), partly occluded objects primed observers' "same" and "different" responses like complete objects; but with short prime durations (50 ms) partly occluded objects primed observers' responses like mosaic objects, or like an intermediate representation. As we discuss below, the primed-matching paradigm has proven extremely versatile, and has been used to address a wide variety of issues concerning amodal completion (e.g., Bruno et al., 1997; Guttman & Sekuler, submitted; Sekuler, 1994; Sekuler et al., 1994; van Lier & Wagemans, 1999). However, the primed-matching paradigm does have its limitations. First, basic shape priming is difficult to detect for short stimulus durations, so the technique is not sensitive to very rapid time courses. Second, basic shape priming can be difficult to detect reliably when response times are short, so individual observers cannot be tested extensively because practice speeds response times. Finally, even in conditions where it is appropriate to use the primed-matching paradigm, it is important to show that the results are not simply an artifact of one particular experimental method.

Fortunately, other converging methods, such as shape discrimination tasks, do exist. Like the primed-matching paradigm, shape discrimination tasks provide researchers with an objective method of determining how an occluded object is processed by the visual system, and also allow us to explore the microgenesis of completion (e.g., Murray et al., in press; Ringach & Shapley, 1996). For example, Figure 3 illustrates the stimuli and task used by Murray *et al.* (in press). In one condition, the shapes to be judged were complete (left panel); in another, the contours defining the shapes were fragmented (right panel); and in a third condition, the contours were also fragmented, but occluders were present in the gaps between fragments (center panel). Phenomenologically, observers reported the occluded shape to be much more similar to the complete shape than to the fragmented shape. Murray *et al.* obtained a more objective measure of the similarities among these shapes by comparing performance on a shape discrimination task. Observers were asked to make a simple shape judgement: Is the rectangle longer vertically or horizontally? One would expect observers to be quite good at this task for complete stimuli, because observers are highly sensitive to small deviations from perfect symmetry in quadrilateral figures (Regan & Hamstra, 1992). One would also expect performance to be markedly impaired in the fragmented condition because much of the stimulus has been deleted, and because observers were required to distribute their attention over several perceptual units rather than focusing on a single object (Baylis & Driver, 1993; Behrmann et al., 1998; Duncan, 1984). The critical question in this task is how observers perform in the occluded condition, compared to the other two

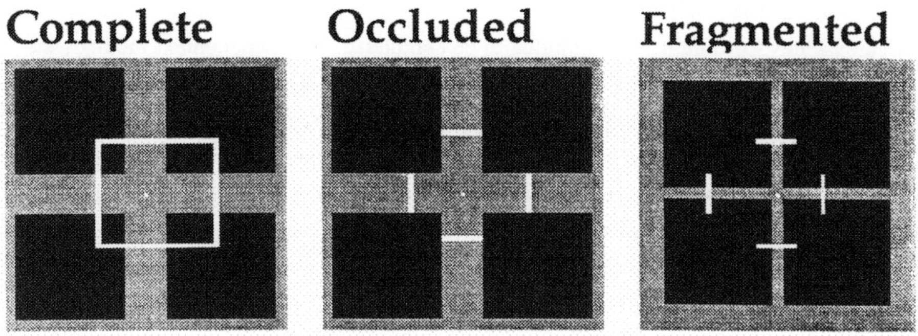

Figure 3. Stimuli from Murray et al. (in press). In each condition, the observer's task is to determine whether the white target pattern is longer vertically or horizontally (in all the stimuli shown, the correct answer is "horizontal"). The target pattern is either a complete rectangle, an occluded rectangle, or a fragmented pattern that contains the same visible line segments as the occluded rectangle, but lacks the T-junctions that give the impression that the line segments belong to a single partly occluded rectangle.

conditions. If the visual system treats the occluded object as though it is complete, then performance should be quite good. However, if the visual system treats the occluded object as a group of unrelated line segments, as in the fragmented condition, then performance should be poor. Like Sekuler and Palmer (1992), Murray *et al.* found that the results depended on the stimulus duration. For short durations (15-30 ms), performance in the occluded condition was as poor as performance in the fragmented condition. For longer durations (75 ms and longer), performance in the occluded condition was almost as good as performance in the complete condition. Hence their results supported the idea that although the visual system does in fact treat partly occluded objects as though they are complete, completion requires a measurable amount of time.

CONTEXT EFFECTS

Although studies have generally been consistent in concluding that completion requires time, the estimate of precisely how much time is required has varied considerably from one study to the next. Sekuler and Palmer (1992) estimated that 100-200 ms was required for completion; Ringach and Shapley's (1996) estimates ranged from 120-170 ms; Murray *et al.*'s (in press) estimate was approximately 75 ms; Guttman and Sekuler's (submitted) estimates ranged from less than 75 ms to over 400 ms; and Bruno *et al.* (1997) reported finding no measurable minimum time for completion. Clearly, completion does not require a fixed amount of time, but varies considerably depending on the *context* of completion.

We define context in the broadest sense, as the spatial, temporal, and attentional circumstances surrounding the stimulus to be completed. As such, context includes the size and shape of a stimulus, the presence or absence of additional cues for depth and grouping beyond occlusion cues, and the recent history of an object (e.g., as described by an object file Kahneman, Treisman, & Gibbs, 1992). We are only beginning to understand the full extent to which these contextual factors affect visual completion, but such an understanding is crucial for the development of accurate, biologically plausible computational models of grouping. Here we describe some results that constrain the development of such models.

Context affects completion time

As described above, it is well established that amodal completion takes time, but estimates of the time required for completion are variable. Two factors that play a role in determining time to completion are (1) the amount of occlusion, and (2) the presence of depth cues other than occlusion cues.

Amount of occlusion. As the amount of occlusion increases, completion could be affected in two ways, described by the *temporal limit hypothesis* and the *spatial limit hypothesis* (Guttman & Sekuler, submitted; Shore & Enns, 1997). The temporal limit hypothesis states that visual completion is constrained by temporal factors. Specifically, as the amount of occlusion increases (as in Figure 4, top panel), so too should the time required for completion. The temporal limit hypothesis is consistent with models of completion based on the propagation of contours (e.g., Grossberg & Mingolla, 1985; see Mingolla, this volume, for details).

Alternatively, visual completion may be constrained by spatial factors, regardless of processing time. The spatial limit hypothesis states that as the amount of occlusion increases beyond some limit, completion no longer occurs. Intuitively, this hypothesis makes sense: In the limit of total occlusion, there is no visible object for the visual system to complete. The theoretical support for the spatial limit hypothesis comes mainly from the influential relatability theory of Kellman and Shipley (1991; 1992). This theory, components of which have received much empirical support (Field, Hayes, & Hess, 1993; Kellman, Yin, & Shipley, 1998; Shipley & Kellman, 1990; Shipley & Kellman, 1992), suggests that completion occurs only when the visible segments of occluded contours are *relatable*, meaning that the tangents to the contours at points of occlusion meet at an angle of no more than 90 degrees, and can be connected by a curve containing no inflection points or discontinuities. This theory can be seen as a modern instantiation of the Gestalt notion of good continuation: Local regions of occlusion are identified based on the presence of T-junctions (Helmholtz, 1910/1962; Ratoosh, 1949), and the contours bounding the occluded

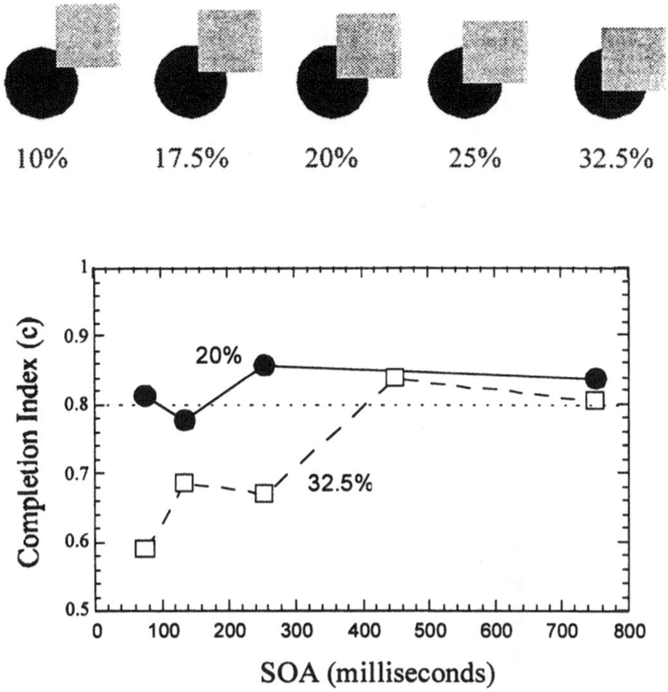

Figure 4. Top panel: A circle partly occluded by a square, with varying amounts of contour occlusion (10% to 32.5%). Occluded contours are relatable in all but the most highly occluded circle. Bottom panel: Results from Guttman & Sekuler (submitted), showing the strength of occlusion as a function of time for two amounts of contour occlusion (20% and 32.5%). In both cases, objects were effectively completed, but different amounts of time were required to reach the asymptote.

surfaces are connected by the simplest continuous contour. Consider, for example, a circle partly occluded by a square (Figure 4, top panel). When 25% or less of the circle's contour is occluded, the occluded contours are relatable. When more than 25% of the circle's contour is occluded, the occluded contours are not relatable, and completion should not occur.

Several studies have investigated how the amount of occlusion affects completion (Guttman & Sekuler, submitted; Rauschenberger & Yantis, 2001; Shore & Enns, 1997). The results of these experiments provide converging evidence that supports the temporal limit hypothesis. Shore and Enns showed observers scenes containing complete shapes, occluded shapes, and mosaic shapes. For each image, observers made a speeded judgment about whether a target shape was a (possibly notched) circle or square. Observers were fast at correctly classifying complete shapes, and were slow at correctly classifying mosaic shapes.

However, the time taken to correctly classify occluded shapes varied as a function of the amount of occlusion. For shapes occluded by less than 25%, classification times were similar to those for complete shapes, whereas for shapes occluded by more than 25%, classification times were much slower, and statistically indistinguishable from those for mosaic shapes. Although this result could be seen as supporting the spatial limit hypothesis (because no evidence of completion was found for occlusion over 25%), it is also consistent with the temporal limit hypothesis (because the visual system may simply require more time than was allowed for completion of highly occluded objects).

Using a visual search paradigm, Rauschenberger and Yantis (2001) also found results consistent with changes in completion as a function of the amount of occlusion. Following previous researchers (Davis & Driver, 1997; He & Nakayama, 1992; Rensink & Enns, 1998), Rauschenberger and Yantis assumed that if the visual system represents an occluded circle as a mosaic (i.e., as a notched circle), then it should "pop out" of a set of distractors comprising complete circles, and search times should not vary much as a function of the distractor set size (so-called "parallel search", e.g., Palmer, 1995; Treisman, 1988; but see Palmer (1995)). Conversely, if the occluded circle is represented as complete, then it should be quite difficult to detect among a field of circle distractors, and significantly larger set-size effects should be found (so-called "serial search", Treisman, 1988). Rauschenberger and Yantis found that whether occluded circles popped out of circle backgrounds depended on both the amount of occlusion and the time for which the display was viewed before masking. When circles were occluded by less than 10%, search was "serial" even when stimuli were displayed for only 100 ms. When circles were occluded by 25%, search was "parallel" when stimuli were presented for 100 ms, but search was "serial" when stimuli were presented for 250 ms. Finally, when circles were occluded by 37%, search was parallel for both 100 ms and 250 ms presentations. These results are consistent with the idea that time to completion increases as a function of the amount of occlusion, at least up to 25%, which is the limit predicted for these stimuli by Kellman and Shipley's (1991; 1992) relatability hypothesis. Beyond this amount, Rauschenberger and Yantis found no clear evidence of completion, although the longest duration they tested (250 ms) may simply not have been long enough to reveal the effects of completion for a highly occluded object.

More recently, Guttman and Sekuler (submitted) used the primed-matching paradigm to test the hypothesis that even highly occluded objects can be completed, given enough time. In their study, the pattern of priming for occluded objects varied as a function of both the amount of occlusion in the prime and the amount of processing time for the prime. Figure 4 (bottom panel) summarizes the results from two of their conditions (20% contour occlusion and 32.5% contour occlusion), plotting the value of a completion index c as a function of prime-to-test SOA. With their completion index, a value of c=1 indicates that priming of the occluded object was identical to that of complete objects, and a value of $c=0$ indicates that priming of the occluded object was identical to that of mosaic objects. Values greater than 0.8 on this scale are taken to indicate effective (though not perfect) completion. With 20% occlusion, *c* reached this critical value for even the shortest SOA tested (75 ms). With 32.5% occlusion, *c* once again reached the critical value, but only after a much longer time. This is a crucial result, because it shows for the first time that highly occluded object *can* be completed when given enough time, even when the condition of relatability is *not* met.

Taken as a group, these studies provide strong support for the temporal limit hypothesis. Thus, although spatial limits may exist as well, those limits are not defined by the condition of relatability – a fact that must be taken into account in the further development of computational models of completion and grouping. Guttman and Sekuler suggested that a modified notion of relatability may prove useful for understanding the role of spatial limits in visual completion. In their scheme, the curvature of contours leading into a discontinuity guides completion (Takeichi et al., 1995) in addition to the tangents at the points of occlusion (Kellman & Shipley, 1991; Kellman & Shipley, 1992). Guttman and Sekuler further suggested that the influence of relatability on visual completion may depend on other factors that affect how informative an object's visible contours are about its occluded contours, such as the length of the contours leading to points of occlusion, and the consistency of their curvature. Thus, although the original notion of relatability cannot completely explain the results of the experiments described in this section, a modified notion of relatability in combination with other factors may well be an important component of future models.

Presence of additional depth cues. The amount of occlusion is not the only factor that can affect the time to completion of partly occluded objects. Recent behavioral and physiological work suggests that time to completion decreases with the addition of depth cues that are consistent with the depth ordering indicated by occlusion cues (Bruno et al., 1997; Sugita, 1999).

Bruno *et al.* (1997) correctly noted that in Sekuler and Palmer's (1992) primed-matching study, the occluder was presented in the same stereoscopic depth plane as the occluded figure. Thus occlusion and the resulting relative depth assignment of objects was specified *only* by discontinuities (T-junctions) at points of occlusion. Although stereopsis plays little role in many viewing situations, it is certainly an important cue to depth for nearby objects. Thus it is important to understand the role that stereoscopic depth cues play in amodal completion. In an elegant experiment, Bruno *et al.* again used the primed-matching paradigm, but examined the effect of consistent stereoscopic depth cues. When no consistent stereoscopic depth cues were presented, Bruno *et al.* replicated Sekuler and

Palmer's results: Some measurable time was required before an occluded prime yielded a pattern of priming similar to that of a complete prime. However, when Bruno *et al.* added stereoscopic depth cues that were consistent with the depth ordering indicated by occlusion, occluded primes yielded a pattern of priming similar to that of a complete prime, even at the shortest SOA tested (50 ms). Although one could interpret this result as indicating that completion required *no* time in the presence of consistent stereoscopic depth cues, a more plausible interpretation is that the process is simply speeded beyond the point where it can be detected using the primed matching paradigm (as noted earlier, the primed-matching paradigm is not ideal for revealing very rapid completion processes).

Recent physiological evidence points to a mechanism that could explain the reduced time to completion in the presence of consistent stereoscopic depth cues. Sugita (1999) found that some orientation selective neurons at the earliest level of processing in the visual cortex (V1) responded to partly occluded contours as though they were complete. This result suggests that neurons as early as V1 have the computational power to complete partly occluded contours. However, these neural responses are observed only when the occluder is presented stereoscopically in front of the occluded contour. If the occluder is presented in the same stereoscopic depth plane as the occluded contour, these same neurons cease to respond to the occluded contours. With respect to Bruno *et al.*'s (1997) results, this suggests that fast completion times in the presence of consistent stereoscopic depth information may have been mediated by early levels of visual processing in the cortex, perhaps as early as V1. On the other hand, slower completion times in the absence of consistent stereoscopic depth cues may have been mediated by later regions of visual cortex. It is difficult to evaluate this hypothesis, because relatively little physiological research has been done on amodal completion, compared to possibly related phenomena such as illusory contours (e.g., Grosof, Shapley, & Hawken, 1993; Sheth, Sharma, Rao, & Sur, 1996; von der Heydt, Peterhans, & Baumgartner, 1984). However, at least one study suggests that shape selective neurons in the inferotemporal cortex show the same shape selectivity in the presence of occlusion (without stereoscopic depth cues) as when the shapes are fully visible, although the relevant neurons' overall rate of responding decreased as a function of increasing occlusion (Kovacs, Vogels, & Orban, 1995). Interestingly, there also appeared to be an inverse correlation between the rate of responding and the time to peak firing (Vogels, personal communication). This result is qualitatively consistent with the effect of the amount of occlusion on time to completion, as discussed in the last section, although additional studies are clearly required to quantify this relationship more precisely.

Context affects completion strength. Just as the speed of amodal completion can vary from one context to another, so too can the asymptotic *strength* of completion vary. As described previously, Murray *et al.* (in press) found that at long stimulus durations, observers were approximately as good at judging the aspect ratio of a partly occluded rectangle (Figure 3, middle panel) as they were at judging the aspect ratio of a complete rectangle (Figure 3, left panel). Furthermore, at long stimulus durations observers were much better at judging the aspect ratio of an occluded rectangle than they were at judging the aspect ratio of fragmented rectangle (Figure 3, right panel). Murray *et al.* formulated a measure of amodal completion, similar to that described earlier, in which the strength of completion was $c=1$ (full completion) if observers' aspect ratio discrimination thresholds were the same in the occluded and complete conditions, and the strength of completion was $c=0$ (no completion) if observers' thresholds were the same in the occluded and fragmented conditions. They used this measure to investigate the time course of amodal completion, and in particular to determine whether motion cues affected the speed or strength of completion.

Murray *et al.* found that the speed of completion did not depend on whether the rectangle was in motion, even though under many circumstances motion is a strong cue for completion and grouping (Kellman & Shipley, 1991). Regardless of whether the rectangle was static or moving, Murray *et al.* found that completion occurred quickly, taking approximately 75 ms. However, the asymptotic strength of completion *did* depend on motion cues. If the rectangle was in motion, the strength of amodal completion rose rapidly and asymptoted at approximately 1.0, meaning that at long durations, thresholds were the same in the occluded and complete conditions. If the rectangle was stationary, the measure of completion rose rapidly and asymptoted around 0.8 (similar to the values of completion strength found for static objects by Guttman & Sekuler, submitted). In other words, even for relatively long stimulus durations (up to 220 ms), thresholds were always slightly lower in the complete condition than in the occluded condition. Hence, Murray *et al.*'s results demonstrate that context can affect the asymptotic strength of completion, and that this effect can be dissociated from effects on the speed of completion.

Context affects completion form

Another way that context affects completion is by influencing how shapes are perceived to continue behind occluding surfaces. These effects have at least two sources: (1) the spatial structure of a scene can affect the form of completion, and (2) past perceptual events can also influence the form of completion.

Spatial structure. The most striking example of how different spatial structures can lead to different visual completions is illustrated by the debate over the relative roles of *local* versus *global* processes in completion. According to local models, completion is based only on attributes of contours and surfaces at or near points of occlusion. The most common instantiation of this model leads to a "good continuation" solution, in which contours are completed by the simplest possible continuous curve (e.g., Kellman & Shipley, 1991; Kellman & Shipley, 1992; see also the chapters in this volume by Kellman, Guttman, & Wickens, and by Shipley & Cunningham). One advantage of this type of model is that it is computationally tractable, and the hypothesized interactions among input units along a contour are consistent with the physiology of early visual cortical processing. Not surprisingly, such models have gained considerable momentum over the past decade.

According to global models, completion is based on attributes of surfaces and contours of the entire object to be completed (and in some cases on attributes of nearby objects as well). One example of a global model, although it is not a process model, is Structural Information Theory (SIT; Buffart & Leeuwenberg, 1981; Buffart, Leeuwenbert, & Restle, 1981; see van Lier, this volume, for an overview). SIT predicts a *Prägnanz* solution to the problem of visual completion: The globally simplest, most regular completion is favored over others. Although early phenomenological approaches supported global models (e.g., Dinnerstein & Wertheimer, 1957), it is unclear how global completions might be computed from known neuronal responses, and consequently less research has focused on global models.

For most of the stimuli described so far, the local and global completion solutions are identical (e.g., a circle completed behind a square). However, in more realistic stimuli, ambiguities are likely to occur, and local and global processes may lead to qualitatively different completions (e.g., Davi, Pinna, & Sambin, 1992). Recently, some of the objective experimental paradigms described earlier have been used with such ambiguous stimuli. The results of these studies suggest that, despite our difficulty in modeling global completion processes, global as well as local processes play a role in completion (Sekuler, 1994; van Lier & Wagemans, 1999; van Lier, Leeuwenberg, & van der Helm, 1995). Thus, these results support so-called "hybrid" models that suggest that completion is influenced by both the local and the global spatial structure of a stimulus (e.g., van Lier, van der Helm, & Leeuwenberg, 1994).

Sekuler and colleagues (1994) used the primed-matching paradigm to explore the conditions under which local or global processes dominate completion. In their stimuli (Figure 5), local models predicted one completion, and global models predicted another. Their results were consistent with previous reports based on subjective methods (e.g., Boselie & Leeuwenberg, 1986; Buffart & Leeuwenberg, 1981; Buffart et al., 1983; Dinnerstein & Wertheimer, 1957), which found that global processes can in fact play a significant role in completion. In a follow-up study, Sekuler (1994) identified some of the factors that determine the influence of local and global processes, and proposed a qualitative model of completion in which costs and benefits lead to a weighted solution based on both local and global processes. In this weighted hybrid model, the costs of global solutions are relatively

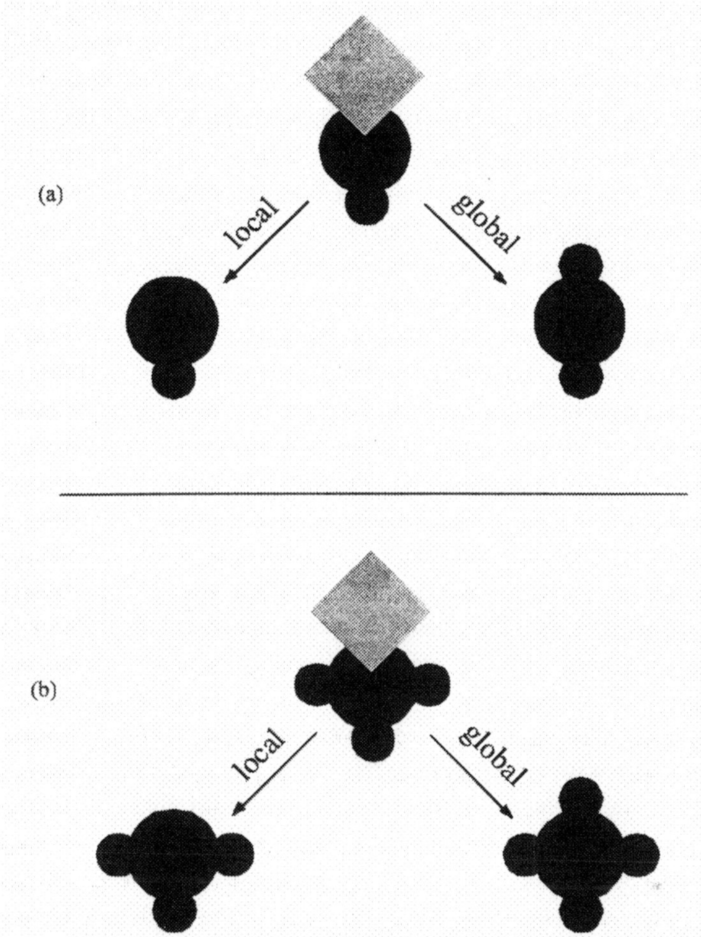

Figure 5. Stimuli used in studies examining the relative roles of local and global processes in amodal completion. In both panels, the top figure shows the occlusion stimulus, and the two lower figures show two possible completions: one based on local processes (left) and the other based on global processes (right).

high compared to those of local solutions because local solutions are easily computed even at the earliest levels of the visual cortex, whereas global solutions are not. Consequently, the benefits must be significant for global processes to play a major role. For a specific example, consider the shapes in Figure 5. The local solution to the occluded shape in Figure 5a yields one-fold bilateral symmetry (about the vertical axis), whereas the global solution yields two-fold bilateral symmetry (about the vertical and horizontal axes). In this case, the additional costs of the global solution add only horizontal symmetry, which has been shown to be a significantly weaker form of symmetry than vertical symmetry (Corballis & Roldan, 1975; Goldmeier, 1972; Mach & Szasz, 1886/1959; Palmer & Hemenway, 1978; Pashler, 1990; Sekuler, 1994; Wagemans, Van Gool, & d'Ydewalle, 1991; see Wenderoth, 1996, for a recent review). Thus, the benefits here do not outweigh the costs, and results from the primed-matching paradigm suggest that local processes do in fact dominate completion for this stimulus (Sekuler, 1994). A much greater contrast is seen between the local and global solutions to the occluded shape in Figure 5b. Here, the local solution yields one-fold bilateral symmetry (about the vertical axis), but the global solution yields four-fold bilateral symmetry (about the vertical, horizontal, and two diagonal axes). Thus, the benefits here are larger than in the previous example, and results from the primed-matching paradigm suggest that the stimulus global processes do dominate completion of this stimulus (Sekuler, 1994). In general, a large weight will be assigned to the global solution when the global completion is much more regular than the local completion. For example, with completely irregular shapes we only ever expect to find evidence for local completion. It is important to note that because the high cost of a global solution is factored into this qualitative model, the global solution is not favored when it requires a very complex completion. For example, we do not expect the visual system to complete the intricate features of a face behind an occluder.

The notion that amodal completions are based on weighted combinations of different processes (the weighted hybrid model) has two important implications. First, it suggests that when conflicts occur between local and global completion solutions, the internal representation of the completed object does not map directly onto one or the other solution, but is somewhere in between. Support for this idea can be found in the results of Sekuler (1994; see also van Lier et al., 1995). Sekuler found that although global processes dominated completion (i.e., occluded objects led to better priming for globally regular objects than for locally completed objects), the amount of priming could differ markedly between occluded primes and complete global primes. This result is consistent with the notion that the internal representation of the occluded object lies between the local and global solutions, but is biased toward the global solution.

A second implication of the weighted hybrid model is that the fidelity of internal representations should vary depending on context. For example, when local and global processes lead to the same solution, one would expect relatively stable representations. When local and global processes lead to conflicting solutions, one would expect less stable representations. In addition, one might expect greater stability for representations that have heavier weightings for local solutions, simply because of the low cost of local solutions compared to global solutions. Recent work using the dot-localization paradigm has provided support for this idea (Kellman et al., 2000). Kellman and colleagues presented observers with partly occluded shapes similar to those in Figure 5b. As described earlier, these shapes have different local and global solutions. In one condition, observers were asked to adopt a 'local' mindset, and to imagine what the object would look like if completed according to a local process. In another condition, observers were asked to adopt a 'global' mindset, and to imagine what the object would look like if completed according to global processes. In both conditions, after the observer viewed the occluded object for some time, a dot appeared superimposed on the occluder. Observers were asked to indicate whether the dot appeared inside or outside the imagined boundary of the completed object, and an error was computed relative to where the boundary actually would have been for either the local or global solution. Kellman *et al.* found that observers had much higher errors in the dot-localization task when they adopted the global mindset than when they adopted the local mindset. Based on these results, Kellman *et al.* suggested that the representation of the global solution is spatially less well-defined than that of the local solution. This interpretation is entirely consistent with the idea that representational fidelity varies with context, and in this case the context is defined by the spatial structure of the stimulus. The dot-localization technique may prove to be quite useful in determining finer scale properties of amodal (and other) completions than can be resolved using paradigms such as primed-matching. For example, we suggested above that even highly occluded, non-relatable contours can be completed when the visual system is given enough time. However, it may be that the fidelity of the completed representation, as assessed by the dot-localization paradigm, varies as a function of the amount of occlusion.

Past perceptual events. Even if the visual system uses a weighted hybrid method to complete occluded objects, it is likely that the relative weights assigned to the local and global processes of amodal completion vary with context. For example, an observer's past experience may be a critical factor for determining the relative weights of local and global processes in completion. This experience might include long term familiarity effects as well as short term priming effects. Consider a task in which observers perform some initial practice trials in which they judge whether two patterns have the same shape or different shapes. In different conditions, 80%, 50%, or 20% of the practice trials might contain highly symmetric shapes that suggest a global completion, with the remainder of the shapes less symmetric and suggesting a local completion. If following these practice trials the observer views occluded stimuli that could be completed either globally or locally, one might expect that observers who viewed a greater proportion of globally completed shapes in the practice session would assign greater weight to global processes. In a preliminary experiment using the primed-matching paradigm and only 100 practice trials, we did indeed find a trend in this direction. Additional work clearly is needed to determine the amount of practice that would produce a significant effect, and whether the effect of past experience depends on shape tokens or types (e.g., Kahneman et al., 1992).

Although additional work is required to determine the effect of previous experience on the shape of a completed contour, it is already clear that experience can influence the extent to which completion occurs. The best evidence of this comes from an experiment conducted by Joseph and Nakayama (1999). Joseph and Nakayama presented observers with an ambiguous apparent motion stimulus, in which motion could be seen in either the horizontal or vertical directions (Figure 6a). The motion is ambiguous in this stimulus because the distance between horizontal elements is the same as the distance between vertical elements. Previous work by Shimojo and Nakayama (1990) showed that when an occluder is placed in this scene (Figure 6b), the stimulus becomes perceptually less ambiguous, and observers show a bias to perceive motion behind the occluder (i.e., vertically in Figure 6b). Shimojo and Nakayama suggested that this effect resulted from the perceptual continuation of an occluded object behind the occluder. This continuation decreases the effective distance between vertical elements, biasing the apparent motion in that direction. In their extension of this work, Joseph and Nakayama asked whether the amount of bias in this apparent motion task depends on how an observer has previously perceived the elements in the scene. In other words, does the recent context in which an observer has seen an object influence the

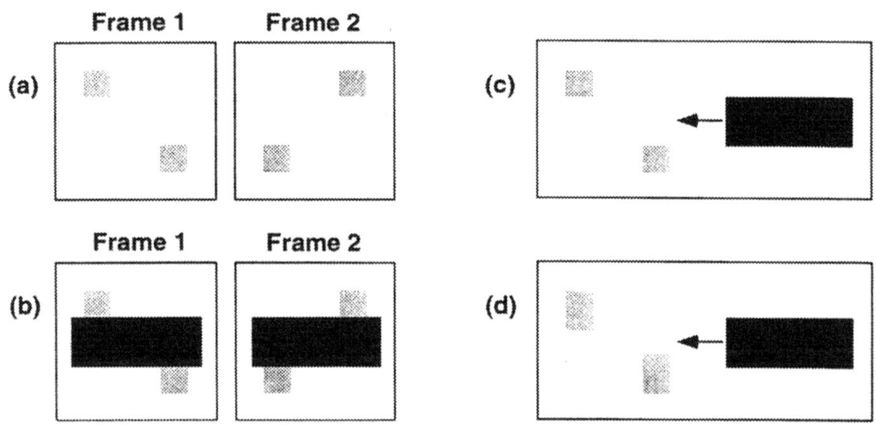

Figure 6. (a) Two frames from an ambiguous apparent motion stimulus in which vertical and horizontal distances between elements are equated. From frame 1 to frame 2, observers may report the squares moving vertically or horizontally. (b) Illustration of stimuli similar to those tested by Shimojo & Nakayama (1990). The moving elements are identical to those in (a), but a horizontally oriented occluder is placed in the middle of the display. Here, observers are much more likely to report vertical motion than in the more ambiguous display of (a). (c) An example of a preview scene from Joseph & Nakayama (1999). Here, observers first view two short elements that are later seen in an apparent motion display (as in (b)). During the preview, the occluder moves into the scene from the right. (d) The same as (c), but with long elements in the preview scene.

completion of that object? In Joseph and Nakayama's study, observers saw previews of the moving elements, whose size was either the same as elements abutting the occluding surface (short elements; Figure 6c) or whose size was consistent with elements continuing behind the occluding surface (long elements; Figure 6d). Later, when judging the perceived direction of the ambiguous apparent motion display, observers showed a greater bias to see motion behind the occluder if they had seen the longer preview elements. Previews of long elements increased the amount of continuation behind the occluder, and these preview effects lasted for at least one second in all observers tested, and even longer in some subjects (at least six seconds in one case). These results show that the recent history of an object can influence the way in which the visual system interprets and processes occlusion cues.

It is important to note, however, that previous experience with an object does not always dominate stimulus-derived information. Using an object-based attention task adapted from Egly, Driver, and Rafal (1994), and Moore, Yantis, and Vaughan (1998), Pratt and Sekuler (in press) showed that a preview of a truncated object does not always prevent completion in the presence of strong grouping cues, even when the occluded stimulus is shown for a relatively short duration. This result shows that a full model of completion (and of grouping more generally) must incorporate interactions among internal factors (such as the effect of past experience) and stimulus-derived factors (such as stimulus structure).

How Does Amodal Completion Affect Perceptual Processing?

What changes with completion: efficiency or internal noise?

As we have just discussed, context can affect amodal completion in a variety of ways, and amodal completion can affect performance in a wide range of perceptual tasks. However, the studies described so far do not speak to the issue of *how* amodal completion affects performance. Performance in any perceptual task is constrained by two factors: (1) the efficiency with which an observer uses relevant information from a stimulus (i.e., calculation efficiency), and (2) random variations in the observer, such as random variations in sensory encoding (i.e., internal noise). In this context, the question becomes: Does amodal completion affect performance in perceptual tasks by changing calculation efficiency, by changing internal noise, or both? Noise masking experiments allow us to measure the influence of each of these factors on an observer's performance in a perceptual task, and hence to characterize an observer's performance in more detail than can be achieved by gross measures of performance, such as percent correct or discrimination thresholds (Burgess & Colborne, 1988; Pelli & Farell, 1999).

In a noise masking experiment, one measures discrimination thresholds in a task, in several levels of external white Gaussian noise. The function that plots discrimination thresholds versus external noise power is called a *noise masking function*. Empirically, noise masking functions are always found to be approximately linear. A well-established body of results, largely derived from signal detection theory, shows that the x-intercept of the noise masking function can be regarded as a measure of the noise in the observer's early encoding of the stimulus, and the slope gives a measure of how efficiently the observer uses the stimulus to perform the task (Burgess & Colborne, 1988; Pelli & Farell, 1999).

Recently, Murray and colleagues (2000) applied noise masking methods to a task developed by Ringach and Shapley (1996). In Ringach and Shapley's study, observers discriminated between 'fat' and 'thin' Kanizsa squares (left and right columns of Figure 7). Fat and thin stimuli are distinguished from one another by a small difference in the orientation of the notched circle inducers at the corners of the square. In one condition, observers discriminated between fat and thin stimuli that had luminance-defined contours connecting the inducers (real condition, Figure 7). In a second condition, observers discriminated between fat and thin amodally completed Kanizsa squares that looked like squares seen through four holes in an occluding surface (occluded condition, Figure 7). In a third condition, all the inducers faced in the same direction (fragmented condition, Figure 7). Locally, the occluded and fragmented stimuli were very similar, and were distinguished only by the orientations of the inducers. Ringach and Shapley showed that, at long stimulus durations, discrimination performance was similar in the real and occluded conditions, and significantly worse in the fragmented condition. It is understandable that performance in the real condition should be better than in the fragmented condition, because the stimulus in the real condition contains more contour that the observer can use to perform the task. But why are performance levels so different in the occluded and fragmented conditions? Here, the same amount of physical information is available in both tasks (eight luminance-defined inducer edges), so naïvely we might expect that performance would be roughly the same.

Murray *et al.*'s noise masking experiments answered this question with respect to the two fundamental limits to performance: calculation efficiency and internal noise. Murray *et al.* found that observers showed no consistent differences between the occluded and fragmented tasks in the amount of internal noise that limited their performance. However, observers did show large differences between the two tasks in terms of the efficiency of their decision strategy (calculation efficiency): Observers were much more efficient in the occluded condition than in the fragmented condition, and in fact they were at least as efficient in the occluded condition as in the real condition. Hence Murray *et al.*'s results answer the question of how amodal completion brings about such large changes in observers' performance: Completion changes the efficiency of the computation that observers use to

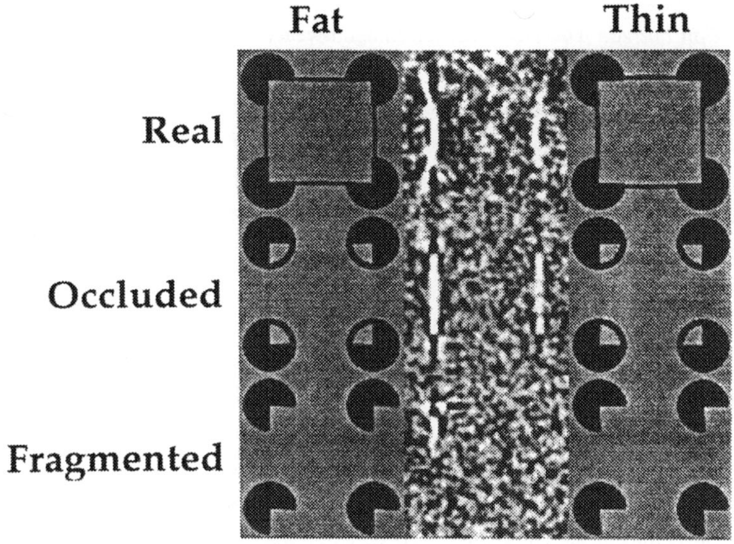

Figure 7. Fat and thin Kanizsa squares (left and right columns), and behavioral receptive fields (center column) for real, occluded, and fragmented stimuli. See text for details.

make their perceptual decisions, but does not change the levels of internal noise. This result strongly constrains the classes of models that can explain the role of amodal completion in visual processing, and the role of grouping more generally.

Mapping behavioral receptive fields for amodal completion

Murray *et al.*'s (2000) results show that amodal completion can affect the efficiency of observers' strategies in perceptual tasks. However, their results say nothing about *how* observers' strategies differed across the three tasks they examined. What is it that makes an observer more efficient in the occluded condition than in the fragmented condition? Ringach and Shapley (1996) suggested that the answer may involve the parts of the stimulus observers use to perform the task. For example, observers may have used all four sides of the amodally completed square to perform the task in the occluded condition, but only a single inducer in the fragmented condition. This hypothesis can be tested using another noise masking technique: *response classification.*

In a response classification experiment, the observer performs a discrimination task on stimuli embedded in Gaussian white noise, and over many trials one measures the correlation between the noise contrast at each stimulus pixel and the observer's responses (Ahumada & Lovell, 1971; Beard & Ahumada, 1998). The resulting map of correlations shows the influence of each noise pixel on the observer's responses, and is called a *classification image*. The classification image reveals which stimulus regions the observer used to perform the task, and can be thought of as a behavioral receptive field.

Gold, Murray, Bennett, and Sekuler (2000) used the response classification method to investigate observers' strategies in the task developed by Ringach and Shapley (1996). The middle panel of Figure 7 shows the classification images that Gold *et al.* obtained in the real, occluded, and fragmented conditions. Gold *et al.* found that in the fragmented task observers used one or two edges of a single inducer, whereas in the occluded task observers used whole sides of the amodally completed square, including both inducer edges and the physically empty regions between the inducers. Furthermore, Gold *et al.* found that classification images in the occluded condition were similar to classification images in the real condition. The similarity between the observers' strategy in the occluded and real conditions suggests that occluded, amodally completed contours are perceptually on a par with real, luminance-defined contours, in the sense that observers adopt the same strategy in a perceptual task regardless of whether the stimuli to be discriminated are defined by amodally completed contours or by luminance contours.

This is a surprising result, as it shows that in the occluded condition observers allowed their decisions to be affected by large regions between the inducers that contained no information as to the correct response, which is a strategy one might expect to be quite inefficient. Yet, both Ringach and Shapley (Ringach & Shapley, 1996) and Murray *et al.* (2000) found that performance was *better* in the occluded condition than in the fragmented condition. This paradox is resolved by Murray *et al.*'s finding that, despite appearances, the classification images in the occluded condition do in fact reflect a more efficient strategy than the classification images in the fragmented condition. They showed this by cross-correlating the observers' classification images with the classification image that would be obtained from the ideal observer for this task (i.e., a hypothetical observer that makes optimal use of all of the available stimulus information). This analysis showed that the cross-correlation of the occluded classification image with the ideal occluded classification image was in fact higher than the cross-correlation of the fragmented classification image with the ideal fragmented classification image. This result implies that observers made more efficient use of the informative stimulus regions (i.e., the luminance-defined inducer edges) in the occluded condition than in the fragmented condition. One can get a sense of this difference by comparing the classification images for occluded and fragmented conditions (Figure 7). Whereas observers used information from only one inducer in the fragmented condition, observers used information from several inducers in the occluded condition.

We suggest that amodal completion is not an end in itself, but a means to a greater end. Amodal completion shifts observers' strategies through grouping, so that spatially disparate fragments of a stimulus are processed as a perceptual unit, thus improving an observer's ability to extract relevant information from a stimulus.

SUMMARY

Amodal completion is a critical component of object recognition. Research over the past few decades has provided convincing objective evidence that the visual system does in fact treat partly occluded objects as though they are complete, and the results from these studies can be taken as a case study for the more general problem of grouping. These studieshave shown that biologically plausible, computational models of grouping are constrained by several empirical facts concerning the completion of partly occluded objects.

1. Amodal completion takes time. Several different paradigms have been used to objectively measure the time course of completion.

2. Time-to-completion depends on context. Time-to-completion is influenced by factors such as the amount of occlusion, and the presence of consistent stereoscopic depth cues.

3. Strength of completion depends on context. One can derive an objective measure of the strength of completion, and this measure can vary independently of time-to-completion. For example, in some cases, the addition of motion cues may increase the strength of completion without affecting time-to-completion.

4. The form of completion depends on context. Both the spatial structure of an object and past perceptual experience can influence the form of completion. Local and global processes can both play a role in completion, but their relative weights depend on the context. Under some circumstances, past experience with a particular object may also influence whether and how that object is completed.

5. Completion affects processing efficiency. Noise masking studies have shown that amodal completion affects the efficiency of visual processing without affecting the level of internal noise. The increased efficiency is reflected in a change in the behavioral receptive field revealed by the response classification method. For examples, observers sometimes use more of an amodally completed stimulus than of a very similar fragmented stimulus. This suggests that completion is not as an end in itself, but a means toward an end: Amodal completion, and grouping more generally, enables the observer to use stimuli more efficiently to perform perceptual tasks.

REFERENCES

Ahumada, A., Jr., & Lovell, J. (1971). Stimulus features in signal detection. *Journal of the Acoustical Society of America, 49*(6), 1751-1756.

Baylis, G. C., & Driver, J. (1993). Visual attention and objects: evidence for hierarchical coding of location. *Journal of Experimental Psychology: Human Perception and Performance, 19*(3), 451-470.

Beard, B. L., & Ahumada, A., Jr. (1998). A technique to extract relevant image features for visual tasks. In B. E. Rogowitz & T. N. Pappas (Eds.), *SPIE Proceedings: vol. 3299. Human Vision and Electronic Imaging III* (pp. 79-85). Bellingham, WA: SPIE.

Behrmann, M., Zemel, R. S., & Mozer, M. C. (1998). Object-based attention and occlusion: evidence from normal participants and a computational model. *Journal of Experimental Psychology: Human Perception and Performance, 24*(4), 1011-1036.

Beller, H. K. (1971). Priming: effects of advance information on matching. *Journal of Experimental Psychology, 87*(2), 176-182.

Boselie, F., & Leeuwenberg, E. (1986). A test of the minimum principle requires a perceptual coding system. *Perception, 15*(3), 331-354.

Brown, J. M., & Weisstein, N. (1991). Conflicting figure-ground and depth information reduces moving phantom visibility. *Perception, 20*(2), 155-165.

Bruno, N., Bertamini, M., & Domini, F. (1997). Amodal completion of partly occluded surfaces: is there a mosaic stage? *Journal of Experimental Psychology: Human Perception and Performance, 23*(5), 1412-1426.

Buffart, H., & Leeuwenberg, E. (1981). Coding theory of visual pattern completion. *Journal of Experimental Psychology: Human Perception and Performance, 7*(2), 241-274.

Buffart, H., Leeuwenberg, E., & Restle, F. (1983). Analysis of ambiguity in visual pattern completion. *Journal of Experimental Psychology: Human Perception and Performance, 9*(6), 980-1000.

Burgess, A. E., & Colborne, B. (1988). Visual signal detection. IV. Observer inconsistency. *Journal of the Optical Society of America A, 5*(4), 617-627.

Corballis, M. C., & Roldan, C. E. (1975). Detection of symmetry as a function of angular orientation. *Journal of Experimental Psychology: Human Perception and Performance, 1*(3), 221-230.

Corballis, P. M., Fendrich, R., Shapley, R. M., & Gazzaniga, M. S. (1999). Illusory contour perception and amodal boundary completion: evidence of a dissociation following callosotomy. *Journal of Cognitive Neuroscience, 11*(4), 459-466.

Davi, M., Pinna, B., & Sambin, M. (1992). Amodal completion versus induced inhomogeneities in the organization of illusory figures. *Perception, 21*(5), 627-636.

Davis, G., & Driver, J. (1997). A functional role for illusory colour spreading in the control of focused visual attention. *Perception, 26*(11), 1397-1411.

Dinnerstein, D., & Wertheimer, M. (1957). Some determinants of phenomenal overlapping. *American Journal of Psychology, 70*, 21-37.

Duncan, J. (1984). Selective attention and the organization of visual information. *Journal of Experimental Psychology: General, 113*(4), 501-517.

Egly, R., Driver, J., & Rafal, R. D. (1994). Shifting visual attention between objects and locations: evidence from normal and parietal lesion subjects. *Journal of Experimental Psychology: General, 123*(2), 161-177.

Field, D. J., Hayes, A., & Hess, R. F. (1993). Contour integration by the human visual system: evidence for a local "association field". *Vision Research, 33*(2), 173-193.

Gerbino, W., & Salmaso, D. (1985). Un'analisi processuale del completamento amodale. *Giornale Italiano di Psicologia, 12*, 97-121.

Gibson, J. J. (1966). *The senses considered as perceptual systems*. Boston: Houghton Mifflin.

Giersch, A., Humphreys, G. W., Boucart, M., & Kovacs, I. (2000). The computation of occluded contours in visual agnosia: evidence for early computation prior to shape binding and figure-ground coding. *Cognitive Neuropsychology, 17*(8), 731-759.

Gold, J. M., Murray, R. F., Bennett, P. J., & Sekuler, A. B. (2000). Deriving behavioural receptive fields for visually completed contours. *Current Biology, 10*(11), 663-666.

Goldmeier, E. (1972). Similarity in visually perceived forms. *Psychological Issues, 8*(1), 1-136.

Grosof, D. H., Shapley, R. M., & Hawken, M. J. (1993). Macaque V1 neurons can signal 'illusory' contours. *Nature, 365*(6446), 550-552.

Grossberg, S., & Mingolla, E. (1985). Neural dynamics of form perception: boundary completion, illusory figures, and neon color spreading. *Psychological Review, 92*(2), 173-211.

Guttman, S., & Sekuler, A. B. (submitted). Visual completion: spatial and temporal limits. Manuscript submitted for publication.

He, Z. J., & Nakayama, K. (1992). Surfaces versus features in visual search. *Nature, 359*(6392), 231-233.

He, Z. J., & Nakayama, K. (1994a). Apparent motion determined by surface layout not by disparity or three- dimensional distance. *Nature, 367*(6459), 173-175.

He, Z. J., & Nakayama, K. (1994b). Perceived surface shape not features determines correspondence strength in apparent motion. *Vision Research, 34*(16), 2125-2135.

He, Z. J., & Nakayama, K. (1994c). Perceiving textures: beyond filtering. *Vision Research, 34*(2), 151-162.

Helmholtz, H. v. (1910/1962). *Treatise on physiological optics (3rd ed.)*. New York: Dover Publications.

Joseph, J. S., & Nakayama, K. (1999). Amodal representation depends on the object seen before partial occlusion. *Vision Research, 39*(2), 283-292.

Kahneman, D., Treisman, A., & Gibbs, B. J. (1992). The reviewing of object files: object-specific integration of information. *Cognitive Psychology, 24*(2), 175-219.

Kanizsa, G. (1979). *Organization in vision : essays on gestalt perception*. New York: Praeger.

Kanizsa, G., & Gerbino, W. (1982). Amodal completion: seeing or thinking? In J. Beck (Ed.), *Organization and representation in perception*. Hillsdale, N.J.: L. Erlbaum Associates.

Kellman, P. J., & Shipley, T. F. (1991). A theory of visual interpolation in object perception. *Cognitive Psychology, 23*(2), 141-221.

Kellman, P. J., & Shipley, T. F. (1992). Perceiving objects across gaps in space and time. *Current Directions in Psychological Science, 1*, 193-199.

Kellman, P. J., Temesvary, A., Palmer, E. M., & Shipley, T. F. (2000). Seeing between the lines: contour interpolation without perception of interpolated contours. [ARVO abstract #2320] *Investigative Ophthalmology and Vision Science, 41*(4).

Kellman, P. J., Yin, C., & Shipley, T. F. (1998). A common mechanism for illusory and occluded object completion. *Journal of Experimental Psychology: Human Perception and Performance, 24*(3), 859-869.

Kersten, D., Shen, L., Ugurbil, K., & Schrater, P. (1999). fMRI study of perceptual grouping of a bistable target [ARVO abstract #4319]. *Investigative Ophthalmology and Vision Science, 40*(4).

Kovacs, G., Vogels, R., & Orban, G. A. (1995). Cortical correlate of pattern backward masking. *Proceedings of the National Academy of Sciences, USA, 92*(12), 5587-5591.

Mach, E., & Szasz, T. S. (1886/1959). *The analysis of sensations and the relation of the physical to the psychical*. New York: Dover Publications.

Moore, C. M., Yantis, S., & Vaughan, B. (1998). Object-based visual selection: evidence from perceptual completion. *Psychological Science, 9*, 104-110.

Murray, R. F., Gold, J. M., Sekuler, A. B., & Bennett, P. J. (2000). Effect of visual completion on calculation efficiency [ARVO poster #2326]. *Investigative Ophthalmology and Vision Science, 41*(4), S440.

Murray, R. F., Sekuler, A. B., & Bennett, P. J. (in press). Time course of amodal completion revealed by a shape discrimination task. *Psychonomic Bulletin and Review*.

Nakayama, K., Shimojo, S., & Silverman, G. H. (1989). Stereoscopic depth: its relation to image segmentation, grouping and the recognition of occluded objects. *Perception, 18*(1), 55-68.

Palmer, J. (1995). Attention in visual search: distinguishing four causes of a set-size effect. *Current Directions in Psychological Science, 4*(4), 118-123.

Palmer, S. E., & Hemenway, K. (1978). Orientation and symmetry: effects of multiple, rotational, and near symmetries. *Journal of Experimental Psychology: Human Perception and Performance, 4*(4), 691-702.

Pashler, H. (1990). Coordinate frame for symmetry detection and object recognition. *Journal of Experimental Psychology: Human Perception and Performance, 16*(1), 150-163.

Pelli, D. G., & Farell, B. (1999). Why use noise? *Journal of the Optical Society of America A, 16*(3), 647-653.

Pratt, J., & Sekuler, A. B. (in press). The effects of occlusion and past experience on the allocation of object-based attention. *Psychonomic Bulletin and Review*.

Ratoosh, P. (1949). On interposition as a cue for the perception of distance. *Proceedings of the National Academy of Sciences, 35*, 257-259.

Rauschenberger, R., & Yantis, S. (2001). Masking unveils pre-amodal completion representation in visual search. *Nature, 410*(6826), 369-372.

Regan, D., & Hamstra, S. J. (1992). Shape discrimination and the judgement of perfect symmetry: dissociation of shape from size. *Vision Research, 32*(10), 1845-1864.

Rensink, R. A., & Enns, J. T. (1998). Early completion of occluded objects. *Vision Research, 38*(15-16), 2489-2505.

Ringach, D. L., & Shapley, R. (1996). Spatial and temporal properties of illusory contours and amodal boundary completion. *Vision Research, 36*(19), 3037-3050.

Rosch, E. (1975a). Cognitive representations of semantic categories. *Journal of Experimental Psychology: General, 104*, 192-233.

Rosch, E. (1975b). The nature of mental codes for color categories. *Journal of Experimental Psychology: Human Perception and Performance, 1*, 303-322.

Sekuler, A. B. (1994). Local and global minima in visual completion: effects of symmetry and orientation. *Perception, 23*(5), 529-545.

Sekuler, A. B., & Palmer, S. E. (1992). Perception of partly occluded objects: A microgenetic analysis. *Journal of Experimental Psychology: General, 121*(1), 95-111.

Sekuler, A. B., Palmer, S. E., & Flynn, C. (1994). Local and global processes in visual completion. *Psychological Science, 5*(5), 260-267.

Sekuler, A. B., & Sekuler, R. (1993). Representational development of direction in motion perception: a fragile process. *Perception, 22*(8), 899-915.

Sekuler, A. B., & Sekuler, R. (1999). Collisions between moving visual targets: what controls alternative ways of seeing an ambiguous display? *Perception, 28*(4), 415-432.

Sheth, B. R., Sharma, J., Rao, S. C., & Sur, M. (1996). Orientation maps of subjective contours in visual cortex. *Science, 274*(5295), 2110-2115.

Shimojo, S., & Nakayama, K. (1990). Amodal representation of occluded surfaces: role of invisible stimuli in apparent motion correspondence. *Perception, 19*(3), 285-299.

Shipley, T. F., & Kellman, P. J. (1990). The role of discontinuities in the perception of subjective figures. *Perception and Psychophysics, 48*(3), 259-270.

Shipley, T. F., & Kellman, P. J. (1992). Strength of visual interpolation depends on the ratio of physically specified to total edge length. *Perception and Psychophysics, 52*(1), 97-106.

Shore, D. I., & Enns, J. T. (1997). Shape completion time depends on the size of the occluded region. *Journal of Experimental Psychology: Human Perception and Performance, 23*(4), 980-998.

Stone, L. S., Beutter, B. R., & Lorenceau, J. (2000). Visual motion integration for perception and pursuit. *Perception, 29*(7), 771-787.

Sugita, Y. (1999). Grouping of image fragments in primary visual cortex. *Nature, 401*(6750), 269-272.

Takeichi, H., Nakazawa, H., Murakami, I., & Shimojo, S. (1995). The theory of the curvature-constraint line for amodal completion. *Perception, 24*(4), 373-389.

Treisman, A. (1988). Features and objects: the fourteenth Bartlett memorial lecture. *Quarterly Journal of Experimental Psychology A, 40*(2), 201-237.

van Lier, R., & Wagemans, J. (1999). From images to objects: global and local completions of self-occluded parts. *Journal of Experimental Psychology: Human Perception and Performance, 25*(6), 1721-1741.

van Lier, R. J., Leeuwenberg, E. L., & van der Helm, P. A. (1995). Multiple completions primed by occlusion patterns. *Perception, 24*(7), 727-740.

van Lier, R. J., van der Helm, P. A., & Leeuwenberg, E. (1994). Integrating global and local aspects of visual occlusion. *Perception, 23*(8), 883-903.

von der Heydt, R., Peterhans, E., & Baumgartner, G. (1984). Illusory contours and cortical neuron responses. *Science, 224*(4654), 1260-1262.

Wagemans, J., Van Gool, L., & d'Ydewalle, G. (1991). Detection of symmetry in tachistoscopically presented dot patterns: effects of multiple axes and skewing. *Perception & Psychophysics, 50*(5), 413-427.

Wenderoth, P. (1996). The effects of dot pattern parameters and constraints on the relative salience of vertical bilateral symmetry. *Vision Research, 36*(15), 2311-2320.

Yantis, S. (1995). Perceived continuity of occluded visual objects. *Psychological Science, 6*, 176-186.

From Fragments to Objects – Segmentation and Grouping in Vision
T.F. Shipley and P.J. Kellman (Editors)

10

Perceptual Organization as Generic Object Recognition

David W. Jacobs, NEC Research Institute, 4 Independence Way, Princeton, NJ 08540, USA

Abstract

We approach some aspects of perceptual organization as the process of fitting generic models of objects to image data. A generic model of shape encodes prior knowledge of what shapes are likely to come from real objects. For such a model to be useful, it must also lead to efficient computations. We show that models of shape based on local properties of objects can be effectively used by simple, neurally plausible networks, and that they can still encode many perceptually important properties. We also discuss the relationship between perceptual salience and viewpoint invariance. Many gestalt properties are the subset of viewpoint invariant properties that can be encoded using the smallest possible sets of features, making them the ecologically valid properties that can also be used with computational efficiency. These results suggest that implicit models of shape used in perceptual organization arise from a combination of ecological and computational constraints. Finally, we discuss experiments demonstrating the role of convexity in amodal completion. These experiments point out some of the limitations of simple local shape models, and indicate the potential role that the part structure of objects also plays in perceptual organization.

Introduction

This paper presents an overview of our recent work on perceptual grouping. We will describe an approach to grouping that has evolved with a number of collaborators, largely at the NEC Research Institute. While we will stress those particular aspects of a solution that we have developed, we will also try to place these results into a broader context in an effort to explain a general perspective shared by many computer scientists.

In this view, perceptual organization is primarily the process of recognizing generic objects. It is the process of isolating and representing the objects in an image without the use of knowledge of specific objects, but based only on information about the properties possessed by objects in general. The results of perceptual organization are then used to trigger more specific models of objects, providing additional information that can be used to further interpret the scene. This view stresses the importance of our knowledge about objects in correctly interpreting images. It also supposes that information about specific objects cannot be directly triggered by the image; that before these models can be selected one must have a general sense of what objects are in the scene and what properties they have. The central tenets of this approach are that our knowledge about objects can be divided between the general and the specific, and that the process of perceptual organization is primarily the process of fitting general models of objects to the image.

In some images it may be possible to completely isolate the objects using only our very general knowledge of what an object is like. In other images we may derive only fragmentary and incomplete representations from perceptual organization, representations that are made more complete and unambiguous only with the subsequent use of more specific knowledge. In some cases perceptual organization processes may even fail completely, and image interpretation may only be possible after top-down information is used to trigger specific object models. However, in studying perceptual organization we attempt to focus on situations in which generic object models are sufficient to organize the image. We suppose that on many perceptual tasks, such as judgements about illusory contours, saliency, and grouping behind occluders, the role of generic models can be isolated. We do not claim that every aspect of perceptual organization can be understood as a process of generic object recognition. We do believe, though, that many of the phenomena can be fruitfully modeled in this way.

To illustrate our view of perceptual organization as a process of object recognition, we will first give an example of how this could work in the case of grouping behind an occluder. This example will be intuitive and informal; we will later present psychophysics addressing this problem. Figure 1-left shows three shapes disappearing behind an occluder. Figures 1-middle and 1-right show two possible ways of organizing these shapes into the boundaries of two objects. Intuitively, we find the interpretation shown in Figure 1-middle to be more reasonable. Our view is that the brain is making use of a general model of the shapes of objects in making this judgement. By this we mean that although objects come in all sorts of shapes, some shapes are more likely to be the boundaries of an object than are others. The brain has an implicit model that allows it to determine the likelihood that an object boundary

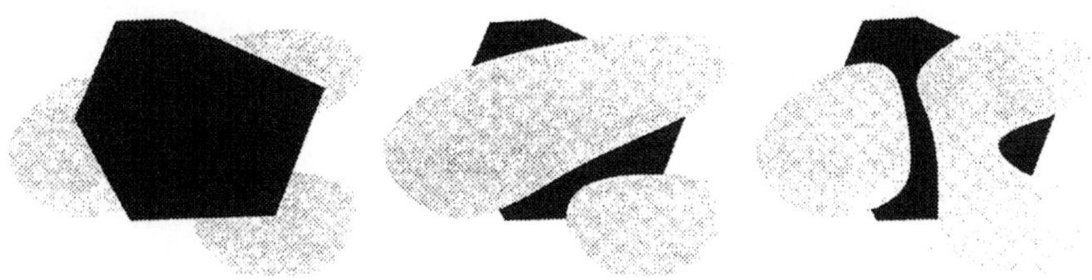

Figure 1. On the left, some shapes disappearing behind an occluder. In the middle and right figures we show possible ways of completing these shapes.

will have a particular shape. In a judgment such as the one depicted in Figure 1, we select the interpretation that yields the most likely boundary shape with the best fit to the image information.

Our view is closely related to many previous and concurrent views on perceptual organization and object recognition. The earliest approaches to recognition in computer vision suggest the idea that recognition of objects proceeds by organizing an image using generic information about shape, then using a bottom-up description of shape to trigger specific models, and then performing more detailed analysis with these specific models. This is essentially the view taken in Roberts, (1966), the first piece of work in the field of computer vision. Lowe, (1985) influentially fleshed out this approach in many ways, suggesting, for example, that Gestalt grouping cues provide the generic information about shape needed to organize the image.

Lowe described grouping as the process of finding small, salient feature sets likely to come from a single object. Kanizsa, (1979), emphasized that illusory contour formation is part of the process of perceiving surfaces, which is more akin to generic object recognition. This view has been elaborated in models of illusory contour formation developed by computer scientists (eg., Brady and Grimson, 1981; Williams and Hanson, 1996; Nitzburg and Mumford, 1990; Kumaran, Geiger, and Gurvits, 1996). Moreover, Mumford has stressed the relationship between the shape of subjective contours and object models, and the views that we express in this chapter have been strongly influenced by Mumford's view. Zhu, (1999), has also emphasized the use of generic models in perceptual organization, extending this approach in a number of interesting ways. The view in the computational world that image understanding results from matching a general model of shape to an image goes back at least to Grenander, (1981). So we feel that the basic framework of our approach is a natural one for computer scientists to take when they approach the problem of perceptual organization.

This approach differs from some others by emphasizing perceptual organization as a process that relates a model of the world to an image. Grouping cues are derived from the nature of 3D objects and their projection into 2D. In contrast, some other approaches to perceptual organization have stressed the search for regularities in a 2D image, without relating these regularities to 3D objects. For example, Gestalt views on "good form" have been interpreted as the visual system having the goal of producing the simplest interpretation of an image, in terms of finding an efficient representation or coding of the image (this approach is summarized in Pomerantz and Kubovy, (1986), and more recently developed in Van der Helm and Leeuwenberg, (1996)). Leyton, (1986), and Palmer, (1983), have stressed perceptual organization as the process of finding 2D relations within the image in terms of group transformations or invariances. These sorts of interpretations do not need to directly invoke the properties of 3D objects, but focus more on the goal of finding efficient representations of images. It is certainly possible to incorporate occlusions and other 3D phenomena into these views, as demonstrated in Van Lier's article in this volume. But, in contrast to these approaches, our view emphasizes the relations between 3D models of objects and 2D images, rather than relations within the 2D image.

Our view also differs from others in emphasizing probabilistic interpretations rather than rules. Every possible organization of an image has some probability of being correct, depending on how well it fits our generic models of shapes and how well it fits the image. The computational challenge to the visual system in this view is to try to find the most probable interpretation. Often, in other approaches, non-probabilistic grouping rules are formulated that determine perceptual organization. Of course, these rules can be seen as the limiting cases of probabilistic inferences. Therefore, these approaches may be different sides of the same coin; but there is a significant difference in emphasis.

When we attempt to model perceptual organization as a problem of object recognition, two key questions naturally emerge. First, what type of models do we have of the generic objects that we recognize during the process of perceptual organization? And how is this knowledge encoded by neurons? Second, how do we match these models to portions of the image? It is well known in computer vision that the process of finding a good fit between an image and an object model can be computationally demanding. How is this process solved efficiently by the brain? One of our chief claims is that the answers to these two questions are intimately interconnected. The types of generic models that we use in perceptual organization are strongly influenced by the efficiency with which these models can be used.

First we will discuss the problem of modeling generic objects. We will argue that a good model should be both ecologically valid, and computationally useful. We will then discuss a class of models of contour shape that describe contours in terms of their local properties. We will point out in that such models can encode many Gestalt properties. But these models are also useful because they facilitate efficient, neurally plausible computations. In the section "Efficient Computation" we provide a specific example of how these models can be used to compute the shape and salience of illusory contours. Overall, the goal of that section is to illustrate how we can conceptualize perceptual organization as the process of matching a generic object model to an image.

In the next section we consider this interaction more explicitly. We add one new constraint, which is that generic object models should also focus on 2D image properties that can be related to the 3D properties of objects. This has previously been argued by a number of researchers, particularly emphasizing the role of viewpoint invariant properties in perceptual organization. We describe results that show that viewpoint invariance alone is not sufficient to explain perceptual salience, that it can do so only when combined with constraints that require perceptually salient properties to also be especially efficient to use computationally.

These sections hopefully present a picture of how local models of contour can be used to perform perceptual organization according to Gestalt principles. Unfortunately, such models do not appear to be adequate to explain all perceptual organization phenomena. To make this point, we describe experiments that show that convexity plays a role in amodal completion (grouping behind an occluder). While some aspects of convexity can be captured by the local shape models that we discuss, we also show effects that cannot. Rather, to explain these effects we seem to need models that also take account of the part structure of objects. We do not feel that these results undermine the general approach that we take to perceptual organization, but they do point out some remaining challenges in fully fleshing out this approach. For our purposes, it is not enough just to point out that convexity is important to perceptual organization, we must also show how it can be encoded in a model of generic objects that can be used in efficient, neurally plausible computation. This remains to be done.

In general we do not present a complete story of how perceptual organization works. The view that we present casts perceptual organization as the solution to an extremely difficult problem. Building and using effective generic models of a complex world is probably as difficult as any task faced by biological systems. A complete story must show what these models capture about the world, how they are constructed and encoded in the brain, and how they are efficiently used to interpret images. The intuition that perceptual organization is a process of generic object recognition is very natural to people who approach vision computationally, and it shows up in much computational work. Our goal in this chapter is to explain why we think this view is plausible, how we have attempted to gather evidence for this view, and how we have also attempted to attack some of the basic problems that must be solved to understand perceptual organization if this view is correct.

GENERIC MODELS OF SHAPE

We will focus only on the perceptual organization of contours in this paper. We model this process as finding the best fit between prior knowledge and the image. Prior knowledge includes models of objects' shapes and other aspects of the image formation process, such as projection and occlusion. The image provides data about which local intensity patterns indicate the presence of object boundaries, and what occlusion processes might explain the absence of object boundaries. In this section we focus on what object models should be like. In other sections we will touch on issues such as how these models will interact with image intensity information and occlusion processes.

We use a generic object model to tell us how likely contour fragments are to come from the boundary of a single object. This can be used in a process that joins those fragments in an image that give rise to boundaries that match the shapes of real objects. To be ecologically valid, a generic model of object shape must accurately capture the properties of a large number of objects. However, there are inevitable tradeoffs between the power of a shape model, and its usability. We will consider a particularly usable class of shape models in this section, those that are *low-order Markov models* (see also Henderson, et al, in this volume for a discussion of the use of Markov models in gaze control). We will explain this jargon, and show that a number of properties of object shape can be captured by such models. We will then discuss how these models can be efficiently represented by a simple neural net, and used to perform perceptual organization by recognizing generic objects.

In this article we focus primarily on modeling the shape of the boundary of objects. We consider a statistical model of boundary shape that can tell us, for any hypothesized shape, how likely this is to be an object boundary. First, though, to lend concreteness to our discussion, let us examine how a generic object model could be used to perform perceptual organization tasks. We will not discuss specific mechanisms or algorithms in this section, but rather, how in principle a generic shape model can guide modal and amodal completion, and saliency judgements. By modal completion we mean perceptual grouping that gives rise to illusory contours. By amodal completion we mean grouping behind an occluder, in which no illusory contour is perceived. By saliency judgements we mean the perception that certain contour fragments in an image appear to give rise to a perceptually salient contour that joins them.

Consider, for example, illusory contour displays such as the one shown in Figure 2. In such displays, a closed boundary is perceived in which portions of the boundary are delineated by significant gradients in intensity. In other parts of the boundary, there is no intensity gradient, though an illusory gradient is perceived. We can view this as the perceptual process of joining together edge fragments to form the boundary of a shape. In our view, one of the factors that determines which inducing elements will be joined into a surface boundary is the likelihood that the resulting shape is an object boundary; that is, how well it fits our model of object shape.

In amodal completion (Figure 1) there is no percept of a specific object shape where that shape appears occluded. However, one can similarly hypothesize that the strength of an amodal connection will be based on the likelihood of the boundary shape that must be supposed in order to connect two object fragments. One can suppose either that a particular shape is hypothesized and its likelihood is assessed using the generic shape model, or that the

Figure 2. An example of an illusory contour figure (left) and its possible interpretation (right).

strength of an amodal completion is based on the likelihood of a set of many possible shapes that complete the object boundary.

In saliency judgements (Figure 3) fragments in a cluttered scene appear joined together into longer contours. Such judgements have been studied, for example, in Shashua and Ullman (1988), Field, Hayes and Hess, (1993), and Kovacs and Julesz (1993). What is interesting in these figures is that there are a huge number of ways that these fragments can be joined up to form contours, but only a small number of these possibilities are perceptually salient. Again, we maintain that one of the factors determining the salience with which a collection of fragments will be seen joined into a contour is how well these fragments can be fit to a prior, generic model of object shape.

In all these judgements, the visual system does not recognize a specific known object, but rather joins fragmentary data into a shape that may be completely novel. To view this as

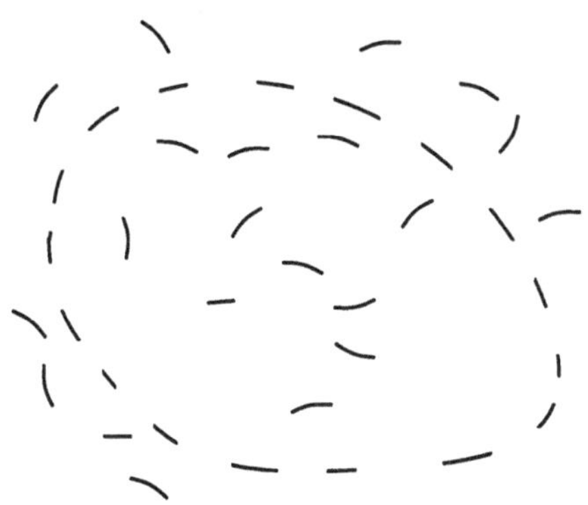

Figure 3. An example of a salient contour that emerges by grouping of edge fragments.

fitting a model to the data, the model must be generic in the sense of applying to almost any possible shape, telling us how likely that shape is to come from an object. This is what we mean by a statistical model that captures generic properties of objects.

LOW ORDER MARKOV MODELS OF BOUNDARY SHAPE

We first focus on properties that can be naturally computed using only local information about boundary shape. As we will see, such local measures lead to efficient computational schemes that can be encoded in simple, neurally plausible networks. As an example of a local model of boundary shape, imagine that we evaluate the likelihood that a shape is an object boundary by sliding a small window over the length of the shape (see Figure 4). At any one time, we only consider the portion of the shape that is visible through this window, and form a judgement about how likely this piece of the shape is to belong to an object boundary. We then combine information over the entire shape by just adding up all these local estimates of likelihood. This is a very simple method, with some obvious advantages. It means that our model of object shape is very compact; it doesn't need to be able to judge an arbitrarily large shape, only a small fragment of a shape. And it means that the problem of determining the likelihood of a shape can be decomposed into many independent small problems of measuring the likelihood of small fragments of shape. On the other hand, it is clear that such a simple model is not powerful enough to capture all aspects of shape that are important in perceptual organization. For example such a model cannot detect whether a shape is symmetric (see Jacobs, forthcoming, for a discussion of how

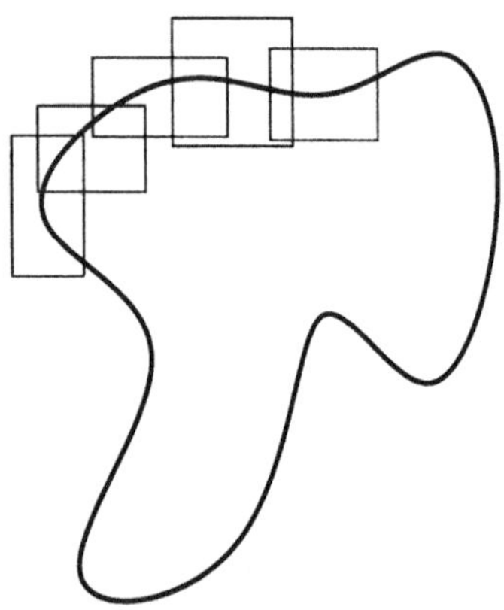

Figure 4. In a local model of contour shape, the likelihood of a contour is found by sliding a small window around the contour, accumulating evidence.

symmetry fits into our view of perceptual organization). In the section "Convexity" we discuss other limitations of a local shape model. In this section we show that a local shape model can be powerful enough to encode many of the properties of shape that seem to be used by the visual system in perceptual grouping. This will allow us to develop a computational model that handles many, though not all, aspects of shape in perceptual organization.

The notion of a local model of shape can be formalized mathematically as a low order, Markov model. We now describe this, a bit informally. Let's suppose that our shape is composed of a finite number of points that are strung together, such as a list of adjacent pixels along the contour. Then if we have a Markov model of shape, it just means that the probability of each point appearing with certain properties depends only on the properties of a specified set of neighbors, which can be inside a local window on the contour. If we say this model is low order, we mean that this window isn't too big. With a Markov model, the probability that the entire shape is an object boundary is just the product of the individual probabilities derived from each window. That is, the Markov model makes assumptions about which portions of this probability are conditionally independent[1]. If we consider the log of this probability, which is monotonically related to it, then we can find this by just taking the sum of the log of each local probability. The advantageous mathematical properties of Markov models have been widely recognized, and they have been extensively applied in computer vision by, for example, Geman and Geman, (1984), and Mumford and Shah, (1985). Mumford (1994), in particular, considers the problem of modeling object contours using a diffusion process that is a simple, low order Markov process. Zhu, (1999), discusses many facets of the use of Markov models for shape description, including how these models may be learned.

We will describe shape models in which the probability that a point is on a boundary depends only on very local information. At times it is useful to think of the boundary as a discrete set of points, and at times it is useful to think of it as a continuous curve. In the first case, given two adjacent points on a contour, the direction between them approximates the tangent to the curve. Given three adjacent points, we can make a discrete approximation to the curvature of the curve based on the magnitude of the change in the tangent direction. With four points, we can determine the change in curvature to, for example, detect inflection points in the curve. If, on the other hand, we think of the boundary as a continuous curve, then rather than basing our measure of likelihood on a small number of points, we can base it on the first few derivatives of the curve. That is, we can base it directly on the tangent,

---

[1] Though not relevant to our current discussion, a key part of the power of Markov models is that global properties can often be described through the propagation of local properties. Because these local neighborhoods overlap, one neighborhood can influence a distant one through intermediate neighborhoods.

curvature, or change in curvature. These are simply the limit of the properties that we can approximate using a small number of points, as these points get closer together.

We can see that the Gestalt property of *good continuation* can be encoded as a low order Markov property of curves (Mumford, 1994). It has been noted that a curve that exhibits good continuation can be described as a curve with minimal amounts of curvature (eg., Ullman, 1976; Horn, 1981). This can be measured as the *energy* of the curve, given by the equation:

$$\int_{t\in\Gamma} \kappa^2(t)dt$$

where $\kappa(t)$ represents the curvature at a point t on the curve, Γ. In the discrete case, we can think of this measure as expressing a model of contours in which the probability of a point on the curve having a particular tangent direction depends only on the tangent at the previous point. The curvature is the normalized change in the tangent. Mumford suggests a stochastic model of contours in which the curvature is drawn from a Normal distribution with zero mean. In this case, the probability of a contour decreases as its energy increases; in fact the negative log of the probability of a curve is its energy. This tells us that models of illusory contour formation that consider the curve of least energy connecting two inducing elements can also be thought of as computing the likelihood of a shape drawn from a Markov model. This Markov model is just a generic model of shape that says shapes tend to be smooth. Figure 5 provides an illustration of contours drawn from this, and from other random processes.

This contour model has one parameter, the variance of the Normal distribution on curvature. This controls how rapidly the orientation of a curve changes. Intuitively, if the variance is close to zero, the model will generate contours that are almost straight lines and that change direction very slowly. When variance is large, contours will become much more wiggly, and reverse directions quickly.

Closure is another Gestalt property that can be encoded as a local property of a contour. A curve is closed if and only if every point on the curve has neighbors on both sides.

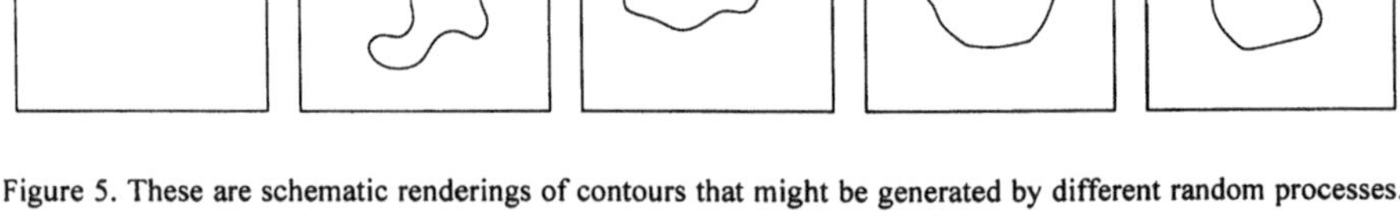

Figure 5. These are schematic renderings of contours that might be generated by different random processes. On the left, is a contour whose probability is inversely related to its energy, and where large curvatures are unlikely. Next, a contour from a similar process, but with large curvatures less unlikely. In the middle, a contour like this, but restricted to be closed. Next, a closed contour in which large curvatures are unlikely, but discontinuities in curvature, though rare, are not impossible. Finally, a closed contour in which inflection points have zero probability.

An endpoint of the curve can be located locally. If we want to enforce the property that object boundaries must be closed, we can say that such endpoints have zero probability of occurring. This gives us a model of shape in which object boundaries are always closed.

For a generic model of shape to be useful, it must assign a reasonable probability to the boundaries of objects that really occur. The model based on the energy of the curve has the disadvantage of not producing boundaries with corners. This is because the curvature of a contour is not defined at a discontinuity. When we discretely sample a boundary with a corner, we will assign a very high curvature at the location of the corner. This curvature will diverge to infinity as the sampling rate increases. This leads to the undesirable property that shapes with corners have zero probability of occurring. If we wish to use a shape model, for example, to produce illusory contours with corners, as seen in Koffka cross stimuli (eg., Figure 6, Sambin, 1974), the model must produce shapes with corners.

Figure 6. A figure of the Koffka cross, in which subjects tend to see illusory contours with corners.

Thornber and Williams, (1997), show that we can handle this by allowing a discontinuity to occur at any point on a contour, with some fixed, small probability. They use this to model the formation of illusory contours having corners. This is similar to the *line process* that is used in Markov Random Fields (eg., Geman and Geman, 1984; Blake and Zisserman, 1987).

Such a shape model now has two parameters that indicate how curvy the contours are that it generates, and how often they generate discontinuities. By adjusting these parameters, we can generate different sorts of shapes. For example, we can set curvature variance to zero, but allow for occasional discontinuities so that the contour never changes direction except at discontinuities. In this case, the shape model produces polygons. Or, we can set variance high and make discontinuities rare, so that we get rather wiggly shapes. In the world, the surface properties of a shape may change from one part of a shape to another. For example, much of a person's body may have a very smooth shape, while one's hair may have a much more wiggly shape. The models we have described until now will assign low probabilities to such shapes, because if the parameters are chosen to make a smooth shape likely, they will make a wiggly shape unlikely, and vice versa. Shapes that have varying characteristics may be produced by a *non-stationary* Markov process. In such a process the parameters of the model are also allowed to change stochastically. So as we move along the contour, just as there is some small chance that a discontinuity will occur, there is also a small chance that the smoothness parameter will change, so that a wiggly or smooth shape becomes more likely from that point on, until the parameters change again.

As a final shape property, we note that some aspects of convexity can also be captured by local shape models. This is because the transition on a contour from convex to concave, called an *inflection* point, is a local property of a shape. If we make inflection points unlikely, then when part of a contour is convex, the ensuing parts of the contour will also be likely to be convex. This produces contours with long stretches that are either all convex or all concave. If inflection points are assigned zero probability, then all contours we generate will either be completely convex or completely concave (eg., holes). In the section "Convexity" we will consider further whether this kind of local model of convexity is adequate to model human sensitivity to convexity in contours.

In completion problems, fragments of contours are connected together into the boundaries of surfaces in spite of the presence of gaps. To determine the likelihood that a particular set of fragments come from a real object boundary, we therefore need not only a model of object shape, but also a model that can tell us how likely a particular gap is to separate two contour fragments that come from the same object. For example, in amodal completion, a gap in the visible boundary of an object is caused by occlusion by another object. In Jacobs, (1989), we analyzed the distribution of gap lengths to which randomly positioned objects give rise, providing a model of gap lengths for amodal completion. While the results depend somewhat on the particular sort of objects used to generate occlusions, we showed both experimentally and analytically that for a number of cases occlusions tend to be shorter rather than longer. This tells us that a hypothesized completion involving shorter gaps will be more likely than one with longer gaps, which is also just a direct application of the Gestalt principle of grouping by proximity. Elder and Zucker, (1994), have also performed psychophysics to measure quantitatively the effect that gap length has on the perceptual salience of a completion, and they have modeled the results.

Grouping by proximity can also be captured using a low order Markov model of shape. This too was done by Mumford, (1994). To do this, when we look at a local window of a shape that is being completed across a gap, we assign some probability to the gap continuing across that small length. These local probabilities accumulate multiplicatively, so that in crossing a long gap we pay a penalty that is the product of many local penalties. This represents the idea that it is increasingly unlikely for a contour to continue to remain hidden from view over a longer and longer stretch of the image.

We can build a model of contour shape and contour gaps that capture a number of Gestalt properties, such as good continuation, closure, convexity, and proximity. A visual system can use such a model to solve completion problems. In a contour completion problem, an image contains a number of contour fragments. The problem is to choose some of these fragments to join together so that they are perceived as the boundary of a surface. Using shape and gap models we can, for example, for any hypothesized grouping of fragments, determine whether the possible shape of the object fitting these fragments, and the associated gaps in it, are likely. This gives us a basis for choosing a preferred completion as the one that is most likely to be the boundary of an object. Such a view explains perceptual completion as the visual system solving a probabilistic inference problem, whose goal is to identify the surfaces of objects in a scene.

This view raises many questions, however. In particular, how can an efficient and neurally plausible system solve this inference problem? In the next section we will demonstrate how some completion problems can be efficiently solved when we adopt a low order Markov model of shape and contour gaps. We will then more carefully address the question of whether such a model can be adequate to capture properties of human perceptual organization.

EFFICIENT COMPUTATION

We will now show concretely how a parallel, neurally plausible system can use Markov shape and occlusion models to compute the shape and salience of illusory contours. This section primarily summarizes the work in Williams and Jacobs, (1997a, 1997b).

We will describe the process of illusory contour formation using Kanizsa's famous example (Figure 2) as an illustration. In this case, a square is perceived as lying on top of and partially occluding four disks, although in fact, only four black three-quarter disks are physically present in the image. The visual system explains the missing edges of the square as due to the square's intensity nearly matching that of the background.

The image consists of twelve smooth curves in the form of four circular arcs, one for each three-quarter disk, and eight line segments. The junctions between the line segments and circular arcs are sharp corners, which serve as a clue of the possible occlusion of one shape by another. This indicates that it is possible that the images of the three-quarter disks are each formed by an object with a straight edge lying on top of an object with a circular arc. Creating an interpretation of the entire image can be viewed as the process of joining edge fragments into smooth surfaces that are most consistent with the image and our prior models of surface shape and occlusion, and determining which of these surfaces lie on top of which. Such an approach is developed in, for example, Williams and Hanson, (1996), or Nitzburg and Mumford, (1990).

In this section we describe a solution to only one piece of this problem. Given two edge fragments, we determine some measure of the likelihood that they should be joined together in a single contour, and the shape and salience of the possible completion between them. To do this, we compute a *stochastic completion field*. This tells, for every position and orientation in the image, the likelihood that there is an edge there, given both our priors and information about the position and orientation where illusory contours begin and end. Given the starting and ending points of an illusory contour, the stochastic completion field resembles, both in shape and salience, the percept of the illusory contour. Given different possible ways of connecting edge fragments into surfaces, the stochastic completion field tells us the relative likelihood of these different completions. We therefore see it as a precursor to illusory contour formation.

So we are faced with the following problem. Given the position and orientation where a contour is supposed to begin and end, which we call *source* and *sink* positions respectively, we wish to compute, for every other position and orientation, $\mathbf{p} = (x,y,\theta)$, in the image, the likelihood that the contour passes through there. We do this using a simple parallel network. First, we break the problem of whether a contour passes through $\mathbf{p}$ into two subproblems, illustrated in Figure 7. These are finding the likelihood that a contour leaving the source point would pass through $\mathbf{p}$, and the likelihood that the contour would continue on to a sink point. That is, one wants to consider all possible contours from the source to the sink, weighted by their likelihood according to a low order Markov model, and measure the proportion that pass through each (x,y,θ). This can be expressed as the product of the likelihood that the contour will reach (x,y,θ) and the likelihood that it will go on to a sink, because our model of likelihood is local; the likelihood of one part of the contour does not depend on the shape of the previous part of the contour.

We therefore compute a *source field*, giving for each (x,y,θ) the likelihood that a contour reaches that position from a source, and a similar *sink field*, and take the product of these two. We now describe how to compute the source field, noting that the sink field is computed in exactly the same way, since the model of contour probability is the same for both. We will describe this computation in intuitive, non-rigorous language, and refer the interested reader to Williams and Jacobs, (1997a, 1997b), for a precise and rigorous description of the algorithm.

First, we consider a somewhat idealized setting in which we ignore issues of discrete sampling. The algorithm proceeds iteratively, at the k'th iteration finding for each position and orientation $\mathbf{p}$ the probability that a contour of length k will leave the source and end at $\mathbf{p}$. This can be determined by looking at the probability that a contour reached each neighboring point of $\mathbf{p}$ on the k-1'th iteration, and combining this with the probability that the contour would proceed to $\mathbf{p}$. This can be done because our measure of probability is Markov. Consequently, the probability of a contour can be determined by taking the product of local probabilities. Each step from one point to the next on the contour is another local

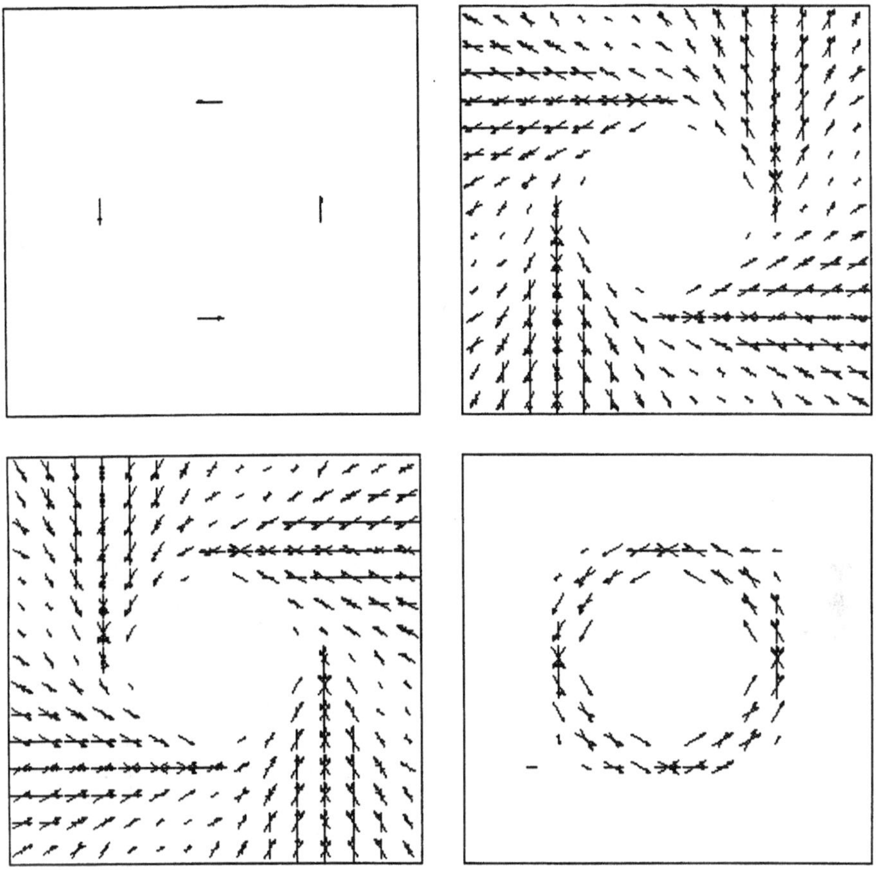

Figure 7. This figure shows an example of source and sink fields when a contour is supposed to pass through four points equally spaced on a circle (top left). The top right shows the source field computed. The length of each vector indicates the probability that a contour passing through an initial position will reach the position and orientation of the vector. The bottom left shows the sink field. The bottom right is the product of the two, the stochastic completion field.

neighborhood, with another probability independent of previous ones. Finally, these probabilities are summed for all values of *k*, which implicitly assumes that the same contour is unlikely to pass twice through the same point.

In our experiments, our local measure of the likelihood contains a term to represent the smoothness, or good continuation of the contour, and a term to measure the likelihood of gaps. The good continuation term is based on a Normal distribution of curvature, as described above. Given a prior position and orientation for a curve, the orientation indicates the direction the curve is moving in, that is, it tells us the position of the next point on the curve. So a point will precede **p** only if it is at an adjacent location, with an orientation pointing towards **p**. Furthermore, the difference between the orientation of the preceding point and the orientation of **p** tells us how much the orientation of the curve has changed. Our good continuation prior tells us how likely any particular change in orientation is, penalizing large changes more than small.

This description of our algorithm is radically oversimplified, because we have ignored the issue of how one can perform these computations with a discrete set of computational units. In this case, only a discrete set of (x,y,θ) positions can be directly represented. Moreover, if we represent one particular (x,y,θ) position, the place that this position points to may not be directly represented. For example, if one unit represents the position $(17,23,\pi/8)$, this points to contour locations with $(x,y) = (17+cos(\pi/8), 23+sin(\pi/8))$. But this location may lie in between points that are directly represented by units. To handle this problem, we use a continuous formulation of how the probability distribution representing the location of contours diffuses in position/orientation space given by a set of partial differential equations in Mumford, (1994). These equations describe the likelihood of the contour position being at any particular place after any particular arc length as diffusing through the space of positions and orientations, and is exact for the continuous case. We then use numerical techniques designed to solve partial differential equations on a discrete grid. This allows us to accurately and stably approximate the computation of these probabilities using computational units that represent a discrete set of positions and orientations. The basic structure of this algorithm is as described above, with each computational unit updating its probability based on its neighbor's values. However, when one unit does not point exactly to another, a contour through it must be considered to have some probability of reaching each of its neighbors on the next step, depending on how closely it points to each of them. Moreover, if some units are more than one step away, the contour must be given some probability of reaching these units, and some probability of staying in the same position at the next step, in order for its path to be accurately represented on average. This provides a stochastic representation of the contour's path through the network. Williams and Jacobs, (1997b) contains details of this method. More recently, Zweck and Williams, (2000), describes a more accurate way of solving this partial differential equation with a related method, but using a wavelet basis to represent positions and orientations.

The length of gaps also plays a role in illusory contour formation (see, eg., Shipley and Kellman, 1992). Two phenomena, at least, seem relevant here. First, if the inducing elements have fixed size but are moved further apart, the salience of the illusory contour drops. Second, if the image is scaled so that the inducing elements become further apart but also grow larger, illusory contour strength does not change, for some range of scales. We will only describe how our model accounts for the first sort of phenomena. A good deal of work addresses overall scale invariance; Thornber and Williams (1998) in particular address this issue within the framework described here.

In modeling illusory contour formation, the entire contour from the source to the sink is a gap, in the sense that a contour is hypothesized even though no intensity edge is present in the image. As described above, models of how gaps are formed suggest that longer hypothesized gaps should be less likely than shorter ones. Mumford, (1994), suggests a model in which the probability of a gap of some length is set to a constant, and the probability of a longer gap is just the product of the probability of shorter gaps (ie., the probability falls off exponentially with length). Again, the probability of a gap can be measured locally, and these can be combined readily. Williams and Jacobs, (1997b), add to this the idea that the likelihood of an illusory contour crossing a gap in the image can be modulated by local brightness information. This means, for example, that we can make it unlikely for an illusory contour to cross an edge in the image. Edges are known to interfere with illusory contour information (eg., Rock and Anson, 1979, Ramachandran et al., 1994). Moreover, if a figure continues to fade into the background even across an edge that is present in the background, this would mean that the figure and background would have to change intensity in the same way, at the same position, an unlikely coincidence. On the other hand, if an "illusory" contour at some point actually follows a faint edge, we can reduce the penalty for gaps to the extent that this local information indicates that an edge may be present.

It is easy to integrate this gap penalty into our previous computational scheme. The local penalty for moving from one contour position to another is now modulated by the local intensity pattern, penalizing movement across a gap, penalizing even more movement across an edge, and penalizing less movement along an edge.

Some experimental results are shown with this system in Figures 8, 9, and 10. The first two figures show results for simple illusory contour stimuli, while Figure 10 shows how the stochastic completion field can be modulated by local intensity patterns. Williams and Jacobs, 1997a, 1997b contain many more experimental results.

We want to stress that although we have described this algorithm very informally, it computes illusory contour strength directly as the probability that positions and orientations lie on the boundary of an object, given our generic model of object shape and of the formation of gaps in object boundaries, and subject to initial information about the position where the illusory contour may begin and end. In this sense, we have a precise, generic model of objects, and we interpret illusory contour formation as the recognition of the most likely position of generic objects.

We consider this to be a neurally plausible model because its computational requirements are modest and roughly matched to those of visual cortex. Our method requires computational units for a discrete sampling of every position and orientation in the image. Such an array of neurons is known to be present in visual cortex. These units only need to compute weighted sums of their neighbor's values. Fixed weight links between each unit and

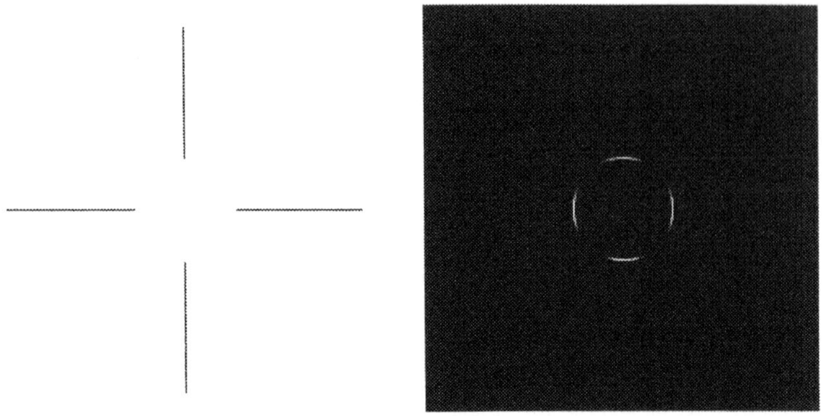

Figure 8. On the left, an Ehrenstein figure. On the right, the stochastic completion field computed from it. Intensity at a pixel is proportional, on a log scale, to the probability at that position, summed over all orientations, for ease of visualization.

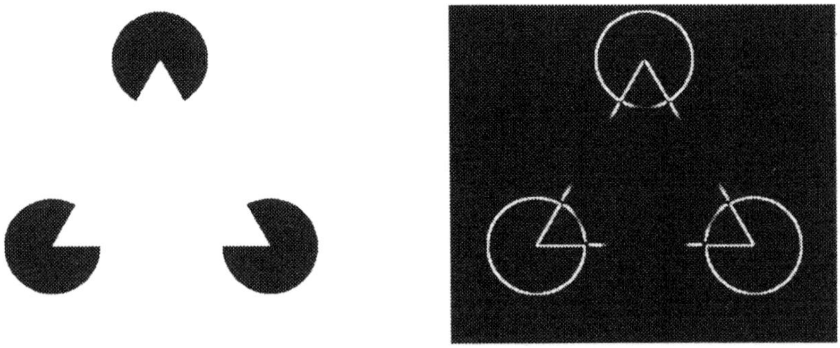

Figure 9. The stochastic completion field for a Kanizsa figure.

its neighbors encode the probability of a contour passing from one unit to its neighbor. This requires a minimal amount of computation and connectivity in the network, probably much less than is actually present. This means that there are many simple ways of mapping our system into regions of the brain.

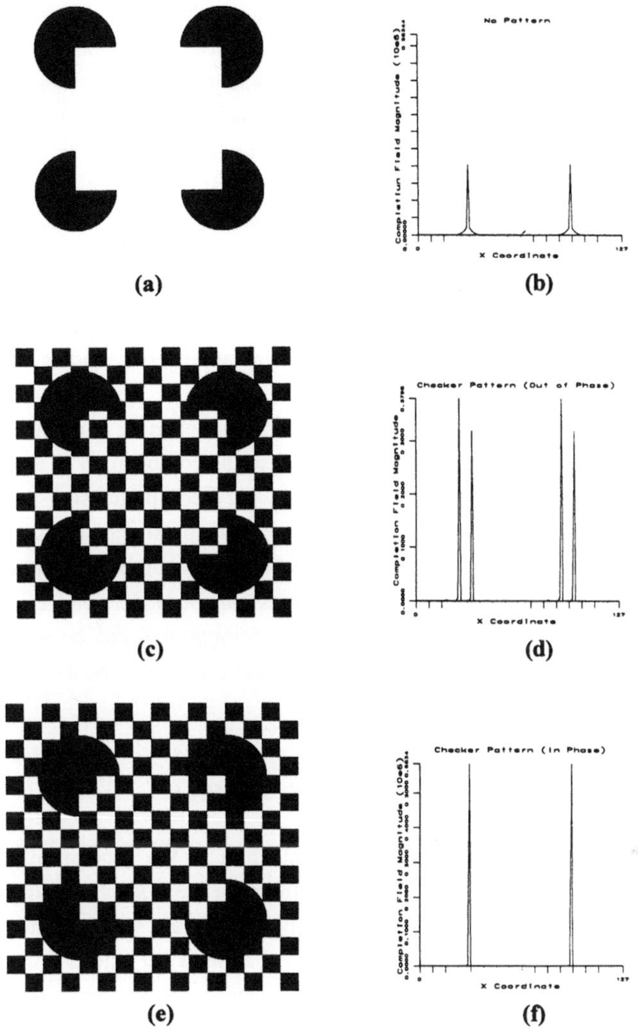

Figure 10. **(a)** Kanizsa Square. **(b)** Stochastic completion field magnitude along the line $y = 64$. **(c)** Kanizsa Square with out-of-phase checkered background (see Ramachandran *et al.*, 1994). **(d)** The enhancement of the nearest contrast edge is not noticeable unless the magnitudes are multiplied by a very large factor (i.e., approximately 1,000,000). **(e)** Kanizsa Square with in-phase checkered background. **(f)** The peak completion field magnitude is increased almost threefold, and the distribution has been significantly sharpened.

Our model is distinguished by using both an explicit use of a model of shape and occlusion and simple computational mechanisms. For example, Shashua and Ullman, (1988), proposed a method of computing the salience of contour fragments to which ours is quite related, in that both use a simple network of elements that each represent position and orientation. They pose their computation as a dynamic program, in which each element can update its value based only on its neighbors. Our method is different, however, in several key ways. First, we explicitly compute a likelihood measure based on a contour model, whereas Shashua and Ullman proposed a more ad-hoc cost function. Second, by posing likelihood propagation as a partial differential equation and solving it in this way, we are able to avoid many discretization artifacts. Alter and Basri, (1997), discuss in detail a number of limitations of Shashua and Ullman's scheme that arise from their ad-hoc cost function and discretization problems. Third, by computing the product of a source and sink field, we ensure that only contours are considered that close a gap between the hypothesized starting and ending of an occlusion. Shashua and Ullman rely on a more ad-hoc approach to finding closed contours, which they recognize to be important for salience.

Heitger and von der Heydt, (1993), propose a model using convolutions with large support, and can be interpreted as something closer to the combination of a source and sink field. Grossberg and Mingolla, (1985), present a very comprehensive model based on convolution that attempts to account for a great many perceptual phenomena. These models are more directly inspired by neurophysiological data. Our model is different in starting from the premise that perceptual organization processes can be understood as generic object recognition, and in showing that each step of the computation can be derived from that premise. This allows us to show how a neurally inspired computation can be interpreted as the solution to a perceptual problem.

THE EFFECT OF PROJECTION ON SHAPE MODELS

If we wish to describe perceptual organization as the process of generic object recognition then we must take account of one of the most basic facts about recognition; it is the identification of 3D objects in 2D images. Properties that are most important to include in an object model are therefore not just properties that arise in 3D objects, but properties that are also preserved when these objects appear in 2D images. At the same time, we have tried to demonstrate the advantage of modeling objects in a way that can be captured with computationally simple mechanisms, such as low order Markov models. In this section we argue that the Gestalt properties (some are illustrated in Figure 11) can be seen as resulting from the conjunction of three important criteria; they are relevant aspects of 3D shape, they are preserved under projection, and they are computationally simple to use. This section describes work discussed in greater detail in Jacobs, (forthcoming).

First, many Gestalt properties of shape are readily connected to regularities in the shape of real objects. For example, the visible boundaries of objects are closed, connected

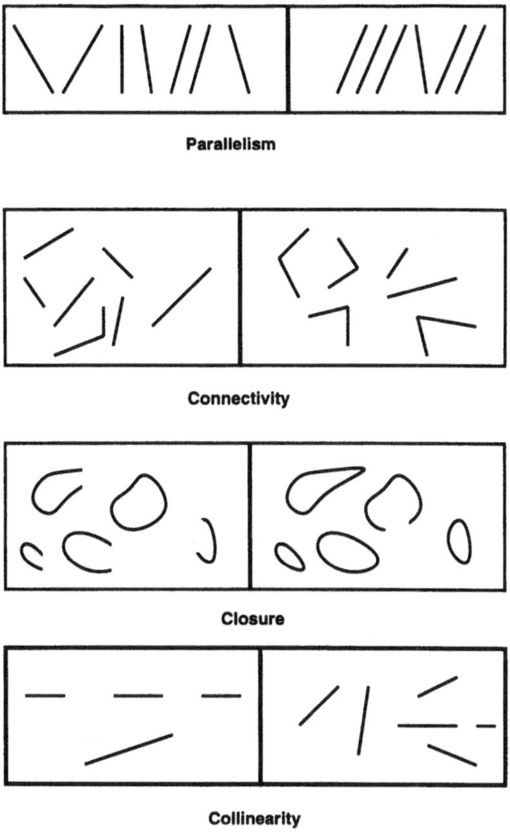

Figure 11. We show the contrast between the presence and absence of some Gestalt properties. For example, one closed figure is shown in a field of open figures, and one open figure is shown in a field of closed figures.

curves. Closure, and the connectivity of edges are Gestalt grouping cues. Rough parallelism, and more general types of symmetry are often present in natural objects. Hoffman and Richards, (1984), have argued that convexity is perceptually important because real objects tend to have convex parts joined at points of concavity. This explanation for Gestalt properties goes back to the Gestaltists themselves. For example, Köhler, (1929), writing for a general audience, describes how: "the common origin of the parts of one object is likely to give them common surface characteristics." That is, the Gestalt principal of grouping by homogenous surface properties arises from regularities present in natural objects. The Gestaltists viewed Gestalt grouping as central to the process of identifying objects without using specific, learned models, and viewed Gestalt properties as arising from the general properties of objects.

Second, it has been noted that Gestalt properties are not just related to the structure of real objects, they are also related to the nature of projection from 3D to 2D. Lowe, (1985), for example, points out that many Gestalt properties are invariant to projection. Therefore, Gestalt properties are ones produced by real objects when they appear in 2D, and also provide clues about the 3D structure of objects, which can be used in their recognition. Biederman, (1985, 1987), makes viewpoint invariant properties (VIPs) the basis of his Geon theory of object recognition, arguing that the set of VIPs present in object parts provide a simple index that allows them to quickly trigger the appropriate models in memory.

Informally, we say that a property is viewpoint invariant when a 3D object with this property always, or almost always produces it in an image, and a 3D object lacking this property always, or almost always produces an image that lacks it. For example, closure is a VIP because a closed 3D curve will always appear closed in an image. An open curve will only appear closed from the special viewing direction in which the beginning and end of the curve happen to line up at the same point in the image. Because this definition is symmetric, whenever a property is a VIP its negation is also, so it is really the contrast between properties such as closure or openness that is a VIP. For convenience, however, we will often refer to just half of this contrast.

Many Gestalt properties are VIPs. For example, closure, connectivity, collinearity, and the presence or absence of discontinuities in curves are preserved under projection. Parallelism is invariant under scaled orthographic projection (an approximation to perspective which applies when parallel lines do not have great depth relative to the viewer, and their convergence is not noticeable). Convexity is a VIP when figure/background are distinguished on the contour. And we show (Jacobs, forthcoming) that when a viewer is standing upright, horizontal and vertical lines are VIPs.

However, Jacobs, (forthcoming), also shows that viewpoint invariance alone is not sufficient to distinguish perceptually salient properties. There are an infinite number of possible VIPs, most of which are not perceptually salient. The simplest reason for this is that any non-trivial viewpoint invariant description of a set of objects gives rise to a VIP. And any planar object can be described in a way that is invariant to projection, using standard methods of geometry. The cross-ratio is a classic description of four parallel lines that is invariant to perspective projection (see, eg., Cutting, (1986), for extensive discussion of the cross-ratio and its relation to perception). But this can be extended to produce a viewpoint invariant description of any set of planar points or lines. Given a viewpoint invariant description of a set of planar features, we can then show that this produces a VIP, since some planar objects always produce images that fit this description, while all other objects never, or almost never do.

What distinguishes Gestalt properties, among this infinity of VIPs, is that they are *minimal*, which means in a specific technical sense they are the VIPs that use the smallest number of image features, and are easiest computationally to incorporate into a generic object model. We will illustrate this using the simple example of sets of points. In this simplified case, we suppose that an object consists of a set of 3D points, and that an image consists of the projection of these points into a 2D image, using scaled orthographic projection (an approximation to perspective that is valid when there is insufficient depth visible in a scene for parallel lines to appear to converge). In this case, for any set of four points, there is a projection invariant description of the points that gives rise to a VIP. However, when we consider smaller sets of points this is not the case. When we consider sets of just three points, only collinear point sets give rise to VIPs. Non-collinear configurations of points do not have invariant descriptions. So in this case, collinearity vs. noncollinearity is a minimal VIP. Also, whether any of these points are identical is a VIP. So, for example, we have discussed the fact that closure of a curve may be seen as derived from the property of whether or not the curve's end points are identical. Therefore, closure is a minimal VIP. Similarly, the connectedness of two curves or lines is a minimal VIP based on identity. So by minimal we refer to the small number of VIPs that emerge when we consider only small sets of features at one time.

Other Gestalt properties can also be shown to be minimal VIPs. This includes properties of curves, such as smoothness (ie., good continuation) in contrast to discontinuity, which is a minimal VIP when we consider only a small number of the derivatives of the curve. Convexity is also a minimal VIP of curves for which figure and background is distinguished. And parallelism and the presence of trihedral vertices are minimal VIPs. Furthermore, for an upright viewer, horizontal and vertical lines are also minimal VIPs.

Minimal VIPs are built using the smallest possible number of features. In the case of properties that are based on the local derivatives of a curve, minimal VIPs will be the ones that require the smallest local neighborhood to compute. That is, they are the viewpoint invariants that can be captured by generic models of curves that are Markov models of the lowest order. The order of the Markov model needed to build a generic model is crucial in determining the amount of computational resources needed by the visual system. For example, in the system we described above, we needed a computational unit for each position and orientation in the plane. This is because the likelihood of a contour fragment is encoded in the link between two units, and could be determined by considering only two adjacent positions and orientations of the contour. This allowed us to capture the change in orientation, ie., the curvature, but no higher order properties. If our Markov model had looked at the change in curvature as well, it would have needed a link between two units each representing position, orientation and curvature, for this link to represent a likelihood based on the comparison between two curvatures. In general, the number of computational units would grow exponentially with the order of the Markov model for shape used. By modeling only the minimal VIPs the visual system is therefore able to focus on those VIPs that provide economical representations and computations.

Other minimal VIPs, such as parallelism, are not captured by the Markov model of shape described above, because parallel lines need not be contained in a local portion of a contour. However, the computational advantages of a property based on only two lines is evident, since parallel lines can be readily searched for, or neighborhoods for local models can be defined containing nearby pairs of lines, which can then be judged for parallelism. In general, minimal VIPs can be identified using small amounts of search or small local neighborhoods can be defined to allow their identification.

Our discussion so far does not include some perceptually salient properties, such as symmetry, which is not minimal, and proximity, which is not a viewpoint invariant. A more complete treatment of perceptually salient properties is given in Jacobs, (forthcoming). In brief, we point out that symmetry is derived from minimal viewpoint invariant properties, such as the parallelism of lines connecting symmetric points, and the collinearity of the midpoints of these lines. Wagemans, et al. (1991, 1993), discuss a model of symmetry detection that uses these properties. Wagemans (1999) discusses how the relative salience of different forms of symmetry can be explained by the relative computational difficulty of detecting them. We also discuss the *quasi-invariance* of properties such as proximity, which provide strong probabilistic information about 3D structure, even though they are not completely invariant.

Minimal viewpoint invariants therefore seem to provide the vocabulary with which we can express properties of generic shape that are computationally useful and preserved under projection. These two factors alone do not determine how a perceptual grouping system will work, however. For example, the visual system tends to perceive largely convex shapes as figure and concave shapes as background, as elegantly demonstrated by Kanizsa and Gerbino, (1976) (see Figure 12). However, it is the contrast between convexity and concavity that is a minimal viewpoint invariant; neither property is distinguished in this regard. Presumably convexity is more salient as figure because real objects are more often composed of convex

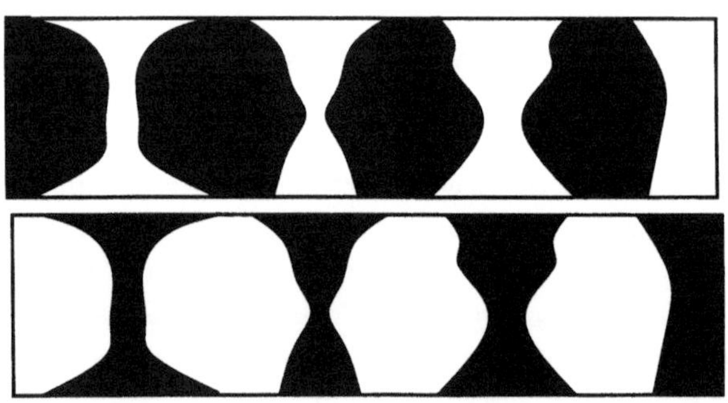

Figure 12. Adapted from Kanizsa and Gerbino, 1976, this figure illustrates how largely convex regions can appear as figure, while the symmetric regions are perceived as background.

parts than concave ones. That is, we hypothesize that perceptual salience arises in properties that reflect the structure of objects in the 3D world, that are preserved under projection, and that also can be used with computational efficiency.

CONVEXITY

At this point, it would be nice if we could claim that perceptual organization is explained as generic objection recognition using a low order Markov model of shape. After all, we can argue that not only does such an object model capture many Gestalt grouping properties, but these properties seem exactly to be qualities that are viewpoint invariant and that can be expressed with simple shape models. And we have computationally effective mechanisms for computing with such shape models.

However, while what we have presented so far may cover one aspect of perceptual organization, it is not a complete answer. In this section we will show that Markov models of contours are not adequate to fully capture the role that shape plays in grouping. We do this by looking in detail at one grouping cue, convexity. Our models of convexity are inspired by the idea that prior models of shape should take account of the part structure of objects. Of course, there is a long history behind the idea that part descriptions can play an important role in perception, and in particular in object recognition (eg., Binford, 1971; Marr, 1982; Biederman, 1985, 1987). It is therefore not surprising that part structure should play an important role in a generic shape model used in perceptual grouping. Moreover, it appears that to express this part structure, we will need more powerful shape models than those that can be provided by local Markov models of contour.

This section addresses two issues. First, we show evidence that convexity plays a role in grouping behind an occluder (amodal completion). Second, we show data that cannot be explained using only Markov contour models, and argue that generic models of shape need to be more powerful to explain human performance. Specifically we suggest that they should also capture the part structure of objects. This section summarizes work described in more detail in Liu, Jacobs, and Basri, (1999, 2000).

To begin, let's consider how the Markov model of shape discussed above might predict the strength of amodal completion. If the two regions are joined behind the occluder, there must be some portion of object boundary joining them. We will refer to curves that can join the two regions as *connecting curves* (see Figure 13). We can hypothesize that the likelihood that possible connecting curves come from the boundary of an object determines the strength of this grouping. If this likelihood is determined using our previous Markov model based on the curve of least energy, then the *energy model* predicts that the lower the energy of the connecting curves, the stronger a grouping. Exact predictions would require a choice of specific parameters of the model, but we will use stimuli in our experiments in

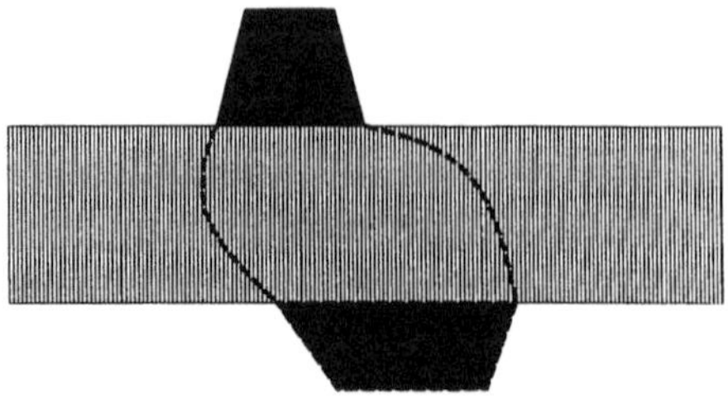

Figure 13. Two elements are separated by a possible occluder. The dashed curves indicate two possible *connecting curves* joining them.

which the predictions are the same for any parameters.

A second model, due to Kellman and Shipley, (1991), can also be applied to predict strength of amodal completion in this case. They call two line segments *relatable* if they can be joined by a connecting curve that has no inflections and that curves by less than ninety degrees. What we will call the relatability model predicts that amodal completion will be stronger when the portions of the region boundary that need to be joined together are relatable. This is similar to the energy model in favoring connecting curves that tend to have less curvature, although the details of how this is done are different. It is also different in disallowing inflections, which are the transitions from convexity to concavity on a contour. This partially captures the idea that convexity should play a role in amodal completion.

Convexity and Amodal Completion

In a first set of experiments, we explore whether convexity has an effect on the strength of amodal completion that these two models cannot predict. To do this, we need a method for judging this strength. We use a stereoacuity task. In this task, stereo is used to place an occluding rectangle in front of the top and bottom regions. These regions are each planar and fronto-parallel. The subject's task is to judge whether these two planar regions are also coplanar, or whether they are slightly displaced in depth. We hypothesize that when the two regions are strongly grouped this will create a bias to perceive them as coplanar. We expect this to be true because we expect that a prior model of 3D shape will suggest that a single object often has planar parts, biasing the subject to discount as noise slight deviations from coplanarity. When the two regions are perceived as coming from two different objects, this bias disappears, as our model of shape does not include the supposition that distinct objects have coplanar regions. Mitchison and Westheimer, (1984) describe related experiments that show that connecting two vertical bars makes discriminating depth differences between them more difficult, although they offer a different sort of explanation for this. Yin, Kellman, and Shipley (1996) also present a related paradigm.

In our experiments, subjects are presented with two such stimuli side by side, as shown in

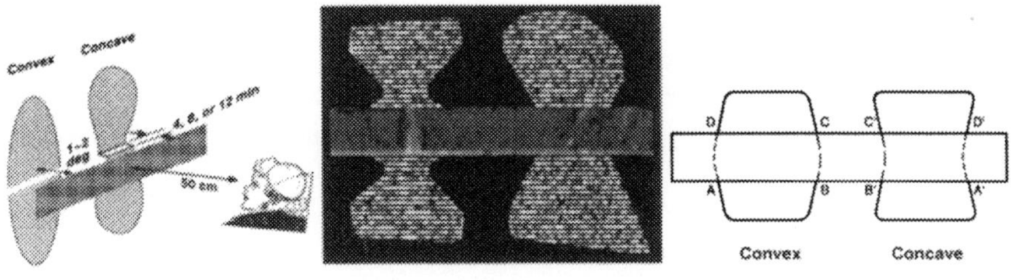

Figure 14. Left: schematic illustration of the experiment. The subject viewed the stimulus in stereo. Middle: example stimulus. The horizontal bar in the middle is the occluder and is closest to the subject. The configuration on the left is called convex, because the simplest completion behind the occluder forms two convex boundary curves. The one on the right is called concave. Right: illustration schematic of contour completion behind the occluder. In this illustration, contour segments AD are identical to $A'D'$, and BC identical to $B'C'$. This example illustrates the condition in which the contour completions for the convex and concave configurations are identical. The example in the middle illustrates another condition, in which the contour completions for the convex configuration are less smooth (curvature > *90* degrees) than the concave (curvature < *90* degrees).

Figure 14. On one side, the separated regions are coplanar, and on the other they are displaced in depth. The subject is required to detect which pair are coplanar. Further details are discussed in Liu, Jacobs, and Basri, (1999).

In one experiment, we test the hypothesis that perceptual grouping impedes stereoacuity. In these experiments, the shapes of the regions on the left and right are identical. However, in one case, the "occluder" was shrunk so that a gap was visible between it and the regions, or the occluder was pushed to the background, so that it could not actually function as an occluder, and the top and bottom regions could not be connected. When grouping was prohibited in this way, stereoacuity did indeed improve, suggesting that stronger grouping inhibited coplanarity judgement.

Next, we use this method to judge the effect of convexity on grouping strength. In Figure 14 on the right we show two sets of groups in which the connecting contours joining the regions have the same possible shapes. The difference is that in one set, the connecting curves are convex, while in the other they are concave. The relatability and energy models treat convex and concave curves as the same, since they do not distinguish which side of the curve is figure and which side is background. Therefore, they cannot predict differential performance on these stimuli.

In a third experiment, we made the change in angle required to connect the convex curves even greater than that required for the concave curves (Figure 14, middle). In this case, the convex connections are not relatable, and require greater curvature, so that both the relatability and energy models will predict that the concave pair will be more strongly joined.

In fact, in both cases, subjects found it more difficult to identify a displacement in depth for the convex pairs, revealing a bias to see the regions that can be joined convexly as coplanar. We infer that these convex connections lead to stronger grouping, showing that convexity does indeed play a role in amodal completion. This effect of convexity is not captured by the possible presence of inflection points, since none of the connecting curves require inflections. We also performed control experiments, in which the same shaped regions were used but grouping on both sides was disrupted by placing the occluder behind the regions. In this case, the difference in stereoacuity between the convex and concave pairs disappeared.

Convexity Beyond Local Shape Methods

These experiments suggest that convexity plays a role in amodal completion. But they do not show whether the effects of convexity can be captured by a local shape model that is a variation on the ones that we have tested. As we discussed, a local shape model can take account of convexity. To do this, the model must represent which side of the curve is figure, and which side is background. But once this is done, a model can penalize local regions that are concave. This expresses a prior that objects will tend to have contours that are more often convex than concave. Such local models could explain all the results we have so far discussed. Moreover, they can predict any results in which convex connections are favored over non-convex ones.

But it is possible to identify effects that cannot be captured by local contour models, but that can be explained by relationships related to convexity. In Jacobs, (1989), we suggest that convexity plays a role in grouping because objects are often composed of convex parts (Hoffman and Richards, 1984, originally stressed the significance of the convex part structure of objects, while Kanizsa and Gerbino, 1976, had shown its importance in figure-ground determination). For objects composed of the union of convex parts, one can distinguish between different sorts of convexity relationships between contour fragments, based on how these fragments might be related within the same object. For example, if two regions can be joined together into a single convex part, we call this a type I convexity relation. This is just the standard notion of convexity. If regions cannot be joined convexly, but could come from overlapping convex parts of the same object, we call this type II convexity. A third relationship, called type III, occurs when regions can only come from the same object if an intermediate, unseen convex part connects them. Jacobs, (1989), predicts that regions with a lower type relationship will group together more strongly. In addition, we can introduce a convexity relationship intermediate between type I and type II, which we call type I.5, in which one region could come from a convex protrusion on another.

We can make these relationships more precise in terms of the convex extension of each region (see Figure 15). This extension is the portion of the figure that the region might occupy if we extend it without introducing concavities. We can view this as the most likely location for the rest of the part, assuming convexity. Yin, Kellman and Shipley, (1997),

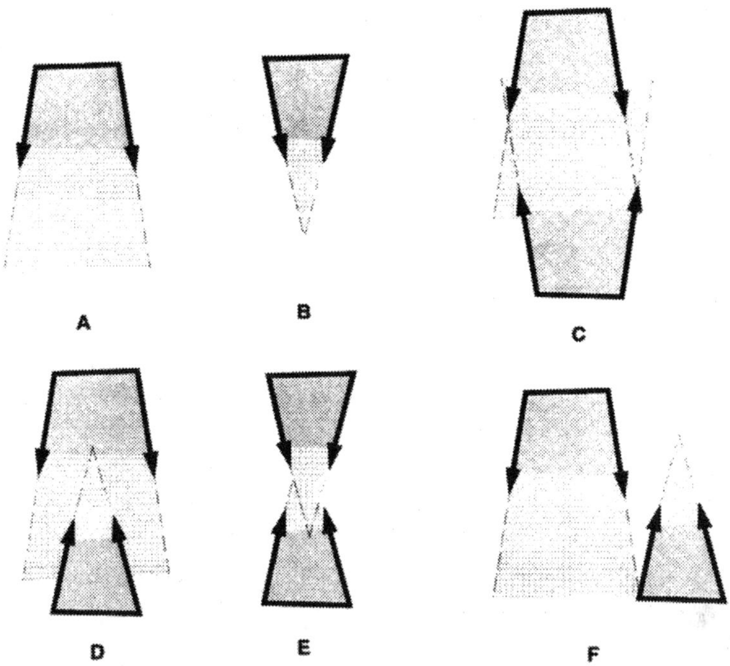

Figure 15. In Figures A and B, the cross-hatched region illustrates the convex extension of an element, the largest convex region containing that element. C shows two elements with a type I convexity relation, in which each element's endpoints are contained in the convex extension of the other. D illustrates a type I.5 relationship, in which only one element's endpoints lie in the convex extension of the other. E shows a type II relationship, in which the convex extensions intersect and the regions can be adjacent convex parts, and F shows a type III relationship.

discuss how these types of extensions can play a role in grouping regions that have visible boundaries with regions visible through a hole, so their boundaries cannot be seen. Here we focus on the suggestion of Jacobs, (1989), that these extensions play a role in grouping when two regions have visible boundaries. One might suppose that regions with a lower type relationship group together more strongly in part because the likely position of their occluded portions more strongly coincide.

Type relationships allow predictions that cannot be made using a model of shape that looks only at small local portions of the contour at one time. To see this, consider the region pairs in Figure 16. On the left, two regions have a type III relationship. In the center, they have a type II relationship. The right pair has a type I.5 relationship. So the convexity model predicts better grouping for the regions on the right, then the center, then the left. However, the possible connecting curves of all pairs are identical, even taking account of the convexity of local portions of contour.

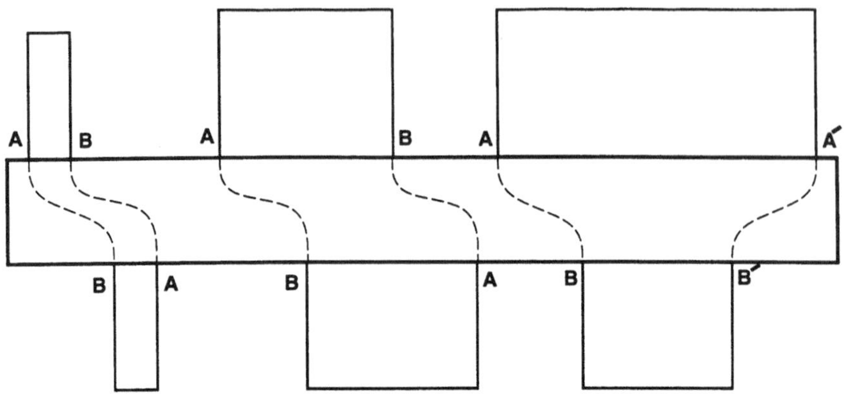

Figure 16. This illustration shows three pairs of regions. For each pair, the regions can form a surface if the left-most lines are connected to each other, and the right most lines are connected. Every pair of lines contains exactly the same geometric relation. Each line labeled A is displaced from the corresponding line labeled B in exactly the same way. So the set of possible connecting curves from each A to the corresponding B is the same (A' and B' have the same relationship, reflected). However, the pairs have different types of convexity relationships. The pair on the left is type III, in the center is type II, and on the right is type I.5.

Experimentally, we find that in stimuli of this sort, subjects do have a harder time judging non-coplanarity when regions have a type I.5 relationship than when they have a type II relationship. We also find that such regions with a type II relationship group together more strongly than those with a type III relationship. This suggests that convexity does indeed play a role in grouping that is not captured by local shape models. Note that in Figure 16 the pair of regions on the right is perfectly symmetric. This was not the case in the actual experiments. Liu, Jacobs, and Basri, (1999, 2000), discuss details of the experiments, including more detailed discussion of the difference between the three sets of stimuli and other possible explanations for the grouping we observed.

It has been our goal in this section to show that convexity plays a role in grouping. Moreover, one cannot simply say that completions with convex contours are preferred over completions with concave ones. Rather, a variety of convexity relationships play a role in grouping, and these relationships depend on the shape of regions, not just of the contours that can connect them. It therefore remains a challenge to us to show how we can formulate precise generic models that capture this, perhaps based on a description of objects as often composed of convex parts, and to imbed these generic models in neurally plausible algorithms.

CONCLUSION

In this chapter we have presented a view that many perceptual organization problems are solved by a process of generic object recognition. In this view, humans fit a model of objects that captures generalities about shape to the available data in the image. The image is decomposed in a way that provides the best fit between the model and the image data. The key problems of perceptual organization, then, are the same as the key problems of object recognition: How do we represent our knowledge of objects? and How do we efficiently align these representations with clues about object location found in the image?

We suggest that generic representations of shape are determined by three principles. First, the representation should capture the properties of 3-D shapes. For example, shapes are volumes bounded by surfaces. And shapes are often composed of parts that are largely convex. Second, the representation should focus on those properties that are preserved under projection to 2D, or at least in which 2D image properties can be used to infer the presence of relevant 3D properties. Indeed we find that many Gestalt properties are invariant to viewpoint. Third, the representation should be built up from small, easily handled chunks of the image. In fact, we find that Gestalt properties are based on minimal viewpoint invariants, and therefore use the fewest number of possible features. Some properties, such as good continuation can be modeled using simple Markov models of shape that we show facilitate efficient computation. Other relationships involve a small number of image units that are not spatially local. For example the types of convexity that we have discussed are based on the relationship between two parts of the object. Parallelism is based on pairs of lines. Pairwise relationships like these may also be handled with computational efficiency. Therefore, these three principles seem sufficient to determine many properties that play a role in grouping.

These principles, along with an overriding view of perceptual organization as generic object recognition do not constitute a theory. They are just an approach, within which one can attempt to formulate specific theories. Moreover, all of these principles have played a role in previous work on perception. Our goal in this paper is to articulate the connections between them, and to show concrete ways in which this viewpoint points towards certain problems as the most pressing ones. In particular, we need to understand what possible representations of shape are expressive enough to capture the information about objects that people actually use in perceptual organization, while also being manageable computationally.

ACKNOWLEDGMENTS

Clearly the viewpoints expressed here have been strongly influenced by a number of other researchers, including especially my collaborators Ronen Basri, Zili Liu, and Lance Williams, and other members of the NEC vision group, including Tao Alter, James Elder, John Oliensis, and Karvel Thornber. Lance has especially been a key influence in developing my views on perceptual organization, and many of the views that I express here I owe to our conversations. Irv Biederman also played an important role in helping me develop my views on minimal viewpoint invariants.

REFERENCES

Alter, T., & Basri, R. (1997). Extracting salient curves from images: an analysis of the saliency network. *International Journal of Computer Vision, 27, 1*, 51-69.

Biederman, I. (1985). Human Image Understanding: Recent Research and a Theory. *Computer Graphics, Vision, and Image Processing, 32*, 29-73.

Biederman, I. (1987). Recognition-by-components: a theory of human image understanding. *Psychological Review, 94, 2*, 115-147.

Binford, T. (1971). Visual perception by computer. *IEEE Conference on Systems and Control.*

Blake, A. & Zisserman, A. (1987). *Visual Reconstruction.* MIT Press, Cambridge, Mass.

Brady, M., & Grimson, W E L. (1981). The perception of subjective contours. Technical report, Massachusetts Institute of Technology, 1981.

Cutting, J. (1986). *Perception with an Eye for Motion.* Cambridge, MA: MIT Press.

Elder, J., & Zucker, S. (1994). A Measure of Closure. *Vision Research, 34, 24*, 3361-3370.

Field, D., Hayes, A., & Hess, R. (1993). Contour integration by the human visual system: evidence for a local "association field". *Vision Research, 33, 2*, 173-193.

Geman, S., & Geman, D. (1984). Stochastic relaxation, gibbs distributions, and the bayesian restoration of images. *IEEE Transactions on Pattern Analysis and Machine Intelligence, 6*, 721-741.

Grenander, U. (1981). *Lectures in Pattern Theory.* Springer-Verlag.

Grossberg, S., & Mingolla, E. (1985). Neural dynamics of form perception: boundary completion, illusory figures, and neon color spreading. *Psychological Review, 92*, 173-211.

Heitger, R., & von der Heydt, R. (1993). A computational model of neural contour processing, figure-ground segregation and illusory contours. *Internal Conference Computer Vision*, 32-40.

Hoffman, D. & Richards, W. (1984). Parts of Recognition. S. Pinker, (Ed), *Visual Cognition.* Cambridge, MA: MIT Press.

Horn, B K P. (1981). The curve of least energy. Technical report, Massachusetts Institute of Technology.

Jacobs, D. (1989). Grouping for recognition. MIT AI Memo 1177.

Jacobs, D. (forthcoming). What makes viewpoint invariant properties perceptually salient?

Kanizsa, G. (1979). *Organization in Vision.* New York, NY: Praeger.

Kanizsa, G., & Gerbino, W. (1976). Convexity and Symmetry in Figure-Ground Organization. M. Henle, (Ed), *Vision and Artifact*. New York, Springer Publishing Company.

Kellman, P.J., & Shipley, T F. (1991). A theory of visual interpolation in object perception. *Cognitive Psychology, 23*, 141-221.

Köhler, W. (1929). *Gestalt Psychology*. New York, NY: Liveright.

Kovacs, I., & Julesz, B. (1993). A Closed Curve is Much More than an Incomplete One: Effect of Closure in Figure-Ground Segmentation. *Proc. Nat. Acad. Sci., USA, 90*, 7495-7497.

Kumaran, K., Geiger, D., & Gurvits, L. (1996). Illusory surfaces. *Network: Computation in Neural Systems, 7*.

Leyton, M. (1986). A theory of information structure II. A theory of perceptual organization. *Journal of Mathematical Psychology, 30*, 257-305.

Liu, Z., Jacobs, D., & Basri, R. (1999). The Role of Convexity in Perceptual Completion. *Vision Research, 39*, 4244-4257.

Liu, Z., Jacobs, D., & Basri, R. (2000). Convexity in Perceptual Completion. In *Perceptual Organization for Artificial Vision Systems*, edited by K. Boyer and S. Sarkar, Kluwer Academic Publishers, 73-90.

Lowe, D. (1985). *Perceptual Organization and Visual Recognition*, The Netherlands: Kluwer Academic Publishers.

Marr, D. (1982). *Vision*. San Francisco: W.H. Freeman and Company.

Mitchison, G.J. & Westheimer, A. (1984). The perception of depth in simple figures. *Vision Research, 24*, 1063-1073.

Mumford, D. (1994). Elastica and Computer Vision. C. Bajaj (Ed), *Algebraic Geometry and its Applications*, Bajaj. New York: Springer-Verlag.

Mumford, D. & Shah, J. (1985). Boundary detection by minimizing functionals, I, *Proc. IEEE Conf. on Computer Vision & Pattern Recognition.*

Nitzburg, M. & Mumford, D. (1990). The 2.1-D sketch. *International Conference on Computer Vision*, 138-144.

Palmer, S. (1983). The psychology of perceptual organization: a transformational approach. In J. Beck, B. Hope, and A. Rosenfeld (Eds.), *Human and Machine Vision*. New York: Academic Press.

Pomerantz, J.R., & Kubovy, M. (1986). Theoretical Approaches to Perceptual Organization. In K.R. Boff, L. Kaufmann, & J.P. Thomas (Eds.), *Handbook of perception and human performance: Vol. II. Cognitive processes and performance* (pp. 36.1-36.46). New York: Wiley.

Ramachandran, V., Ruskin, D., Cobb, S., Rogers-Ramachandran, D., & Tyler, C. (1994). On the perception of illusory contours. *Vision Research, 34, 23*, 3145-3152.

Roberts, L. (1966). Machine perception of three-dimensional solid objects. *Optical and*

Electro-optical Information Processing, edited by J. Tippett, Cambridge, MA: MIT Press.

Rock. I., & Anson, R. (1979). Illusory contours as the solution to a problem. *Perception. 8*, 665-681.

Sambin, M. (1974). Angular margins without gradients. *Italian Journal of Psychology, 1*, 355-361.

Shashua, A., & Ullman, S. (1988). Structural saliency: The detection of globally salient structures using a locally connected network. *2nd Intl. Conf. on Computer Vision*, 321-327.

Shipley, T., & Kellman, P. (1992). Strength of visual interpolation depends on the ratio of physically specified to total edge length. *Perception and Psychophysics, 52, 1*, 97-106.

Thornber, K. & Williams, L. (1997). Characterizing the Distribution of Completion Shapes with Corners Using a Mixture of Random Processes. *Int. Workshop on Energy Minimization Methods in Computer Vision and Pattern Recognition*, 19-34.

Thornber, K. & Williams, L. (1998). Orientation, scale and discontinuity as emergent properties of illusory contour shape. *Neural Information Processing Systems (NIPS).*

Ullman, S. (1976). Filling-in the gaps: The shape of subjective contours and a model for their generation. *Biological Cybernetics, 25*, 1-6.

Van der Helm, P., & Leeuwenberg, E. (1996). Goodness of visual regularities: a nontransformational approach. *Psychological Review, 103, 3*, 429-456.

Wagemans, J. (1999). Toward a better approach to goodness: comment on Van der Helm and Leeuwenberg (1996). *Psychological Review, 106, 3*, 610-621.

Wagemans, J., Van Gool, L., & d'Ydewalle, G. (1991). Detection of symmetry in tachistoscopically presented dot patterns: effects of multiple axes and skewing. *Perception and Psychophysics, 50, 5*, 413-427.

Wagemans, J., Van Gool, L., Swinnen, V., & Van Horebeek, J.(1993). Higher-order structure in regularity detection. *Vision Research, 33, 8*, 1067-1088.

Williams, L., & Hanson, A. (1996). Perceptual completion of occluded surfaces. *Computer Vision and Image Understanding, 64*, 1-20.

Williams, L., & Jacobs, D. (1997a). Stochastic Completion Fields: A Neural Model of Illusory Contour Shape and Salience. *Neural Computation, 9*, 837--858.

Williams, L., & Jacobs, D. (1997b). Local Parallel Computation of Stochastic Completion Fields. *Neural Computation, 9*, 859-881.

Yin, C., Kellman, P. J., & Shipley, T. F. (1996). Surface completion influences depth discrimination. *ARVO Abstracts. Investigative Ophthalmology & Visual Science*, volume 37.

Yin, C., Kellman, P.J., & Shipley, T.F. (1997). Surface completion complements boundary interpolation in the visual integration of partly occluded objects. *Perception, 26*, 1459-1479.

Zhu, S. (1999). Embedding Gestalt Laws in the Markov Random Fields. *IEEE Transactions on Pattern Analysis and Machine Intelligence, 21, 11*, 1170-1187.

Zweck, J., & Williams, L. (2000). Euclidean Group Invariant Computation of Stochastic Completion Fields Using Shiftable-Twistable Functions. *European Conference on Computer Vision.*

From Fragments to Objects – Segmentation and Grouping in Vision
T.F. Shipley and P.J. Kellman (Editors)

11

SIMPLICITY, REGULARITY, AND PERCEPTUAL INTERPRETATIONS: A STRUCTURAL INFORMATION APPROACH

Rob Van Lier, NICI, University of Nijmegen, PO Box 9104, 6500 HE Nijmegen, The Netherlands

Upon opening our eyes we start interpreting our visual surrounding. Within a fraction of a second, the light falling on the retinae is transformed into an understandable world. This output of the visual system is so convincing that it can easily be confused with the thing that is perceived, but in fact it is nothing more than a reflection of it. Notwithstanding this basic uncertainty, we mostly agree on what we perceive. On the whole it appears that -- although each visual pattern can be interpreted in many different ways -- just one specific interpretation is preferred. In the history of visual science, students of perception have searched for organizational grouping principles that determine how an arbitrary visual pattern is interpreted. The notion of simplicity advocated in this chapter attempts to combine various aspects of perceptual grouping within one framework and is a central issue within the Structural Information Theory (SIT), initiated by Leeuwenberg (1969, 1971) and further developed since then. In this chapter, a brief introduction to the notion of simplicity and SIT's regularity based quantifications is given. Furthermore, applications of SIT to various stimulus domains (series, surfaces, objects) are illustrated.

FROM PRÄGNANZ TO SIMPLICITY

In perception research, consideration of simplicity can be traced back to the early Gestalt psychologists (e.g. Wertheimer, 1912; Köhler, 1920; Koffka, 1935). To predict perceived interpretations of visual patterns, these psychologists formulated various so-called Gestalt laws, such as good continuation, closure, and proximity. It appeared, however, to be virtually impossible to predict which rule applies to what pattern. Moreover, there was no a priori hierarchy between the separate laws: in principle, each law could overrule -- or could be overruled by -- another law. In order to cope with these problems, Koffka (1935) formulated the law of Prägnanz. This law can be regarded as an attempt to integrate the Gestalt laws, and stresses an overall tendency toward "good" forms. Nevertheless, even on the basis of this general law, predictions of perceived interpretations could hardly be made, as no clear specifications were provided. An important step forward was the formulation of the global-minimum principle by Hochberg and McAlister (1953). The global-minimum principle states that for a given pattern its simplest possible interpretation will be perceived. Hatfield and Epstein (1985) made a distinction between three types of simplicity: procedural simplicity, phenomenal simplicity, and descriptive simplicity. Procedural simplicity requires that the preferred interpretation is attained by the most economical process. The notion of phenomenal simplicity endorses the idea that the preferred interpretation contains a maximum of regularity. Finally, the notion of descriptive simplicity states that the description of the preferred interpretation is as compact as possible. The above notions do not exclude each other. Actually, the latter two are more or less integrated in the claim within SIT that the simplest description reflects the interpretation with the highest degree of regularity. Hatfield and Epstein (1985) further remarked that the global-minimum principle is an empty concept if it does not have an operationalization, that is, it needs a measure of simplicity. Indeed, in order to test the global-minimum principle, a quantifiable measure of simplicity is required (cf. Boselie & Leeuwenberg, 1986).

Quantification of simplicity

Formalization of regularity. Several descriptive systems, or coding systems, have been proposed by various scientists (e.g. Simon & Kotovsky, 1963; Vitz, 1966; Vitz & Todd, 1969; Leeuwenberg, 1969, 1971; Restle, 1979, 1982; Jones & Zamostny, 1975; Deutsch & Feroe, 1981). Although not all coding systems were designed for visual patterns, each of them transposes a pattern into a symbolic representation. Within SIT, a visual pattern is represented by a symbol series referring to, for example, lengths and angles in the contour of a visual pattern. Then, by means of coding rules, the initial series can be reduced to a shorter series or code. This reduction proceeds by extracting as much regularity as possible from an initial series. These regularities are based on identities between the elements in the symbol series.

Theoretical considerations (Van der Helm, 1988; Van der Helm & Leeuwenberg, 1991; Van der Helm & Leeuwenberg, 1996) have led to a formalization of the concept of regularity, which, in turn, affected the quantification of simplicity. The starting point of this formalization is the concept of accessibility, stating that appropriate coding rules are characterized by so-called holographic regularity and transparent hierarchy. Holographic regularities are regularities constituted by identity structures in which all substructures express the same kind of regularity. As a consequence, the structure of the regularity is invariant under growth (e.g., a repetition is a holographic regularity because it can be expanded by adding additional elements, preserving its repetition character). The concept of transparent hierarchy holds that different regularities can be combined only if their groupings are hierarchically compatible, i.e., the grouping by one regularity builds on the grouping by the other regularity. These concepts are extensively discussed and clarified in Van der Helm and Leeuwenberg (1991) and Van der Helm, Van Lier, and Leeuwenberg (1992), and Van der Helm (2000). Considering all possible regularities in a pattern, it appears that only a few regularities possess the qualities of holography and transparency (Van der Helm & Leeuwenberg, 1991). These regularities form the kernel of the set of coding rules that have been used since SIT's conception (Leeuwenberg, 1969; 1971), namely Iteration, Symmetry, and Alternation (e.g., the symbol series aaaa can be encoded into 4*(a) by means of the Iteration rule; the series abba into S[(a)(b)] by the Symmetry rule; and the series akal into <(a)>/<(k)(l)> by the Alternation rule). In addition, Van der Helm and Leeuwenberg (1986, 1991) showed that, by means of the concept of accessibility plus a mathematical technique called the shortest path method, the simplest code can be found without generating each and every possible code separately. SIT's basic concepts of holographic regularity and transparent hierarchy provide a coherent approach to the problem of defining regularity. Until the development of the concept of accessibility, the transformational approach, based on mathematical Group theory, was the only formalism available to specify kinds of regularity. The latter approach has been applied to phenomena of perceptual organization by various researchers (cf., Garner, 1974; Palmer, 1991). By that approach, regularity is assessed by groups of transformations that leave a visual pattern invariant. Van der Helm and Leeuwenberg (1996) compared the transformational approach and the formalization of regularity as specified within SIT. The authors concluded that with respect to repetition the two approaches hardly differ from each other, whereas they differ essentially with respect to symmetry. For example, within the transformational approach, mirror symmetry is an all-or-nothing property, whereas within SIT it is a graded property as it is represented in a point-by-point fashion (a difference which can be related to various phenomena such as noise insensitivity in symmetric dot patterns). Furthermore, the authors related the difference between repetition and symmetry to so-called 'objectness', comprising a more dominant role of repetition in the case of multiple objects and a more dominant role of symmetry in the case of a single object (cf. Baylis & Driver, 1995). Another example on which the holographic and the SIT approach differ is the perceived goodness of symmetric patterns. Whereas according to the transformational approaches, a 3-fold symmetry would result in a better pattern than a 2-fold symmetry, the SIT approach does not predict a simple increase in perceived goodness (and would actually predict the opposite in this particular case, see Van der Helm and Leeuwenberg, 1996). Van der Helm and Leeuwenberg (1996) found some scattered evidence that supported their predictions. Since SIT and the transformational approach make diverging predictions about a number of perceptual phenomena, the relative merits of the two theories should soon be evident.

Information load. Before the accessibility criterion was incorporated into SIT, several measures of Structural Information were considered. The measure that was most commonly used was meant to reflect the amount of memory space needed for the storage of a given code. Roughly all parameters and operations in a structural code were counted to determine the amount of Structural Information. Van der Helm et al. (1992) argued, however, that this measure was conceptually troublesome as incomparable entities contributed to the complexity of that code (see also Hatfield & Epstein, 1985). In addition, our view is that the semantic implication of a code (i.e., an interpretation) should not be judged on the basis of the required memory space but, in psychologically more meaningful way, on the basis of the semantic content of the code, i.e., the description of regularity. The accessibility criterion, mentioned above, paved the way to a better-defined information load. This new information load considers all parameters at all hierarchical levels in a structural code. To exemplify such hierarchical codes consider the minimum codes of the symbol series 'ababab' and 'abcab', being '3*(ab)' and 'S[(ab),(c)]', respectively. The information load of the first code equals 3: 'a' and 'b', and the group 'ab', which is considered as a parameter at a higher code level. The second code yields an information load of 4: 'a', 'b', 'c', and the group 'ab' (by means of contrast, the latter encoding can be compared with the encoding of the series 'abcba' into S([(a)(b),(c)], with the parameters 'a', 'b', and 'c', having an information load of 3). An algorithm has been developed that can achieve the code with the lowest information load, given an initial series (PISA; Van der Helm, 1988).

As an example of how the information load can be used to predict perceived organization, let us consider a case of perceptual grouping in serial patterns. In Van der Helm et al. (1992), subjects had to indicate their preferred organization of a symbol series, by way of a paired-comparison (see Figure 1A). Two possible organizations of the series were given by means of a grouping of symbols (Figures 1B and 1C). While the black and white dots in A can be represented by the series 'ababb', the groupings shown in B and C reveal specific encodings of that series, i.e. '2*(ab) b', and 'S[(a),(b)] 2*(b)', respectively. According to the information measure outlined above, the I-load of the first code equals 4 (based on the parameters 'a', 'b', another 'b' and the group 'ab'), whereas the I-load of the second code equals 3 (based on the parameters 'a', 'b', and another 'b'). On the basis of this difference, the latter

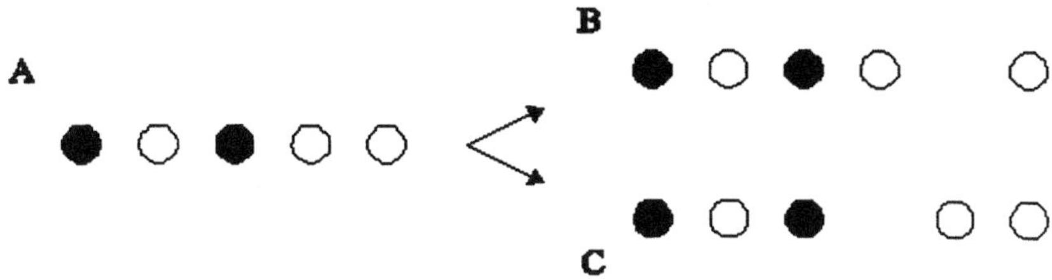

Figure 1. Two possible groupings within a symbol series (A). Generally C is preferred to B, which agrees with SIT.

organization is predicted to be preferred (which, in fact, was in line with the actual preferences). Notice that if all parameters and operators contributed to the information load, the prediction would be reversed; in this case the I-loads would be 4 and 5, respectively. Notice further that the new information load, by way of accounting for descriptive hierarchy, generally favors clustering in smaller units.

Obviously, the minimum code does not necessarily express all identities in a pattern. This is a consequence of the specific coding language, which allows only specific combinations of regularities within one code. This 'underspecification' might be considered (at first glance) as a drawback of the coding system. However, it should be realized that demanding the description of all identities within one code would result in mere template codes without any classification implications. As a matter of fact, the description of subsets of identities is essential for the classification of patterns (cf. Collard & Buffart, 1983). Yet, nondescribed identities may have a perceptual role as well, as their description allows alternative interpretations of the same pattern. For example, the series 'aaba' can be encoded into 'aS[a,b]', expressing the identity of the second and fourth element, and into '2*(a)ba', expressing the identity of the first and second element. In neither case are all possible identities accounted for. Because of this "incompleteness", Collard and Buffart (1983) suggested that identities which remain unexpressed in the minimum code are expressed in complementary codes revealing different interpretations of the same pattern. The perceptual relevance of such alternative codes has been demonstrated in various experiments on the salience of pattern interpretations (Mens & Leeuwenberg, 1988). The rivalry between different interpretations leads us to the following topic.

Diversity and integration by simplicity

Local versus global completions. In line with the minimum principle, it is assumed that the perceptual system generates multiple interpretations and that the simplest one is selected. Herbart (1850) already suggested such a competition between different interpretations. According to Herbart the dominant percept may vary in strength, depending on the attractiveness of the competing interpretations. We will illustrate this rivalry by means of some research in the amodal completion domain. When looking around we notice that objects usually occlude parts of themselves and parts of other objects. In those cases, the perceptual system seems to complete the occluded part. Two completion tendencies are often distinguished, namely local and global tendencies. Local completions merely depend on local shape characteristics at regions of occlusion (e.g., Kellman & Shipley, 1991; Wouterlood & Boselie, 1992). Global completions take into account global figural regularities, such as symmetry or repetition (e.g., Buffart, Leeuwenberg & Restle, 1981). In Van Lier, Van der Helm, and Leeuwenberg (1995) and Van Lier, Leeuwenberg and Van der Helm (1995), we focussed on both local and global completion tendencies. In these studies, patterns were examined for which the local completion tendency proceeded by means of linear continuation of the occluding contours (i.e., the completion itself was as simple as possible), whereas the global completion tendency resulted in the most regular shape (i.e., the simplest completed shape). Patterns can be constructed for which, on the one hand, local and global strategies converge to the same shape and, on the other hand, local and global strategies diverge to different shapes. In Figure 2, an example is given of both type of patterns. Clearly, the latter type of patterns seem to be much more ambiguous than the former type of patterns.

In Van Lier, Van der Helm, and Leeuwenberg (1995), participants were asked to draw their spontaneous pattern interpretation, (like in, e.g., Buffart, Leeuwenberg, & Restle, 1981;

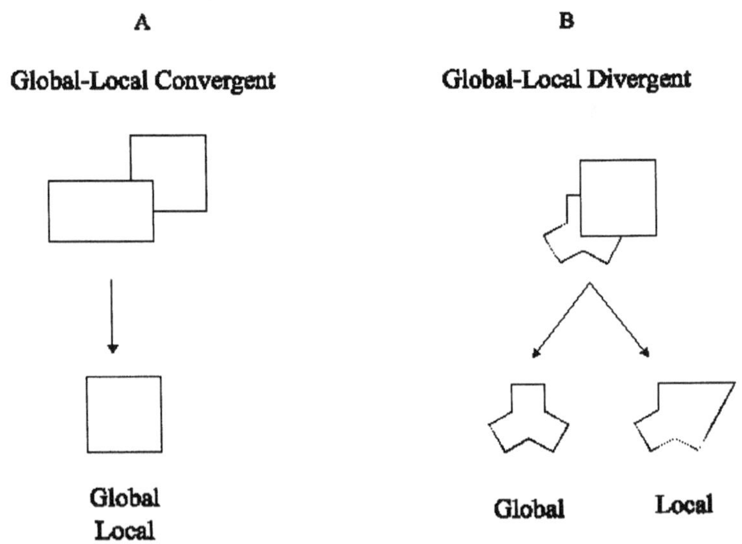

Figure 2. Two types of completion patterns. In A, Global and local strategies converge to the same completion. In B, Global and local strategies diverge to the different completions.

Boselie, 1988; Boselie & Wouterlood, 1989) whereas a second experiment concerned the simultaneous-matching task, partly adopted from Gerbino and Salmaso (1987). The results revealed an interdependency of the strengths of local and global completions and supported the notion that the preference for a specific completion is the outcome of a competition between these completions. Additionally, in Van Lier, Leeuwenberg, and Van der Helm (1995), converging evidence was found for the generation of multiple completions (using the so-called primed-matching paradigm; an experimental method which is based on the facilitating effect of a prime on the matching of a pair of representationally similar successive test items; see Beller, 1971; Sekuler & Palmer, 1992; Bruno, Bertamini, & Domini, 1997). Comparable results confirming the special status of local and global completions were obtained by Sekuler (1994) and Sekuler, Palmer and Flynn (1994).

On the one hand, these results demonstrated that a strict local approach to visual occlusion does not always correctly predict the perceived interpretations. On the other hand, some cases of local completion were evident, so the observed tendencies challenged SIT's simplicity approach. In the next section, I review SIT's integrative approach dealing with both local and global aspects.

SIT's integrative approach. In Van Lier, Van der Helm and Leeuwenberg (1994) we have argued that both the simplicity of the shapes and their relation with the pattern must be considered in determining the complexity of an interpretation. In our view, this relational aspect is of decisive importance in achieving an interpretation. To that end, a distinction was made between the memory complexity and the perceptual complexity of an interpretation. Whereas the memory complexity specifies the amount of information that is required to store an interpretation in memory, the perceptual complexity is based on the relationship between the pattern and its interpretation. The perceptual complexity can be considered as a selection criterion related to the difficulty of achieving a specific interpretation for a given visual pattern (as proposed in Van Lier et al., 1994). SIT's integrative approach is based on the observation that both local and global aspects jointly determine the perceptual complexity. These aspects are embedded in three different types of structure, indicated by the internal structure, the external structure, and the virtual structure, respectively. As outlined below, for each pattern interpretation the complexities of each of these structures can be determined in terms of structural information.

The internal structure of an interpretation deals with the perceived shapes themselves. To determine the complexity of the internal structure, the shape is mapped to a symbol series. Heuristically, this can be done by tracing the contour of the shape after having labeled all edges and angles such that equal edges and equal angles obtain equal symbols. Second, the symbol series is reduced by extracting the maximum amount of regularity from such a series. For example, a square can be represented by the symbol series, or primitive code, 'kakakaka' (with 'k' referring to, e.g., the edges and 'a' to the angles) which can be reduced by applying the Iteration rule (revealing '4*(ka)', with $I_{internal}$=3). In general it holds that the more regular the shapes are, the simpler is its description, and the lower the complexity of the internal structure (compare, for example, the primitive code of a rectangle which could be 'kalakala', revealing the minimal code: 2*(<(k)(l)>/<(a)>), with $I_{internal}$=4).

The external structure refers to the positional relation between the perceived shapes. The account of the external structure can be considered as related to Rock's avoidance-of-coincidence principle. Rock (1983), argued that the visual system seeks interpretations in which positional coincidences are avoided. As an example, consider Figure 2A once more. The preferred occluded-square interpretation can be explained on the basis of a tendency toward the simplest shape but one may also argue that the preferred interpretation avoids a coincidental meshing of borders as would, for example, be the case if there was no completion (i.e., the so-called 'mosaic' interpretation, in which an L-shape is adjacent to a rectangle). Notice that applying the avoidance-of-coincidence principle to the pattern in Figure 2B, does not reveal which completion (global or local) would be predicted to be preferred. The simplest-shape tendency and the avoidance-of-coincidence principle do not always lead to the same predictions. In Figure 3 (inspired by Kanizsa, 1985), for example, patterns A-C are all perceived as a black square occluding a second shape. The latter could be a regular octagon (D) or a more complex shape (E). Now, the preference for interpretation D appears to be weakest in pattern A and strongest in pattern C, leaving pattern B in an intermediate position. This phenomenological difference in completion strength seems to vary

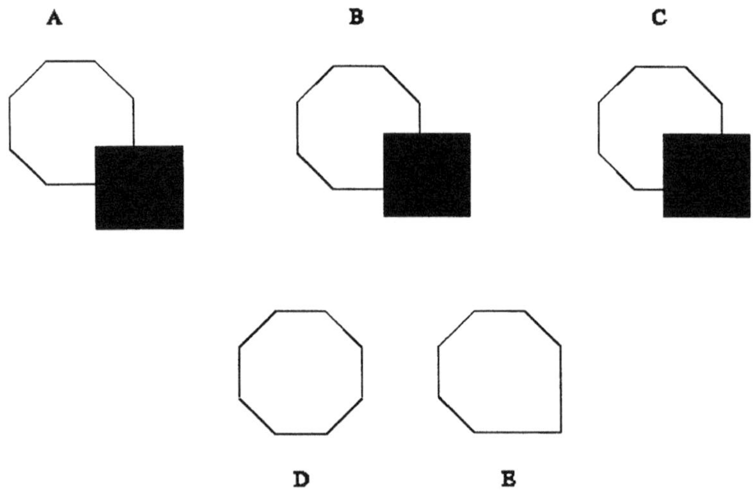

Figure 3. Patterns A-C can all be interpreted as a square occluding a second shape (as in D and E). Apparently, interpretation D is less prevalent in A and most prevalent in C, whereas for interpretation E the reverse holds. This agrees with the tendency to avoid coincidences between the contours of the shapes.

with the degree of coincidence between the location of the edges of the square and the location of the corners of the octagon (notice that the numbers of times the edges and corners are at the same location decreases going from A to C, see Van Lier, Van der Helm, & Leeuwenberg, 1995).

To illustrate the relationship between inter-object regularity and perceived (im)probability further, consider the following example. In Figure 4, four configurations of two matches are depicted as they may show up after a random throw. Many observers would rate the configurations on the left to be far more probable the result of a random throw, than the configurations on the right. In fact there is no such an unequivocal difference in probability of occurrence between these configurations. What differs, however, is that there are more configurations like A than there are like D. That is, the class of all 'A-like' configurations is much larger than the class of all 'D-like' configurations. The number of configurations within a class is determined by the regularities within that class. The more regular the positions, the smaller the class, the less likely a specific configuration seems to be the result of a random throw. In this example, the positional regularity between the matches can be conceived as a perceptual obstacle with respect to the two-matches interpretation. In Van Lier et al. (1994), $I_{external}$ was determined for various types of junctions and their dissociations (with respect to the configurations A-D of Figure 4, for example, $I_{external}$ would be 0, 1, 2 and 3, respectively). In general, it holds that the more coincidental is a specific junction between elements belonging to different objects, the higher is the complexity of the external structure (notice that this analysis is in line with the notion that connection between surfaces is a very powerful grouping factor, e.g., Saiki & Hummel, 1998; Van Lier & Wagemans, 1998).

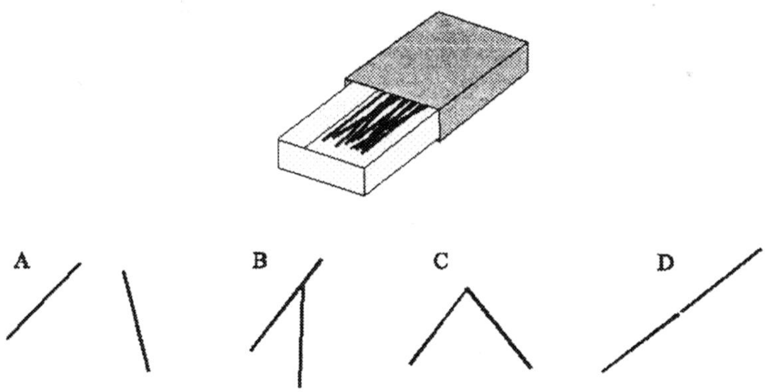

Figure 4. Four configurations of matches (e.g., after an arbitrary throw). The fact that there are more configurations like A than there are configurations like D explains the difference in perceived probability of occurrence. The perceived probability can be related directly to the regularity between the matches.

Finally, the virtual structure deals with the occluded (non-visible) parts of the perceived shapes. More specifically, it concerns the elements that are not present in the proximal stimulus, but are present in the interpretation of that stimulus. For the pattern in Figure 2B, the global completion has the simplest shape, yet seems to be disfavored because of the larger number of occluded structural elements (with regard to Figure 2B, for example, $I_{virtual}$ would be 5 for the global completion and 1 for the local completion). In Van Lier et al. (1994) and Van Lier, Van der Helm, and Leeuwenberg (1995) we have argued that the more structural elements of a specific surface interpretation are occluded, the less likely it is that the interpretation will be preferred.

So, resuming, regularities in the internal structure support a specific interpretation, whereas regularities in the external structure weaken that interpretation. Additionally, a specific completion is weakened by an increase in the complexity of the virtual structure. To a certain extent, $I_{internal}$, $I_{external}$, and $I_{virtual}$ correspond to three well-known tendencies in the domain of visual occlusion, namely the simplicity of shape, the avoidance of coincidence, and the good-continuation principle (the latter as far as completion is concerned). In Van Lier et al. (1994), we have tested the hypothesis that the sum of the perceptual complexities of the three structures, i.e. the total perceptual complexity (I_{total}) of the most preferred interpretation of a pattern is lower than that of any other interpretation of that same pattern. This was done on a set of 144 patterns stemming from different studies (Boselie, 1988; Boselie & Wouterlood, 1989; Buffart et al., 1981). It appeared that of these patterns the most preferred interpretation had the lowest $I_{internal}$ in 53% of all cases, the lowest $I_{external}$ in 65% of all cases, and the lowest $I_{virtual}$ in 49% of all cases. Only in 3% of all cases all three structures had the lowest complexity. However, I_{total} was the lowest for the most preferred interpretation in 95% of all cases. In Figure 5, various examples are given. The regions in the Venn-diagram diagram provide a way to classify completion patterns according to their most preferred completion tendencies in terms of the three separate structures. For example, for pattern A, only $I_{internal}$ would predict the most preferred interpretation correctly, whereas for pattern B, both $I_{internal}$ and $I_{external}$ would predict correctly, etc. It should be noted, however, that for each and every pattern the inter-pattern comparison on I_{total} determines the most preferred interpretation. Thus, for example, a high value for $I_{virtual}$ for a specific interpretation does not imply that this specific interpretation is unlikely (see also Van Lier, 2000). One may argue that the summation of the complexities is rather arbitrary and that possibly weighing factors could have been added. In Van Lier et al. (1994), however, we have shown that this simple summation of terms revealed good predictions (revealing an Ochamian parsimony-justification for this specific choice). Further on in this chapter (section 'simplicity versus likelihood'), an additional argument will be given in favor of the summation of the terms.

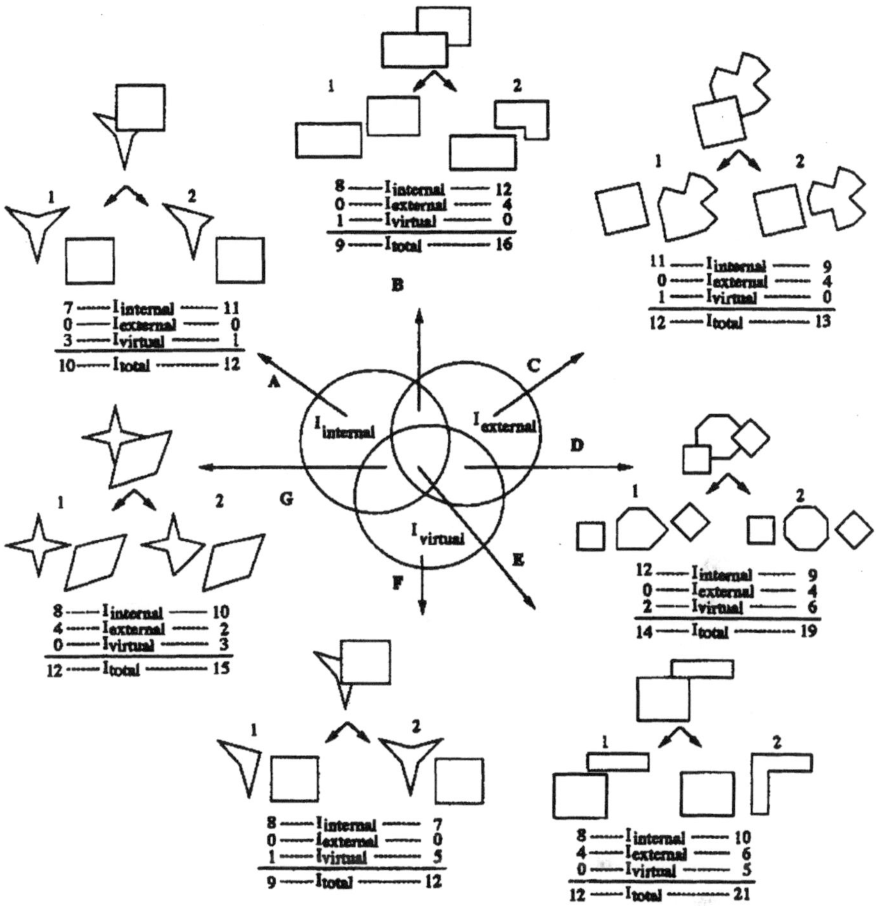

Figure 5. Various patterns with possible interpretations. The circles in the Venn-diagram indicate whether the complexity (I) for a specific structure (internal, external, virtual) is lowest for the most preferred interpretation (labeled with number 1). For each region an example is given. In each of these cases Itotal is lowest for the most preferred interpretation (adapted from Van Lier et al., 1994).

From 2D surfaces to 3D objects

SIT's structural descriptions are not restricted to series or surfaces but apply to 3D objects as well (e.g. Leeuwenberg 1971; Leeuwenberg & Van der Helm, 1991; Leeuwenberg, Van der Helm, and Van Lier, 1994; Van Lier, 1999a, Van Lier, Leeuwenberg, & Van der Helm, 1997; Van Lier & Wagemans, 1999). Again, in line with the notion of simplicity in visual shape, and in analogy with the implications on the previous domains, the simplest object description is predicted to be selected by the visual system. To illustrate SIT's object descriptions, consider Figure 6 (for a more detailed explanation see e.g. Leeuwenberg & Van der Helm, 1991).

The vase-like object (Figure 6A) can be described by means of two components: a circular component (O-shape) and an S-shaped component (S-shape). Now, moving the S-shape along the O-shape (Figure 6-A1), under a specific angle of connection between the two shapes, would mimic the contours of the vase. If, the other way around, the O-shape is moved along the S-shape, an S-shaped tube would evolve (Figure 6-B1). Notice that the vase could. in principle, also be reconstructed with, for example, the S-shape as path (Figure 6-A2). In such a case, however, the O-shape would have to vary its size while moving along the S-shape. Moreover, the angle of connection between the shapes would vary. Therefore, the latter description is much more complex and less preferable. In a similar way, the description depicted in Figure 6-B2 would be much less preferable. Within SIT, the component that serves as path in the simplest reconstruction is referred to as the superstructure (O-shape in Figure 6A, S-shape in Figure 6B), whereas the components that have to be moved along that path (S-shape in Figure 6A, O-shape in Figure 6B) are referred to as subordinate structures. This hierarchical relationship between descriptive components is a crucial aspect of SIT's

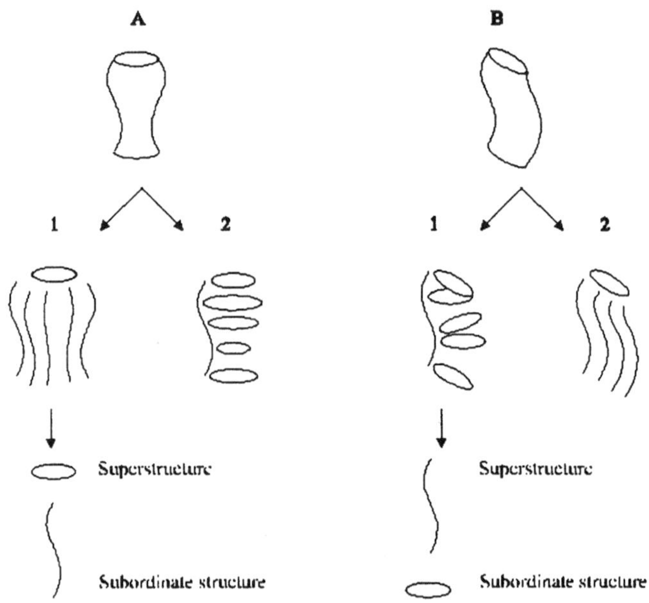

Figure 6. According to SIT, objects A and B can be described by the same components (an S-shape and an O-shape). For A, the simplest description is achieved when taking the O-shape as superstructure and the S-shape as subordinate structure (as in A1), whereas for B the situation is reversed (as in B1; see text).

object representations.

It is important to notice that the descriptive components in principle may have any possible shape, as long as they describe the object with a minimum of structural variation -- or stating it otherwise, with a maximum of structural constancy -- as possible. The descriptive components are therefore not given a priori but in fact stem from the simplest representation. Notice further that the super-subordinate assignment proceeds irrespective of the actual relative size of the components. These characteristics contrast with other structural description models, perhaps most noticeably with the Recognition By Components model (RBC; Biederman, 1987). In the latter approach, descriptive components of certain simple objects, called geons, are defined a priory by means of so-called nonaccidental properties (i.e., properties of the 2D projection that generally do not arise from projections of arbitrary oriented 3D objects). In Leeuwenberg et al. (1994), object classifications according to RBC and SIT were compared with each other. Whereas within RBC the selection of the internal axis of an object depends on metrical considerations (e.g., the direction of the longest elongation), within SIT such considerations do not play a role. Leeuwenberg et al. (1994) demonstrated that that judged similarities between objects largely rely on structural aspects, leaving a secondary, non-dominant, role for metrical aspects (more specifically it was shown that such judgements followed classifications based on constancy and symmetry of the descriptive parts rather than their size). Additionally, Van Lier et al. (1997) investigated whether the descriptive components at the superstructural level perceptually dominate the components at the subordinate level (i.e. the superstructure-dominance hypothesis, see also Leeuwenberg & Van der Helm, 1991). From the experiments, in which the primed matching paradigm (as in, e.g., Sekuler & Palmer, 1992) was used, it appeared that, amongst others, the matching of objects was facilitated much more if their superstructure was primed than if their subordinate structure was primed. We concluded that this supported the notion that there is an internal superstructure dominance, which can be assessed during the construction of an object representation. Other experiments (e.g., Van Bakel, 1989; see also Leeuwenberg & Van der Helm, 1991) have supplied converging evidence on the differential status of superstructures and subordinate structures. The results suggested that the perceived unity in visual stimuli primarily depends on the unity of the superstructure (more specifically, it appeared that a subdivision or segmentation in the superstructure affected unity judgements more strongly than a subdivision or segmentation in the subordinate structure did). Ongoing research aims at a further investigation of the generalizability of these findings.

Additionally, the results of SIT's integrative approach on surfaces as outlined previously, support future investigations on the applicability of the integrative model on 3D object perception. Recent research on preferred completions of self-occluded 3D object parts (Van Lier & Wagemans, 1999) has already shown the impact of intrinsic object regularities on a set of 3D objects in which the differential effect of the external structure and the virtual structure were minimized. The combined impact of the three structures can be illustrated by

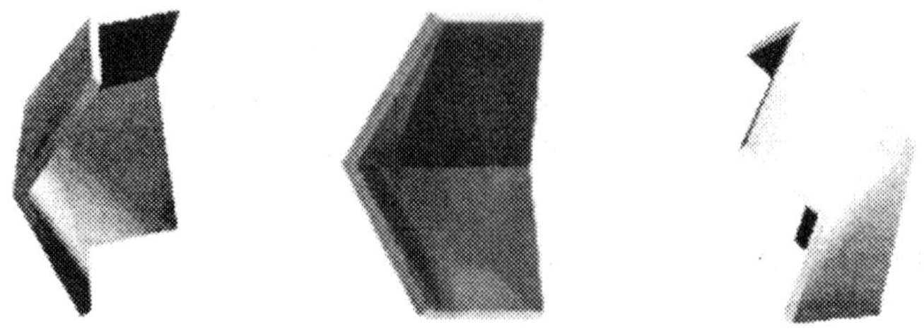

Figure 7. Three possible views of the same object. The internal structure (a viewpoint independent aspect) is the same for all views, whereas the external and the virtual structure (being viewpoint dependent aspects) vary across the images.

means of the three images in Figure 7.

The images A to C (Figure 7) in fact comprise one and the same object, viewed from three different orientations. Therefore, the internal structure (dealing with the object itself) does not vary between the images. This is not the case for the external structure and the virtual structure. In Figure 7B, for example, the external structure (dealing with the spatial positioning of the object) disfavors the 3D interpretation, due to the very specific object orientation, inducing coincidental alignments of object parts. Furthermore, the virtual structure (dealing with the object parts that are not visible) varies between images. An interesting aspect of such a 2D-to-3D extension is the fact that SIT's integrative approach actually accounts for viewpoint independent aspects and viewpoint dependent aspects. That is, the internal structure can be considered as viewpoint independent as it merely describes intrinsic object characteristics, whereas both the external structure and the virtual structure are of a viewpoint dependent nature as they evidently depend on the positional relationship between the observer and the objects. Recent discussions in the literature have made clear that both viewpoint independent aspects and viewpoint dependent aspects need to be accounted for in explanatory models of object perception. For example, Biederman and Gerhardstein (1993) suggested that, within the RBC model on object perception, viewpoint independence does not hold in case of accidental views or in case of occlusion of crucial object parts. In terms of the integrative approach, these two restrictions on viewpoint independency conceptually fit with the account of the external structure and the virtual structure, respectively. More specifically, accidental viewpoints would lead to high $I_{external}$ values (because of the coincidental image regularities) and the occlusion of complex parts would lead to high $I_{virtual}$ values. In general, the approach implies that intrinsic object regularities increase object identification, whereas accidental views or views in which large parts are (self-)occluded decrease object identification. Current research (Van Lier, 1999b) aims at the further development of SIT's integrative approach, and the underlying regularity-based simplicity metric, as an account of both viewpoint independent and viewpoint dependent aspects. In this way, the proposed extension of the integrative approach links some well-known opposing tendencies in 2D surface occlusion and completion research with those of 3D object recognition, based on the notion of global simplicity.

Global Simplicity: Further Observations

Simplicity versus Likelihood. A theoretical problem which deserves some attention here and which links up with the previous issue is whether perception is simplicity-based or likelihood-based. The likelihood principle, originally formulated by Von Helmholtz (1867/1962), states that the preferred perceptual organization reflects the most likely object or event. Several researchers (Mach, 1886; Sober, 1975; see also Hatfield & Epstein, 1985; Chater, 1996) have argued that the likelihood principle and the minimum principle could be two sides of the same coin, as in many cases the most likely interpretation is the simplest interpretation and vice versa. Although we do not agree with this exchangeability of concepts (e.g., Leeuwenberg and Boselie, 1988; Leeuwenberg et al., 1994; Van der Helm, 2000; Van Lier, 1996) there is an interesting parallel between SIT's integrative approach (Van Lier et al. 1994, Van Lier, 2000) and Bayesian likelihood inferences as recently shown by Van der Helm (2000). According to the latter, the probability of a certain event can be considered as being based on an a priori probability and a conditional probability. An analogous distinction can be made in SIT's integrative approach (Van Lier et al., 1994; Van Lier, 1999b). That is, the viewpoint independent component (i.e., the internal structure) is to be considered as the a priori argument whereas the viewpoint dependent components (i.e., the external structure and the virtual structure) are to be considered as conditional arguments. More specifically, Van der Helm (2000) argues that whereas the likelihood principle can be considered to be based on the maximization of the probability (p) for a certain hypothesis (H) and data (D) according to the equation $p(H|D)= p(H)$ x $p(D|H)$ (focusing on the numerator in Bayes rule), the simplicity principle is based on the minimization of the complexity or information load (I) according to the equation $I(H|D) = I(H) + I(D|H)$, where H can be read as 'the interpretation' and D as 'the proximal stimulus'. These equations merge into each other under the substitution $I = -\log p$ (e.g., Pomerantz & Kubovy, 1986) or $p = 2^{-I}$ (Leeuwenberg & Boselie, 1988; although care should be taken as both p and I are expressed in different ways in the latter equations, see also Van der Helm, 2000). Notice that the foregoing provides supplementary support (beside mere parsimony) --from a rather unexpected side-- for taking the mere sum of the complexity values in the determination of the I_{total}. As indicated, this does not mean that there would be a conceptual equivalence between the approaches. The intuitive (im)probability of a specific positional relation between objects (or between observer and objects) actually depends on regularity-based categorization but not the other way around (see also Leeuwenberg & Boselie, 1988; Van Lier et al. 1994; Van der Helm, 2000). In everyday life, however, the probability of occurrence is such a compelling subjective experience that it is often taken as a cause rather than as an effect. Regarding the nonaccidental properties, we do not deny their effects, but, again, we do deny that probability is the appropriate concept for explaining them.

Local prevalence, global simplicity. Before concluding this chapter it seems expedient to briefly return to the concepts of local and global. Although the terms local and global are frequently used in the literature, some care should be taken with these concepts as there is no unique definition of them. For example, Navon (1977) refers with the term global to the low resolution structure of a pattern in contrast to the fine-grained local details at high resolution levels (cf. Robertson, 1996). Somewhat related to this, the local-global distinction often refers to the span of certain pattern properties. In this way, the occurrence of a specific junction type can be considered as a local cue, whereas a bilateral symmetry can be considered as a more global property, as it covers a greater part of a pattern. As argued in the previous sections, both local and global figural aspects influence the preferred percept, whereas predictions of preferred interpretations were always based on a global measure of simplicity. These predictions concern, for example, grouping of serial symbols, completion of surfaces, and the dominance of object components. In Figure 8, from each of these stimulus domains, an example is presented once more. Below each pattern, two plausible 'solutions' are given. The qualifications "global" and "local" are given on the basis of merely metric stimulus properties. For pattern A, the grouping in A' has the largest component and has been qualified as global, whereas A" is qualified as local. For pattern B, completion B' is qualified as global, as it is the more symmetric one, whereas B" is qualified as local. For pattern C, the dominance

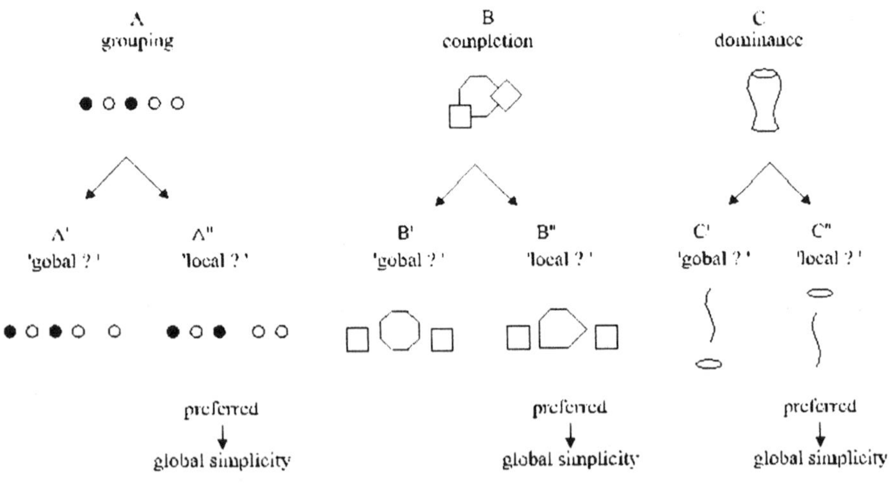

Figure 8. Three examples to illustrate that preferences may be labeled 'local' on an intuitive basis but are, in fact, predicted by a global measure of simplicity.

relationship in C' is qualified as global, as it considers the largest contour component as a superstructure, whereas C" is referred to as local. Notice, however, that for each pattern the 'local solution' is predicted on the basis of global simplicity. So, at an intuitive level there seems to be a discrepancy between the local prevalence and global simplicity whereas, in fact, the 'local solutions' are in line with the global predictions. The notions of local and global as indications of figural aspects are, instead of a priori explanatory concepts, best to be considered as a-posteriori assignments.

FUTURE RESEARCH AND CONCLUDING REMARKS

The SIT approach is still in a state of flux and will be further developed in the coming years. As mentioned, the extension of SIT's integrative approach to 3D objects, incorporating viewpoint independent and viewpoint dependent aspects, is one of the current research lines (Van Lier, 1999b). To explicate this extension a little further, it can be said that, in addition to the simplicity of the perceived shape, the goodness of the 2D image for a specific 3D object -- i.e., the goodness of view-- will be taken into consideration. Whereas both accidental views and occlusions tend to produce relatively simple 2D images (imagine, for example, a bucket seen from above), good views generally reveal rather complex images. One of the current issues concerns the relation between, on the one hand, the goodness of view, and, on the other hand, the difference between the complexity of the actual image of an object and the complexity of a general viewpoint image of that object (in which most of its structure is visible in a nonaccidental way, i.e., no coincidental 2D image regularities).

The above extension from 2D to 3D implies a gradual incorporation of more natural stimuli. A further step in that direction concerns the extension of the domain to quasi-regular shapes (as in Van Lier, 1999a). The patterns in Figure 9, for example, clearly reveal a limited class of plausible interpretations. Although the exact metrical values of edges and angles are all different, it appears that preferred completions reveal the same 'fuzzy' characteristics as the visible part. Alternative descriptions that capture such characteristics for both 2D and 3D shapes (as proposed in Van Lier 1999a) will be a topic of further research.

SIT is first of all a quantitative, representational, approach to perception. Its formalization of regularity, combined with the notion of simplicity, allows classification and prediction of perceptual interpretations. An advantage of SIT is that it is applicable to a wide range of stimuli, treating various perceptual phenomena from the same point of view. It will be clear, however, that SIT is not a process theory. That is, within SIT, perceptual organization is primarily attributed to the simplicity of representation and not to certain process assumptions (e.g., Leeuwenberg & Van der Helm, 1991). It's approach to perceptual organization phenomena provides a way of thinking about perceptual issues that is firmly rooted in the Gestalt tradition and until the present day builds further on those initial ideas

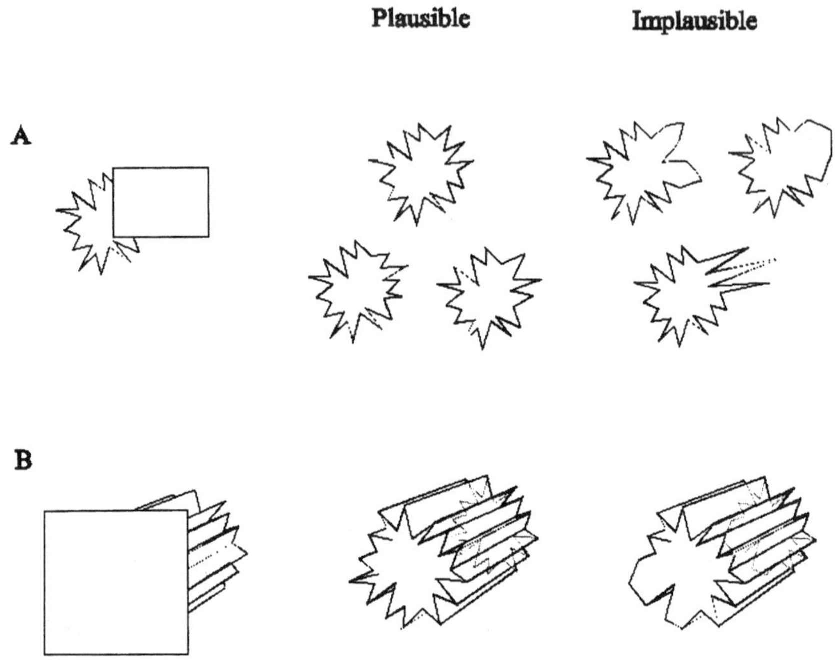

Figure 9. Plausible interpretations of A and B are clearly not restricted to a few exemplars but may actually extent to a whole class of interpretations.

(see also Palmer, 1999). Hopefully, the open questions mentioned in this chapter, will lead to further investigations into SIT.

ACKNOWLEDGMENTS

The text of this chapter is partly based on the author's PHD-thesis. Part of the research reviewed in this chapter has been made possible by the Netherlands Organization for Scientific Research (NWO). The writing of this chapter has been made possible by a grant from The Royal Netherlands Academy of Arts and Sciences (KNAW). RVL thanks Emanuel Leeuwenberg and Peter Van der Helm for their support.

REFERENCES

Baylis, G. & Driver, J. (1995). Obligatory edge assignment in vision: The role of figure and part segmentation in symmetry detection. *Journal of Experimental Psychology:*

Human Perception and Performance, 21, 1323-1342.

Beller, H. (1971). Priming: Effects of advance information on matching. *Journal of Experimental Psychology, 87,* 176-182.

Biederman, I. (1987). Recognition by components: A theory of human image understanding. *Psychological Review, 94,* 115-147.

Biederman, I., & Gerhardstein, P. (1993). Recognizing depth-rotated objects: Evidence and conditions for three-dimensional viewpoint invariance. *Journal of Experimental Psychology: Human Perception and Performance, 19,* 1162-1182.

Boselie, F, & Leeuwenberg, E. (1986) A test of the minimum principle requires a perceptual coding system. *Perception, 15,* 331-354.

Boselie, F. (1988). Local versus global minima in visual pattern completion. *Perception & Psychophysics, 43,* 431-445.

Boselie, F., & Wouterlood, D. (1989). The minimum principle and visual pattern completion. *Psychological Research, 51,* 93-101.

Bruno, N., Bertamini, M., & Domini, F. (1997). Amodal completion of partly occluded surfaces: Is there a mosaic stage? *Journal of Experimental Psychology: Human Perception and Performance, 23,* 1412-1426.

Buffart, H., Leeuwenberg, E., & Restle, F. (1981). Coding theory of visual pattern completion. *Journal of Experimental Psychology: Human Perception and Performance, 7,* 241-274.

Chater, N. (1996). Reconciling simplicity and likelihood principles in perceptual organization. *Psychological Review 103,* 566-581.

Collard, R, & Buffart, H. (1983) Minimization of structural information: A set-theoretical Approach. *Pattern Recognition, 16,* 231-242.

Deutsch, D, & Feroe, J. (1981) The internal representation of pitch sequences in tonal music. *Psychological Review, 88,* 503-522.

Garner, W. (1974). *The processing of information and structure.* Potomac, MD: Erlbaum.

Gerbino, W., & Salmaso, D. (1987). The effect of amodal completion on visual matching. *Acta Psychologica, 65,* 25-46.

Hatfield, G., & Epstein, W. (1985). The status of the minimum principle in the theoretical analysis of visual perception. *Psychological Bulletin, 97,* 155-186.

Herbart, J. (1850) *Lehrbuch zur Psychologie* (Leipzig: Leopold Voss Verlag).

Hochberg, J., & McAlister, E. (1953). A quantitative approach to figural 'goodness'. *Journal of Experimental Psychology, 46,* 361-364.

Jones, M, & Zamostny, K. (1975). Memory and rule structure in the prediction of serial patterns. *Journal of Experimental Psychology: Human Learning and Memory, 104,* 295-306.

Kanizsa, G. (1985). Seeing and thinking. *Acta Psychologica, 59,* 23-33.

Kellman, P. J., & Shipley, T. F. (1991). A theory of visual interpolation in object perception.

Cognitive Psychology, 23, 141-221.

Köhler, W. (1920) *Die Physischen Gestalten in Ruhe und im stationären Zustand.* Braunschweig: Vieweg.

Koffka, K. (1935). *Principles of Gestalt psychology*. New York: Harcourt, Brace & World.

Leeuwenberg, E. (1969). Quantitative specification of information in sequential patterns *Psychological Review, 76,* 216-220.

Leeuwenberg, E. (1971). A perceptual coding language for visual and auditory patterns. *American Journal of Psychology, 84,* 307-349.

Leeuwenberg, E, & Boselie, F. (1988). Against the likelihood principle in visual form Perception. *Psychological Review, 95,* 485-491.

Leeuwenberg, E., & Van der Helm, P. (1991). Unity and variety in visual form. *Perception, 20,* 595-622.

Leeuwenberg, E., Van der Helm, P., & Van Lier, R. (1994). From geons to structure. A note on object representation. *Perception, 23,* 505-515.

Mach, E. (1886) *Beiträge zur Analyse der Empfindungen.* Jena: Gustav Fisher.

Mens, L., & Leeuwenberg, E. (1988). Hidden figures are ever present. *Journal of Experimental Psychology: Human Perception and Performance, 14,* 561-571.

Navon, D. (1977). Forest before trees: the precedence of global features in visual perception. *Cognitive Psychology, 9,* 353-383.

Palmer, S. (1991). Goodness, Gestalt, Groups, and Garner: Local symmetry subgroups as a theory of figural goodness. In G. Lockhead, & J. Pomerantz (Eds.), *The Perception of Structure.* (pp. 23-39). WashingtonDC: APA.

Palmer, S. (1999). *Vision Science: Photons to Phenomenology.* Cambridge, MA: MIT Press.

Pomerantz, J. & Kubovy, M. (1986). Theoretical approaches to perceptual organization. In K. Boff, L. Kaufman, J. Thomas (Eds), *Handbook of Perception and Human Performance.* (pp.1-46). New York: John Wiley.

Restle, F. (1979). Coding theory of the perception of motion configurations. *Psychological Review, 86,* 1-24.

Restle, F. (1982). Coding theory as an integration of gestalt psychology and information processing theory. In J. Beck (Ed), *Organization and representation in perception* (pp. 31-56). Hillsdale, NJ: Lawrence Erlbaum.

Robertson, L. (1996). Attentional Persistence for features of hierarchical patterns. *Journal of Experimental Psychology: General, 125,* 227-249

Rock, I. (1983). *The logic of perception.* Cambridge MA: MIT Press.

Sekuler, A. (1994). Local and global minima in visual completion: Effects of symmetry and orientation. *Perception, 23,* 529-545.

Sekuler, A., & Palmer, S. (1992). Perception of partly occluded objects: A microgenetic analysis. *Journal of Experimental Psychology: General, 121,* 95-111.

Sekuler, A., Palmer, S., & Flynn, C. (1994). Local and global processes in visual completion.

Psychological Science, 5, 260-267.

Simon, H., & Kotovsky, K. (1963) Human acquisition of concepts for sequential patterns. *Psychological Review, 70,* 534-546.

Sober, E. (1975) *Simplicity.* London: Oxford University Press.

Van Bakel, A. (1989) *Perceived unity and duality as determined by unity and duality of superstructure-components of pattern codes.* Masters Thesis, University of Nijmegen.

Van der Helm, P. (1988). *Accessibility and simplicity of visual structures.* PhD Thesis, University of Nijmegen.

Van der Helm, P. (2000). Simplicity versus Likelihood: From Surprisals to Precisals. *Psychological Bulletin, 126,* 770-800.

Van der Helm, P., & Leeuwenberg, E. (1986). Avoiding explosive search in automatic selection of simplest pattern codes. *Pattern Recognition, 19,* 181-191.

Van der Helm, P., & Leeuwenberg, E. (1991). Accessibility, a criterion for regularity and hierarchy in visual pattern codes. *Journal of Mathematical Psychology, 35,* 151-213.

Van der Helm, P., & Leeuwenberg, E. (1996). Goodness of visual regularities: A non-transformational approach. *Psychological Review, 103,* 429-456.

Van der Helm, P., Van Lier R., & Leeuwenberg, E. (1992). Serial pattern complexity: Irregularity and hierarchy. *Perception, 21,* 517-544.

Van Lier, R. (1996) *Simplicity of visual shape: A structural information approach.* PhD-Thesis, University of Nijmegen.

Van Lier, R. (1999a). Investigating global effects in visual occlusion: From a partly occluded square to the back of a tree trunk. *Acta Psychologica* (Special issue: 'Object Perception and memory') *102*, 203-220.

Van Lier, R. (1999b). From image to object: An integration of global and local aspects. Internal report (Project proposal), University of Nijmegen.

Van Lier, R. (2000) Separate features versus one principle: A comment on Shimaya (1997). *Journal of Experimental Psychology: Human Perception and Performance,26,* 412-417.

Van Lier, R., Van der Helm, P., & Leeuwenberg, E. (1994). Integrating global and local aspects of visual occlusion. *Perception, 23,* 883-903.

Van Lier, R., Van der Helm, P., & Leeuwenberg, E., (1995). Competing global and local completions in visual occlusion. *Journal of Experimental Psychology: Human Perception and Performance, 21,* 571-583.

Van Lier, R., Leeuwenberg, E., & Van der Helm, P. (1995). Multiple completions primed by occlusion patterns. *Perception, 24,* 727-740.

Van Lier, R., Leeuwenberg, E., & Van der Helm, P. (1997). In support of hierarchy in object representations. *Psychological Research, 60,* 134-143.

Van Lier, R., & Wagemans, J. (1998). Effects of physical connectivity on the representational unity of multi-part configurations. *Cognition, 69*, B1-B9.

Van Lier, R., & Wagemans, J. (1999). From images to objects: Global and local completions of self-occluded parts. *Journal of Experimental Psychology: Human Perception and Performance, 25,* 1721-1741.

Vitz, P. (1966) Preference for different amounts of visual complexity. *Behavioral Science, 11,* 105-114.

Vitz, P., & Todd, R. (1969) A coded element model of the perceptual processing of sequential stimuli. *Psychological Review, 76,* 433-449.

Von Helmholtz, H. (1867) *Handbook on Physiological Optics* Vol. III. Translation (1962) from the 3rd German edition (New York: Dover Publications)

Wertheimer, M. (1912) Experimentelle Studien über das Sehen von Bewegung. *Zeitschrift für Psychologie, 12,* 161-265.

Wouterlood D., & Boselie, F. (1992). A good-continuation model of some occlusion phenomena. *Psychological Research*, 54, 267-277.

From Fragments to Objects – Segmentation and Grouping in Vision
T.F. Shipley and P.J. Kellman (Editors)

12

COMPUTATIONAL NEURAL MODELS OF SPATIAL INTEGRATION IN PERCEPTUAL GROUPING

Heiko Neumann[†] *and Ennio Mingolla*[‡]

[†] *Fakultät für Informatik, Abteilung Neuroinformatik, Universität Ulm,*
[‡] *Department of Cognitive and Neural Systems, Boston University*

ABSTRACT

Recent developments in the neural computational modeling of perceptual grouping are described with reference to a newly proposed taxonomy to formalize mechanisms of spatial integration. This notational framework and nomenclature is introduced in order to clarify key properties common to all or most models, while permitting unique attributes of each approach to be independently examined. The strength of spatial integration in the models that are considered is always some function of the distances and relative alignments in perceptual space of the centers of units representing orientational features or energy in a visual scene. We discuss the significance of variations of the constituents of an activation function for spatial integration, and also consider the larger modeling framework in which this function is applied in each approach. We also discuss the relationship of feedforward and feedback mechanisms and the issues of self-organization as core principles underlying the establishment of spatial integration mechanisms. The relationship of the grouping models to models of other visual competencies is considered with respect to prospects for future research.

INTRODUCTION

Recent years have seen burgeoning interest in spatial integration mechanisms for perceptual grouping, with psychophysical, physiological, brain imaging, and computational perspectives all playing important roles. This chapter examines formal approaches to a particular aspect of grouping related to the Gestalt concept of *good continuation* (Koffka, 1935) that have garnered increasing attention since Field, Hayes, and Hess (1993) popularized the notion of an "association field," a figure-eight shaped zone aligned with perceptual contour segments, along which facilitatory perceptual interactions with other contour segments tend to occur. We examine prior expositions of the figure-eight idea and more recent developments, with the focus on studies that have included sufficient formal specification to afford computer implementation and simulation of the key grouping mechanism and its ancillary machinery, such as early filters.

Our focus is on models intended to address psychophysical and physiological data, as opposed to pure computer vision approaches. The key behavioral properties of spatial integration include enhancement or suppression of detectability of contour segments depending on particular geometric relationships among local orientations and positions of contour segments to be grouped, as are described in Section 2. Important constraints from neural data include the results of pioneering studies of von der Heydt, Gilbert, and their collaborators concerning the physiology and anatomy of cells with long-range horizontal connections in cortical areas V1 and V2.

Even with such restrictions on scope, a number of models remain to be examined, and our classification is based on several factors. These include the type of formalism employed, such as relaxation labeling or systems of ordinary differential equations. We also compare functional properties of models, particularly with respect to their treatment of feedback, whether in the form of recurrent horizontal connections among network nodes, or in the form of processing loops involving nodes of different layers. The common thread in the models we address is that some key stage or process in the model accomplishes spatial integration using some sort of figure-eight based mechanism or process. We next make precise the significance of this construct, before examining several models' treatment of it in detail, by describing each model's formalization of spatial integration and presenting some key simulation results. A concluding discussion outlines outstanding questions for further modeling studies.

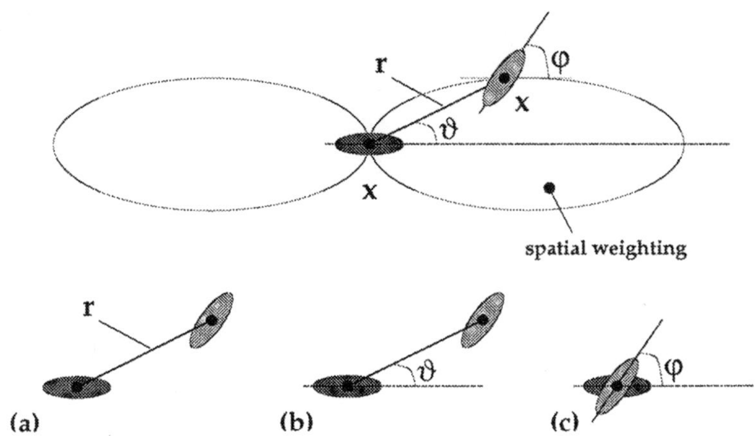

Figure 1. The "bipole icon" for modeling feature integration in spatial grouping (top). The quantity to be assessed is the "contribution" of activation in a oriented unit, denoted by the light ellipse, to the activation of another unit, denoted by the dark ellipse. The figure-eight shape of a bipole expresses relations among three fundamental quantities (bottom): (a) the distance, $\mathbf{r}$, between the centers of the two ellipses, (b) the angle, ϑ, formed by a ray passing through the centers of the two ellipses and the orientation axis of the dark ellipse, and (c) the difference in orientation, φ, of the principle axes of the two ellipses.

MECHANISMS OF SPATIAL INTEGRATION

The bipole icon

The geometry of spatial integration is summarized in the bipole[1] icon of Figure 1. Imagine that some pattern of contrast, such as an edge, occurs in a scene in the region of, and in the orientation denoted by the long axis of, the light ellipse (at location $\mathbf{x}'$). How should the influence of that edge on the representation of contour strength in the region of the dark ellipse be calculated? Whatever the details of the computation, the fundamental quantities to be considered are: (1) the distance, $\mathbf{r}$, between the centers of the two ellipses; (2) the angle, ϑ, formed by a ray passing through the centers of the two ellipses and a ray along the principle axis of the dark ellipse; and (3) the difference in orientation, φ, of the principle axes of the two ellipses. The characteristic "figure-eight"

[1]The term "bipole" was introduced by Grossberg and Mingolla (1987) to describe a unit in a neural network model described by Cohen and Grossberg (1984b), Grossberg (1984), and Grossberg and Mingolla (1985a, 1985b) as a "cooperative cell".

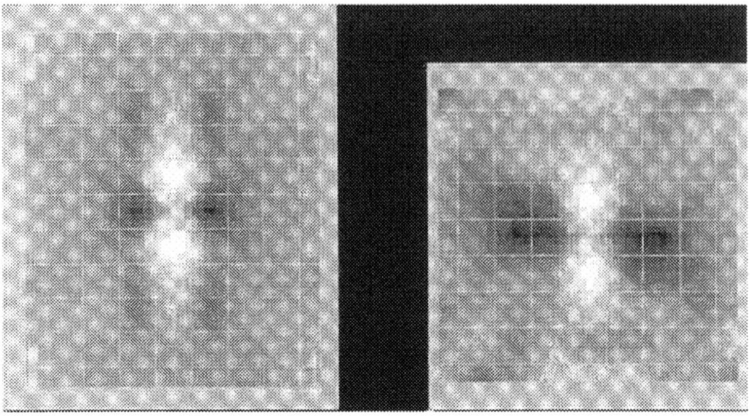

Figure 2. Left panel: This plot summarizes psychophysical data from 450 trials of one observer in a tilt illusion experiment. The observer controlled the orientation of a central line segment displayed in juxtaposition with two symmetrically flanking lines whose actual orientation was 5 degrees from the vertical. The observer's task was to make the central line appear vertical. The data show regions for which attractive (light) and repulsive (dark) tilt illusions were obtained. Right panel: Summary of excitatory and inhibitory zones of influence for flanking stimuli on single cells of vertical orientational preference whose receptive fields are centered in the diagram. See Kapadia *et al.* (2000) for details. (This is Figure 12a of Kapadia *et al.* (2000), reproduced with permission. Efforts to convert the original figure from color to grayscale may have introduced unintended artifacts. Although the overall bipole shape of excitatory regions is representative, readers should consult the original source if possible.)

shape in the figure expresses the region of relatively high coupling strength for the influence of contour segments remote from the central ellipse on a unit whose positional and orientational preferences are denoted by the ellipse at the center (*cf.* Lesher, 1995).

The bipole icon can be interpreted in several rubrics. Most generally, it expresses the basic functional task that must be achieved in contour integration. That task is to assess the influence that a contour segment at one location should have on the likelihood of a contour being perceived at a second location – specifically, at a place "pointed to by" or "consistent with" the first segment. Instead of likelihood, we might also speak of the contour at the former location modulating the perceived strength or salience of a contour at another. In this respect, the icon summarizes functional relationships in the processing of visual input by our perceptual system. Before examining anatomical and physiological correlates of the bipole shape, we first turn to psychophysical evidence.

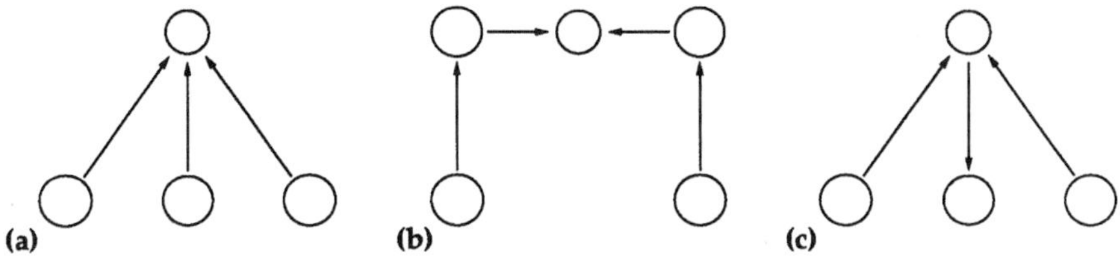

Figure 3. Different principles of how remote activities influence localized spatial activation patterns of a target cell through integration: (a) bottom-up (feedforward) convergence, (b) lateral integration in a neural layer, and (c) recurrent integration utilizing localized feedback processing.

Psychophysical and physiological data

Recent investigations by Kapadia *et al.* (2000) arrived at a bipole shape in a summary data plot for an experiment in which observers were asked to adjust the orientation of a test line of dimension 8 × 1 minutes in the presence of flanking lines. Figure 2 summarizes regions for which flanking lines placed in individual grid squares affect the perceived orientation of a line in the central square, with light regions coding zones of attraction and dark regions coding zones of repulsion in the perceived orientation of a vertical line. The height of each square corresponds to the arc length of a test or flanking line (8 minutes).

That the region of orientational attraction in the left panel of Figure 2 takes the shape of a bipole is both a hint about the human visual system's perceptual processing and a fact in need of explanation. One possible hypothesis is that our visual systems contain neurons at some layer whose pattern of connections with neurons that synapse upon them from earlier layers is itself that of a bipole. Note that this is not a logical necessity. That is, the pattern of psychophysical data of Figure 2 could be the result of processing by the subjects' entire visual systems, no individual component of which need have the structure of a bipole. The final pattern of data could instead be the result of many interacting components of unknown character. That is, the receptive field of a cell is the result of all factors that bear on a cell's potential, including bottom-up, top-down, and lateral excitatory and inhibitory connections. (See Figure 3.) Kapadia *et al.* (2000) made progress on this question by performing electrophysiological recordings of activity of units in V1 of macaques, using stimuli analogous to those used in the psychophysical task performed by human subjects. The zones of attraction and repulsion in the single-unit studies bear a striking resemblance to those found psychophysically. (See Figure 2.)

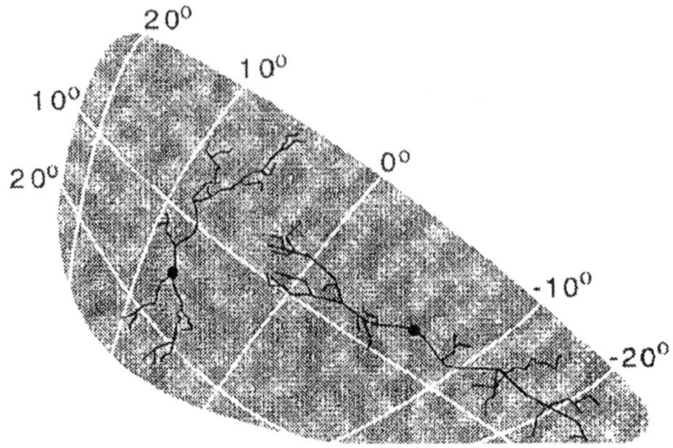

Figure 4. Summary of specificity of horizontal connections between V1 cells of layer 2/3. Axon arborizations from two example cells are shown over a combined map of visual space and orientation preference (dark regions: cells with 90 deg. orientation preference; light regions: cells with 0 deg. preference). Horizontal connections are reciprocal such that layer 2/3 cells receive input from other cells in layer 2/3 with the same orientation selectivity. The cell shown above that was found in a dark region of the map projects to other areas with the same orientation preference (90 deg.). Moreover, those cells that were selectively contacted lie along a line that is orthogonal to the 0 deg. meridian. The other cell shown was found in a light region of the map and projects to spatially distant cells with the same orientation preference (0 deg. in this case) and that lie along a line parallel to the 0 deg. meridian. (This is Figure 12 of Bosking *et al.* (1997), reproduced with permission.)

Anatomical data

Recent anatomical data support the "bipole hypothesis" – the claim that the figure-eight shaped region of excitatory interactions in perceptual contour integration is mediated primarily by direct anatomical linkages that form a figure-eight shape in retinotopic coordinates (Grossberg and Mingolla, 1985a, 1985b, 1987). Early work had already shown that horizontal connections among single cells in V1 connect cells of like orientational preference (Gilbert and Wiesel, 1979, 1983; Martin and Whitteridge, 1984; Rockland and Lund, 1982). More recently Bosking *et al.* (1997) have used a double-labeling technique to demonstrate directly that such connections in tree shrew are also preferentially made among cells whose receptive field centers in retinotopic space are in positions aligned with the orientational preference of the cell making the long-range connections. That is, a vertically tuned cell will make long-range connections with cells that are also vertically tuned and that code positions above or below, but not to the side of, its receptive field center. (See Figure 4.)

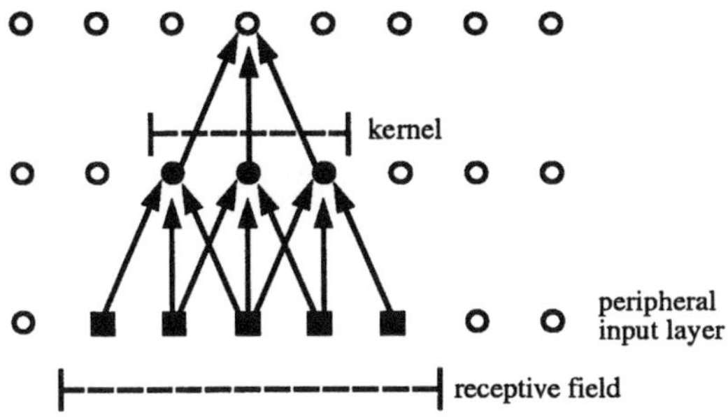

Figure 5. Feedforward input convergence onto a target cell v_i over a cascade of neural layers. The arrows connecting the top two rows of open circles stand for pathways to provide input for the target cell. These pathways may have different efficacies and can be modeled as *kernels* of different weight coefficients. The kernels thus define the structure of direct connections to cell v_i. The squares at the "input layer" (e.g., retina) code the *receptive field* (RF) of v_i. The RF of a cell thus determines, functionally, where in the periphery a stimulation will yield a response at the cell. The RF is always defined in the coordinates of the peripheral sensor, e.g. the retina.

Bipoles in modeling

Before proceeding, then, it is useful to review some points concerning usage of terms in computational modeling, psychophysics, and physiology. A physiologist may use electrode recordings to determine a cell's receptive field. Recently, there has been an explosion of interest cells with so-called "nonclassical receptive field" properties – that is, cells whose firing can be modulated by stimulus manipulations well outside the classical receptive field. (See Spillmann and Werner (1996) for a review.) Note, however, that whether classical or nonclassical, a cell's receptive field is, by definition, a functional property – the result of all interactions from receptors through any "top-down" feedback that might bear on a cell's potential. The present paper, on the other hand, examines computational variations of a hypothesis concerning how a specific bipole pattern of connectivity exists among relatively tightly-coupled neural units. This pattern of connectivity is described in formal terms by a *kernel*, or set of weights, coding the strength of connection between a spatial array of units in a network to a particular designated unit. (See Figure 5.)

The direct analogue of a kernel in vivo, however, is difficult or impossible to assess for most cortical neurons. To precisely determine all the cells that send input to a particular neuron, and with what "weight," would be an heroic undertaking. Note that Figure 4 shows the pattern of axonal connections radiating outward from a single neuron, which is

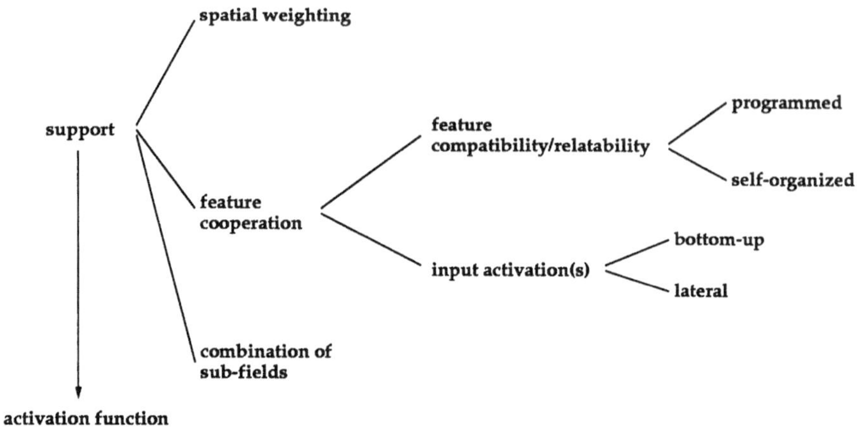

Figure 6. Taxonomy of contributions to the formal definition of spatial integration mechanisms. Their functionality can be organized in a tree structure of elements. The *spatial weighting* defines the structure of lateral spatial connectivity, or kernel. The *feature compatibility* function defines the representation of relatable visual structure, or context. This encodes the model of the expected most likely visual arrangement in the environment. The product of spatial weighting and compatibility function defines the total coupling strength for support measures in the space-feature domain. The definition of individual components are described in the text.

the dual of the set of connections terminating at a neuron (*cf.* Grossberg and Mingolla, 1985b, Figures 32 and 33). In any event, since the pioneering work of von der Heydt, Peterhans, and Baumgartner (1984) first provided evidence for bipole shaped receptive fields, the idea that a structural bipole kernel underlies the functional receptive field properties has featured in many models. We next explore the variations employed in detailed instantiations of such kernels in several key modeling studies.

ELEMENTS OF SPATIAL INTEGRATION FOR GROUPING

Dimensions of integration

Grouping mechanisms invoke principles of selective integration of more localized measurements along any of several possible feature dimensions. The primary goal of this section is to describe the elements of spatial integration mechanisms and their formal description. Figure 6 depicts a taxonomy of the elements which contribute to the definition of the support and final activation function computed as a mechanism of feature integration and grouping.

In all, the result of integration of items defines the *support* of a localized target feature measurement at a given spatial location based on the configuration of other measurements. Based on the bipole structure of left and right sub-fields, the support can be defined as a function

$$\text{support}_{xy,feature} = \left\{\text{left-input}_{xy,feature}\right\} \circ \left\{\text{right-input}_{xy,feature}\right\} \tag{1}$$

where '$\circ$' denotes some operation to define the *combination of sub-fields*. Subscripts xy denote spatial locations in a 2-D retinotopic map and $feature$ identifies the feature dimension involved in the grouping process. In the bipole model the segregated lobes of the integration field define the support of a target item. The *activation* of the corresponding target cell results as a function of the support such that

$$\text{activation}_{xy,feature} = f\left(\text{support}_{xy,feature}\right). \tag{2}$$

The formal description of the mechanisms underlying the computation of activations 'left-input' and 'right-input', respectively, necessitates the detailed specification of the interaction of activities in grouping.

A *spatial weighting*, or kernel, function specifies the mutual influence between two localized features. Items that are closely spaced are in general more likely to be grouped than candidates that are located far apart. The underlying spatial neighborhood function often selectively facilitates a sector of a spatial surround to define an anisotropic coupling that is compatible with the feature domain. Elementary features along dimensions such as, e.g., (tangential) orientation, motion direction, and disparity provide the dimensions of the visual representation space. The feature *relatability* (or *compatibility*; see Parent and Zucker (1989) and Kellman and Shipley (1991)) between stimulus items is defined along these dimensions. Herein, the most typical or likely appearance of meaningful structure is somehow encoded to represent "what feature goes with what". The resulting model representation is encoded in the spatial weights of the connectivity pattern of a target cell with its surround and thus defines a spatial filter (*cf.* Grossberg, 1980). In the following treatment, we will particularly focus on grouping mechanisms for static shape or form processing and, therefore, consider only *orientation* as the relevant feature dimension. (See Figure 1.)

In most models the connectivity pattern of the relatable features is pre-specified, or *programmed*, based on a framework of geometric measures. These are encoded in closed-form mechanisms that define a static efficacy between tuples, e.g. pairs, of feature measurements at given locations. In this sense, they are designed *a priori* in order to achieve a given functionality. To date, few approaches investigate the possible *self-organization* of such lateral interactions in a neural architecture. Note that the spatial weighting function and the feature relatability define the components of the net *coupling strength.* This separable function specifies a metric for the similarity measure in the $< xy, feature >$-space and thus defines the distance function for the clustering of a visual pattern according to a relatability measure. This measure contributes to the definition of *feature cooperation.* In order to get activated, *input activations* are necessary to gather any support. Here, two different types of interactions can be distinguished: (1) a convergent feedforward mechanism is defined when the *bottom-up* input is integrated at the target location, whereas (2) a mechanism of (non-linear) *lateral* interaction is defined when activity is horizontally integrated within a neural layer (compare Figures 3a and 3b).

Taken together, the support – which corresponds to the activity derived from the feature integration process using the bipole mechanism – is usually computed by the following scheme assembled from the elements that were introduced above:

$$\begin{aligned} \text{support}_{\mathbf{x}\theta} &= \sum_{\mathbf{x}'\phi} \left\{ \text{act}_{\mathbf{x}'\phi} \cdot \text{relate}_{\theta\phi} \cdot \text{weight}^{\text{left}}_{\mathbf{x}\mathbf{x}'\theta} \right\} \circ \\ & \sum_{\mathbf{x}'\phi} \left\{ \text{act}_{\mathbf{x}'\phi} \cdot \text{relate}_{\theta\phi} \cdot \text{weight}^{\text{right}}_{\mathbf{x}\mathbf{x}'\theta} \right\} \end{aligned} \tag{3}$$

where 'weight' denotes the spatial weighting kernel, 'relate' the feature relatability, and 'act' the input activations (Figure 6). The small circle denotes some nonlinear combination of terms. Coordinates in the space-feature domain are denoted by bold Latin letters (spatial) and by Greek letters (orientation features). Here, $\mathbf{x} = (x, y)$ and θ correspond to the location and orientation of the target feature, respectively. Other parameters refer to the specific location $< \mathbf{x}', \phi >$ in the space-orientation neighborhood. (See Figure 1.)[2] The precise definition of these components varies for different models.

Outline of core models and their components

Several computational models for feature integration and grouping have been published. We here focus on those approaches which we believe are most influential with respect to (1) the explanation of empirical data and (2) their importance for subsequent scientific developments. In particular, we outline the Boundary Contour System (BCS) model developed by Grossberg and colleagues, the relaxation approach for feature compatibility labeling developed by Zucker and colleagues, and the filter model developed by von der Heydt, Peterhans and colleagues based on their results of neurophysiolog-

[2]Note that in these definitions the feature orientations θ and ϕ are measured against an oriented coordinate axis. In Figure 1 a gauge coordinate system is assumed such that the axis of orientation of the target cell serves as the reference. For completeness, the angles which define the relations between quantities can be computed as $\vartheta = \tan^{-1}(y' - y/x' - x) - \theta$ and $\varphi = \phi - \theta$.

ical investigations. New contributions of other recent models are then introduced and discussed.

For clarity we first establish a coherent usage of variables and names for different types of elements in each model. The following table shows the three generic categories for the definition of the components in different schemes of feature integration. The elementary categories in all models are weighting functions, activations and parameters (constants) of the activation dynamics. Further necessary elements in the formal description will be specified in addition.

weighting functions		*activations*	*parameters*
oriented kernels (bipole)	isotropic kernels		
$\text{weight}^{\text{left}}$, $\text{weight}^{\text{right}}$	Λ (space), Ψ (orientation)	c, u, v, w, x, y, z	α, β, ...

Boundary Contour System (BCS)

The following section follows the description of the BCS given by Mingolla, Ross, and Grossberg (1999). The BCS consists of a series of boundary detection, competition, and cooperation stages as shown in the block diagram in Figure 7. Stage 1 models the contrast enhancement resulting from on-center, off-surround (ON channel) and off-center, on-surround (OFF channel) interactions at the retina and LGN. These ON and OFF cells compensate for variable illumination by computing locally normalized contrast ratios throughout the image.

At Stage 2, these ON and OFF cells generate half-wave rectified outputs which together drive the activation of oriented simple cells. Simple cells compute a measure of the local image gradient magnitude and orientation. Like-oriented simple cells sensitive to opposite contrast polarities or directions-of-contrast pool their activations at complex cells. Complex cells are hereby rendered insensitive to direction-of-contrast (dark-to light vs. light-to-dark), as are all subsequent BCS processing stages.

Next, complex cell activations compete at Stage 3 processing. Competition occurs through on-center off-surround processing across both image space (spatial competition) and across orientation space (orientational competition). Spatial and orientational competition captures the functional implications of lateral inhibition across a cortical map in which nearby cells tend to be sensitive both to contrasts at neighboring (or overlapping) image locations and similar boundary orientations. Functionally, competition sharpens boundary localization and orientational tuning of individual complex cell filters. It also endows the complex cells with a property of *endstopping* that enables them to respond more vigorously near the ends of a line than at its middle. This competition is also driven by feedback from Stage 4 long-range boundary cooperation, thereby suppressing weaker boundary activations while enhancing the contrast and the completion of stronger and more globally consistent boundary activations.

Long-range boundary cooperation at Stage 4 accomplishes the grouping together of consistent boundaries and the completion of camouflaged boundaries. This cooperation is achieved by bipole cells which realize a type of statistical AND gate, since they fire if both halves of their receptive fields are sufficiently activated by appropriately oriented input contrasts from the complex cells of Stage 3.

The cooperative-competitive (CC) feedback loop between Stage 3 and Stage 4 acts to complete and enhance spatially and orientationally consistent boundary groupings while inhibiting inconsistent ones. This feedback process simultaneously achieves the addition of sharp completions and the suppression of noise. Furthermore, excitatory and inhibitory feedback are balanced such that boundary strength sensitivity is preserved and boundary activations are not driven to saturation. The robust preservation of sensitivity to the analog strength of inputs that support long-range completion of boundary signals over gaps in the image – that is, regions of the image where local image data would not signal a boundary – is an important innovation of recent versions of the BCS (Grossberg *et al.*, 1997; Mingolla *et al.* 1999; Ross *et al.* 2000). Previous versions of the BCS tended to sacrifice sensitivity to input strength as a cost of the advantages of context-sensitive long-range grouping in a feedback system. The present architecture combines the nonlinear choice properties necessary to determine whether and where to coherently link boundary segments with sensitivity to input contrast magnitudes in the completed boundary signals.

The BCS boundaries act as barriers to diffusion of the ON and OFF contrast signals within the FCS. Cohen and Grossberg (1984a), Grossberg and Todorović (1988), Neumann (1996), Pessoa, Neumann, and Mingolla (1995), and Neumann, Pessoa, and Mingolla (1998) developed the FCS model to simulate data about human brightness perception. The combination of BCS boundary completion and FCS surface diffusion mechanisms is an early exemplar of a class of image processing procedures known as inhomogeneous or geometry-driven diffusion. Unlike most such approaches, however, BCS/FCS algorithms do not require that diffusion rates be limited by initial image data, or by iterative updates of any transformations of image data that are influenced by diffusion. Instead, the boundary signals that limit diffusion are computed by a self-equilibrating process that is both buffered from the effects of the diffusion process and capable of generating barriers to diffusion that are based on contextual image data at

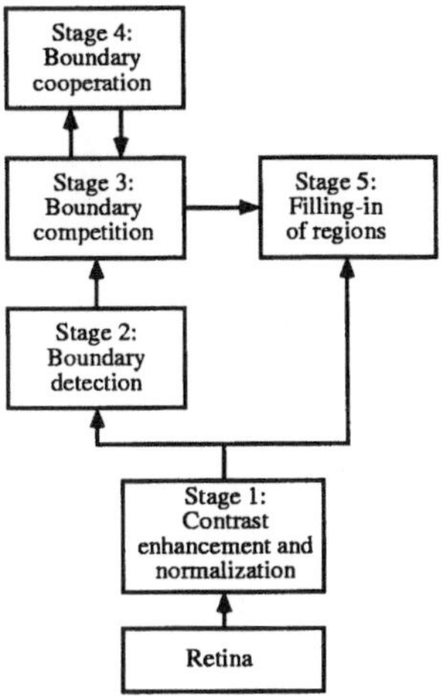

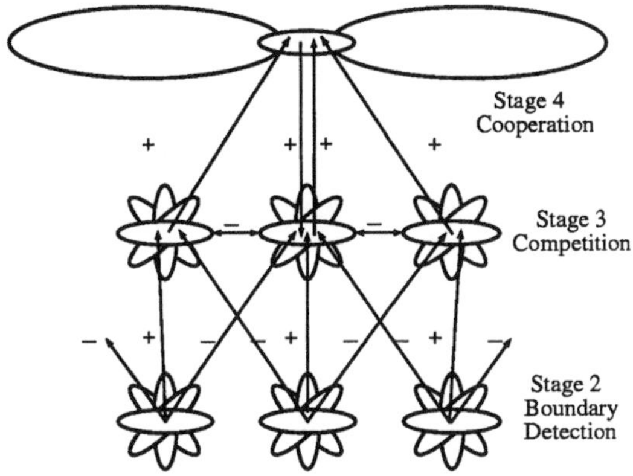

Figure 7.The left panel shows the macrocircuit of the BCS-FCS model. The right panel shows details of the stage of oriented contrast detection (OC Filter) and of the stages of the competitive-cooperative (CC) Loop of recurrent boundary processing in the BCS. See text for details.

some distance from a pixel location, rather than simply on local measures of image gradients.

Description of the modeling framework. The key elements in the definition of the spatial integration mechanisms of the BCS proposed by Grossberg and Mingolla (1985b) are summarized below. Since several instances of the precise definition of components have been published, we simply describe one selected scheme and mention the alterations.

(1) *Spatial weighting functions (bipoles)*

The weighting functions for the spatial integration are defined by two separate collinearly oriented kernels for the gauge orientation θ. These kernels are defined by a polar separable function denoted by

$$\begin{aligned} \text{weight}^{\text{left}}_{\mathbf{xx}'\theta} &= \left[W^{rad}_{\mathbf{xx}'} \cdot W^{ang}_{\mathbf{xx}'\theta}\right]^+ \quad \text{and} \\ \text{weight}^{\text{right}}_{\mathbf{xx}'\theta} &= \left[-W^{rad}_{\mathbf{xx}'} \cdot W^{ang}_{\mathbf{xx}'\theta}\right]^+, \end{aligned} \tag{4}$$

respectively, with $[x]^+ = \max[x, 0]$. The radial and angular distance weightings are defined by

$$W^{rad}_{\mathbf{xx}'} = \text{elongated-Gaussian}(\mu, dist), \quad \text{with} \quad dist = \left((x-x')^2 + (y-y')^2\right)^{1/2},$$

$$W^{ang}_{\mathbf{xx}'\theta} = \pm\cos^T(Q_{\mathbf{xx}'} - \theta), \text{ with } Q_{\mathbf{xx}'} = \tan^{-1}((y'-y)/(x'-x)). \quad (5)$$

The parameter μ in the radial weighting denotes the spatial offset of the Gaussian, T. The sign changes distinguish the left and right lobes of the bipole sub-fields. (See Figure 7.)

(2) *Feature cooperation*
The *relatability* of two segregated features in orientation space is encoded in a weighting pattern that represents a model of the most likely underlying geometrical shape that occurs in the visual world. This representation has been sampled at discrete locations. Maximal relatability is defined by orientations tangent to the model segment at the sample locations. Most often shape segments such as straight lines, circular arcs, splines, or parabolic curves have been used. The simplest model utilizes the deviation from the orientation of the virtual line between sample points and the orientation in the neighborhood. More formally, we get

$$\text{relate}^{straight}_{\mathbf{xx}'\theta\phi} = \cos^R(Q_{\mathbf{xx}'} - \phi), \text{ with } Q_{\mathbf{xx}'}, \quad (6)$$

with R denoting a tuning constant (*cf.* Grossberg and Mingolla, 1985b). For a circular shape model the relatability can be formalized by the co-circularity constraint

$$\text{relate}^{circ}_{\mathbf{xx}'\theta\phi} = \cos^R(2Q_{\mathbf{xx}'} - (\theta + \phi)), \quad (7)$$

with R again denoting the tuning of the selectivity (*cf.* Gove *et al.*, 1995; Parent and Zucker, 1989; and several later models).[3]

The *input activation* is represented by a dipole field composed of antagonistic ON and OFF responses in an orientation field, whereby a horizontally tuned ON cell at one location is equivalent to a vertical OFF, and vice versa, and similarly for other pairs of perpendicular orientations. Pairs of cells with mutually orthogonal orientation preferences incorporate a push-pull mechanism for fast reset processes. Their activity (from the previous neural layer) is denoted by

$$y_{\mathbf{x}\theta}, \quad \bar{y}_{\mathbf{x}\theta} = y_{\mathbf{x}\theta_\perp}. \quad (8)$$

Such pairs of neurons enter in a mutually inhibitory fashion into the integration mechanism.

[3]Note that in order to fulfill the relatability constraint of Kellman and Shipley (1991), additional constraints must be taken into account, namely $\theta < Q_{\mathbf{xx}'} < \phi$ (or instead $\theta > Q_{\mathbf{xx}'} > \phi$) and $|\theta - \phi| \leq 90°$.

(3) *Support and activation function* The support is computed by the combination of sub-fields and their result from integrated activities. We get

$$
\begin{aligned}
z_{\mathbf{x}\theta} &= g\left(\sum_{\mathbf{x}'\phi}\left[y_{\mathbf{x}'\phi}-\bar{y}_{\mathbf{x}'\phi}\right]^{+}\cdot \text{relate}_{\mathbf{x}\mathbf{x}'\theta\phi}\cdot \text{weight}^{\text{left}}_{\mathbf{x}\mathbf{x}'\theta}\right)+ \\
& \quad g\left(\sum_{\mathbf{x}'\phi}\left[y_{\mathbf{x}'\phi}-\bar{y}_{\mathbf{x}'\phi}\right]^{+}\cdot \text{relate}_{\mathbf{x}\mathbf{x}'\theta\phi}\cdot \text{weight}^{\text{right}}_{\mathbf{x}\mathbf{x}'\theta}\right),
\end{aligned}
\tag{9}
$$

with $g(s) \simeq s/(\alpha+s)$. When $\alpha \to 0$, this function approximates a step or switch and thus allows for setting a threshold such that the target cell responds only if it receives input from both lobes. As a consequence, the mechanism acts like an AND gate, despite additively combining the lobes of a bipole.

The activation of a bipole cell enters a stage of center-surround feedback competition which in turn completes the closed-loop computation of the competitive-cooperative (CC) mechanism. This leads to the dynamics

$$
v_{\mathbf{x}\theta} = \frac{h(z_{\mathbf{x}\theta})}{1+\sum_{\mathbf{x}'} h(z_{\mathbf{x}'\theta})\cdot \Lambda^{FB}_{\mathbf{x}\mathbf{x}'}}, \quad \text{with} \quad h(s)=\max[s-L,0], \quad \text{and} \tag{10}
$$

$$
\frac{d}{dt}w_{\mathbf{x}\theta} = -w_{\mathbf{x}\theta}+I+x_{\mathbf{x}\theta}+v_{\mathbf{x}\theta}-w_{\mathbf{x}\theta}\sum_{\mathbf{x}'} x_{\mathbf{x}'\theta}\cdot \Lambda^{FF}_{\mathbf{x}\mathbf{x}'}, \tag{11}
$$

with L denoting a threshold firing level, $x_{\mathbf{x}\theta}$ denoting the initial oriented contrast activity from cortical complex cells, and I is a tonic input. The kernels Λ denote the weighting functions for the spatial competitive interactions in the feedback (FB) and feedforward (FF) pathways. The distributions of w-activity are then transformed via a stage of dipole competition to generate responses $y_{\mathbf{x}\theta}$.

This network incorporates additive feedback processing and thus can generate activities at locations that lack any initial driving input from the input layers. Thus, according to the classification of Crick and Koch (1998), the recurrent network incorporates a *strong loop*. Like-oriented flanking items of proper spacing enable the bipole mechanism to generate an inward directed completion of the activity distribution and thus create illusory contours. Figure 8 shows the action of the spatial completion process.

Characteristic simulations. Figure 9 illustrates how the property of analog sensitivity allows the completion of illusory contours by BCS feedback circuits to vary in strength as a function of the "support ratio" of inducers, which is the length of an illusory contour compared to the total (real plus illusory) contour length (Shipley and Kellman, 1992). Note that illusory contour strength increases as an inverted-U shaped function

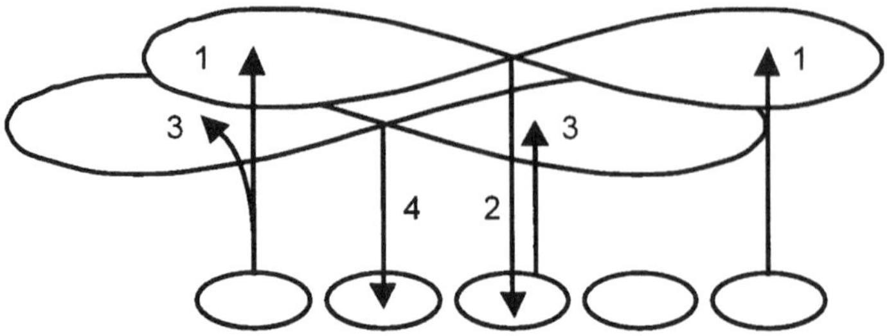

Figure 8. Principle of the feedback mechanism to generate a spatially continuous arrangement of activity in boundary completion processes. Initially, like-oriented contrast cells feed the lobes of a bipole cell at the integration stage (1); activity is fed back to the input layer creating an activation in the middle of the gap (2); these activities in turn are integrated by other bipole cells (3) which in turn also generate new activities (4). This process of rapid completion is finished after two cycles of iteration generating a spatially continuous boundary representation.

of line density, as reported by Lesher and Mingolla (1993). These results were predicted by an analysis of the interaction of short-range inhibition and long-range excitation in the CC Loop. While the addition of arcs to a display containing few inducers initially increases illusory contour strength, inhibition reduces the effective input to the BCS's bipole completion mechanisms as line ends become too crowded.

Figure 10 illustrates how the bipole spatial integration mechanisms of the BCS can improve performance of image processing algorithms designed to enhance the interpretability by humans of images derived from artificial sensors (Mingolla *et al.*, 1999). Pixel intensities in synthetic aperture radar images span five orders of magnitude, with a relatively few high intensity pixels and a large majority of low intensity ones. Typically, a compressive logarithmic transformation of intensities is used simply to display image data (e.g., on an 8-bit grayscale). Form-sensitive processing by algorithms based on the BCS and FCS models results in imagery with reduced graininess, higher contrast, and greater ease of use than conventional alternatives. The comparison of Figure 10e and Figure 10f, in particular, illustrates the advantages of using bipole completion mechanisms in the CC Loop to enhance favored boundaries, while suppressing less coherent bottom-up boundary signals caused by noise.

Recent work on the BCS model. The original BCS has been extended and elaborated in recent years, as part of a larger model of earlier vision known as the FACADE (Form And Color And DEpth) model (Grossberg, 1994). An important theme of this work has been the identification of specific neuron types in the laminae of cortical ar-

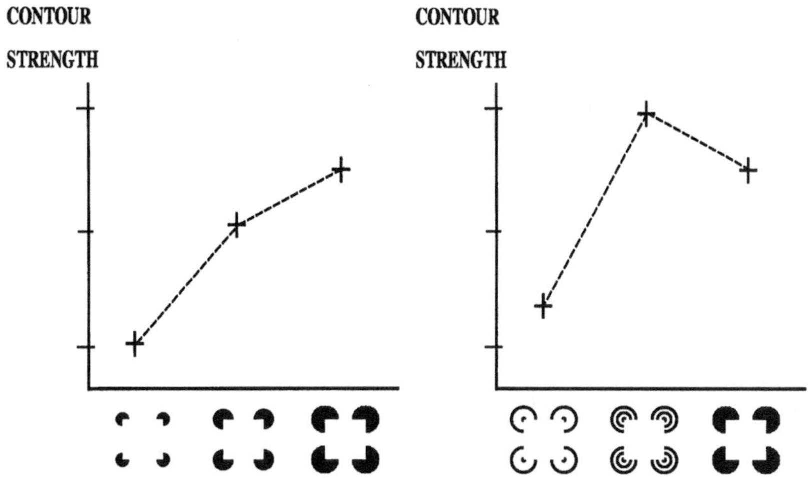

Figure 9. Model simulations of psychophysical data: (Left) In response to the edge inducers, illusory contour strength increases with support ratio. Support ratio is the ratio of real to total contour length. (Right) For the line end inducers, contour strength is an inverted U function of the number and density of line end inducers. Contour strength was determined by computing the average cell activity along the path of the illusory portion of the contour. (Reprinted with permission from Grossberg *et al.*, 1997.)

eas V1 and V2 that instantiate the bipole property (Grossberg, 1999; Grossberg *et al.*, 1997; Ross *et al.*, 2000). Since long-range lateral connections in cortex are axonal, a key question underlying this research is how inward completion, or interpolation without extrapolation, can be achieved in a circuit whose main long-range connections are outward. This work has also shown how *analog-sensitive* completion can be instantiated in a feedback network. Analog sensitivity refers to the modulation of the perceptual "strength" of completion as a function of variations of contrast, distance, or orientation of inducing elements.

Additional work on the bipole property has shown how a model of laminar mechanisms in areas V1 and V2 can explain difficult recent psychophysical and physiological data concerning how variations of inducer contrast can produce facilitatory or inhibitory effects on single cell activity, while subserving perceptual completion (Grossberg, 1999; Grossberg and Raizada, 2000). These same circuits are also shown to be involved in attentional modulation of activity in early cortical areas such as V1 or V2.

Other work has developed algorithms based on bipole mechanisms and BCS/FCS interactions for processing of synthetic aperture radar images (Mingolla *et al.*, 1999).

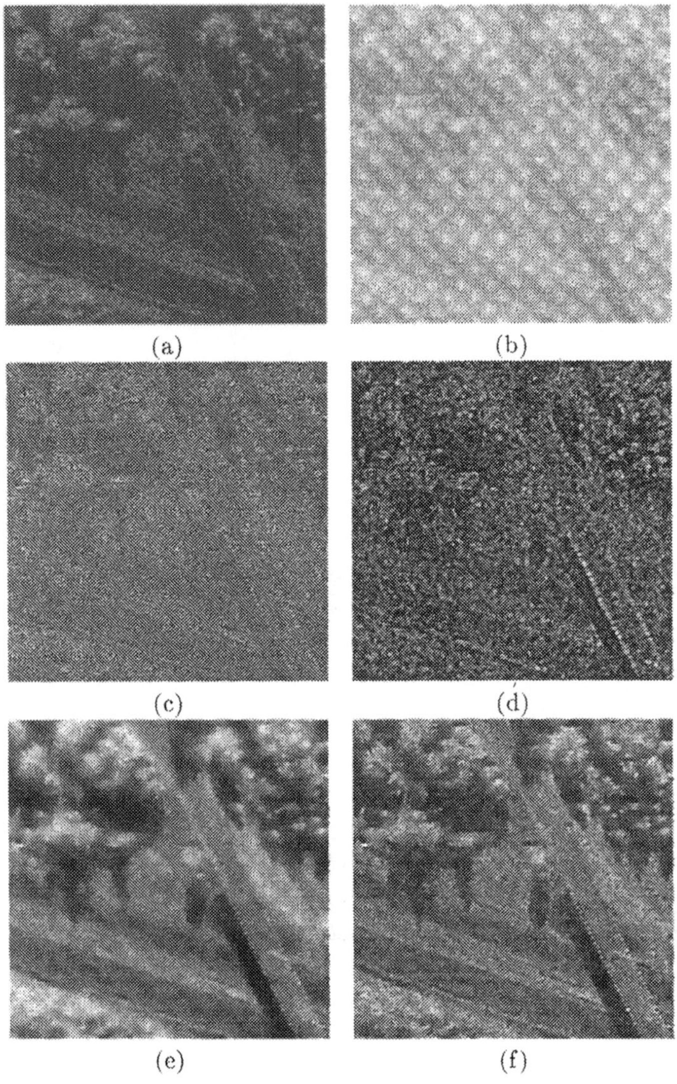

Figure 10. (a) Unprocessed synthetic aperture radar (SAR) image of an upstate New York scene consisting of a highway with a bridge overpass. (b) Logarithm-transformed SAR image. (c) Normalized contrast enhancement of (a), output of Stage 1 of BCS of Figure 7a. (d) BCS boundaries, output of Stages 3 and 4 of BCS. (e) Filling-in of featural signals from Stage 1, using Stage 2 boundaries only. (f) Filling-in of featural signals from Stage 2, using bipole-completed boundaries from Stages 3 and 4. See text for details. (Reprinted with permission from Mingolla *et al.* (1999).)

Another study has shown how bipole mechanisms and related receptive field properties can be self-organized through developmental tuning (i.e., learning) in networks exposed to visual inputs containing image gradients (Grossberg and Williamson, 2001). Bipole mechanisms also underlie a treatment of T-junctions that supports amodal and modal completion and figure/ground separation (Kelly and Grossberg, 2000).

Relaxation labeling for contour finding

Relaxation labeling schemes have been developed in the context of optimization to find consistent interpretations for measurement problems with uncertainty. To introduce concepts, consider a set of entities and the relations between them. This can be described as a graph $\mathcal{G}(\mathcal{N}, \mathcal{E})$ where the set of nodes (or cells), $\mathcal{N}$, represent the entities (e.g., objects or features) and the links, $\mathcal{E}$, represent the relations between pairs of nodes. To each of the nodes will be associated a label from a given set, $\mathcal{L} = \{l\}$, with $l = 1, ..., m$. The association of a set of labels to each node is guided by constraints which describe the mutual consistency between labelings for n-tuples of entities in certain (spatial) arrangements. In spatial vision, locations on a discrete grid can be considered as nodes $\mathcal{N}$ which are connected to their neighbors via the set of links $\mathcal{E}$ (in a given connectivity structure).

Description of the modeling framework. In the case of boundary finding, the labeling problem can be formulated as one of finding the most likely set of orientations at the boundary positions. In order to deal with the sparsity of edge locations, the set of orientation labels is extended by a "no-line" label to account for the non-responsiveness of cells at locations that are not elements of a boundary. Initial likelihoods (or responses) are generated by oriented filters that measure the presence of local structure at different orientations in the input image. These responses need to be normalized against the maximum response in the image. This allows the treatment of filter responses as probabilities for assigning orientation labels to locations. The relatability of orientations (in the image graph) is measured by a compatibility function defined over n-tuples of orientations. In order to keep the complexity of this function at a reasonable level, only pairs of labels are evaluated. The individual strengths for orientation measures at a given image location are iteratively updated through the support that is gathered from relatable activities in a spatial neighborhood.

The elements of the relaxation model by Parent and Zucker (1989) are as follows:

(1) *Spatial weighting function*

The weighting is only specified indirectly by the requirement of having pathways of equal length along different curved shape outlines. The path lengths of neigh-

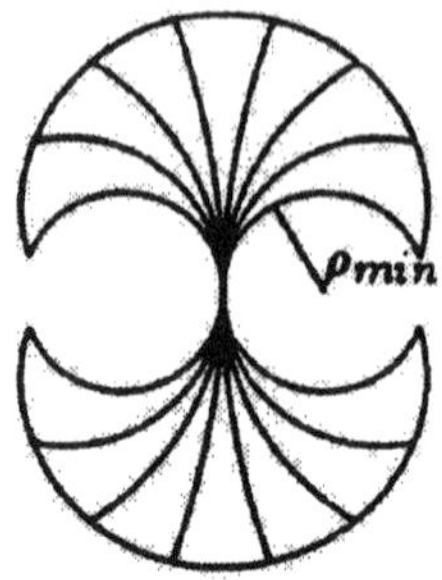

Figure 11. This figure outlines the configuration of the spatial integration field to measure compatibilities between contrast orientations measured at different locations in Parent and Zucker's (1989) model. The target cell is located at the center with matching orientation as this vertically oriented "halbert" shape. The curved sectors drawn in each hemi-field, or lobe, denote the different curvature sectors depicting the range of uncertainty for the curvature classes assigned to each tangent orientation. (This is Figure 13 from Parent and Zucker (1989), reproduced with permission.)

borhood support define an "extent" predicate

$$P^{length}_{\mathbf{xx}'\theta} = \begin{cases} 1 & \text{if path length } ((\mathbf{x},\theta) \text{ to } (\mathbf{x}',\phi)) \text{ is closer than max. arc length} \\ 0 & \text{otherwise} \end{cases} \tag{12}$$

(compare the geometry depicted in Figure 11); here θ again identifies the orientation of the target cell at the center, and ϕ refers to the orientation of a related cell in the spatial neighborhood). This predicate function is augmented by an intra-pixel length correction factor $length(\mathbf{x},\mathbf{x}')$ to compensate for any discretization effects in the orientation space. The spatial coupling is then defined by

$$\text{weight}^{\text{left}}_{\mathbf{xx}'\theta} = P^{length,\text{left}}_{\mathbf{xx}'\theta} \cdot length(\mathbf{x},\mathbf{x}') \text{ and} \tag{13}$$

$$\text{weight}^{\text{right}}_{\mathbf{xx}'\theta} = P^{length,\text{right}}_{\mathbf{xx}'\theta} \cdot length(\mathbf{x},\mathbf{x}'). \tag{14}$$

(2) *Feature cooperation*

The *relatability* of two tangent orientations is defined by a co-circularity constraint corresponding to Eqn. 7 above and is denoted here by the function $c_{\mathbf{xx}'\theta\phi}$. An additional function is defined for the partitioning of the spatial neighborhood function into curved strips of shape segments (Figure 11). The rationale for this

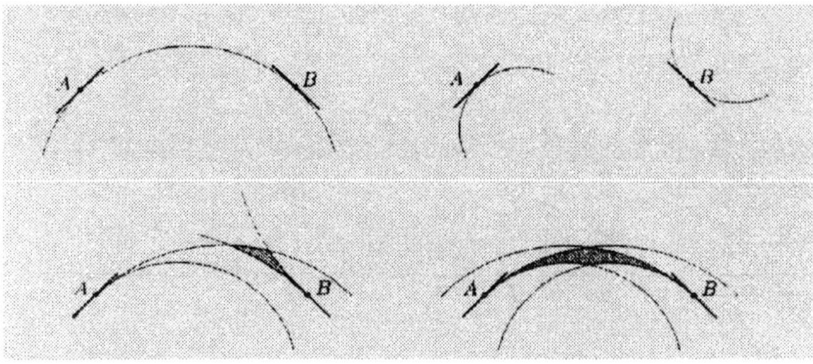

Figure 12. This sketch outlines the configurations of spatially related, or compatible, contrast orientations. The usefulness of a curvature constraint is highlighted in the top row in which two identical contrast configurations (at points A and B) belong to the same contour segment (left) or to different segments (right). The bottom row shows a sketch of how the compatibility between curvature classes can be expressed by an intersection measure of overlap between sectors of the spatial integration fields (grey regions). Incompatible curvatures tend to reduce the area of intersection (left) while compatible ones maximize this measure (right). (These are Figures 11 and 12 from Parent and Zucker (1989), reproduced with permission).

partition is sketched in Figure 12 (top) showing that two identical spatial configurations of tangents are related if they are part of the same boundary segment (thus having the same curvature). Conversely, if the tangents appear to belong to two segregated parts it is likely that they do not share the same curvature class $\mathcal{K}_k(\cdot)$. The local assignment of a curvature class is defined by an additional predicate

$$K^k_{\mathbf{xx}'\theta} = \begin{cases} 1 & \text{if } \rho^k_{\min} \leq \rho_{\mathbf{xx}'\theta} \leq \rho^k_{\max} \text{ (radius of curvature)} \\ 0 & \text{otherwise} \end{cases}, \qquad (15)$$

where $\rho_{\mathbf{xx}'\theta}$ denotes an estimate of local curvature derived from local tangent orientations.

Two tangent orientations are mutually relatable if they belong to compatible curvature classes. This constraint is displayed in Figure 12 (bottom) showing the consistency of curvature classes as the overlap sections (grey regions) of the curvature sectors. This constraint is again encoded by a binary predicate function

$$C^{kk'}_{\mathbf{xx}'\theta\phi} = \begin{cases} 1 & \text{if } \mathcal{K}_k(\theta) \sim \mathcal{K}_{k'}(\phi) \\ 0 & \text{otherwise} \end{cases} \qquad (16)$$

where '$\sim$' means compatibility between curvature classes. The pairwise relatability of tangent orientations is then finally evaluated by

$$\text{relate}_{\mathbf{xx}'\theta\phi} = c_{\mathbf{xx}'\theta\phi} \cdot K^k_{\mathbf{xx}'\theta\phi} \cdot C^{kk'}_{\mathbf{xx}'\theta\phi}. \qquad (17)$$

The *input activation* is generated by a field of neural line detectors that measure the presence of oriented line-like structure. Before entering the next stage of integration, their activity $y_{\mathbf{x}\theta}$ undergoes a stage of lateral non-maximum suppression in a discrete 3 X 3 position-orientation neighborhood, $\mathcal{N}_{3\times3}$. This filtering can be expressed as

$$M_{\mathbf{x}\theta} = \begin{cases} 1 & \text{if } y_{\mathbf{x}\theta} \text{ is a lateral maximum} \\ 0 & \text{otherwise} \end{cases} \tag{18}$$

to form a binary label.

(3) *Support and activation function*

The support is computed by the combination of sub-fields and their result from integrated activities. We get

$$z_{\mathbf{x}\theta} = \max_{k=1,k_{\max}} \sum_{\mathbf{x}'\phi} y_{\mathbf{x}'\phi}\, M_{\mathbf{x}'\phi} \cdot \text{relate}_{\mathbf{x}\mathbf{x}'\theta\phi} \cdot \left(\text{weight}^{\text{left}}_{\mathbf{x}\mathbf{x}'\theta} + \text{weight}^{\text{right}}_{\mathbf{x}\mathbf{x}'\theta}\right). \tag{19}$$

The final activation is computed in a stage of normalizing and remapping the support for a given target cell, i.e.

$$v_{\mathbf{x}\theta} = \frac{z_{\mathbf{x}\theta} - z_{\min}}{z_{\max} - z_{\min}}. \tag{20}$$

This network utilizes an activation dynamics in which the normalized support values $v_{\mathbf{x}\theta}$ is fed back to the layer of the current input activities.[4] A discrete time iterative update rule follows which can be described as

$$y^{t+1}_{\mathbf{x}\theta} = f\left(y^{t}_{\mathbf{x}\theta}, v_{\mathbf{x}\theta}\right), \tag{21}$$

where $f(\cdot)$ denotes some function that takes into account the normalized total support for all orientations at a given location.

Variants of the model and further details. The relaxation scheme reviewed above can be considered as an elaborated version of earlier simplified schemes of relaxation labeling (e.g., Zucker, 1985; Zucker, Hummel, and Rosenfeld, 1977; Zucker and Parent, 1984). The previous models did not include any geometric definition of pairwise compatibilities between two activations, nor did they include any definition of curvature classes. The generic support function is defined as

$$z_{\mathbf{x}\theta} = \sum_{\mathbf{x}'} \left(\text{weight}^{\text{left}}_{\mathbf{x}\mathbf{x}'\theta} + \text{weight}^{\text{right}}_{\mathbf{x}\mathbf{x}'\theta}\right) \cdot \sum_{\phi} y_{\mathbf{x}'\phi} \cdot \text{relate}_{\mathbf{x}\mathbf{x}'\theta\phi}. \tag{22}$$

[4] In the context of (probabilistic) relaxation labeling, the current activity of a cell selective for a given orientation denotes the probability of proper assignment of a given label (orientation) at a particular location.

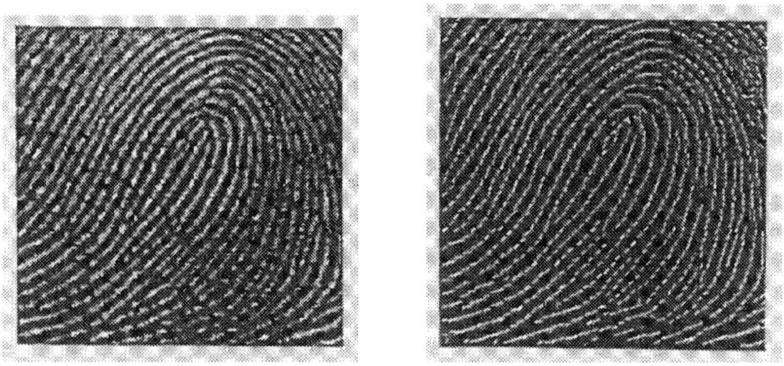

Figure 13 This figure shows the processing results for a fingerprint image (left). Tangent fields are shown after two iterations of the relaxation process (right). (This is Figure 19 from Parent and Zucker (1989), reproduced with permission.)

The relatability function 'relate' is usually defined so that the values are in the interval [-1, 1] – with negative relatabilities for incompatible orientations and with positive relatabilities for compatible arrangements. The activation is generated by the update rule

$$y_{\mathbf{x}\theta}^{t+1} = \frac{y_{\mathbf{x}\theta}^{t}\left[1 + z_{\mathbf{x}\theta}\right]}{\sum_{\phi} y_{\mathbf{x}\phi}^{t}\left[1 + z_{\mathbf{x}\phi}\right]}. \tag{23}$$

In all, the activation is normalized locally against the total support gathered for different orientations. (Compare Eqns. 20 and 21; see Zucker, Hummel, and Rosenfeld, 1977). The scheme proposed by Parent and Zucker (1989) thus investigates the elaboration of the spatial relatability function by formalizing the co-circularity constraint and by incorporating the compatibility of curvature classes of pairs of orientations.

In order to make the relaxation process more sensitive to the image structure, Zucker and Parent (1984) proposed a mechanism to better evaluate the responses of oriented line detectors of different sizes and to measure the deviations of observed responses from expected ones. The expectations have been computed off-line for frequently occurring image structures. The relatability in this model is expressed as

$$\text{relate}_{\mathbf{x}\mathbf{x}'\theta\phi} = 1 - \sum_{S} \| y_{\theta\phi;S}^{expect} - y_{\theta\phi;S}^{obs} \|, \tag{24}$$

where S denotes the scale, or filter size, *expect* represents the pre-computed model responses, *obs* denotes the currently measured, or observed, activities, and $\|\cdot\|$ defines a proper norm. It is assumed that the y responses are normalized, thus having magnitudes

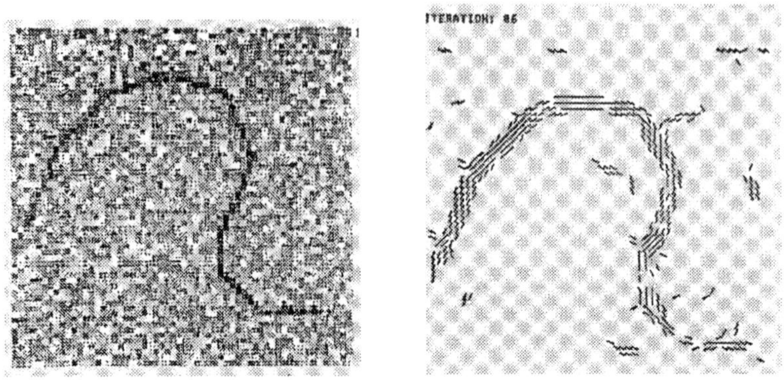

Figure 14. Left panel: drawing of a curved dark line on a light background. (The image is corrupted with noise). Right panel: result of the relaxation process for finding the tangents of the noisy contour after six iterations. Note that this process does not include any mechanism of lateral inhibition, or non-maximum suppression. (This is Figure 14.4 from Zucker and Parent (1984), reproduced with permission).

in the range $[0,1]$. Identical responses between expectation and observation lead to maximum relatability, i.e. $\text{relate}_{\mathbf{xx}'\theta\phi} = 1$, whereas dissimilar responses extinguish the measure of relatability. In other schemes, e.g. in Parent and Zucker (1989) and Grossberg and Mingolla (1985), the expected visual structure is encoded in the weighting pattern of the matching field, which leads to a correlative metric to measure similarity between model expectations and observations.

Characteristic simulations. Applications of the relaxation labeling approach are shown in Figures 13 and 14. The first case shows the result for a noisy image of a finger print, whereas the second case shows the extraction for an isolated line on a noisy background. These examples demonstrate the reduction of uncertainty of localized measures based on the integration via an association field and also demonstrate its robustness against noise. The iterative update mechanism is designed to increase the certainty of consistent measurements against the inconsistent ones at each spatial location independent from any other support measure. This leads to a potential broadening of the response field of the grouping or curve enhancement (compare Figure 14). In order to compensate for this, the non-maximum suppression ($M_{\mathbf{x}\theta}$, Eqn. 18) is utilized to achieve a proper thinning. Alternatively, the activity distribution can be post-processed by a separate thinning algorithm.

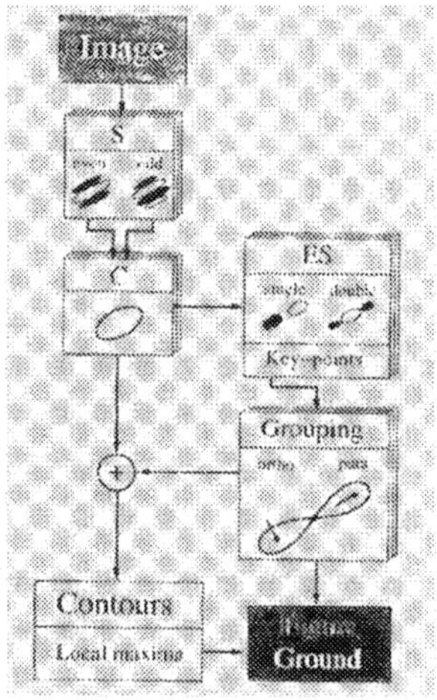

Figure 15. Elementary stages of the contour grouping model proposed by Heitger and coworkers. Details of the processing stages and the logic of the computational scheme are described in the text. (This is Figure 2 from Heitger *et al.* (1998), reprinted with permission.)

Filter model for the forward integration of end-stop responses

Based on the results of electrophysiological investigations of the response properties of V2 contour cells (e.g., Peterhans and von der Heydt, 1989; von der Heydt and Peterhans, 1989), Heitger *et al.* (1998) suggested a computational model of a mechanism for contour grouping. (See also Heitger and von der Heydt (1993) for a first description of the scheme.) Figure 15 presents an overview of the elementary processing stages. The architecture consists of a set of hierarchically organized filtering stages. Oriented contrast is measured at the stage of simple and complex cells. The result of oriented end-stop (ES) detection from complex cell responses feeds into a segregated grouping pathway. The definition of the proposed grouping mechanism is mainly influenced by the goal to make the scheme sensitive to figure-ground direction. The rationale for this design principle is the observation that partial occlusions or surface borders often generate abrupt terminations of surface items – preferentially at the side of the partially occluded surface (i.e., the background; compare also Finkel and Edelman (1989)). Also Baumann, van der Zwan, and Peterhans (1997) found evidence that cells of V2 that respond to illusory contours are sensitive to the direction of contrast that is compatible with the occlusion direction. In the computational scheme, model ES cells signal the possible directions of the occluding surface at corners and line ends. (Compare

Grossberg and Mingolla's (1985a, 1985b) treatment of "end cuts.") Two independent grouping rules were introduced to deal with different occlusion features, namely *ortho* grouping at line ends and *para* grouping for discontinuities in contour orientation, e.g. at corners. In order to generate a dense representations of boundary activation, complex cell responses to luminance contrasts are added to the interpolated contours between ES cells.

Description of the modeling framework. The elements central for the definition of the grouping model of Heitger *et al.* (1998) are the following:

(1) *Spatial weighting function*
The model utilizes the same scheme of bipolar weighting functions as those originally proposed by Grossberg and Mingolla (1985b). The weighting functions are separable in polar space such as those described in Eqn. 4 defining the spatial kernels $\text{weight}^{\text{left}}_{\mathbf{xx}'\theta}$ and $\text{weight}^{\text{right}}_{\mathbf{xx}'\theta}$.

(2) *Feature cooperation*
The *relatability* of oriented spatially separate ES responses is defined by a rule-based scheme that incorporates an implicit notation of curvature consistency. In order to distinguish between directions of figure and ground, the scheme requires that only those corners and line-ends cooperate which point in the same direction.

Para and ortho grouping. Figure 16 sketches the logic of the grouping strategy. In a nutshell, para groupings occur for ES responses at corners oriented towards the location of the target grouping cell between two relatable items. The relatability is indicated by the orientation of ES cells orthogonal to the grouping direction: Same orientations cooperate, opposite orientations do not. Similarly, ortho groupings can be established between responses of like orientations, ES cells of opposite orientation are not relatable. In order to keep a specificity to figure-ground direction, separate cooperation fields are established for each individual termination direction.

Orientation variability and curvature. The scheme is designed so that the association fields only integrate responses of ES cells in individual lobes of different orientations. The partitioning and combination of the integration (or association) field is a spatial variant of the curvature classes introduced by Parent and Zucker (1989). Four "curvature classes" are distinguished that are depicted in Figure 17.[5] In this scheme, the integrated responses from

[5]In the original definition a weighted sum of pairs of bipoles at different orientations is proposed (Heitger *et al.*, 1998). However, a simple rearrangement of terms leads to the scheme outlined above.

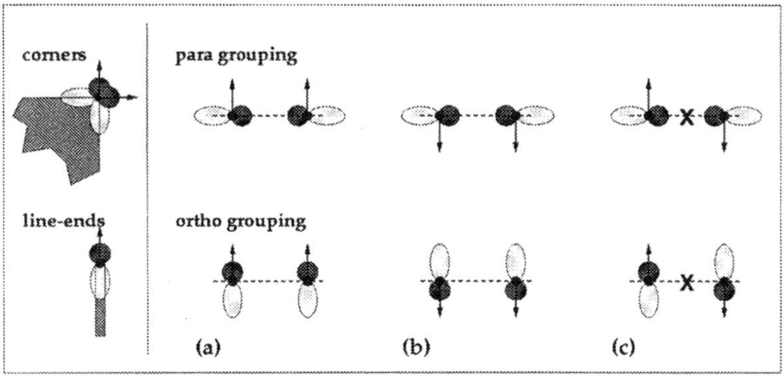

Figure 16. The sketches show the idealized responses of ES cells at sharp corners and line-ends, respectively, which in turn serve as input for the subsequent grouping stage in the Heitger et al. model. The authors distinguish two types of spatial integration mechanisms, namely 'para' and 'ortho', depending on the input features. Panels (a) and (b) show cases of compatible ES-orientation which are allowed to group. Panel (c) shows the cases of opposite ES-orientation where no grouping occurs according to the model's rules.

either side of a grouping cell are not simply added as in Zucker's proposal but a non-linear AND-gate combination is used, similar to the Grossberg and Mingolla (1985b) scheme, as is next described.

The *input activation* to the grouping scheme is generated by a field of oriented ES cells. In order to account for any orientation variability the ES responses are summed over nearest neighbor orientations. We get

$$\bar{w}_{\mathbf{x}\theta} = \sum_{k\in\{-1,0,1\}} w_{\mathbf{x}\theta+k\Delta\theta}. \tag{25}$$

Responses assigned to ortho- and para-grouping, respectively, are computed separately for both figure-ground directions $\uparrow$ and $\downarrow$. The following equations have been proposed (for notational simplicity, we omit subscripts for location and orientation):

$$x^{\uparrow}_{ortho} = \bar{w}^{\uparrow}\,, \quad x^{\downarrow}_{ortho} = \bar{w}^{\downarrow} \tag{26}$$

and

$$\begin{aligned} x^{\uparrow\,\text{left}}_{para} &= p^{\uparrow}\cdot w^{\text{left}}\,, \quad x^{\uparrow\,\text{right}}_{para} = p^{\uparrow}\cdot w^{\text{right}} \\ x^{\downarrow\,\text{left}}_{para} &= p^{\downarrow}\cdot w^{\text{left}}\,, \quad x^{\downarrow\,\text{right}}_{para} = p^{\downarrow}\cdot w^{\text{right}}\,, \end{aligned} \tag{27}$$

with $p^{\uparrow} = \bar{w}^{\uparrow}/(\bar{w}^{\uparrow}+\bar{w}^{\downarrow})$ and $p^{\downarrow} = \bar{w}^{\downarrow}/(\bar{w}^{\uparrow}+\bar{w}^{\downarrow}) = 1-p^{\uparrow}$. These responses of ortho

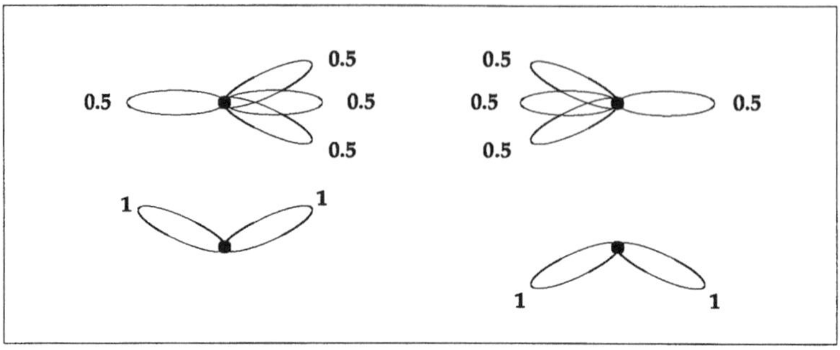

Figure 17. The figures show the integration (or association) field that has been partitioned into sectors of individual lobes. The association fields shown at the top support nearly straight horizontal completion allowing slight boundary curvatures to either side of the grouping cell location. The fields shown at the bottom realize grouping of left or right curvature segments. The numbers indicate the individual weights of contribution from each lobe.

and para contributions are linearly interpolated. We get the activities

$$\begin{aligned} y^{\uparrow\,\text{left}} &= (1-\alpha)x^{\uparrow}_{ortho} + \alpha x^{\uparrow\,\text{left}}_{para}, \quad y^{\uparrow\,\text{right}} = (1-\alpha)x^{\uparrow}_{ortho} + \alpha x^{\uparrow\,\text{right}}_{para} \\ y^{\downarrow\,\text{left}} &= (1-\alpha)x^{\downarrow}_{ortho} + \alpha x^{\downarrow\,\text{left}}_{para}, \quad y^{\downarrow\,\text{right}} = (1-\alpha)x^{\downarrow}_{ortho} + \alpha x^{\downarrow\,\text{right}}_{para}, \end{aligned} \tag{28}$$

where the interpolation is controlled by the "cornerness" index $\alpha = 2\sum_{\phi}(w_{\phi} \cdot w_{\phi_{\perp}})^{1/2} / \sum_{\phi}(w_{\phi} + w_{\phi_{\perp}})$ which gives a value $\alpha \approx 1$ for corners and $\alpha \approx 0$ for line-ends.

(3) *Support and activation function*

The support is computed by the multiplicative combination (AND-gating) of bipole lobes. We get

$$z^{\uparrow}_{\mathbf{x}\theta} = \sum_{k} \left[\sum_{\mathbf{x}'\phi} \left(y^{\uparrow}_{\mathbf{x}'\phi} \cdot \text{weight}^{k,\text{left}}_{\mathbf{x}\mathbf{x}'\theta} \right) \cdot \sum_{\mathbf{x}'\phi} \left(y^{\uparrow}_{\mathbf{x}'\phi} \cdot \text{weight}^{k,\text{right}}_{\mathbf{x}\mathbf{x}'\theta} \right) \right], \tag{29}$$

were k denotes the different "curvature classes" that were represented by the differently oriented lobes (Figure 17). The grouping response for the opposite figure-ground direction $z^{\downarrow}_{\mathbf{x}\theta}$ are computed analoguously. The boundary representation is computed by pooling the activities of complex cells c and both grouping activations selective for opposite figure-ground directions

$$u_{\mathbf{x}\theta} = c_{\mathbf{x}\theta} + m\left(z^{\uparrow}_{\mathbf{x}\theta} + z^{\downarrow}_{\mathbf{x}\theta}\right). \tag{30}$$

The constant m regulates the relative importance of luminance contrast and grouping strength. The responses are spatially blurred and thus positionally uncertain.

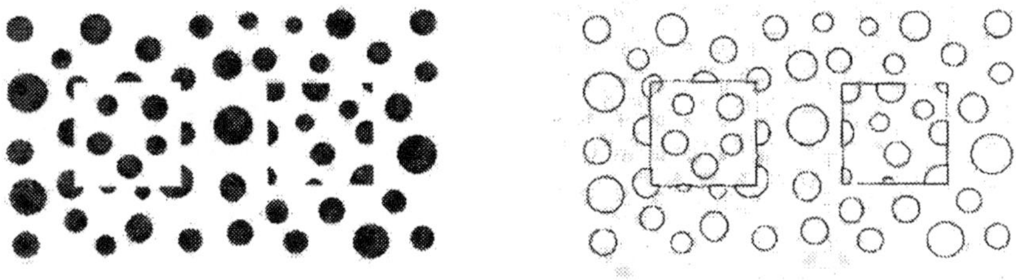

Figure 18. Contour grouping based on selective integration of ES responses using the scheme of Heitger and coworkers. Input pattern (left) with an occlusion pattern generated by a near surface and an occlusion generated by a hole in the ground revealing a far surface (from Kanizsa, 1979). Final contour representation (right) from oriented contrast responses and grouping of ES responses along the illusory contours that were induced by the occlusions. Due to the selectivity of the grouping scheme to the orientation of ES directions, figure-ground direction is signaled correctly (not shown here). (These panels are Figures 16 (a) and (b) from Heitger *et al.* (1998), reprinted with permission.)

A stage of non-maximum suppression is applied to the pooled boundary responses generating $u_{\theta_{\max}}$.

The selection of the direction of figure and ground is based on a voting scheme. The direction of the background is assigned to the side that contributes more ES responses in the grouping (see Figure 18). This is simply calculated by $D = z^{\uparrow}_{\theta_{\max}} - z^{\downarrow}_{\theta_{\max}}$ and then taking the sign of the result.

Variants of the model and further details. The present grouping scheme is an elaboration of an earlier one sketched by Peterhans and von der Heydt (1991), who proposed that pairs of ES cells with distant receptive fields that signal the same end direction are connected by gating cells. (See the description in Lesher (1995)). Gating cells of opposite directions are pooled together with complex cells of orthogonal orientation that signal real contrasts. The non-linear grouping of pairs of ES cell responses requires a precise definition of the width of the connectivity pattern to span certain gap sizes. In order to successfully group across different gap sizes, several gating cells must exist at each spatial position that integrate ES responses from different distances. A formalized representation of such an integration scheme (for one direction) is given by

$$z^{\uparrow}_{\mathbf{x}\theta} = \sum_{offset} y^{\uparrow}_{\mathbf{x}-offset,\theta} \cdot y^{\uparrow}_{\mathbf{x}+offset,\theta}, \tag{31}$$

where $offset$ denotes the distance from the target location along θ (the integration for $z^{\downarrow}_{\mathbf{x}\theta}$ is computed in an analoguous fashion). This simplified version in Eqn. 31

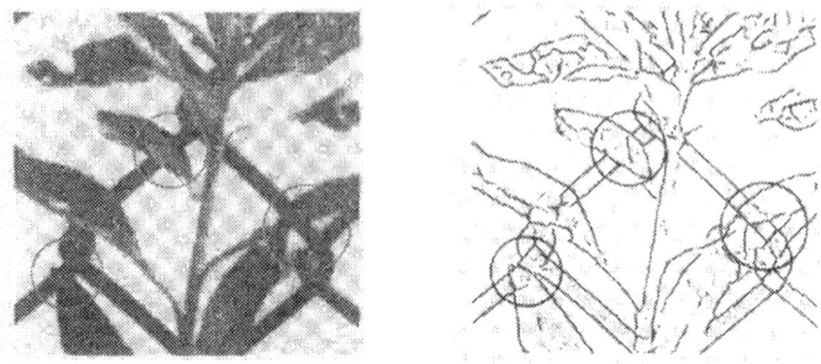

Figure 19. Performance of the model for a natural scene. Input image that contains leaves which partially occlude the wires of a metal fence (left). Complete contour map of contrasts and grouping responses (right). Critical regions of contour completions at occlusions are highlighted by circles. (These panels are Figures 17 (a) and (c) from Heitger *et al.* (1998), reprinted with permission.)

is a special case of the scheme that utilizes a bipole mechanism (compare Eqn. 29). The summation is absorbed by the use of spatial weighting functions $\text{weight}^{k,\text{left}}_{\mathbf{xx}'\theta}$ and $\text{weight}^{k,\text{right}}_{\mathbf{xx}'\theta}$, respectively. Also, more flexibility has been introduced in the elaborated scheme by integration from cells of different orientations ϕ and neighboring lobes of the bipole in order to deal with curved boundaries.

Characteristic simulations. Processing results of the filtering and grouping scheme are shown in Figs. and . The first case shows the result for two occlusion patterns in opposite figure-ground relation (left). Illusory contours are generated along the abrupt terminations that are caused by surface occlusions (middle). Figure-ground direction is correctly predicted (though not shown in Figure 19) through the voting of the directions of ES cells. The proposed voting principle that assigns the background direction according to the sign of the magnitude D (see above) is successful in many cases. However, figure-ground direction cannot always be determined by local rules alone as proposed by Heitger and colleagues. (See Lesher (1995), Figure 4b and discussion.) Figure 19 shows the application of the Heitger *et al.* (1998) scheme for a real world image in which partial occlusions were interpolated depending on their relative widths.

Other models

The models (and their variants) outlined above define different classes of approaches for feature integration based on local mechanisms. The *BCS mechanism* emphasizes the

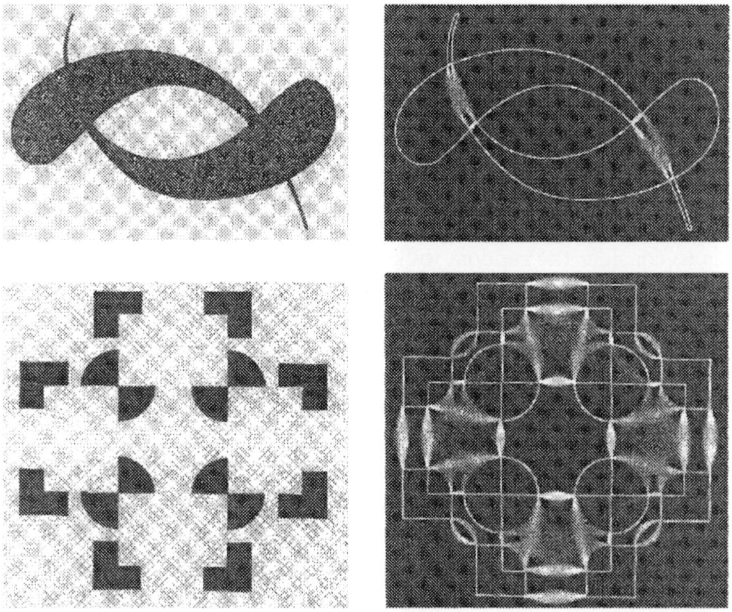

Figure 20. Simulation results for two input configurations (left) that produce percepts of illusory contours and the corresponding results generated by Williams and Jacobs' model (right). The activities were summed over orientations and represent the integrated edge maps formed by the sum of complex cell responses and the result of contour interpolation by stochastic completion fields. (These are Figures 10 and 11 from Williams and Jacobs (1997a), reprinted with permission.)

role of feedback in order to sharpen completed contours, amplify consistent information and explain asymmetries and conflicting effects in the perception of real and illusory boundaries. The *relaxation labeling* approach emphasizes the enhancement of noisy measures in a consistent and salient arrangement to generate smooth curves. The process is guaranteed to converge to a stable equilibrium. The *filter scheme*, finally, emphasizes the fast forward integration of selected stimulus features utilizing parallel channels of selective processing and the subsequent integration of segregated representations into one final result. Below, we discuss some models that have been developed more recently by highlighting their new features and computational competences in comparison with the models discussed above.[6]

[6]It should be emphasized here that we do not review a number of grouping and integration models that appeared in the computational vision literature, unless they aim to deal explicitly with the explanation of perceptual data.

Completion fields

Williams and colleagues have proposed a framework that investigates the shape of grouping fields and utilized the derived weightings for simulating illusory contour generation (Thornber and Williams, 1996; Williams and Jacobs, 1997a, 1997b). The key idea is to consider the random walk of particles in a discrete lattice of the sampled space-orientation domain. The goal is to determine the probability density function for elements of a contour path between two end points (which in turn are assumed to be generated by ES neurons as in the model of Heitger *et al.* (1998). The stochastic process underlying the random walk is divided into the components of a source field and a sink field. Each of them denote the probability densities that a particle at a given spatial location (x, y) and orientation θ (the initial condition) reaches another point (i, j, ϕ) on the space-orientation lattice. The stochastic completion field is finally the product of the source and the sink field. Its strengths represent the likelihood of smooth paths connecting a pair of points (i.e., ES responses).

The strength of boundary interpolation can be computed by the spatial convolution of impulse functions on the space-orientation lattice with the kernels of the stochastic completion field. In terms of our framework developed in this chapter, this kernel denotes the weighting function of the *spatial weighting* and the *relatability.* Unlike previous formulations, here the two contributions do not occur in a separable fashion, but, instead appear as a joint distribution of likelihoods. This is due to the formulation of the underlying process as a stochastic walk on the 3-D lattice of spatial locations and orientations. The width of the spatial kernel can be controlled by the decay of particle activation in the corresponding Fokker-Planck equation. Also, the opening of the 'figure-eight' shape of the completion field is varied by the variance of the normal distribution which controls the "straightness" of the interpolated boundary (Williams and Jacobs, 1997a).

The *combination of subfields*, or lobes, is additive since the stochastic process which computes the path probabilities between two end points finally yields a symmetric convolution kernel. The *support* is therefore computed by the convolution of the input ES responses with the kernels derived from the stochastic completion fields. Figure 20 shows the simulation results for the generation of boundary completions for input images that contain illusory contour arrangements. The results show the final integrated edge map that is defined by complex cell responses for physical contrasts and the activities generated by the interpolation process. (Compare Heitger and von der Heydt, 1993; Heitger *et al.*, 1998.) The generated activity distributions vary with the length

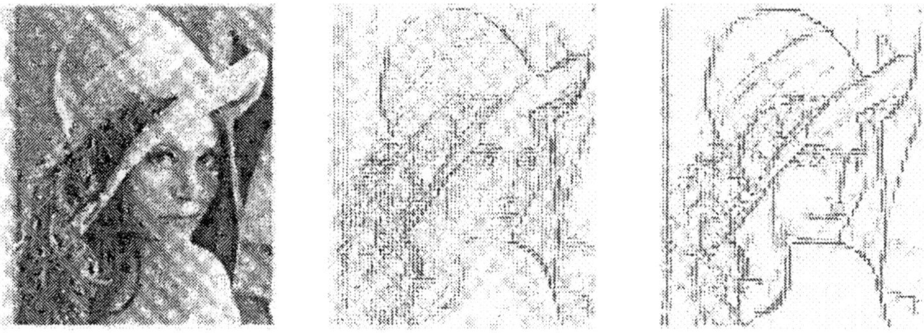

Figure 21. Demonstration of contour enhancement and reduction of noise responses for a natural test image using Li's model (left); initial responses of oriented contrast detectors show a mixture of strong edge response and weak spurious responses for fine structure and homogeneous regions (middle); thresholded model output is generated by the average activity from 24 cycles of oscillator membrane potential (right) showing enhanced activities along significant object boundaries. (This is Figure 5b of Li (1998), reproduced with permission.)

of the boundary gaps and the shape of the interpolated contour. Note that the authors make no particular attempt to distinguish between the representation of boundaries for modal and amodal completions.

Contour integration and segmentation

Li (1998, 1999a, 1999b) proposed a model of spatial boundary integration in V1 based on a network of coupled oscillators that are defined by pairs of inhibitory interneurons and excitatory cells. Li's model also utilizes oriented weighting functions for lateral interaction between orientation selective cells. Each cell receives net input by laterally integrating activities in a spatially weighted neighborhood. The *combination of sub-fields*, or lobes – according to the scheme depicted in Figure 6 – is additive, leading to the *spatial weighting* $\text{weight}_{\mathbf{xx}'\theta} = \text{weight}^{\text{left}}_{\mathbf{xx}'\theta} + \text{weight}^{\text{right}}_{\mathbf{xx}'\theta}$. The selectivity of the excitatory integration field for *feature compatibility* measurement, $\text{relate}_{\mathbf{xx}'\theta\phi}$, is similar to the scheme specified in Eqn. 6. The opening angle of the spatial weighting function is approximately ±45 deg. around the orientation axis of the target cell. An inhibitory influence is generated from cells at laterally offset positions and an orientation preference that is similar to the one of the target cell. The segregated fields of excitatory and inhibitory connectivity patterns are thus explicit representations of the feature compatibility function that has been proposed by Parent and Zucker (1989). A similar computational model utilizing coupled oscillators was investigated earlier by Grossberg and Somers (1991). (See Ellias and Grossberg (1975) for an analysis of the dynamic properties of such networks.) This model, however, utilized only one-dimensional chains of oscillators in order to study binding properties as observed in previous physiological findings of stimulus-evoked synchronized oscillatory firing by Eckhorn *et al.* (1998) and Gray *et al.* (1989). Here, the influence of different coupling architectures on the synchronization of cell firing when probed with a single oriented bar in comparison to spatially disconnected bars was studied.

The main focus of Li's investigations lies in the study of how V1 horizontal long-range integration could functionally account for the enhancement of co-circular contour arrangements in cluttered scenes (Li, 1998), the enhancement of texture region boundaries (Li, 1999a) and pop-out effects in visual search (Li, 1999b). Emphasis was devoted to the mathematical analysis and stability behavior of such a network of non-linear coupled oscillators. Simulation results demonstrate the functionality of, e.g., contour enhancement in artificial and natural scenes (see Figure 21). In comparison to the core models described above, Li's model shares several properties with those of Zucker (e.g., Parent and Zucker, 1989) and the BCS (e.g., Grossberg and Mingolla, 1985b; Grossberg, Mingolla, and Ross, 1997; Ross, Grossberg, and Mingolla, 2000) and, consequently, leads to contrast contour enhancement properties as shown by previous models. The enhanced selectivity to texture boundaries, however, seems to be mainly contributed by the pronounced inhibitory action of cells with same orientation preference. These are integrated from lateral spatially offset positions but not from regions that overlap the field of mutually excitatory interactions along the axis of the target cell's orientational preference. This provides the machinery to signal local orientation contrast, e.g., near the borders of texture regions, and also to sharpen the activity distribution along a ridge of activations.

Boundary finding as model matching

Neumann and coworkers have investigated the role of context effects that are generated by the arrangements of contrast responses that are generated along boundaries and that are integrated by a process of long-range interaction (Hansen *et al.*, 2001; Neumann and Sepp, 1999). The main focus lies on the investigation of the functionality of recurrent cortico-cortical interaction. Adaptive resonance theory, or ART (Carpenter and Grossberg, 1988; Grossberg, 1980) proposes that the coincidence between a spatial distribution of activation at an early processing stage and the predictions from categorical representations of model shape patterns at a higher stage enables the weight adaptation of the connectivities between the associated areas. Similarly, inspired by

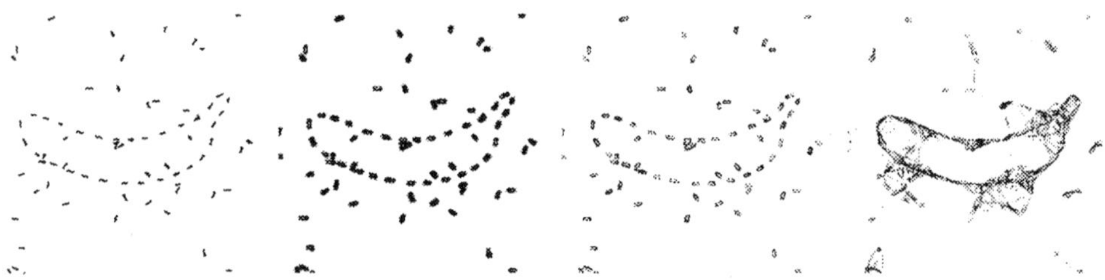

Figure 22. The figure shows the equilibrated results of boundary processing for a fragmented shape outline (left) with Neumann and Sepp's model. The second panel shows the spatial arrangement of model complex cell responses from the initial stage of oriented contrast detection. The third and fourth panels show the responses of cells at the stage of model V1 and the boundary cells of model V2, respectively. (This is Figure 5 from Neumann and Sepp (1999), reprinted with permission.)

basic principles of pattern recognition, descending pathways between cortical areas are suggested to carry flexible templates which are subsequently compared with the features of the sensory input (Mumford, 1991, 1994). Following these ideas, Neumann and Sepp's approach considers initial filter responses from oriented contrast detectors as feature measurements that are fed forward to a stage of long-range integration for matching. This (model) matching, according to the description given earlier, utilizes a pattern of weighted connectivities which represent the most likely patterns of contrast orientations along boundary segments of expected shape outlines. The degree of match generates a signature whose activity is used to modulate those initial activations at the feature detection stage that are consistent with the model expectation.

In all, the model incorporates components which also appear in the three core models introduced above: The *spatial weightings*, $\text{weight}_{\mathbf{xx}'\theta}^{\text{left,right}}$ are similarly defined as in Eqn. 5. The *feature compatibility* function incorporates an excitatory as well as an inhibitory weight field. Co-circular tangent orientations are supportive as they define a measure of feature relatability, $\text{relate}_{\mathbf{xx}'\theta\phi}^{+}$, similar to the scheme of Parent and Zucker (1989) that was also adopted by Gove *et al.* (1995). Instead of incorporating an additional symbolic predicate of curvature consistency (Parent and Zucker, 1989), the integration is supplied by a measure of non-relatability between pairs of contrast orientation, $\text{relate}_{\mathbf{xx}'\theta\phi}^{-}$, which helps to enhance the selectivity of the support function by incorporating more global aspects of contour arrangements. The *combination of subfields* utilizes a mechanism of disinhibition of activities generated by the individual lobes of the bipole when input is generated from *both* lobes. The proposed mechanism utilizes a network of cross-channel inhibition in which equilibrium activity at the output stage results in

$$z_{\mathbf{x}\theta} = LR\frac{2/\zeta + L + R}{1/\zeta + (L+R)/\zeta + LR}, \tag{32}$$

with

$$\begin{aligned} L &= \sum_{\mathbf{x}'\phi} y_{\mathbf{x}'\phi} \cdot \text{relate}_{\mathbf{xx}'\theta\phi} \cdot \text{weight}^{\text{left}}_{\mathbf{xx}'\theta} \quad \text{and} \\ R &= \sum_{\mathbf{x}'\phi} y_{\mathbf{x}'\phi} \cdot \text{relate}_{\mathbf{xx}'\theta\phi} \cdot \text{weight}^{\text{right}}_{\mathbf{xx}'\theta}. \end{aligned} \tag{33}$$

The constant ζ controls the efficacy of the interactions between the bipole lobes. This mechanism incorporates a measure of feature conjunction using an explicit AND-gating functionality like the model proposed by Heitger *et al.* (1998). The *support function*'s functionality combines the feedforward integration (similar to Heitger *et al.* (1998) but without segregated feature representations) and recurrent feedback processing (similar to Grossberg and Mingolla (1985b)). This unifies different approaches that were based on different architectural principles and provides a computational theory of contour integration for surface boundary finding. Simulation results have demonstrated that the model, though it contains only a minimum number of rather simple computational stages, is able to replicate such diverse perceptual effects as, e.g., the integration of fragmented shapes, the modulation of complex cell responses by texture surround effects, and the generation of illusory contours for both Kanizsa and abutted grating illusions. Figure 22 shows the result of boundary enhancement through the action of top-down modulation by the result of contour matching.

Long-range integration for contour detection

Pettet *et al.* (1998) investigated a single layer network architecture which adaptively integrates contour paths in a field of randomly oriented distractors. Elementary items were generated by oriented Gabor patches of a given spatial frequency and constant phase (*cf.* Field *et al.* (1993)). The pop-out of an arrangement of aligned and co-oriented items was related to the increase in activation of network cells by the mutual facilitation of elements which form a (closed) contour.

The input to the stage of spatial integration is generated by a mechanism that comprises an adaptive decision-like processing element. Namely, a 0-1 activity distribution is generated where the 1's were generated by those cells located at the position of a Gabor item with corresponding orientation. The support is subsequently evaluated by a separable function of spatial weighting and relatability. The *spatial weighting* is defined by a radially symmetric function of distance with Gaussian fall-off. The spatial *relatability* $\text{relate}_{\mathbf{xx}'\theta\phi}$ is evaluated on the basis of two Gaussian functions of total curvature and *change* in curvature, respectively, of a fitting spline through a pair of cells and their oriented RFs (*cf.* Figure 1).

The spatial weighting, $\text{weight}_{\mathbf{xx}'\theta}$, unlike the previously described approaches, is isotropic and thus imposes no preferential orientation for the grouping of oriented items in relation to θ. Furthermore, the model proposed by Pettet *et al.* (1998) assumes that lateral interaction extends over the entire field of the stimulus display. This leads to an adaptive scheme in which the efficacy of mutual interactions in the spatial integration process is adjusted to the display size.

The *support* is calculated simply by the sum of weighted input from cells with unit activation and the product weighting of $\text{weight}_{\mathbf{xx}'\theta} \cdot \text{relate}_{\mathbf{xx}'\theta\phi}$. The *activation function*, finally, is defined by the non-linear dynamics of laterally coupled cells in an excitatory layer.

DISCUSSION

In this chapter we have introduced a framework and taxonomy to describe computational neural mechanisms of spatial integration in perceptual grouping. Based on this conception we presented key models as well as some derived from them using this taxonomy. It turns out that many similarities exist between several approaches, but also some differences that need to be further evaluated in order to quantify their functional significance.

All models may be coarsely classified according to the architectural principles involved in the generation of spatial integration and grouping, namely feedforward and feedback mechanisms. A related question refers to the mechanisms that help to establish the neural wiring underlying the observed functionality of grouping. The following questions turn out to be of central importance in order to reveal the principles and mechanisms of spatial long-range integration mechanisms in early and mid-level vision:

(1) What are the core principles underlying the establishing of spatial integration and grouping?

(2) What are the constraints and underlying mechanisms for establishing long-range interactions?

Core principles of grouping

Concerning the first issue, it can be stated that there still is an ongoing debate on the role of feedforward and feedback mechanisms involved in spatial grouping and the dominance of their individual contributions in visual processing. Advocates of a *feedforward*-dominated principle often argue on the basis of time constraints of the brain mechanisms involved compared with the observed physiological data. For example, the time course of generating illusory contour responses related to stimulus onset argues in favor of a mechanism that is mainly feed-forward by simply integrating segregated local items, according to von der Heydt and Peterhans (1989) and Peterhans and von der Heydt (1989). This view has been further fueled by more recent experimental investigations of Thorpe *et al.* (1996) who investigated the lower bounds on time needed by subjects to signal the presence of an object category in a visual scene.

On the other hand, proponents of the view that *feedback* mechanisms play a major role in grouping begin by admitting that relatively noise-free tasks can support "one-pass," essentially feedforward processing within an architecture capable of feedback, and then go on to argue on that recurrent processing allows more flexibility and robustness in shape boundary finding that relies on noisy estimates (Grossberg *et al.* 1997; Zucker, 1985). For example, Grossberg (1994) has argued that feedback mechanisms help to disambiguate and further tune the activities generated to outline the surface of a fragmented shape. Recently, Neumann and Sepp (1999) have combined these seemingly diverging architectural frameworks and have shown that grouping can occur in a "rough-and-ready" fashion by a feedforward mechanism. If there are several initial candidate groupings, feedback helps to further tune and sharpen the spatial responses based on more global information and stimulus context.

The investigation of the differences in the temporal persistence of illusory and contrast boundaries further argues in favor of feedback mechanisms (Francis *et al.*, 1994; Francis and Grossberg, 1996). It was demonstrated empirically that the occluding surface region of a Kanizsa square (which is delineated by illusory contours) has a longer perceptual persistence in comparison to a region that is bounded by a physical contrast (Meyer and Ming, 1988). The neural representation of surface regions seems to be very similar irrespective of the type of boundary Mendola *et al.* (1999). It is therefore reasonable to assume that the main effect of perceptual persistence is due to the mechanisms of boundary generation. It was suggested that boundary activation that is fed by contrast detectors is immediately switched off after withdrawal of the contrast input, whereas the illusory boundaries still receive recurrent facilitation by top-down activation and therefore cause the boundary activation to persist longer Francis *et al.* (1994). In further support of the feedback hypothesis, Ringach and Shapley (1996) found evidence for two masking regimes for stimuli containing illusory contours, the second of which extended more than 300 msec beyond stimulus onset.

Aspects of *temporal coding* principles based on oscillator mechanisms or spiking neurons may play another important role in grouping tasks. Several empirical studies (Eckhorn *et al.*, 1988; Engel *et al.*, 1991; Gray *et al.*, 1989) indicate that distributed representations of related scene fragments are linked by temporally correlated, or synchronized, neural activation. It is claimed that perceptual grouping based on temporal binding implements the principles of Gestalt grouping allowing the desired flexibility in the dynamic linking and segregation that alternative mechanisms such as convergent coding principles or population coding seem to lack (Gray, 1999). Several studies demonstrate that γ-band activity (30-60 Hz) signals the relatedness of stimulus features in a robust fashion (Frien *et al.*, 1994), although this property holds only over small cortical distances of 3-5 millimeters (Saam and Eckhorn, 2000). The temporal coding hypothesis studied in isolation appears, however, to be incomplete. The temporal establishment of grouping addresses the signaling of binding, but not the "how" or "what" of its computation (Shadlen and Movshon, 1999). These questions form the core of this chapter. In all, therefore, our contribution provides a necessary framework to classify several approaches and also help to identify potentially new mechanisms to further improve the computational as well as the explanatory power of grouping models.

Establishing long-range interactions

Early in this chapter we introduced the underlying anatomical, physiological and behavioral basis of grouping. On the behavioral level, it has been demonstrated that the capability of organizing visual patterns, as in the case of illusory contours, is developed postnatal within the first seven months (Bertenthal *et al.*, 1980).[7]

Oriented long-range connections seem to provide the basis for smooth boundary grouping. The oriented fiber connections of an oriented target cell link with other cells of similar orientation preference that are arranged along a line defined by the target cell's orientation (see Figure 4). It remains, however, as an open issue, how these long-range interactions are established and how the stimulus properties of real world scenes constrain the parameters of the relatability function. Possible constraints and underlying mechanisms for establishing oriented lateral long-range connections have been modeled on different levels:

(1) Principles of stochastic motion are utilized to investigate the oriented diffusion of particles by Williams and Jacobs (1997a). The key to this modeling approach

[7]This observation seems to run against the results of more recent studies where babies were shown to group items into units according to the Gestalt laws of organization (Farroni *et al.*, 2000). The stimuli used in both studies differed significantly, however: Whereas the first investigation utilized Kanizsa figures where illusory boundaries need to be generated in order to form surface-related units, the latter study used square items of different luminances that can be spontaneously grouped into columns.

lies in the computation of likely paths that interpolate between pairs of separated items. This basic idea can be generalized, however, such that a neural growth process tends to send axonal arbors along a direction tangential to the target cell's orientation. The growth may be driven along a gradient that decreases with distance and deviation from the reference orientation.

(2) The statistical nature of oriented contrast and boundaries in natural scenes has been investigated to derive coefficients for the co-occurrence of separated pairs of oriented items (Geisler *et al.*, 2001). These authors evaluated the statistics of the triplets defined by the fundamental quantities that were displayed in Figure 1 (bottom). The results demonstrate that the most frequently occurring contrast orientations (at given distances and orientation differences from a target cell) resemble a structure similar to the bipole icon. This information provides a key to understanding the underlying structure and extent of long-range connection utilized for grouping and integration that is based on the statistics of natural scenes. The importance of investigating the co-occurrence of oriented structure in natural scenes is further highlighted by related studies. For example, Krueger (1998) studied the second order statistics of responses generated by oriented filters that resemble the structure of cortical simple cells. The results demonstrate a significantly increased likelihood for the joint occurrence of collinear as well as parallel structure in images of real scenes. This concurs with the structure of the grouping field derived by Geisler *et al.* (2001). More recently and in a similar vein, Sigman *et al.* (2001) investigated the probability of co-occurrence of responses from oriented filters along a co-circular path. A correlation energy measure again shows that this is indeed the case, adding further evidence for the significance of long-range correlations between oriented contrast items in natural scenes.[8]

(3) The mechanisms of neural self-organization have been modeled in order to demonstrate that the long-range connections can be established in a stable fashion (Grossberg and Williamson, 2001). Their results directly relate to the observation discussed before that fragments of boundary structures appear with certain probabilities in natural scenes. The model investigates the stable development of neural layer 2/3 connections in cortical areas V1 and V2.

[8]It is worth adding a note about some simplifying assumptions that have been utilized in order to derive the probability measures. All approaches mentioned above utilize some sort of a binarization process in order to reduce the computational load for getting the resulting statistics. These processes, however, can in principle vary the structure of the probability distributions. It might, therefore, be useful to utilize the full power spectra instead and measure co-occurrences on the basis of oriented energy (compare Keil and Cristobal (2000)).

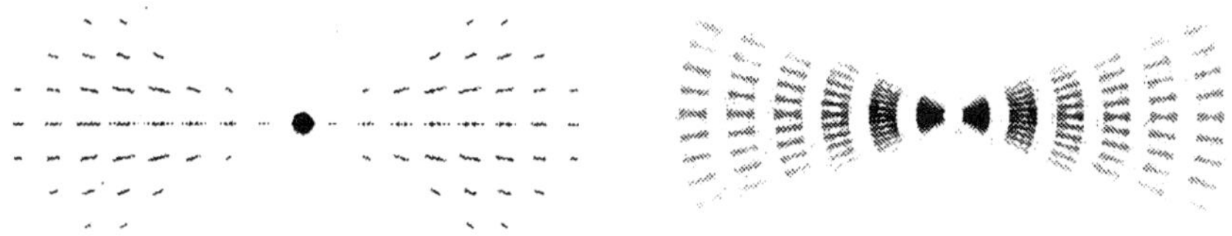

Figure 23. The left panel represents the earliest graphical representation of a bipole icon, or grouping support function, in the literature. Here the lengths of line segments graphically code the coupling strength between an array of filters centered at the positions of particular segments and having the orientational preferences indicated by those segments, and the bipole cell, which has a horizontal orientational preference and a receptive field center at the center of the diagram. The panel on the right uses a grayscale code, where darker lines stand for higher coupling strengths, and a similar position and orientation code. The represented values were derived by a computational and psychophysical *tour de force*. Although the precise values vary, the overall distributions of the two figures, one derived intuitively years ago and the other created more recently by careful measurement, are in remarkable agreement with respect to the dimensions described in Figure 1. (The left panel is Figure 32a of Grossberg and Mingolla (1985b) and the right is Figure 3e of Geisler *et al.* (2001); both are reproduced with permission.)

In all, these different lines of investigation shed light on the nature of the processing problems in grouping and long-range integration as well as the adaptive mechanisms to adjust the neural machinery to solve the problem of binding together separate visual elements.

CONCLUSION

The core of this chapter focuses on the computational mechanisms of spatial long-range integration. In our discussion in the previous section we identified the topics of key investigation, namely, the computational role of different principles in neural architecture, the precise coding of spatial relatedness or binding, as well as the self-organization of the wiring patterns. We have demonstrated that the common framework of all computational models is based on some variation of the structure of the bipole kernel (depicted in Figure 1) and a number of additional computational principles in evaluating related activities in feature space. The bipole kernel itself graphically visualizes the oriented fan-like connectivity between sites in a space-orientation feature space. Its initial definition was based largely on the investigation of geometrical concepts, namely the differential geometry of plane curves. The particular shape and its parametrization, however, was derived largely by intuition. Figure 23 (left) reviews the structure of the fan-in efficacies in the original bipole kernel proposed by Grossberg and Mingolla (1985b). It shows the three-dimensional weighting kernel in the space-orientation domain for a horizontally oriented target cell.

Later, several investigations shed some light on the underlying structure of such long-range mechanisms, both structurally and functionally. Bosking *et al.* (1997), for example, demonstrated the selective connectivity of axon fiber connections in striate cortex. Functionally, Field *et al.* (1993) derived the bipole distribution of a grouping support function on the basis of their psychophysical investigation of the conditions for pop-out of spatial arrangements of oriented items in a field of distractors. Only recently, these different aspects in model definition and related empirical methods received a grounding through the investigation of the statistics of visual scene properties. Geisler *et al.* (2001) measured the co-occurrence of oriented contrasts in natural scenes. It turns out that the frequencies of the naturally occurring pairs of edges (at given distances and orientations) resemble the structure of the bipole kernel (compare Figure 23, right).

The findings of Geisler *et al.* (2001) "justify" the definition of such a kernel structure based on the statistics of the natural environment. They further provide constraints for proper parameterizations of bipole mechanisms. The plain statistics of joint co-occurrence of contrast edges in static images may only be a first step in revealing the underlying basis of grouping. Since objects and surfaces in the natural environment occur in a depth order, partially occluding each other and being in motion, the next step may be to investigate statistical distributions of even higher order, including feature dimensions such as disparity and motion direction. In all, this demonstrates that there is still a need for ongoing investigation in order to explain the principles and mechanisms of binding contour fragments and to explain how these "units" will be linked into surfaces and objects involving later stages of processing.

ACKNOWLEDGMENTS

The authors thank Thorsten Hansen, Matthias Keil, and Gurumurthy Swaminathan for helpful comments on earlier drafts, and Cynthia Bradford for assistance in manuscript preparation. H.N. was supported in part by a grant of the Volkswagen-Stiftung (VW I/75967) and E.M. was supported in part by the Defense Advanced Research Projects Agency and the Office of Naval Research (ONR N00014-95-1-0409). Email: hneumann@neuro.informatik.uni-ulm.de, ennio@cns.bu.edu

REFERENCES

Baumann, R., van der Zwan, R., and Peterhans, E. (1997). Figure-ground segregation at contours: A neural mechanism in the visual cortex of the alert monkey. *European Journal of Neuroscience, 9*, 1290-1303.

Baumgartner, G., von der Heydt, R., and Peterhans, E. (1984). Anomalous contours: A tool in studying the neurophysiology of vision. *Experimental Brain Research (Supplement), 9*, 413-419.

Bertenthal, B.I., Campos, J.J., and Haith, M.M. (1980). Development of visual organization: The perception of illusory contours. *Child Development, 51*, 1072-1080.

Bosking, W.H., Zhang, Y., Schofield, B., and Fitzpatrick, D. (1997). Orientation selectivity and the arrangement of horizontal connections in tree shrew striate cortex. *Journal of Neuroscience, 17*(6), 2112-2127.

Bullier, J., McCourt, M., and Henry, G. (1988). Physiological studies on the feedback connection to the striate cortex from cortical areas 18 and 19 of the cat. *Experimental Brain Research, 70*, 90-98.

Carpenter, G.A. and Grossberg, S. (1988). The ART of adaptive pattern recognition by a self-organizing neural network. *Computer, 21*, 77-88.

Cohen, M. A., and Grossberg, S. (1984a). Neural dynamics of brightness perception: Features, boundaries, diffusion, and resonance. *Perception and Psychophysics, 36*(5), 428-456.

Cohen, M. A. and Grossberg, S. (1984b). Some global properties of binocular resonances: Disparity matching, filling-in and figure-ground synthesis. In P. Dodwell and T. Caelli (eds.), *Figural synthesis*. Hillsdale, NJ: Erlbaum.

Crick, F. and Koch, C. (1998). Constraints on cortical and thalamic projections: The no-strong loop hypothesis. *Nature, 391*, 245-250.

DeYoe, E. and van Essen, D. (1988). Concurrent processing streams in monkey visual cortex. *Trends in Neurosciences, 11*, 219-226.

Eckhorn, R., Bauer, R., Jordan, W., Brosch, M., Kruse, W., Munk, M., and Reitboeck, H.J. (1988). Coherent oscillations: A mechanism of feature linking in the visual cortex? *Biological Cybernetics, 20*, 69-98.

Eckhorn, R., Reitboeck, H.J., Arndt, M., and Dicke, P. (1990). Feature linking via synchronization among distributed assemblies: Simulations of results from cat visual cortex. *Neural Computation, 2*, 293-307.

Ellias, S.A. and Grossberg, S. (1975). Pattern formation, contrast control, and oscillations in the short term memory of shunting on-center off-surround networks. *Biological Cybernetics, 20*, 69-98.

Engel, A.K., König, P., and Singer, W. (1991). Direct physiological evidence for scene segmentation by temporal coding. *Proceedings of the National Academy of Sciences USA, 88*, 9136-9140.

Farroni, T., Valenza, E., Simion, F., and Umilta, C. (2000). Configural processing at birth: Evidence for perceptual organization. *Perception, 29*, 355-372.

Field, D.J., Hayes, A., and Hess, R.F. (1993). Contour integration by the human visual system: Evidence for a local "association field". *Vision Research*, *33*, 173-193.

Finkel, L. and Edelman, G.M. (1989). Integration of distributed cortical systems by reentry: A computer simulation of interactive functionally segregated visual areas. *Journal of Neuroscience*, *9*, 3188-3208.

Francis, G. and Grossberg, S. (1996). Cortical dynamics of boundary segmentation and reset: Persistence, afterimages, and residual traces. *Perception*, *25*, 543-567.

Francis, G., Grossberg, S., and Mingolla, E. (1994). Cortical dynamics of feature binding and reset: Control of visual persistence. *Vision Research*, *34*, 1089-1104.

Frien, A., Eckhorn, R., Bauer, R., Woelbern, T., and Kehr, H. (1994). Stimulus-specific fast oscillations at zero-phase between visual areas V1 and V2 of awake monkey. *NeuroReport*, *5*, 2273-2277.

Geisler, W.S., Perry, J.S., Super, B.J., and Gallogly, D.P. (2001). Edge co-occurrence in natural images predicts contour grouping performance. *Vision Research*, *41*, 711-724, 2001.

Gilbert, C. (1992). Horizontal integration and cortical dynamics. *Neuron*, *9*, 1-13.

Gilbert, C. and Wiesel, T.N. (1979). Morphology and intracortical projections of functionally identified neurons in cat visual cortex. *Nature*, *280*, 120-125.

Gilbert, C. and Wiesel, T.N. (1983). Clustered intrinsic connections in cat visual cortex. *Journal of Neuroscience*, *3*, 1116-1133.

Gilbert, C. and Wiesel, T.N. (1989). Columnar specificity of intrinsic horizontal and corticocortical connections in cat visual cortex. *Journal of Neuroscience*, *9*, 2432-2442.

Gilbert, C. and Wiesel, T.N. (1990). The influence of contextual stimuli on the orientation selectivity of cells in primary visual cortex of the cat. *Vision Research*, *30*, 1689-1701.

Gove, A., Grossberg, S., and Mingolla, E. (1995). Brightness perception, illusory contours, and corticogeniculate feedback. *Visual Neuroscience*, *12*, 1027-1052.

Gray, C.M. (1999). The temporal correlation hypothesis of visual feature integration: Still alive and well. *Neuron*, *24*, 31-47.

Gray, C.M., König, P., Engel, A., and Singer, W. (1989). Oscillatory responses in cat visual cortex exhibit inter-columnar synchronization which reflects global stimulus properties. *Nature*, *338*, 334-337.

Grossberg, S. (1973). Contour enhancement, short term memory, and constancies in reverberating neural networks. *Studies in Applied Mathematics*, *LII*, 213-257.

Grossberg, S. (1980). How does a brain build a cognitive code? *Psychological Review*, *87*, 1-51.

Grossberg, S. (1984). Outline of a theory of brightness, color, and form perception. In E. deGreef and J. van Buggenhaut (eds.), *Trends in mathematical psychology*. Amsterdam: North Holland.

Grossberg, S. (1994). 3-D vision and figure-ground separation by visual cortex. *Perception and Psychophysics*, *55*, 48-120.

Grossberg, S. (1995). How does the cerebral cortex work? Learning, attention, and grouping by the laminar circuits of visual cortex. *Spatial Vision, 12*, 16-185.

Grossberg, S. (1999). The attentive brain. *American Scientist, 83*, 438-449.

Grossberg, S. and Mingolla, E. (1985a). Neural dynamics of form perception: Boundary completion, illusory figures, and neon color spreading. *Psychological Review, 92*, 173-211.

Grossberg, S. and Mingolla, E. (1985b). Neural dynamics of perceptual grouping: Textures, boundaries, and emergent segmentation. *Perception and Psychophysics, 38*, 141-171.

Grossberg, S. and Mingolla, E. (1987). Neural dynamics of surface perception: Boundary webs, illuminants, and shape-from-shading. *Computer Vision, Graphics, and Image Processing, 37*, 116-165.

Grossberg, S., Mingolla, E., and Ross, W.D. (1997). Visual brain and visual perception: How does the cortex do perceptual grouping? *Trends in Neurosciences, 20*, 106-111.

Grossberg, S. and Raizada, R.D.S. (2000). Contrast-sensitive perceptual grouping and object-based attention in the laminar circuits of primary visual cortex. *Vision Research, 40*, 1413-1432.

Grossberg, S. and Somers, D. (1991). Synchronized oscillations during cooperative feature linking in a cortical model of visual perception. *Neural Networks, 4*, 453-466.

Grossberg, S. and Williamson, J.R. (2001). A neural model of how horizontal and interlaminar connections of visual cortex develop into adult circuits that carry out perceptual grouping and learning. *Cerebral Cortex, 11*, 37-58.

Hansen, T., Sepp, W., and Neumann, H. (2001). Recurrent long-range interactions in early vision. In S. Wermter (ed.) *Emergent neural computational architectures based on neuroscience.* Heidelberg: Springer, 129-141.

Heitger, F. and von der Heydt, R. (1993). A computational model of neural contour processing: Figure-ground segregation and illusory contours. Proc. 4th Int. Conf. on Computer Vision (ECCV '93), Berlin, Germany, 32-40.

Heitger, F., von der Heydt, R., Peterhans, E., Rosenthaler, L., and Kübler, O. (1998). Simulation of neural contour mechanisms: Representing anomalous contours. *Image and Vision Computing, 16*, 407-421.

Hubel, D.H. and Wiesel, T.N. (1968). Receptive fields and functional architecture of monkey striate cortex. *Journal of Physiology, 195*, 215-243.

Hupé, J.M., James, A.C., Payne, B.R., Lomber, S.G., Girard, P., and Bullier, J. (1998). Cortical feedback improves discrimination between figure and background by V1, V2 and V3 neurones. *Nature, 394*, 784-787.

Kanizsa, G. (1968). Percezione attuale, esperienza passata è l'"esperimento impossibile". In G. Kanizsa and G. Vicario (eds.) *Ricerche sperimentali sulla percezione.* Trieste: Università degli Studi.

Kanizsa, G. (1976). Subjective contours. *Scientific American, 234*, 48-52.

Kanizsa, G. (1979). *Organization in vision: Essays on Gestalt perception.* New York: Praeger.

Kapadia, M.M., Ito, M., Gilbert, C.D., and Westheimer, G. (1995). Improvement in visual sensitivity by changes in local context: Parallel studies in human observers and in V1 of alert monkeys. *Neuron, 15*, 843-856.

Kapadia, M.M., Westheimer, G., and Gilbert, C.D. (2000). The spatial distribution of contextual interactions in primary visual cortex and in visual perception. *Journal of Neurophysiology, 84*(4), 2048-2062.

Keil, M.S. and Cristobal, G. (2000). Separating the chaff from the wheat: Possible origins of the oblique effect. *Journal of the Optical Society of America A, 17*, 697-710.

Kellman, P.J. and Loukides, M.G. (1987). An object perception approach to static and kinetic subjective contours. In S. Petry and G.E. Meyer (eds.) *The perception of illusory contours.* New York: Springer.

Kellman, P.J. and Shipley, T.F. (1991). A theory of visual interpolation in object perception. *Cognitive Psychology, 23*, 141-221.

Kelly, F. and Grossberg, S. (2000). Neural dynamics of 3-D surface perception: Figure-ground separation and lightness perception. *Perception and Psychophysics, 62*(8), 1596-1618.

Koffka, K. (1935). *Principles of Gestalt psychology.* London: Routledge & Kegan Paul Ltd.

Krüger, N. (1998). Collinearity and parallelism are statistically significant second order relations of complex cell responses. *Neural Processing Letters, 8*, 117-129.

Lesher, G.W. (1995). Illusory contours: Toward a neurally based perceptual theory. *Psychonomic Bulletin and Review, 2*, 279-321.

Lesher, G.W. and Mingolla, E. (1993). The role of edges and line-ends in illusory contour formation. *Vision Research, 33*, 2253-2270.

Li, Z. (1998). A neural model of contour integration in the primary visual cortex. *Neural Computation, 10*, 903-940.

Li, Z. (1999a). Visual segmentation by contextual influences via intra-cortical interactions in the primary visual cortex. *Network, 10*, 187-212.

Li, Z. (1999b). Contextual influences in V1 as a basis for pop-out and asymmetry in visual search. *Proceedings of the National Academy of Sciences USA, 96*, 10530-10535.

Martin, K.A.C. and Whitteridge, D. (1984). Form, function and intracortical projections of spiny neurones in the striate visual cortex of the cat. *Journal of Physiology (London), 353*, 463-504.

Mendola, J.D., Dale, A.M., Fischl, B., Liu, A.K., and Tootell, R.B.H. (1999). The representation of illusory and real contours in human cortical visual areas revealed by functional magnetic resonance imaging. *Journal of Neuroscience, 19*, 8560-8572.

Meyer, M. and Ming, C. (1988). The visible persistence of illusory contours. *Canadian Journal of Psychology, 42*, 479-488.

Mingolla, E., Ross, W., and Grossberg, S. (1999). A neural network for enhancing boundaries and surfaces in synthetic aperture radar images. *Neural Networks, 12*, 499-511.

Mumford, D. (1991). On the computational architecture of the neocortex II: The role of cortico-cortical loop. *Biological Cybernetics, 65*, 241-251.

Mumford, D. (1994). Neuronal architectures for pattern-theoretic problems. In C. Koch and J.L. Davis (eds.) *Large-scale neuronal theories of the brain.* Cambridge: MIT Press.

Neumann, H. (1996). Mechanisms of neural architecture for visual contrast and brightness perception. *Neural Networks, 9*, 921-936.

Neumann, H., Pessoa, L., and Mingolla, E. (1998) A neural architecture of brightness perception: Non-linear contrast detection and geometry-driven diffusion. *Image and Vision Computing, 16*, 423-446.

Neumann, H. and Sepp, W. (1999). Recurrent V1-V2 interaction in early visual boundary processing. *Biological Cybernetics, 81*, 425-444.

Parent, P. and Zucker, S. (1989). Trace inference, curvature consistency, and curve detection. *IEEE Transactions on Pattern Analysis and Machine Intelligence, 11*, 823-839.

Peterhans, E. and von der Heydt, R. (1989). Mechanisms of contour perception in monkey visual cortex. II. Contours bridging gaps. *Journal of Neuroscience, 9*, 1749-1763.

Peterhans, E. and von der Heydt, R. (1991). Subjective contours – bridging the gap between psychophysics and physiology. *Trends in Neurosciences, 14*, 112-119.

Pettet, M.W., McKee, S.P., and Grzywacz, N. (1998). Constraints on long range interactions mediating contour detection. *Vision Research, 38*, 865-879.

Ringach, D. L., and Shapley, R. (1996). Spatial and temporal properties of illusory contours and amodal boundary completion. *Vision Research, 36*(19), 3037-3050.

Rockland, K. S., and Lund, J. S. (1982). Widespread periodic intrinsic connections in the tree shrew visual cortex. *Science, 215*(4539), 1532-1534.

Ross, W.D., Grossberg, S., and Mingolla, E. (2000). Visual cortical mechanisms of perceptual grouping: Interacting layers, networks, columns, and maps. *Neural Networks, 13*, 571-588.

Saam, M. and Eckhorn, R. (2000). Lateral spike conduction velocities in the visual cortex affects spatial range of synchronization and receptive field size without visual experience: A learning model with spiking neurons. *Biological Cybernetics, 83*, L1-L9.

Shadlen, M.N. and Movshon, J.A. (1999). Synchrony unbound: A critical evaluation of the temporal binding hypothesis. *Neuron, 24*, 67-77.

Shipley, T.F. and Kellman, P.J. (1992). Strength of visual interpolation depends on the ratio of physically specified to total edge length. *Perception and Psychophysics, 52*, 97-106.

Sigman, M, Cecchi, G.A., Gilbert, C.D., Magnasco, M.O. (2001). A common circle: Natural scenes and Gestalt rules. *Proceedings of the National Academy of Sciences USA, 98*, 1935-1940.

Spillmann, L. and Werner, J.S. (1996). Long-range interactions in visual perception. *Trends in Neurosciences, 19*(10), 428-434.

Thorpe, S., Fize, D., and Marlot, C. (1996). Speed of processing in the human visual system. *Nature, 381*, 520-522.

Ullman, S. (1995). Sequence seeking and counter streams: A computational model for bidirectional information flow in the visual cortex. *Cerebral Cortex, 1*, 1-11.

von der Heydt, R., Peterhans, E., and Baumgartner, G. (1984). Illusory contours and cortical neuron responses. *Science, 224*, 1260-1262.

von der Heydt, R., Heitger, F., and Peterhans, E. (1993). Perception of occluding contours: Neural mechanisms and a computational model. *Biomedical Research, 14*, 1-6.

von der Heydt, R. and Peterhans, E. (1989). Mechanisms of contour perception in monkey visual cortex. I. Lines of pattern discontinuity. *Journal of Neuroscience, 9*, 1731-1748.

Thornber, K.K. and Williams, L.R. (1996). Analytic solutions of stochastic completions fields. *Biological Cybernetics, 75*, 141-151.

Williams, L.R. and Jacobs, D.W. (1997a). Stochastic completions fields: A neural model of illusory contour shape and salience. *Neural Computation, 9*, 837-858.

Williams, L.R. and Jacobs, D.W. (1997b). Local parallel computations of stochastic completions fields. *Neural Computation, 9*, 859-881.

Zucker, S. (1985). Early orientation selection: Tangent fields and the dimensionality of their support. *Computer Vision, Graphics, and Image Processing, 32*, 74-103.

Zucker, S.W. and Parent, P. (1984). Multiple-size operators and optimal curve finding. In A. Rosenfeld (ed.) *Multiresolution image processing and analysis.* Berlin: Springer, 200-210.

Zucker, S., Hummel, R.A., and Rosenfeld, A. (1977). An application of relaxation labeling to line and curve enhancement. *IEEE Transactions on Computers, 26*, 394-403.

From Fragments to Objects – Segmentation and Grouping in Vision
T.F. Shipley and P.J. Kellman (Editors)

13

PART-BASED REPRESENTATIONS OF VISUAL SHAPE AND IMPLICATIONS FOR VISUAL COGNITION

Manish Singh[†] *and Donald D. Hoffman*[‡]
† Department of Psychology and Center for Cognitive Science, Rutgers University, New Brunswick, NJ 08903 USA
‡ Department of Cognitive Science, University of California, Irvine, 92697 USA

ABSTRACT

Human vision organizes object shapes in terms of parts and their spatial relationships. Converging experimental evidence suggests that parts are computed rapidly and early in visual processing. We review theories of how human vision parses shapes. In particular, we discuss the minima rule for finding part boundaries on shapes, geometric factors for creating part cuts, and a theory of part salience. We review empirical evidence that human vision parses shapes into parts, and show that parts-based representations explain various aspects of our visual cognition, including figure-ground assignment, judgments of shape similarity, memory for shapes, visual search for shapes, the perception of transparency, and the allocation of visual attention to objects.

INTRODUCTION

Our visual world is replete with structure, in the form of objects and surfaces. The inputs to our visual systems, however, contain no objects or surfaces—only discrete arrays of intensity values that can vary dramatically with small changes in viewing conditions. The objects and surfaces we see thus need to be constructed by our visual systems from these inputs. A critical aspect of this construction is parsing the input arrays into regions that are likely to have arisen from distinct objects; in other words, the formation of 'perceptual units.'

Entire objects, however, are not the only perceptual units. Indeed, the objects we see are not unstructured wholes—they themselves have further part structure. We perceive a table, for example, as a coherent perceptual object; but also as a spatial arrangement of clearly defined parts: four legs and a top. Hence, 'perceptual units' exist at many levels: at the level of whole objects, at the level of parts, and possibly smaller parts nested within larger ones (Palmer, 1977; Marr & Nishihara, 1978). Moreover, as we will see, mechanisms of part segmentation interact with mechanisms of object and surface segmentation in a number of ways.

Many theorists believe that, because human object recognition is often sensitive to viewpoint, shape descriptions employed by human vision are not part-based. However, this belief is based on the assumption that a part-based approach is synonymous with (or, at least, commits one to) a volumetric, object-centered, approach to shape representation in which a set of basic 3D parts is specified in advance (e.g., Marr & Nishihara, 1978; Biederman, 1987). This assumption if false. Parts are equally consistent with, and just as useful for, 2D (image-based) and 2-$^{1}/_{2}$ D (surface-based) representations as they are for 3D (volumetric) representations. And using parts does not entail that one must commit to a fixed repertoire of primitive shapes.

In this chapter we argue, both on computational and empirical grounds, that the human representation of visual shape is in fact part-based. Human vision parses shapes into component parts, and it organizes them using these parts and their spatial relationships. This places strong constraints on theories of human visual shape description.

From a computational perspective, parts are useful for many reasons. First, many objects are articulated: they consist of parts that move non-rigidly with respect to each other. Fingers, for instance, can move independently. A template for an outstretched hand correlates poorly with a template for a pointing hand. A part-based description allows one to decouple the shapes of the parts from the spatial relationships between the parts—hence providing a natural way to represent and recognize articulated objects. Second, one never sees all of an object in one view: the back of an object is not visible due to self-occlusion, and its front may be occluded by other objects. Representing shapes by parts allows the recognition process to proceed with those parts that are visible.

From an empirical perspective, recent evidence suggests that parts are computed quickly, automatically, and in parallel over the visual field (Baylis & Driver, 1994; 95a; 95b; Hulleman, te Winkel, & Boselie, 2000; Wolfe & Bennett, 1997, Xu & Singh, 2001). With ambiguous shapes flashed for just 50 ms and followed by a mask, parts affect the perception of figure and ground (Hoffman & Singh, 1997). Hence, whatever further transformations of shape into other representational formats may take place later in visual processing, these are likely to be influenced by the early formatting of shapes into parts. Indeed, we show that parts explain a remarkable variety of visual phenomena, including the following.

1. Phenomenology. In Figure 1, we see hill-shaped parts with dashed lines in the valleys between them. Turn the figure upside down, and new hills appear; the dashed lines lie on top of the new hills.

Figure 1. This display is seen as hills separated by dashed lines. If you turn the page upside down, convex and concave reverse—leading to a switch in perceived part boundaries. As a result, the dashed lines now appear to lie on top of hills, rather than along the boundaries between hills.

2. Similarity. Of the two half moons on the right of Figure 2, the bottom looks more similar to the half moon on the left (Attneave, 1971; Hoffman, 1983)—even though the top, not the bottom, has the same wiggle as the one on the left.

Figure 2. Which of the two half moons on the right is more similar to the one on the left? Most observers pick the bottom one, even though it is the one on top, not bottom, whose wiggly contour is identical to the one on the left.

3. Figure-ground. In Figure 3, the staircase on the right looks upside down, whereas the one on the left can be seen either as right side up or as upside down (Hoffman & Singh, 1997).

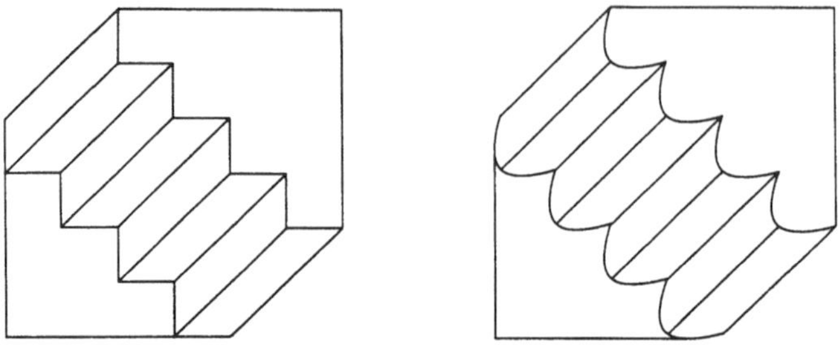

(a) (b)

Figure 3. The staircase on the left can be seen as either right-side up, or as upside down. The staircase on the right, however, is more likely to be seen in the upside-down interpretation.

4. Transparency. In Figure 4, the display on the left looks transparent, but the one on the right does not (Singh & Hoffman, 1998).

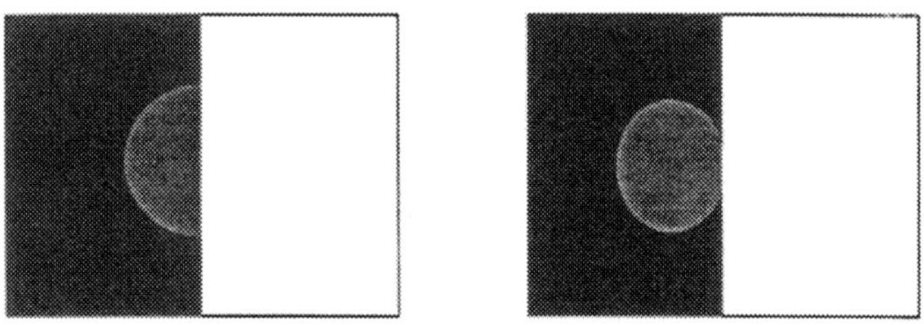

(a) (b)

Figure 4. The display on the left is readily seen as a partially transmissive, i.e., transparent, disk over a bipartite background. The display on the right is more difficult to see as containing a transparent overlay.

5. Symmetry. Symmetry (Figure 5a) within an object is easier to detect than repetition (Figure

(a) (b)

Figure 5. Observers are faster and more accurate at detecting symmetry within a figure—as in (a)—rather than repetition within a figure—as in (b).

5b; Baylis & Driver, 1994).

6. Pop out. A shape with a concave corner pops out among a set of distractors with convex corners (see Figure 6a), but not vice versa (Figure 6b) (Hulleman, te Winkel, & Boselie, 2000).

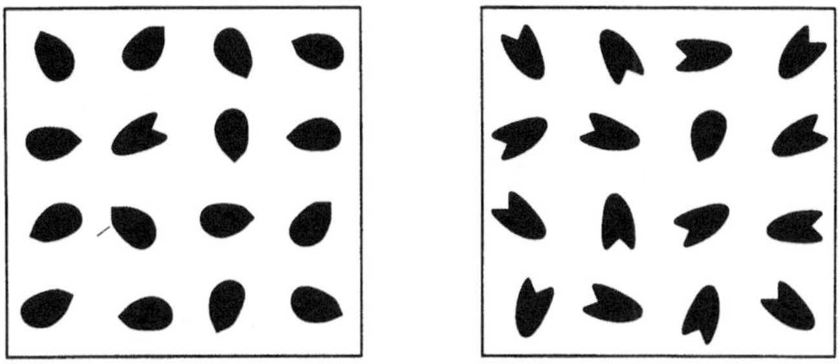

(a) (b)

Figure 6. (a) A shape with a concave corner pops out among distractors with convex corners. (b) However, the reverse visual search is slow and inefficient.

7. Recognition memory. Some "parts" of shapes are better remembered than others (Braunstein, Hoffman & Saidpour, 1989).

8. Attention. The allocation of visual attention to an object can be part-based, so that attention shifts more readily within a part than across parts of an object (Singh & Scholl, 2000; Vecera, Behrmann, & McGoldrick, 2000; Vecera, Behrmann, & Filapek, 2001; Barenholtz & Feldman, 2001).

We begin by discussing the *minima rule* for finding part boundaries on shapes (Hoffman & Richards, 1984), and review experimental work that demonstrates its psychological reality. However, part boundaries alone do not define parts. So next we consider how human vision uses part boundaries defined by the minima rule, together with other geometric factors, to create cuts on shapes that specify parts. In particular, we discuss the role of cut length (Singh, Seyranian, & Hoffman, 1999), part-boundary strength (Hoffman & Singh, 1997), good continuation, and local symmetry (Singh, Seyranian, & Hoffman, 1996) in determining part cuts. We then review work on part salience, i.e., geometric factors that make some parts more visually salient than others. In discussing the implications of perceptual part structure for visual cognition, we demonstrate that part salience can influence the assignment of perceived figure and ground (Hoffman & Singh, 1997). We show how the minima rule and part salience allow us to refine and extend figural conditions for the perception of transparency proposed by the Gestalt psychologists Metelli and Kanizsa (Singh & Hoffman,

1998). We review results of visual-search experiments that demonstrate that part structures consistent with the minima rule are computed rapidly and early in visual processing (Xu & Singh, 2001). And, we review results of attentional-cueing experiments that reveal that part structure and part salience modulate the allocation of visual attention to multi-part objects (Singh & Scholl, 2000). We end with a discussion of an alternative approach to parts and shape description involving curve evolution and shocks, and relate it to our geometric-constraints approach.

DEFINING BOUNDARIES BETWEEN PARTS

Geometric Considerations

Physically speaking, any subset of an object may be considered to be a part of that object. But human observers clearly find some parts more natural, and others rather contrived. For instance, the legs and the top of a table are clearly seen as distinct natural parts; whereas the upper half of a leg along with a small adjoining piece of the top seems rather contrived. Similarly, the partitioning shown in Figure 7b looks quite natural, whereas the one in Figure 7c looks contrived. How does the visual system compute such psychologically natural parts?

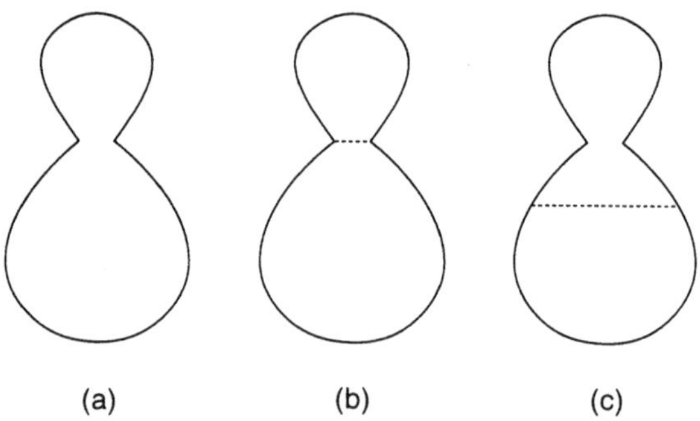

Figure 7. Although any subset of an object is physically a "part" of it, human observers clearly find some parts perceptually natural (b), whereas others seem rather contrived (c).

From a computational perspective, computed parts must satisfy certain principles in order to be useful (Sutherland, 1968; Marr & Nishihara, 1978; Hoffman & Richards, 1984). They must be stable over small generic perturbations of viewpoint, and over small generic changes in object shape. They must be computable from retinal images. And they must be defined for all shapes, and not just a small class of shapes. These principles suggest that to define parts we must use the intrinsic geometry of shapes.

There are two primary approaches that theorists have taken in defining parts. One theoretical approach defines, in advance, a set of shape primitives that are the possible parts. Proponents of this approach postulate that human vision parses shapes by finding these primitives in images; hence it uses the shape primitives both to find parts and to describe them. Examples of shape primitives that have been proposed include *polyhedra* (Roberts, 1965; Waltz, 1975; Winston, 1975), *superquadrics* (Pentland, 1986), *generalized cones and cylinders* (Binford, 1971; Marr, 1977; Marr & Nishihara, 1978), and *geons* (Biederman, 1987). Although each set of primitives works well on a special class of objects, none can capture the variety of object parts we see—since part shapes that are not in the predefined set of primitives cannot be represented adequately. Nevertheless, if well motivated, shape primitives may be useful as qualitative descriptors of parts for recognizing objects at the basic level, such as *car*, rather than at a superordinate level, such as *vehicle*, or a subordinate level, such as *BMW 325i*. Biederman (1987), for example, uses nonaccidental properties (Binford, 1981; Lowe, 1987; Witkin & Tenenbaum, 1983), i.e., 3D properties that generically survive projection onto an image plane[1] (like straight versus curved), to motivate his set of geons—because human vision is more sensitive to differences in nonaccidental properties than to metric differences. However, the list of geons only includes a small subset of those shapes that follow from the principle of nonaccidental properties. No geon, for instance, has a rounded tip—even though the difference between a rounded tip and a truncated or pointed tip is nonaccidental. Similarly, no geon can have a cross section that changes its shape or rotates as it sweeps along the axis, or even be at any angle other than 90 degrees to the axis. Indeed, there is as yet no complete, well-motivated, set of shape primitives—and it remains unclear whether there can be.

A different approach to parts, and one that we espouse, is to postulate that human vision uses general computational rules, based on the intrinsic geometry of shapes, to parse visual objects. This approach separates the issue of finding parts from the issue of describing them. For example, Hoffman & Richards (1984) have argued that mechanisms which find parts are more basic, and operate regardless of the shapes of the parts (i.e., independently of whether or not the parts belong to any particular class of shape primitives). They motivate their minima rule, by the principle of transversality, from differential topology.

Principle of Transversality: Two generic 3D shapes intersect almost surely in a concave crease.[2]

---

[1] Strictly speaking, nonaccidental properties are simply spatiotemporal regularities that are unlikely to arise by chance alone: "In its bare form, the argument says that what *looks* parallel or rigid really *is* parallel or rigid because the spurious appearance of parallelism is extremely unlikely to arise among causally unrelated curves" (Witkin & Tenenbaum, 1983, p. 505). 3D properties that generically survive projection onto an image plane are a special case of this general definition.

[2] Something is true "almost surely" if it is true everywhere except (possibly) on a set of measure zero. See, e.g., Guillemin & Pollack (1974).

Figure 8 demonstrates this principle: When the two shapes on the left are joined at random, their intersection creates a concave crease (i.e., a crease that points *into* an object—marked on the right by the dashed contour). If we now view the composite shape on the right as a single object, the two original shapes are natural parts of this object, and the concave crease defines their part boundary. Hence transversality motivates the following rule for parsing 3D shapes.

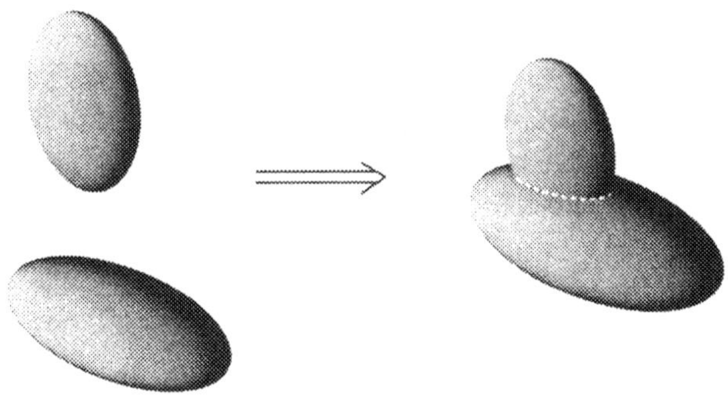

Figure 8. The principle of transversality: When two 3D shapes intersect, they generically create a concave crease at the locus of intersection.

Rule of Concave Creases: Divide 3D shapes into parts at concave creases.

The Schröder staircase in Figure 9 illustrates the rule of concave creases. When you see the "upright staircase" interpretation, the two dots lie on the same step of the staircase. And this step is bounded on both sides by concave creases. Now if you reverse figure and ground, and see the "inverted staircase" interpretation, the two dots lie on different steps. These steps are nevertheless bounded by the new concave creases.

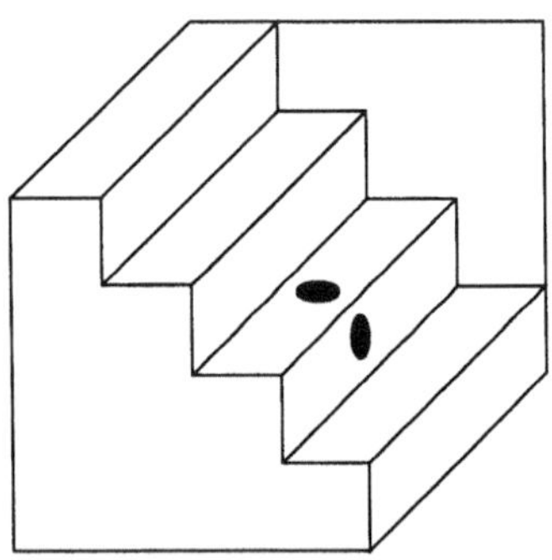

Figure 9. Are the two dots on the same step, or on different steps? When you see the staircase as upright, the two dots appear to lie on the same step. When you see the staircase as upside down, the dots appear to lie on different steps. Note that, in both interpretations, the boundaries between steps lie along the perceived concave creases.

As we saw in Figure 1, however, smooth surfaces with no creases can also be seen as having parts. It is easy to generalize the rule of concave creases so that it applies to smooth surfaces as well. Just note that if one smooths a surface in the neighborhood of a concave crease then, intuitively, the concave crease becomes a locus of negative minima of curvature (i.e., a concave region with locally highest magnitude of curvature). This intuition can be made precise using the tools of differential geometry (Bennett & Hoffman, 1987). Similarly, if a branch or limb grows out of a main body, its boundary lies along a locus of negative minima (Leyton, 1987). Such considerations lead to the minima rule for 3D shapes.

Minima Rule for 3D shapes: Divide 3D shapes into parts along negative minima of the principal curvatures, along their associated lines of curvature. [3]

The minima rule can explain the parts we see in Figure 1. The sinusoidal curves are lines of curvature on the ruled surface. And the dashed lines are the loci of negative minima of the principal curvatures along these lines of curvature. As the minima rule predicts, these dashed lines are the part boundaries we perceive. If you turn the page upside down, then figure and ground reverse (owing to a preference by human vision to see figure below). This turns concave into convex, and hence negative minima into positive maxima, and vice versa. And the new part boundaries we see are the new negative minima, as predicted by the minima rule.

By considering 2D silhouettes as projections of 3D shapes, and using the tools of differential geometry, we obtain the minima rule for 2D silhouettes.

Minima Rule for Silhouettes: Divide silhouettes into parts using points of negative minima of curvature on their bounding contour as boundaries between parts.

This rule explains an interesting effect described by Attneave (1971). Draw a random curve down the middle of a disk (as in Figure 10 on the left) and pull the two halves apart (as in Figure 10 on the right). The wiggles on the two halves look different, even though they are, by construction, identical. The reason, according to the minima rule, is that because border-ownership (or figure-ground) is reversed in the two halves, these induce different parsings on the identical wiggle. For the half disk on the left, the negative minima of curvature are labeled m_1 and m_2, and these are, by the minima rule, the boundaries between parts. For the half disk on the right, however, the points m_1 and m_2 are not negative minima, but positive maxima of curvature (since they now lie in convex, rather than concave, regions). The negative minima,

---

[3] Recall that for any point on a surface, there are associated two canonical directions: one in which the surface curves the most, and the other in which the surface curves the least. These are called, respectively, the directions of greatest, and least, curvature. The curvatures in these two directions are called the principal curvatures, and the curves obtained by always moving along these directions are called the lines of curvature (Do Carmo, 1976).

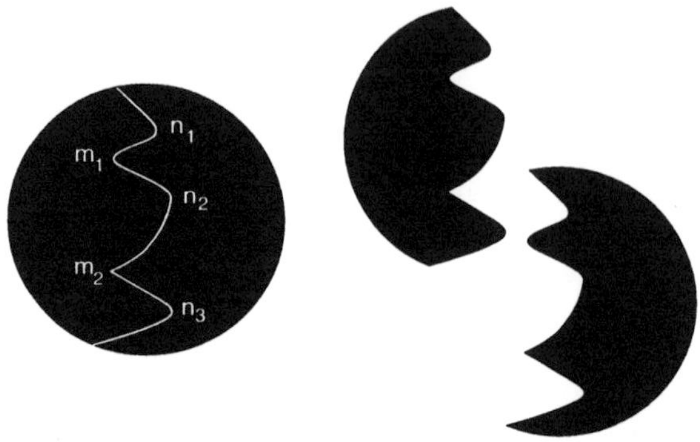

Figure 10. The wiggle drawn down the middle of the disk appears different, depending on whether it is seen as belonging to the half moon on the left, or the half moon on the right. Note that the part boundaries are different for these two half moons, because switching figure and ground switches convex and concave. Whereas the negative minima of curvature lie at points m_1 and m_2 for the left half moon, they lie at the points n_1, n_2, and n_3 for the right half moon.

and hence the part boundaries, for this half are labeled n_1, n_2, and n_3. The wiggles on the two half disks therefore have different parts. Since these parts are the basic units of our perceptual representations of shape, the two half disks receive different representations, and hence they look different.

It is also instructive to relate the minima rule to Attneave's (1954) claim that information along a contour is concentrated on points of 'maxima of curvature.' Attneave used 'curvature' to mean magnitude of curvature (i.e., as an unsigned quantity). Hence his statement about the importance of 'maxima of curvature' translates, in our framework, to the visual importance of both negative minima *and* positive maxima of curvature. In the context of parsing, however, the minima rule distinguishes between these two types of extrema, and assigns a special status to the negative minima (i.e., those points of locally highest curvature that lie in concave regions). Indeed, we shall see ample evidence that the visual system treats negative minima quite differently from positive maxima of the same magnitude of curvature.

Psychophysical Evidence

Consider again the large half moon on the left of Figure 11. Which of the two half moons on the right looks most similar to it? In an experiment with such stimuli, Hoffman (1983) found that subjects chose the bottom one, or its analogue, 94% of the time. Note, however, that the half moon at the top has the same wiggle as the one on the left, whereas the half moon at the bottom does not. In fact, the wiggle at the bottom was created by taking the one on the left, mirror reversing it, and then swapping two of its parts.

So why does the half moon at the bottom look more similar to the one on the left? Note that it has the same parts as the one on the left—even though two of these parts have been

Figure 11. Most observers see the bottom half moon as being more similar to the one on the left, even though it is the one on top whose wiggle is identical to it. Note, however, that the half moon at the bottom has the same parts as the one on the left—even though two of them have been swapped.

swapped. The half moon at the top, however, does not. Even though it has the same wiggle as the large shape on the left, it induces an opposite assignment of figure and ground on it; hence the visual system carves it differently into parts. It has different parts, so it looks different.

It has long been observed (at least as far back as Mach; see Baylis & Driver, 1994; 1995), that humans are more sensitive to symmetry in a pattern than to repetition (compare Figure 12a with 12b). This observation has since been confirmed by researchers (Baylis & Driver, 1994; Bruce & Morgan, 1975; Corballis, 1974). Indeed, Baylis & Driver (1994) found that human vision detects symmetry, but not repetition, in parallel. This advantage for symmetry has been something of a paradox because repetition involves simply a translation of the curves to be compared, whereas symmetry involves a translation *plus* a reflection. Hence any account based on a point-by-point comparison of the two curves should predict an

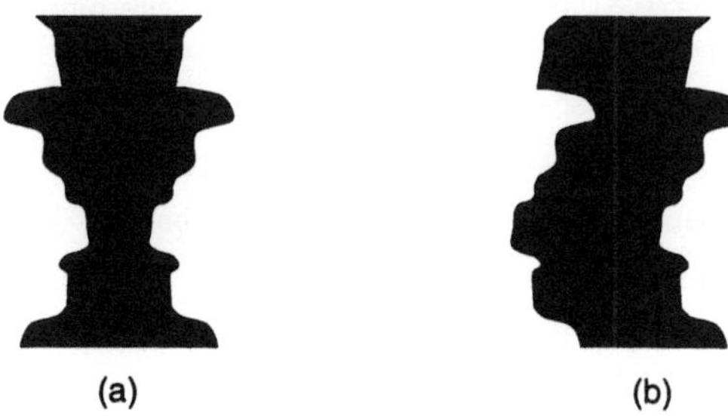

Figure 12. Human observers can detect symmetry (a) but not repetition (b) in parallel. This is surprising because repetitions involve only a translation, whereas symmetry involves a reflection and a translation. Note, however, that the symmetric figure has matching parts on the two sides, whereas the repeated figure has mismatching parts.

advantage for repetition, not symmetry.

Baylis & Driver (1995a) noted that in a symmetric shape, such as Figure 12a, the two sides have matching negative minima of curvature—and hence matching parts. In a repeated pattern, such as Figure 12b, however, the two sides do not have matching negative minima, because they get opposite assignments of figure and ground. Hence the two sides have mismatching parts. Therefore, if human vision represents the two sides in terms of their parts, as per the minima rule, and then compares them at the level of parts, one would expect it to be more sensitive to symmetry (as in Figure 12a) than to repetition (as in Figure 12b).

In support of their claim, Baylis & Driver (1995a) argued that one should be able to reverse the advantage for symmetry using displays such as Figure 13, in which symmetries have mismatching parts (13a) and repetitions have matching parts (13b). It is easy to create such displays because, as we noted above, the parts on a curve depend on which side 'owns' the curve, and is hence assigned the status of 'figure,' rather than 'ground.' For these new displays, Baylis & Driver (1995a) found that subjects were faster and more accurate at detecting repetition than symmetry. Hence it is matching versus mismatching parts that determines the speed and accuracy of such judgments—not symmetry versus repetition per se.

Figure 13. When the symmetric curves are made to have mismatching parts, and the repeated curves are made to have matching parts, then repetition becomes easier to judge than symmetry. Hence it is matching parts that give symmetry its advantage in displays such as Figure 12. (Adapted from Baylis & Driver, 1995.)

Combined with their earlier study (Baylis & Driver, 1994) which showed that human vision detects symmetry (with matching parts) in parallel—but not repetition (with mismatching parts)—these results suggest that human vision computes parts in parallel. These experiments also demonstrate that human vision compares shapes, not by a process of point-by-point matching of contours, but by a process of matching parts. Hence the basic units of shape description are intermediate-level parts, and not individual pixels and edge segments, or unstructured wholes.

Evidence for the early computation of part boundaries also comes from visual search experiments. In such experiments, subjects search for a target object in a field of distractor objects. If the time to find the target is independent, or nearly independent, of the number of distractors, then the target is said to "pop out" of the field of distractors. In a series of experiments on visual search, Wolfe & Bennett (1997) found that preattentive processing for *overall* shape is limited. They found, however, that a shape having a salient negative minimum of curvature (Figure 14, top) pops out among distractors that do not (Figure 14, bottom), but not vice versa. This kind of asymmetry has traditionally been interpreted as a sign of preattentive processing (Treisman & Souther, 1985), suggesting that part boundaries are computed preattentively—or at least rapidly and early in visual processing.

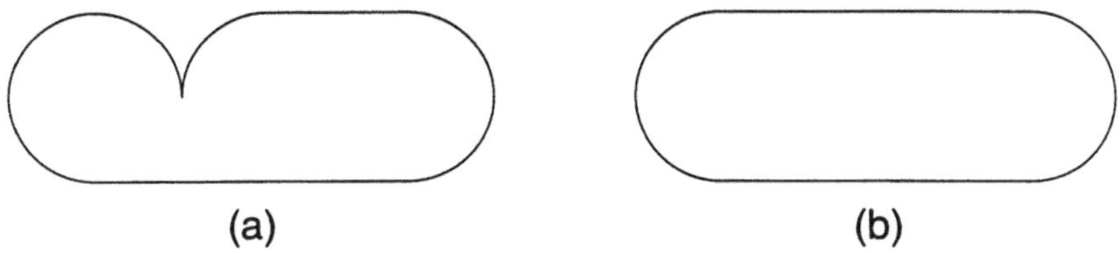

Figure 14. A shape with a sharp negative minimum (a) pops out among distractors that lack a negative minimum (b)—but not vice versa. (Adapted from Wolfe & Bennett, 1997.)

One might attribute Wolfe & Bennett's (1997) results to the fact that the shape in Figure 14a has a point of high curvature, whereas the shape in Figure 14b does not. To control for this factor, Hulleman et al. (2000) conducted visual search experiments with shapes as in Figure 15. The shape in Figure 15a has a negative minimum of curvature, whereas the one in Figure 15b has a positive maximum of curvature. These two extrema of curvature are equally sharp; they differ only in that one lies in a concave region, whereas the other lies in a convex region. Hulleman et al. (2000) found that the shape with the negative minimum of curvature (as in Figure 15a) pops out among distractors, each with a positive maximum of curvature (as in Figure 15b)—but not vice versa (recall Figure 6). Hence not all points of high curvature are

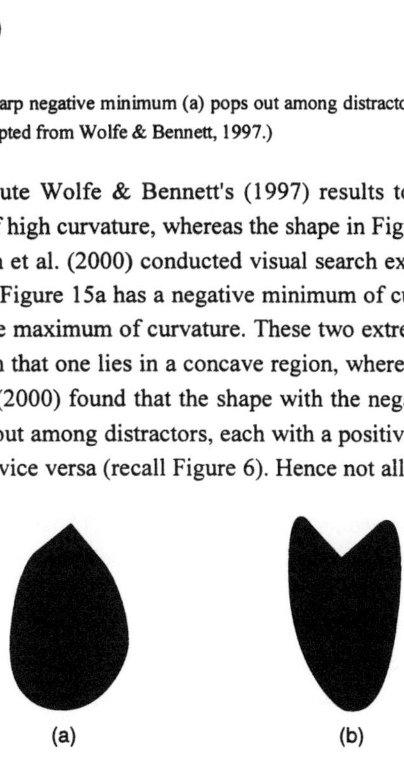

Figure 15. A shape with a sharp negative minimum of curvature (b) pops out among distractors that have a positive maximum of curvature (a)—but not vice versa—even though the two curvature extrema are equally sharp. (Adapted from Hulleman, te Winkel, & Boselie, 2000.)

processed rapidly, only those that lie in concave regions—in other words, negative minima.[4]

Further evidence for the minima rule comes from the experiments of Braunstein et al. (1989). Their subjects viewed 3D surfaces of revolution presented in structure from motion, i.e., as computer-generated dot displays set in motion (see Figure 16a). After viewing a surface for 20 seconds, subjects had to choose, from four alternatives, a part that belonged to the object just viewed. Of these four alternatives, one was a part defined by negative-minima boundaries, one was a "part" defined by positive-maxima boundaries (i.e., points of locally

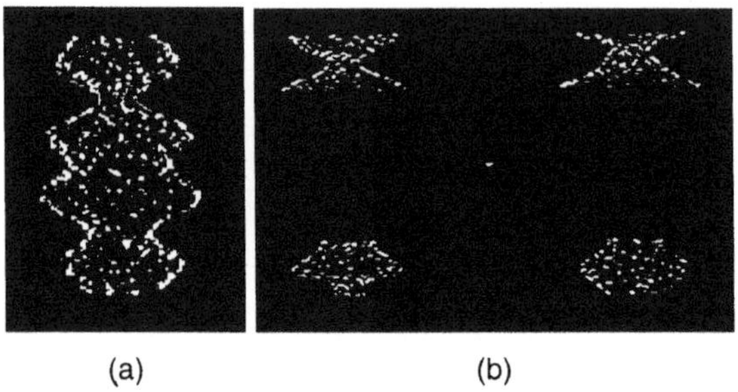

Figure 16. When asked to indicate which of four "parts" (shown in b) was in the initial display (a), subjects are twice as likely to respond with negative-minima parts than positive-maxima parts. (Adapted from Braunstein, Hoffman, & Saidpour, 1989.)

highest curvature in convex regions), and the other two were distractors (see Figure 16b). 77% of the subjects responded more frequently with negative-minima parts than with positive-maxima parts, and 65% of all correct responses were negative-minima responses. Hence subjects were twice as likely to remember parts defined by negative minima, than those defined by positive maxima. This demonstrates that parts also affect recognition memory for shapes.

In a different experiment, subjects had to mark part boundaries on 3D surfaces, using a joystick to move a red line on the computer monitor. The surfaces had relatively narrow points defined by circular concavities (of low curvature), as well as (sharp) negative minima (see Figure 17). 81% of all responses were made at negative minima of curvature, 10% at positive maxima, and 9% at other places—again supporting the minima rule. (We will later discuss the roles of cut length and boundary strength in parsing, as well as the status of circular concavities.)

Biederman and Blickle (cited in Biederman, 1987) asked subjects to identify objects in

---

[4] Although Wolfe & Bennett's and Hulleman et al.'s experiments suggest that part *boundaries* are computed pre-attentively, they do not in themselves show that parts or part structures are also computed pre-attentively. We will return to this issue later (see section on "Implications for Visual Cognition.")

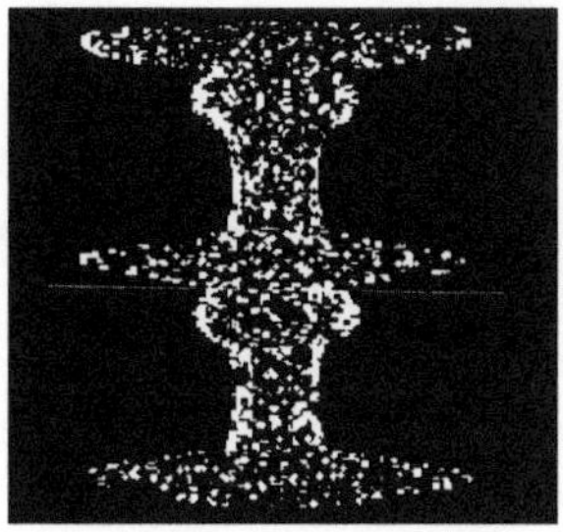

Figure 17. Subjects are more likely in these display to place part boundaries at the sharp negative minima of curvature than at relatively narrow points with low-curvature. (Adapted from Braunstein, Hoffman, & Saidpour, 1989.)

line drawings that had some of their contours deleted. They deleted contours in one of two ways: one which allowed for the recovery of the object's parts (see Figure 18b), and the other which did not (see Figure 18c). They found that subjects had no difficulty identifying objects in the recoverable-parts condition, with error rates approaching zero for long (5s) exposures. But subjects were largely unable to identify objects in the nonrecoverable-parts condition, even with long exposures. They found this difference despite the fact that the proportion of contour deleted in the two conditions was comparable. Although these results do not support any particular set of shape primitives, they do indicate that recovering parts is important for recognition. They also support the minima rule because many of the nonrecoverable-parts stimuli were in fact created by deleting regions around negative minima of curvature (see Figure 18c).

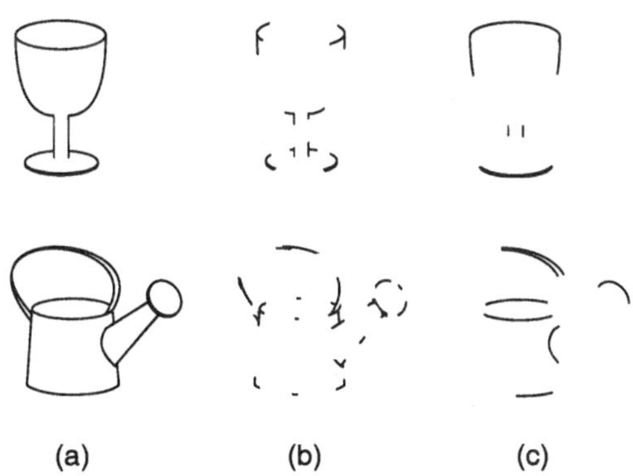

Figure 18. Subjects can easily recognize objects when contours are deleted in a way that allows parts to be recovered, as in (b). However, recognition becomes extremely difficult when contours are deleted in regions around negative minima—which makes it difficult to recover the parts. (Adapted from Biederman, 1987.)

Biederman & Cooper (1991) first presented their subjects with contour-deleted line drawings. They deleted contours in one of two possible ways: either by deleting every other feature (i.e., edge or vertex), or by deleting every other part. The first manipulation resulted, roughly, in the deletion of half of each part (see Figure 19a), whereas the second resulted in the deletion of half of the parts in the drawing (see Figure 19c). In a subsequent block, they showed subjects contour-deleted images that were either identical to the ones in the first block, or complementary to them (Figures 19b and d). Subjects had to name the line drawings with basic-level names as quickly as possible. Having seen a line drawing earlier produces an advantage in speed and accuracy the second time through, i.e., *priming*. In the feature-deletion case, the level of priming was as high for complementary images as for identical images—since all parts could be recovered in either case. But in the part-deletion case, the level of priming was much lower for complementary images, in which altogether different parts were seen. Biederman & Cooper (1991) concluded that all of the visual priming in object naming is due to the activation of part-based representations, and none due to the activation of specific edges and vertices. This again points to the importance of parts in object identification and naming, though not to any specific set of pre-defined parts.

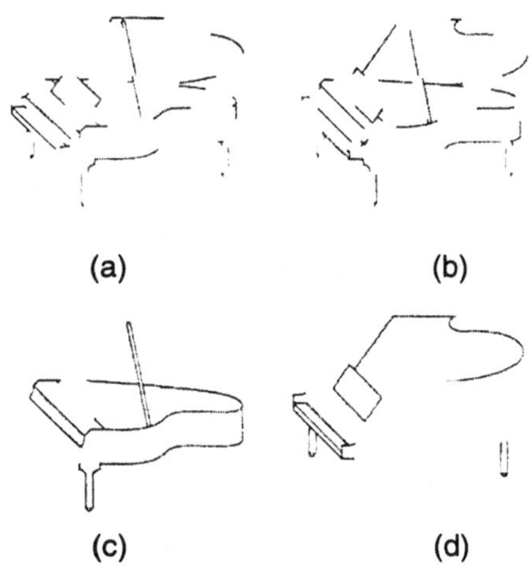

Figure 19. Priming with complementary contours is as effective as priming with identical contours, when roughly half of the contours in each part is deleted—so that all parts can be recovered in each case (a and b). However, priming with complementary contours is much less effective when the contours of half of the parts are deleted (c and d). (Adapted from Biederman & Cooper, 1991.)

Somewhat indirect evidence for part-based descriptions of shape comes from the experiment of Todd, Koenderink, van Doorn, & Kappers (1996). These researchers studied the effects of changing viewing conditions on perceived 3D structure. They presented observers with images depicting smoothly curved surfaces (male and female torsos) that were lit either frontally or obliquely. Observers made judgments of local surface orientation at a large number of probe points over these surfaces. From these local measurements, these researchers could estimate the 3D structure perceived by the observers (Koenderink, van Doorn, & Kappers, 1992). Their results showed that surfaces perceived in monocular and stereoscopic conditions were related by an affine stretching, and similarly, surfaces perceived under frontal and oblique illumination contained a strong affine component (with stereoscopic viewing and oblique illumination eliciting greater perceived depths). In addition, they found that the change in illumination condition did not lead to a *uniform* stretching of the entire surface, but rather, to a stretching that was piecewise uniform. In other words, different "pieces" of the surface appeared perceptually stretched by different amounts—and these "pieces" corresponded to the natural and namable parts of the human torso. We will see further evidence for part-based representations, and their role in visual cognition, in the following sections.

FROM PART BOUNDARIES TO PART CUTS

The minima rule defines precise part boundaries on shapes. As we have seen, for a 2D shape these part boundaries are points of negative minima of curvature on the outline of the shape. The minima rule does not, however, define part cuts: It does not tell how to pair negative minima of curvature to create cuts that parse the shape into parts (Beusmans et al., 1987; Siddiqi & Kimia, 1995). For example, for the cross on the left in Figure 20, the minima rule gives the four negative minima as part boundaries, but is silent on how to join these to give cuts. Note that this cross is naturally perceived as a large vertical body with two small parts on the sides. The cross on the right also has four negative minima. However, it is naturally perceived as a small core surrounded by four small parts.

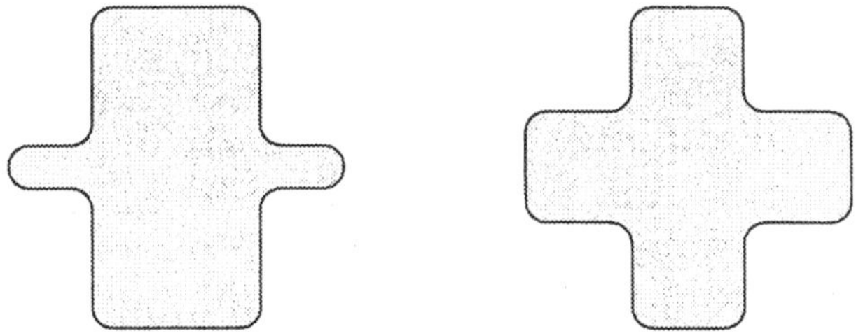

Figure 20. Although negative minima of curvature define part boundaries, they do not determine part cuts. Both shapes in this figure have four negative minima. However, the shape on the left is naturally segmented using two part cuts (into a large vertical body and two parts on the sides), whereas the one on the right is naturally segmented using four part cuts (into a central core and four parts).

In addition, the minima rule does not tell when to use part boundaries other than negative minima of curvature. The shape in Figure 21a, for example, is naturally parsed using the two cuts shown in 21b. Each of these two cuts terminates at one end in a negative minimum of curvature, but at the other end, in a point of zero curvature. Simply joining the two negative minima, on the other hand, produces perceptually unnatural parts (Figure 21c).[5] Clearly, some rules are needed, in addition to the minima rule, to define part cuts—and hence the parts themselves.

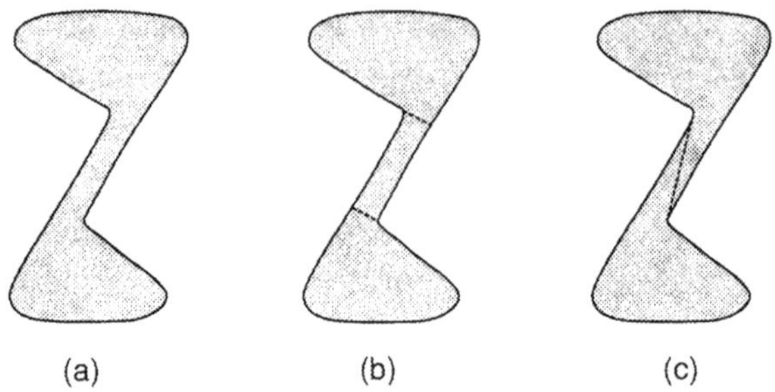

Figure 21. The natural part cuts for the shape in (a) are shown in (b). Note that each of these cuts joins a negative minimum of curvature to a point of zero curvature. Simply joining the two negative minima, on the other hand—as in (c)—leads to a perceptually unnatural parsing. Thus geometric constraints in addition to the minima rule are needs to define cuts, and hence the parts themselves. (Adapted from Singh, Seyranian, & Hoffman, 1999.)

For our current purposes, we take a part cut to be a straight-line segment which joins two points on the outline of a silhouette such that (1) at least one of the two points has negative curvature, (2) the entire segment lies in the interior of the shape, and (3) the segment crosses an axis of local symmetry (Brady & Asada, 1984).[6] Condition (1) builds on the intuition behind the minima rule that concave regions with high magnitude of curvature are important for parsing. However, it allows for the possibility that other geometric factors may also play a role in parsing, thereby pulling part cuts slightly away from negative minima of curvature. Condition (3) ensures the region being separated by the cut is natural enough to be considered for parthood. In Figure 22, for example, the segment <u>*ab*</u> crosses an axis of local symmetry, whereas the segment <u>bc</u> does not. As a result, <u>*ab*</u> is a legitimate potential cut, but

[5] This example also shows that any scheme that creates part cuts by joining *consecutive* negative minima along a contour will give unnatural cuts.

[6] Local symmetry is a weak form of symmetry that allows for the axes of symmetry to be curved, and to span only local subregions of the shape rather than the entire shape. The axes of local symmetry provide, in effect, the skeletal axial structure of any given silhouette. See the section on 'Local Symmetry' for details.

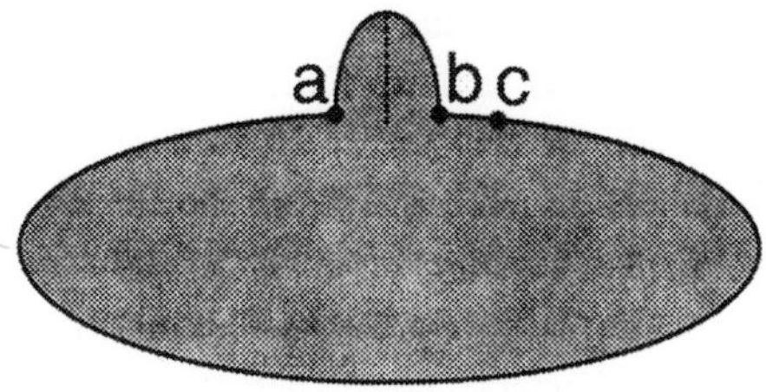

Figure 22. Only points along the contour of a shape that are separated by an axis of local symmetry are valid candidates for being the end points of a part cut. Thus the join of a and b is a legitimate part cut, whereas the join of b and c is not.

bc is not.

In this section, we consider four geometric factors that determine how human vision creates part cuts. These factors are: the length of a cut, the strength of its boundary points, good continuation, and local symmetry. We consider also the role of 'simple descriptions.'

Cut Length

Consider the elbow in Figure 23a. Cut *pq* on this elbow looks far more natural than cut *pr*. In Figure 23b, we have made the areas of the two segments equal, and *pq* is still the preferred cut, suggesting that the area of the parts is not determining the cuts in these figures. Instead, examples like these suggest that human vision prefers to divide shapes into parts using the shortest cuts possible.[7]

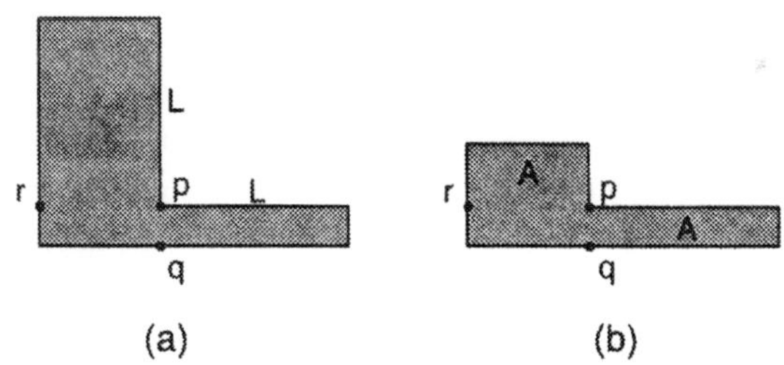

Figure 23. The role of cut length in determining part cuts. The cut pq in (a) appears far more natural than the cut pr. This is also true in (b) where the areas of the two candidate parts have been equated.

---

[7] These cuts must, of course, satisfy conditions (1)—(3) above. In Figure 22, for example, cut bc is shorter than cut ab—but it is nevertheless unnatural because it does not cross an axis of local symmetry.

This "short-cut rule" (Singh, Seyranian, & Hoffman, 1999) is motivated using the geometry of transversal intersections in three dimensions. Consider first the simple case of two cylinders with unequal radii. If these cylinders intersect *completely* (i.e., in a way that produces *two,* rather than a single, concave creases), these creases always encircle the thinner cylinder and never the thicker cylinder (see Figure 24). If this intersection is now projected onto an image plane, these concave creases project onto the shorter cuts, and not the longer ones. Hence a silhouette of this intersection is naturally parsed using these shorter cuts. Furthermore, as the ratio of the radii (larger to smaller) of the two cylinders increases—say, by keeping the radius of the thicker cylinder fixed, and decreasing the radius of the thinner one—complete intersections become more and more likely (indeed, the probability of obtaining a complete intersection approaches 1). Hence, the probability assigned to the shorter cuts should increase as the ratio of their radii gets more extreme.

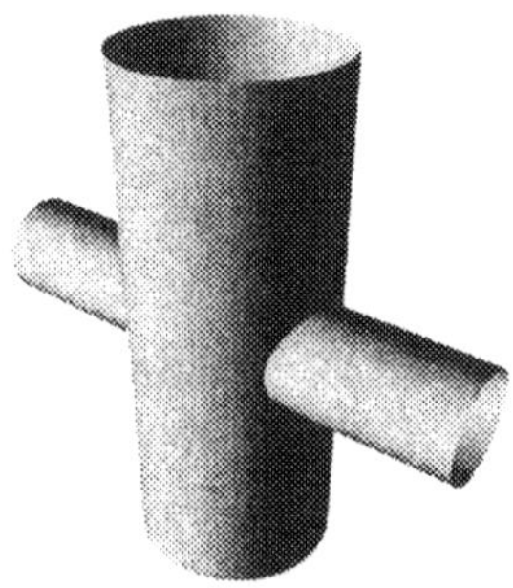

Figure 24. Motivating the visual system's preference for shorter part cuts using the transversal intersection of volumes in 3D. When two cylinders of unequal radii intersect completely, the concave creases always encircle the thinner cylinder, and never the thicker one. (Adapted from Singh, Seyranian, & Hoffman, 1999.)

Now, given a silhouette produced by a 3D shape of unknown geometry, the principle of genericity (e.g., Freeman, 1994) assigns high probability to those 3D interpretations in which the shape is about as deep as it is wide in the image. Therefore, as in the case of the cylinders above, the concave creases will encircle the thinner shape, and hence project onto the shorter cuts. Thus the silhouette is naturally parsed using these shorter cuts.

In a series of experiments using crosses and elbows Singh, Seyranian & Hoffman (1999) studied subjects' preferences for making part cuts, as a function of relative cut lengths and relative part sizes induced by the cuts. They found that subjects strongly and consistently prefered to parse shapes using shorter cuts, rather than longer ones. However, subjects did not show a consistent preference for either smaller or larger parts. In addition, their results demonstrated that the short-cut rule can create part boundaries that are not negative minima of curvature (see, for example, the two elbows in Figure 23, and the shape in Figure 21).

Siddiqi & Kimia (1995; Siddiqi et al. 1996) proposed a method for parsing shapes, called 'necks.' A neck is a part cut "which is also a local minimum of the diameter of an inscribed circle" (p. 243). Although this method prefers locally shorter cuts, it measures distances only along diameters of circles that can be inscribed within the shape. This requirement turns out to be too restrictive. Figure 25, for example, shows a shape with a natural cut that should be made; but this cut is not captured by the definition of a neck. The problem is that the circle whose diameter is the cut cannot be inscribed in the shape. The short-cut rule, on the other hand, considers distances between *all* pairs of points on the silhouette outline, as long as these are separated by an axis of local symmetry (recall the three

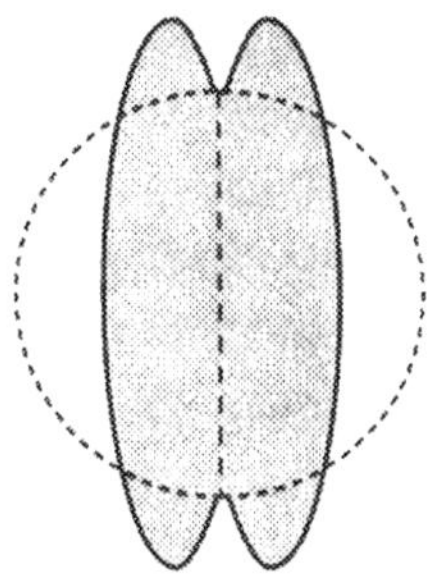

Figure 25. Siddiqi & Kimia's definition of "neck" fails to capture cases in which a circle of locally minimal diameter cannot be inscribed within the shape.

conditions that part cuts must satisfy). For example, in Figure 23, the short-cut rule explains the preference for the cut *pq* over the cut *pr*, but necks fail to explain this preference.

Boundary Strength

Negative minima of curvature are attractors of part cuts: A cut which passes through a negative minimum is typically preferred to one which passes near, but not through, it. All negative minima are not created equal, however: Some are more salient than others (Hoffman & Singh, 1997). Figure 26a, for example, shows a 2D shape with two part boundaries of extremely high strength, together with a natural part cut that joins them. If this part cut is displaced just slightly, as in Figure 26b, it looks clearly wrong. Figure 26c shows a similar silhouette, but with weak part boundaries. Note that the displaced part cut in Figure 26d does not look nearly as wrong as in Figure 26b, even though the displacements are equal in magnitude. Examples such as these suggest that sharper extrema of curvature are more powerful attractors of part cuts.[8]

Boundary strength can interact with the short-cut rule in the following way: For weak

[8] We will discuss precise geometric factors that determine the strength of part boundaries in the section on "Part Salience."

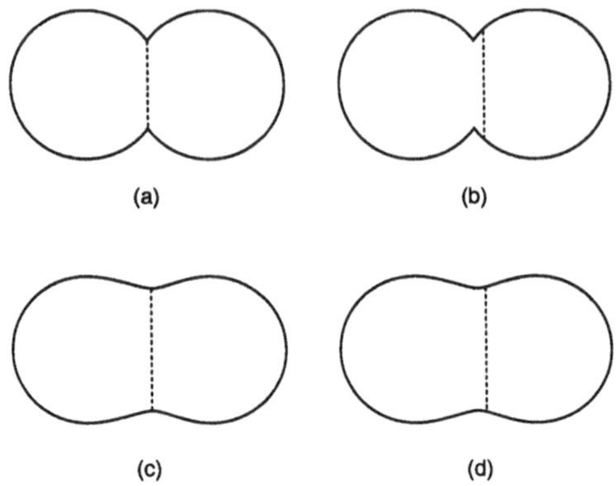

Figure 26. Sharper negative minima are stronger attractors of parts cuts than weaker negative minima. In (b), a slight deviation of the part cut from negative minima looks clearly wrong. However, in (d) a deviation of identical magnitude appears less contrived.

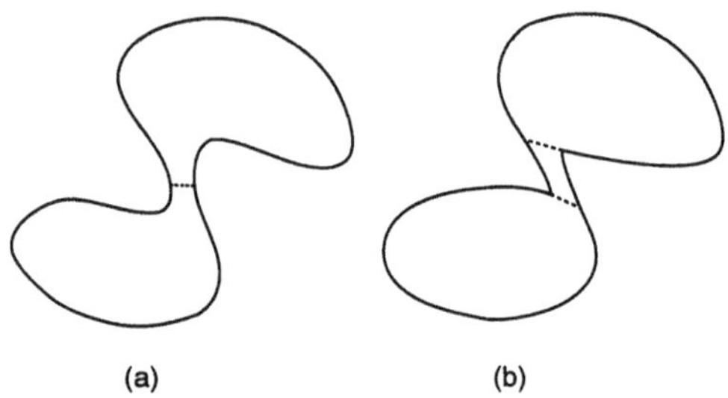

Figure 27. (a) When negative minima are weak, other factors such as cut length can sometimes pull part cuts away from negative minima. (Adapted from Siddiqi & Kimia, 1995). (b) However, when negative minima are sharp, they force the cuts to pass through them—even if this means making two cuts instead of one.

part boundaries, the preference for short cuts can sometimes pull part cuts away from negative minima of curvature, as in Figure 27a (figure modified from Siddiqi & Kimia, 1995). Note, however, that if the part boundaries are sharp, they force the part cuts to pass through them, even if this means making slightly longer cuts, or making two cuts instead of one (see Figure 27b).

Another interaction between boundary strength and the short-cut rule can be seen in Figure 28a. This shape has a narrow region in the middle defined by concave arcs of circles. Each of these arcs is a *region* of negative minima of curvature—so the minima rule by itself does not specify any unique boundary point on them. Furthermore, these concave arcs have low curvature, and hence low boundary strength. At the endpoints of these arcs are negative minima of curvature with high boundary strength. The cuts joining these sharp negative

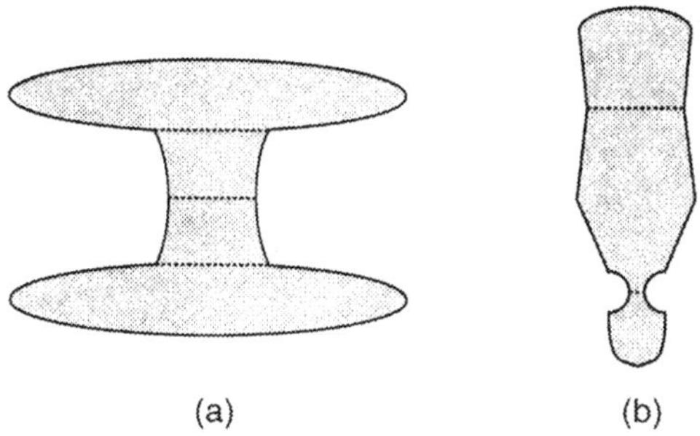

Figure 28. Demonstrating the interaction between cut length and the strength of part boundaries. In (a), the cuts at the sharp negative minima are preferred to the shorter cut at the low-curvature arcs of circles. (Adapted from Braunstein et al., 1989.) In (b), the cut at the arcs of circles is preferred because it is both shorter and involves boundaries with higher salience.

minima are slightly longer than the 'neck' cut in the middle; but these cuts are nevertheless preferred by subjects (Braunstein et al., 1989). So, in this example, the short-cut rule loses to boundary strength. In other cases, the short-cut rule can also win over boundary strength (for example, if the shorter cut joining the two weak boundaries in Figure 28a were to be made extremely short).

Boundary strength and the short-cut rule can also cooperate, rather than compete. In Figure 28b, the 'neck' cut at the bottom is short and joins two circular part boundaries with high curvature—and hence high boundary strength. The cut at the top, on the other hand, is longer and joins negative minima with low boundary strength. Hence, subjects in this case prefer the bottom cut. Siddiqi et al. (1996) claim that this provides an example of 'necks' winning over the minima rule. But, in fact, neither cut violates the minima rule, and the bottom cut wins simply because *both* the short-cut rule and boundary strength are in its favor.[9]

Good Continuation

Consider the shape in Figure 29. Here the parsing induced by the shorter cuts (shown in Figure 29b) appears less natural than the one induced by the longer cuts (shown in Figure 29c). However, there is another factor at play here, in addition to minimizing cut length: In Figure 29c each cut continues the directions of two tangents at the negative minima of

[9] As we mentioned earlier, circular concavities are appropriately thought of as regions, rather than points, of negative minima of curvature. Moreover, circular concavities are nongeneric in that almost any perturbation will induce an isolated point of negative minimum of curvature. Hence, it is not surprising that human vision treats circular concavities no differently than negative minima of curvature.

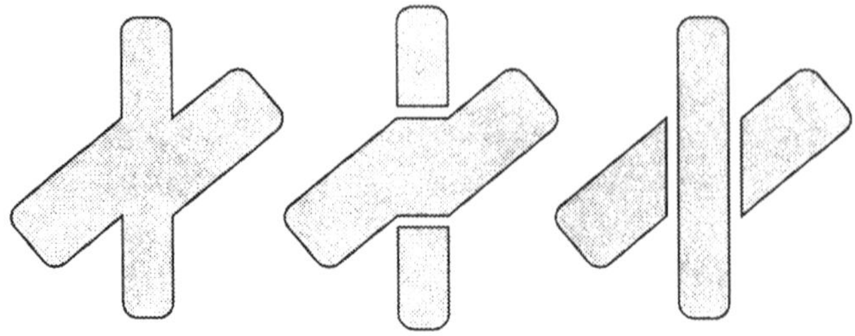

Figure 29. An example of the role of good continuation in parsing. The horizontal cuts in (b) appear less natural than the vertical cuts in (c), even though the vertical cuts are longer.

curvature—but not in Figure 29b. Hence good continuation between a pair of tangents (one at each of the two part boundaries) is an important geometric factor for determining part cuts.

Recognizing the role of good continuation in parsing shapes, Siddiqi & Kimia (1995) proposed a scheme for parsing known as "*limbs*:" A limb is a part-line going through a pair of negative minima with co-circular boundary tangents on (at least) one side of the part-line" (p. 243). In other words, Siddiqi & Kimia define good continuation between two vectors by requiring that both be tangent to the same circle. This requirement is much too restrictive, however, since the slightest perturbation of either vector will result in the violation of co-circularity. Indeed, given two random vectors in a plane, the probability is zero that they will be co-circular (Singh, Seyranian & Hoffman, 1999). Hence, this definition almost never applies to real parts.

Although the requirement of co-circularity fails, the intuition of good continuation holds, and other formalizations may be used to capture this intuition. For example, in the context of illusory contour formation, the requirement of contour *relatability* (Kellman & Shipley, 1991) is often used to determine good continuation between two tangents: The extensions of these tangents must intersect, and their exterior angle of intersection must be acute. As it stands, relatability is an all-or-none property, but it is easily extended to a graded measure of good continuation (see Singh & Hoffman, 1999). Intuitively, this graded measure has two components:

II. The smoothness of the smoothest possible curve that can be interpolated between the two tangents (captured by *variation in curvature*), and

III. The absolute value of the angle through which this smoothest curve turns between the first tangent and the second tangent (captured by *total curvature*).

The smoother the curve, and the smaller the angle it needs to turn through, the better is the continuation between the two tangents. Recently, psychophysical evidence in support of these two measures of good continuation has been provided by Kubovy & Gephstein (2000).

Two additional considerations, however, constrain the role of good continuation in determining part cuts. First, good continuation can play a role in defining part cuts in which only one of the two part boundaries is a negative minimum of curvature. In this case, only the tangent at the negative minimum constrains good continuation—not the tangent at the other part boundary. For example, the perceptually natural cuts in Figure 30a simply continue the directions of (one of) the segments that goes into each negative minimum of curvature. Since the definition of "limb" requires two negative minima, this has the consequence that many parts that are defined by a single negative minimum of curvature—including arms, elbows, and knees—fail to be "limbs" according to Siddiqi & Kimia's definition.

Second, parts are often defined by smooth negative minima of curvature. At each such negative minimum, there is, by definition, only one tangent. And requiring good continuation between these two tangents can give counterintuitive results. For example, in Figure 30b, a curve that smoothly continues the tangent at one negative minimum into the tangent at the other negative minimum is a poor candidate for the "good continuation" of either part—even though these two tangents are co-circular. This suggests that, for smooth part boundaries, the tangents that constrain good continuation should not be the ones at the negative minima, but at the inflection points closest in arc length to the smooth negative minima. These inflections are likely to provide a stable estimate of the tangent direction of the contour on each side of the negative minimum (see Figure 30c).[10]

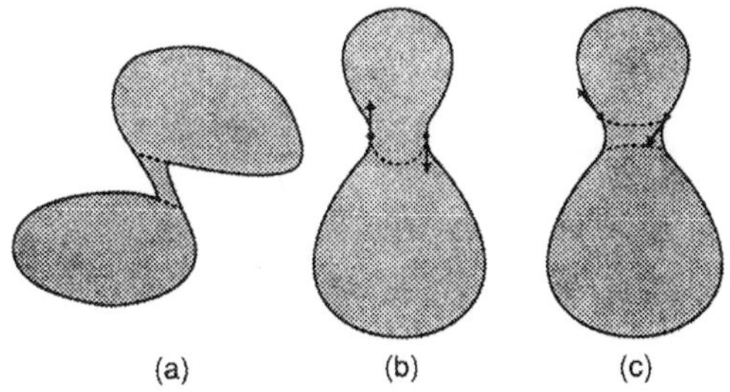

Figure 30. The figure in (a) demonstrates that good continuation plays a role in also defining those part cuts, only one of whose boundary points is a negative minimum of curvature. (b) In the case of smooth negative minima, computing good continuation from tangents at the negative minima themselves yields unintuitive results. (c) In this case, the tangents that constrain good continuation should be the ones at the inflection points closest to the negative minima.

[10] It is also possible, however, that when part boundaries are highly smoothed, good continuation simply becomes less relevant, because the estimation of the tangent direction on each side of the negative minimum becomes significantly more difficult.

Local Symmetry

The relevance of local symmetry for segmenting shapes was first noted by Blum (1973). The Symmetry Axis Transform (SAT; see below for a precise definition) was put forward as a formalism for local symmetry, and it was suggested that a shape should be divided into parts at branch points of axes of local symmetry. For example, the two branch points in the axes of local symmetry of the "dog bone" in Figure 31a partition it into five parts. Unfortunately, the SAT scheme gives the same axes to a rectangle (Figure 31b), and therefore provides an unintuitive part structure for it (as acknowledged by Blum & Nagel, 1978).

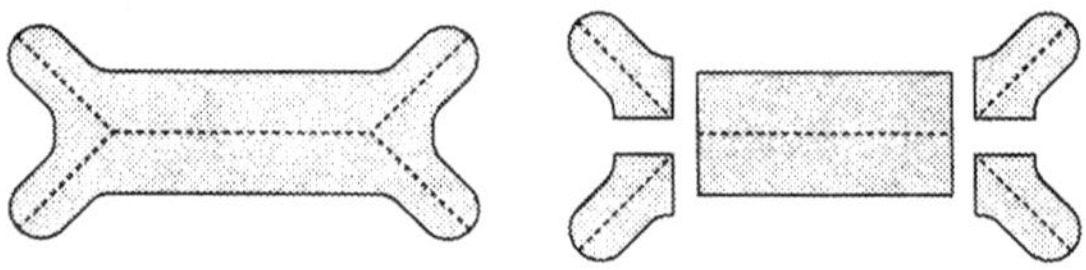

(a)

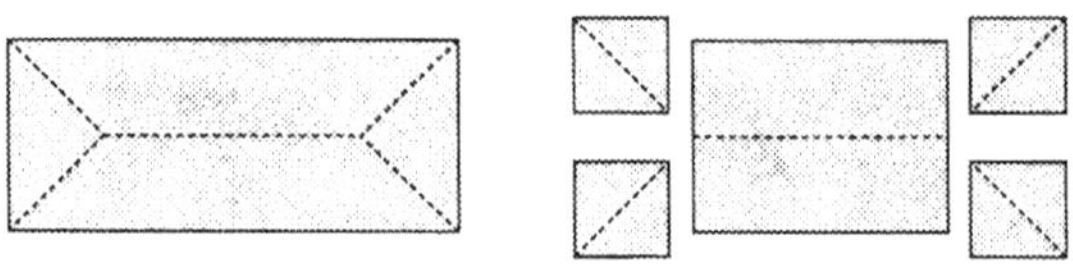

(b)

Figure 31. (a) The parsing of the "dog bone" into parts at the branch points of the Symmetric Axis Transform. (Adapted from Blum, 1973.) (b) Unfortunately, this parsing rule gives the same part structure to a rectangle.

To motivate our own intuitions on the relevance of local symmetry to part cuts, consider the two points *A* and *B* in Figure 32a: It is, in part, because these two negative minima of curvature are locally symmetric to each other that they form such a natural candidate pair for a cut. As another example, consider the smooth elbow in Figure 32b. There is only one negative minimum of curvature on the shape (located at the point *A*), and so the minima rule tells us that one endpoint of a part cut must be point *A*. However, the minima rule does not dictate where the other endpoint of this cut will lie. One could imagine, for example, the cut passing through any of the points between B_1 and B_3. The most natural cut appears to be the one through B_2. Interestingly, B_2 is the point (of all the points between B_1 and B_3) that is *furthest* from *A*. Hence, in this case, some factor other than minimizing cut length is at work. We suggest that this factor is the local symmetry between B_2 and *A*. Note, similarly, that the natural cuts in Figure 32c are determined by points that are locally symmetric to each of the two negative minima of curvature.

What is local symmetry? Local symmetry may be thought of as a weak form of symmetry. For example, take an object that is perfectly symmetric (Figure 33a), and imagine a process that curves or bends its axis of symmetry (Figure 33b). Observers still see some "symmetry" in the resulting shape. This is one aspect of what local symmetry is intended to capture. Note, though, that this shape has an axis of symmetry that spans the entire shape. The notion of local symmetry allows, in addition, for axes that span only local subshapes of the entire shape, as illustrated in Figure 33d. What the axes of local symmetry provide, in effect, is the skeletal axial structure of any given 2D shape.

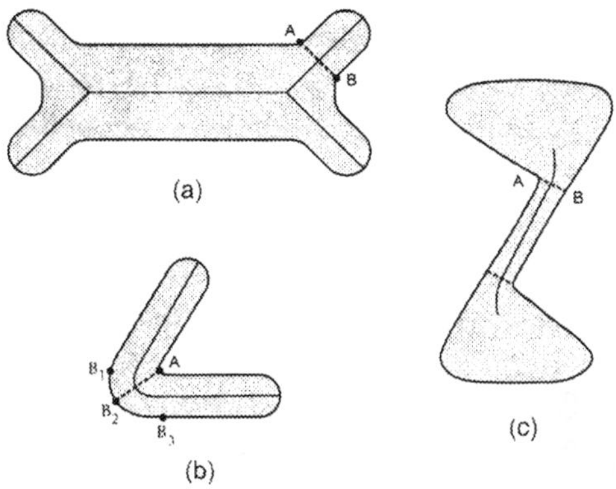

Figure 32. Demonstrating the role of local symmetry in determining part cuts. There is a strong perceptual preference for cuts that join locally-symmetric pairs of boundary points.

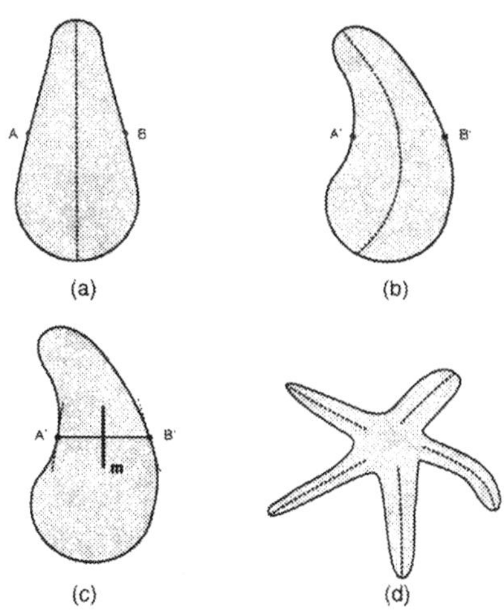

Figure 33. Clarifying the notion of local symmetry. Curving the axis of a symmetric shape(a) leads to a weaker form of symmetry (b). The axis of local symmetry locally reflects the tangent at A' into the tangent at B' (c). The axes of local symmetry span local subshapes, providing a skeletal structure of the shape (d).

There are at least two respects, therefore, in which the notion of local symmetry can be said to be "local." First consider the two points A and B in Figure 31a that are symmetric with respect to each other. In what sense can their corresponding points, A' and B', in the transformed shape (Figure 33b), be said to be locally symmetric? Imagine a mirror being placed at the point where the curved symmetry axis intersects the join of A' and B' (see Figure 33c). And suppose that the mirror is oriented perpendicular to this join. Then not only will this mirror reflect the point A' into the point B', but it will also reflect the tangent to the curve at A' to the tangent to the curve at B' (Leyton, 1992). In other words, the curve in an (infinitesimal) neighborhood of the point A' is reflected into the curve in an infinitesimal neighborhood of the point B': hence the "local" symmetry. The other sense in which local symmetry is "local" is simply that no global symmetry axis is required: one may have local axes spanning local subshapes (as in Figure 33d).

Many different schemes for local symmetry have been put forward to capture these intuitions. The most prominent among them are the SAT scheme mentioned above (Blum, 1973; Blum & Nagel, 1978) and Smoothed Local Symmetry (SLS; Brady, 1983; Brady and Asada, 1984).

Blum's SAT is obtained by considering maximal disks that lie entirely in the interior of a given shape, and taking the locus of their centers as an axis (as in Figure 34a). This scheme has a number of shortcomings (Brady, 1983; Leyton, 1992). For example, in Figure 32b, the

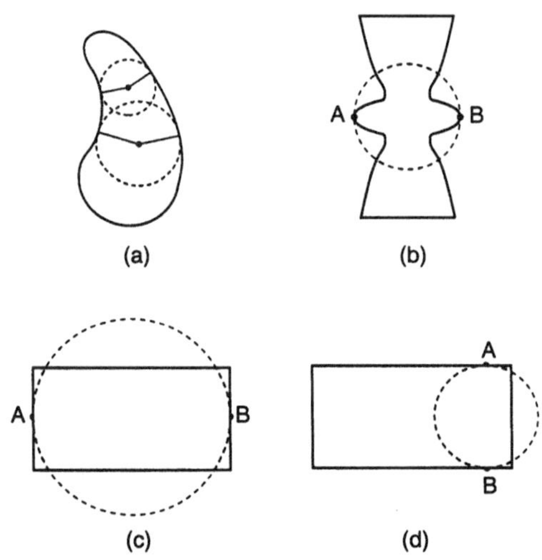

Figure 34. (a) Blum's SAT is defined by taking the locus of the centers of circles that can be inscribed within the shape. (b)–(d) demonstrate some shortcomings of Blum's definition. The requirement that the circle must lie within the shape means that the pairs of points A and B shown in these displays are not locally symmetric according to this definition.

points A and B are clearly symmetric. However, it is impossible to draw a circle that lies entirely in the interior of the shape and is tangent to it precisely at A and B. For the same reason, the SAT scheme does not give the minor axis of a rectangle (Figure 34c), nor does it give all of the major axis (Figure 34d). In fact, as we noted above (in Figure 31), the SAT of the rectangle is the same as that of the "dog bone.'"

Brady's SLS scheme is formulated as follows: two points A and B are said to be locally symmetric if their tangents make equal angles with the line segment that joins them (Figure 35a). The axis of symmetry is then defined by taking the locus of the *midpoint* of the join $\underline{AB}$ (Figure 35b). The SLS scheme maintains all the advantages of the SAT, but eliminates its shortcomings. In particular, it does not require the circle that is simultaneously tangent to the contour at points A and B to lie in the interior of the shape (the existence of such a circle is guaranteed by the SLS construction; see Leyton, 1992). We adopt Brady's SLS formalism for local symmetry.

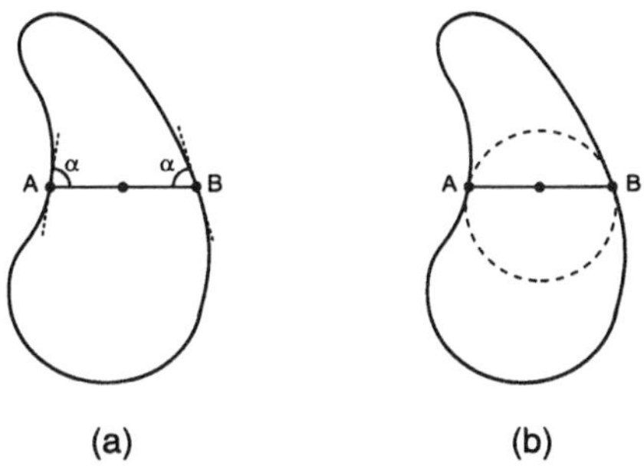

Figure 35. Two points are locally symmetric according to Brady's SLS scheme if the tangents at these points make equal angles with their join. The axis of local symmetry is then defined by the locus of midpoints of the joins of such pairs of points. This scheme preserves all the advantages of Blum's SAT, but does not require a circle to be inscribed within the shape.

Given that pairs of points that enjoy local symmetry yield more natural cuts than those that do not, how should we motivate a formal definition of this term. Consider two points x and y on the shape in Figure 36a. Let $s(x)$ denote the point on the shape that is locally symmetric to x. Then the arc-length distance (i.e., distance measured along the contour) between the points y and $s(x)$, denoted $||y - s(x)||_a$, measures how much the point y deviates from local symmetry to x. [11] Similarly, the arc-length distance between the points $s(y)$ and x,

---

[11] In general, if the point y has n points locally symmetric to it, namely, $s_1(x), ..., s_n(x)$, the point that is relevant in evaluating the cut xy is clearly the one that is closest, in arc-length distance, to y (see Figure 36c). In this case, the term $||y - s(x)||_a$ needs to be replaced by $min_i\{||y - s_i(x)||_a\}$.

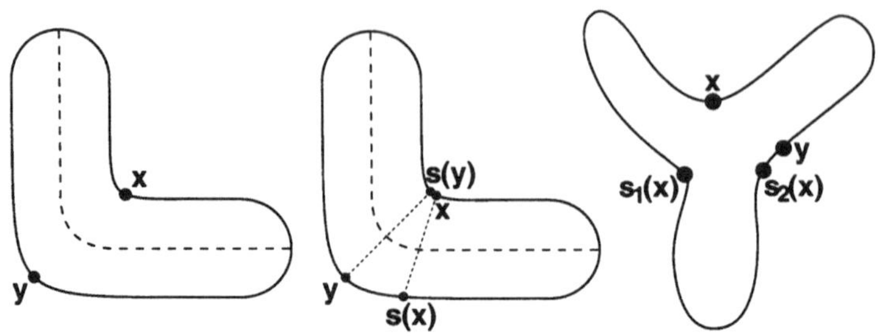

Figure 36. Computing the extent to which two points on a shape deviate from being locally symmetric.

denoted $||x - s(y)||_a$, measures how far the point $\underline{x}$ deviates from local symmetry to y (see Figure 36b). In general these two distances are not equal. Their mean, then, provides a measure of how much the pair $\{x,y\}$ deviates from local symmetry (Singh, Seyranian, & Hoffman, 1996).

Simple Descriptions: Number of parts and convexity

The idea behind parsing shapes is to allow for efficient descriptions of these shapes in terms of simpler components. Hence the most natural parsings are those that lead to the simplest parts, and the simplest descriptions in terms of parts. This suggests two constraints: (1) Other things being equal, parsings with fewer parts should be preferred to those with more parts. If a simple description of a shape has already been achieved with a small number of parts, there is no need for further parsing. (2) Parsings that create parts with *no* negative minima on their outlines should be preferred to parsings that create parts *with* negative minima—since the presence of negative minima is indicative of further part structure. The simplest shapes are convex shapes—whose outlines have positive curvature throughout (see,

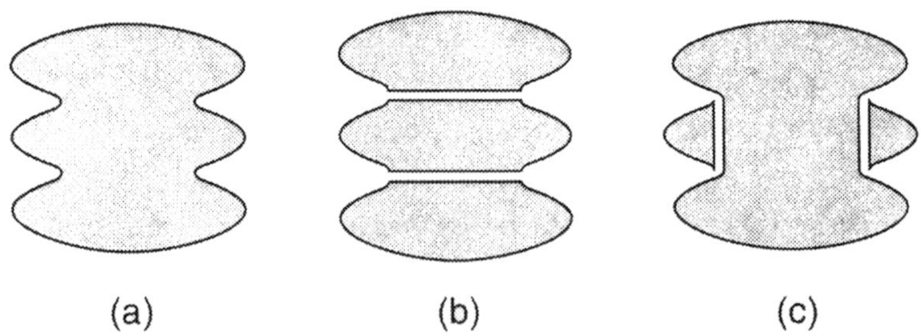

Figure 37. The parsing depicted in (b) is more natural than the one in (c) even though it requires longer part cuts. Note that the parts in (b) have no further negative minima, whereas the central part in (c) has four negative minima and can thus be parsed further.

e.g., Rosin, 2000, for the role of convexity in parsing). If the outline of a shape has regions of negative curvature, especially if these regions contain salient negative minima of curvature, this usually indicates that the shape can be further parsed to give simpler subshapes. As an example, consider the shape in Figure 37a. The parsing in 37b looks more natural than the one in 37c, even though it involves making slightly longer cuts. The reason is clear: The resulting central "part" in 37c has four negative minima of curvature, and can be parsed further into three different parts; whereas the parsing in 37b leads to parts with no further part structure.

PART SALIENCE

As the shape in Figure 38a indicates, perceptual parthood is a graded—rather than an all-or-none—notion. In other words, parts are not all created equal. For example, in Figure 38a, the part labeled **A** is more visually salient than the part labeled **B**. Three main geometrical factors determine the perceptual salience of a part (Hoffman & Singh, 1997): (1) its protrusion, (2) its relative area, and (3) the strength of its boundaries. Salience of a part increases as its protrusion, relative area, or boundary strength increases. In this section we briefly consider protrusion and relative area, and then discuss in more detail the strength of part boundaries. We restrict attention to 2D shapes; the theory for 3D shapes is more complex and discussed elsewhere (Hoffman & Singh, 1997).

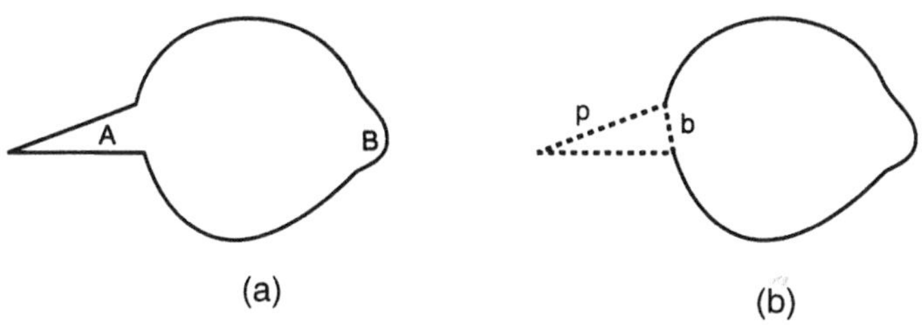

Figure 38. Perceptual parthood is a graded, rather than an all-or-none, notion. Some parts (such as A) are clearly more perceptually salient than others (such as B).

The protrusion of a part is, roughly, how much the part sticks out. This can be made more precise using terminology illustrated in Figure 38b. Here the outline of part **A** is divided into a base b and a perimeter p. The protrusion of **A** is simply the ratio p/b (Hoffman & Singh, 1997). This definition of protrusion is scale invariant (i.e., it gives the same value if the entire shape is uniformly shrunk or expanded), and it gives larger values to parts long and narrow than to parts short and wide. The greater the protrusion of a part, the greater is its visual salience. In Figure 38a, part **A** has greater protrusion than part **B**.

The effect of relative area on visual salience has long been recognized by Gestalt psychologists (e.g., Rubin, 1958). The relative area of a part is the area of that part divided by the total area of the whole object, a definition that is scale invariant. Again, the greater the relative area of a part, the greater is its salience. In Figure 38a, part **A** has greater relative area than part **B**.

The strength of a part boundary depends first on how "sharp" the boundary is; sharper boundaries have greater strength, and lead to more salient parts. Concave corners, such as those that define part *A* in Figure 38a, are sharper than smooth boundaries, such as those that define part *B*. Intuitively, the difference is in degree of curvature. Concave corners have infinite curvature whereas smooth boundaries have finite curvature. And various smooth boundaries can differ in their magnitudes of curvature, leading to differences in their strengths. The only caveat here is that curvature is not a scale invariant quantity, so that curvature simpliciter is not an appropriate measure of boundary sharpness. But this is easily fixed by using relative curvatures, or by introducing a normalization factor (Hoffman & Singh, 1997). We can state this as the following hypothesis:

Hypothesis of normalized curvature: The salience of a part boundary increases as the magnitude of normalized curvature at the boundary increases.

One rationale for this hypothesis follows from the principle of transversality. Recall that two shapes will generically intersect transversally, and that a transversal intersection creates concave corners at each point of intersection. These concave corners are the boundaries where one shape stops and the next shape begins, and are therefore part boundaries on the composite body formed by the two intersecting shapes. Boundaries that are not concave corners can be obtained from these corner boundaries by various amounts of smoothing. The greater the smoothing, the lower is the (magnitude of) curvature of the resulting boundary, and the further from the primary transversal case. This is illustrated in Figure 39a, where two rectangular shapes, A and B, intersect transversally at points *p* and *q*. If we smooth the transversal intersection at *p* just a little, to obtain curve *1*, we induce an extremum of curvature with a higher magnitude of curvature; if we smooth a lot, to obtain

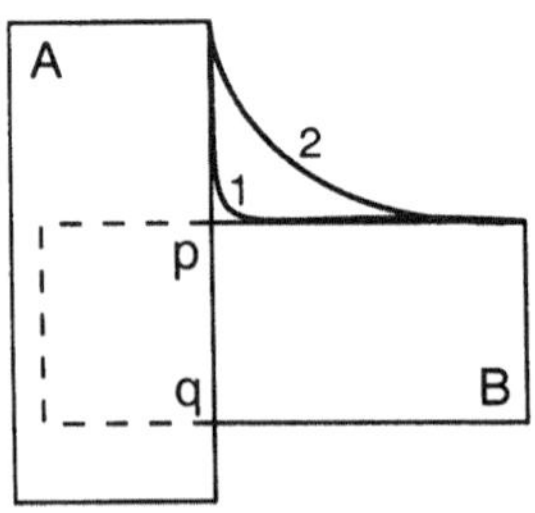

Figure 39. Demonstrating the role of curvature in determining the perceived salience of a part boundary. Greater degrees of smoothing of a transversal intersection lead to negative minima of curvature with lower magnitudes of curvature.

curve *2*, we induce an extremum of curvature with a lower magnitude of curvature (Bennett & Hoffman, 1987). In short, lower-curvature boundaries are further from (i.e., more smoothed from) the original transversal case than higher-curvature boundaries, and therefore have lower salience as boundaries.

We can be more precise about the smoothing in Figure 39 and its effect on the magnitude of curvature at the induced smooth part boundary. We represent the transversal intersection at point p in Figure 39 by the equation $xy = 0$. Various hyperbolic smoothings of this transversal intersection can be written $xy - \varepsilon = 0$, where $\varepsilon > 0$ parametrizes the hyperbolic smoothings such that larger values of $\underline{\varepsilon}$ correspond to greater smoothings. The curvature on the smoothing $xy - \varepsilon = 0$ is given by

$$\kappa(x,\varepsilon) = \frac{-2\varepsilon x^{-3}}{\sqrt{1+\varepsilon^2 x^{-4}}}$$

and the extremum of curvature is given by

$$\kappa_{ext}(\varepsilon) = \frac{1}{\sqrt{2\varepsilon}},$$

so that as $\varepsilon \to 0$, i.e., as the smoothing decreases, the magnitude of curvature at the extremum increases (Bennett & Hoffman, 1987).

Because curvature is a purely local notion, however, it fails to capture another determinant of perceived boundary strength, namely, the angle through which the contour turns in a neighborhood of the negative minimum (Hoffman & Singh, 1997). All concave-corner boundaries, for example, have infinite curvature, but their perceptual salience varies greatly as a function of the angle through which the contour turns around the boundary: Sharp corners require the contour to turn through a large angle (Figure 40a), whereas shallow corners require small turning angles (Figure 40c). This notion can also be generalized to smooth negative minima by considering them to be the result of smoothing concave corners of different turning angles. Given a smooth part boundary, a stable estimate of the turning angle is obtained by measuring the angle through which the contour turns between the nearest inflection point on each side of the negative minimum—a region we term the *locale* of the boundary (Hoffman & Singh, 1997). This yields the following hypothesis:

Hypothesis of Turning Angle: The salience of a negative-minimum boundary increases as the magnitude of the turning angle around the boundary increases.

As is clear from Figure 40, the curvature at a negative minimum and its turning angle can vary independently of each other. Smooth negative minima with the same turning angle can have different magnitudes of local curvature, and vice versa. Both variables must thus be taken into account to determine the perceived boundary salience (see the section on "Parts and Transparency" for an experimental design involving both variables).

Implications for Visual Cognition

In earlier sections, we have seen how parts can explain many aspects of our visual phenomenology. In this section, we consider in more detail how mechanisms that compute part structure and part salience interact with mechanisms of object and surface segmentation, and with the allocation of visual attention.

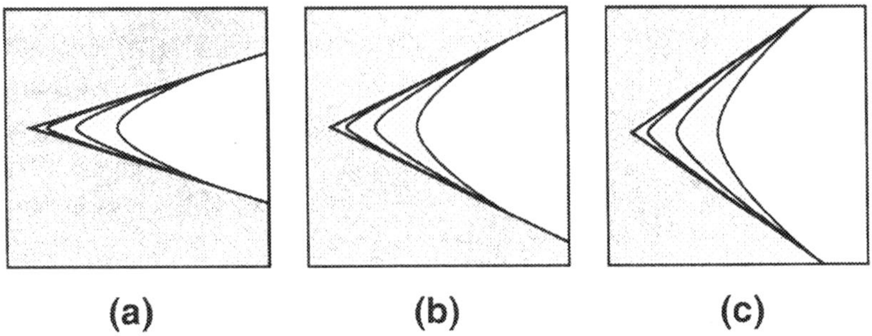

Figure 40. The turning angle captures how much the tangent must turn in a neighborhood of the part boundary. This parameter can vary independently of the magnitude of curvature at the point of negative minimum.

Parts and Figure-Ground Assignment

An important early function of human vision is to parse the retinal image into regions that are likely to correspond to distinct objects. To do so, the visual system must decide which of the two sides of a given image contour corresponds to an object, and hence 'owns' that contour, and which corresponds to the underlying background. We hypothesize that this choice of figure and ground is intimately related to the salience of parts created on both sides of the contour (Hoffman & Singh, 1997).

Hypothesis of salient figures: Other things being equal, that choice of figure and ground is preferred which leads to the most salient parts for the figure object.

Many factors, of course, affect the perception of figure and ground, such as symmetry (Bahnsen, 1928; Hochberg, 1964), size and contrast (Rubin, 1958; Koffka, 1935), and convexity (Kanisza & Gerbino, 1976; Stevens & Brookes, 1988). Part salience is another factor. To see how it works, consider the curve in Figure 41a. It has two possible choices of figure and ground, one in which the right side of the curve is seen as figure, which would lead to the parts shown in Figure 41b, and one in which the left side is seen as figure, which would lead to the parts shown in Figure 41c. Although both sets of parts have the same value of

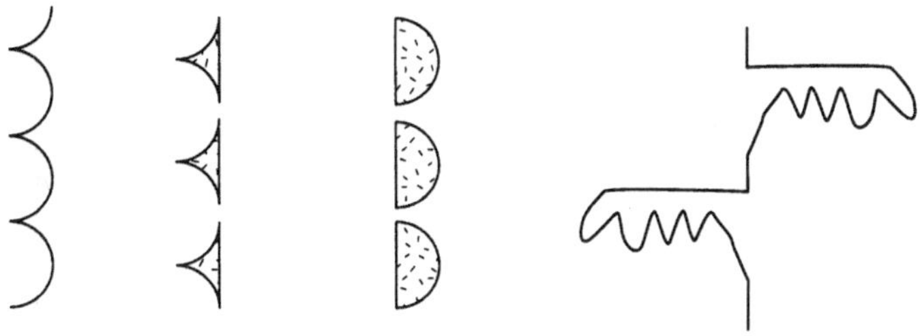

Figure 41. Illustrating the Hypothesis of Salient Figures. The left of the display in (a) is more likely to be seen as figure because it leads to more salient parts (c), than the parts obtained if the right side were taken to be figure (b). This rule can lead to globally inconsistent assignments of figure and ground (d).

protrusion, the parts in Figure 41c are more salient than the parts in Figure 41b because the parts in 41c have sharper boundaries and greater area. Thus the hypothesis of salient figures predicts that the parts in Figure 41c will be seen more frequently—and hence the left side of the contour in Figure 41a is more likely to be seen as figure.

It has often been argued that no shape description occurs (or even, can occur) prior to the assignment of figure and ground—and that only the figure side of a contour is ever given a shape description (e.g., Koffka, 1935; Baylis & Driver, 1995; Palmer 1999). Contrary to this, the hypothesis of salient figures suggests that human vision analyzes *both* sides of a visual contour, and it does so prior to assigning one of them as "figure." This analysis takes place at least to the extent that both sides of a contour are segmented into parts, and the perceptual salience of these parts is compared (indeed, such analysis is a critical component of the process of assigning border ownership). Moreover, according to the hypothesis, the assignment of figure and ground need not be globally consistent—because, e.g., the left side of a contour may have more salient parts along some portion of a contour, but the right side may have more salient parts along other portions (see Figure 41d).

One experimental test of the theory of part salience used three stimuli shown in Figure 42 (Hoffman & Singh, 1997). In Figure 42a is the standard Schröder staircase. In Figures 42b and 42c the staircase is modified so that the steps for the inverted figure-ground interpretation are more salient. As you can see, the inverted interpretation is most easily seen in Figures 42b and 42c, as predicted by the theory of part salience. Subjects were shown these figures using brief 50 millisecond flashes followed by a mask, and were asked to report whether they saw the two dots as on the same step or on different steps. From these reports it was possible to determine which choice of figure and ground the subjects saw. The results showed a significant effect of part salience in the predicted direction.

Another experimental test used three stimuli shown in Figure 43 (Hoffman & Singh, 1997). Figure 43a is the standard face-goblet figure, which can be seen either as a goblet in the

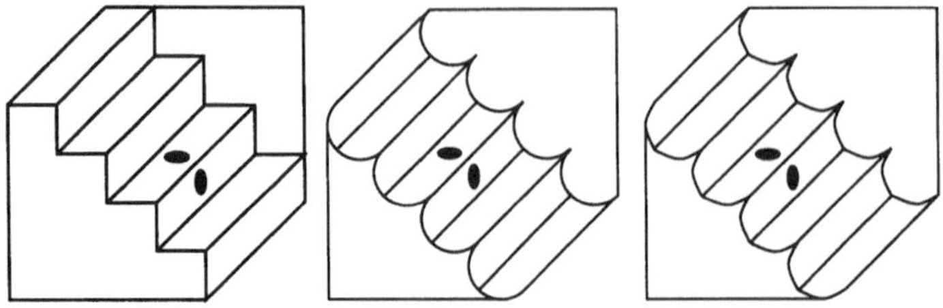

Figure 42. (a) depicts the standard Schröder staircase which can be seen either in the upright or the inverted interpretation. There is usually a bias to see the upright interpretation. This bias is reversed in (b) and (c), which are more likely to be seen in the inverted interpretation, since this choice yields more salient parts for the figural side.

center or as two faces looking at each other. In Figure 43b the face-goblet figure is modified so that the parts of the faces have the most salient part boundaries (sharp corners) and the parts of the goblet have less salient part boundaries (smoothed boundaries). Figure 43c shows the opposite modification. The theory of part salience predicts a roughly equal balance of face interpretations and goblet interpretations in Figure 43a, a preference for seeing the faces in Figure 43b, and a preference for seeing the goblet in Figure 43c. Subjects were shown these stimuli using 250 millisecond displays followed by a mask, and were asked to report which interpretation, faces or goblet, they saw. The results again showed a clear effect of part salience in determining figure and ground.

A simple demonstration of the power of part salience to influence choice of figure and ground is shown in Figure 44 (Hoffman & Singh, 1997). The dot in this figure can in principle be seen as either lying in a valley or as lying on top of a hill. The hypothesis of part salience predicts that we should see the dot lying on top of a hill. You can check the prediction for yourself; and you can see if it still holds as you turn the page upside down.

Figure 43. (a) Rubin's standard "face-vase" illusion, which can be seen either as a vase or as two faces. One can bias the display either toward the face interpretation (b), or toward the vase interpretation (c), by modulating the relative salience of the parts on the two sides of the curves.

Figure 44. The dot is seen as lying on top of a hill, rather than in a valley. This is consistent with the fact that assigning figure to the left side of the repeated curves leads to more salient parts.

Parts and Transparency

The visual parsing that we have considered so far involved a "sideways" parsing of the image into regions that correspond to distinct parts of objects. In other words, one *side* of a perceived part boundary is assigned to one part, and the other *side* to another part. The perception of transparency, on the other hand, provides a striking example of parsing in depth. Here a single intensity value in the image must be parsed into two distinct surfaces along the same line of sight—one of which is seen *through* the other. For example, the dark gray patch in Figure 45 is parsed perceptually into two surfaces: an underlying black surface, and an overlying mid-grey transparent filter. Similarly, the light grey patch in Figure 45 is parsed into an underlying white surface, and a mid-grey filter. Thus, in order to construct the percept of transparency, the visual system must *scission* (Koffka, 1935) or decompose the luminance in a given image region and assign the different components to distinct surfaces. In this section, we show that

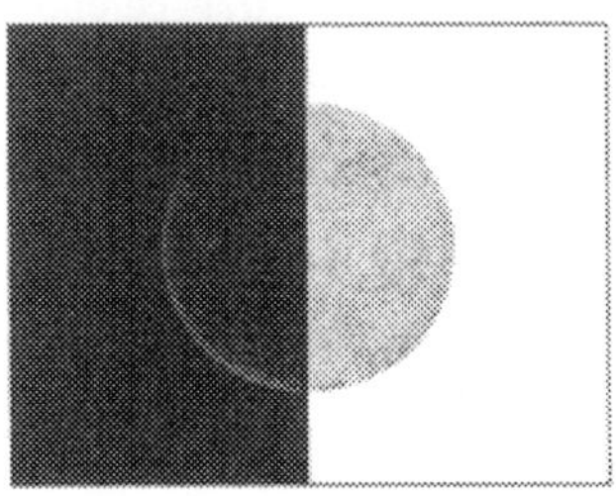

Figure 45. Computing perceived transparency requires the depthwise segmentation of an image region (e.g., the mid-grey half disks) into two surfaces—one seen through the other.

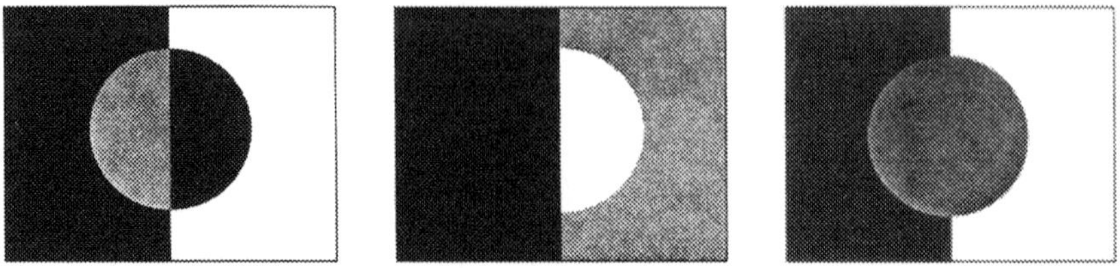

(a) (b) (c)

Figure 46. Illustrating the luminance conditions for perceptual transparency. (a) The central region must preserve contrast polarity with respect to the surround. (b) the central region must have lower contrast. (c) Occlusion is a limiting case of transparency.

this parsing in depth interacts in an interesting way with the "sideways" parsing into parts.

When does the visual system initiate the scission of an image region to create the percept of transparency? Two main kinds of image conditions have been studied that lead to perceptual transparency: (a) photometric conditions, involving relative luminance (or color) values, and (b) figural conditions, involving geometric or configural factors.

In the context of simple displays like Figure 45, two luminance conditions are critical (Metelli, 1974; Gerbino, Stultiens, Troost, & de Weert, 1990; Beck, Prazdny, & Ivry, 1984; Anderson, 1997). First, the two grey patches in the center must have the same contrast polarity as the two halves of the surround. For example, in Figure 46a, the contrast polarity of the two grey patches has been reversed and, as a result, the central region no longer scissions into multiple layers. Second, the central region (consisting of the two grey patches) must have a lower “contrast” than the surround. This lowering in "contrast" has typically been defined in terms of lowered reflectance differences (Metelli, 1974), lightness differences (Beck et al., 1984), and luminance differences (Gerbino et al., 1990) across a contour. However, Singh & Anderson (2001) have recently shown that the critical variable is Michelson contrast.[12] The central region in Figure 46b, for example, has been given higher contrast and, as a result, the central region no longer appears transparent. (Note, however, that now the surrounding region may appear transparent.) A limiting case of transparency occurs when the contrast in the central region is zero: now the central regions appear simply as an opaque occluding surface (see Figure 46c).

In addition to these luminance conditions, figural conditions for transparency have also been studied—mostly by the Gestalt psychologists Kanizsa (1979) and Metelli (1974). These

[12] The fact that the visual system uses Michelson contrast has the perceptual consequence that observers systematically underestimate the opacity of darkening transparent filters and overestimate the opacity of lightening transparent filters (see Singh and Anderson, 2001, for details).

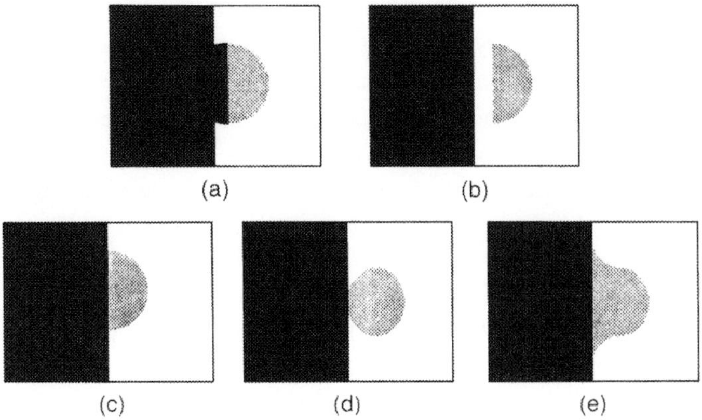

Figure 47. Demonstrating the role of figural conditions in initiating percepts of transparency. (a) The border between the two grey patches must be continuous with the boundary separating the bipartite background. (b) The two grey patches must unite into a single surface. There must be no discontinuous jumps (c) or tangent discontinuities (d,e) along the contour of the putative transparent surface. Note that, although (d) and (e) both involve tangent discontinuities, the presence of negative minima has a more deleterious effect on perceived transparency.

figural conditions may be divided naturally into two kinds. The first requires continuity of contours (and, more generally, textures) on the underlying surface. For example, if the grey patches are shifted together so that their mutual border no longer aligns with the black-white border (see Figure 47a), the percept of transparency is lost. This is consistent with the fact that although transparent filters reduce the contrast across underlying contours, they cannot produce large shifts in the positions of these contours.

The second kind of figural condition requires continuity and grouping of the image regions that define the putative transparent surface. In the extreme, if the two grey patches are separated—so that they no longer unite into a single surface—they no longer appear transparent (see Figure 47b). The percept of transparency is also lost in Figures 47c and 47d, even though there could be a transparent filter with the odd shape shown in Figure 47c or in Figure 47d. One reason why transparency is not seen is provided by the principle of genericity. According to this principle, the visual system rejects unstable scene interpretations of image data. In Figures 47c and 47d, the interpretation of transparency is unstable because it assumes a special (or "accidental") placement of the transparent filter in front of the bipartite background, and a special vantage point of the observer—thus resulting in the precise alignment of the discontinuities on the filter with the contour separating the bipartite background. As a consequence, a slight displacement of either the transparent filter or the observer's vantage can lead to a large change in the image.

In addition, the evidence presented above, that part boundaries are computed early in visual processing, suggests another explanation (Singh & Hoffman, 1998). In both Figures 47c and 47d the luminance boundary between the two grey regions precisely aligns with the part boundaries between the regions. If the visual system permits different parts of an object to have different reflectances, then the luminance change from light grey to dark grey would be interpreted as a reflectance change on an opaque surface—thus leading to a suppression of the percept of transparency. Hence, the visual system might operate according to the following "part-coloring rule": Interpret changes in image color that align with part boundaries as changes in surface reflectance.

We thus have two different accounts for the loss of transparency in Figures 47c and 47d—one based on the principle of genericity, and the other on the part-coloring rule. The relative contributions of these two explanations can be separated using a display like Figure 47e. In this display, we have tangent discontinuities of the same magnitude as in Figure 47d, and these are also precisely aligned with the luminance boundary—hence leading to a non-generic interpretation of transparency. However, these tangent discontinuities are not part boundaries because they lie in convex, rather than concave, regions. Therefore, whereas the part-coloring rule distinguishes between Figure 47d and Figure 47e—predicting a greater loss of transparency in Figure 47d—the genericity principle does not.

Singh and Hoffman (1998) tested the predictions of the part-coloring rule and genericity rule in an experiment in which observers rated the perceived transparency of displays like the ones shown in Figures 48 and 49. Using the notion of part salience reviewed in the previous section, Singh and Hoffman designed the figures to differ in three independent dimensions: the sign of curvature at the extrema (convex or concave), the turning angle at the extrema (42°, 72°, 102°, 132°), and the degree of smoothing of the extrema (corner, small smoothing, large smoothing). They compared the ratings of transparency for these figures to the ratings of transparency for a figure whose central gray region had no curvature extrema at all (i.e., a disk). They found that ratings for the positive-maxima cases (convex corners and smoothed convex corners) were significantly lower than ratings for the disk, supporting the prediction of the genericity rule. Moreover they found that ratings for the negative-minima cases (concave corners and smoothed concave corners) were significantly lower than those for the positive maxima—indicating that the part-coloring rule operates in addition to the genericity rule. They also found that ratings decreased with increasing salience of the extrema, supporting the predictions of the salience theory of the previous section.

The genericity and part-coloring rules also predict that if we misalign the extrema from the color changes in the image, then ratings of transparency should go up. This was tested in a second experiment by Singh and Hoffman (1998), using stimuli such as those shown in Figure 49. They found that for both convex and concave extrema, ratings of transparency increased as the misalignment between the extrema and color changes increased, supporting the predictions of both the genericity and part-coloring rules.

Hence the "sideways" parsing of an image region into parts interacts with the parsing

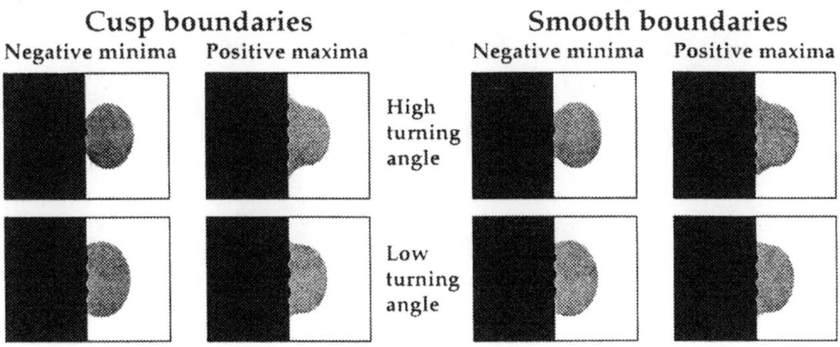

Figure 48. The stimuli used in Singh & Hoffman's (1998) Experiment 1 to test the role of perceived part structure on perceptual transparency.

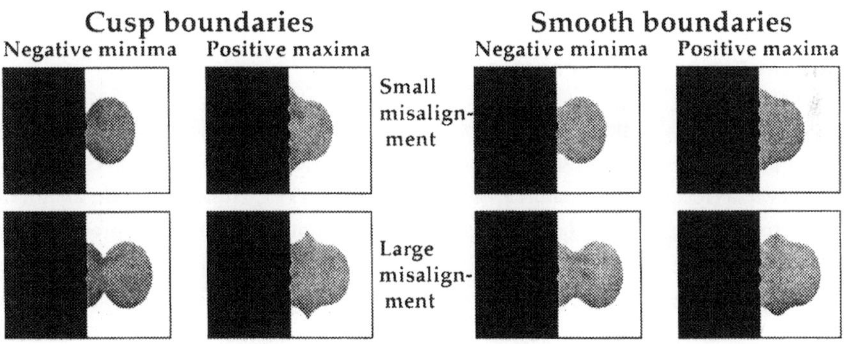

Figure 49. The stimuli used in Singh & Hoffman's (1998) Experiment 2 to study the role of the precise alignment of the extrema of curvature with the bipartite background.

in depth that leads to the perception of transparency, via the part-coloring rule: If the change in luminance in an image region coincides with the boundary between two distinct parts, the visual system tends to assign this to a reflectance change, thereby allowing the two parts to have distinct colors. This, in turn, leads to a suppression in the percept of transparency. The displays in Figure 50 again demonstrate this rule at work: Whereas Figures 50b–c are easily seen as containing transparency, Figure 50a is not. (Figures 50d–e demonstrate that this difference is not simply due to differences in the contour length of the putative transparent filter.)

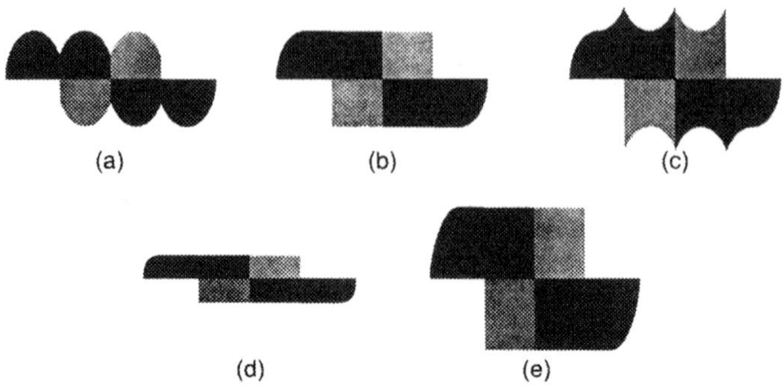

Figure 50. Another demonstration of the interaction between the sideways segmentation of a shape into parts, and the depth-wise segmentation into multiple layers involved in transparency. Relative to (b) and (c), the display in (a) is least likely to be seen as containing transparency. The displays in (d) and (e) demonstrate that this effect cannot be attributed simply to differences in the contour length of the putative transparent filter.

Parts and Pre-attentive Processing

We reviewed experiments earlier, demonstrating that a target shape having a negative minimum of curvature pops out among distractors that do not have a negative minimum—but not vice versa (recall Figs 14 and 15; Wolfe & Bennett, 1997; Hulleman et al., 2000). Such an asymmetry has traditionally been interpreted to be a sign of pre-attentive processing, or of a basic feature (Treisman & Souther, 1985; Treisman & Gormican, 1988; Duncan & Humphreys, 1992; Wolfe & Bennett, 1997; Wolfe, 1998). Although more recent work has disputed whether *any* visual search can really be considered to be free from attentional demands (see, e.g., Joseph, Chun, & Nakayama, 1996), it is nevertheless true that pop-out and search asymmetry are indicative of features that are computed rapidly and early in visual processing.

In particular, the above experiments suggest that negative minima (and, more generally, perceptually salient concavities) are computed pre-attentively, or at least rapidly and early in visual processing. They leave open the question, however, of whether part structures themselves are computed early. As we have seen, on a 2D shape, negative minima are points on the bounding contour of the shape—whereas determining part structures requires computing *part cuts* that divide the shape into parts. Some evidence for the early computation of parts comes from Baylis & Driver's (1994; 1995) experiments on judging symmetry and repetition (recall Figs 12 and 13). Note, however, that because this experimental method can only use shapes that are near-symmetric or near-repeated, it is unclear how the results generalize to arbitrary shapes. Furthermore, this method does not allow for a comparison of the perceptual naturalness of alternative part structures. It does not, in fact, uniquely point to negative minima of curvature as the critical loci of part boundaries. For example, the shapes in Figure 12a and Figure 13b have not only matching negative minima on the two sides, they also have matching positive maxima and matching inflection points. Hence, the advantage enjoyed by these shapes could, in principle, be due to the matching positive maxima or inflections as well.

To get at the issue of early processing of part structure, Xu & Singh (2001) used the visual search paradigm. However, unlike previous visual search studies—which have used different shapes for targets and distractors—they used the same shape, but parsed in two different ways. One of these parsings was always consistent with the minima rule, the other not (an example of a shape used is shown in Figure 51). Xu & Singh argued that, if parsing at negative minima occurs automatically, then the bottom "part" in Figure 51b would be parsed further, yielding the effective parsing shown on the right. As a result, the non-minima-parsed shape (Figure 51b) would end up having an additional feature that the minima-parsed shape (Figure 51a) does not have. Hence, the search for the non-minima-parsed shape should be fast and efficient, whereas the reverse search for the minima-parsed shape should be slow and inefficient (defined, as it is, by the *absence* of a feature). Note that the lengths of the cuts, the orientations of the cuts, and the areas of the parts created are all equated in the two parsings, so any search asymmetry cannot be attributed to these factors.

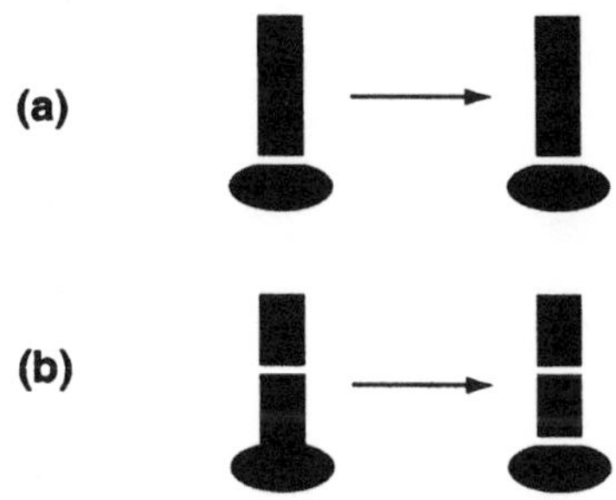

Figure 51. One of the shapes used by Xu & Singh (2001) to test whether part structures consistent with the minima rule are computed pre-attentively. The targets and distractors for visual search consisted of two different parsings of the same shape—one had cuts at negative minima (a), the other had cuts elsewhere (b). If parsing at negative minima occurs automatically, the stimulus in (b) should be parsed further, hence yielding an additional feature that can guide visual search.

This is exactly what their data revealed. When subjects searched for a non-minima-parsed target among minima-parsed distractors (see Figure 52a), search slopes satisfied all criteria for a pop-out (or feature) search (search slopes were 5.5 ms/item for target-present trials, and 6.7 ms/item for target-absent trials). This indicates that when a part cut appeared at a non-negative-minima location on the target shape, it was considered as a unique feature among the cuts that occurred at negative minima on the distractor shapes. However, when

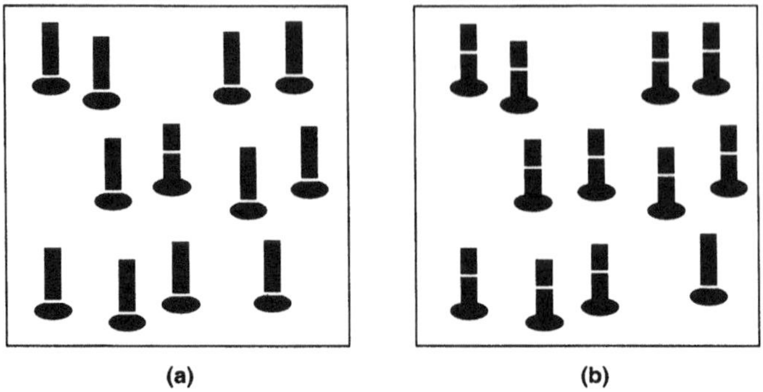

Figure 52. Stimuli from Xu & Singh's (2001) experiment. Subjects search for either (a) a target parsed with non-minima cuts among distractors parsed with minima cuts, or (b) vice versa. As predicted, the first search was a pop out, whereas the second was slow and inefficient.

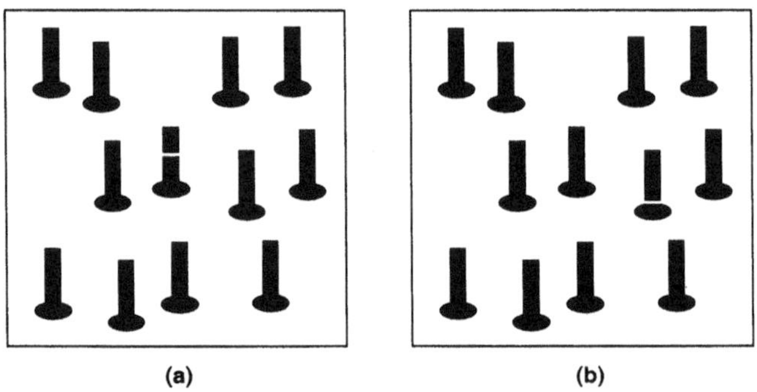

Figure 53. Stimuli from a subsequent experiment by Xu & Singh (2001). Subjects searched either for (a) a non-minima parsing, or (b) a minima parsing among unparsed shapes. As expected, both searches were pop out. (In both cases, the cut on the target shape acts as unique feature.) Nevertheless, the search for the minima-parsed target was slower by about 100ms.

subjects searched for a minima-parsed target among non-minima-parsed distractors (see Figure 52b), the search became slow and inefficient (slopes were 19.3 ms/item for target present, and 32.2 ms/item for target absent). Thus, the automatic parsing at negative minima in the distractor shapes made the negative-minima cut in the target shape much less prominent.

To provide further evidence that parsing at negative minima occurs early in visual processing, Xu & Singh (2001) conducted another experiment in which subjects searched for parsed shapes among unparsed shapes (Figure 53). In different blocks, subjects searched either for a minima-parsed shape or a non-minima-parsed shape. Since the target can be distinguished from the distractors by the presence of a cut, quite independent of its location, the parsed shape was expected to pop out in both cases. Xu & Singh argued, nevertheless, that if parsing at negative minima occurs automatically in early stages of visual processing, a cut located at negative minima would still be less efficacious as a feature that distinguishes the target from the unparsed distractors. Indeed, their results showed that although the search for a parsed shape among unparsed shapes was fast and efficient in both cases, the search for the minima-parsed shape was nevertheless significantly slower. This result was most striking for target-absent displays. In these cases, both search displays were identical (since the parsed target shape was absent in both cases). Nevertheless, it took subjects 100 ms longer to determine the absence of a cut when they were looking for it at negative minima, than when they were looking for it elsewhere. The fact that parsing at negative minima influenced visual search even when the search was already fast and efficient thus provides further evidence that such parsing must occur very early in visual processing.

Beyond these specific findings, Xu and Singh's experiments also provide a general methodology for studying how the visual system parses shapes into parts. In particular, to compare the perceptual naturalness of two different ways of parsing a given shape, one conducts visual search experiments using one parsing as the target and the other as distractors; and then reverses their roles. Any asymmetry between these two searches can be interpreted as a difference in the perceptual naturalness of the two parsings—assuming that other local factors have been controlled for.

PARTS AND ATTENTIVE PROCESSING

A great deal of recent work has indicated that it is insufficient to characterize visual attention in purely spatial terms, for example, as a 'spotlight' that can move around the visual field, enhancing visual processing within the spatial region 'lit' by the spotlight (e.g., Posner, Nissen, & Ogden, 1978). A number of experiments have demonstrated that visual attention can be object-based as well. In other words, attention shifts more readily within a single object than across separate objects—so that attending to one location on an object tends to enhance processing resources for the entire object. One source of evidence for object-based attention comes from the attentional-cueing paradigm. Egly, Driver, & Rafal (1994), for example, presented participants with a display containing two vertically elongated rectangles. They cued one end of a rectangle, and asked participants to make speeded responses to the (possible) appearance of a probe. On most of the trials, the probe appeared at the cued location. However, on a critical subset of trials, the probe appeared elsewhere. Amongst these "invalid-cue trials," participants were faster at detecting probes that appeared on the opposite end of the same rectangle, than those that appeared on the same end of the other rectangle. Since both of these locations were equidistant from the (invalid) cue, this response-time advantage for the same-object trials indicated that visual attention shifts more readily within a single object, than across two different objects. Moore, Yantis, & Vaughan (1998) extended this finding to amodally completed objects, using a discrimination version of the attentional-cueing paradigm. They placed a third rectangle that partially occluded the middle portions of the two elongated rectangles (so that the two rectangular objects could only be defined after amodal completion had taken place) and asked participants to make speeded responses to whether the probe was a **T** or an **L.** They again found a response-time advantage for same-object trials relative to different-object trials.

We have argued that 'perceptual units' exist not only at the level of objects, but also at the level of parts within an object. If object parts do indeed constitute perceptually natural units in visual representation, might we not expect a part-based advantage, analogous to the object-based advantage revealed by attentional cueing? To address this question, Singh & Scholl (2000) used (the discrimination version of) the attentional-cueing paradigm, on 3D rendered objects that had two parts (see Figure 54). On each trial, one of four locations was cued, followed by three characters: a probe (either **T** or **L)** and two distracters (rotated **F**'s). On 80% of the trials, the cue was valid (i.e., it correctly predicted the probe location), and on 20% of the trials, the cue was invalid (i.e., the probe did not appear at the cued location). On half of the invalid-cue trials, the probe appeared on the same part as the cue; on the other half,

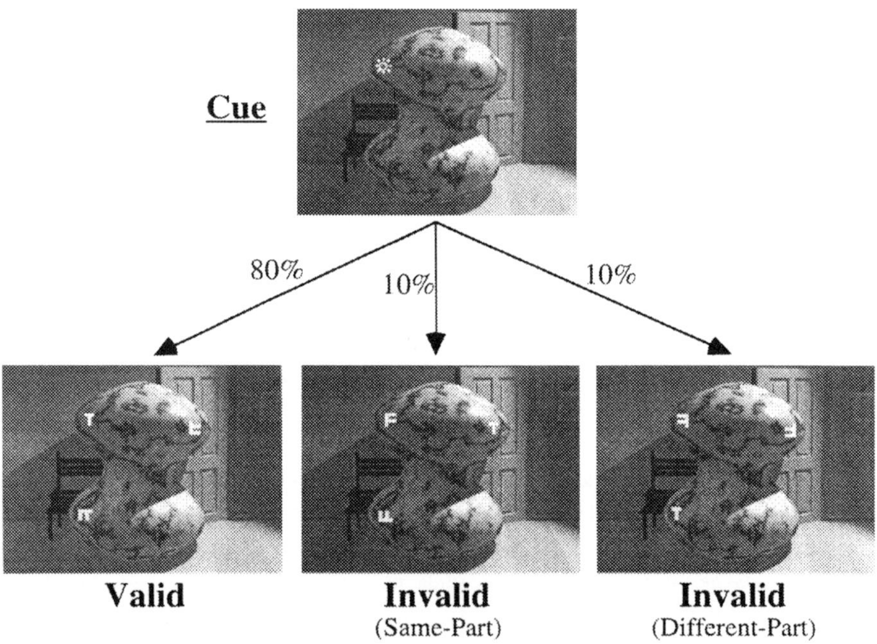

Figure 54. A schematic of the trial sequence used in Singh & Scholl's (2000) attentional-cueing experiment. (The cue and probes are not to scale.) The experiment demonstrated that the allocation of visual attention to an object can be part-based.

the probe appeared on the other part. Since the same-part and different-part probe locations were equidistant from the (invalid) cue, any systematic difference in response-time between these two types of trials would provide evidence for a part-based effect.

Singh & Scholl (2000) performed this attentional-cueing experiment with three different objects. All were two-part objects, but they differed in the perceptual salience of their parts. In one case (the "high-salience" object), the boundary between the two parts was a crease (i.e., surface tangent discontinuity), in the other two cases (the "mid-salience" and "low-salience" objects), the part boundary was smooth, and the turning angle at the boundary was shallower (see Figure 55). They found that, for all three salience levels, the mean RT's were significantly faster for same-part trials than for different-part trials. Moreover, the magnitude of this part-based effect was modulated by the salience of the parts, so that the effect size for "low-salience" object (30.6 ms) was less than half that for the "high-salience" object (65.8 ms).[13]

Figure 55. The three shapes used in Singh & Scholl's attentional-cueing experiment. These differ in the perceptual salience of the part structure. Part salience was found to modulate the magnitude of the part-based cueing effect.

These results provide evidence for part-based attention: Visual attention shifts more readily within a part, than across parts of a single object. Moreover, geometric factors that determine perceived part salience modulate the strength of this part-based cueing effect. Finally, these results indicate that attentional cueing can be used as a tool—providing an objective performance measure—to study perceptual part structure.

Similar results have also been obtained on 2D shapes using a different experimental paradigm in which participants are asked to report, or to compare, two attributes of either the same part or of two different parts of an object. Participants are faster (Barenholtz & Feldman,

---

[13] Note that the magnitude of the part-based effect for the high-salience object is larger than the object-based effect obtained by Egly et al. (1994) and Moore et al., (1998). It has been shown recently that that 3D rendered shapes yield larger effects (Atchley & Kramer, 2000). Indeed, this was a primary motivation for using 3D stimuli—since starting with an object-based effect of ~30-40ms would not leave much room to study the effect of parts, and part salience.

2001) or more accurate (Vecera, Behrmann, & McGoldrick, 2000; Vecera, Behrmann, & Filapek, 2001) when the two attributes are on the same part, than when they are on two different parts. In addition, the experiments of Barenholtz & Feldman (2001) demonstrate that this part-based advantage cannot be attributed simply to the magnitude of the curvature of the object contour that intervenes between the two features to be compared. In particular, the effect is greatly reduced if the two features are separated by a convex contour (i.e., no part boundary) of the same curvature magnitude as a concave contour (i.e., with a part boundary).

PARTS AND ILLUSORY CONTOURS

Consider the displays in Figure 56a–c. Each of these displays could be seen, in principle, either as the projection of a single object with multiple parts, or as the projection of two distinct objects—one partly occluding the other. Surprisingly, even though these displays are chromatically homogeneous, and therefore lack any T-junctions to signal occlusion, each of 56a–c is seen as *two* overlapping objects. Because of the tendency of such displays to *split* perceptually into two distinct objects, they have been termed "spontaneously-splitting figures" or "self-splitting objects" (Kanizsa, 1979; Kellman & Loukides, 1987). Constructing this percept of two overlapping objects requires that one of the two objects (the occluding object) be modally completed in front, and the other (occluded object) be amodally completed behind it.

When does the visual system split a single figure of homogenous color into two distinct objects? And, how does it assign relative depth ordering to these objects? It is clear that certain image properties *must* be satisfied in order for the perceptual split to occur. For

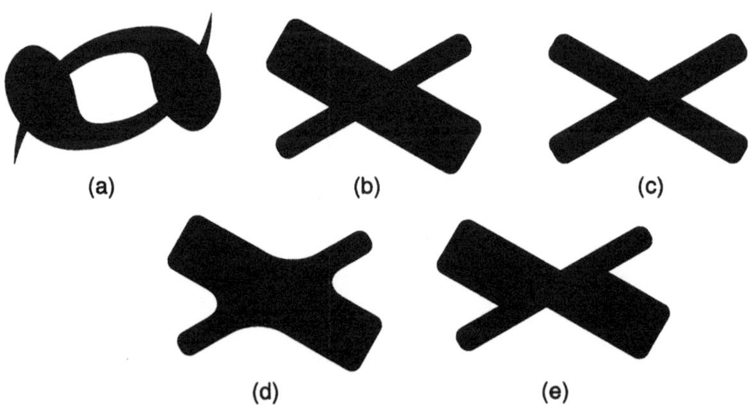

Figure 56. (a)—(c) tend to be seen as two overlapping objects— even though these figures lack any T-junctions to signal occlusion. Smoothing the negative minima (d), or disrupting the good-continuation between one set of contours (e), switches the percept to that of a single object with multiple parts.

example, if the negative minima are smooth (Figure 56d), rather than tangent discontinuities, the display is seen as a single object with parts, rather than two objects separated in depth. This makes sense because the display is no longer consistent with a generic view of an object interposed between the viewer and a second object (Shipley & Kellman, 1992). Similarly, if the good continuation (or relatability) between one of the two sets of contours is disrupted, the display is again seen as a single object (Figure 56e).

Concerning the second question, note that the figure (or portion of the figure) that requires the shorter contour completions is the one that is perceived to be modally completed in front (see Figs 56a–b). For the cross in Figure 56b, for example, observers are more likely to see the thicker bar as being in front of, and occluding, the thinner bar. For the cross in Figure 56c, on the other hand, both bars require equally long completions and this leads to a perceptual bistability: One switches between seeing one bar in front, and seeing the other one in front.

The tendency of human vision to see modal completions as short as possible is known as Petter's rule (Petter, 1956). This rule has often been motivated by the heuristic that closer objects tend to project larger retinal images (e.g., Stoner & Albright, 1993). However, Petter's rule cannot be explained by a "larger is closer" heuristic because relative lengths of interpolated contours can vary independently of relative areas of the corresponding figures (Tommasi, Bressan, & Vallortigara, 1995). Moreover, Petter's rule works even when it contradicts the "larger is closer" hypothesis (Singh, Hoffman, & Albert, 1999).

However, given that it is initially ambiguous whether a display such as Figure 56b is the silhouette of a single object with multiple parts or of two objects separated in depth, it is likely that the visual system applies the same segmentation rules in both cases (Singh, Seyranian, & Hoffman, 1999). In particular, when presented with such a silhouette, the visual system finds the negative minima of curvature and pairs them according to the short-cut rule. Depending on whether the silhouette is interpreted to be a single object (Figures 56d–e) or multiple objects (Figure 56a–c), these pairings are then taken to be either part cuts or modal completions. In this way, Petter's rule can be understood in terms of the same visual mechanisms that create parts cuts—and it thus inherits the ecological motivation for the short-cut rule.

AN ALTERNATIVE APPROACH TO PARTS AND SHAPE DESCRIPTION: CURVE EVOLUTION AND SHOCKS

An alternative approach to parts and shape description has been proposed by Kimia and colleagues (e.g., Kimia, Tannenbaum, & Zucker, 1995). Although we have previously mentioned some shortcomings in the definitions of limbs and necks as proposed by Siddiqi & Kimia (1995) and Siddiqi, Tressness, & Kimia (1996), there is actually a more general framework on which these intuitions are based. In this section, we briefly review this framework and contrast it with our geometric-constraints approach to parts.

This framework involves deriving a structural description of 2D shapes from the singularities (or "shocks") of a curve evolution process in which every point on the shape's contour moves inward at constant speed. This process is identical to Blum's grassfire (SAT) transformation, and the final skeletal structure obtained is the same as Blum's medial axis.[14] However, in addition to storing the final skeletal structure, Kimia et al. also classify the singularities that are formed, and store the order of shock, as well as the location and time of its formation. These together are taken as a representation of the 2D shape.

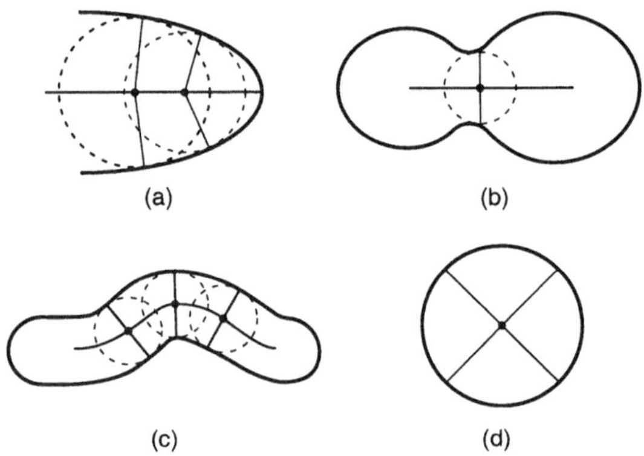

Figure 57. Different orders of "shocks" obtained from the singularities of a curve evolution process. (Adapted from Kimia, Tannenbaum, & Zucker, 1995.)

Figure 57 shows examples of different orders of shocks. In particular, at loci of 1-shocks, the radius around the axis varies monotonically (a "protrusion"), whereas 3-shocks occur in regions where the radius function is constant, i.e., the contours on the two sides are parallel ("bends"). 2-shocks correspond to local minima of the radius function ("necks"), and 4-shocks corresponds to local centers of mass ("seeds").

Critical to the context of parsing, however, note that the notion of "protrusion" as a connected locus of 1-shocks does not distinguish between a part such as the one shown in Figure 58a, and a convex region that ends in a positive maximum of curvature, as shown in

---

[14] Kimia et al. study a more general class of shape deformations, which are describable in terms of two basic kinds: (1) deformations in which a curve evolves at a constant speed in a direction normal to the curve ("reaction"), and (2) deformations in which the speed of evolution is proportional to the curvature at a given point ("diffusion"). However, for the purpose of computing shocks and shock-graphs, they use only the first kind.

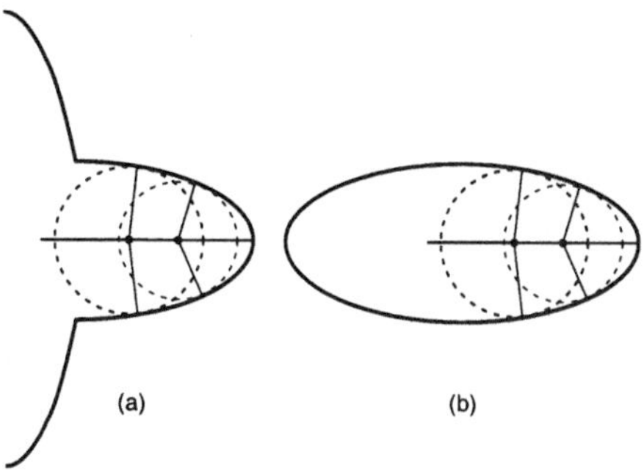

Figure 58. The notion of "protrusion" as a connected locus of first-order shocks does not distinguish between a part (a) and a convex region ending in a positive maximum (b). Making this distinction requires the notion of a negative minimum of curvature.

Figure 58b. (This is reminiscent of the shortcoming of Blum's proposal that shapes should be parsed at the branch points of the axes of local symmetry. Recall that the medial axis gives the same skeletal structure to a rectangle and a dog-bone shape, and is therefore unable to find parts solely on this basis; see Figure 31). Making the distinction between parts and convex tips requires the notion of a negative minimum of curvature—so that the shock-based approach also needs to incorporate negative minima to fully capture part structure. Indeed, it is likely that this consideration is what motivated Siddiqi & Kimia (1995) to define a notion of "limb" using further geometric criteria—which, as we noted earlier, turn out to be too restrictive.

Based on the geometry of shocks, Kimia et al. proposed a "shape triangle" which contains three different continua along which shapes can be defined: a parts-protrusions continuum, a bends-parts continuum, and a bends-protrusions continuum (see Figure 59). For

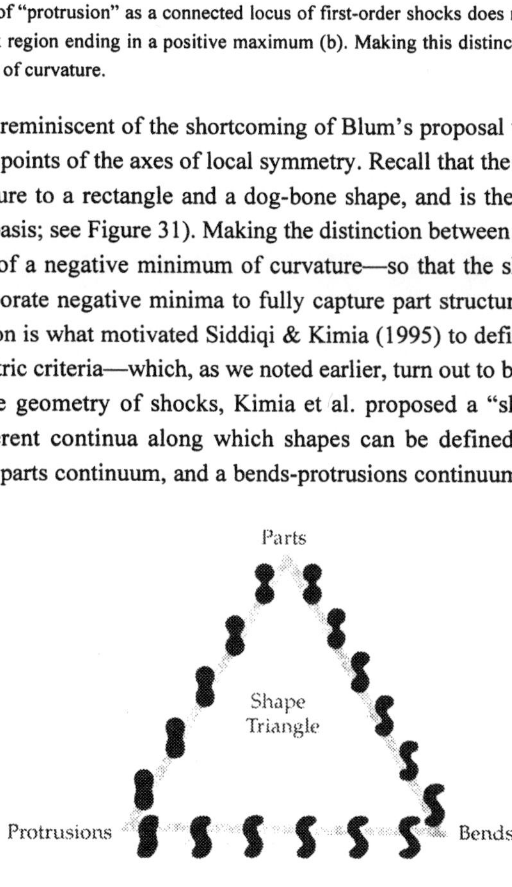

Figure 59. Kimia et al.'s shape triangle embodies three different continua along which a shape can vary. These continua are also captured by the geometric constraints of cut length, local symmetry, and part-boundary strength.

example, along the parts-protrusions continuum, the ratio of minimum ("neck") width to maximal width is gradually increased so that the shape looks more like a vertical body with small "protrusions" on the sides, rather than parts stacked vertically, one on top of the other. Within our framework, protrusions and bends are different varieties of parts with varying perceptual salience and/or involving different ways of pairing part boundaries (i.e., neg min to neg min, or neg min to pos max). For example, in moving from "parts" to "protrusions," the length of the horizontal cuts increases relative to the vertical ones, and as a result, the vertical cuts become more likely to be perceived. Furthermore, the salience (e.g., the strength of the part boundaries and protrusion) of the parts gradually decreases. Hence, one moves from a part structure consisting of salient parts stacked on top of each other to one consisting of a main vertical body with low-salience parts on the sides. Similarly, along the parts-bends continuum, the local symmetry between pairs of negative minima is gradually offset, so that the negative minima on one side of the curve eventually become locally symmetric to the positive maxima on the other side, rather than the negative minima. Hence, using the two variables of cut length and local symmetry, one can span the space defined by the three continua that define the shape triangle (see Figure 60a).

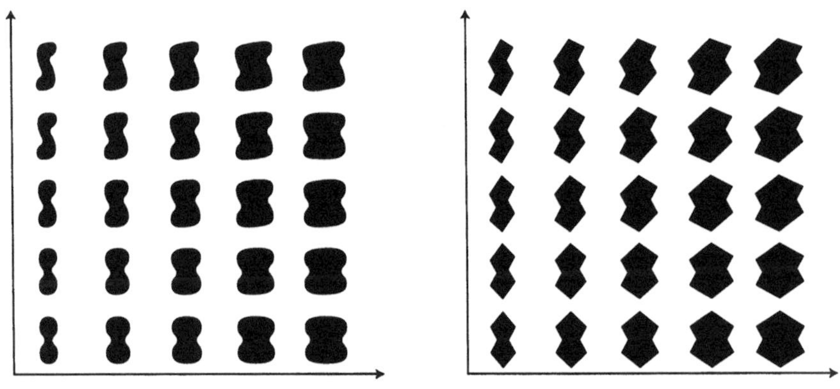

Figure 60. Each diagram represents a two-parameter space involving changes in cut length and local symmetry. The two diagrams portray different levels of strength of curvature extrema.

Note, moreover, that moving along the part-protrusion continuum, and the bend-protrusion continuum involves a change in another variable that is not made explicit within the shape triangle, namely, the curvature at the extrema of curvature (see Siddiqi, Kimia, Tannenbaum, & Zucker; Figure 6). Within our geometric-constraints framework, the strength of curvature extrema is a further variable that is orthogonal to cut length and local symmetry (recall the section on part salience). Figure 60b, for example, shows sharp-extrema versions of the shapes shown in Figure 60a (in the two-parameter space spanned by local symmetry and cut length). Note that although low-curvature "bends" have the appearance of a single-part object, "bends" with sharp corners are more likely to appear as distinct parts.

Thus, within the geometric-constraints approach, cut length, local symmetry and the strength of part boundaries interact to determine perceived parts and their visual salience: Human vision prefers shorter cuts, cuts that join locally-symmetric negative minima, and cuts that join points of high magnitude of curvature. These geometric constraints capture the important aspects of perceived part structure. We argue that the visual system employs simple geometric constraints such as these, rather than compute detailed shock graphs. In particular, visual search tasks that require distinguishing "parts," "protrusions," and "bends" (e.g., Siddiqi et al., 2000) can be performed on the basis of the visual system's sensitivity to simple geometric properties such as cut length, strength of curvature and local symmetry—rather than on specific differences in computed shock graphs.

From the point of view of shape description, the shock-based approach does represent a great deal more information than the geometric-constraints approach—which provides simply the locations of the part boundaries and part cuts on a shape, and the relative visual salience of the resulting parts. From the point of view of parsing, however, we have noted that loci of first-order shocks do not distinguish between convex tips and parts (recall Figures 58 and 31)—and thus need to incorporate the notion of negative minima in order to make this distinction. Moreover, the number of possible shock types undergoes a combinatorial explosion with the addition of the third dimension—so that basing 3D-shape description on a classification of shock types becomes very difficult. The geometric-constraints approach, on the other hand, generalizes easily and naturally to three-dimensional surfaces and volumes, because the notions of negative minima, strength of curvature extrema, cut length, and local symmetry all have natural counterparts in 3D.

CONCLUSIONS

We have reviewed evidence that the human visual representation of shape is part-based, and we have discussed several geometric factors that determine how human vision parses shapes into parts, and determines their perceived salience. Moreover, we have shown that mechanisms of part segmentation interact with mechanisms of object and surface segmentation in a number of ways: in assigning border ownership, in computing surface structure in transparency, and in dividing spontaneously-splitting figures. Finally, we have reviewed evidence suggesting that part segmentation is carried out rapidly and early in visual processing, and that the allocation of visual attention to objects can be part-based.

REFERENCES

Atchley, P. & Kramer, A. (2000). Object and space-based attentional selection in three-dimensional space. *Visual Cognition, 8*, 1-32.

Attneave, F. (1954). Some informational aspects of visual perception. *Psychological Review, 61*, 183-193.

Attneave, F. (1971). Multistability in perception. *Scientific American, 225, 6*, 63-71.

Anderson, B.L. (1997). A theory of illusory lightness and transparency in monocular and binocular images: the role of junctions. *Perception, 26*, 49-453.

Bahnsen, P. (1928). Eine untersuchung ueber symmetrie und asymmetrie bei visuellen wahrnehmungen. *Zeitschrift fuer Psychologie, 108*, 355-361.

Barenholtz, E., & Feldman, J. (2001). Interpretation of part boundaries and the movement of attention. Poster presented at the *1st Annual Meeting of the Vision Sciences Society*, Sarasota, Florida (May 2001).

Baylis, G.C., & Driver, J. (1994). Parallel computation of symmetry but not repetition in single visual objects. *Visual Cognition, 1,* 377-400.

Baylis, G.C., & Driver, J. (1995a). One-sided edge asignment in vision. 1. Figure-ground segmentation and attention to objects. *Current Directions in Psychological Science, 4*, 140-146.

Baylis, G.C., & Driver, J. (1995b). Obligatory edge assignment in vision - The role of figure and part segmentation in symmetry detection. *Journal of Experimental Psychology: Human Perception and Performance, 21,* 1323-1342.

Beck, J., Prazdny, K., & Ivry, R. (1984). The perception of transparency with achromatic colors. *Perception & Psychophysics, 35,* 407-422.

Bennett, B.M. & Hoffman, D.D. 1987. Shape decompositions for visual recognition: the role of transversality. In W. Richards and S. Ullman (Eds.), *Image Understanding* 1985-86, Norwood, New Jersey: Ablex Publishing, 215-256.

Beusmans, J., Hoffman, D.D., & Bennett, B.M. (1987). Description of solid shape and its inference from occluding contours. Journal of the Optical Society of America, A, 4, 1155-1167.

Biederman, I. (1987). Recognition-by-components: A theory of human image understanding. *Psychological Review, 94*, 115-147.

Biederman, I., & Cooper, E.E. (1991). Priming contour-deleted images: evidence for intermediate representations in visual object recognition. *Cognitive Psychology, 23,* 393-419.

Binford, T.O. (1971, December). Visual perception by computer. *IEEE Systems Science and Cybernetics Conference*, Miami, FL.

Binford, T. O. (1981). Inferring surfaces from images. *Artificial Intelligence, 17*, 205-244.

Blum, H. & Nagel, R.N. (1978). Shape description using weighted symmetric axis features. *Pattern Recognition, 10*, 167-180.

Brady, M., & Asada, H. (1984). Smoothed local symmetries and their implementation. *The International Journal of Robotics Research, 3*, 36-61.

Braunstein, M.L., Hoffman, D.D., & Saidpour, A. (1989). Parts of visual objects: an experimental test of the minima rule. *Perception, 18*, 817-826.

Bruce, V. and Morgan, M. J. (1975). Violations of symmetry and repetitions in visual patterns. *Perception, 4*, 239-249.

Casati, R. & Varzi, A. (1999). Parts and places. Cambridge, MA, MIT Press.

Corballis, M. C. & Roldan, C. E. (1974). On the perception of symmetrical and repeated patterns. *Perception and Psychophysics, 16*, 136-142.

Do Carmo, M. (1976). *Differential geometry of curves and surfaces*. Englewood Cliffs, NJ, Prentice-Hall.

Driver, J., & Baylis, G.C. (1995). One-sided edge assignment in vision. 2. Part decomposition, shape description, and attention to objects. *Current Directions in Psychological Science, 4*, 201-206.

Egly, R., Driver, J., & Rafal, R. (1994). Shifting visual attention between objects and locations: Evidence for normal and parietal lesion subjects. *Journal of Experimental Psychology: General, 123*, 161-177.

Freeman, W. T. (1994). The generic viewpoint assumption in a framework for visual perception. *Nature, 368*, 542-545.

Gerbino, W., Stultiens, C. I., Troost, J. M., & de Weert, C. M. (1990). Transparent layer constancy. *Journal of Experimental Psychology: Human Perception & Performance, 16*, 3-20.

Hochberg, J. (1964). *Perception*. Englewood Cliffs, NJ: Prentice-Hall.

Hoffman, D.D. (1983a). *Representing shapes for visual recognition*. PhD Thesis, Massachusetts Institute of Technology.

Hoffman, D.D. (1983b). The interpretation of visual illusions. *Scientific American, 249, 6*, 154-162.

Hoffman, D. D. (1998). *Visual Intelligence: How we create what we see.* New York: Norton.

Hoffman, D.D., & Richards, W.A. (1984). Parts of recognition. *Cognition, 18*, 65-96.

Hoffman, D. D. & Singh, M. (1997). Salience of visual parts. *Cognition, 63*, 29-78.

Hulleman, J., te Winkel, W., & Boselie, F. (2000). Concavities as basic features in visual search: Evidence from search asymmetries. *Perception & Psychophysics, 62*, 162-174.

Joseph, J. S., Chun, M. M., & Nakayama, K. (1996). Attentional requirements in a "preattentive" feature search task. *Nature, 379*, 805-807.

Kanizsa, G. (1979). Organization in vision: essays on Gestalt perception. NewYork: Praeger.

Kanisza, G., & Gerbino, W. (1976). Convexity and symmetry in figure-ground organization. In M. Henle (Ed.), *Art and artefacts* (pp. 25-32). New York: Springer.

Kellman, P. J. & Loukides, (1987). An object perception approach to static and kinetic subjective contours. In S. Petry & G. E. Meyer (Eds.), *The perception of illusory contours* (pp. 151-164). New York: Springer-Verlag.

Kellman, P. J. & Shipley, T. F. (1991). A theory of visual interpolation in object perception. *Cognitive Psychology, 23*, 141-221.

Kimia, B. B., Tannenbaum, A. R. & Zucker, S. W. (1995). Shapes, shocks, and deformations. 1. The components of two-dimensional shape and the reaction-diffusion space. *International Journal of Computer Vision, 15*, 189-224.

Koffka, K. (1935). *Principles of gestalt psychology*. New York: Harcourt, Brace and World.

Koenderink, J. J., Van Doorn, A. J., & Kappers, A. M. (1992). Surface perception in pictures. *Perception & Psychophysics, 52*, 487-496.

Kubovy, M., & Gephstein, S. (2000). From good continuation to best continuation. Talk given at the *41st Annual Meeting of the Psychonomic Society*, New Orleans, LA.

Leyton, M. (1987). Symmetry-curvature duality. *Computer vision, graphics, and image processing, 38*, 327-341.

Leyton, M. (1992). *Symmetry, causality, mind.* Cambridge, MA: MIT Press.

Lowe, D. (1985). Perceptual organization and visual recognition. Amsterdam: Kluwer.

Marr, D. (1977). Analysis of occluding contour. *Proceedings of the Royal Society of London, B, 197*, 441-475.

Marr, D. & Nishihara, H.K. (1978). Representation and recognition of three-dimensional shapes. *Proceedings of the Royal Society of London, B, 200*, 269-294.

Metelli, F. (1974). The perception of transparency. *Scientific American, 230,* 90-98.

Metelli, F., Da Pos, O., & Cavedon, A. (1985). Balanced and unbalanced, complete and partial transparency. *Perception & Psychophysics, 38,* 354-366.

Moore, C., Yantis, S., & Vaughan, B. (1998). Object-based visual selection: Evidence from perceptual completion. *Psychological Science, 9,* 104-110.

Palmer, S. E. (1977). Hierarchical structure in perceptual representation. *Cognitive Psychology, 9*, 441-474.

Palmer, S. E. (1999). *Vision Science: From photons to phenomenology.* Cambridge, MA: MIT Press.

Pentland, A.P. (1986). Perceptual organization and the representation of natural form. *Artificial Intelligence, 28,* 293-331.

Petter, G. (1956). Nuove ricerche sperimentali sulla totalizzazione percettiva. *Rivista di Psicologia, 50,* 213-227.

Posner, M. I., Nissen, M. J., & Ogden, W. C. (1978). Attended and unattended processing modes: The role of set for spatial location. In H. J. Pick and I. J. Saltzman (Eds.), *Modes of perceiving and processing information* (pp. 137-157). Hillsdale, NJ: Erlbaum.

Rosin, P. L. (2000). Shape partitioning by convexity. *IEEE Transactions on Systems, Man, and Cybernetics—Part A: Systems and Humans, 30,* 202-210.

Rubin, E. (1958). Figure and ground. In D.C. Beardslee (Ed), Readings in perception, Princeton, New Jersey: Van Nostrand, 194-203. (Reprinted from *Visuell wahrgenommene figuren*, 1915, Copenhagen: Gyldenalske Boghandel.)

Scholl, B. J. (2001). Objects and attention: The state of the art. *Cognition, 80,* 1-46.

Shipley, T. F., & Kellman, P. J. (1990). The role of discontinuities in the perception of subjective figures. *Perception & Psychophysics, 48,* 259-270.

Siddiqi, K. & Kimia, B.B. (1995). Parts of visual form: computational aspects. *IEEE Transactions on Pattern Analysis and Machine Intelligence, 17,* 239-251.

Siddiqi, K., Kimia, B. B., Tannenbaum, A. R., & Zucker, S. W. (2000). On the Psychophysics of the Shape Triangle. *Vision Research*, In Press.

Siddiqi, K., Tresness, K.J., & Kimia, B.B. (1996). Parts of visual form — Psychophysical aspects. *Perception, 25,* 399-424.

Singh, M. & Anderson, B. L. (2001). Toward a perceptual theory of transparency. *Psychological Review*, in press.

Singh, M. & Hoffman, D. D. (1998). Part boundaries alter the perception of transparency. *Psychological Science, 9,* 370-378.

Singh, M. & Hoffman, D. D. (1999). Completing visual contours: The relationship between relatability and minimizing inflections. *Perception and Psychophysics, 61,* 943-951.

Singh, M., Hoffman, D. D., & Albert, M. K. (1999). Contour completion and relative depth: Petter's rule and support ratio. *Psychological Science, 10,* 423-428.

Singh, M, & Scholl, B. (2000). Using attentional cueing to explore part structure. Poster presented at the *Annual Symposium of Object Perception and Memory*, New Orleans, Louisiana (November 2000).

Singh, M., Seyranian, G. D., & Hoffman (1996). Cuts for parsing visual shapes. *Institute for Mathematical Behavioral Sciences, Technical Report MBS96-33.*

Singh, M., Seyranian, G. D., & Hoffman (1999). Parsing silhouettes: The short-cut rule. *Perception and Psychophysics, 61,* 636-660.

Stevens, K.A. & Brookes, A. (1988). The concave cusp as a determiner of figure-ground. *Perception, 17,* 35-42.

Stoner, G. R. & Albright, T. D. (1993). Image segmentation cues in motion processing: Implications for modularity vision. *Journal of Cognitive Neuroscience, 5,* 129-149.

Sutherland, N.S. (1968). Outlines of a theory of visual pattern recognition in animals and man. *Proceedings of the Royal Society of London, B, 171,* 297-317.

Todd, J. T., Koenderink, J. J., van Doorn, A. J., & Kappers, A. M. L. (1996). Effects of changing viewing conditions on the perceived structure of smoothly curved surfaces. *Journal of Experimental Psychology: Human Perception & Performance, 22,* 695-706.

Tommasi, L., Bressan, P., & Vallortigara, G. (1995). Solving occlusion indeterminacy in chromatically homogeneous patterns. *Perception, 24,* 391-403.

Treisman, A., & Gormican, S. (1988). Feature analysis in early vision: Evidence from search asymmetries. *Psychological Review, 95,* 15-48.

Treisman, A., & Souther, J. (1985). Search asymmetry: A diagnostic for preattentive processing of separable features. *Journal of Experimental Psychology: General, 114,* 285-310.

Vecera, S.P, Behrmann, M., & McGoldrick, J. (2000). Selective attention to the parts of an object. *Psychonomic Bulletin & Review, 7,* 301-308.

Vecera, S.P, Behrmann, M., & Filapek, J.C. (2001). Attending to the parts of a single object: Part-based selection limitations. *Perception & Psychophysics, 63,* 308-321.

Waltz, D. (1975). Generating semantic descriptions from drawings of scenes with shadows. In P. Winston (Ed.), *The psychology of computer vision* (pp. 19-91). New York: McGraw-Hill.

Winston, P.A. (1975). Learning structural descriptions from examples. In P.H. Winston (Ed.), *The psychology of computer vision* (pp. 157-209). New York: McGraw-Hill.

Witkin, A.P., & Tenenbaum, J.M. (1983). On the role of structure in vision. In J. Beck, B. Hope, & A. Rosenfeld (Eds.), *Human and machine vision* (pp. 481-543). New York: Academic Press.

Wolfe, J. M. (1998). What can 1 million trials tell us about visual search? *Psychological Science, 9,* 33-39.

Wolfe, J. M., Bennett, S. C. (1997). Preattentive object files: Shapeless bundles of basic features. *Vision Research, 37*, 25-43.

Xu, Y., & Singh, M. (2001; Manuscript submitted for publication). Pre-attentive computation of part structure: Evidence from visual search.

V.

SPATIOTEMPORAL UNIT FORMATION

Visual segmentation and grouping processes serve thought and behavior by delivering representations of coherent objects and spatial arrangements. Particularly remarkable is the fact that we can obtain a stable and coherent world from dynamically changing inputs, due to motion of objects or of the observer. Although the processes of segmentation and grouping have been more often studied in static, spatial arrays, the spatiotemporal versions of these abilities may be most important for action in ordinary environments.

It might seem that the facts of occlusion in 3-D environments coupled with constant changes given by motion would produce visual chaos. Yet most often, we effortlessly parse the temporal steam of events in such a way that objects and the layout are recovered and coordinated action is possible. Perhaps this is not surprising. Since at least the pioneering work of J.J. Gibson, perception researchers have been aware that motion and change are not only sources of complexity but rich sources of information. In research on segmentation and grouping the task is to understand these sources of information, along with the processes and mechanisms by which they are exploited. The chapters in this section address several aspects of spatiotemporal segmentation and unit formation. In developing models of how segmentation over time occurs, the research presented here draws upon classic and recent approaches to understanding segmentation. An observer's knowledge and past experience might help in identifying boundaries; in the spatiotemporal case, these may be *event* boundaries. John Henderson takes up such issues in attempting to answer the question: How does the visual system use regularities in past experience with the environment to deal with the spatially discontinuous inputs from a moving eye? Maggie Shiffrar considers how our knowledge of human action may influence the perceived unity of the complex motions associated with walking. A different starting point is that observers rely on some aspect of the world, some relationship in the ambient optic array, that provides information for event boundaries. Nicola Bruno as well as William Prophet, Donald Hoffman, & Carol Cicerone offer analyses of what properties might be useful in processing the events associated with occlusion. Maggie Shiffrar and Thomas Shipley & Douglas Cunningham offer treatments that combine the two general approaches to ask: How are spatially localized events integrated with other spatially removed events? While research in this area is in its infancy relative to work on static segmentation and unit formation, the reader will see that cognitive scientists and psychologists are developing accounts that may ultimately serve as models for perception in natural scenes where objects and observers can move.

From Fragments to Objects – Segmentation and Grouping in Vision
T.F. Shipley and P.J. Kellman (Editors)

14

GAZE CONTROL FOR FACE LEARNING AND RECOGNITION BY HUMANS AND MACHINES

John M. Henderson[1,4], Richard Falk[1,4], Silviu Minut[2], Fred C. Dyer[3,4], and Sridhar Mahadevan[2,4], [1]Department of Psychology, [2]Department of Computer Science, [3]Department of Zoology, and [4]Cognitive Science Program, Michigan State University, East Lansing, Michigan, 48824-1117, USA

OVERVIEW

In this chapter we describe an ongoing project designed to investigate gaze control in face perception, a problem of central importance in both human and machine vision. The project uses converging evidence from behavioral studies of human observers and computational studies in machine vision. The research is guided by a formal framework for understanding gaze control based on Markov decision processes (MDPs). Behavioral data from human observers provide new insight into gaze control in a complex task, and are used to motivate an artificial gaze control system using the Markov approach. Furthermore, the efficacy of a Markov approach to gaze control for face recognition in machine vision is tested. The general goal of the project is to uncover key principles of gaze control that cut across the specific implementation of the system (biological or machine).

INTRODUCTION

The Problem of Gaze Control

The majority of work in human and machine vision to date has made the simplifying assumption that visual acuity during stimulus input is equally good across the image to be processed. A property of human perception, though, is that high acuity vision is restricted to a small (2°) foveal region surrounding fixation, with acuity dropping off precipitously from the fixation point (Anstis, 1974; Riggs, 1965). The human visual system takes advantage of this high-acuity region by rapidly reorienting the eyes via very fast (saccadic) eye movements (Buswell, 1935; Henderson & Hollingworth, 1998, 1999; Rayner, 1998; Yarbus, 1967). Recent work in computer vision and robotics (Kuniyoshi et al., 1995; Brooks et al., 1998) suggests that outfitting artificial vision systems with a central high-acuity region can similarly provide important computational advantages in computer vision. However, foveated vision systems require that the direction of gaze be controlled so that the foveal region is appropriately directed within the image based on the properties of the stimulus and the goals of the agent (human or machine), a complex real-time learning and control problem. The interdisciplinary project described in this chapter is an attempt to integrate the study of human and machine gaze control, with the ultimate goal of shedding light on the underlying principles and properties of gaze control within the important context of face perception.

Gaze Control in Human Vision. The human visual system takes advantage of the high resolving power of the fovea by reorienting the fixation point around the viewed scene an average of three times each second via saccadic eye movements. Saccades are ballistic, very fast sweeps (velocities of up to 900°/s; Carpenter, 1988) of gaze position across the scene during which visual information acquisition is severely limited due to *saccadic suppression* (Matin, 1974; Volkmann, 1986). Fixations are brief epochs (averaging about 300 ms; Henderson & Hollingworth, 1998) in which the fovea is directed at a point of interest, gaze position remains relatively still, and pattern information is acquired from the scene. Given the importance of foveation in human vision, the control of fixation placement over time (gaze control) is a critical sequential decision-making problem. Furthermore, gaze control appears to have important consequences for other cognitive processes beyond the timely and efficient acquisition of visual information. For example, Ballard and colleagues have suggested that fixation is necessary for enabling computations that require the binding of cognitive and motor processes to external objects (Ballard, 1996; Ballard, Hayhoe, Pook, & Rao, 1997; also Henderson, 1996; Milner & Goodale, 1995). An important issue in the study of vision and visual cognition therefore is the nature of the process that controls sequential decision-making for saccadic eye movements during dynamic visual and cognitive tasks.

Gaze Control in Computer Vision. Most classical computer vision methods process images at constant resolution. In contrast, in human vision the magnitude and complexity of the input is reduced by a decrease in the resolution of the visual field from the fovea to the periphery. This decrease in resolution across the retina leads to loss of information, but the human visual system compensates for the loss by employing an efficient gaze control mechanism, directing the fovea to different points in the image to gather more detailed information as it is needed. Thus, rather than analyzing an enormous amount of detailed visual information at once, a computationally expensive proposition, the brain processes detailed information sequentially, turning vision in part into a sequential decision-making process. Only recently has the importance and the potential of foveated vision been discovered in computer vision, and work in this direction is very early in development (e.g., Kuniyoshi 1995, van der Soiegel 1989, Bandera 1996). As these foveated vision systems develop, algorithms will be required to control the timely placement of the artificial fovea over the external scene.

A central component of a successful general theory of gaze control will be an account of how the perceiving agent– whether it be a human or a machine– can decide where to fixate at each point in time. This problem of sequential decision-making for gaze control is formidable. The world offers a dizzying array of stimuli to which the agent could direct the fovea. Compounding the problem, the consequences of particular alternative actions (foveating Feature A rather than Feature B, C, D... N) may not become apparent until a sequence of related fixations has been taken, and yet the perceiving agent may need to estimate the likely payoff of a particular fixation (or sequence of fixations) in advance. Furthermore, for a perceiving agent, decisions about fixation position need to be made in quick succession, leaving little time to sort through the space of all possible fixation placements and associated outcomes. Finally, a well-designed agent should be able to modify its fixation behavior through learning, raising the problem of how to assign credit to the correct decision and how to store the associated information in memory.

The Problem of Face Perception

Face Perception in Human Vision. Faces are arguably the most important and salient visual stimulus a human ever encounters. Faces are central in human social interaction, providing critical information about the age, gender, emotional state, intention, and identity of another. There is substantial evidence that the perception of faces by human observers may be "special" in at least two ways. First, the computational processes responsible for face perception appear to be qualitatively different from those involved in the recognition of other kinds of objects or complex scenes. This view is supported by behavioral data showing that faces are preferentially attended by young infants when compared to similarly complex visual stimuli or even scrambled faces (Bruce, 1988; Johnson, Dziurawiec, Bartrip, & Morton, 1991). When placed in complex scenes, faces preferentially draw the attention of adult viewers (Yarbus, 1967). Inverting a face disrupts face recognition to a greater degree than does inverting other types of objects (Yin, 1969). Second, the neural systems that underlie face perception appear to be partially independent of those systems that underlie object perception more generally. For example, single cell recording from neurons in the temporal cortex of monkeys has revealed a population of cells that respond selectively to faces, and in some cases to specific faces (Desimone, 1991). Evidence from human neuropsychology has provided examples for a double dissociation between object and face recognition, with some patients showing intact face recognition and impaired object recognition (prosopagnosia), and other patients showing the opposite pattern (visual object agnosia; e.g., Moscovitch et al., 1997; Newcome et al., 1994). Recent functional neuroimaging studies similarly provide evidence that face recognition is supported by a neural module in the fusiform gyrus of the human cortex that is not active during perception of other types of objects (Ishai et al., 1997; Kanwisher et al., 1997; McCarthy et al., 1997), though it has also been suggested that this area may be more generally devoted to the analysis of exemplars of a well-learned object class (Diamond & Carey, 1986; Gauthier et al., 1997). Together, these converging sources of evidence strongly support the hypothesis that the human visual system contains specialized neural and computational systems that are devoted to face perception. However, the specific nature of those computations remains very much unresolved.

Face Perception in Computer Vision. Face recognition is a well-studied problem in computer vision, but is not completely solved. The problem is typically posed in the following way: Suppose we have a database of images of *N* people. In general, all images are the same size, and there are several images for each person. Given a test image (i.e., an image of a person whose identity is not known), one must detect whether or not the person is in the database, and if it is, correctly identify that person. The traditional approach is to treat each image as a (high dimensional) vector by concatenating the rows of pixels that compose it (e.g. see Pentland et al., 1994). The dimensionality of the vector, *K*, equals the total number of pixels in the image; each dimension is a measure of the gray-scale level (or color) of a particular pixel in the image. Analyzed in this way, each image in the database defines a point in a *K*-dimensional Euclidean space. If it turns out that images of the same person are closer to each other in this space than they are close to images of other people, a clustering algorithm can be used to form decision boundaries. Thus, to classify a test image it suffices to determine the class of its nearest neighbors or, in other words, to determine the cluster to which that image belongs. Although appealing, this basic scheme is difficult to implement, for reasons of dimension. An image as small as 60 x 80 pixels yields a vector of dimension 4800. If the database contains a few hundred images, it is difficult if not impossible to find the nearest neighbors in reasonable time.

A considerable number of techniques that try to reduce the dimensionality of the problem are known, each with its own strengths and weaknesses. These include Principal

Component Analysis (Pentland et al., 1994), Neural Networks (Mitchell, 1997) and Markov models (Samaria et al., 1994). From a purely computational point of view, any method is acceptable as long as it produces high classification rates, e.g., see recent work on probabilistic face matching (Mogaddam et al., 1998). Such methods do not have to imitate nature. However, there must be a good reason nature chose, through evolution, certain algorithms over others. Thus, from the perspective of computer vision, it is of interest to discover the nature of the algorithms used by the human brain, and to come to understand why those algorithms have been selected. Furthermore, the superiority of the algorithms used by the human visual system (whatever they may be) over standard face recognition (and more generally, computer vision) algorithms is obvious. Of the frameworks used to reduce the dimensionality of the face recognition problem, the one that appears most promising in uncovering the algorithm used by nature, given the characteristics of the human foveal vision system, is a foveated vision approach. Our work thus begins with the following fundamental questions: How important is foveal vision in human face learning and recognition, and would it provide any benefits in machine face learning and recognition?

AN INVESTIGATION OF GAZE CONTROL IN FACE LEARNING AND RECOGNITION

We have recently undertaken an initial investigation designed to integrate the study of gaze control for face learning and recognition across humans and artificial agents. This investigation entailed a behavioral study of gaze control with human participants, and the implementation of a face learning and recognition system within a Hidden Markov Model (HMM) framework. In this section we will summarize the work so far and the promise it holds for the future.

Behavioral Study: Human Gaze Control During Face Learning and Recognition

In an initial behavioral study (Falk, Hollingworth, Henderson, Mahadevan, & Dyer, 2000), we asked 16 participants to view full-color images of human faces in two phases, a study phase in which the participants were asked to learn the faces of twenty previously unknown undergraduate women, and a recognition phase in which the participants were asked to distinguish these learned faces from distracter faces, drawn from the same pool, that had not been learned. In addition, during the recognition phase, half of the previously learned and half of the new (distracter) faces were presented upright, and half were presented upside-down. The purpose of this latter manipulation was to examine whether differences in gaze control to upright and inverted faces might be related to fixation position or scanning sequence.

The method of the experiment was as follows: In the Study Phase, 16 participants viewed a series of 20 upright faces for 10 sec each, with the order of faces and conditions randomized within the block. The participants then viewed a series of 10 pictures of naturalistic scenes for 10 sec each, with the order of scenes randomized within the block. This scene viewing phase constituted a period of time over which the learned faces had to be remembered. In the Recognition Phase, the same 16 participants viewed 10 new upright faces. 10 new inverted faces, 10 previously learned upright faces, and 10 previously learned inverted faces. Each face was presented until the participant responded, or for 20 sec maximum. All four types of face stimuli were presented in a single block, with order of stimuli (and hence condition) randomized within that block. Assignment of particular faces to particular learning and recognition conditions (learned or distracter, upright or inverted) was counterbalanced over participants.

The face stimuli used in the study were generated from photographs of undergraduate women with dark hair. The photographs were scanned into a computer and cropped so that each picture included only the face and hair. Hair was also cropped so that its style was relatively uniform across the set of stimuli (See Figure 1 for an example). Faces that included distinctive features such as eyeglasses, jewelry, moles, and so on were not used. Each cropped face was pasted onto a uniform gray background. All images were presented at a resolution of 800 by 600 pixels by 15 bit color (32,768 colors) and appeared photographic in quality. The faces subtended 7.56° horizontally by 10.47° vertically on average at a distance of about 1 meter; thus, they appeared at a natural size for a human face at this viewing distance.

The viewer's eye position over the course of face learning and recognition was precisely tracked using a Generation 5.5 Stanford Research Institute Dual Purkinje Image Eyetracker (Crane, 1994; Crane & Steele, 1985). Eye position was sampled at 1000 Hz, with spatial resolution better than 10' of arc.

Summary of Results: Study Phase. Figure 1 presents the scan pattern (the sequence of

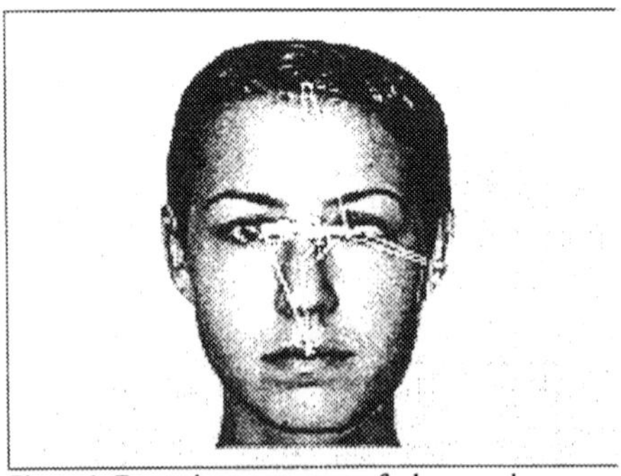

Figure 1. Example scan pattern of a human observer in the behavioral experiment. Dots represent fixations, and lines represent saccades.

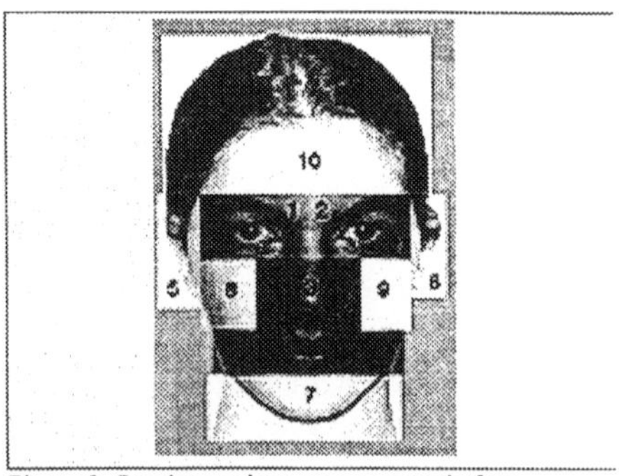

Figure 2. Scoring regions on an example face stimulus from the behavioral experiment.

fixations and saccades) of a single participant viewing a single face during the study phase. The straight lines represent saccades, and the dots represent fixations. This scan pattern is typical: Participants tended to focus on the salient features of the faces, including the eyes, the nose, and the mouth.

To quantitatively examine the data, each face was divided into ten scoring regions, consisting of the two eyes, the nose, the mouth, the two ears, the chin, the two cheeks, and the forehead, as shown in Figure 2. All fixations for each participant were then assigned to one of these regions. Figure 3 shows the mean percentage of times each facial region was entered at least once during a trial. As can be seen, both eyes were fixated at least once in over 95% of all trials. The nose, mouth, and forehead were also examined with a high degree of regularity, whereas the cheeks, ears, and chin were rarely fixated over the course of 10 seconds of viewing time. Thus, consistent with prior face viewing studies, participants generally distributed the majority of their fixations on or near important facial features (e.g., Buswell, 1935; Walker-Smith, Gale, & Findlay, 1977; Yarbus, 1967).

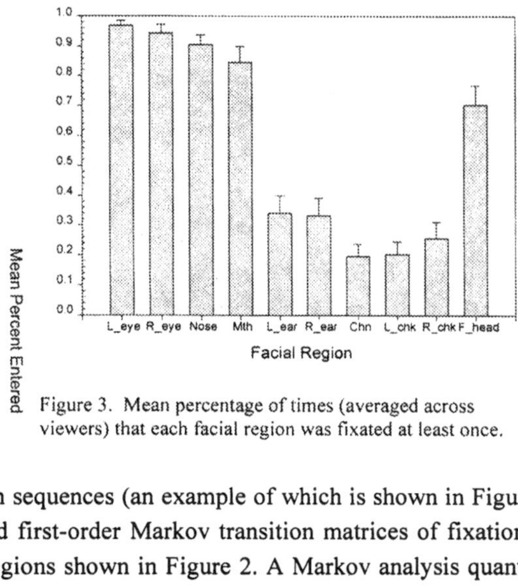

Figure 3. Mean percentage of times (averaged across viewers) that each facial region was fixated at least once.

Fixation sequences (an example of which is shown in Figure 1 above) were analyzed using zero- and first-order Markov transition matrices of fixation sequences from the pre-defined face regions shown in Figure 2. A Markov analysis quantitatively characterizes the distribution of gaze transitions from one fixation position to the next. The goal of the Markov analysis was to determine if the location of fixation position n, and hence perceptual and cognitive processing during fixation n, influences the spatial placement of fixation $n+1$. The zero-order matrix captures the probability of fixating a given region (zero-order Markov matrix), and the first-order Markov matrix captures the probability of moving to a given region from another given region. If the location of the current fixation significantly influences the placement of the subsequent fixation, then the first-order matrix should deviate from that predicted by the base probabilities represented by the zero-order matrix. The method used for computing the zero- and first order matrices was modified from that given by Liu (1998).

Table 1 provides a summary of the Markov matrix analysis. Chi-squared tests of deviations of observed fixation positions from those that would be expected based on the marginal (zero-order) matrices showed systematic deviations from base probabilities, suggesting that there was a degree of regularity in the fixation sequences. A non-zero number in the difference matrix in Table 1 indicates a reliable difference between the predicted first-order matrix and the observed first-order matrix as determined by the Chi-Square analysis. A plus sign in the difference matrix indicates that there were more observed transitions in that cell than would be predicted from the zero-order matrix. A minus sign indicates fewer transitions than would be predicted. As Table 1 demonstrates, in several instances position of fixation *n* significantly affected the selection of fixation *n+1* position. For example, notice that along the diagonal axis there is almost a uniform influence of current fixation position. This result shows that the tendency to refixate the currently fixated facial region was typically higher than the baseline fixation rate for that region. Second, there were a large number or transitions from one eye region to the other, suggesting a greater likelihood of moving to an

		Target Region									
	Region	L_Eye	R_Eye	Nose	Mouth	L_Ear	R_Ear	Chin	L_Chk	R_Chk	F_Head
	L_Eye	+	+				-	-		-	
	R_Eye		+	-		-		-	-		
Source Region	Nose		-	+	+		-				-
	Mouth		-					+			-
	L_Ear		-	-		+					
	R_Ear	-		-			+				
	Chin	-	-					+			-
	L_Chk		-								
	R_Chk	-									-
	F_Head	-		-	-						+

Table 1. Deviations of fixation transition frequencies observed in the first-order Markov matrix from the frequencies predicted by the zero-order Markov matrix. Positive (+) indicates more observed fixations than predicted. Negative (-) indicates fewer observed fixations than predicted.

eye if the other eye was presently fixated. These data provide additional evidence that the eyes are a particularly important or salient facial features for gaze targeting during face learning.

Summary of Results: Recognition Phase. In the Recognition Phase, participants viewed the 20 previously learned faces and 20 new faces drawn from the same pool. Half of the new and old faces were presented upright, and half were presented upside-down. Participants viewed each face freely and indicated, via button press, whether the current face was new or was one of the faces viewed during the learning phase. When the participant pressed the response button, the current face was removed from the computer screen and, following a brief calibration screen, the next face was displayed.

Overall accuracy in the Recognition Phase, collapsed over new and old faces, was about 73% correct. As expected from the face recognition literature, accuracy was influenced by the orientation of the face in the Recognition Phase, with accuracy of about 79% in the upright condition and 66% in the inverted condition. Average viewing time during the Recognition Phase was about 2.3 seconds, with participants taking about 560 ms longer to respond to new than to learned faces, and about 144 ms longer to respond to inverted than to upright faces.

Interestingly, although viewing time in the Recognition Phase was about an order of magnitude shorter than in the Learning Phase, the distribution of fixations over the faces in these two phases was remarkably similar (Falk, Hollingworth, Henderson, Mahadevan, & Dyer, 2000). This similarity can be seen in Figure 4, which shows the proportion of total time

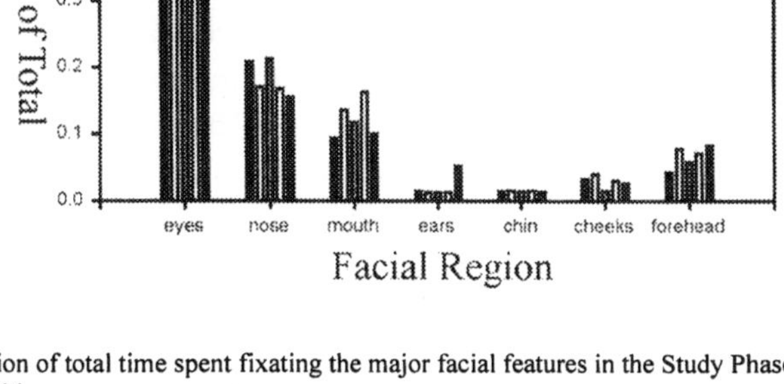

Figure 4. Proportion of total time spent fixating the major facial features in the Study Phase and the four Recognition conditions.

spent on the major features defined in Figure 2. As can be seen, the same features received the same proportion of total fixation time in the Learning and Recognition Phases. Also clear in Figure 4 is the fact that inversion in the Recognition Phase had little influence on the distribution of fixation time over the faces. A similar pattern is observed when proportion of fixation time rather than proportion of discrete fixations is used as the dependent measure (Falk et al., 2000). These data suggest that, at least insofar as the overt selection of facial features for visual analysis is concerned, the face inversion effect is not due to a transition from more wholistic face processing to more local, feature-based processing.

We can draw four main conclusions from this behavioral study. First, selection of facial features through overt orienting of the eyes is observed during both face learning and recognition. Although we don't have evidence here that gaze control is strictly necessary for face learning and recognition, it is striking that when allowed to view faces freely, human observers moved their eyes over the face, making clear choices about which features to orient to and which to ignore. Second, as shown by the results of the Markov analysis, the selection of a fixation site during learning is driven, in part, by the specific feature that is currently under fixation. Thus, there is some sequential dependency to gaze control decisions. Third, the facial features selected for fixation during recognition are very similar to those selected for fixation during learning. It is tempting to conclude that feature processing during learning influences this selection during recognition, though we do not yet have direct evidence for this proposition. Fourth, the facial features selected for fixation during recognition of an upright face are very similar to those selected for fixation during recognition of an inverted face. This finding is intriguing, because one might have expected that recognition of upright faces, hypothesized to be supported by wholistic pattern processing, would lead to less feature-specific analysis than would inverted faces, which are hypothesized to be supported by feature-based analysis (Farah, Tanaka, & Drain, 1995; Tanaka & Farah, 1993).

Computational Study: Gaze Control for Face Recognition using Hidden Markov Models

Formal Framework: A Probabilistic Model of Sequential Decision Making. We have seen in the previous section that human gaze control is regular and efficient. It is deeply puzzling how to endow machines with similar fluidity and accuracy. What is needed is a formal framework that both accounts for patterns of human gaze and allows for the development of algorithms for gaze control in artificial foveated visual systems. The long-term goal of our project is to investigate whether Markov decision processes (MDPs) can be the basis of such a framework.

MDPs are a well-developed formal framework for studying sequential decision making, originally proposed in the operations research literature (Bellman, 1957; Howard, 1960; Puterman, 1994). In recent years, MDPs have become a unifying formalism for studying a range of problems in artificial intelligence and robotics, from planning in uncertain environments (Kaelbling, 1998), to learning from delayed reward (Mahadevan et al., 1992). The MDP framework comprises a range of different models, from the simple case of *Markov chains* where states are observable and there is no choice of action, to the intermediate cases of *hidden-Markov models* (HMMs) where states are not observable but there is no action choice, to *Markov decision processes* (MDPs) where states are observable but there is a choice of action, and finally to the most complex case of *partially-observable MDPs* (POMDPs) where states are not observable and the agent has a choice of action in any state. In our project to date, we have focused first on the HMM case, since the underlying states during the process of face recognition are not themselves observable, but have to be inferred from fixation points during recognition. Our goal is to use the simpler HMM case as a jumping-off point to the more complex POMDP problem of allowing the agent choice of what the next fixation point should be. One advantage of starting with the HMM case is that the principal algorithms for learning an HMM model (the well-known Baum Welch, forward-backward, and Viterbi algorithms) all extend nicely to the POMDP case.

In a recent study we tested the potential of the HMM formalism in face recognition (Minut, Mahadevan, Henderson, & Dyer, 2000). HMMs are in one important respect not a good model of human gaze control, since humans clearly do not follow a fixed, predetermined sequence of action when scanning faces. However, HMMs are appealing because they do not require us to specify the nature of the underlying states of the system (which are not known for human gaze control), only the actions available to it (shifts of gaze), and the (probabilistic) effects of the actions on the information available to the system. Furthermore, it should eventually be possible to build on the HMM framework to introduce more flexible selection of action, hence turning it into a POMDP.

We used a database consisting of 27 women and 19 men with 6 images per person, as shown in Figure 5. Each image was 512x512 pixels. We defined 10 regions of interest for each face, loosely based on the human fixation patterns we observed in the behavioral study, and we built a left to right HMM corresponding to these regions (see Figure 6).

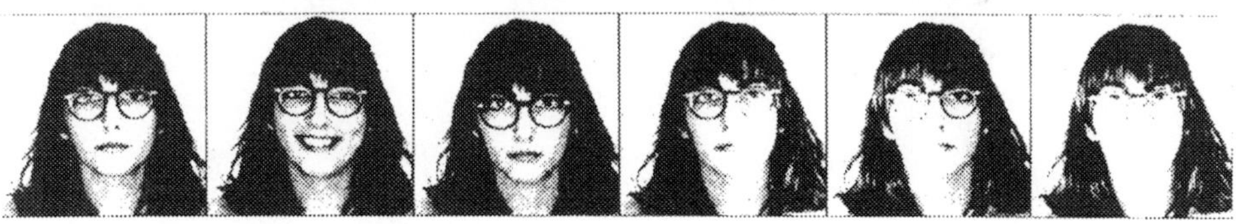

Figure 5. Face stimuli used in the HMM study.

The goal of this experiment was to build an HMM for each class (person) in the database, using input from a foveated vision system. To this end we produced for each image an observation sequence that consisted of 30 observation vectors. Each observation vector was produced by foveating on the same image multiple times. The system fixated 3 times in each of the 10 regions, and moved to the next region in sequence. This order was of course

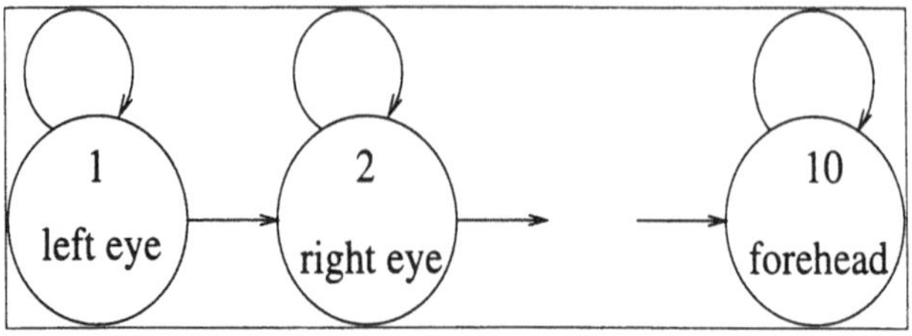

Figure 6. Regions of interest for the HMM study.

arbitrarily imposed by us and does not agree with the patterns that human subjects seem to follow. The HMM was built when all of its parameters had been learned (i.e. all the state transition probabilities and all the observation density functions). The parameters were learned (updated) incrementally, as new observation sequences were processed. The HMMs for different classes had the same states, but different parameters. Each HMM was built based on 5 images for each class, with the 6th image used for testing of recognition performance. Thus, recognition was tested using images that had not been seen during learning.

In this study, our simulated fovea was a software-defined square patch centered at the desired fixation point, of the same resolution as the original unfoveated image. We surround this patch with rings of "superpixels'" which double in size as we move from the center towards the periphery of the image. A superpixel is simply a small square patch whose size is a few (physical) pixels. All pixels that make up a superpixel have the same graylevel value, namely the average of the pixels in the same region in the original image. Within a ring, all superpixels have the same size. Their size doubles only when one moves from one ring to another. Furthermore, each ring contains the same number of layers of superpixels. (Figure 7 shows a 512 x 512 image (1:4 scale), fixation on the left eye.). A second dimensionality reduction is then achieved by applying a standard compression technique (DCT) to the image (Figure 8 shows the reduced image obtained by mapping each superpixel to a single physical

Figure 7. Example of a face representation with fixation positioned on the left eye.

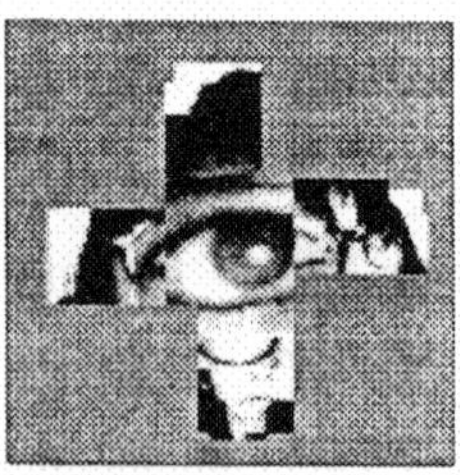

Figure 8. Reduced image obtained by mapping superpixels to a single physical pixel.

pixel).

HMMs have been used recently to model faces (Nefian & Hayes, 1999; Samaria & Young, 1994). However, those implementations did not make use of foveated vision. Instead, the observations for each image were produced by first dividing the image into horizontal (overlapping) stripes, and then computing the DCT coefficients in each stripe. The images used were already small (about 100 x 100 pixels), 25 times smaller than our images. Any attempt to run the HMM algorithms using observations coming from 512 x 512 images would be futile. In order to compare our method with Samaria's we had to reduce the size of our images through subsampling (vs foveation) in order to achieve constant resolution.

In this study ten regions of each face were foveated (three fixations in each region), and we varied the number of states in the HMMs from 3 to 10, comparing foveated vision and subsampling. Interestingly, peak performance for foveated vision was observed at about 6-7 states, rather than 10, as expected based on the number of regions used (see Figure 9). Since the fixation points are spread rather uniformly in the ten regions across the image, it is unlikely that the states arose due to clustering, and it is very intriguing why the HMM algorithms, purely mathematical in nature, came up with an optimum of 6-7 states. This may suggest that the states of the recognition process do not correspond to regions in the image. It is also interesting to note that the optimal number of states for subsampling is different (and higher) than the optimal number of states for the HMMs built through foveation

Although our purpose was not necessarily to produce a better recognizer, but rather to determine if the HMM framework using foveated vision could produce at least reasonable results, it is interesting that we achieved higher accuracy using foveation than with subsampling (see Figure 9). In addition, the sequential decision-making framework represented by the HMM approach has other advantages. For example, it provides a method that allows incremental learning of new classes. That is, new faces can be added to the database without recomputing the representations of all other learned faces. We are encouraged that performance benefits may be derived from incorporating foveal vision and sequential information acquisition into an artificial face learning and recognition system.

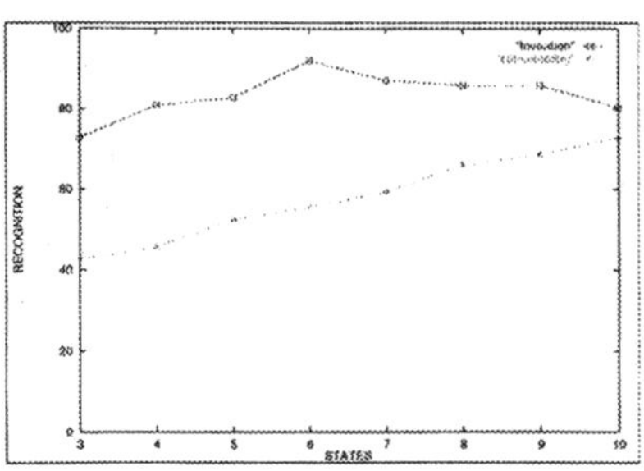

Figure 9. Recognition performance with foveation versus subsampling.

The MDP Approach to Gaze Control for Face Perception. The MDP approach to sequential decision making provides an appealing framework within which to study human gaze control for face perception. First, these models provide a formalism that can be used to generate specific hypotheses about the decision processes supporting gaze control. Second, these models can be formulated at the appropriate temporal and spatial grain size, with an action conceptualized as a "macro" that specifies the goal of the saccadic system in a hierarchical control structure. Conceptualizing gaze control at this grain size is consistent with current cortical control models (Pierrot-Deseilligny et al., 1995), and makes the decision process far more tractable (Precup et al., 1997). In addition, recent work on foveated vision and gaze control in machine vision and robotics suggests that the MDP approach may provide new insights into decision-making for fixation placement and the manner in which gaze control is learned and optimized to support new perceptual tasks (Bandera et al., 1996; Darrell, 1995; Rimey & Brown, 1991).

Although there has been some work on the applicability of Markov models to human scan patterns, this work has predominantly been descriptive and motivated by a theory of perceptual memory (the scan path theory, Noton & Stark, 1971) that has not been strongly supported by the behavioral data (Groner et al., 1984; Stark & Ellis, 1981). Furthermore, little work has specifically attempted to integrate Markov analyses of gaze control with face learning and recognition (though see Althoff & Cohen, 1999). Finally, prior work applying Markov models to human gaze control has focused on the sequence of fixation placement. Another important aspect of gaze control is the duration of each fixation. Fixation durations in scene viewing have a mean of about 300 ms, but there is considerable variability around this mean (Henderson & Hollingworth, 1998). A substantial proportion of this variability is accounted for by the fact that an important function of gaze control is to gain information about the world, as suggested by the findings that fixation durations are shorter for semantically constrained objects (Friedman, 1979; Henderson et al., 1999; Loftus & Mackworth, 1978) and objects that have been fixated previously (Friedman, 1979).

Human eye movements are examples of actions whose primary purpose is to gain information, not to change the state of the world. Information gathering actions can be contrasted with most motor actions, which have the purpose of affecting the world in some way. Information-gathering actions naturally arise in partially observable environments, where the agent does not have complete knowledge of the underlying state. POMDPs are an approach to extending the MDP model to modeling incomplete perceptions, as well as to treat naturally actions that change the state as well as collect information (Kaelbling et al., 1998). Here, in addition to states and actions, there is a finite set of observations O (much smaller than the set of states), where an individual observation may be a stochastic function of the underlying state. POMDPs can be viewed as MDPs over a much larger set of belief states, which are a vector of estimates of the probability that the agent is in each of the underlying real states. Given a belief state, the agent can update the belief state on the basis of new observations and actions in a purely local manner. However, finding optimal policies (sequences of decisions leading to the desired outcome) in a known POMDP model is intractable, even for problems with as few as 30 states (Littman, 1996). The ultimate goal of our work is to determine how humans are able to solve POMDPs in restricted situations, such as face recognition, by exploiting particular properties of the image (e.g., faces are symmetrical, and the main features of a face remain invariant over age or ethnicity). We assume that careful investigations of human gaze control will provide insights into how artificial gaze control systems can meet these same challenges. These insights will not only lead to a better theoretical understanding of gaze control in humans and machines, but also result in practical algorithms for robots.

CONCLUSION

The ability to control the direction of gaze in order to properly orient the fovea to important regions of the external world is important for all mammals, including humans. This ability is especially critical in the case of face perception, where the need to quickly determine the identity, kinship, intention, and emotional state of another is central to all social interaction and presumably, to survival. In human vision, evidence suggests that the ability to learn and recognize faces uses dedicated neural and cognitive systems that have evolved to support it. In machine vision, face perception is an important test-bed for computational theories of vision, is necessary for constructing robotic systems that can interact socially with humans, and has important practical applications in the construction of computer security systems that operate via person identification. The promise of foveated vision systems with appropriate gaze control for artificial vision is in its infancy, but holds great promise.

Our current work is designed to extend our study of gaze control during face learning and recognition. We are particularly interested in finding answers to these questions: How are potential fixation targets selected by human observers? What stimulus and cognitive factors determine which specific target is fixated next, and how do these factors interact? Is the specific ordinal sequence of fixations important, and if so, what advantages are conferred by choosing one sequence of fixation sites over another? We are addressing these questions by using converging methods from behavioral studies of human gaze control and MDP studies using computational modeling and implementation of artificial gaze control.

ACKNOWLEDGMENTS

The research summarized in this chapter was conducted by the Michigan State University Sequential Decision Making in Animals and Machines (SIGMA) Laboratory, and was supported by the Knowledge and Distributed Intelligence Program of the National Science

Foundation (ECS-9873531). We would like to thank the other members of the SIGMA Lab for their invaluable suggestions and insights. We also thank Tim Shipley and Shaun Vecera for commenting on an earlier version of this chapter. Further information about the project can be found at www.cogsci.msu.edu/sigma/.

REFERENCES

Altoff, R. R., & Cohen, N. J. (1999), Eye-movement-based memory effect: A reprocessing effect in face perception. *Journal of Experimental Psychology: Learning, Memory, and Cognition 25:* 997-1010.

Anstis, S. M. (1974). A chart demonstrating variations in acuity with retinal position. *Vision Research, 14*, 589-592.

Ballard, D. H. (1996). In K. Akins (Ed.). *Perception: Vancouver Studies in Cognitive Science.* (111-131). Oxford: Oxford Univ. Press.

Ballard, D. H., Hayhoe, M. M. Pook, P. K., & Rao, R. P. N. (1997). Diectic codes for the embodiment of cognition. *Behavioral and Brain Sciences, 20*, 723-767.

Bandera, C., Vico, F., Bravo, J., Harmon, M., & Baird, L. (1996). Residual Q-learning Applied to Visual Attention, *Proceedings of the 13th International Conference on Machine Learning*, July 3rd-6th, Bari, Italy, 20-27.

Bellman, R. (1957). *Dyamic Programming*, Princeton University Press.

Brooks, R. A. et al. (1998). Alternative Essences for Artificial Intelligence, *Proceedings of the AAAI Conference*, Madison, Wisconsin.

Bruce, V. (1988). *Recognizing faces*. Hove, England: Erlbaum.

Buswell, G. T. (1935). *How people look at pictures*. Chicago: University of Chicago Press.

Carpenter RHS. (1988). *Movements of the Eyes.* London: Pion.

Crane, H. D. (1994). The Purkinje image eyetracker, image stabilization, and related forms of stimulus manipulation. In D. H. Kelley (Ed.), *Visual science and engineering: Models and applications* (pp. 15-89). New York: Macel Dekker.

Crane, H. D., & Steele, C. M. (1985). Generation-V dual-Purkinje-image eyetracker. *Applied Optics, 24*, 527-537.Desimone, R. (1991). Face-selective cells in the temporal cortex of monkeys. *Journal of Cognitive Neuroscience, 3*, 1-8.

Darrell, T. (1995). Reinforcement Learning of Active Recognition Behaviors. *Advances in Neural Information Processing Systems, 8, pp. 858-864.*

Desimone, R. (1991). Face-selective cells in the temporal cortex of monkeys. *Journal of Cognitive Neuroscience, 3*, 1-8.

Diamond, R., & Carey, S. (1986). Why faces are and are not special: An effect of expertise. *Journal of Experimental Psychology: General, 115*, 107-117.

Falk, R. J., Henderson, J. M., Hollingworth, A., Mahadevan, S., & Dyer, F. C. (2000,

August). Eye movements in human face learning and recognition. In L. R. Gleitman and A. K. Joshi (Eds.), *Proceedings of the Twenty-Second Annual Conference of the Cognitive Science Society*. Mahwah, NJ: Lawrence Erlbaum Associates.

Farah, M.J., Tanaka, J.W., & Drain, H.M. (1995). What causes the face inversion effect? *Journal of Experimental Psychology: Human Perception and Performance, 21,* 628-634.

Friedman, A. (1979). Framing pictures: The role of knowledge in automatized encoding and memory for gist. *Journal of Experimental Psychology: General, 108*, 316-355.

Gauthier, I., Anderson, A. W., Tarr, M. J., Skudlarski, P., & Gore, J. C. (1997). Levels of categorization in visual object studied with functional MRI. *Current Biology, 7*, 645-651.

Groner, R., Walder, F., & Groner, M. (1984). Looking at faces: Local and global aspects of scanpaths. In A. G. Gale & F. Johnson (Eds.), *Theoretical and applied aspects of eye movement research.* North Holland: Elsevier Science Publishers.

Henderson, J. M. (1996). Visual attention and the attention-action interface. In K. Aikens (Ed.), *Perception: Vancouver Studies in Cognitive Science (Vol V.).* Oxford: Oxford University Press.

Henderson, J. M., & Hollingworth, A. (1998). Eye movements during scene viewing: an overview. In G. W. Underwood (Ed.), *Eye guidance while reading and while watching dynamic scenes* (269-295). Amsterdam: Elsevier.

Henderson, J. M., & Hollingworth, A. (1999). High-level scene perception. *Annual Review of Psychology, 50*, 243-271.

Henderson, J. M., Weeks, P. A., Jr., & Hollingworth, A. (1999). Eye movements during scene viewing: Effects of semantic consistency. *Journal of Experimental Psychology: Human Perception and Performance, 25*, 210-228.

Howard (1960), *Dynamic Programming and Markov Processes.* Cambridge, MA: MIT Press.

Ishai, A., Ungerleider, L. G., Martin, A., Maisog, J. M., & Haxby, J. V. (1997). FMRI reveals differential activation in the ventral object vision pathway during the perception of faces, houses, and chairs. *NeuroImage, 5*, S149.

Johnson, M. H., Dziurawiec, C., Bartrip, J., & Morton, J. (1991). Newborns' preferential tracking of faces and its subsequent decline. *Cognition, 40*, 1-19.

Kaelbling, L., Littman, M., & Cassandra, T. (1998). Planning and Acting in Partially Observable Stochastic Domains, *Artificial Intelligence*.

Kanwisher, N., McDermott, J., & Chu, M. M. (1997). The fusiform face area: A module in human extrastriate cortex specialized for face perception. *Journal of Neuroscience, 17*, 4302-4311.

Kuniyoshi et al. (1995). A foveated wide angle lens for active vision, *IEEE International Conference on Robotics and Automation*, Japan, pp. 2982-2985.

Liu, A. (1998). What the driver's eye tells the car's brain. In G.J. Underwood, Ed., *Eye*

Guidance in Reading and Scene Perception, Oxford: Elsevier, pp. 431-452.

Littman, M. (1996). *Algorithms for Sequential Decision Making*, Ph.D. dissertation, Brown University, Department of Computer Science, Providence, RI, March.

Loftus, G. R., Mackworth, N. H. (1978). Cognitive determinants of fixation location during picture viewing. *Journal of Experimental Psychology: Human Perception and Performance, 4,* 565-572.

Mahadevan, S. and Connell, J. (1992). Automatic Programming of Behavior-based Robots using Reinforcement Learning, *Artificial Intelligence.*

Matin, E. (1974). Saccadic suppression: A review and an analysis. *Psychological Bulletin, 81,* 899-917.

McCarthy, G., Puce, A., Gore, J., & Allison, T. (1997). Face-specific processing in the fusiform gyrus. *Journal of Cognitive Neuroscience, 9*, 605-610.

Milner, A., & Goodale, M. (1995). The visual brain in action. Oxford: Oxford University Press.

Minut, S., Mahadevan, S., Henderson, J. M., & Dyer, F. C. (2000). Face recognition using foveal vision. In. S-W. Lee, H. H. Bulthoff, & T. Poggio (Eds.), *Biologically motivated computer vision.* Berlin: Springer-Verlag.

Mitchell, T. (1997). *Machine Learning.* McGraw-Hill.

Moghaddam, B. et al. (1998). Beyond Eigenfaces: Probabilistic Matching for Face Recognition, *International Conference on Automatic Face and Gesture Recognition.*

Moscovitch, M., Winocur, G., & Behrmann, M. (1997). What is special in face recognition. Nineteen experiments on a person with visual object agnosia and dyslexia but normal face recognition. *Journal of Cognitive Neuroscience, 9*, 555-604.

Nefien, A., and Hayes, M. 1999. Face recognition using an embedded HMM. *IEEE Conference on Audio and Video-based Biometric Person Authentication.* Washington, D.C. 1999.

Newcome, F., Mehta, Z., & de Haan, E. H. F. (1994). Category specificity in visual recognition. In M. J. Farah & G. Ratcliff (Eds.), *The neuropsychology of high-level vision* (pp. 103-132). Hillsdale, NJ: Erlbaum.

Noton, D., & Stark, L. (1971). Scanpaths in eye movements during pattern perception. *Science, 171*, 308-311.

Pentland, A. et al. (1994). View-based and Modular Eigenfaces for Face Recognition, *IEEE Conference on Computer Vision and Pattern Recognition.*

Pierrot-Deseilligny, C., Rivaud, S., Gaymard, B., Muri, R., & Vermersch, A. (1995). Cortical control of saccades. *Neurological Reports, 37*, 557-567.

Precup, D., Sutton, R., & Singh, S. (1997). Planning with closed-loop macro actions, *Working Notes of the AAAI Fall Symposium on Model-Directed Autonomous Systems.*

Puterman, M. (1994). *Markov Decision Processes: Discrete Stochastic Dynamic Programming*, Wiley.

Rabiner, Lawrence R. (1989) *A Tutorial on Hidden Markov Models and Selected Applications in Speech Recognition.*

Rayner, K. (1998). Eye movements in reading, visual search and scene perception: 20 years of research. *Psychological Bulletin, 124,* 372-422.

Riggs, L. A. (1965). Eye movements. In C. H. Graham (Ed). *Vision and Visual Perception* (pp. 321-349). New York: Wiley.

Rimey, R. D., & Brown, C. M. (1991). Controlling eye movements with hidden Markov models. *International Journal of Computer Vision, November,* 47-65.

Samaria, F., & Young, S. (1994), HMM based architecture for face identification. *Image and Computer Vision 12*

Stark, L., & Ellis, S. R. (1981). Scanpaths revisited: Cognitive models direct active looking.

Tanaka, J. W., & Farah, M.J. (1993). Parts and whole relationships in face recognition. *Quarterly Journal of Experimental Psychology, 46A*, 225-245.

Van der Spiegel, J. et al. (1989). A Foveated Retina-like Sensor using CCD Technology. In Mead, C. and Ismail, M. Analog VLSI Implementations of Neural Systems, Kluwer Academic Publishers, pp. 189-212.

Volkmann, F. C. (1986). Human visual suppression. *Vision. Research, 26*, 1401-1416.

Walker-Smith, G.J., Gale, A.G., & Findlay, J.M. (1977). Eye movement strategies in face perception. *Perception, 6*, 313-326.

Yarbus, A. L. (1967). *Eye movements and vision.* New York: Plenum Press.

Yin, R. K. (1969). Looking at upside-down faces. *Journal of Experimental Psychology, 81*, 141-145.

From Fragments to Objects – Segmentation and Grouping in Vision
T.F. Shipley and P.J. Kellman (Editors)

15

THE VISUAL INTERPRETATION OF OBJECT AND HUMAN MOVEMENT

Maggie Shiffrar, Department of Psychology, Rutgers University, Newark NJ 07102 USA

ABSTRACT

The visual interpretation of object motion requires the integration of motion information within the same object and segmentation of motion signals across different objects. How does the visual system balance these two requirements simultaneously? A series of experiments using a variety of methodologies suggests two answers to this question. Firstly, simple form cues direct the integration and segmentation of motion signals during the analysis of object motion. This suggests that motion perception is not a modular process. Secondly, motion analyses may differ significantly across different object categories. Behavioral, neurophysiological, and imaging studies suggest that the visual perception of human movement may benefit from a convergence of motor and visual processes in a manner that differs from other types of motion perception. Thus, interpretation of an object's motion depends upon local form cues and object category.

INTRODUCTION

While sipping a cup of tea at an outdoor café, I scan my environment. In doing so, I observe trees gently bending with the wind, my rotating tea cup, cars zipping down the street, and people rushing by. In order to make sense of these different motions, my visual system must simultaneously perform two apparently conflicting tasks. On one hand, my visual system must separate motion signals belonging to different objects. It would be an error for me to confuse the motion of a car with the motion of a pedestrian. On the other hand, my visual system must also combine motion signals belonging to the same object. While a pedestrian's swinging arms usually move in opposing directions, their motion signals must be combined before I can visually understand the movements of an entire person. These simultaneous processes of integration and segmentation are what allow us to interpret the motion of objects in our world.

The goal of this chapter is two-fold. Firstly, we will investigate the cues that the visual system uses to direct and balance the integration and segmentation processes. Secondly, we will examine whether these cues and processes are used in all visual motion analyses or whether different analyses are preferred for different object categories.

The Aperture Problem

As it is often best to start at the beginning, let's first consider why the accurate integration and segmentation of motion information poses a challenge to the visual system. Initial motion measurements are made by neurons having several important characteristics (e.g., Hubel & Wiesel, 1968; Movshon, Thompson, & Tolhurst, 1978). Firstly, neurons in the early stages of the visual system have relatively small receptive fields and as such can only respond to changes within very small regions of an observer's field of view. As a result, in order to interpret the motion of a real object, motion information must be combined across much larger regions of retinal space. Secondly, early motion sensitive neurons are conjointly sensitive to direction and orientation. This combined sensitivity means that different combinations of object orientation and direction can give rise to the same neuronal response. In other words, directionally sensitive neurons with small receptive fields will sometimes give the same response to very different motions. Thus, the activity of any particular neuron provides only ambiguous motion information.

This ambiguity, illustrated in Figure 1 (A and B), is commonly referred to as the aperture problem. The aperture problem can arise whenever the motion of a smooth luminance edge must be estimated from the activity of a receptor having a small receptive field. To understand this problem from a spatial perspective, first consider that the motion of any line can be decomposed into the portion that is parallel to the line and the portion that is perpendicular to the line. Because a neuron can not track or "see" the ends of the line if those ends fall outside of its receptive field, the neuron can not measure any of the motion that is parallel to the line's orientation (that is, along the length of the line). As a result, a neuron can only detect the perpendicular component of the line's motion. Because only this perpendicular component of motion can be measured, all motions having the same perpendicular motion will appear to be identical even if these motions differ significantly in

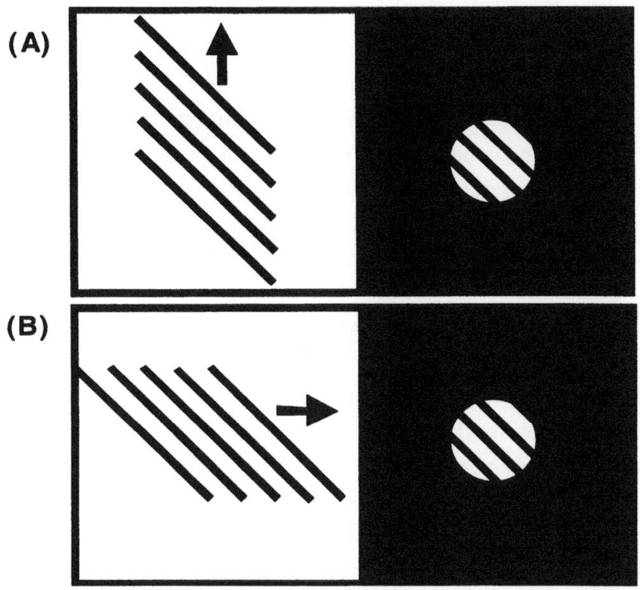

Figure 1. The aperture problem. (A) On the left, a diagonal line translates upward. Each line segment shows the position of a single translating line at a different time. On the right, the vertically translating line is viewed through a small window or aperture. Such apertures can be used to represent the receptive field of a neuron. (B) On the left, a diagonal line translates rightward. Again, each line segment illustrates the position of the translating line at a different time. On the right, the rightwardly translating line is viewed through an aperture. Notice that the upward (A) and rightward (B) motions appear to be identical when they are viewed through an aperture that hides the end points of the line.

their parallel component. Thus, a neuron will give the same response to many different motions. Because all known visual systems, whether biological or computational, have neurons with receptive fields that are limited in size, this measurement ambiguity has been extensively studied (e.g., Hildreth, 1984; Wallach, 1935).

How can observers interpret object motion when early motion measures are inherently ambiguous? While the interpretation of a single translating line is ambiguous, the possible interpretations of its motion are limited to a large family of related motions. All of the members of this family differ only in the component of translation that is parallel to the line's orientation. Members of two hypothetical families are illustrated by the groups of three arrows in Figure 2. Each of the three arrows depicts one possible motion. Arrow orientation indicates the line's potential direction of translation while the arrow length indicates the corresponding speed of translation. Notice that the arrows all line up along a dashed line. This dashed line, known as the constraint line, depicts the entire family of motions that is consistent with the motion measured from a single translating line or grating. The visual system can solve the aperture problem by taking advantage of this regularity in possible motions. To do so, individually ambiguous motion estimates from two differently oriented lines must be combined. As long as two differently oriented lines are rigidly connected to each other, and therefore actually moving in the same direction, their corresponding constraint lines will intersect at a single point. This point, known as the intersection of constraints or IOC, defines the only possible motion interpretation that is shared by the two rigidly connected translating lines. Thus, when the visual system is correct in assuming that two lines are rigidly connected to each other, then the motion of an object defined by those lines can be uniquely interpreted.

Experimental support for this IOC approach comes from studies examining the visual perception of and neural response to spatially overlapping edges and gratings. In their influential behavioral experiments, Adelson and Movshon (1982) asked subjects to report whether superimposed sinusoidal gratings (illustrated on the right hand side of Figure 2) appeared to move as a coherent whole. When the luminance contrast and the spatial frequency of the two gratings were similar, subjects perceived a single translating plaid pattern. The perceived direction of translation was the same as the IOC solution for the two gratings, as shown in Figure 2. On the other hand, when the two gratings differed significantly in their spatial frequency or contrast, subjects reported the perception of two independently translating gratings that slid over one another. These results suggest that when overlapping stimuli are structurally similar, the visual system assumes that they belong to the same object, and as a result, combines their component motions according to the IOC solution (Adelson & Movshon, 1982).

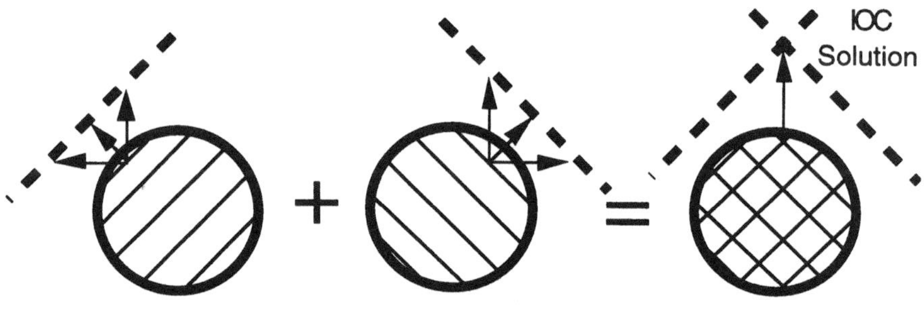

Figure 2. The Intersection of Constraints solution to the aperture problem. Because of the aperture problem, the true motion of a line or grating viewed within an aperture could be any one of an infinitely large family of different motions defined by its constraint line (shown here as a dashed line). The visual system can overcome this ambiguity by considering the motion measurements from two or more differently oriented lines. That is, while the measured motion of a single translating line is consistent with infinitely many interpretations, measurements of differently oriented lines can be combined to uniquely interpret the line motion. This unique solution is defined by the point of intersection of two different constraint lines (shown on the right) and is known as the intersection of constraints or IOC solution.

Neurophysiological evidence suggests that at least some MT neurons may perform an IOC analysis. In collecting this evidence, Movshon and his colleagues began by determining how the responses of MT neurons were tuned to the direction of translating sinusoidal gratings (Movshon et al., 1985). They then examined how these responses to one-dimensional gratings could be used to predict responsiveness to two-dimensional plaid patterns formed by superimposing two one-dimensional gratings (Figure 2). One class of neurons only responded to the directions of the individual gratings. A second class of neurons, making up approximately 25% of MT neurons, responded maximally to the direction of motion predicted by the intersection of constraints solution. These findings suggest that MT neurons may solve the aperture problem with an IOC approach (for discussion, see Grzywacz & Yuille, 1991 and Shiffrar, 2000).

The above discussion provides just one example of how the visual system might solve the aperture problem for superimposed gratings presented within a single receptive field or region of visual space. Two important aspects of the visual interpretation of object motion remain to be addressed. Firstly, the projected images of physical objects can be much larger than the receptive fields of V1 neurons. Thus, to interpret object motion, the visual system must integrate motion signals across disconnected spatial locations. Secondly, real world visual scenes contain objects that have many different features. Such features can produce motion signals of differing degrees of ambiguity. For example, while the motion of a smooth edge is ambiguous, the motion of an edge with an orientation discontinuity, such as a corner or line ending, can be measured with greater certainty because there is no ambiguity in the motion of a unique point. The following sections address these two key issues in turn.

MOTION INTEGRATION ACROSS SPACE

How does the visual system link motion signals across differently oriented edges? Previous theories assumed that overlapping, plaid patterns would be analyzed and perceived in the same way as spatially separated contours (e.g., Adelson & Movshon, 1982; Burt & Sperling, 1981). However, subsequent behavioral tests have not supported this hypothesis. When subjects view differently oriented edges through disconnected windows or apertures, they experience systematic difficulties in their ability to link motion signals across the disconnected edges (Shiffrar & Pavel, 1991; Lorenceau & Shiffrar, 1992). For example, when viewing a simple, rigidly rotating polygon through a set of apertures, subjects can not combine motion measurements accurately across the polygon's edges (Shiffrar & Pavel, 1991). Instead, subjects perceive non-rigid movement. Even when subjects know that they are viewing a square rigidly rotating behind four stationary apertures, subjects still perceive either disconnected rotating line segments or a pulsating elastic figure (Additional discussion of this phenomenon can be found in Nicola Bruno's chapter in this volume). Thus, although theories of motion perception are based on the assumption that the visual system overcomes the ambiguity of individual motion measurements by combining those measurements, observers are often unable to perform this crucial task. Moreover, this finding also has important implications for another classic theory of unit formation. The object rigidity constraint proposes that the visual system overcomes the ambiguity of motion measurements by selecting image interpretations that are consistent with rigid objects (Ullman, 1979). The rotating polygon displays used in this study were always consistent with the interpretation of a rigid object. However, observers interpreted these displays as non-rigid.

What is the cause of subjects' inability to integrate velocity estimates across the different sides of a rotating object? In classic motion integration studies (e.g., Adelson & Movshon, 1982), edges undergo translation rather than rotation (Shiffrar & Pavel, 1991). Therefore, to insure that the differences in motion integration within and across spatial locations suggested by the above study did not result from differences in the type of motion used, motion integration across translating edges was examined (Lorenceau & Shiffrar, 1992). To that end, subjects in another series of experiments viewed a diamond figure rigidly translating behind a set of spatially separated apertures, as shown in Figure 3A. In a two-alternative forced choice procedure, subjects performed a direction discrimination task constructed so that the diamond's direction of translation could only be determined from an integration of the motion measurements across the diamond's visible edges. When the translating diamond was centrally presented at high luminance contrast, subjects performed at

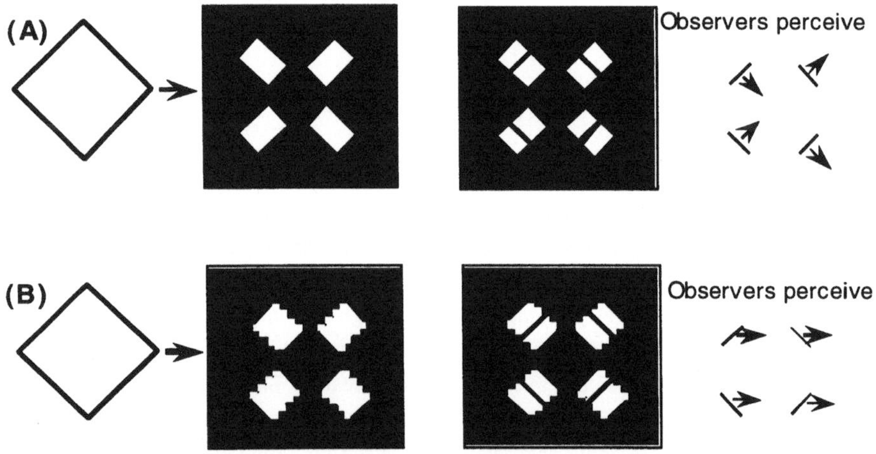

Figure 3. (A) A diamond translates rightward behind four rectangular windows. The four visible line segments appear to move in different directions. (B) However, if the shape of the window edges is changed so that positional noise is added to the visible line endings, the same four edges now appear to translate coherently as a unitary diamond shape.

chance levels in the direction discrimination task. That is, even though subjects knew they were viewing a translating diamond, they could not link motion signals across the diamond's sides and determine its direction of motion. Instead, under these conditions, the visual system interpreted the display as four independently translating object fragments.

When considered together, the results of the above studies clearly suggest that the integration of motion signals within the same visual areas differs from the integration of motion signals across disconnected spatial locations. How does the visual system integrate motion information across different spatial locations? Remember that outside of the laboratory, visual scenes usually contain multiple objects. To identify moving objects in natural scenes, the visual system must integrate motion measurements originating from the same object while segmenting motion measurements arising from different objects. Because the ends of lines (or terminators) and the ends of surfaces (or corners) are simple form cues that signal object boundaries, such discontinuities may determine when motion measurements are linked across edges. This hypothesis was tested in a series of studies.

If contour discontinuities determine whether motion integration or segmentation occurs, then manipulations of discontinuity visibility should significantly alter the visual interpretation of dynamic images. In the previously described translating diamond display, the four stationary apertures were positioned so that only one segment of each of the diamond's four sides could be viewed. The apertures were rectangular so that the visible length of each segment remained constant as the diamond moved. This created eight (two per segment) high contrast terminators that smoothly translated back and forth along the obliquely oriented aperture sides. The visibility of these terminators was manipulated in three different ways (Lorenceau & Shiffrar, 1992). In the first experiment, the luminance contrast of each visible segment's terminators (relative to the background) was varied independent of the luminance of the central, homogeneous portion of the same segments. Again, subjects performed the same direction discrimination task while the luminance contrast of the visible terminators varied across blocks of trials. Performance was significantly influenced by terminator contrast. When terminator visibility was low, because terminators were presented at low luminance contrast, performance was high suggesting that motion integration across space was facilitated. However, as terminator contrast increased and terminators became more visible, performance dropped. Since accurate performance requires motion integration, this performance decrease suggests that motion segmentation increased with terminator visibility. This pattern of results strongly suggests that terminator visibility determines whether motion information is integrated or segmented; that is, whether the visual system interprets displays as objects or fragments.

The results of two additional studies further support this conclusion. Image visibility can also be manipulated with positional noise. To determine whether terminator visibility, per se, controls motion integration, varying amounts of positional noise were added to the translating, high contrast diamond display shown in figure 3A. In the first translating diamond display, four rectangular apertures were used. In this experiment, a variable amplitude sine wave was simply added to each aperture edge, as indicated in Figure 3B. With this simple modification, positional jitter was added to each terminator such that the terminators appeared to follow irregular paths instead of the smooth, linear path used in the previous studies. Will the addition of this positional jitter decrease the ability of terminators to force motion segmentation? Yes. As positional jitter increased, performance in the same direction discrimination task also increased (Lorenceau & Shiffrar, 1992). Thus, decreased terminator visibility, per se, facilitates motion integration across space.

Finally, it is important to recall that image visibility naturally varies across retinal space. When the location of a constant size display is shifted towards an observer's visual periphery, positional uncertainty increases (Burbeck & Yap, 1990). As a result, the visibility of a contour terminator should decrease with increasing retinal eccentricity. If so, then the likelihood of motion integration should increase with increasing display eccentricity. To test this hypothesis, the same translating diamond display was peripherially presented to subjects. Under these peripherial conditions, ceiling levels of performance, and thus, motion integration across space, were found. Thus, the balance between motion integration and motion segmentation depends upon those factors that determine terminator visibility.

When considered together, these results have important implications for our understanding of and scientific approach to the interpretation of object motion. In the past, the domain of visual science has avoided the study of dynamic image discontinuities because such discontinuities are inherently non-linear. As such, they may be costly to compute under noisy conditions. For example, it can be difficult to solve the correspondence problem for a dynamic feature presented within noise or at low luminance contrast because the number of potential false correspondences increases with increasing noise and decreasing contrast. However, the results of the above studies clearly suggest that these discontinuities can control the motion integration and segmentation processes. Thus, whether the visual system selects a wholistic, object based interpretation or a segmented, fragment based interpretation of a visual scene depends upon low level form cues.

Underlying Integration Mechanism

Classic physiological models of the visual interpretation of object motion are based on a two stage process. In the first stage, directionally selective simple cells in the primary visual cortex (area V1) measure the motion of translating luminance edges. In the second stage, these local velocity estimates are combined (Movshon et al., 1985). The results of the previously discussed behavioral studies suggest that contour discontinuities, such as line endings and corners, may determine when local velocity estimates are combined. If so, by what visual mechanism do discontinuities direct motion integration? To address this question, a series of experiments measuring the perceived direction of translating line segments was conducted (Lorenceau, Shiffrar, Wells, & Castet, 1993). The perceived direction of translating oblique lines was measured across variations of line length, luminance contrast, and display duration. This resulted in the identification of systematic errors in the perceived direction of translation. The pattern of errors suggested a model of motion perception involving two distinct classes of receptors. One class of receptors appears to measure the velocity of straight edges while the second class measures the velocity of edge terminators. Electrophysiological evidence supports the existence of these two general classes of receptors. That is, end stopped cells might be suited for the measurement of moving line endings or terminators while directionally selective simple cells could process edge motion (e.g., Hubel & Wiesel, 1968; Orban, Kato, & Bishop, 1979).

If there are indeed two classes of receptors, how might they interact? To address this question another series of studies was undertaken to characterize the competition between different receptor types (Castet et al., 1993). Psychophysical measures of the perceived speed of translating line segments were made under a variety of spatial and temporal conditions. The results suggest that a simple averaging process, weighted according to the perceptual spaliency of the two feature types, could be used to model motion integration along continuous contours.

Across spatially discontinuous contours, the motion integration process remains competitive. To determine how observers interpret more realistic, multi-featured dynamic images, subjects were asked to judge the perceived coherence of images containing an ambiguously translating grating and an unambiguously translating random dot pattern (Shiffrar, Li, & Lorenceau, 1995). The results of these studies suggest that the visual system takes into account the degree of uncertainty associated with each motion measurement. Less ambiguous velocity estimates dominate the interpretation of more ambiguous estimates, even across significant spatial separations.

While discontinuities may control motion integration, an unrestricted reliance on such motion signals would result in image segmentation errors. This might occur, for example, if a discontinuity from one object completely determined how the motion of a different object was interpreted. One way in which the visual system appears to limit this problem is by facilitating the integration of motion signals across collinear edges (Barchilon Ben-Av & Shiffrar, 1995) and corners. For example, as predicted by Kellman and Shipley (1991), motion integration across a pair of edges is facilitated when those edges form a corner as compared to a T-junction even though the orientations of the edges are the same in both cases (Shiffrar, Pavel, & Lorenceau, 1995). Such structural biases in motion integration may assist the visual system in successfully juggling the need for integration within but segmentation across objects.

Subcortical Grouping Mechanisms?

Margaret Livingstone and David Hubel proposed that the magnocellular pathway of the geniculostriate system is responsible for "deciding which visual elements, such as edges and discontinuities, belong to and define individual objects in the scene" (Livingstone & Hubel, 1988). In other words, these researchers predicted that the information gathered by subcortical mechanisms controls whether the visual system interprets images as unrelated fragments or coherent objects. Because neurons in the magnocellular pathway vigorously respond to luminance differences but not to color differences (according to Livingstone & Hubel, 1988), this system should be inactive when objects are defined only by color differences. Therefore, one can manipulate the relative activity of the magnocellular system, and hence its ability to perform its predicted linking function, through manipulations of the brightness or luminance of a color display. Using this logic, the "magno-linking" hypothesis was tested (Shiffrar & Lorenceau, 1996). The translating polygon stimulus, described reviously, was presented to subjects at isoluminance and at increasing levels of luminance contrast.

According to Livingstone and Hubel's magno-linking hypothesis, performance in the direction discrimination task should increase as luminance contrast increases. The results of a series of experiments follow the opposite pattern. That is, subjects' performance, and hence motion linking, increased with decreasing luminance contrast. Because observers were better able to link motion signals across the disconnected edges of a translating diamond near isoluminance than at higher luminance contrasts, these results do not support the magno-linking hypothesis. Instead, we hypothesized that terminator visibility determined motion linking. At low luminance contrasts, the localization of contour terminators would be difficult. If terminators can not be readily identified, then they can not cause image segmentation and as a result, motion integration dominates. To test whether motion integration is enhanced whenever terminators are difficult to localize, we manipulated stimulus duration and edge width with these same variable contrast diamond displays. Terminator localization should be best whenever the visual system has enough time to actually find the discontinuities and whenever the terminators are large. Consistent with these predictions, direction discrimination performance was best with small contours and brief display durations. Thus, when terminators are difficult to identify, because they are small, only briefly shown, or at low luminance contrast, motion integration is facilitated and performance in this task is optimal. Thus, the motion linking process can be interpreted as a competition between unambiguous terminator velocities and ambiguous contour velocities (Lorenceau & Shiffrar, 1992).

A GENERAL PURPOSE PROCESSOR?

The previous studies indexed some of the information and mechanisms that the visual system uses to interpret the motion of simple shapes. Are the cortical mechanisms that were tapped during these studies involved in the analysis of all other visual stimuli? In other words, is the visual system best conceived of as a general-purpose machine that processes all images in the same manner? Or is the visual system designed to solve some tasks differently or better than others?

To function adaptively within our environment, individuals are obviously at an advantage when they can readily and accurately interpret moving objects such as crashing waves, swaying trees, and rolling rocks. However, all objects may not contribute equally to an organism's ability to function within its physical environment. For example, all animals must accurately interpret the movements of their prey, predators, and conspecifics. Animals who fail to rapidly perform such analyses would likely be attacked, starve, and/or interact inappropriately with relatives and mates. On the other hand, animals with inferior skills in the visual analysis of rock rolling would probably suffer less significant repercussions.

Modern urban life renders the need for catching prey and avoiding predators less relevant (unless of course you are a rat or a cockroach). However, not all humans live in cities or suburbs. The livelihood of many humans outside of these areas still depends upon their visual abilities to understand and predict the movements of their prey and predators. Moreover, while current city dwellers may not require these skills, their early ancestors certainly did. If the visual system has evolved to be maximally sensitive to those environmental factors upon which our survival depends (Shepard, 1984), then one would expect to find that human observers are particularly sensitive to the movements of animals.

There is also reason to believe that of the category of animal movements, the visual analysis of human movement may be particularly important. As social animals, all humans, whether urban or desert dwellers, must interact with other humans for physical and social support. Some researchers have proposed that visual analyses can be best understood in relation to the motor outputs they subserve (e.g., Milner & Goodale, 1995). Obviously, the visual perception of a waving friend and a wind blown shrub are normally associated with different motor responses on the part of the observer. I might wave back to a friend, but I would never wave back to a shrub. Thus, the intimate connection between human social behavior and human movement perception may render some separation between human and non-human motion analyses. If no man (or presumably woman) is an island, then the visual analysis of human movement might define our existence as social beings. If the visual analysis of human movement is so important, has our visual system evolved special mechanisms to direct the integration and segmentation of bodily movements? The following section will provide an overview of the research that addresses this question.

THE INTEGRATION OF HUMAN MOVEMENT ACROSS TIME

According to traditional neurophysiological theories, object identification is thought to occur in the ventral or "what" pathway while spatial relationships are thought to be analyzed separately in the dorsal or "where" pathway (e.g., Baizer, Ungerleider & Desimone, 1991). Numerous behavioral studies are consistent with the hypothesis that the visual system performs object recognition, that is determines what an object is, independently from spatial analyses including where or how the object moves (e.g., Burt & Sperling, 1981; Krumhansl, 1984). The perceptual phenomenon of apparent motion is frequently used to support this proposed separation of form and motion analyses. In classic demonstrations of apparent motion, two stationary dots are presented sequentially. Under appropriate spatio-temporal conditions, the two stationary dots are perceived as a single moving dot. While there are an infinite number of possible paths connecting the two dots, observers almost always perceive motion along the shortest path. Researchers have concluded that an object's identity does not influence the perception of its movement since observers perceive the shortest path of apparent motion even when that path requires a non-rigid deformation of object form (Shepard, 1984).

If the visual analysis of human movement differs from other motion analyses, then the presentation of biological forms might influence the visual perception of apparent motion. When humans move, their limbs tend to follow curved rather than straight trajectories. Will observers of human movement be more likely to perceive apparent motion paths that are consistent with the movement limitations of the human body or paths that traverse the shortest possible distance? This hypothesis has been tested with stimuli consisting of photographs of a human model in different positions created so that the biomechanically possible paths of motion conflicted with the shortest paths (Shiffrar & Freyd, 1990, 1993).

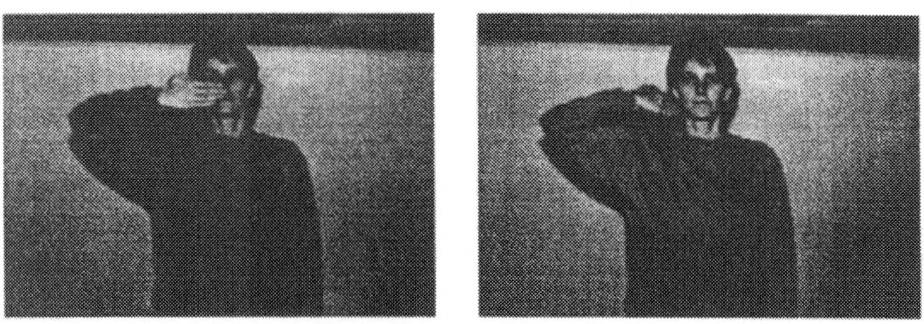

Figure 4. A sample apparent motion stimulus from Shiffrar and Freyd (1990). When these two photographs are shown sequentially, subjects perceive the hand moving through the woman's head at short SOAs. As SOA increases, subjects increasingly report the perception of the woman's hand moving around her head.

For example, one stimulus, shown in Figure 4, consisted of two photographs in which the first displayed a standing woman with her right arm positioned in front of her head while the second photograph showed this same arm positioned behind the woman's head. The shortest path connecting these two arm positions would involve the hand moving through the head while a biomechanically plausible path would entail the hand moving around the head. When naive subjects viewed such stimuli through a tachistoscope, their perceived paths of motion changed with the Stimulus Onset Asynchrony (SOA) or the amount time between the onset of one photograph and the onset of the next photograph. At short SOAs, subjects reported seeing a linear path--the shortest, physically impossible motion path. That is, under these conditions, subjects would report clearly seeing the woman's hand move through her head. However, with increasing SOAs, observers were increasingly likely to see paths that were consistent with normal human movement (Shiffrar & Freyd, 1990). In this case, subjects reported that the woman's hand move around her head.

In a second study, we found that when subjects viewed a different set of human model photographs created so that the shortest movement path was a biomechanically plausible path and longer movement paths were physically impossible (that is, the reverse of that described above), observers always reported seeing the shortest path (Shiffrar & Freyd, 1993). Thus, subjects do not simply report the perception of longer paths with longer presentation times. Instead, the perception of normal human movement, per se, becomes increasingly likely over extended temporal intervals.

Does the perception of non-human objects in apparent motion also change with temporal display rates? To answer this important question, we designed apparent motion displays consisting of pairs of photographs of inanimate control objects, such as clocks and erasers, positioned so that their locations and orientations replicated the positions and orientations of the limbs and torso of the human model used in the previously described human apparent motion studies. Thus, these objects were positioned so that the shortest paths of apparent motion required the perception of some physically impossible motion such as a stapler passing through an eraser. As before, naïve subjects viewed these picture pairs in a tachistoscope and reported their perceived paths of apparent motion across variations in SOA. When viewing these photographs of inanimate objects, subjects consistently reported perceiving the shortest possible path of apparent motion across all SOAs. That is, subjects perceived objects passing through one another at all display rates. There was no tendency for subjects to report the perception of physically possible events, such as one object moving around another object, at slower rates of picture alternation. This pattern of results suggests two conclusions. Firstly, during short temporal intervals, both objects and actions are interpreted as following the shortest path of apparent motion even when that path is physically impossible. This finding suggests that under some temporal conditions, human actions and moving objects may be similarly analyzed. On the other hand, when temporal display rates are extended, the perception of human action and moving objects differ since observers perceive physically possible human movements but physical impossible object movement. These results support the hypothesis that human movement may be analyzed by processes that differ from those underlying the analysis of object movement.

If so, then what structural aspect(s) of or cues to the human form lead to this "special" analysis? Or, asked another way, are non-human objects always excluded from these apparently specialized human movement analyses? If sensitivity to human movements extends to the perception of human movement relative to an object filled physical world, then observers might perceive paths of apparent motion that are consistent with normal human movements about inanimate objects. On the other hand, if our sensitivity to human motion reflects the activity of a system that analyses human movement in isolation, then observers might only perceive paths of apparent motion consistent with the ways in which humans move relative to themselves. These questions were addressed by a near replication of the above apparent motion experiments again involving paired photographs of a human model in different poses (Heptulla-Chatterjee, Freyd, & Shiffrar, 1996). The poses always depicted the model moving one limb about either side of some part of her body. In the experimental condition, each picture pair was modified by a replacement of the part of the body about which the limb moved with a similarly positioned, inanimate object having roughly the same size and orientation. In both experimental and control conditions, subjects simply reported the perceived path of apparent motion as the SOA was varied. Our results showed nearly identical functions relating path to SOA were found in both conditions. When combined with other results from this series of studies, these findings indicates that the tendency to see biomechanically consistent paths of apparent motion with increasing temporal duration is not limited to the movement of human limbs about the human body. Instead, our visual sensitivity to human movement appears to be general and incorporates how human bodies move with respect to inanimate objects (Heptulla-Chatterjee et al., 1996).

Is the presentation of realistic images of the human body necessary for the perception of apparent human motion? In other words, do any particular physical cues to the human body, such as skin, eyes, hair, or body shape, trigger the processes underlying the visual analysis of human movement? To answer this question, we created a new set of stimuli depicting the global structure of the human body out of a non-human material. Stimuli were created by videotaping a wooden mannequin posed in approximately the same positions as the human model in our previous work (Shiffrar & Freyd, 1990; 1993). When subjects viewed these simplified, non-biological renditions of the human form (literally, stick figures made of wood), they still reported paths of apparent motion consistent with the human body even though a human body was not actually present. However, when a pair of such simulated human limbs was presented in isolation (that is, not within the more global context of an entire human body), observers always reported the shortest path of apparent motion. Taken together, these results suggest that the hierarchy of limb position and orientation cues consistent with a complete human form may be sufficient for the apparently "specialized" human movement analyses (Heptulla-Chatterjee et al., 1996). Thus, sensitivity to human motion can be evoked by form cues that are not inherently 'animate' or 'biological' in nature.

BIOLOGICAL MOTION INTEGRATION ACROSS SPACE

The previous apparent motion studies suggest that the integration of human movement across time may differ from the temporal integration of non-human movements. If the analysis of human movement truly differs from the analysis of non-human movements, then these two analyses or mechanisms may also differ in their spatial constraints. Is the integration of human movement across space different from the spatial integration of non-human movements? This question was addressed with an adaptation of the polygon moving behind apertures display described earlier (Shiffrar & Pavel, 1991; Lorenceau & Shiffrar, 1992). In this experiment, the moving polygon was replaced with a translating car, opening and closing scissors, or a walking human. Subjects simply viewed one of these three items moving behind a set of specially constructed apertures for six seconds and reported what they observed (Shiffrar, Lichtey, and Heptulla-Chatterjee, 1996). The apertures were constructed so that only straight edges, that is, no corners or end points, were visible. The subjects verbally reported what they saw and an audiotape of their descriptions was given to a naïve scorer who categorized the subjects' descriptions as either reflecting local segmentation (independently moving line segments) or global integration (a whole object or being). If human movement is analyzed over a greater spatial extent than non-human motions, then observers should be more likely to identify human figures than inanimate objects moving behind apertures.

The results of a series of five experiments clearly indicated that when a walking human figure was viewed through apertures, subjects readily and accurately identified the walker. Recognition of the walker was orientation specific, robust across a range of stimulus durations and benefited from limb orientation cues. On the other hand, when observers viewed moving, non-human objects (the scissors or cars) through the same apertures under the same conditions, they were unable to recognize these objects. Instead, subjects described these non-human displays as sets of line segments moving incoherently. Such descriptions suggest that subjects could not group motion information across the apertures—just as with the rotating square and translating diamond displays described much earlier. The results of control studies, which manipulated aperture visibility, demonstrated that the car and scissors displays were recognizable and therefore could have been interpreted in the same global manner as the walker. Finally, recognition of the walking figure behind apertures was at or near ceiling levels of performance only when the spatial and temporal parameters of the display corresponded to realistic walking speeds (Barclay, Cutting, & Kozlowski, 1978). These results provide important behavioral data supporting the hypothesis that there may be striking differences in the integration of human and non-human motion across space.

BIOLOGICAL MOTION INTEGRATION ACROSS SPACE AND TIME

One way to interpret the above results is in terms of the temporal or spatial extents of the window within which biological motions can be grouped into a single perceptual unit. Using these apparent motion and multiple aperture displays, it appears that the visual system is capable of grouping information across either space or time during the analysis of human movement in a manner that differs from the analysis of non-human objects in motion. If the visual system is exquisitely tuned for the analysis of human movement, then one might predict that the visual analysis of human movement should be possible even when it requires simultaneous grouping over both space and time. To test this idea, a display classically associated with the visual analysis of human movement was used.

Extending a technique first devised by Etienne Jules Marey (1895/1972), Johansson created "point light walker" displays by filming human actors with small light sources attached to their major joints. By adjusting the lighting, the resultant film showed only a dozen or so moving points of light, as illustrated in Figure 5A. Nevertheless, observers of these films report a clear and compelling perception of the precise actions performed by the point light defined actors. Importantly, observers rarely recognize the human form in static displays of these films (Johansson, 1973). Subsequent research has demonstrated that our perception of the human form in such displays is rapid (Johansson, 1976), orientation specific (Bertenthal & Pinto, 1994; Pavlova & Sokolov, 2000; Sumi, 1984), tolerates random contrast variations (Ahlström, Blake, & Ahlström, 1997), and extends to the perception of complex actions (Dittrich, 1993), social dispositions (MacArthur & Baron, 1983), gender (Kozlowski

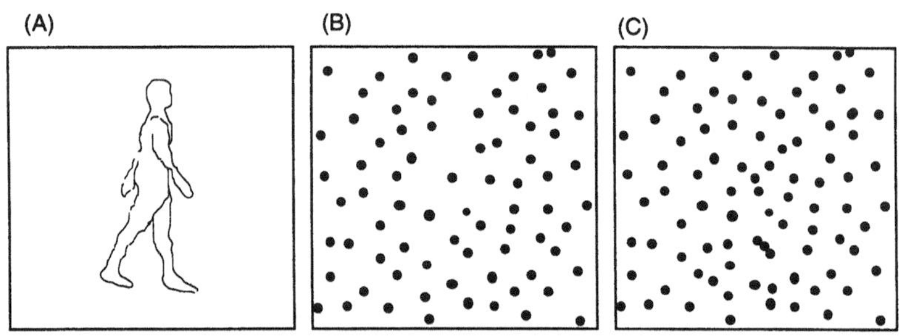

Figure 5. (A) A point light walker. The outline of the walker is not presented during experiments. (B) The walker is placed in a mask of similarly moving points. Here the walker points are shown in gray while the mask points are black. (C) In experiments, the walker and mask points have the same color and luminance. As you can see, when presented statically, the walker is not visible. However, when display C is set in motion, observers can rapidly locate the walker.

& Cutting, 1977; 1978), and sign language (Poizner, Bellugi & Lutes-Driscoll, 1981).

By manipulating two characteristics of point light walker displays, one is able to test whether human movement can be simultaneously integrated across both space and time. Masked point light walkers are commonly used to test for motion integration across space. With this manipulation, observers view displays containing a point light walker that is masked by the addition of superimposed moving point lights, as illustrated in Figure 5C. This mask can be constructed from multiple point-light walkers that are positionally scrambled so that the spatial location of each point is randomized. The size, luminance, speed, and motion trajectory of each point remains unchanged. Thus, the motion of each point in the mask is identical to the motion of one of the points defining the walker. As a result, only the spatially global configuration of the points distinguishes the walker from the mask. The fact that subjects are able to detect the presence as well as the direction of an upright point light walker "hidden" within such a scrambled walker mask implies that the mechanism underlying the perception of human movement operates over large spatial scales (Bertenthal & Pinto, 1994).

As described previously, apparent motion paradigms are commonly used to test for the integration of visual information across time. By varying the amount of time between displays, researchers can assess the size of the temporal window within which motion integration occurs.

Thus, to determine whether the visual system can integrate human movement over both space and time (without the help of disambiguating form cues), subjects performed a direction discrimination task with point light walkers (Thornton, Pinto, & Shiffrar, 1998). The point light walkers were presented within scrambled walker masks and under conditions of apparent motion. On half of the trials, the walker faced leftward and on the remaining trials, the walker faced rightward. The walker figure did not translate across the screen but rather appeared to walk in place as if on a treadmill. The results indicate that observers could accurately determine the walker's direction when the walker was simultaneously masked and presented under long range apparent motion conditions (that is, with inter-stimulus intervals greater than 50 msec). Thus, the spatial-temporal window within which human movement information can be integrated is particularly large. These results add strong support to the proposal that the visual system's ability to intepret human movement is truly exquisite. These findings support the hypothesis that the visual system might be constructed so as to interpret human movement with unusually high precision even under extremely noisy conditions. This conclusion suggests that the visual system may not be best understood as a general processor that devotes equal processing resources to all object categories.

Underlying Mechanisms

The previously described behavioral research provides a hint to the possible neurophysiological mechanisms underlying the visual perception of human movement. A behavioral signature of high level visual processes is their dependence upon global display characteristics. More specifically, most models of the visual system are hierarchical in nature (e.g., Van Essen & DeYoe, 1995; Zeki, 1993). Visual analyses at the lower levels of this hierarchy are thought to occur within brief temporal intervals and small spatial neighborhoods. The results of these low level or "local" analyses are then passed onto and processed by higher level or more "global" mechanisms which process information across larger spatiotemporal extents. While local and global are difficult to define as absolute terms, most studies of the visual perception of human movement have defined local analyses as the computations conducted on individual points (joints) or point pairs (limbs). Global analyses are conducted over larger areas and generally involve half to an entire point light walker. In the temporal domain, local motion processes are thought to be restricted to a window of 50 ms or less (Baker & Braddick, 1985), while global motion processes may operate over much longer intervals.

The results of the masked point light study (Thornton et al., 1998), combined with those from the other studies described above, strongly suggest that the mechanisms that underlie our ability to perceive and interpret human movements may be located at relatively high levels of the visual system. If so, then what is the nature of the high level mechanism(s) involved in the visual perception of locomotion? Neurophysiological and case studies suggest that the superior temporal polysensory area (STP) may play an important role in the visual perception of human movement (McLeod, Dittrich, Driver, Perrett, & Zihl, 1996; Oram & Perrett, 1994; Perrett, Harries, Mistlin, & Chitty, 1990; Vaina, Lemay, Bienfang, Choi, & Nakayama, 1990). Area STP of the macaque is a particularly interesting high-level visual area because it receives input from both dorsal ("where/how") and ventral ("what") visual pathways and as such, may be the integration site for form and motion information (Baize et al., 1991). Importantly, single cell recordings in the anterior portion of this area indicate that it contains cells that appear to be selectively attuned to precise combinations of primate forms and movements (Perrett et al., 1990). Neurons in this area have been shown to respond to Johansson point light walker displays (Oram & Perrett, 1994). Importantly, these same cells are unresponsive to inanimate control objects that move. They are also unresponsive to the monkey's own movements (Hietanen & Perrett, 1993).

Case studies of patients with extrastriate lesions sparing the temporal lobe demonstrate that individuals can lose their ability to perceive simple motion displays, such as clouds of coherently translating points, while retaining the perception of point light walker displays (Vaina et al., 1990; McLeod et al., 1996). In human subjects, brain imaging studies conducted by Bonda, Petrides, Ostry, and Evans (1996) revealed neural responses in the superior temporal sulcus tied to the perception of point-light displays of human dance. Thus, the analysis of human and non-human primate human movement clearly appears to involve processes located in the superior temporal polysensory area.

A second line of research suggests a different, but perhaps complimentary, approach to our understanding of the visual analysis of human movement. Human movement differs from all other movements since it is the only movement that we both produce and perceive. The visual perception of human movement may involve a functional linkage between the perception and production of human motor activity (Viviani & Stucchi, 1992; Viviani, Baud-Bovy, & Redolfi, 1997). In other words, the perception of human movement may be constrained by knowledge of human motor limitations (Shiffrar, 1994; Shiffrar & Freyd, 1990, 1993). Consistent with this, increasing physiological evidence increasingly suggests that the motor system plays a crucial role in this visual process. For example, "mirror" neurons in monkey premotor cortex respond both when a monkey performs a particular action and when that monkey observers another monkey or a human performing that same action (Rizzolatti, Fadiga, Gallese, & Fogassi, 1996). Since mirror neurons appear to represent hands, arms, and faces, these neurons may be dedicated to the interpretation of manual and facial gestures involved in communication. This conjecture is strongly supported by brain imaging data which demonstrate that Broca's area, the human equivalent of the premotor cortex and normally considered to be a critical language area, is selectively activated during the observation of finger tapping (Iacoboni et al., 1999). Additional support for the role of premotor areas comes from the finding that when humans are asked to observe the actions of another human so that they can later imitate those actions, PET activity is found in those brain regions involved in motor planning (Decety, Grezes, Costes, Perani, Jeannerod, Procyk, Grassi, & Fazio, 1997). Thus, visual observation of another individual's movement can lead to activation within the motor system of the observer.

Motor system activity during the perception of human movement may also depend upon whether the observer is physically able to perform the observed action. This conclusion comes from a study in which PET activity was recorded while subjects viewed two frame apparent motion of a human model in different poses (Stevens, Fonlupt, Shiffrar & Decety, 1999). These displays replicated those used by Shiffrar and Freyd (1990, 1993) since the picture pairs were created such that the biomechanically possible paths of human movement conflicted with the shortest, physically impossible paths. When these picture pairs were presented slowly (with SOAs of 400ms or more), subjects perceived biomechanically possible paths of apparent human motion. Under these conditions, PET scans indicated significant bilateral activity in the pimary motor cortex and cerebellum. However, when these same picture pairs were presented more rapidly (with SOAs less than 300 ms), subjects then perceived impossible paths of human movement, and motor system activity was no longer found (Stevens et al., 1999). This latter pattern of results was also found with object based control stimuli under both rapid and slow presentation rates. Importantly, subjects in this experiment were never given instructions to imitate the observed actions, either during or after the experiment. Instead, subjects remained stationary and simply viewed two frame apparent motion sequences. Thus, there is no reason to believe that activity of the motor system was associated with an overt preparation to act. When considered together, these results suggest that the visual perception of human movement may benefit from disambiguating motor system input as long as the movement under analysis is humanly possible.

The above results suggest that the visual analysis of human movement depends upon a neural circuit that includes STPa, premotor cortex, and primary motor cortex. Each of these areas is directly or indirectly connected with each of the other areas (e.g., Rizzolatti, Luppino, & Matelli, 1998). Thus, these three areas may function as a coherent whole during the visual analysis of human movement. On the other hand, each area might specialize in the analysis of a particular category of movements. Because nearly every physiological study of these areas has differed in display type, movement type, and task type, it is not yet possible to determine how this circuit functions. However, one thing is clear. This circuit represents a potentially powerful coupling between the visual and motor systems.

CONCLUSIONS

The visual interpretation of moving objects requires the visual system to perform a balancing act of sorts. On one hand, the visual system must group motion measurements together in order to determine an object's motion. On the other hand, the visual system must also simultaneously segment motion information. Grouping is necessary because initial motion measurements can only record the velocities of small bits or subregions of an object in a manner that is often ambiguous. Segmentation is needed to confine grouping within objects. Without segmentation processes, someone sipping a cup of tea at an outdoor café would not be able to appreciate the movements of the cars, pedestrians, and tea cup. Instead, all of the motion signals arising from these independent events would be grouped together into one giant and uninformative motion-soup.

The ultimate goal of all of the studies described here was to determine how the visual system balances the processes of integration and segmentation during the analysis of object motion. One of the take home messages from these studies is that the visual system solves this balancing act by ignoring the theoretical separation of form and motion processes to which vision researchers have clung for many years. For example, much effort has been expended in search of a solution to the so-called aperture problem. The aperture problem is only a problem if the visual system is strictly modular such that motion analyses are conducted independently of form analyses. If motion analyses can not take advantage of disambiguating form cues, then all motion signals must be weighted equally and the aperture problem becomes a very big problem indeed. However, the previously outlined studies suggest that this is not the case. Instead, the visual system appears to side step many aspects of the aperture problem by simply analyzing motion and form cues together. To that end, simple form cues, such as contour discontinuities, determine how motion measurements are interpreted. When contour discontinuities are not easily or immediately localized, motion information is combined. When discontinuities are visible and suggest the presence of one or more object boundaries, motion information is segmented across those regions. Thus, simple form cues can determine when we perceive independently moving fragments and when we perceive coherently moving objects. It follows that, while theoretical models of the visual system may be modular, the visual analyses themselves may not be.

Another conclusion that can be drawn from these studies is that the visual system may not be constructed so as to process all object categories similarly. Instead, the visual analysis of human movement may be profoundly different from other motion analyses. Evidence from numerous apparent motion and multiple aperture studies support this claim. Once again, simple form cues may direct this processing difference. When global orientation cues suggest the presence of an upright human form, motion integration across space and time can be facilitated. Thus, the visual system may be best understood as a task dependent system that is optimally designed to interpret those events that have the greatest potential impact on an organism's livelihood. Integrated form and motion processes may be one step towards such optimal visual processing, at least as it relates to the interpretation of object motion.

Whether our visual systems have evolved a specialized mechanism that is strictly dedicated to the analysis of human movement has yet to be determined. Nonetheless, the implications of this apparently straight-forward psychophysical question are profound. If our ability to correctly perceive another individual's actions depends upon shared motor experience, then concepts such as empathy can be understood from a fundamentally new perspective. Are children relatively poor at inferring feelings from actions simply because they do not have sufficient motor experience to visually interpret, and thereby adequately appreciate, the movements of others? Do the motor experiences associated with physical abuse change the way in which victims and perpetrators visually perceive otherwise innocuous human movements? When police officers repeatedly practice drawing their guns, does that motor experience change the way in which they visually interpret similar arm movements by others? These questions illustrate just some of the ways in which understanding motion integration across different object and event categories can have important implications for how we relate to our world.

ACKNOWLEDGMENTS

Preparation of this chapter was supported by NIH grant EY12300. Many thanks go to Jeannine Pinto for numerous helpful comments.

REFERENCES

Ahlström, V., Blake, R., & Ahlström, U. (1997). Perception of biological motion. *Perception, 26*, 1539-1548.

Adelson, E. H. & Movshon, J. A. (1982). Phenomenal coherence of moving visual patterns. *Nature, 300*, 523-525.

Baizer, J., Ungerleider, L., & Desimone, R. (1991). Organization of visual inputs to the inferior temporal and posterior parietal cortex in macaques. *Journal of Neuroscience, 11*, 168-190.

Baker, C. & Braddick, O. (1985). Temporal properties of the short-range process in apparent motion. *Perception, 14*, 181-192.

Barchilon Ben-Av, M. & Shiffrar, M. (1995). Disambiguating velocity estimates across image space. *Vision Research, 35*, 2889-2895.

Barclay, C., Cutting, J., & Kozlowski, L. (1978). Temporal and spatial factors in gait perception that influence gender recognition. *Perception & Psychophysics, 23*, 145-152.

Bertenthal, B. I., & Pinto, J. (1994). Global processing of biological motions. *Psychological Science, 5*, 221-225.

Bonda, E., Petrides, M., Ostry, D. & Evans, A. (1996). Specific involvement of human parietal systems and the amygdala in the perception of biological motion. *Journal of Neuroscience, 16*, 3737-3744.

Burbeck, C. A., & Yap, Y. L. (1990). Two mechanisms for localization? Evidence for separation dependent and separation independent processing of position information. *Vision Research, 30*, 739-750.

Burt, P., & Sperling, G. (1981). Time, distance, and feature trade-offs in visual apparent motion. *Psychological Review, 88*, 171-195.

Castet, E., Lorenceau, J., Shiffrar, M., & Bonnet, C. (1993). Perceived speed of moving lines depends on orientation, length, speed and luminance. *Vision Research, 33*, 1921-1936.

Decety, J., Grezes, J., Costes, N., Perani, D., Jeannerod, M., Procyk, E., Grassi, F., & Fazio, F. (1997). Brain activity during observation of actions: Influence of action content and subject's strategy. *Brain, 120*, 1763 - 1777.

Dittrich, W. H. (1993). Action categories and the perception of biological motion. *Perception, 22*, 15-22.

Heptulla-Chatterjee, S., Freyd, J., & Shiffrar, M. (1996). Configural processing in the perception of apparent biological motion. *Journal of Experimental Psychology: Human Perception & Performance, 22*, 916-929.

Grzywacz, N. & Yuille, A. (1991). Theories for the visual perception of local velocity and coherent motion. In M.S. Landy and J. A. Movshon (Eds.), *Computational Models of Visual Processing* (pp. 231-252.). Cambridge, MA : MIT Press.

Hietanen, J. & Perrett, D. (1993). Motion sensitive cells in the macaque superior temporal polysensory area I. Lack of response to the sight of the animal's own limb movement. *Experimental Brain Research, 93*, 117-128.

Hildreth, E. (1984). *The measurement of visual motion*. Cambridge, MA: MIT Press.

Hubel, D. & Wiesel, T. (1968). Receptive fields and functional architecture of the monkey striate cortex. *Journal of Physiology, 195*, 215-243.

Johansson, G. (1973). Visual perception of biological motion and a model for it's analysis. *Perception & Psychophysics, 14*, 201-211.

Johansson, G. (1976). Spatio-temporal differentiation and integration in visual motion perception. *Psychological Review, 38*, 379-393.

Kellman, P., & Shipley, T. F. (1991). A theory of visual interpolation in object perception. *Cognitive Psychology, 23*, 141-221.

Kozlowski, L. T., & Cutting, J. E. (1977). Recognizing the sex of a walker from a dynamic point-light display. *Perception & Psychophysics, 21*, 575-580.

Kozlowski, L. T., & Cutting, J. E. (1978). Recognizing the sex of a walker from point-lights mounted on ankles: Some second thoughts. *Perception & Psychophysics, 23*, 459.

Krumhansl, C. (1984). Independent processing of visual form and motion. *Perception, 13*, 535-546.

Livingstone, M. & Hubel, D. (1988). Segregation of form, color, movement, and depth:anatomy, physiology, and perception. *Science, 240*, 740-749.

Lorenceau, J. & Shiffrar, M. (1992). The role of terminators in motion integration across contours. *Vision Research, 32*, 263-273.

Lorenceau, J., Shiffrar, M., Wells, N., & Castet, E. (1993). Different motion sensitive units are involved in recovering the direction of moving lines. *Vision Research, 33*, 1207-1218.

Marey, E. J. (1972). *Movement*. New York: Arno Press & New York Times. (Original work published 1895).

MacArthur, L. Z., & Baron, M. K. (1983). Toward an ecological theory of social perception. *Psychological Review, 90*, 215-238.

McLeod, P., Dittrich, W., Driver, J., Perrett, D., & Zihl, J. (1996). Preserved and impaired detection of structure from motion by a "motion blind" patient *Visual Cognition, 3*, 363-391.

Milner, A. D., & Goodale, M. A. (1995). *The visual brain in action*. New York: Oxford University Press.

Movshon, J. A., Adelson, E. H., Gizzi, M. S., & Newsome, W. T. (1985). The analysis of moving visual patterns. In C. Chagas, R. Gattas, & C. G. Gross (Eds.), *Pattern recognition mechanisms* (pp. 117-151). Rome: Vatican Press.

Movshon, J.A., Thompson, I.D., & Tolhurst, D. J. (1978). Receptive field organization of complex cells in the cat's striate cortex. *Journal of Physiology, 283*, 79-99.

Oram, M. & Perrett, D. (1994). Responses of anterior superior temporal polysensory (STPa) neurons to "biological motion" stimuli. *Journal of Cognitive Neuroscience, 6,* 99-116.

Orban, G.A., Kato, H., & Bishop, P. O. (1979). Dimensions and properties of end-zone inhibitory areas in receptive fields of hypercomplex cells in cat striate cortex. *Journal of Neurophysiology, 42,* 833-849.

Pavlova, M. & Sokolov, A. (2000). Orientation specificity in biological motion perception. *Perception & Psychophysics, 62,* 889-899.

Perrett, D., Harries, M., Mistlin, A. J., & Chitty, A J. (1990). Three stages in the classification of body movements by visual neurons. In H. B. Barlow, C. Blakemore, & M. Weston-Smith (Eds.), *Images and understanding,* (pp. 94-107). Cambridge, England: Cambridge University Press.

Poizner, H., Bellugi, U., & Lutes-Driscoll, V. (1981). Perception of American Sign Language in dynamic point-light displays. *Journal of Experimental Psychology: Human Perception and Performance, 7,* 430-440.

Rizzolatti, G., Fadiga, L., Gallese, V., & Fogassi, L. (1996). Premotor cortex and the recognition of motor actions. *Cognitive Brain Research, 3,* 131-141.

Rizzolatti, G., Luppino, G., & Matelli, M. (1998). The organization of the cortical motor system: new concepts. *Electroencephalography and Clinical Neurophysiology, 106,* 283-296.

Shepard, R. N. (1984). Ecological constraints on internal representation: Resonant kinematics of perceiving, imagining, thinking, and dreaming. *Psychological Review, 91,* 417-447

Shiffrar, M. (1994). When what meets where. *Current Directions in Psychological Science,* 3, 96-100.

Shiffrar, M. (2001). Movement and event perception. In B. Goldstein (Ed.), *The Blackwell Handbook of Perception.* (pp. 237-272). Oxford: Blackwell.

Shiffrar, M., & Freyd, J. J. (1990). Apparent motion of the human body. *Psychological Science, 1,* 257-264.

Shiffrar, M., & Freyd, J. J. (1993). Timing and apparent motion path choice with human body photographs. *Psychological Science, 4,* 379-384.

Shiffrar, M., Li, X., & Lorenceau, J. (1995). Motion integration across differing image features. *Vision Research, 35,* 2137-2146.

Shiffrar, M., Lichtey, L., & Heptulla-Chatterjee, S. (1997). The perception of biological motion across apertures. *Perception & Psychophysics, 59,* 51-59.

Shiffrar, M. & Lorenceau, J. (1996). Improved motion linking across edges at decreased luminance contrast, edge width and duration. *Vision Research, 36,* 2061-2067.

Shiffrar, M. & Pavel, M. (1991). Percepts of rigid motion within and across apertures. *Journal of Experimental Psychology: Human Perception and Performance, 17,* 749-761.

Shiffrar, M., Pavel, M. & Lorenceau, J. (1995). What is a corner? *Investigative Ophthalmology and Visual Science, 36,* 1921.

Stevens, J., Fonlupt, P., Shiffrar, M., & Decety, J. (2000). New aspects of motion perception: Selective neural encoding for apparent human movements. *Neuroreport, 11,* 109-115.

Sumi, S. (1984). Upside-down presentation of the Johansson moving light-spot pattern. *Perception, 13,* 283-286.

Thornton, I., Pinto, J., & Shiffrar, M. (1999). The visual perception of human locomotion. *Cognitive Neuropsychology, 15,* 535-552.

Ullman, S. (1979). *The interpretation of visual motion.* Cambridge, MA: MIT Press.

Vaina, L., Lemay, M., Bienfang, D., Choi, A., & Nakayama, K. (1990). Intact "biological motion" and "structure from motion" perception in a patient with impaired motion mechanisms: A case study. *Visual Neuroscience, 5,* 353-369.

Van Essen, D. C., & DeYoe, E. A. (1995). Concurrent processing in primate visual cortex. In M. Gazzaniga (Ed.), *The Cognitive Neurosciences* (pp. 383-400). Cambridge, MA: MIT Press.

Viviani, P., Baud-Bovy, G., & Redolfi, M. (1997). Perceiving and tracking kinesthetic stimuli: Further evidence of motor-perceptual interactions. *Journal of Experimental Psychology: Human Perception and Performance, 23,* 1232-1252.

Viviani, P. & Stucchi, N. (1992). Biological movements look constant: Evidence of motor-perceptual interactions. *Journal of Experimental Psychology: Human Perception and Performance, 18,* 603-623.

Wallach, H. (1935). Uber visuell wahrgenommene Bewegungsrichtung. *Psychologische Forschung, 20,* 325-380.

Zeki, S. (1993). *A vision of the brain.* Cambridge: Cambridge University Press.

From Fragments to Objects – Segmentation and Grouping in Vision
T.F. Shipley and P.J. Kellman (Editors)

16

CONTOURS FROM APPARENT MOTION: A COMPUTATIONAL THEORY

William D. Prophet, Donald D. Hoffman, and Carol M. Cicerone
Department of Cognitive Science, University of California, Irvine, 92697 USA

ABSTRACT

Human vision readily constructs subjective contours from displays of kinetic occlusion and color from motion. To construct these contours from kinetic displays it is argued that human vision must solve the point-aperture problem, a problem more general and more difficult than the well-known aperture problem. In the aperture problem one is given a contour and its orthogonal velocity field, and must compute the full velocity field; in the point-aperture problem one is given neither the curve nor any components of its velocity field, and must construct both the curve and its full velocity field. We formalize the point-aperture problem and present, in special cases, two simple algorithms for its solution.

1 INTRODUCTION

In 1911 Pleichart Stumpf introduced the *aperture problem* to explain why rotating spirals appear to expand or contract. The problem, as Stumpf pointed out, is that if one views a moving curve through an aperture sufficiently small that the curve can be well approximated by a line, then only the component of motion perpendicular to the curve can be detected, and other components are lost. Therefore, to obtain a global motion for the curve one must construct one of these other components, perhaps by combining the locally-detected perpendicular components. The aperture problem is illustrated in Figure 1.

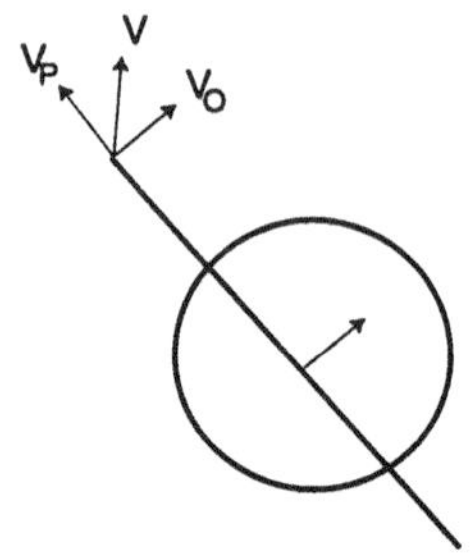

Figure 1. The aperture problem. A small aperture, depicted by the circle, attempts to measure the velocity, V, of a contour passing through it. Due to its limited extent, the aperture can only measure V_O, the component of V orthogonal to the contour. The parallel component, V_P, is invisible to the aperture and must be constructed by later visual processes.

Many researchers have studied the aperture problem with psychophysical experiments (Wallach 1935; 1976; Metzger 1953; Musatti 1975; Scott and Noland 1966; Marr and Ullman 1981; Adelson and Movshon 1982; Hildreth and Koch 1987; Nakayama and Silverman 1988a; 1988b) and with computational theories (Yuille and Grzywacz 1988; Hildreth 1984; Waxman and Wohn 1988; Todorović 1993). The aperture problem assumes that one is given a contour and the orthogonal component of its motion; only one other component of the velocity field along the contour must be constructed. Displays of kinetic occlusion and color from motion (Andersen and Braunstein 1983; Andersen and Cortese 1989; Bruno and Bertamini 1990; Cicerone and Hoffman 1991, 1997; Cicerone et al. 1995; Gibson 1979; Gibson et al. 1969; Kaplan 1969; Kellman and Cohen 1984; Palmer, Kellman, and Shipley 1997; Rock and Halper 1969; Shipley and Kellman, 1993, 1994, 1997; Wallach 1935; Yonas, 1987) often contain no contours, yet human vision readily constructs subjective contours and their motions from these kinetic displays. To do so, human vision must solve what we will refer to as the "point-aperture problem", a problem more general than the aperture problem. In this paper, we formalize the point-aperture problem and present, in special cases, two simple algorithms for its solution. Our formalization does not address the issue of whether subjective contours seen in static displays arise from the same visual mechanisms as in kinetic displays. Henceforth we will use the term "subjective contour" to be equivalent to the percept of a clearly recognizable contour not present in the physical stimulus.

We begin by describing how to construct displays of color from motion, in which the point-aperture problem arises. The display consists of multiple frames. In each frame a few hundred small colored dots are placed at random on a white background. From frame to frame dots never change their location, but change their color as follows. Dots within a virtual disk are colored green and all other dots red. In each successive frame the virtual disk is translated a prescribed distance and again only dots within the virtual disk are colored green. The result is a sequence of frames in which the dots do not move, but in which some dots systematically change colors from red to green or from green to red. The first and last frames of a movie created by such frames is shown in Figure 2, with the green dots depicted by the smaller black dots and the red by the larger ones. Within a second or two of viewing this movie, observers see a subjective green disk that glides over the stationary field of dots (Cicerone and Hoffman 1991, 1997). This effect is known as *color from motion*. If the green dots are of higher luminance than the red ones then viewers see a subjective contour surrounding the subjective green disk. By changing the shape of the virtual region (within which color assignments of dots change) to, say, a square, viewers can be made to see subjective borders in the shape of a square with color spreading throughout.

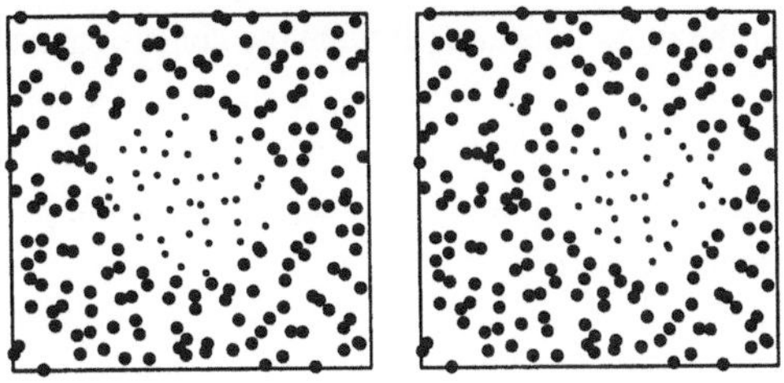

Figure 2. The first and last frames from a display of color from motion that leads observers to perceive a translating subjective disk. No dots change position from frame to frame of the display, but some dots do change color according to an algorithm described in the text.

To construct subjective contours in such displays, observers must solve the point-aperture problem.

> **Point-aperture Problem:** Given a finite set of stationary points and given, as a function of discrete time, which points are to one side of a (virtual) moving contour and which to the other, construct the shape and complete velocity field of the (virtual) contour.

It is helpful to compare this with a succinct statement of the aperture problem.

Aperture Problem: Given a contour and its orthogonal velocity field, construct its complete velocity field.

The aperture problem is a special case of the point-aperture problem. To solve the aperture problem and construct a complete velocity field one need only compute a second component of the velocity field along a given contour. By contrast, to solve the point-aperture problem one must first construct a contour and then compute at least two components of the velocity field along this contour.

In the aperture problem a curve passes through a window so small that only the local differential properties of the curve, viz., the local tangent line and its orthogonal velocity component, can be measured. In the point-aperture problem this window shrinks to a point, precluding the measurement of local differential properties and reducing the available information to one bit: whether the point is to one side of the (virtual) curve or the other at discrete moments in time. This difference is illustrated in Figure 3.

This major difference in what can be measured leads to a corresponding difference in the subsequent constructive tasks. For the aperture problem the constructive task is to compute a total velocity field by integrating the given orthogonal components along the given curve. For the point-aperture problem the constructive task is to compute not only a velocity field but also the curve itself by integrating the bits of information given at discrete points in space and discrete instances in time. Just as there are many ways to solve the aperture problem, there are many ways to solve the point-aperture problem, of which two are described here.

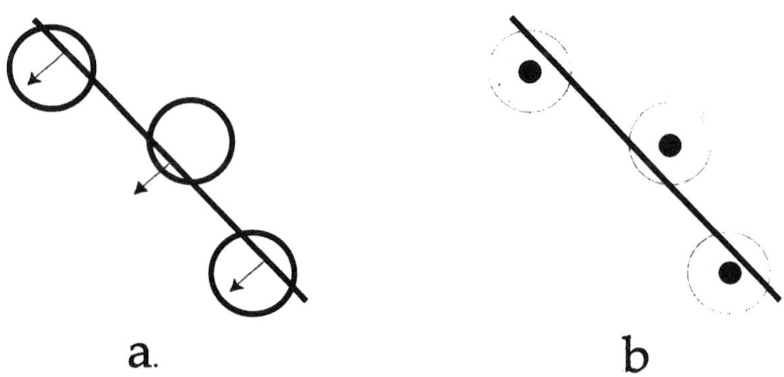

Figure 3. The point-aperture problem compared to the aperture problem. (a) Several apertures measuring the orthogonal velocity of a contour. (b) These apertures now restricted to regions so small that neither the local contour nor its orthogonal velocity can be measured.

2 Phenomenological Motivations

The point-aperture problem, like the aperture problem, is ill posed mathematically: without further constraints one cannot find unique, smoothly varying solutions. A variety of different constraints, leading to a variety of different solutions, can be chosen. In order to obtain a solution which is perceptually plausible, the phenomenology and psychophysics of color-from-motion displays were used as guides for choosing constraints.

Contour Formation Depends on Luminance Contrast

Early work (Liebmann, 1927) showed that the perception of motion is degraded in equiluminant displays. Miyahara and Cicerone (1997) created color-from-motion displays containing regions differing in chromaticity but not in luminance. Viewers still see a spreading of color, but the subjective contour is attentuated. This suggests that the construction of these subjective contours depends primarily on luminance and not on chromaticity information (Miyahara & Cicerone, 1997).

Variable Distinctness

As mentioned above, we see subjective contours in color-from-motion displays with randomly-placed dots. In such displays the density of dots is typically not uniform but varies from one region to another. The clarity of the subjective contour varies with this density: the contour is strongest in regions of high density and weakest in regions of low density. Therefore, the construction of a segment of subjective contour depends primarily on the image data in the neighborhood of that segment (Andersen & Cortese, 1989; Shipley & Kellman, 1993).

Spatial Smoothness

The subjective contour is typically smooth and has no inflections that are not suggested by the data points. Therefore, in the construction of subjective contours, human vision seems to employ a constraint of spatial smoothness (Shipley & Kellman, 1994). This is similar to a constraint like Grimson's "no news is good news": we create no "complications" in the contour without explicit evidence demanding the complication (Grimson, 1981).

Isolated Spatial Discontinuities

The subjective contours that we see in displays of color from motion can have sharp corners. We can, for example, see a subjective square with four sharp corners. A smoothness constraint would never, of course, construct sharp corners. This indicates that a corner-producing process, antagonistic to the smoothness constraint, must also be at work in our construction of subjective contours. Algorithms have been studied for some time that incorporate both a smoothness constraint and a process that creates corners (e.g., Weiss, 1990), although the issue is still unresolved.

Concave Segments

The convex hull (Hocking and Young, 1961) has proved useful in many vision algorithms. However, it is easy to create displays of color from motion in which viewers see a subjective contour that has clear concavities. For example it is easy to create displays in which viewers see a subjective contour in the shape of a banana. This suggests that human vision does not construct subjective contours by an algorithm requiring a convex hull. A more general approach to the construction of subjective contours is needed.

Temporal Smoothness of Shape

In displays of color from motion, the dots never move, only color assignments of individual dots change. Nonetheless, a subjective contour is seen to move over these static dots. Although the arrangement of dots within the subjective contour changes radically from frame to frame, as illustrated in Figure 2, the subjective contour does not change shape, unless the dot density becomes too sparse to support contour formation. For instance, in some displays of color from motion, viewers see a disk of unchanging shape moving over the field of dots. This suggests that human vision may tend to minimize the variation in time of the shape of the subjective contour (Shipley & Kellmanm, 1997).

Temporal Smoothness of Motion

In displays of color from motion, viewers often see the motion of the subjective contour as smooth. However, as mentioned above, there is no motion of dots in these displays, rather only changes in dot colors. This suggests that, in constructing the motion of the subjective contour, human vision uses a constraint of smoothness of motion.

Isolated Motion Discontinuities

It is easy to create displays of color from motion in which viewers see a subjective contour move in a particular direction with uniform velocity, and then suddenly change direction, before once again moving with uniform velocity. This indicates that smoothness of motion is not the only constraint being used in human vision. If we think of the visual system as trying to minimize some functional in its construction of the motion of these subjective contours, then we can think of this functional as having two penalty terms. One term penalizes smooth portions of the motion for high variations in acceleration, a second term penalizes isolated points of motion discontinuity. Abrupt changes of direction are seen in those circumstances in which there is less penalty for inserting a motion discontinuity than for constructing a smooth motion with high variation in acceleration.

Nested Curves

Displays can easily be created in which observers see an annulus with both an outer and inner subjective contour. This demonstrates that the visual processes which construct these subjective contours are sophisticated enough that they can construct several contours at once (Cunningham, Shipley, & Kellman, 1998).

Tolerance for Color Inhomogeneity in the Test Region

In the displays of color from motion discussed so far, all dots on the "inside" have been one color, say green, and all dots on the "outside" have been another color, say red. Displays in which the chromaticities of test dots are assigned probabilistically can also be created (Cicerone & Hoffman, 1997). Each dot inside the virtual disk has a higher probability of being green but some probability of being red, while each dot outside has a higher probability of being red, but some probability of being green. Over a range of probabilities in such displays, viewers can still see a subjective contour despite a high degree of color inhomogeneity. This suggests that, to handle this color inhomogeneity, there may be a process prior to the point-aperture problem in which the visual system uses spatial or temporal windows to compute statistics to determine "inside" versus "outside" decisions for each dot. For example, green dots outside the filter may be consistent with a background of multicolored dots, against which a green object or filter must be detected.

Volumetric Interpretations

It is possible to create a color-from-motion display in which one perceives a boundary not just in two dimensions, but in three. If the motion of a rotating virtual ellipsoid is simulated, and the dots inside its virtual occluding contour are colored differently from those outside, a dynamic color spreading over the surface of a three-dimensional ellipsoid will be seen, and the boundary contour will appear to be the occluding contour of this ellipsoid (Cortese and Andersen, 1991, first showed this in the achromatic case; Cicerone and Hoffman, 1991, in the chromatic case). This indicates that human vision can solve the point-aperture problem by constructing subjective contours in three dimensions.

Partial Invariance

The perceived shape of the subjective contour does not, in general, change if the entire color-from-motion display is translated. Similarly we find that the perceived shape is scale and rotation invariant as others have with similar stimuli (e.g., Shipley & Kellman, 1993). This suggests that human vision respects these invariances in constructing subjective contours.

3 FORMALIZATION

In this section we formalize the point-aperture problem.

Point-Aperture Problem: Given a set $P = \{p_1, \ldots, p_n\}$, $p_i \in \Re^2$, and given at each time $t \in \{1, \ldots, m\}$ a copy P_t of P partitioned into subsets I_t and O_t, construct for each t a piecewise smooth plane curve α_t that *divides* I_t and O_t , and construct a velocity field V_t on α_t.

The set P represents the dots in a color-from-motion display. Each copy P_t is called a "frame" of the display. The sets I_t and O_t are called, respectively, the dots "inside" (of higher luminance) and "outside" (of lower luminance). A curve α_t *divides* I_t and O_t if any plane curve joining any $p_i \in I_t$ with any $p_j \in O_t$ crosses α_t.

The point-aperture problem is ill-posed: At each time t there are infinitely many curves α_t which divide I_t and O_t. Therefore we need further constraints.

One constraint mentioned in the last section is temporal smoothness: When subjects view displays of color from motion, they report that the curves α_t appear to deform smoothly rather than arbitrarily, by deformations that are small or zero. This suggests the following approach: stack the frames P_t evenly in sequence, in effect making the time coordinate t a depth coordinate. Then construct a *surface,* S, surrounding the points I_t. The curves $\alpha_1, \ldots, \alpha_m$ are obtained as intersections of S with the sequence of planes $t = 1, \ldots, m$. The velocity fields $V_1, \ldots, V_m$ are obtained by computing appropriate partial derivatives on S.

Thus the point-aperture problem is solved by constructing a single surface. Given this formulation, an extensive literature on surface construction can be immediately applied (e.g., Blake 1989; Szseliski 1990; Weiss 1990).

The construction process, whether of a sequence of curves or of a single surface, depends most critically on those dots that change luminosity from one frame to the next. These are dots that have just been crossed by the boundary defining the luminosity change, so they provide maximal information about its location. They are therefore called "border dots".

At each time t, $1 < t \leq m$, the border dots B_t are those dots in I_t that were not in I_{t-1} together with those dots in I_{t-1} that were not in I_t. That is, B_t is the symmetric difference of I_t and I_{t-1},

$$B_t = I_t \bigtriangleup I_{t-1} = (I_t - I_{t-1}) \cup (I_{t-1} - I_t).$$

As can be seen, B_t is the union of two sets. The first, $I_t - I_{t-1}$, contains the dots accreted at time t; this set we label A_t. The second, $I_{t-1} - I_t$, contains the dots deleted at time t; this set we label D_t. Thus the border dots B_t can be written as the union of the accreted and deleted dots at time t.

$$B_t = A_t \cup D_t.$$

These two sets play different roles in the process of constructing a curve or surface: the deleted dots must be just outside the constructed curve or surface, whereas the accreted dots must be just inside it.

In the next sections we present two different methods for solving the point aperture problem: the back-projection and border-surface algorithms. Both algorithms generate a set of border dots that must then be used to construct a curve or surface which passes near these dots. The back projection method is for the special case of a rigid object undergoing translation without rotation, and the border-surface method works in the more general case that allows deformation.

4 Rigid Translations: The Back-Projection Method

In this section we solve the point-aperture problem for the special case of a rigid object undergoing uniform translation without rotation. The color-from-motion display first described in the introduction, in which a disk is seen to move over a field of dots, is an example of such a case. Another example is kinetic occlusion, also described earlier. For kinetic occlusion the border dots at time t are those points accreted or deleted at time t.

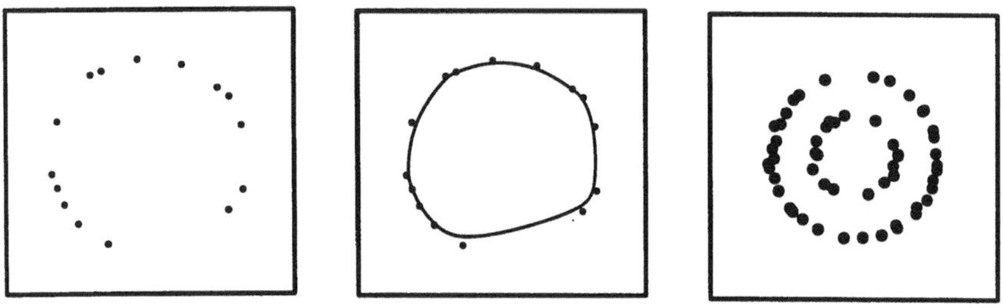

(a) (b) (c)

Figure 4. Border frames determined by the back-projection algorithm. (a) The border frame determined from 10 frames of a color-from-motion display depicting a moving disk. The first and last frames of the display are shown in Figure 2. (b) The curve α, constructed as a sequence of cubic spline curves that pass near these border points. Human vision almost certainly uses a more sophisticated approach than cubic splines. (c) The border frame determined from 5 frames of a color-from-motion display depicting a moving annulus.

A simple algorithm for this case is the "back-projection method" defined as follows: Given a sequence of partitioned frames $P_1, \ldots, P_m$ with inside dots $I_1, \ldots, I_m$, let the coordinates of each dot $p_i \in P$ be $p_i = (x_i, y_i)$. Compute the mean translational velocity, T, of the inside regions by subtracting the center of mass of I_1 from that of I_m and dividing by m.

$$T = \left(\frac{\sum_{p_j \in I_m} x_j, \sum_{p_j \in I_m} y_j}{m|I_m|} \right) - \left(\frac{\sum_{p_j \in I_1} x_j, \sum_{p_j \in I_1} y_j}{m|I_1|} \right),$$

where $|A|$ is the size of set A. For each set of border dots, B_k, create a translated set of dots $\tilde{B}_k$, by translating back each border dot $p_i \in B_k$ by the vector $-(k-1)T$. Then create a "border frame", B, by taking the union of these $\tilde{B}_k$:

$$B = \bigcup_k \tilde{B}_k.$$

Construct a (piecewise) smooth curve, α, based on the dots in B, by using say the spring interpolation method of Weiss (1990). The velocity field along α is T. The value of the functional that is minimized to obtain α represents the strength of the percept of the contour α.

The back-projection algorithm for determining the border frame B was implemented and run in Monte Carlo simulations.

In the first example the back-projection algorithm was given seven frames of a color-from-motion display in which is seen a disk undergoing uniform translation along the x axis. The first and last frames of this display are shown in Figure 2. The border frame determined by the algorithm is shown in Figure 4a. As can be seen in this figure, the points of the border frame fit nicely around a circle of the appropriate radius. Thus this border frame provides a good data set for interpolating a boundary curve, as shown in Figure 4b. If the color-from-motion display is altered so that an annulus is seen rather than a disk, then one obtains nested border frames, as shown in Figure 4c.

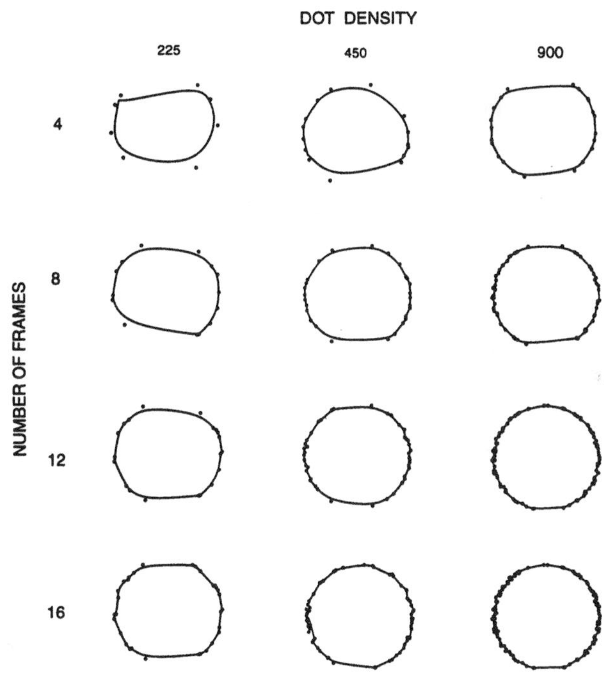

Figure 5. Border dots and interpolating cubic splines for three levels of dot density and four levels of frames. Derived from a display of color from motion that depicts a translating disk. Not represented in this figure is the perceptual strength of the interpolated contours.

With fewer frames, or fewer dots per frame, the border set can become sparse. In this case the back-projection algorithm predicts that one will perceive a well-defined boundary only in those regions for which there are adequate border dots. This is illustrated in Figure 5, which shows the border dots and interpolating cubic splines (Foley and van Dam, 1982) for three levels of dot density and four levels of frames. This fits with the observation noted earlier that the illusory boundary seen in a color-from-motion display can appear better defined in some regions than in others.

In the second example the algorithm used seven frames of a color-from-motion display in which is seen a square undergoing uniform translation along the line $y = x$. The first frame of this display is shown in Figure 6a, with the green dots depicted as smaller than the black ones. The border frame determined by the algorithm is shown in Figure 6b. As can be seen in this figure, the points of the border frame fit reasonably close to a square of the appropriate size. Thus this border frame also provides a good data set for interpolating a boundary curve.

The Monte Carlo trials were based on color-from-motion displays depicting a disk undergoing uniform translation. Figure 2 shows frames typical of these displays. Seventeen hundred displays were generated at random (points chosen according to a uniform distribution), with the number of dots in each display varying from 16 to 400. Each display consisted of four frames in which the disk translated 4.17% of its radius per frame.

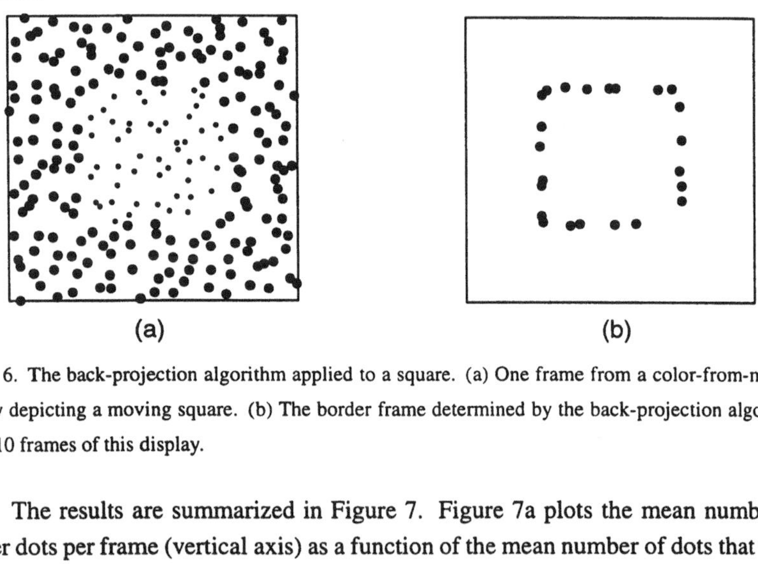

Figure 6. The back-projection algorithm applied to a square. (a) One frame from a color-from-motion display depicting a moving square. (b) The border frame determined by the back-projection algorithm using 10 frames of this display.

The results are summarized in Figure 7. Figure 7a plots the mean number of border dots per frame (vertical axis) as a function of the mean number of dots that were within the disk. As expected, the number of border dots per frame increases as the total number of dots within the disk increases. Figure 7b plots the mean distance of border dots from the origin computed by the algorithm, again as a function of the mean number of dots that were within the disk. The distribution of values obtained by the algorithm approximates the actual value 0.24. As the mean number of dots within the disk increases, the algorithm's estimate of the disk's translation velocity becomes more stable, leading to a more accurate computation of the border frame. As can be seen in Figure 7c, the variance of the distribution decreases with increasing dot density.

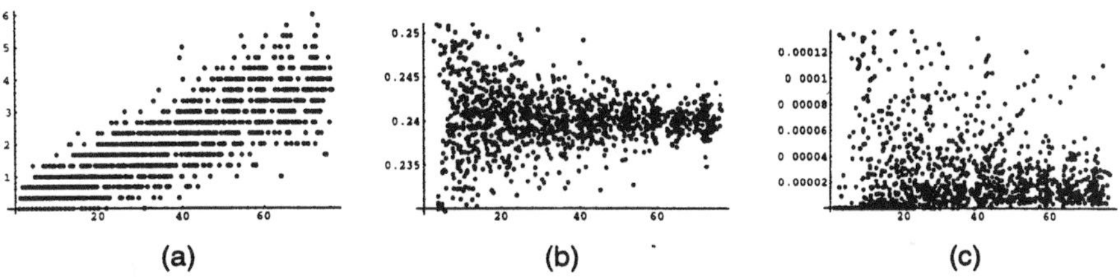

Figure 7. Monte Carlo test of the back-projection algorithm. The results are shown for 1700 displays depicting moving disks. (a) Mean number of border dots per frame, plotted as a function of mean number of dots within the disk. (b) Mean distance of border dots from the origin, plotted as a function of mean number of dots within the disk. The correct value was 0.24. (c) The variance in distance of border dots from the origin, plotted as a function of mean number of dots within the disk.

Thus, the back-projection method is an effective algorithm to solve the point-aperture problem for kinetic occlusion and for color-from-motion displays depicting rigid bodies that translate but do not rotate.

5 DEFORMATIONS: THE BORDER SURFACE METHOD

The back-projection method of the last section cannot handle the more general case in which a color-from-motion display represents an object that deforms or rotates as it translates. A border frame does not work in this more general case, because its construction depends on the assumption that α does not deform as it translates.

In this case the "border dots" can be constructed as follows. As before, a sequence of partitioned frames $P_1, \ldots, P_m$ with inside dots $I_1, \ldots, I_m$ are given, and the coordinates of each dot $p_i \in P$ can be represented by $p_i = (x_i, y_i)$. To each dot in border set B_t, $1 < t \leq m$, an appropriate depth coordinate is attached, giving the "embedded border set"

$$B'_t = \bigcup_{p_j \in B_t} (x_j, y_j, ct),$$

where $c \in \Re^+$ is a scale factor for converting time into a depth dimension. The embedded border sets are stacked to create the final "border dots"

$$B = \bigcup_{t=2}^{m} B'_t.$$

A piecewise-smooth surface, S, is constructed using B as the data points, with a method such as that of Weiss (1990) or Blake (1989). The intersection of S with the plane $z = t$ gives the boundary curve at time t, viz., α_t. The boundary α_t will in general deform as t varies, and its center of mass will translate. The velocity field, T, along α_t is given by the time derivative

$$T(s) = \frac{dS}{dt}|_{\alpha_t(s)},$$

where s is a natural parameter, such as arc length, along α_t.

An example of this method is shown in Figure 8. Part (a) shows the first and last frames of a display in which a disk appears to expand as it translates to the right (green dots are depicted as larger than the black dots). Part (b) shows a stereo view of the border dots computed by the border-surface method. As expected, these dots appear to lie on the surface of a truncated cone. The conical surface which can be seen in this figure demonstrates that the border dots can be a sufficiently rich data set to support the interpolation of the proper surface.

6 DISCUSSION

We have seen that displays of kinetic occlusion and color from motion raise an interesting computational problem for the visual system, a problem we have called the **point-aperture problem:**

> Given a finite set of stationary points and given, as a function of discrete time, which points are to one side of a moving contour and which to the other, construct the shape and complete velocity field of the contour.

We have argued that this problem is more general than the aperture problem, because neither the contour nor its orthogonal velocity field are given. Human vision solves this problem nonetheless.

We have presented two algorithms for solving the point-aperture problem. The back-projection algorithm assumes that the contour translates rigidly at constant velocity and does not rotate. This algorithm uses the green test dots—used to recover the object of interest—to estimate the center of mass of this object and to track it over frames. Using the center of mass seems a plausible way that human vision might work. The results of our simulations with this model (shown in Figures 4–6) indicate some interesting psychophysical predictions, namely that (1) as dot density decreases, subjective borders should become less clear perceptually; (2) as dot density increases, sharp corners should be more visible; (3) as dot density decreases, motion from frame to frame should appear less smooth; and (4) in principle, any rigid, nonrotating shape should be perceivable.

The border-surface method goes one step beyond the back-projection method by allowing contours to deform, rotate, and translate nonuniformly. Although this method applies more generally than the back-projection method, it is not an algorithmic generalization. In particular it does not use a center of mass, because for objects that can rotate and change scale the center of mass cannot help to compute an interpolating contour: reverse translations of the center of mass do not lead to a consistent set of border points for interpolation. Rather than a two-dimensional contour interpolation, this method works in a three-dimensional space-time framework to interpolate a surface by tagging sets of border dots with a time coordinate represented as depth. This algorithm makes all the same psychophysical predictions as the back-projection method, but in addition predicts that nonrigid and rotating shapes can be perceived (Figure 8).

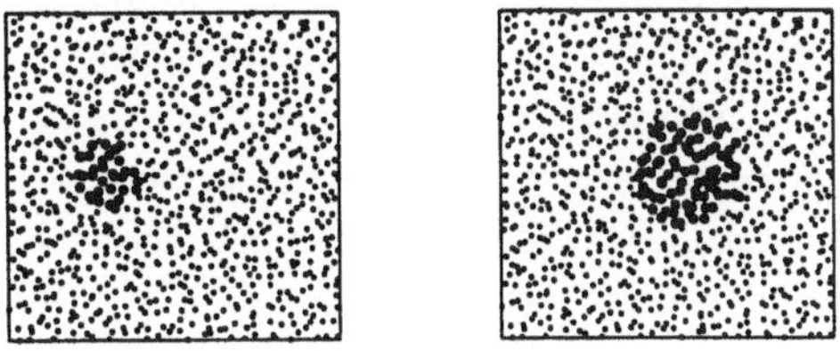

(a)

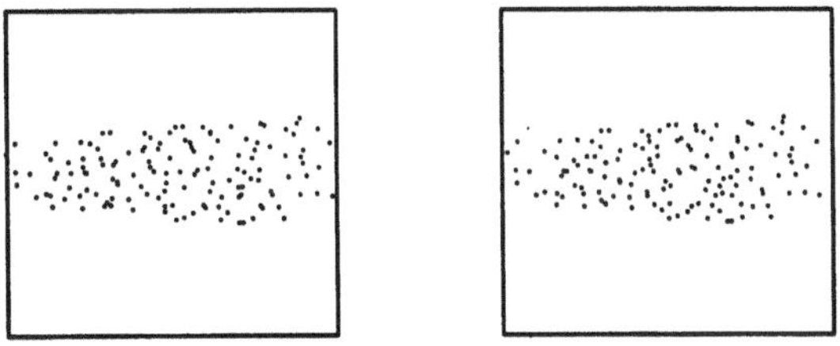

(b)

Figure 8. The border-surface algorithm applied to a growing disk. (a) First and last frames of a color-from-motion display depicting a translating and growing disk. (b) A stereo view of the border-surface points computed by the algorithm. The main axis of the 3D cylinder represents the passage of time.

As noted above displays of color from motion in which the color of dots is assigned probabilistically can be created (Cicerone & Hoffman, 1997). Each dot inside is, say, green; while each dot outside has a higher probability of being red, but some probability of being green. Over a range of probabilities in such displays, viewers can still see a subjective contour despite a high degree of color inhomogeneity. This suggests that, to handle this color inhomogeneity, there may be a process prior to the point-aperture problem in which the visual system uses spatial and/or temporal windows to compute statistics to determine "inside" versus "outside" decisions for each dot. For example, green dots outside the filter may be consistent with a background of multicolored dots, against which a green object or filter must be detected. Once this decision is made, the results can then be fed into the point-aperture algorithms as presented here.

Our approach differs from the related work of Basri, Grove, and Jacobs (1998) and of Lindenbaum and Bruckstein (1988): They assume that portions of the bounding contour of the object are visible and can be obtained in single static images. As we noted in the introduction, we assume that no portion of the bounding contour is visible in any static image, and that the bounding contour must be constructed entirely from properties of the sequence of images.

It is of some interest to find neural correlates of the illusory boundaries perceived in displays of color from motion. Studies with standard illusory boundaries are encouraging. Using single cell recordings, von der Heydt, Peterhans, and Baumgartner (1984) found that almost half of the neurons in area V2 of macaque visual cortex can respond to the presence of moving illusory contours. They have subsequently studied this effect in great detail (Peterhans and von der Heydt 1989; 1991; Peterhans, von der Heydt, and Baumgartner 1986; von der Heydt and Peterhans 1989a; 1989b). All these studies used illusory contours generated by abutting line gratings or by two parallel bars with aligned rectangular notches. Using similar stimuli, Redies, Crook, and Creutzfeld (1986) found that some complex cells in visual areas 17 and 18 of the cat also respond to illusory contours, although Gregory (1987) failed to replicate this finding. And Grosof, Shapley, and Hawken (1993) found complex and simple cells in V1 of macaques that respond to illusory contours. In each of these studies the experimenters moved real contours to produce the effect of illusory contours. It would be of interest to see if cells in V1 or V2 can respond to illusory contours formed without any motion of any "real" contours, i.e., by displays of color from motion. If so, this would challenge most current neural network models of illusory contours, which rely on edges and their orientations to construct the illusory contours (Peterhans et al. 1986; Finkel and Edelman 1989; Finkel and Sajda 1992; 1994; Sajda and Finkel 1992a; 1992b; 1995; Kellman and Shipley 1991;

Grossberg and Mingolla 1985a; 1985b; 1987a; 1987b; Grossberg 1994). Displays of color from motion demonstrate that human vision does not require real motion, oriented edges, or discontinuities to see illusory contours. Perhaps the same is true of some of its neurons.

An interesting open question is the precise form of the functional to be optimized in the construction of such curves and surfaces.

ACKNOWLEDGEMENTS

For helpful discussions we thank Andrea van Doorn, Heiko Hecht, Jan Koenderink, Manish Singh, Lothar Spillmann, and Dejan Todorović. This work was supported by a grant from the Zentrum fur interdisziplinäre Forschung der Universität Bielefeld, Germany (D.D.H.) and by PHS-NIH/NEI Grant EY71132 (C.M.C.).

REFERENCES

Adelson, E.A. & Movshon, J.A. (1982). Phenomenal coherence of moving visual patterns. *Nature, 300,* 523–525.

Andersen, G.J., & Braunstein, M.L. (1983). Dynamic occlusion in the perception of rotation in depth. *Perception & Psychophysics, 34,* 356–362.

Andersen, G.J., & Cortese, J.M. (1989). 2-D contour perception resulting from kinetic occlusion. *Perception & Psychophysics, 46,* 49–55.

Blake, A. (1989). Comparison of the efficiency of deterministic and stochastic algorithms for visual reconstruction. *IEEE Transactions on Pattern Analysis & Machine Intelligence, 11,* 2–12.

Bruno, N. and Bertamini, M. (1990). Identifying contours from occlusion events. *Perception & Psychophysics, 48,* 331-342.

Cicerone, C.M. & Hoffman, D.D. 1991. Dynamic neon colors: Perceptual evidence for parallel visual pathways. *University of California, Irvine, Mathematical Behavior Sciences Memo 91–22.*

Cicerone, C.M., & Hoffman, D.D. (1997). Color from motion: dicoptic activation and a possible role in breaking camouflage. *Perception, 26,* 1367–1380.

Cicerone, C.M., Hoffman, D.D., Gowdy, P.D., and Kim, J.S. (1995). The perception of color from motion. *Perception & Psychophysics, 57,* 761–777.

Cortese, J.M., & Andersen, G.J. (1991). Recovery of 3-D shape from deforming contours. *Perception & Psychophysics, 49,* 315–327.

Cunningham, D.W., Shipley, T.W., & Kellman, P.J (1998). Interactions between spatial and spatiotemporal information in spatiotemporal boundary formation. *Perception & Psychophysics, 60,* 839–851.

Finkel, L.H., & Edelman, G.M. (1989). Integration of distributed cortical systems by reentry: A computer simulation of interactive functionally segregated visual areas. *Journal of Neuroscience, 9,* 3188–3208.

Finkel, L.H., & Sajda, P. (1992). Object discrimination based on depth-from-occlusion. *Neural Computation, 4,* 901–921.

Finkel, L.H., & Sajda, P. (1994). Constructing visual perception. *American Scientist, 82,* 224–237.

Foley, J., Van Dam, A. (1982). *Fundamentals of interactive computer graphics.* Reading, MA: Addison-Wesley.

Giblin, P.J., Pollick, F.E., and Rycroft, J.E. (1994). Recovery of an unknown axis of rotation from the profiles of a rotating surface. *Journal of the Optical Society of America A, 11,* 1976–1984.

Gibson, J.J. (1979). *The Ecological Approach to Visual Perception.* Boston, MA: Houghton Mifflin.

Gibson, J.J., Kaplan, G.A., Reynolds, H.N. Jr., and Wheeler, K. (1969). The change from visible to invisible: A study of optical transitions. *Perception & Psychophysics, 5,* 113–116.

Grimson, W.E.L. (1981). *From Images to Surfaces: A Computational Study of the Human Early Visual System.* Cambridge, MA: MIT Press.

Gregory, R.L. (1987). Illusory contours and occluding surfaces. In S. Petry & G.E. Meyer (Eds.), *The perception of illusory contours* (pp 81–89). New York: Springer-Verlag.

Grosof, D.H., Shapley, R.M., and Hawken, M.J. (1993). Macaque V1 neurons can signal "illusory" contours" *Nature, 365,* 550–552.

Grossberg, S. (1994). 3-D vision and figure-ground separation by visual cortex. *Perception & Psychophysics, 55,* 48–121.

Grossberg, S., & Mingolla, E. (1985a). Neural dynamics of form perception: Boundary completion, illusory figures, and neon color spreading. *Psychological Review, 92,* 173–211.

Grossberg, S., & Mingolla, E. (1985b). Neural dynamics of perceptual grouping: Tetures, boundaries, and emergent segmentations. *Perception & Psychophysics, 38,* 141–171.

Grossberg, S., & Mingolla, E. (1987a). Neural dynamics of surface perception: Boundary webs, illuminants, and shape from shading. *Computer Vision, Graphics, & Image Processing. 37,* 116–165.

Grossberg, S., & Mingolla, E. (1987b). The role of illusory contours in visual segmentation. In S. Petry & G.E. Meyer (Eds.), *The perception of illusory contours* (pp 116–125). New York: Springer-Verlag.

Heitger, F., & von der Heydt, R. (1993). A computational model of neural contour processing: Figure-ground segregation and illusory contours. In *IEEE 4th International Conference on Computer Vision* (pp 32–40). Los Alamitos, CA: IEEE Computer Society Press.

Kellman, P.J., & Cohen, M.H. (1984). Kinetic subjective contours. *Perception & Psychophysics, 35,* 237–244.

Kellman, P.J., & Shipley, T.F. (1991). A theory of visual interpolation in object perception. *Cognitive Psychology, 23,* 141–221.

Koenderink, J. (1995). Personal communication, November 23.

Kaplan, G.A. (1969). Kinetic disruption of optical texture: The perception of depth at an edge. *Perception & Psychophysics, 6,* 193–198.

Liebmann, S. (1927). Über das Verhalten farbiger Formen bei Helligkeitsgleichheit von Figure und Grund. *Psychologische Forschung, 9,* 300–353.

Marr, D., & Ullman, S. (1981). Directional selectivity and its use in early visual processing. *Proceedings of the Royal Society of London Series B, 211,* 151–180.

Metzger, W. (1953). *Gesetze des Sehens, 2nd ed.* (Frankfurt: Waldemar Kramer).

Miyahara, E., & Cicerone, C.M. (1997). Color from motion: separate contributions of chromaticity and luminance. *Perception, 26,* 1381-1396.

Musatti, C.L. (1975). Stereokinetic phenomena and their interpretation. In G B Flores D'Arcais (Ed.), *Studies in Perception: Festschrift for Fabio Metelli.* Milan:

Martello-Giunti.

Nakayama, K., & Silverman, G.H. (1988). The aperture problem – I. Perception of nonrigidity and motion direction in translating sinusoidal lines. *Vision Research, 28,* 739–746.

Nakayama, K., & Silverman, G.H. (1988). The aperture problem – II. Spatial integration of velocity information along contours. *Vision Research, 28,* 747–753.

Palmer, E., Kellman, P.J., & Shipley, T.F. (1997). Spatiotemporal relatability in dynamic object completion. *Investigative Ophthalmology & Visual Science, 38,* 256.

Peterhans, E., & von der Heydt, R. (1989). Mechanisms of contour perception in monkey visual cortex: II. Contours bridging gaps. *Journal of Neuroscience, 9,* 1749–1763.

Peterhans, E., & von der Heydt, R. (1991). Elements of form perception in monkey prestriate cortex. In A. Gorea, Y. Fregnac, Z. Kapoula, & J. Findlay (Eds.), *Representations of vision—Trends and tacit assumptions in vision research* (pp 1–12). Cambridge, UK: Cambridge University Press.

Peterhans, E., von der Heydt, R., and Baumgartner, G. (1986). Neuronal responses to illusory contour stimuli reveal stages of visual cortical processing. In J.D. Pettigrew, K.J. Sanderson, & W.R. Levick (Eds.), *Visual Neuroscience* (pp 343–351). Cambridge, UK: Cambridge University Press.

Pollick, F.E. (1994). Perceiving shape from profiles. *Perception & Psychophysics, 55,* 152–161.

Redies, C., Crook, J.M., and Creutzfeldt, O.D. (1986). Neuronal responses to borders with and without luminance gradients in cat visual cortex and dorsal lateral geniculate nucleus. *Experimental Brain Research, 61,* 469–481.

Rock, I., & Halper, F. (1969). Form perception without a retinal image. *American Journal of Psychology, 82,* 425–440.

Sajda, P., & Finkel, L.J. (1992a). Cortical mechanisms for surface segmentation. In F. Eeckman & J. Bower (Eds.), *Computation and neural systems 1992* (p 10). Boston, MA: Kluwer.

Sajda, P., & Finkel, L.J. (1992b). Simulating biological vision with hybrid neural networks. *Simulation, 59,* 47–55.

Sajda, P., & Finkel, L.J. (1995). Intermediate-level visual representations and the construction of surface perception. *Journal of Cognitive Neuroscience, 7,* 267–

291.

Scott, T.R., & Noland, J.H. (1965). Some stimulus dimensions of rotating spirals. *Psychological Review, 72,* 344–357.

Shipley, T.F., & Kellman, P.J. (1993). Optical tearing in spatiotemporal boundary formation: When do local element motions produce boundaries, form, and global motion? *Spatial Vision, 7,* 323–339.

Shipley, T.F., & Kellman, P.J. (1994). Spatiotemporal boundary formation: Boundary, form, and motion perception from transformations of surface elements. *Journal of Experimental Psychology: General, 123,* 3–20.

Shipley, T.F., & Kellman, P.J. (1997). Spatiotemporal boundary formation: The role of local motion signals in boundary perception. *Vision Research, 37,* 1281–1293.

Stumpf, P. (1911). Über die Abhängigkeit der visuellen Bewegungsempfindung und ihres negativen Nachbildes von den Reizvorgängen auf der Netzhaut. *Zeitschrift für Psychologie, 59,* 321–330.

Szeliski, R. (1990). Fast surface interpolation using hierarchical basis functions. *IEEE Transactions on Pattern Analysis & Machine Intelligence, 12,* 513–528.

Todd, J.T., & Norman, J.F. (1991). The visual perception of smoothly curved surfaces from minimal apparent motion sequences. *Perception & Psychophysics, 50,* 509–523.

Todorović, D. (1993). Analysis of two- and three-dimensional rigid and nonrigid motions in the stereokinetic effect. *Journal of the Optical Society of America A, 10,* 804–826.

von der Heydt, R., Peterhans E., and Baumgartner G. (1984). Illusory contours and cortical neuron responses. *Science, 224,* 1260–1262.

von der Heydt, R., & Peterhans, E. (1989a). Cortical contour mechanisms and geometrical illusions. In D.M. Lam & C.D. Gilbert (Eds.), *Neural mechanisms of visual perception* (pp 157–170). The Woodlands, Texas: Portfolio Publishing.

von der Heydt, R., & Peterhans, E. (1989b). Mechanisms of contour perception in monkey visual cortex: I. Lines of pattern discontinuity. *Journal of Neuroscience, 9,* 1731–1748.

Wallach, H. (1935). Über visuell wahrgenommene Bewegungsrichtung. *Psychologische Forschung, 20,* 325–380.

Wallach, H. (1976). The direction of motion of straight lines. In H. Wallach (Ed.), *On Perception.* New York: Quadrangle.

Waxman, A.M., & Wohn, K. (1988). Image flow theory: a framework for 3-D inference from time-varying imagery. In C.M. Brown (Ed.), *Advances in Computer Vision: Vol. 1* Hillsdale, NJ: Erlbaum.

Weiss, I. (1990). Shape reconstruction on a varying mesh. *IEEE Transactions on Pattern Analysis & Machine Intelligence, 12,* 345–362.

Yonas, A., & Granrud, C.E. (1985). The development of sensitivity to kinetic, binocular, and pictorial depth information in human infants. In D.J. Ingle, M. Jeannerod, and D.N. Lee (Eds.), *Brain Mechanisms and Spatial Vision* (pp 113–145). Dordrecht, the Netherlands: Martinus Nijhoff.

Yuille, A.L., & Grzywacz, N.M. (1988). A computational theory for the perception of coherent visual motion. *Nature, 333,* 71–74.

From Fragments to Objects – Segmentation and Grouping in Vision
T.F. Shipley and P.J. Kellman (Editors)

17

BREATHING ILLUSIONS AND BOUNDARY FORMATION IN SPACE-TIME

Nicola Bruno, Dipartimento di Psicologia, Università di Trieste, via S. Anastasio 12, 34134 Trieste, Italy

ABSTRACT

Human observers are remarkably adept at detecting and identifying surface boundaries despite incomplete optical information. There is a general consensus that this ability is instantiated by mechanisms of visual interpolation across spatio-temporally sparse elements, a process that may be termed spatiotemporal boundary formation (SBF). If adequate information is available, SBF generally produces veridical boundaries. In some special cases, however, SBF fails. Such failures are theoretically relevant in that they provide crucial information about underlying processing constraints. In the chapter, I define and analyze a class of motion illusions (the "breathing" illusions). In breathing illusions, rigidly rotating surfaces appear to pulsate or deform, even though a straightforward process of geometrical interpolation across space would reconstruct the veridical surface boundary. It is generally believed that such nonrigid outcome depends on a failure to apply a rigidity constraint across spatiotemporal discontinuities. The chapter reviews measurement methods and main findings in the area, and discusses the theoretical implications of breathing illusions for the current theory of SBF.

INTRODUCTION

Many animals have evolved skin patterns that resemble those present in their ecological niches. Under appropriate conditions, when such animals stand still in front of a background, observers (and predators) fail to detect them. Camouflage usually breaks down, however, when a camouflaged animal moves. The sudden revelation of the previously unseen shape is a prototypical example of a cognitive process known as spatiotemporal boundary formation, or SBF (Shipley & Kellman, 1994). When the animal stands still, spatial unit formation processes such as those described by the Gestalt laws of similarity, proximity, and good continuation prevent a predator's visual system from segregating the animal from its background. As soon as motion starts, spatiotemporal processes of unit formation cause the silhouette of the animal to become visible. Thus, SBF phenomena consist of surface boundaries seen during a motion sequence, but not in any of the static frames that compose the sequence. The motion sequence may be caused by either object relative motions or by displacements of the viewpoint relative to static objects, or both. Whatever the origin of the relevant optical motions, it is easy to demonstrate (Kaplan, 1969) that SBF requires that two conditions be met. First, the motion of individual pattern elements on the animal's skin must be distinguishable from the motion of other patterns in the image. If patterns belonging to both regions all move randomly, boundary formation does not occur. Second, as the animal moves over the ground surface, patterns on the latter must undergo some coherent transformation (in the example, progressive occlusion and disocclusion of local patterns).

Perhaps the most striking aspect of SBF is the appearance of a clear, crisp contour in regions of spatially homogenous luminance. This contour appears as the boundary of an occluding figure having a color in the surface-mode of appearance (Katz, 1935). The surface-character of the figure color may be described as perceived opacity and solidity. (Cunningham, Shipley, & Kellman, 1998). In addition, the emerging figure appears brighter than the background. Finally, SBF tends to yield the impression that the emerging surface is somewhat detached from its background, as if there was some empty space between the layers. This latter impression may be more or less compelling depending on the stimulus conditions. A number of investigators have noted that SBF may be considered as a prototypical case of *modal* completion, and that the modal character of the emerging occluding surface is accompanied by the *amodal* completion of the perceptually underlying surface or surfaces. In what is perhaps the first investigation of SBF, Sampaio (1943), a student of Belgian psychologist Albert Michotte, showed observers a simple animation involving progressive occlusion and disocclusion. In the animation, a black disk moved horizontally across an homogeneous field. For the first portion of the motion path, the whole disk was always visible. But, as it moved on a sequential transformation began: The area of the disk that had passed across a line was deleted progressively, until the whole disk had disappeared (Figure 1). Geometrically, what Sampaio did was to destroy geometrical

Figure 1. A example of the motion sequence that produces the "screen" effect.

congruence and projective identity for the disk, generating a sharp transition from a regular to an irregular figure, and then sequentially destroying congruence and identity for successive versions of the truncated disk. However, this is not what observers reported. Quite unanimously, observers described the event as depicting a disk passing behind a surface, a "screen". The screen had a clear, crisp boundary (modal completion) which appeared in the physically homogeneous background, and the disk continued to be perceived as a circular figure despite its partial occlusion (amodal completion). Both kinds of completion seem to be invariably present in SBF -- a direct consequence of the occlusion interpretation that always accompanies the appearance of a SBF surface.

VARIETES OF SBF

This bulk of this chapter is devoted to an exploration of the theoretical implications of a particular class of illusions observed in SBF. To introduce and define this class of illusions, a brief review of SBF phenomena is in order. Examples of SBF can be classified according to the manipulation used to generate the appropriate spatiotemporal structure in the optic array. In principle, this operation leads to a potential classification into four categories: (1) manipulations of texture discontinuities, such as accretions and deletions, relative motion, changes in element shape, color, and so on (see Shipley & Kellman, 1994); (2) manipulations of the shape of filled surfaces, (3) manipulations of the length and position of lines, and (4) manipulations of combinations of two or more of the above.

Texture Manipulations

In a seminal demonstration, Kaplan (1969) presented two regions of homogeneous texture side by side, and moved them as if they corresponded to two separate surfaces at different depths. This motion sequence (see Figure 2) produces a characteristic transformation at the implicit edge, known as accretion and deletion of texture. Accretion of texture takes place due to sequential uncovering by a trailing edge, whereas deletion takes

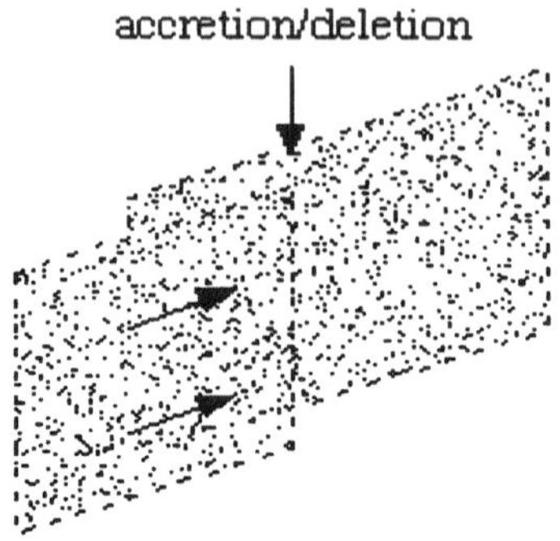

Figure 2. Generating a boundary from accretion/deletion of texture elements.

place due to sequential covering by a leading edge. At the loci where accretion and deletion occurs, a crisp, compelling edge appears. As soon as motion is halted, however, the edge stops for a brief moment and then disappears. Concurrently, the appearance of two surfaces separated in depth also vanishes, and a single homogeneous surface reappears. (Interestingly, the disappearance is not instantaneous -- to my knowledge, no measures have been attempted of this "permanence time" nor of the factors that may affect it.).

The discovery of occluding edges specified by accretion and deletion of texture played an important role in the development of the ecological approach to visual perception (Gibson, 1979), because they provided one instance of visual distance that does not need to be cognitively inferred (see Gibson, 1976) but may be picked up directly from the spatiotemporal structure of the optic array. Edges from accretion and deletion are inherently relational -- they can not occur on the basis of any single aspect of the display but require changes over time -- and thereby provided an important case for the ecological theory of perception. The role of accretion and deletion in SBF has been demonstrated in a variety of spatial tasks in adults (Andersen & Braunstein, 1983; Andersen & Cortese, 1989; Bruno & Bertamini, 1990; Kaufmann-Hayoz, Kaufmann & Stucki, 1986) and 5-month old infants (Craton & Yonas, 1988; Granrud, Yonas, Smith, Arterberry, Glicksman & Sorkes, 1984).

Besides accretion and deletion, some investigators have argued that crucial information for retrieving a SBF surface lies in the relative motion of texture elements and a boundary (Thompson, Mutch & Berzins, 1985), a source of information that has been dubbed the "boundary flow" cue (Yonas, Craton & Thompson, 1987). Information from relative motion stems from the basic constraint that, as a textured object sequentially occludes a textured background, elements on the object surface and the object boundaries move in unison. However, Craton & Yonas (1990) reported a series of experiments involving displays with two rigidly translating textures. The textures translated horizontally and were separated by a textureless gap, preventing the accretion and deletion of texture elements. Results suggested that observers were less likely to report the formation of one surface in front of another as the width of the gap increased. If horizontal lines were added to define an illusory contour at the gap, however, observers again reported a surface in front independent of gap width.

These results seem to point to a role of relative motion as information for depth order, but not as information for the formation of the boundary. Some models of spatiotemporal boundary formation have proposed to distinguish between a depth segmentation and a boundary formation stage in SBF (Kellman & Shipley, 1991). To account for the latter stage, Shipley & Kellman (1997) presented an edge-orientation-from-motion (EOFM) model which extracts local boundary orientations from local motion vectors defined by the sequence of disappearances and appearances during accretion and deletion of texture, as well as other kinds of spatiotemporal discontinuities (see also Shipley & Cunningham, this volume). Supporting the notion that the crucial information for SBF in textured displays lies in local discontinuities, Kojima (1998) recently reported that discrimination between spatiotemporally defined vertical and horizontal figures was best at high spatial frequencies whereas it was significantly reduced in low-pass versions of the same displays.

Manipulations of Filled Shapes

Spatiotemporal boundary formation can be induced by sequential transformations of filled surfaces in otherwise homogeneous fields. Suppose that a set of four filled circles is placed on a homogeneous background on the perimeter of a circle, and that a triangle having the same color as the background is rotated over this circle so that its vertices are never in front of more than two circle sat the same time. Although the triangle is invisible in any of the frames that make up the sequence, it becomes clearly visible when the sequence is animated. The sequential transformation of each circle in this kind of animation is similar to that of the original demonstration of the screen effect (Sampaio, 1943). However, in addition to seeing local occlusions at each circle as the triangular "screen" passes in front of them, observers also perceive a whole, modally present figure with a color different from the background. This figure appears to be the outcome of spatiotemporal interpolation and may be considered the SBF analog of Kanizsa's triangle (Kellman & Cohen, 1984).

The temporal and spatial characteristics of such interpolation have not been studied in a systematic fashion so far, although some relevant data can be found in Petersik & McDill (1981). An alternative manipulation of filled shapes has been reported by Klymenko & Weisstein (1986), which described the formation of a boundary of a 3D cube whose vertices were defined by dots. However, it could be argued that such boundaries are of a different kind from SBF in that the inducing motion sequence does not involve breaking projective correspondence. In fact, it is precisely because of the preservation of projective correspondence (no elements appear or disappear over time) that a 3D object emerges from the sequential transformation. The appearance of a border at the edge of the object may then be a direct consequence of the 3D interpretation rather than a form of visual interpolation.

Manipulations of Line Segments

Spatiotemporal boundaries can emerge from appropriate manipulations of line segments. In an early observation, Bradley and Lee (1982) superposed a white equilateral triangle on a black outline equilateral triangle. They also placed three black dots at the vertexes of the white triangle. Finally, they sequentially rotated the white triangle and the three dots, took successive snapshots of the transformations, and used them to construct an animation film (see Figure 3). When the animation was presented to 37 observers, 35 of them reported that the moving illusory triangle was more compelling than the static counterpart. Bradley and Lee took these results as evidence for an involvement of temporal information in the formation of the illusory triangle. In a variation of their basic display, however, they also tried removing the dots and they observed that the triangle appeared to have rounded corners when in certain positions relative to the inducing lines. The significance of this latter observation will be discussed in a later section.

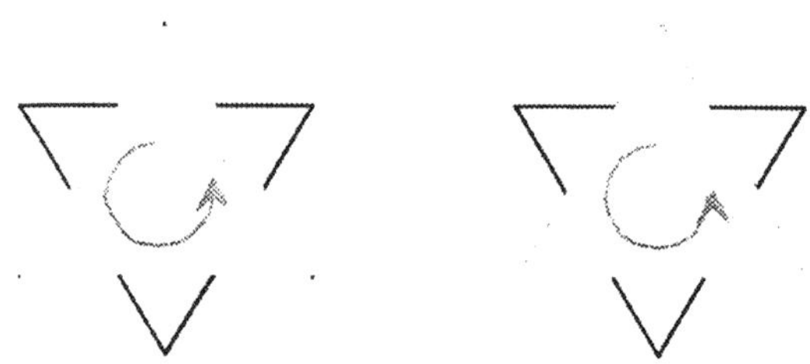

Figure 3. Spatiotemporal boundaries emerge from manipulations of line segments.

Given that the illusory boundary was already visible in the static frames, the observation of Bradley and Lee was not properly an instance of SBF. However, with a straightforward extension of their methodology (Bruno, 1989a,b) I have been able to demonstrate SBF boundaries from changes in length and position of lines as well as from simple changes in length. I employed thin luminous lines radiating from a common center attached on a black cardboard background. In front of the lines, I placed a black cardboard triangle centered on the radiating center. When observed in a dark environment, this pattern consisted of no other optical discontinuity but the set of luminous lines, which had different lengths depending on the position of the invisible triangle in front of them. However, the appearance of the pattern changed as a function of the number of lines employed. With more than 8 equidistant lines, all observers reported seeing an illusory triangle (Kanizsa, 1955). But with less than 5 lines, no observer saw a triangle and they all reported simply lines of different lengths.

I then animated the 5-line display using a rotor. When animated, all observers reported that they could see a clear, crisp boundary despite the fact that in the static views they could see none. In addition, and much to my surprise, the boundary was triangular and rigid when the lines were rotated behind the stationary triangle, whereas it was amoeba-like and nonrigid when the triangle was rotated in front of the stationary lines (Figure 4). The asymmetry was surprising, because the two kinds of events entailed the same physical relative motions. Further studies (Bruno & Bertamini, 1990; Bruno & Gerbino, 1991) demonstrated that the ability to reconstruct the physically correct occluding shape is a function of spatial and temporal factors when the lines move, but of spatial factors alone when the figure moves. Thus, SBF is usually successful in retrieving the implicit occluding edge but it can fail under certain conditions.

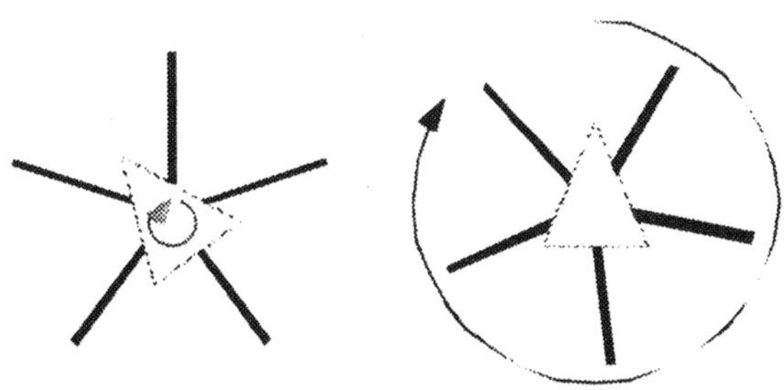

Figure 4. Rotating the figure vs. rotating background lines in a SBF display.

Combinations

In natural vision, occlusion and disocclusion of background elements by a moving surface often involves concurrent temporal transformations of texture, contours, and extended areas. For this reason, it is somewhat surprising that little attention has been devoted to SBF involving combinations of the classes of stimulus transformations described above. In a recent series of experiments (Bernardis & Bruno, 1999), we have started investigating the joint effect of textural transformations and of transformations of extended surface areas.

Experiments involved a square target surface rotating over a cross-like pattern. With a square having the same color as the general background, this pattern is equivalent to that investigated elsewhere (Bruno, 1989; Bruno & Bertamini, 1990; Bruno & Gerbino, 1991) and discussed in the previous section. Accordingly, the retrieval of the correct rotating shape depends on the size of the sequentially occluded cross arms, as demonstrated by a matching experiment. A set of eight small comparison squares was presented next to the experimental pattern. All these squares rotated around their centers 45 deg/s while physically changing their size. The change in size varied from 70% to 0% of the maximum square area, in steps of 10%. At small arm sizes, observers failed to retrieve the veridical, rigid rotating square and instead matched the rotating pattern to squares changing in size. The amount of size change reduced monotonically as arm size was increased, and disappeared when the width of the cross arm was around 50- 60% of the side of the rotating square.

Taking rigidity matches for the standard SBF pattern as a baseline, we then tried several combinations of potential spatiotemporal information for surface boundaries. In the first of these, we added random-dot textures at a number of different densities. When a square defined by random-dot texture is rotated over a stationary background covered with texture having the same density, a rigid square is readily perceived even with very sparse textures (see section on texture information above). In our matching paradigm, we found essentially perfect rigidity matches even with textures as sparse as .004%. Thus, when the same texture patterns are superimposed on the cross pattern, the resulting pattern of temporal occlusion and disocclusion contains rich information about the rigid boundaries of the rotating square. However, and rather surprisingly, the square keeps deforming. In our matching paradigm, we found that adding sparse textures is essentially ineffective in reducing the temporal deformation. Increasing texture density, the temporal deformation reduces somewhat, but is still significant even at 50% densities.

In addition to manipulations of texture, we also investigated the effect of constraint points on the spatial interpolation of the occluding boundary. This we did by adding just four dots to the rotating square in different positions along its contour. Given that the presence of several hundreds of dot patterns in the random dot texture had such a minimal effect on reducing the deformation, one would predict that just four dots would be even less effective. However, the contrary occurs. When four dots are positioned at the vertices of the rotating square, the temporal deformation is significantly reduced even with very small dots and essentially neutralized as soon as the dots become larger. On the other hand, if the dots are positioned at the middle point of the square side, the deformation is as strong as without the constraint dots. Thus, the effect of adding four constraint dots on the temporal deformation of the rotating square appears similar to the effect of constraint dots on the spatial interpolation in static illusory contours (Vezzani, 1999). The theoretical implications of these preliminary findings will be discussed in a later section. Given the diverse findings that are brought together in these later sections, a brief review of the methods that have been used to quantify SBF phenomena is presented first.

MEASUREMENT ISSUES

Methods for quantifying spatiotemporal boundary formation have met with a typical dilemma of research on perceptual representations. On one hand, SBF surfaces can be assessed directly, by asking subjects to rate their vividness or clarity, or by collecting numerical rigidity ratings in the cases where SBF produces illusory deformations (see section on the breathing figure illusion below). Such direct ratings are typically performed as a function of several physical parameters, such as spatiotemporal alignments of inducing elements or surfaces, contrast, and speed. Resulting functions appear to summarize well how the strength of SBF depends on such parameters, but their interpretation is often difficult because of the demand character (Orne, 1962) of these tasks.

Suppose that in one experiment an investigator varied the spatial alignment of inducing elements and asked observers to rate the clarity of the contour of the SBF surface. In such an experiment, one typically gets a monotonic curve whereby the clarity decreases as a function of departure from perfect alignment. It seems plausible to interpret this result as evidence that clear, crisp SBF contours are best obtained from spatially aligned inducers. However, one simply cannot rule out the possibility that what observers do in this task is not to judge the clarity of the SBF contour, but alignment itself. The latter perceptual quality is, after all, clearly available in the stimulus pattern, whereas the former is less clearly defined and it may require a certain amount of expertise to rate.

As an alternative to direct ratings, a number of investigators have sought to employ performance measures. An example of such measure is the ability to distinguish between straight and sinusoidal SBF contours bounding surfaces of equal area (Bruno & Bertamini, 1990). Other examples are the ability to distinguish between a vertical and a horizontal SBF surface (Kojima, 1998) or to identify which of a set of several shapes is induced by a current SBF display (Andersen & Cortese, 1989; Hine, 1987; Shipley & Kellman, 1997).

Performance measures provide an objective, quantitative assessment of dimensions that are presumably related to contour quality and vividness. For instance, it seems reasonable to assume that the more vivid the SBF contour, the better one should be able to discriminate it from other contours and to identify it. However, discrimination may also be possible on the basis of local properties of the inducing elements. If this is the case, then 'objective' performance measures are even more problematic than direct ratings, for in performance paradigms observers are simply told to try to discriminate or identify shapes as well as they can, which may actually encourage them to use inducer features if available. In direct ratings, one at least tells observers to pay attention to a certain aspect of their experience, and can hope that observers will comply with that request. In performance measures, there is simply no way to be assured that observers are basing their responses on the SBF surface unless careful controls are employed.

One such control is the assessment of static versions of the induced figures. If these show a different pattern from the motion versions, one can at least conclude that discrimination was not based on spatial local properties of the inducers. Another approach would be to use the same animation sequence used for the SBF condition but slowed to a frame rate (e.g., 300 msec per frame) where no one reports seeing an SBF contour. It is still possible, however, that observers base their discriminations on temporally local properties, or on a combination of spatial and temporal features. I cannot think of a suitable control for these possibilities at present.

As yet another alternative to both direct reports and performance measures, some investigators have used paradigms involving indirect methods. For instance, Bernardis & Bruno (1999) evaluated the amount of nonrigidity in a SBF figure by asking observers to select, among a graded set of pulsating comparison figures, that which best matched the amount of pulsation seen in the current SBF display. In an earlier paper, Shiffrar & Pavel (1991) measured the amount of nonrigidity by an elegant nulling method, whereby observers changed the amount of perceived nonrigidity by manipulating the actual change in size of a rotating figure.

Such indirect methods combine the objectivity of performance measures with the possibility of directing the observer's attention to the perceptual variable one wishes to measure. However, it may not always be possible to find an appropriate procedure for all kinds of SBF surfaces and this may limit the applicability of the latter approach. In conclusion, direct assessments as well as performance measures are sometimes difficult to interpret. Indirect methods potentially provide unbiased measures of SBF clarity, but they may not always be possible. For these reasons, it seems advisable that theoretical conclusions be supported by converging evidence (Garner, Hacker & Ericksen, 1956) from as many paradigms as possible.

BREATHING ILLUSIONS

The human visual system can use spatiotemporally sparse information efficiently to detect and identify surface boundaries. Presumably, this ability is rooted in constraints originating from the ecology of our visual world (Parks, 1984). Environmental conditions such as transparent layers, fog, mist, reduced illumination, or camouflage can minimize the amount of spatial structure specifying surface boundaries in the optic array. In addition, most surfaces are subjected to partial occlusion by other opaque objects. That humans and other animals (Bravo, Blake & Morrison, 1988) are able to exploit additional constraints from the temporal structure of the optic array to reconstruct otherwise invisible boundaries is therefore useful and adaptive.

However, the ability to reconstruct surface boundaries from spatiotemporal patterns of occlusion and disocclusion is not perfect. In several documented cases, observers are unable to perform the reconstruction correctly because of insufficient spatiotemporal density of the visible elements (Andersen & Cortese, 1989; Bruno & Bertamini, 1990; Hine, 1987). These cases are interesting, in that they provide information concerning what is the minimum amount of information necessary for SBF. Of even greater interest, however, are cases where the available spatial information is potentially sufficient for veridical retrieval of the boundaries, but this is not used or it is misused.

In this section, the claim is developed that there is a class of motion illusions that has precisely such characteristics. These illusions have to do with SBF in rotary patterns similar to those investigated by Bruno & Gerbino (1991), and consist of compelling impressions that the rotating figure, which is actually rigid, pulsates or "breathes" during the rotation. Following a terminology that has somehow made its way into popular science catalogs, I propose to refer to this class as the "breathing" illusions. Animated examples of such illusions can be viewed on the world-wide-web at http://www.illusionworks.com. A web tutorial specifically devoted to spatial effects on motion perception, including examples of breathing figure illusions, may be found at the web site of the Perception Laboratory of the University of Trieste, at http://www.psico.univ.trieste.it/labs/perclab.

Varieties of Breathing Figures

Instances of breathing illusions have been known for about a decade. To the best of my knowledge, the first report of illusory pulsation in a rigidly rotating figure is due to Meyer and Dougherty (1987, 1988), who described an illusion that they called "contours that contract". Their illusion was generated by a white square rotating over a white background and four equidistant black-filled disks (Figure 5). The pattern yields a Kanizsa-type illusory square which is readily perceived in the stationary frames, but appears as a pulsating figure when in rotation. The pulsation is cyclical, with the perceived area reaching its maximum when the corners of the square are visible within the disks, and its minimum when the sides of the square produce perfectly horizontal and vertical cuts on the disks.

Figure 5. Two frames from a sequence generating a "breathing" illusory square.

In a later paper, Meyer & Dougherty (1990) also reported a related illusion obtained by rotating a black square behind four stationary white disks on a white background (Figure 6). The latter pattern produces the same cycle of visibility/invisibility of the square vertices as the original illusion, but with an inversion of the resulting surface stratification (the square is seen as occluded instead of occluding). The perceptual outcome of this manipulation is comparable to that of the original illusion, with the addition of figural bistability. Because of

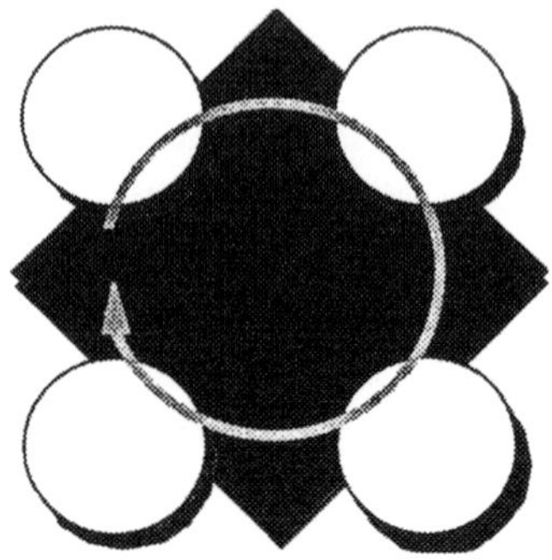

Figure 6. A bistable display perceived as a breathing occluded square or as an unoccluded "oozing" cross (the boundaries of the four disks were not visible in the actual motion sequence).

the figural characteristics of the pattern, most notably those having to do with the Gestalt law of closure, the perceptual interpretation of this pattern oscillates between two possibilities. The first of these consists of four stationary occluding illusory disks and a square behind them. When observers perceive these four illusory occluding disks, they also see that the rotating square breathes as in the original illusion. The second interpretation consists of an irregular object without occluders. If no occluders are perceived, this irregular object changes shape over time and it is perceived as a sort of rubbery or "oozing" cross. The two percepts seem to alternate for all observers although the second is somewhat easier to achieve.

A more exact analog to Meyer and Dougherty's breathing illusory can be created by simply adding a line around the four disks (Shiffrar & Pavel, 1991). Given that the circumference is always visible in these displays, the inversion of the surface stratification is stable in this case, causing the four disks to appear as four holes in a homogeneous surface. Through the four disks, one continuously perceives a square that completes behind the surface. However, the temporal transformations that occur within the four "holes" while the square is rotated "behind" the surface are exactly equivalent to those caused by the occluding surface of Meyer & Dougherty and the same illusory breathing is perceived.

Shiffrar & Pavel (1991) interpreted this finding as evidence that the breathing square illusion of Meyer & Dougherty is due to constraints on the spatial integration of motion signals. According to their proposal, when the corners of the square are not visible within one of the disks, because of the aperture problem the center of rotation for each of the visible contours is misperceived and placed near to, or at, the local center of the rotating side. As a consequence, local motion signals that are oriented toward or away from the actual center of rotation become available. These signals signal a change in size, and this causes the apparent breathing. There is, however, an alternative explanation for their observed equivalence. It could be that the same process of spatial completion is involved in both forms of the illusion. The hypothesis that the modal completion of an illusory border and the amodal completion of a partly occluded border are mediated by the same unit-formation process is supported by a number of observations (Bradley & Petry, 1977; Kellman & Loukides, 1987; Kellman & Shipley, 1991; Petter, 1956; Shipley & Kellman, 1992). In a later section, I speculate that this equivalence of modal and amodal unit formation is actually crucial to an explanation of breathing figure illusions.

The breathing square displays of Meyer & Dougherty are not proper instances of SBF in that one can see an occluding square shape in each of the static views that compose the animation sequence. As such, they differ from the kinetic illusory triangle reported by Kellman & Cohen (1984). However, the relation between the two displays becomes obvious if one substitutes the three filled disks of the Kellman & Cohen animation with three filled rectangles similar to those studied by Bernardis & Bruno (1999). Figure 7, based on observations by Shiffrar and Pavel (1991), illustrates this point.

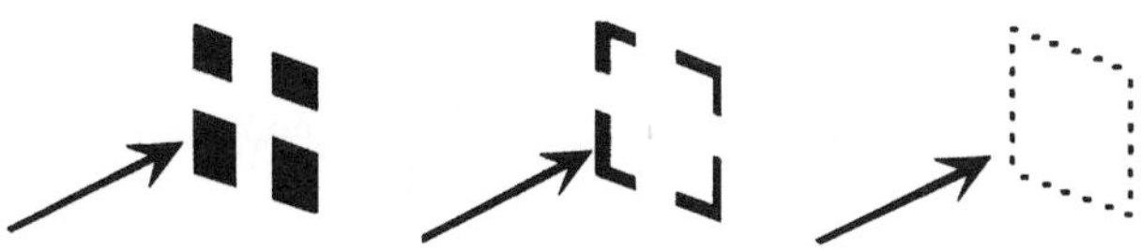

Figure 7. Generating an occluded filled square, an occluded square contour, or a square illusory figure with comparable spatiotemporal discontinuities.

The observation of motion sequences using these displays is especially instructive. When the rectangles are sufficiently wide, the substitution produces the same local transformations over the endings of the rectangles as those that are produced within the disks of Kellman and Cohen. As soon as rectangle width is decreased, however, a point is soon reached where the triangle appears nonrigid. Moreover, if the three rectangles are equidistant from each other, defining three 120 deg sectors, the triangle appears to breath exactly as the square of Meyer and Dougherty. Finally, by decreasing the width of the rectangles even more, one can produce the thin line display studied by Bruno (1989a; b) and by Bruno & Gerbino (1991) and described in the above section on SBF from line manipulations. Thus, all illusory deformations of rigidly rotating surfaces may be viewed as special cases of a general manipulation of the same stimulus dimensions, involving the size and density of the filled elements that are sequentially occluded and revealed. Parametric data collected by Bruno & Bertamini (1990) and, more recently, by Bernardis & Bruno (1999) suggest that the conditions of occurrence for breathing figure illusions depend on both these spatial parameters, whereas they do not depend on rotation velocity.

Ravioli

Meyer and Dougherty (1987) also reported that if their square is replaced with a serrated square, a sort of illusory post-stamp or illusory *raviolo,* the breathing impression disappears. Observations from our laboratory indicate that this fact may not to be true in general. Data collected using the methodology of Bernardis &Bruno (1999) demonstrated that the pulsation is visible in the rotating ravioli, over a range of serration widths and not just when the serrations are so small as to make the corners difficult to perceive, as claimed by some (Shiffrar & Pavel, 1991).

In general, transitions between three, phenomenally distinct percepts can be observed when one measures breathing as a function of serration width. None of these entail a recovery of rigidity proper. With very small serrations, the breathing is clearly visible and the serrations appear to slide over the rotating sides in the opposite direction relative to the rotation direction. The sliding is similar to the so-called "sliding" effect observed when one places a dot on a contour viewed through a circular aperture, suggesting that very small serrations are perceived as elements placed on a straight contour, which becomes their proximal frame of reference independently of the overall rotation of the square, an instance of separation between perceptual systems (Duncker, 1923). With middle-sized serrations, the breathing is also very clear and only slightly less strong than the smaller cases. However, middle-sized serrations do not slide but appear as proper jagged edges. With very large serrations, finally, the spatio-temporal interpolation of the jagged lines fails, and one has a confusing impression of an incomplete figure flashing and then disappearing, occasionally rotating in one direction, occasionally rotating in the other.

Background Superiority

Breathing square illusions share another common element. They are readily experienced when a surface is seen rotating in front of stationary background elements or behind stationary holes, whereas they are much less compelling when exactly the same relative motions are produced by rotating the background element or foreground holes relative to a stationary figure. In a previous paper (Bruno & Gerbino, 1991), I have proposed to call this asymmetry in the perceptual result of displays having equivalent relative motions the "background superiority effect" or BSE for short.

Background-motion superiority in veridically specifying the shape of an occluding figure has been reported by a number of investigators. Bruno & Bertamini (1990) measured shape discriminations from occlusion events involving thin lines as a function of rotation speed and line density. They found that in figure-motion conditions discrimination was essentially a step function of spatial density whereas it did not depend on velocity. In background motion conditions, on the other hand, discrimination performance was superior within comparable spatial conditions, and depended on both spatial density and velocity. Meyer and Dougherty (1991) reported that their "oozing cross" was perceived only when the sequence was generated by rotating the square behind the circles. When the circles themselves were rotated, a rigid square was perceived with only a momentary loss of identity (not of rigidity) when the disks covered the square vertices. Shiffrar & Pavel (1991) measured the strength of the illusory breathing in both figure- and background-motion conditions and found essentially no breathing in the latter. Bruno and Gerbino (1991) analyzed the thin-line display investigated by Bruno (1989a, b) and found that a rotating triangle could yield a number of nonrigid percepts depending on the density of the occluded thin lines, whereas equivalent displays where the lines were moved behind the triangle yielded essentially rigid percepts. Even in related displays that do not yield the breathing illusion, it has been noted that the SBF figure appears sharper and clearer when the background moves (Kellman & Cohen, 1984; Kellman & Loukides, 1987).

Translatory Motion

A final element common to breathing figure illusions is their confinement to rotary displays. If the patterns studied by Meyer and Dougherty and Shiffrar and Pavel are modified to yield a cyclic oscillation along a rectilinear path, the translating square appears rigid. If they are modified to depict translation along the perimeter of a small square centered at the middle of the configuration, the square also appears rigid. Some nonrigidity can be perceived if a figure is translated over thin, sparse line elements, but not if it is translated over a random-dot texture (Bruno & Bertamini, 1990). Even in this case, however, discrimination performance is better with translations than with rotations.

THEORETICAL IMPLICATIONS

In this chapter, a claim is made that several motion illusions should be viewed as members of one general class. The class of breathing illusions consists of a number of compelling percepts of nonrigidity that are perceived when a moving figure is incompletely specified by the spatial structure of the optic array, so that its shape must be retrieved by processes of visual interpolation across spatially sparse elements. In most of the cases discussed above, the impression of nonrigidity consists of a cyclical change in size (i.e. "breathing"). However, alternative percepts are also possible, involving the perception of deforming blobs. Whatever the resulting type of nonrigidity, in all cases nonrigidity is perceived only if the figure moves and only if the motion is a rotation. If the background moves relative to a stationary figure, or if the motion is a translation, then the illusion is absent or greatly reduced.

Relatability Theory

Although instances of breathing figure illusions have been known for some time, their theoretical implications have not been clarified. According to the current theory of SBF, observers reconstruct incompletely defined edges by means of an integration process that connects occlusion discontinuities across space or time, or both. The view that modal and amodal boundaries could be thought of as resulting from perceptual interpolation over space is found in early computational work (Brady & Grimson, 1981; Ullman, 1976). However, the development of a general theory of boundary formation across relatable discontinuities (henceforth: relatability theory) proceeded mostly from visual psychophysics and phenomenological observations (Kellman & Loukides, 1987; Kellman & Shipley, 1991; Shipley & Kellman, 1994, 1997). Relatability theory may be regarded as consisting of three key elements: the assumption of a common unit formation stage for modal and amodal boundary formation, the definition of spatio-temporal discontinuity, and the definition of constraints on interpolation. Let us consider them in detail against the characteristics of breathing figure illusions.

Consider first the hypothesis of a common unit formation stage. According to relatability theory, a common unit formation stage is involved in the formation of both modal and amodal boundaries. The phenomenal difference between these two types of boundaries is not due to the properties of the unit formation process, but to the properties of a second stage having to do with edge classification. If an edge is classified as being an occluding edge, then it becomes a modally perceived (albeit "illusory") surface edge. If it is classified as an occluded edge, then it becomes an amodally completed edge. However, the actual reconstruction of boundary characteristics such as orientation, curvature, and motion is performed by one and the same process. In support of the claim of a single unit formation process underlying modal and amodal boundaries, it has been noted that in a number of displays both kinds of boundaries can form across the same discontinuities. For instance, in Petter's (1955) "spontaneously splitting" black-on-black figures, both a modal occluding boundary and an amodal occluded boundary are perceived, but their placement can flip over time as in a bistable pattern. Similarly, in Bradley & Petry's (1977) illusory Necker cube one sees modal boundaries belonging to an occluding cube, but the same configuration can also appear as an occluded cube seen through several holes. In this latter case, the boundaries of the cube are completed amodally.

Inasmuch as they can be produced both with modal and amodal boundaries, breathing figures are fully consistent with relatability theory in this respect. For instance, in Meyer and Dougherty's (1987) breathing square, the same spatial and temporal discontinuities yield occluding, modal boundaries or, applying Shiffrar and Pavel's (1991) modification, occluded amodal boundaries. Yet, the breathing impression is identical, suggesting that the process that generated boundary properties yielded exactly the same results in both cases. The same considerations apply to the thin line displays studied by Bruno and Gerbino (1991). With training, it is possible to see the lines as thin slits on a homogeneous surface, with a figure moving behind such surface and seen through the slits (Maloney, personal communication). Again, the breathing impression is the same in the two cases.

Consider now the notion of discontinuities. Within the relatability framework, perceptual interpolation is triggered by specific properties in the structure of the optic array. These properties, called discontinuities, are defined separately for spatial and temporal domains. Let us consider them in turn. Spatial discontinuities are abrupt changes of direction in a contour specified by a luminance step. Such changes are identifiable as loci where functions describing contour curvature are not differentiable, that is, loci where the contour is not locally smooth. All t-junctions resulting from the superposition of two surfaces correspond to a spatial discontinuity and generate processes of amodal visual interpolation. However, any abrupt change in direction in a surface contour can function as a discontinuity, even without a t-junction defined by luminance steps. Thus, missing sectors or gaps in inducing surfaces can also trigger interpolation, as in the modal formation of illusory boundaries. Temporal discontinuities are temporal positions marking a sudden breakage of projective identity. Again, such losses of projective identity take place every time a surface undergoes partial occlusion and disocclusion by another opaque surface. However, such losses can take place even with a single surface. In the screen effect, for instance, initial views of the moving disk are projections of the same figure. As soon as the occlusion event begins, however, part of the disk is cut off and the resulting stimulus region is no longer a possible projection of the initial disk. Such interruption of projective identity is a temporal discontinuity.

Are breathing figure illusions consistent with process that interpolate across spatial and temporal discontinuities? At first blush, it would seem that the answer is no. After all, one of the defining characteristics of the class is that simple geometrical interpolation always reproduces the veridical occluding shape when applied to the static frames that compose the breathing animation. Thus, a trivial spatial interpolation process would predict rigidity in both figure- and background motion conditions. It is possible, however, that (potentially veridical) interpolation of spatial discontinuities is affected by a conflicting interpolation solution across temporal discontinuities. This is, in a nutshell, the explanation put forth by Shiffrar and Pavel (1991) for breathing figure illusions. In the next section, however, I argue that there are empirical reasons to conclude that this proposal may not be entirely correct.

Finally, consider constraints on interpolation. Within relatability theory, visual interpolation across spatial and temporal discontinuities is constrained by two factors: pairwise connectability and monotonicity. Pairwise connectability means that interpolation can take place between two discontinuities, provided that no other discontinuity is in between. Monotonicity means that the connection between the two discontinuities must progress continuously, without changing direction or doubling back onto itself. The implications of these constraints for spatial relatability are straightforward. Their meaning for temporal relatability has been less clearly developed, but it seems to imply temporally continuous change of paired temporal discontinuities.

Breathing figure illusions are generally regarded as a consequence of a failure to apply a rigidity constraint against a potential nonrigid alternative, when this alternative is supported by specific processes of spatiotemporal interpolation (Shiffrar & Pavel, 1991). According to this account, the rotation of individual occluding contours is misperceived by observers because of a tendency to locate the center of rotation on the contour itself even when this is physically outside of the area where the contour is visible. Because of the aperture problem, such misperception yields significant motion components oriented away or toward the actual center of the configuration. Interpolating across the corresponding temporal discontinuities generates a nonrigid alternative to the rigid solution yielded by spatial interpolations. For some reason the system fails to apply a rigidity constraint across the temporal and spatial changes, and the perceptual result is a breathing figure.

Spatial vs. Spatiotemporal Interpolation

The explanation put forth by Shiffrar and Pavel (1991) is attractive, in that it ascribes the illusion to known constraints on the processing of local motion (i.e., the aperture problem, see Shiffrar, this volume), thereby providing an elegant proposal for the observed equivalence of the modal and amodal version of the breathing square illusion. Contrary to the above explanation, however, a number of facts suggest that breathing figures are not due to misperceiving the center of rotation. Consider the background superiority effect. Given that figure- and background-motion animations consist of exactly the same sequence of relative motions, it is not clear why center misperception should apply to the former, but not the latter. In fact, the temporal changes that occur as an occluding contour rotates over a stationary surface are identical to those that occur as the stationary surface rotates behind the occluding contour. Thus, the corresponding discontinuities (spatial and temporal) are the same, and local misperception of the center of rotation for contours should take place in both cases. It could be, however, that retrieving a stationary occluding figure lends more readily to a rigid interpretation, if available. This bias may results simply due to the stability of the occluding figure and its boundaries relative to a retinotopic frame of reference. Thus, the two motion conditions are not fully comparable, and the same explanation cannot be applied to both. This appears to be, albeit implicitly, the position of Shiffrar and Pavel (1991). Alternatively, it has been proposed that background motion conditions contain qualitatively different kinematic information about the occluding contour (Bruno & Gerbino, 1991).

Next, recall that compelling breathing illusions can be achieved using thin line displays (Bruno & Gerbino, 1991). Given that any 2D line is a possible projection of some line oriented in space, this type of display contains spatial, but not temporal discontinuities by the current definition. Therefore, either we conclude that temporal interpolation is not involved in the illusion, or we conclude that the definition of temporal discontinuities cannot be purely local. Under a global definition, the thin line displays investigated by Bruno and Gerbino (1991) could be regarded as involving the occlusion of a larger pattern, consisting of lines radiating off a common center. The global changes of this pattern do involve temporal breaking of projective identity, and would therefore constitute a temporal discontinuity by the current definition. However, two recent observations from our lab seem to provide definitive arguments against center misperception. These concern the effects of texture (Bernardis & Bruno, 1999) and of constraint dots (Bruno & Bernardis, in preparation) on the breathing illusion in patterns involving thin line elements.

Recall descriptions of these results in the section on SBF phenomena above. If random dot texture is added to the breathing square pattern, such that the spatiotemporal pattern of accretion and deletion veridically specifies square rotation, the square keeps breathing. This fact is problematic for the explanation based on misperceiving the center of rotation, because textural optic flow unambiguously specifies this center in these displays. On the other hand, adding just four constraint dots on the vertices of the rotating square greatly reduces the breathing. This fact is even more problematic for the center misperception hypothesis, because no local information is available about the center of rotation of each square side in these displays. In conclusion, conditions that should allow accurate perception of the center can fail to stop the breathing, whereas conditions that should be consistent with its misperception can stop it. When considered together, these two results demonstrate a causal dissociation between misperceiving the center of rotation and the breathing impression.

The above facts suggest that breathing illusions are due to constraints on the multiscale interpolation of spatial, not spatiotemporal discontinuities. Consider the case of the breathing square. As the square rotates, it occupies one of two qualitatively different positions relative to the four disks. In one of these, the square covers the disks with its vertices. In the other, it covers them with its sides and its vertices are not specified in the luminance domain. These two positions correspond to different phases of the breathing impression. When the vertices are visible, the square reaches its maximum apparent size. As soon as they disappear, the square appears to shrink reaching its minimum size when the middle point of the side reaches the midpoint of the occluded disk. These phasic changes are consistent with transitions between different spatial interpolations of the discontinuities produced at the disks by the occlusion events. When the vertices are visible, each side is also partly visible and interpolation can be performed along a straight path. Accordingly, a Kanizsa-type illusory square is perceived in the stationary frames. When the side are visible, however, the vertices are not. Each of the visible sides is oriented at 90 deg relative to contiguous sides. Thus, in this position continuous interpolation across spatial discontinuities must be along a curved path. Accordingly, in frames where only the sides are visible one does not tend to perceive a square but a square with rounded corners or, with sufficiently thin occluded elements, an illusory circle.

The fact that thin line inducers produce curve illusory contours has been known for a long time (Ehrenstein, 1941; Sambin, 1987) and has been often regarded as evidence for the constraints proposed by relatability theory (Kellman & Shipley, 1991). However, the implications for the explanation of breathing illusions have not been recognized. Breathing illusions may be simply due to cyclic transitions between different spatial interpolations, which in turn imply figures of different sizes and shapes. This proposal can be put to test by generating a breathing square animation employing four rectangular occluded elements in a crosslike pattern, and paying attention to the phenomenology of the apparent deformation. With relatively thin rectangles, one can indeed perceive a square turning into a circle. As the rectangles get wider, one no longer perceives a circle and the breathing impression weakens (Bernardis & Bruno, 1999). Further tests are also possible. For instance, it is known that adding constraint dots to an illusory circle induced by thin line elements turns the circular figure into a figure with vertices defined by the dots themselves (see Vezzani, 1999). We have found that if constraint dots are added to the breathing square animation to define the vertices of the rotating square, the illusion is greatly reduced relative to comparable textured animations that contain many dots instead of four (Bruno & Bernardis, in preparation). This finding is also consistent with a causal role of purely spatial interpolation.

Finally, discrimination studies suggest that the ability to retrieve the veridical shape from the sequential occlusion of lines or texture elements depends on spatial factors, such as line density, but not on temporal factors, such as rotation velocity (Bruno & Bertamini, 1990). Readers can easily convince themselves of this by again generating a breathing square animation employing four rectangular occluded elements in a cross like pattern. As the rectangles get wider, the reduction in the breathing impression is obvious. As the rotation is sped up within comparable widths, however, no reduction is seen.

Rigidity Constraints

In my initial definition of breathing illusions, I suggested that in these illusions a spatial interpolatory process should always produce a rigid, veridical interpretation. Although this is true in a purely geometrical sense, the above considerations imply that this is not equally true from the standpoint of the edge representations that are produced at early stages of visual processing. These representations entail a temporal transition between shapes having different shapes and sizes. Thus, in terms of these representations there simply is no rigid alternative in these displays. Breathing figures are not a counter example to the validity of a rigidity assumption in motion processing, because the system is not in the position of making a choice between a rigid and a nonrigid alternative in these cases. The nonrigid interpretation is the only interpretation available given the early edge representations, their temporal unfolding, and binocular information about the position in depth of the rotating figure. If the salience of the latter is reduced by closing one eye, sitting far enough from the monitor, or simply by attentively ignoring it, then a rigid alternative exists and it is readily perceived: looming. An interesting test of these implications would be to assess the relative frequency of the looming vs. breathing interpretations, for monocularly viewed animations, as a function of rectangle width. With narrower rectangles, looming should be harder to perceive in that one can easily perceive the change in shape of the rotating figure.

Pursuit Eye Movements

The bulk of this chapter has been devoted to an analysis of breathing illusions within the framework of SBF theory. The examined data supported a causal role of spatial, not spatiotemporal interpolatory processes as claimed by earlier proposals (Shiffrar & Pavel, 1991). In addition, the present analysis suggested that breathing illusions should not be regarded as a counterexample to a rigidity assumption in motion processing. There is, however, one characteristic of the class that could appear as evidence against an explanation based on pure spatial interpolation. This characteristic is the confinement of breathing illusions to figure rotation conditions. Occlusion events involving the same sparse elements give rise to breathing illusions if they result from a rotating figure in front of a stationary background, but not if they result from a rotating background behind a stationary figure.

In an earlier paper, Bruno and Gerbino (1991) suggested that this asymmetry may be due to the nature of the stimulus transformations involved in the two conditions. Consider a breathing figure display with thin-line occluded elements. In figure rotation conditions, the stimulus transformations correspond solely to changes in length of the lines. The visual system has been shown to generally resist interpreting such one-dimensional change as due to occlusion (Rock & Gilchrist, 1975). Accordingly, observers report a deforming shape that closely follows the temporal transitions between spatial interpolations of line endings. In background rotation conditions, however, the stimulus transformations correspond to changes in length and position for each line. This two-dimensional transformation can be used to generate a motion vector oriented along the occluding contour by a simple vector summation operation (Bruno & Gerbino, 1991). Given that their analysis can be readily extended to any occluding element possessing a contour, the asymmetry appears consistent with a spatial explanation of breathing.

Bruno and Bertamini (1990) investigated the role of spatial density and velocity in four kinds of occlusion events: rotations with thin line backgrounds, horizontal translations with thin line background, rotations with textured backgrounds, and horizontal translations with textured backgrounds. They found that contour discriminations improved with spatial density in all conditions, whereas they improved with density and velocity only with translatory displays, texture yielding the most marked improvement and thin lines yielding a somewhat weaker effect. To account for this difference, they speculated that observers might use pursuit eye movements to register contour information. As an illusory surface is translated over background elements, observers can produce a retinal transformation akin to background motion conditions if they maintain fixation on the figure itself. Such ocular pursuit would be most accurate with random dots peppered at all positions around the spatially undefined figure, less accurate with thin lines that occupy only specific positions and essentially impossible for rotary motions given that the eye can perform only limited rotations around its optical axis. The hypothesis of a role of pursuit in SBF is consistent with earlier reports of eye movement effects in anorthoscopic perception (Rock, Halper, Divita & Wheeler, 1986).

Direct tests of the role of pursuit in SBF would require eye-tracking equipment and have not been performed so far. However, indirect tests are possible. In unpublished experiments (Bruno, 1990) using the methodology of Bruno and Bertamini (1990), I investigated contour discriminations as a function of texture density, velocity, and duration. Given that the initiation of smooth pursuit involves latencies of about 100-200 ms (Robinson, 1965; Lightstone, 1973), I predicted that shorter durations would remove velocity effects in figure translation conditions, where pursuit is hypothesized to be critical for SBF, but not in background translation conditions. Three levels of density (12, 18, and 24 dots per cm^2 on a Macintosh screen viewed at an approximate distance of 50 cm), two levels of velocity (7 cm and 1.5 cm/s) and four stimulus durations (150, 300, 450, 600 ms) were investigated in both figure- and background-translation conditions. Percentages of correct identifications of the occluding contours were at chance at 150 ms and improved monotonically with density at longer durations in both conditions. However, the time course of the velocity effect was markedly different as a function of motion conditions. In background motion conditions, higher velocities allowed significantly more accurate identifications at 300 ms, and produced marked improvements at 450 and 600 ms. In figure motion conditions, velocity produced no effect at 300 and 450 ms, whereas it had a weak effect only at 600 ms durations.

These results are consistent with an account of identification as requiring two kinds of perceptual activity: retinal stabilization of the candidate contour, and acquisition of contour information. The first activity involves ocular pursuit, whereas the second implies stimulation of motion detectors. The extent to which an observer needs to perform these activities depends on motion conditions. With background motion, the figure is stationary and appears in correspondence with a fixation mark. Consequently, no pursuit movements are needed to stabilize the contour. All that is needed is to maintain fixation as the contour begins to be revealed by motion components from the moving background. If the motion is sufficiently fast, after approximately 300 ms enough of the contour has been revealed for discrimination. With figure motion, on the other hand, the figure must be pursued to reveal motion components that are informative about contour direction. The initiation of pursuit involves an initial stage of about 200 ms to overcome inertia and begin the movement. Additional time may be needed to fine-tune eye motion in register with stimulus motion (Hallet, 1986). Thus, after another 300-400 ms, enough of the contour is revealed and performance begins to improve with velocity.

Adopting a more general theoretical stance, the potential role of pursuit could be regarded as a form of active exploratory behavior allowing observers to pick up spatiotemporal information. Such information can be retrieved only if the appropriate relationship is established between the perceptual system of an organism and the actual motions occurring in the environment. If this is correct, then SBF and its failures in breathing illusions may be considered as a theoretically important paradigm for investigating interrelations between perception and action (Gibson, 1979, E.J. Gibson, 1988).

ACKNOWLDEGMENTS

The preparation of this chapter was supported by MURST grant n. 991133382. Thanks to Tim Shipley and Maggie Shiffrar for useful comments on an earlier version. Recent empirical findings were collected in collaboration with Paolo Bernardis and presented in part at the XXII European Conference on Visual Perception (ECVP), Trieste, Italy, 22 - 26 August 1999.

REFERENCES

Andersen, G.J. & Braunstein, M.L. (1983). Dynamic occlusion in the perception of rotation in depth. *Perception & Psychophysics*, *34*, 356-362.

Andersen, G.J. & Cortese, J.M. (1989). 2-D contour perception resulting from kinetic occlusion. *Perception & Psychophysics, 46*,49-55.

Bernardis, P. & Bruno, N. (1999). Kinetic illusory figures: interaction of information from accretion and deletion of surface texture and surface contours. *Perception supplement, 28*, 117.

Bradley, D. R. & Lee, K. (1982). Animated subjective contours. *Perception & Psychophysics, 32*, 393-395.

Bravo, M., Blake, R., & Morrison, S. (1988). Cats see subjective countours. *Vision Research, 28*, 861-865.

Bruno, N. (1989a). Occlusion events and the perception of surfaces. Poster presented at the 5th International Conference on Event Perception and Action, Miami University, Oxford, Ohio, June 1989.

Bruno, N. (1989b). Two kinds of occlusion event and the shape of illusory contours. *Contributi di Psicologia, 2*, 85-101.

Bruno, N. & Bertamini, M. (1990). Identifying contours from occlusion events. *Perception & Psychophysics, 48*, 331-342.

Bruno, N. & Gerbino, W. (1991). Illusory figures based on local kinematics. *Perception, 20*, 259-274.

Craton, L.G. & Yonas A. (1988). Infants' sensitivity to boundary flow information for depth at an edge. *Child Development, 59*, 1522-1529.

Craton, L.G. & Yonas A. (1990). Kinetic occlusion: further studies of the boundary flow cue. *Perception & Psychophysics, 47*, 169-179.

Cunningham, D.W., Shipley, T. F. & Kellman, P. J. (1998a). Interactions between spatial and spatiotemporal information in spatiotemporal boundary formation. *Perception & Psychophysics, 60*, 839-851.

Cunningham, D.W., Shipley, T. F. & Kellman, P. J. (1998b).The dynamic specification of surfaces and boundaries. *Perception, 27*, 403-415.

Duncker, K. (1929). Über induzierte bewegung. Psychologische Forschnung, 12, 180-259.

Garner, W.R., Hake H.W., & Ericksen, C.W. (1956). Operationism and the concept of perception. *Psychological Review, 63*, 149-159.

Gibson, J. J. (1976). Three kinds of distance that can be seen, or how Bishop Berkeley went wrong. In G.B. Flores d'Arcais (Ed) Studies in perception: Festschrift for Fabio Metelli, 83-87. Firenze: Giunti.

Gibson, J. J. (1979). *The ecological approach to visual perception*. Boston: Houghton-Mifflin.

Hine, T. (1987). Subjective contours produced purely by dynamic occlusion of sparse-points array. *Bulletin of the Psychonomic Society, 25*, 182-184.

Kanizsa, G. (1955). Margini quasi percettivi in campi con stimolazi oneomogenea. *Rivista di Psicologia, 49*, 7-30.

Kaplan, G. (1969). Kinetic disruption of optical texture: the perception of depth at an edge. *Perception & Psychophysics, 6*, 193-198.

Katz, D. (1991). Die Erscheinungweisen der Farben und ihre Beeinflussungdurch die individuelle Erfahrung. *Zeitschrift für Psychologieund Physiologie der Sinnesorgane, 7*. Engl. Trans. (1935) The world of Color. Kegan Paul.

Kaufmann-Hayoz, R., Kaufmann, F., & Stucki, M. (1986). Kinetic contours in infants' visual perception. *Child Development, 57*, 292-299.

Kellman, P. J. & Loukides, M. G. (1987). An object perception approach to static and kinetic subjective contours. In S. Petry & G. E. Meyer (Eds.) *The perception of illusory contours*. Springer.

Kellman, P. J. & Cohen, M. H. (1984). Kinetic subjective contours. *Perception & Psychophysics, 35*, 237-244.

Kellman, P. J. & Shipley, T. F. (1991). A theory of visual interpolation in object perception. *Cognitive Psychology, 23*, 141-221.

Klymenko, & Weisstein, N. (1986). The resonance theory of kinetic shape perception and the motion-induced contour. In S. Petry & G. Meyer (Eds) The perception of illusory contours. 143-147. Springer.

Kojima, H. (1998). Figure/ground segregation from temporal delay is best at high spatial frequencies. *Vision Research, 38*, 3729-3734.

Meyer, G. & Dougherty, T. (1987). Sawtooth Pac People and the realization of illusory edges: Computational, cognitive, and utilitarian implications. Paper presented at the Meeting of Psychonomic Society, November, Seattle, WA, USA.

Meyer, G. & Dougherty, T. (1988). Sawtooth 'pacpeople', fuzzy illusory edges and contours that contract. *Perception Supplement, 17*, A26-A27.

Meyer, G. & Dougherty, T. (1990). Ambiguous fluidity and rigidity and diamonds that ooze. *Perception, 19*, 491-496.

Orne, M.T. (1962). On the social psychology of the psychological experiment: with particular reference to demand characteristics and their implications. *American Psychologist, 17*, 776-783.

Parks, T E. (1984). Illusory figures: A (mostly) atheoretical review. *Psychological Bulletin, 95*, 282-300.

Petersik, T. J. & McDill, M. (1981). A new bistable motion illusion based upon 'kinetic optical occlusion'. *Perception, 10*, 563-572.

Petter, G. (1956). Nuove ricerche sperimentali sulla totalizzazione percettiva. *Ricerche di Psicologia, 50*, 213-227.

Petry, S. & Meyer, S. (1986). *The perception of illusory contours*. Springer.

Rock, I., & Gilchrist, A. (1975). The conditions for the perception of the covering and uncovering of a line. *American Journal of Psychology, 88*, 571-582.

Rock, I., Halper, F. Divita, J. & Wheeler, D. (1987). Eye movement as a cue to figure motion in anorthoscopic perception. *Journal of Experimental Psychology: Human Perception and Performance, 13*, 344-352.

Sambin, M. (1986). A dynamic model of anomalous figures. In S. Petry & G. Meyer (Eds) *The perception of illusory contours*. 131-142. Springer.

Sampaio, A. C. (1943). La translation des objects comme facteurde leur permanence phenomenale. In A. Michotte (Ed) *Causalitè, permanence et realitè phenomenales*, 33-90, Louvain: publications universitaires.

Shiffrar, M. & Pavel, M. (1991). Percept of rigid motion within and across apertures. *Journal of Experimental Psychology: Human Perception & Performance, 17*, 749-761.

Shipley, T. F. & Kellman, P. J. (1994). Spatiotemporal boundary formation: Boundary, form, and motion perception from transformations of surface elements. *Journal of Experimental Psychology: General, 123*, 3-20.

Shipley, T. F. & Kellman, P. J. (1997). Spatio-temporal boundary formation: the role of local motion signals in boundary perception. *Vision Research, 37*, 1281-1293.

Stappers, P.J. (1989). Forms can be recognized from dynamic occlusion alone. *Perceptual and Motor Skills, 68*, 243-251.

Thompson, W.B., Mutch, K.M., & Berzins, V.A. (1985). Dynamic occlusion analysis in optical flow fields. *IEEE transactions on pattern analysis and machine intelligence.* PAMI-7, 374-383.

Yonas, A., Craton, L.G., & Thompson, W.B. (1987). Relative motion: kinetic information for the order of depth at an edge. *Perception & Psychophysics, 41*, 53-59.

Vezzani, S. (1999). A note on the influence of grouping on illusory contours. *Psychonomic Bulletin & Review, 6*, 289-291.

From Fragments to Objects – Segmentation and Grouping in Vision
T.F. Shipley and P.J. Kellman (Editors)

18

Perception of Occluding and Occluded Objects Over Time: Spatiotemporal Segmentation and Unit Formation

Thomas F. Shipley[†] *and Douglas W. Cunningham*[‡],
† Department of Psychology, Temple University, Philadelphia, PA 19122, USA
‡ Max-Planck Institute for Biological Cybernetics, Spemannstrase 38, 72076 Tübingen, Germany

Perception has tended to be analysed as a static process where inputs from the here and now contribute to an observer's perceptual experience. This may reflect the phenomenal experience of things as happening in the here and now. It may also reflect a lack of conceptual tools for analysing how an ongoing process may be influenced by changes that occur over time. A legacy of the Gestalt psychologists and J.J. Gibson is an awareness that change over time is an important aspect of perception (Gibson, 1966, 1979; Johansson, 1973, 1975). Even in a scene where nothing moves, the phenomenal impression of that scene is that it is all immediately available, even though information is picked up over time. Observers move their eyes and head as they attend to different aspects of a scene (see the chapter by Henderson in this volume for a brief review). Neisser (1976) described the ongoing process of picking up information and using that information to guide the subsequent pickup of information as the "perceptual cycle". Although it is obvious that time, or events, are a part of the environment that we perceive, many areas of perception shy away from considering the issues that arise when an observer or objects in a scene are allowed to move. Consider, for example, one of the more contentious issues in current research on recognition: Are representations viewpoint dependent? In other words, how do we recognize objects given that we can move and might approach an object from different directions at different times? Most models of recognition are static analysers that work with a snapshot(s) -- each a view of the world divorced from temporal context (e.g., Tarr & Bulthoff, 1995 and Biederman & Gerhardstein, 1993). The problem of recognition might be quite different for continuous observation (see for example, Kourtzi & Shiffrar, 1997; Henderson, this volume; Wallis, 1998; Wallis & Buelthoff, 1999, 2001; Wallis & Baddeley, 1997).

The problem of understanding how we see objects has also largely been considered in terms of static observers looking at static objects. Despite years of work on this problem, a solution has proven elusive because of occlusion. The physics of light and objects results in views of the world in which only portions of an object are visible, and frequently multiple portions of one object are spatially separated from each other. Recognizing a chair that has someone sitting in it, a task that is intuitively quite simple and apparently effortless, is quite difficult because the sitter obscures the connections between the pieces of the chair, and few objects can be definitively recognized based on a glimpse of a single part. If solving the problems of segmentation (which surfaces are separate from each other) and edge correspondence (which edges go together) seem daunting in the static domain, the changes that accompany motion would seem overwhelming, leaving the observer without hope of fully integrating them into a coherent percept. Two general approaches have been used to relieve the perceiver of this burden. The ecological approach has claimed that the burden is illusory and only exists for a system that is limited to local changes. The pattern of changes considered across space and over time is neither arbitrary nor complex, and coordinated action is possible when an observer moves. Alternatively, computational approaches propose that a set of constraints reduce the large number of potential answers to the question of "what is out there?" to a small, manageable, set that is usually correct, or close to correct.

As Marr (1982) has observed the two approaches are not mutually exclusive and this chapter represents our attempt to combine the two approaches. Here we focus on a specific aspect of spatiotemporal segmentation and unit formation—how the pattern of changes generated by occlusion are related to distal objects and how they might be used by the perceiver.

A brief walk down a country lane provides an illustration of the issues at hand. When walking past a white cottage with a white picket fence, an observer readily segments the house from the fence. If our observer is interested in architecture, they have no problem admiring the facade despite the appearance and disappearance of parts of the house (windows, doors, porches, etc.) as pickets progressively cover and reveal them. Another observer might be a master fence builder; they could admire the size, shape, and spacing of the pickets despite the similarity of paint used for fence and house. Should either observer stop to admire the house or fence, they would be frustrated by the similarity of features and might find it hard to separate the house from the fence.

Our simple example, which only considers two layers, gives a sense of the challenge faced by the visual system when confronted with the changes in visibility that occur in a fully populated scene. Every edge will progressively hide or reveal a more distant edge as the observer moves, and many of the edges in a scene might themselves move. Despite the flux, both occluding and occluded forms are readily perceived and appear to be stable over time. Because both front and back objects contribute to the pattern of change, a complete account of unit formation over time will naturally account for both. Here we argue for an integrated model that accounts for both types of unit formation.

Historically, completion of the front and back objects have been considered separately, perhaps because the two forms have different appearances. The surfaces that appear at different depths have different phenomenal properties; in our example an observer would say that they could see the edges and surfaces of the fence, while not all of the house could be seen. Instead, the visible pieces of the house are seen to go together, connected behind the fence (Wallach, 1935). Helmholtz (1867/1962) used the term *modal* to refer to the perceptual qualities of visible parts of a scene, and Michotte, Thinès and Crabbé (1964) coined the contrasting term *amodal*, which refers to the perceptual qualities of the hidden regions -- the sections of a figure which have phenomenal presence and spatial extension, but no other sensory qualities (e.g., color). Kellman and Shipley (1991) argued that static amodal and modal completion were governed by the same process. The same may be true for moving forms.

Completion of occluding forms probably does not occur as often as that of occluded forms. Completion of an occluded form is required whenever one object is in front of another while completion of the occluding form would only be required when a portion of the object is in front of a background that is similar in luminance and color. The need to complete occluding forms may arguably arise from some evolutionarily significant cases (such as the detecting predators, like lions and tigers, that blend in with their background). Alternatively, the ability to complete the occluding object may be a consequence of our ability to complete occluded forms. While these two possibilities are not mutually exclusive, some research suggest that the latter is more likely the case (Shipley & Kellman, 1992). Here we briefly review research on completion of occluded and occluding forms in dynamic scenes and then offer a preliminary model of how they might be related.

COMPLETION OF THE OCCLUDED FORM

Michotte

The perception of a stable form despite the projective changes that accompany gradual occlusion was noted by Michotte, Thinès, and Crabbé's (1964) in their discussion of amodal perception. They observed that static occluded objects are generally seen to be amodally complete. For example, a rectangle that has its center occluded is seen to be amodally complete because the visible pieces are seen as parts of a single unit, this despite the absence of a clear modal experience of the central region—an observer would not say that they "saw" the connecting edges or surfaces (see also Wallach, 1935).

Michotte identified an analogous situation when an object moved behind an occluder so that it disappeared, briefly, before reappearing. He referred to the perceived continuation of the object over time as "tunneling"— its path of motion was amodal. Michotte, Thinès, and Crabbé (1964) observed that the pattern of change over time in such a scene provided rich information about the object. In one of their original demonstrations of tunneling, illustrated in Figure 1, a circle is deformed by gradually removing portions of it as if it were being occluded by a surface with a straight edge and the same surface color as the background. Most observers reported seeing a complete circle gradually disappearing from sight behind an occluder. Few, if any, report that the circle changed shape. In order to perceive a whole circle in such displays, the straight edge must be perceived as not belonging to the circle, but as the occluding edge of a second surface (or a slit in a surface). The deformation of the circle simultaneously produces an experience of phenomenal persistence of the circle, defines the shape of the occluder (i.e., the edge that deforms the circle), and determines the depth relation between the occluded and occluding surfaces.

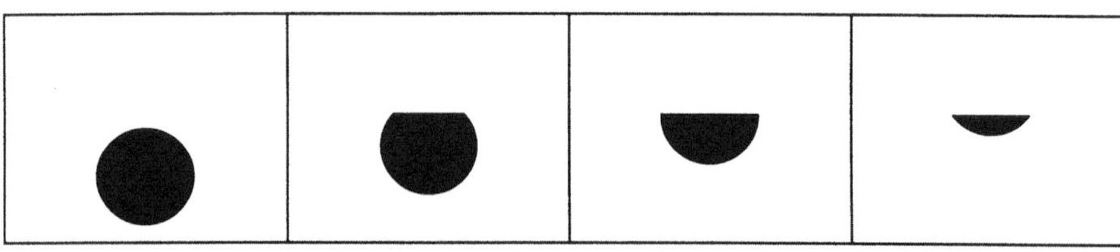

Figure 1. A series of frames illustrating the sequential changes that occur as a circle is progressively hidden by an occluding edge.

Anorthoscopic Perception

The term anorthoscopic perception has been used to refer to perception of a whole form in displays where a figure is moved behind an opaque surface with a small aperture that reveals only a portion, typically a sliver, of the object at any given time. Early demonstrations that forms could be seen under such conditions involved cutting a small slit in a piece of paper and moving an outline form under the slit, or moving the paper with the slit over the form. If the speed of motion falls within a fairly wide range, the form is seen in its entirety (as if the figure were suddenly illuminated by a flash of lightning), and slightly compressed along the direction of motion (Zöllner, 1862 and Plateau, 1836); To the degree that there is any consistent labeling of these aperture viewing displays, these forms tend to be referred to as 'simultaneously perceived'. This description contrasts with other reports where the entire figure does not appear but observers still can make accurate size and shape judgments; such figures are generally referred to as 'successively perceived'.

Differences in phenomenal appearance combined with a dissociation in the stimulus conditions that produce the two appearances led Wenzel (1926, see also Anstis & Atkinson, 1967) to conclude that two separate mechanisms were at work. Subsequently, other differences have been observed, such as Haber and Nathanson's (1968) observation that depth reversals in the Necker cube only occurred when the entire form was simultaneously perceived. Unfortunately almost all of the research and modeling has focused on one or the other type of phenomenal appearance. Not surprisingly, then, two classes of models have been proposed -- (1) a *retinotopic representation* (most commonly referred to as "retinal painting" in this literature) and (2) a *distal representation* (sometimes referred to as "reconstruction" models). The retinotopic representation class of models primarily focuses on simultaneously perceived figures while the distal representation approach concentrates on the perception of successively perceived figures. Unfortunately, this distinction is frequently glossed over leading to attempts to treat all aperture viewed figures as being processed by the same mechanism. The evidence against such a view is quite clear: The two types of representations are served by two different perceptual mechanisms that have different time courses, produce different percepts, and are differentially dependent on the proper tracking of the occluded figure (Morgan, Findlay, & Watt, 1982). Here the work on these two types of representations is reviewed separately.

Retinotopic Anorthoscopic Perception

If an observer moves their eyes with a moving figure, neighboring parts of the figure will affect neighboring areas on the retina. If the consequences of the retinal stimulation persist, they may serve as the basis for the perceptual experience of a whole form despite occlusion. In terms of the retinal painting metaphor, the figure projects a spatially extended figure onto the canvas of the retina. By this account, the shape of the spatiotemporal retinal image should be the same as the shape of the perceived figure: If the retinal image is distorted, then the perceived figure should be as well. A series of experiments by Anstis and Atkinson (1967) supported this hypothesis. They found that the motion of an afterimage, used to track the movement of the subject's eyes (Vierordt, 1868), appeared to move with the same frequency as the perceived figure, even when this motion did not match the frequency and amplitude of the distal figure's motion. In a second experiment, a cutout was moved behind a slit while a bright light shone through the cutout from behind. Thus, the figure was an outline of light that left an afterimage on the retina. The afterimage and the perceived figure were similar in size and shape. Interestingly, the afterimage was blurred but the perceived figure was not. A complete account of this phenomena will presumably include an explanation of this de-blurring effect (for example like that offered by Burr, 1980).

When the orientation and extent of retinal stimulation was controlled by the experimenter, either by using a tracking point or by partially stabilizing the entire display on the retina, compression, elongation, or other distortion could be predicted by the shape of the temporally extended retinal image (as determined by the combination of figure motion and eye motion). For example, if the figure and tracking point moved in opposite directions, the shape of the retinal image should be a mirror image of the actual figure's shape. Under these conditions subjects reported a figure that was left-right reversed. When two images were simultaneously moved in opposite directions through two parallel slits (in this situation one of the figures must be moving in the opposite direction as the eyes), one figure was always seen as reversed while the other was seen in its correct left-right orientation. Finally, there is evidence that the transition from appearance to disappearance play an important role in this form of representation (Sohmiya & Sohmiya, 1992; Wenzel, 1926). They found that two images were seen when a wide slit was used. One image was seen just beyond the edge that revealed the figure, and the other was seen just past the edge that hid the figure. Both images were displaced slightly in the direction that the image was moving. The perceptual mislocalization of a moving target's point of appearance and disappearance is reminiscent of the Fröhlich effect, a mislocalization, in the direction of motion of the initial location of a moving object (Fröhlich, 1923), and representational momentum, a similar mislocalization of the final location (Freyd, 1983).

The term "retinal painting", which appears to date back to Helmholtz (1867/1962), is an unfortunate choice for this process, hopefully it will become clear in this chapter that some post-retinal processing is necessary. Here we use the term retinotopic representation. The process qualifies as a form of representation in that the retinotopic relationships map isomorphically onto some relationships in the proximal stimulus, and some operations can be applied to them (e.g., combining contours to form a whole boundary and recognition on the basis of the outer contour; see Gallistel (1990) for a discussion of the necessary features of a representation). While there may not be a localized "store", the continued activity of neurons when a stimulus is removed may have the same functional consequences (See Enns & Di Lollo chapter in this volume for more on this issue). Some researchers have dismissed retinotopic temporal integration, indeed Rock went so far as to say "the theoretical implications are nil" (Rock & Sigman, 1973, p. 357). Yet, a retinotopic representation can capture some important relations and qualitative properties of the stimulus. For example, such a representation could help us see objects as they move through a cluttered environment, allowing the system to discount temporary occluders.

Temporal Window for Retinotopic Representations

A full characterization of the simultaneous perception of an aperture presented figure will require a description of the decay function that limits retinotopic representations.

Psychophysical estimates for the temporal limit of anorthoscopic perception have yielded a very large range. Haber and Nathanson (1968) asked subjects to adjust the speed of a slit moving over a stationary figure until the entire figure was just barely seen simultaneously. The thresholds varied considerably between individuals, ranging from 174 ms to 474 ms per pass of the figure, but were highly consistent within a given subject. It is possible that the variability was due to a failure to distinguish between distal and retinotopic representations. However, part of the range is consistent with other estimates of the duration information is preserved in the visual system (Burr (1980) gives an estimate of 120 msec). As an alternative approach, one might estimate the duration of activation of this retinotopic representation by measuring the amount of a form that is seen simultaneously -- that is, the amount of an edge, surface, or form that is seen to extend beyond the width of the slit. This portion of the percept may represent the contribution of a retinotopic representation. To address this issue, Morgan, Findlay & Watt (1982) presented a circle made entirely of small dots, plotted one dot at a time on an oscilloscope, as if a slit were moving around the circumference of the circle. This allowed them to control the amount of time that elapsed between the presentation of the first and last dot. They found that the entire circle had to be plotted within 150 ms before the entire figure was seen modally. When more than 150 ms elapsed, only portions of the circle were modally visible. At 400 ms, only a small arc in constant motion in a circular path was seen.

Distal Anorthoscopic Perception

A second visual process complements the one responsible for retinotopic representations. The two have been lumped together by some as anorthoscopic perception because of the type of displays employed. Yet, they are distinct; both integrate over time, but one represent proximal relations while the other represents distal spatial relations. In the simplest demonstration that form perception does not require a retinotopic representation, Haber and Nathanson's (1968) displayed a stationary figure through a moving slit. When subjects were asked to track the slit, the successive glimpses of the figure would be presented to the same section of the retina, nevertheless the figure was seen. Most of the researchers who proposed a reconstruction model of aperture viewing were primarily concerned with demonstrating that extended figures were seen under conditions where there was no extended retinal image. For example, Parks (1970) found that two figures could be seen even when one was moving and the other still: a circle could be seen moving behind a stationary slit, while a stationary circle was seen behind a moving slit. Since an extended spatiotemporal retinal image would require motion or stasis, for the moving and stationary forms respectively, a retinotopic representation cannot explain the perception of both figures. Others have shown that forms may be seen even when eye motion is controlled with a tracking point and no retinotopic representation could be possible (e.g., Rock & Halper, 1969).

Rock and Gilchrist (1975) noted that one of the most important aspects of form perception, whether it be perception of simultaneously presented figures, or figures presented through an aperture, is a description of the phenomenal locations of an object's parts relative to each other. Under this account, first the parts of a figure are perceived, then the spatial relation of each part to each of the others is coded, and then the parts are put together to see the global form (see Girgus, Gellman, & Hochberg 1980 for a similar analysis; Henderson's chapter in this volume provides a computational approach to solving this problem in face perception). Most researchers who have developed accounts of how a distal representation is achieved have proposed reconstruction models where the spatial aspects of a form that are observed over time are combined to yield a representation of the entire form (Parks, 1965 was one of the first to suggest that perception of figures presented through an aperture was the result of reconstruction). Reconstruction of a whole from pieces collected over time would seem to require two basic perceptual operations: *segmentation* of boundaries of the pieces, so that the system can distinguish the boundaries of the occluded form from the boundaries of the occluder, and spatial *alignment* of the pieces viewed over time. These two requirements are considered in turn.

Segmentation

The visible fragment(s) of an object seen through an aperture will be a combination of the object's boundaries and the boundaries of the aperture (Nakayama, Shimojo & Silverman, (1989) referred to these as intrinsic and extrinsic edges, respectively). Rock and Sigman's (1973) work on the effects of figure–ground assignment in anorthoscopic perception provides evidence for a segmentation process that is independent of and precedes perceptual integration. They found that the perceived boundary ownership of the edges of the aperture had a dramatic effect on perception of a figure. In their displays they used the vase region of Rubin's face-vase figure as an aperture. They presented a line in the shape of a sine wave that moved horizontally through this narrow region. The figure-ground relations in this display were rendered unambiguous by adding context that completed the faces, or repeated the vases. When the rest of the head was added (e.g., top, back, and neck) the picture was seen as containing two faces, the area between the faces was seen as an aperture, the line was seen as being behind the faces, and 67% of the subjects saw an extended figure. In contrast, when additional contours were added that completed a vase, the area between the faces was seen as the stem of a vase, the line was seen as being in front of this surface (i.e., not occluded), and only 25% of the subjects saw an extended figure. Presumably, in this latter situation where the sequentially presented line fragments were seen as independent bounded regions, they were not integrated over time. Instead, the sequence was seen as a small line changing orientation and length. More recently, Shiffrar and her colleagues have shown that aperture visibility allows edges to be grouped so that motion signals may be combined across apertures for translating (but not rotating) figures (Shiffrar chapter in this volume, and Lorenceau & Shiffrar, 1992). In general, information that facilitates segmentation appears to facilitate formation of distal anorthoscopic perception.

Alignment

Since knowledge of the direction and speed of motion of the figure can, in principle, be used to derive the correct spatial relations of the successively presented slices of the figure (Rock & Gilchrist, 1975), spatial alignment may be based on motion signals from the occluded and occluding forms (Palmer, Kellman & Shipley, 1997; Kellman, Palmer, & Shipley, 1998). Determining the motion of an edge in an aperture may be difficult as it is impossible to locally determine the component of motion that is parallel to an extended smooth edge (Adelson & Movshon, 1982; Wallach, 1935). We direct the reader to Maggie Shiffrar's chapter in this volume for an excellent review of the "aperture problem". Briefly, two sorts of solutions may be used. If there is one or more unique point on an edge (e.g., a corner), then it's motion can specify the motion of the edge. In the absence of such points, the motion of two edges with differing orientations that move in the same direction can be combined to recover the direction of their motion (Adelson & Movshon, 1982).

If motion signals are used to align fragments over time, any information about the motion of an aperture-viewed figure should aid in the perceptual completion of that figure. Rock and Gilchrist (1975) offered a test of this hypothesis with an induced motion display. They created a display that simulated a sinusoidal curved line moving through a small aperture. The display was designed so that the visible line segment did not change location. Moving the surface with the aperture provided the vertical motion of the line, which was given by vertical changes in the line's location within the aperture. The horizontal motion was given by surrounding the display with a textured background that moved horizontally. This surface induced apparent horizontal motion in the surface with the aperture. Six of the 10 subjects reported seeing an extended form through the slit in this display (about the same number that report seeing extended forms with real motion). Unfortunately, the aperture in this display was wide enough for subjects to see the orientation changes that occurred with the simulated horizontal and vertical motions. As a result, it is not clear that observers were responding on the basis of the induced motion in these displays. It is possible that the orientation changes, in combination with the vertical position changes, were sufficient to provide information about the horizontal motion of the line (Wallach, 1935). Additional discussion on the relationship between aperture motion and line motion is in the section on alignment in perception of the occluding surface.

Additional evidence in support of the use of motion based information comes from Casco and Morgan (1984) who studied the effects of adding motion noise to anorthoscopic displays. They employed a tilted line made up of dots and the subject's task was to identify the direction of the line's tilt. When the slit width was such that only one dot was visible in the aperture at any given time, there was no static information for the slope of the line. Subjects were able to integrate a moving dot seen at one time with another dot seen at a later time to determine slope. When additional static masking dots were added to these displays, subjects could still accurately report the slope of the line. When the masking dots moved, however, subjects could not determine the slope of the line. This impairment became increasingly pronounced with increases in interframe interval. Casco and Morgan (1984) noted that there are two possible aspects of the motion noise that might interfere with the detection of dot motion: (1) the time-averaged density of the dots may be so great that there are too many dots to allow the detection of just one dot; and (2) the apparent motion signals of the motion noise serve to obscure the apparent motion of the dots in the aperture. By reducing the rate of dot replacement and increasing the number of dots, the time-averaged density can be held constant while decreasing the motion of the mask dots. A series of experiments employing this manipulation supported the second account -- the motion of the mask dots appears to interfere with determining the motion of the signal dots and thus makes it difficult to integrate over time.

Finally, a number of researchers following Zöllner (1862) noted that many of the occluded forms seen in these displays are distorted. Fast moving figures seemed to be compressed parallel to the figure's direction of motion, while slow moving figures were seen as elongated (Haber & Nathanson, 1967; Morgan, Findlay & Watt, 1982; Zöllner, 1862). The distortion in the fast moving forms may be a product of a failure to track the form accurately and the resulting retinotopic representation is distorted. The distortion seen in the slower forms may represent a failure to accurately recover the motion of the form and thus a failure to accurately align the pieces in a distal representation.

Temporal Window for Distal Representations

Earlier we noted that there appeared to be a temporal limit on retinotopic representation. When that limit is reached, what happens? A number of researchers have noted that a form's speed can be used to predict its phenomenal appearance (e.g., Zöllner, 1862, and Parks, 1965). Faster speeds are associated with simultaneous appearance while slower ones with successive appearance. Different perceptual processes may be responsible for the perception of the same form at different speeds. An upper speed limit for distal representations makes sense since accurate integration requires accurate velocity information, and as speed increases, velocities become harder to estimate accurately. The retinotopic and distal representations may be complementary. Thus, retinotopic representations allow form perception of fast moving objects, while distal representations may be used for slower forms.

Multiple Apertures

While much of the research relevant to the perception of dynamically occluded objects used a single aperture, there are a few notable studies with multiple apertures. These studies have shown that the relative location and orientation of pieces seen across slits can influence what is seen over time. Shiffrar and colleagues found that edges are more likely to be grouped across apertures when they form an angle that is less than 90 degrees (Shiffrar & Lorenceau, 1992). As was true with a visible aperture, the effect was evident for translation but not rotation. Additionally, when part of a shape is presented in one aperture and another part in a different aperture, the shapes that can be completed with smooth monotonic functions are better discriminated than those where no smooth link is possible (Palmer, Kellman, & Shipley, 2000). This suggests that the constraints that govern static unit formation (such as Kellman and Shipley's (1991) description of relatability) also apply to pieces seen over time. Recognition of familiar motion patterns, or shape fragments, may also influence perception of partially occluded moving forms. Shiffrar, Lichtey, and Heptulla-Chatterjee (1997) found that a stick figure simulating a human walking was seen as a single unit when visible through multiple apertures, while other objects (scissors and a car) were not. In the latter case, the visible lines were seen as independent objects. Note, this effect was only seen when segmentation was difficult (e.g., in displays where the edges of the apertures were not visible and so boundary assignment was ambiguous).

Finally, it appears that absence of information is also information in some cases of multiple apertures. Rock and Sigman (1973) found that the absence of a figure in neighboring slits can affect reports that a figure is present behind the occluder. They added additional apertures that were adjacent to the one where a form was seen. When these additional apertures were empty, but should have had line elements in them if there really was a line behind the occluder, the number of subjects who reported seeing an extended figure dropped. Unfortunately, it is possible that this finding simply reflects a response bias (e.g., subjects do not want to report a percept that does not make sense). A replication with an objective task, like shape identification, is needed to confirm this conclusion.

A simple model of distal anorthoscopic perception

Consider a horizontally moving occluder with two small, vertically and horizontally separated windows and a stationary, vertically oriented object behind the occluder (See Figure 2). Two parts of this object will become visible at different times in the two windows. The object's continuity may be perceived because the first visible fragment persists for some time interval in a storage buffer. When the second fragment becomes visible, it also enters the buffer. Then, the spatial relatability constraints (two edges are relatable if a smooth monotonic function that does not turn past 90 degrees can be constructed) operate on the two

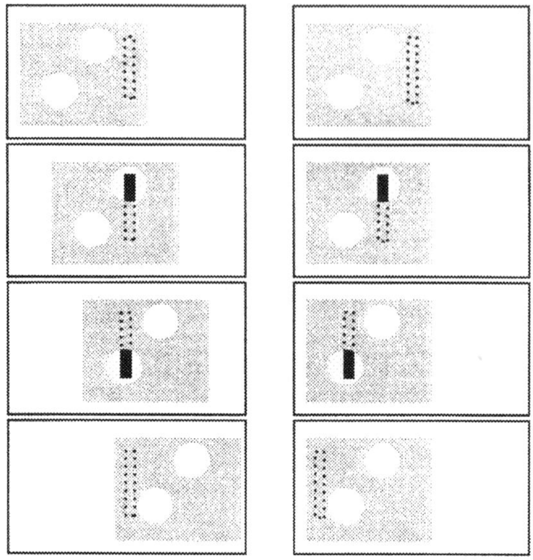

Figure 2. An illustration of a sequence in which parts of an object become visible at different times. The solid forms are the visible parts and the dotted form the invisible parts. Sequential frames are presented vertically. The left column illustrates a stationary object and an moving occluder, and the right column, a stationary occluder and a moving object. After Palmer, Kellman & Shipley (2000).

parts to determine whether they are integrated into a single object. Alternatively, suppose the object, rather than the occluder, moves horizontally. One object part becomes visible through one window at a certain time, and the other part becomes visible at a different place later. Here, persistence alone is not sufficient. Updating occurs if, from the first visible fragment, a velocity signal is obtained, and that signal is used to spatially update the position of the fragment while it remains in the buffer. When the other part of the object becomes visible, the spatial relatability computation is applied to the currently visible part and the spatially updated position of the previously stored part. We call this idea *spatiotemporal relatability* (Palmer, Kellman & Shipley, 1997; Kellman, Palmer, & Shipley, 1998; see also Kellman, in press). The first case may be considered a special case of the second where, for the purposes of spatial alignment, the velocity of the object is zero.

When the aperture is large and unique points are visible on the occluded form, estimating its velocity is relatively easy. When the aperture is small, however, estimating velocity can be hard even when the occluded object is not moving. When only a small portion of an edge is visible, estimating velocity requires segmenting intrinsic from extrinsic edges and using the change in orientation over time of the intrinsic edges. Since velocity estimates can be made locally, it is possible to perceive multiple objects moving in different directions (Parks, 1970).

Recent research by Palmer, Kellman, & Shipley (2000) offer some initial support for a spatiotemporal relatability constraint on unit formation. They employed an indirect measure of unit formation in which subjects were shown displays, like the ones illustrated in Figure 2, with apertures that were horizontally and vertically separated. In these displays portions of an occluded figure were seen at different times, while other portions were never seen (e.g., the portion in the vertical gap between apertures). The occluded forms were irregular forms, and the subject's task was to choose which of two forms was present on each trial. Previous research with shape discrimination tasks (Kellman, Machado, Shipley, & Li, 2001) have found discrimination of subtly different objects (e.g., paper clips bent into slightly different shapes) to be superior to discrimination of corresponding location differences in separate objects (e.g., paper clip fragments placed in slightly different locations). Discrimination may serve as an indirect measure of grouping. Thus, the more the pieces are grouped, the easier it should be to tell the different shapes apart. In one experiment two types of displays were employed, *relatable* displays where the orientation and locations of edges presented over time met the requirements for relatability, and *non-relatable* displays, where the same pieces were used but scrambled so that relatability no longer was present. Subjects were more accurate when the parts seen over time were relatable.

How might edges be segmented in such a display? There are several potential sources of information. Segmentation may occur as a result of static discontinuities in the first derivative of the boundaries in the apertures (Kellman & Shipley, 1991). Indeed, when the pieces were thin sticks, rounding off the visible ends of the pieces resulted in a decrease in discrimination (Palmer, Kellman, & Shipley, 2000). In addition, if the forms are moving fast enough, a retinotopic representation may be available for a portion of a boundary. If a boundary in the retinotopic representation extended beyond boundaries of an aperture that would indicate that the edge continued beyond the boundaries of the aperture. Finally the pattern of change in the visible pieces may provide information—we discuss this source of information in the next section.

COMPLETION OF THE FRONT FORM

In Michotte's demonstration of tunneling, the progressive hiding of a luminance defined surface revealed a surface with the same color as the background (See Figure 1). The transformation provides information about both the continued existence of the more distant form and the presence of an occluding form. Gibson, Kaplan, Reynolds, & Wheeler (1969) asserted that the changes over time at the boundaries of an object are sufficient to define the shape of those boundaries. Gibson's (1968) film, constructed to support this claim, depicts a square with a speckled texture moving over a similarly textured surface. Since there is no static information for the form or its boundaries (e.g., no global difference in luminance, hue, texture, or depth between the inside and outside of the square), neither the surface, nor the boundaries, are visible when the figure is stationary. When the figure moves, however, a well-defined surface bounded by clear edges is seen moving in front of another surface with similar texture. The figure can only be seen when it moves. The edges seen in Gibson's displays, as well those seen in Michotte Thinès and Crabbé's (1964) demonstration, have a phenomenal quality similar to the edges of illusory figures such as the Kanizsa triangle (Kanizsa, 1979). Similarly, in some anorthoscopic displays the boundaries of the slit are not defined in the luminance domain, yet they are still seen. A number of researchers have studied the perception of boundaries in dynamic displays (e.g., Andersen & Cortese, 1989; Bradley & Lee, 1982; Bruno & Bertamini, 1990, 1997; Bruno & Gerbino, 1991; Cicerone & Hoffman 1997; Cicerone, Hoffman, Gowdy & Kim, 1995; Cunningham, Shipley, & Kellman, 1998a, 1998b; Gibson, Kaplan, Reynolds & Wheeler, 1969; Hine, 1987; Kellman & Cohen, 1984; Palmer, Kellman & Shipley, 1997; Kellman, Palmer, & Shipley, 1998; Prazdny, 1986; Rock & Halper, 1969; Shipley & Kellman, 1993, 1994, 1997; Stappers, 1989). Here we review some of the work on perception of occluding forms and discuss the overlap between perception of occluding and occluded forms.

The earliest description of change over time contributing to the perception of an occluding form appears to be in Wertheimer's classic 1912 monograph on apparent motion (see Sekuler, 1996 and Steinman, Pizlo, & Pizlo, 2000 for extended discussions of this work). Among the various perceptual experiences that are evident in a two-frame apparent motion display, Wertheimer describes φ movement as the motion of a surface, with the same color as the background, in front of the luminance defined forms. These forms appear to flicker but do not themselves move. The appearance of such an emergent occluding form from apparent motion displays has been independently reported by a number of researchers (Petersik & McDill, 1981; see also Steinman, Pizlo, & Pizlo, 2000). Steinman, Pizlo, & Pizlo (2000) argued that this observation was particularly important because something is seen, in this case motion, when no surface boundary is seen. While this may be an accurate account for the historical importance of the observation, it is not clear that it is an accurate account of the phenomenology. There is a "thing" quality to the moving form, the surface has substance (Katz, 1935), it has a color, appears to be opaque, and even in some cases form[1]. The boundaries are not absent, they are vague. We have found that the spatial resolution of boundaries in such displays exist on a continuum and depend on the size and density of the changing elements (Shipley & Kellman, 1993, 1994). When the density is low, edges are less clear. Their appearance is similar to the illusory edges defined by blurred inducing elements

[1] Steinman, Pizlo, & Pizlo base their assertion that there is no surface boundary in these displays on the lack of a surface boundary in the static frames. While this is true, the important issue here is whether a bounded form is seen in the kinematic displays. Form is seen in these displays, indeed Steinman, Pizlo, & Pizlo refer to a "dark bar" in their "magni-phi" displays (p. 2262).

(Minguzzi, 1987). Understanding how we perceive a moving occluding boundary in displays like these, where the occluder and background have similar surface properties, requires consideration of the same issues we discussed earlier: segmentation and alignment.

Segmentation

The visible boundaries of an object often do not match the distal boundaries of that object because of occlusion by nearer objects. But, we rarely experience a visible object fragment as a bounded whole. Perceiving the visible patch to be part of a larger, partially visible, object entails segmenting the edges of the occluding form from the occluded form. Similarly, when near and distant objects have similar properties, seeing the near object requires segmenting it's visible edges from the background. In Michotte's tunneling example, like most of the displays studied in anorthoscopic perception, the shape of the visible edges provides static information for segmentation. The sharp corners evident at the point of overlap are reliable indictors of occlusion and as such may serve to initiate segmentation (Kellman & Shipley, 1991; Shipley & Kellman, 1990). While such static discontinuities may be sufficient, moving displays appear to be more than the sum of a series of static snapshots. Bradley and Lee (1982) found that an illusory triangle defined by both static and kinematic information was sharper than one defined by static information alone. For the kinematic condition, the illusory triangle (with dots at each vertex) was rotated around its center so that it progressively hid and revealed portions of a luminance-defined outline of a triangle. Thirty-five of their 37 subjects reported that the illusory triangle was stronger when defined by both kinematic and static information than when it was defined only by static information.

We have studied the role of spatiotemporal information using displays with no static discontinuities, where boundaries are only defined by the pattern of changes over time. We refer to the visual processes responsible for seeing a form in the two types of displays illustrated in Figure 3 as spatiotemporal boundary formation (or SBF). The sequential pattern of change in each is sufficient to define a form. When the pattern of changes was consistent with a circle moving over the array of elements, as is illustrated in Figure 3, subjects reported seeing a moving circle with well defined edges. In unidirectional displays where the elements disappear entirely as the form passes over them, a form with the same color as the background is seen. In contrast, in the bidirectional displays, where elements appear and disappear along all edges, the surface does not have a distinct quality – some subjects describe it as looking like a piece of glass (Shipley & Kellman, 1994; Cunningham, Shipley, & Kellman, 1998a).

The initiating conditions for completion of the occluding surface are probably the same that initiate completion of occluded surfaces since the same optical changes specify the presence of an occluded and occluding surface. In moving displays, this could be some abrupt change; appearance and disappearance would be one example of such a change. The class of changes that results in boundaries is not restricted to accretion and deletion, it appears

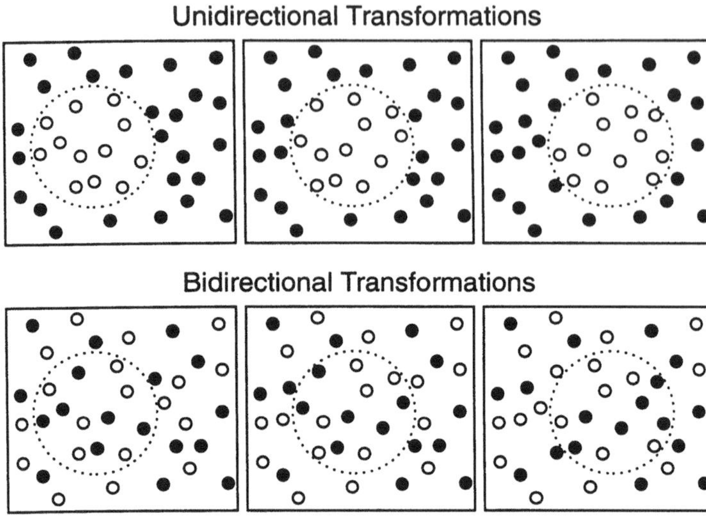

Figure 3. An illustration of two classes of transformations. In unidirectional transformations all elements along a given edge change in the same manner. In bidirectional transformations, elements change in two directions with the net result that there is no static difference between the inside and outside of the moving form.

to be quite large (Shipley & Kellman, 1994). Many changes in an element's appearance, such as changes in color, orientation, or location, also result in the perception of moving bounded forms. When we first established that the set of changes extended beyond accretion and deletion we had a certain embarrassment of riches. It was hard to define the set of changes that served to create forms in such displays because we were having trouble identifying the class of changes that did not work. We finally found such a change and it proved to be quite useful in helping us define the boundaries of the class. The critical transformation was a small change in location. Small changes in locations were seen as deformations of a surface, whereas large changes were seen as a result of a separate surface (Shipley & Kellman, 1993). Abrupt changes over time are invariantly related to occlusion, and they appear to serve the same role in motion displays as discontinuities in the first derivative of luminance specified contours do in static displays. We argued that visual system handles information for surfaces and boundaries differently. The changes that occur over time within a surface are continuous and are present in optic flow. In contrast, the changes that occur at edges are not continuous and could disrupt recovery of form from optic flow. The latter pattern of changes we called *optic tearing*, and argued that they are processed separately from continuous changes. These abrupt changes over time, or spatiotemporal discontinuities, could serve as the starting place for perception of boundaries over time.

Alignment

Since an occluder may move, and we may or may not track it, the changes that occur at different points in time must be spatially aligned to be useful in defining an occluding form. Clues as to how this might be done can be found in Wallach's early work on perception of motion and its relation to form (Wallach, 1935). In Wallach's displays lines moved inside apertures of different shapes. The basic display is illustrated in Figure 4a. The edges of the aperture are indicated here by gray lines; in the actual displays the boundaries of the aperture were not physically defined. With no way of tracking a feature of a line, it is impossible to discern the motion parallel to the orientation of the line, so any given motion is consistent with a class of motions (see the chapter by Shiffrar in this volume for further discussion). Although each line's motion is consistent with a wide range of motions in a square aperture, subjects generally report either horizontal or vertical motion (illustrated here by horizontal and vertical arrows). In general the size, shape, and orientation of the aperture's edges can influence the perceived direction of line motion (Buelthoff, Little, Poggio, 1989; Wallach, 1935). Wallach also noted that in some cases the apparent direction of motion of the lines

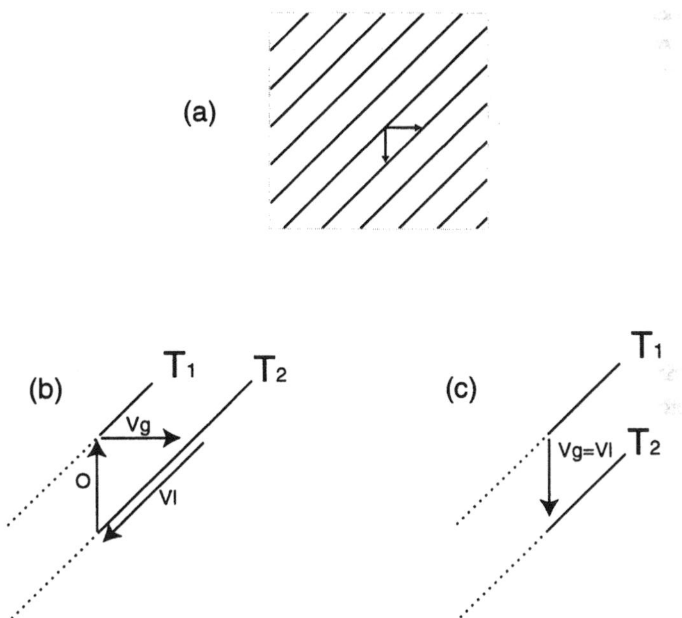

Figure 4. The inherent ambiguity of the motion in an aperture is illustrated for these lines with two arrows. There is nothing to distinguish diagonal downward motion from horizontal motion to the right and vertical motion downwards. When horizontal motion is seen, the motion of the line ends is consistent with gradual accretion by a vertical edge. Whereas, when vertical motion is seen the line ends simply appear to move vertically.

determined whether or not a boundary was seen. In a display with diagonal lines presented in a square aperture, a vertical edge was seen when the lines appeared to move horizontally. In contrast, when the lines appeared to move vertically a horizontal edge was seen, but no vertical edge was seen. Subjects reported both appearances (across subjects and within the same subject over time).

To understand why there would be a relationship between the apparent motion of the lines and the presence of an occluding edge, consider the local motions of the line ends. In the example, the ends of the lines on the left and right sides always move down and the ends on the top and bottom always move rightward. In general the motion of a line end is determined by the true motion of the line and, if present, the orientation of an occluding edge. There is a simple relationship between the three variables (Bruno & Gerbino, 1991; Shimojo & Richards, 1986; see also the chapter by Nicola Bruno in the volume). The local motion signal of a line end will be the vector sum of the true motion of the line and the motion along the occluded edge. Figure 4b illustrates these relationships for a diagonal line moving horizontally. The actual motion of the line is indicated by the arrow labeled Vg. The point on the line that was the line end at T1 moves to the middle of the line at T2; as the line moves, more of the line becomes visible -- the line appears to be growing. The change in length of the line, the local velocity, is indicated by the arrow labeled Vl. The addition of Vg and Vl defines a third vector, which is the orientation of the occluding edge. In contrast, when the line appears to be moving vertically, as in Figure 4c, the global motion of the motion of the line end are identical (Vg=Vl) and no edge is seen. Return to Wallach's lines moving in a square aperture; the appearance of horizontal motion will result in the appearance of changes in the length of lines along the vertical edges of the aperture, these two define an occluding edge and a boundary is seen.

One may think of a local motion signal as the visual system's way of representing the relationship between events that happen at different times. Shipley and Kellman (1994, 1997) argued that the visual system uses motion signals to define boundaries in moving displays. In bidirectional SBF displays there is no static form information. The form that is seen from the sequential element changes is a product of the local motion signals. In addition to directly coding the motion of objects, local motion signals may serve as an efficient representation of the spatial and temporal locations of occlusion events (e.g., appearance and disappearance of texture).

The observations made by Wallach and others (Michotte, Thinès & Crabbé, 1964; Petersik & McDill, 1981; Shipley & Kellman, 1997) support the hypothesis that local motion signals may be used by the visual system for multiple purposes. Across a number of different displays, subjects shown the same sequence of images will report, when an edge is seen, that the occluded elements appear stable, but when an edge is not seen, the elements appear to move. In the first case the local motion signals are consistent with a moving boundary and are responsible for the experience of a moving oriented occlusion edge, in the latter case the local motion signals are phenomenally experienced as motion. If motion signals form the basis of the edges seen in these displays, then those edges should be disrupted by adding motion noise. Indeed, the addition of a few moving elements that are not consistent with the motions defined by the moving edge are sufficient to severely disrupt shape identification (Shipley & Kellman, 1997). Static noise, however, has no effect on shape identification in bidirectional displays (Cunningham, Shipley, & Kellman, 1998a).

Shipley & Kellman developed a model of how local motion signals might be used to identify a moving edge. The model is based on the unique pattern of motion signals that occurs when a moving edge occludes, or otherwise effects the visible qualities of small elements. A sequence of successive occlusion events is illustrated in Figure 5. At any given local region motion will result in the sequential covering, or revealing, of elements. Sequential pairs of abrupt changes in luminance will result in a local motion signal. For example, in Figure 5, the successive disappearances of elements in frames 2 and 3 results in a motion signal, illustrated as an arrow in frame 3, that moves from the first disappearance towards the second. The direction of motion is determined by the location of changes and the magnitude by the spatial and temporal distance between changes. In Figure 5, the spatial separation between the disappearances in frames 3 and 5 is greater than between the disappearances in frames 2 and 3, however, the temporal separation between frames 3 and 5 is twice the separation between frames 2 and 3. The result is the corresponding motion, shown on frame 5, is slower. Shipley and Kellman (1997) proved that for edges moving with a constant velocity, the direction and magnitude of local signals define the orientation of the moving edge when the two vectors are superimposed such that they have a common origin (See bottom of Figure 5). Support for this particular approach comes from a demonstration that edge recovery was sensitive to the sequential location of events. The two-vector model

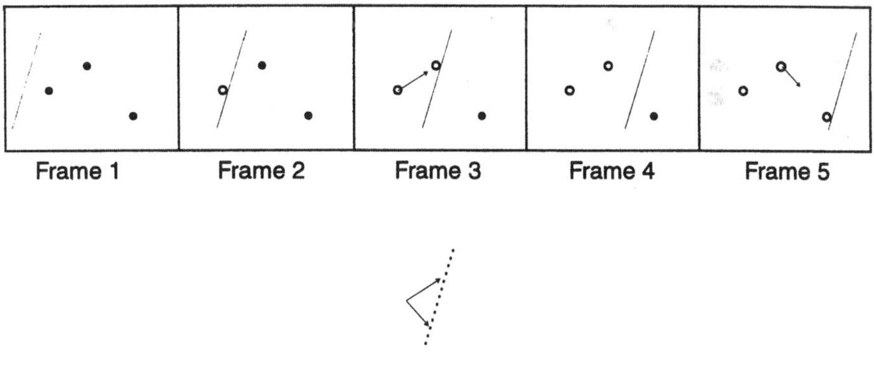

Figure 5. An illustration of an edge sequentially covering three elements. The spatial and temporal separation between element changes define the two local motion vectors shown as arrows. When superimposed, these vectors can define the orientation of the edge that caused the changes.

would be particularly sensitive to any internal noise, or errors, in motion magnitude when the local changes were similar in orientation and magnitude. As predicted, subject's shape identification was quite poor under such conditions (Shipley & Kellman, 1997).

Generally, the more events that occur as a surface moves, the clearer the emergent boundary; both the spatial and temporal density of events influences boundary perception (Anderson & Cortese, 1989; Hine, 1987; Shipley & Kellman, 1994). The clarity of the boundary is relatively stable over time, suggesting that there is some temporal limit on the spatiotemporal integration mechanism, otherwise it would get continuously clearer with extended viewing. When frame durations are increased accuracy decreases to a floor between 100 and 200 msec per frame (Shipley & Kellman, 1994). To precisely determine the temporal limit we conducted an experiment in which we displayed animations at an optimal frame rate (33 msec per frame) for a variable number of frames, followed by a pause of 300 msec which should have exceeded the temporal window (Shipley & Kellman, 2001). The results from two groups of subjects, run on slightly differing sets of durations, are shown in Figure 6. Accuracy steadily improved up to six 33 msec frames. To estimate the limit more precisely, the best linear functions were determined by step-wise fitting two independent

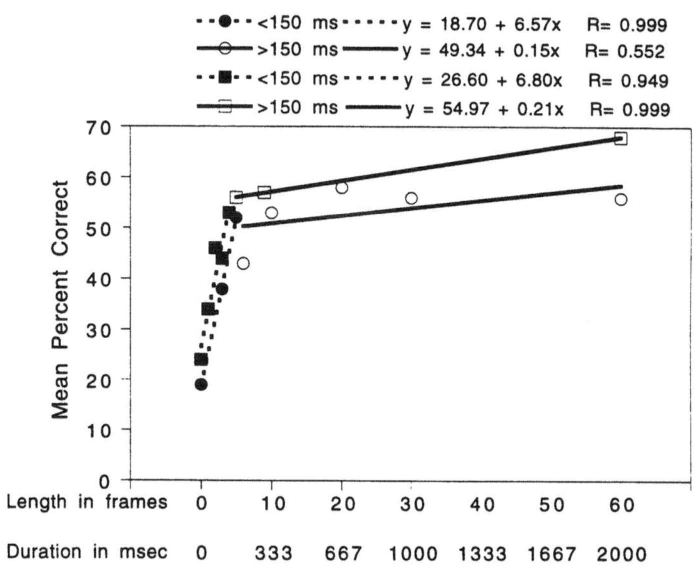

Figure 6. Shape discrimination accuracy plotted as a function of optimal-frame-rate duration. The circles and squares represent two different groups run on differing sets of durations. The solid lines are best linear fits above 150 msec and the dotted line best fit below 150 msec. From Shipley and Kellman (2001).

linear functions to each data set. For both data sets the functions intersect at 150 msec. These findings indicate that alignment over time, however it is achieved, is limited to relatively short temporal intervals.

Finally, one relatively simple mechanism for temporal alignment would employ eye movements: In attending to a moving object one tracks it so that events that are seen at different points in time project to retinotopically appropriate spatial positions. We know relatively little about the relationship between eye position and SBF. There are a few findings that suggest eye movements are important. Wallach (1935) observed that location of fixation affected the perceived motion in displays where motion was ambiguous. Some of these effects may be accounted for by a reduction in the effect of individual line ends when they are present in the periphery (see Shiffrar, this volume and Lorenceau & Shiffrar,1992).

To find out if eye movements were necessary for SBF we collaborated with Frank Durgin on an experiment in which eye movements were explicitly controlled. We instructed subjects to either follow a fixation cross that moved with the SBF form around the screen, or fixate a stationary cross in the center of the screen (Shipley Cunningham & Durgin, 2001). Compliance was monitored with an eye tracker and subjects that did not follow instructions were excluded. We found no difference in accuracy between the two conditions. In this experiment, as in most of our other research, we used a range of element densities, so it is unlikely the null effect was due to a ceiling or floor problem.

Surface appearance

In addition to the boundaries seen in all SBF displays, many displays also contain surfaces. Surfaces are seen in displays where the events along the leading and trailing edges are changes in a consistent direction. An opaque occluding surface (Katz, 1935) is seen when the elements disappear at the leading edge and appear along the trailing edge. These surfaces generally show an enhanced contrast (appearing darker then the background on a dark ground and lighter on a light background). As noted by Hine (1987), a similar effect is seen in static illusory contours. When elements do not disappear completely, a transparent surface is seen. Wallach (1935) may have been the first to note this phenomenon in moving displays. Hoffman and Cicerone and their colleagues have since extensively studied the appearance of transparent colored surfaces in such displays, which they refer to as "color from motion" (Cicerone, Hoffman, Gowdy & Kim, 1995 and the chapter by Prophet, Hoffman, & Cicerone in this volume).

The appearance of a surface does not appear to be directly linked to a surface boundary. As independently noted by a number of researchers, a surface may not be seen when edges are quite vague because the number of changes are small or displays are shown at isoluminance (Petersik & McDill, 1981, Steinman, Pizlo & Pizlo, 2000, Miyahara & Cicerone, 1997), and edges are seen in bidirectional displays where there is no clear surface quality. This suggests that different sources of information serve the different perceptual qualities. However, surface appearance and contour clarity may not be completely independent, the relationship between the two appears to be more complex. In a study of the monocular and binocular contributions to SBF we found an interesting interaction between the two.

Previous research by Cicerone and Hoffman (1997) found that SBF displays generated by splitting the dot array between the eyes showed no loss in effect. They concluded that the lack of effect meant that color-from-motion was the result of a process that was served by binocular neurons. While the spatial location of elements in these displays differed in the monocular images, the pattern of changes was identical in the two images. In collaboration with Frank Durgin, we found that the monocular pattern of change is important. We presented unidirectional and bidirectional displays consisting of white and red dots to subjects with the polarity of dots reversed in the two eyes (e.g., red dots inside and white outside for one eye, and white dots inside with red outside for the other eye). The locations of dots in the two eyes were identical, the monocular images differed only in luminance and color[2]. If the contribution from each eye is weighted equivalently, these displays would all be identical because each element is red in one eye and white in the other. Furthermore, no change over time would be detectable since the only thing that changes is the eye of origin for each red and white element. The surface of the color-reversed displays was markedly different from the normal displays. There was no clear surface character in the color-reversed unidirectional displays; there appearance was like the bidirectional color-reversed display. While the surface character of these displays was disrupted, boundary formation was not. Accuracy for the color reversed unidirectional displays was close to the normal unidirectional accuracies and significantly higher than the bidirectional displays (see Figure 7). The monocular differences between inside and outside in the color reversed unidirectional displays appear to have helped stabilize the boundaries in these displays. This indicates that the SBF mechanisms do not simply use binocular information but rather can use some information that is specific to the eye of origin. That information involves not just the local color changes, but also somehow captures the consistency in the pattern of changes over a spatial region.

What might be the source of information for opacity and surface quality in SBF displays? The information might be static in nature; in unidirectional SBF displays the central region contains elements with a different character than the surrounding region (e.g., no elements are visible inside the form, while elements are visible outside). Alternatively, the source of information might be kinematic (Cunningham, Shipley, & Kellman, 1998a). The spatiotemporal pattern of changes might specify the transparency of the surface just as the pattern across a static boundary specifies transparency (e.g., Mettelli, 1974). Cunningham,

---

[2] Because the red and white dots were presented on a dark background, the sign of the contrast was the same in the two eyes, and as a result subjects had no trouble fusing the images.

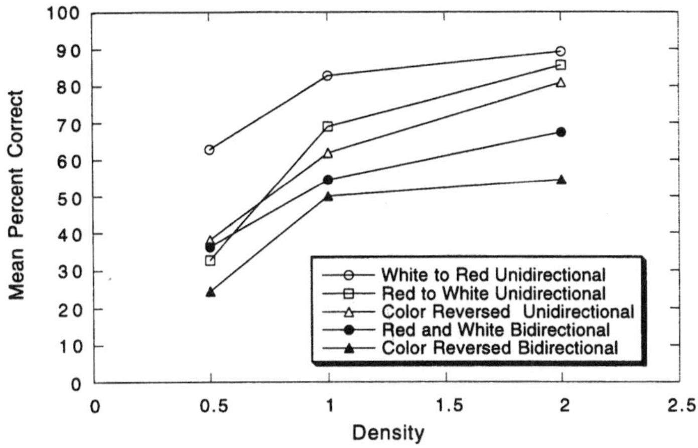

Figure 7. Shape discrimination accuracy plotted as a function of element density for unidirectional and bidirectional displays where elements were the same in both eyes or reversed. From Shipley, Cunningham, and Durgin (2001).

Shipley, and Kellman investigated this hypothesis using unidirectional displays with a large number of additional elements that did not change. These elements effectively masked the static differences across the boundaries of the form. The static mask did not affect the perceived surface quality. Subjects still reported a solid surface, which appeared to move under a layer of dots (the static mask). The pattern of luminance, and perhaps color, changes that occurs over time may serve to inform the visual system about the surface properties of moving objects.

THE SIMPLE MODEL REVISITED

Because perceptual systems evolved to serve the needs of moving organisms, sensitivity to information involving motion and change is fundamental. The visual system has remarkable capacities to generate accurate representations of objects despite receiving spatially discontinuous fragments piecemeal over time. These representations appear to be the product of a system that takes fragments that are visible at one point in time and relates them to fragments seen at another time. If we return to our observers walking down a country lane, we may consider how unit formation allows them to see the pickets and the house.

For a quickly moving observer either pickets or house may be perceived using a retinotopic representation. This would be possible if the observer is moving sufficiently quickly so that fragments from a substantial portions of the house or pickets project to the eye within a relatively short time. By maintaining eye position on some part of the house, or picket, fragments could be integrated over time. Whether the near or far object was seen would be determined by which object maintained it's position on the retina.

For observers taking a more leisurely walk, seeing the house, or pickets, requires first segmenting the picket boundaries from the house boundaries. Segmentation could be based on static properties, such as discontinuities in edge orientation, as well as the spatial pattern of motion signals. The complex pattern of local motion signals at the points of overlap can resolve themselves into motion signals consistent with disappearance and reappearance, and motion of the near and far surfaces. The first sort of signals can provide information for the location and orientation of the occluding edge, in this case a picket, even when no static information is available. The remaining motion signals provide information about the distal movement of the objects and so can serve as the basis for alignment of the pieces seen at different times. If attending to the house, it's fragments may be present in the distal representation with locations that are determined by the motion of the fragment and the temporal interval since the observation. The story would be the same for the pickets because the same process may be applied to the occluding surface. As was true in the static domain, the final percept of a moving form as occluded or occluding (modal or amodal) may depend on depth assignment. When the moving unit is seen in front, its boundaries appear modal, and when it is seen behind, its pieces are amodally unified.

Finally, in the distal representation some parts of an object may not be defined over time. Missing edges and surfaces may be filled in by the visual system. Surfaces may be filled in on the basis of surface properties (e.g., Yin, Kellman, and Shipley, 1997, in press), and edges may be filled in when two fragments are spatiotemporally relatable. Evidence for contour interpolation in dynamic displays comes from a distinct pattern of errors seen in certain SBF displays. At low element densities a hexagon will appear to the majority of subjects as a circle, only when densities are quite high do subjects accurately report seeing a hexagon. The reverse is almost never seen, subject do not mistake the circle for a hexagon (Shipley & Kellman, 1994). At low densities the form's boundary is sparsely defined and the visual system follows the constraints on relatability to fill in the missing boundaries so that the edge is smooth and monotonic.

AKNOWLEDGEMENTS

This chapter is based, in part, on Douglas Cunningham's Preliminary Exam. The writing of this chapter was supported in part by a grant from the National Eye Institute (R01 EY13518) to TFS.

REFERENCES

Adelson, E. H. & Movshon, J. A. (1982). Phenomenal coherence of moving visual patterns. *Nature, 300*, 523-525.

Anderson, G. J., & Cortese, J. M. (1989). 2-D contour perception resulting from kinetic occlusion. *Perception & Psychophysics, 46*, 49-55.

Anstis, S.M., & Atkinson, J. (1967). Distortions in moving figures viewed through a stationary slit. *American Journal of Psychology, 80*, 572-585.

Biederman, I. & Gerhardstein, P.C., (1993). Recognizing depth-rotated objects: Evidence and conditions for three-dimensional viewpoint invariance. *Journal of Experimental Psychology: Human Perception and Performance, 19*, 1162-1182.

Bradley, D. R., & Lee, K. (1982). Animated subjective contours. *Perception & Psychophysics, 32(4)*, 393-395.

Bruno, N. & Bertamini, M. (1990). Identifying contours from occlusion events. *Perception & Psychophysics,48(4)*, 331-342.

Bruno, N. & Bertamini, M. (1997). Amodal completion of partly occluded surfaces: Is there a mosaic stage? *Journal of Experimental Psychology: Human Perception and Performance, 23(5)*, 1412-1426.

Bruno, N., & Gerbino, W. (1991). Illusory figures based on local kinematics. *Perception, 20(2)*, 259-274.

Buelthoff, H., Little, J., & Poggio, T. (1989) A parallel algorithm for real-time computation of optical flow. *Nature, 337(6207)*, 549-553.

Burr, D.C. (1980). Motion smear. *Nature, 284(5752)*, 164-165.

Casco, C., & Morgan, M. (1984). The relationship between space and time in the perception of stimuli moving behind a slit. *Perception, 13(4)*, 429-441.

Cicerone, C.M. & Hoffman, D.D. (1997). Color from motion: Dicoptic activation and a possible role in breaking camouflage. *Perception, 26*, 1367-1380.

Cicerone, C.M., Hoffman, D.D., Gowdy, P.D., & Kim, J.S. (1995). The perception of color from motion. *Perception & Psychophysics, 57*, 761-777.

Cunningham, D. W., Shipley, T. F. & Kellman, P. J. (1998a). The dynamic specification of surfaces and boundaries. *Perception, 27(4)*, 403-416.

Cunningham, D. W., Shipley, T. F., & Kellman, P. J. (1998b). Interactions between spatial and spatiotemporal information in Spatiotemporal Boundary Formation. *Perception & Psychophysics, 60(5)*, 839-851.

Freyd, J.J. (1983). The mental representation of movement when static stimuli are viewed. *Perception & Psychophysics, 33(6)*, 575-581.

Fröhlich, F.W. (1923). Über die Messung der Empfindungszeit. *Zeitschrift für Sinnesphysiologie, 54*, 58-78.

Gallistel, C.R. (1990). *The organization of learning*. The MIT Press:, Cambridge, MA.

Gibson, J. J. (1966) *The senses considered as perceptual systems*. Houghton Mifflin: Boston.

Gibson, J. J. (1979). *The ecological approach to visual perception*. Lawrence Erlbaum: Hillsdale, NJ.

Gibson, J.J. (Producer). (1968). *The change from visible to invisible: A study of optical transitions*. [Film]. State College, PA: Psychological cinema register.

Gibson, J.J., Kaplan, G.A., Reynolds, H.N., & Wheeler, K. (1969). The change from visible to invisible: A study of optical transitions. *Perception & Psychophysics*, *5*, 113-116.

Girgus, J.S. Gellman, L.H., & Hochberg, J. (1980). The effect of spatial order on piecemeal shape recognition: A developmental study. *Perception & Psychophysics, 28(2),* 133-138.

Haber, R.N., & Nathanson, L.S. (1968). Post-retinal storage? Some further observations on Park's camel as seen through the eye of a needle. *Perception & Psychophysics*, *3*, 349-355.

Helmholtz, H. von (1962). Handbook of Physiological Optics, (3rd edit, J.P.C. Southall trans.) New York: Dover, (original work published in 1867).

Hine, T. (1987). Subjective contours produced purely by dynamic occlusion of sparse-points array. *Bulletin of the Psychonomic Society*, *25(3)*, 182-184

Johansson, G. (1973). Visual perception of biological motion and a model for its analysis. *Perception & Psychophysics. 14(2),* 201-211.

Johansson, G. (1975). Visual motion perception. *Scientific American*, *232(6)*, 76-88.

Kanizsa, G. (1979). *Organization in Vision*. Praeger: New York.

Katz, D. (1935). *The world of Color*. (English Translation by R. B. MacLeod and C.W. Fox.) Andover Hants: Kegan Paul International.

Kellman, P.J. (in press). An update on Gestalt Psychology. In B. Landau, J. Jonides, E. Newport & J. Sabini (Eds.), *Essays in Honor of Henry and Lila Gleitman*, MIT Press.

Kellman, P.J. & Cohen, M.H.. (1984). Kinetic subjective contours. *Perception & Psychophysics*, *35*, 237-244.

Kellman, P.J., Machado, L., Shipley, T.F. & Li, C.C. (2001). 3-D determinants of object completion. In preparation.

Kellman, P.J. & Shipley, T. F. (1991). A theory of visual interpolation in object perception. *Cognitive Psychology*, *23*, 141-221.

Kourtzi, Z. & Shiffrar, M. (1997). One-shot view invariance in a moving world. *Psychological Science, 8(6),* 461-466.

Lorenceau, J. & Shiffrar, M. (1992). The role of terminators in motion integration across contours. *Vision Research, 32,* 263-273.

Marr, D. (1982). *Vision*. San Francisco: W.H. Freeman.

Metelli, F. (1974). The perception of transparency. *Scientific American*, *230*, 90-98.

Michotte, A., Thinès, G., & Crabbé, G. (1964). Les complements amodaux des structures perceptives [Amodal completion and perceptual organization]. *Studia Psychologica*. Louvain, Belgium: Publications Universitaires de Louvain.

Minguzzi, G.F. (1987). Anomalous figures and the tendency to continuation. In S. Petry & G. E. Meyer (Eds.) *The Perception of Illusory Contours*. Springer-Verlag: New York.

Miyahara, E. & Cicerone, C.M. (1997). Color from motion: Separate contributions of chromaticity and luminance. *Perception, 26*, 1381-1396.

Morgan, M. J., Findlay, J. M., & Watt R.J. (1982). Aperture viewing: A review and a synthesis. *Quarterly Journal of Experimental Psychology: Human Experimental Psychology, 34A(2)*, 211-233.

Nakayama, K. Shimojo, S., & Silverman, G.H. (1989). Stereoscopic depth: Its relation to image segmentation, grouping, and the recognition of occluded objects. *Perception, 18(1)*, 55-68.

Neisser, U. (1976). *Cognition and Reality*. Freeman: New York.

Palmer, E., Kellman, P. J. & Shipley, T.F. (1997). Spatiotemporal relatability in dynamic object completion. *Investigative Ophthalmology & Visual Science, 38(4)*, 256.

Kellman, P. J., Palmer, E. M., & Shipley, T. F. (1998). Effects of velocity in dynamic object completion. *Investigative Ophthalmology and Visual Science Supplement, 39(4)*, S855.

Palmer, E., Kellman, P.J. & Shipley, T.F. (2000). Modal and amodal perception of dynamically occluded objects. *Investigative Ophthalmology and Visual Science, 41(4)*, 439.

Parks, T.E (1965). Post-retinal visual storage. *American Journal of Psychology*, 78, 145-147.

Parks, T.E. (1970). A control for ocular tracking in the demonstration of post-retinal visual storage. *American Journal of* Psychology, *83*, 442-444.

Petersik, J.T. & McDill, M. (1981). A new bistable motion illusion based on "kinetic optical occlusion'. *Perception, 10*, 563-572.

Prazdny, K. (1986). Illusory contours from inducers defined solely by spatiotemporal correlation. *Perception & Psychophysics, 39(3)*, 175-178.

Rock, I., & Gilchrist, A., (1975). Induced Form. *American Journal of Psychology, 88(3)*, 475-482.

Rock, I., & Halper, F., (1969). Form perception without a retinal image. *American Journal of Psychology, 82*, 425-440.

Rock, I., & Sigman, E. (1973). Intelligence factors in the perception of form through a moving slit. *Perception, 2(3)*, 357-369.

Sekuler, T.R. (1996). Motion perception: A modern view of Wertheimer's 1912 monograph. *Perception, 25*, 1243-1258.

Shiffrar, M., Lichtey, L., & Heptulla-Chatterjee, S. (1997). The perception of biological motion across apertures. *Perception & Psychophysics, 59*, 51-59.

Shimojo, S., & Richards, W. (1986). 'Seeing' shapes that are almost totally occluded: A new look at Parks' camel, *Perception & Psychophysics, 39*, 418-426.

Shipley, T. F. & Kellman, P. J. (1990). The role of discontinuities in the perception of subjective figures. *Perception & Psychophysics, 48(3),* 259-270.

Shipley, T.F. & Kellman, P.J. (1992). Perception of partly occluded objects and illusory figures: Evidence for an identity hypothesis. *Journal of Experimental Psychology: Human Perception & Performance, Vol. 18(1)*, 106-120.

Shipley, T. F., & Kellman, P. J. (1993). Optical tearing in spatiotemporal boundary formation: When do local element motions produce boundaries, form, and global motion? Special Issue: In honor of Bela Julesz. *Spatial Vision, 7(4),* 323-339.

Shipley, T.F., & Kellman, P.J., (1994). Spatiotemporal boundary formation: Boundary, form, and motion perception from transformations of surface elements. *Journal of Experimental Psychology: General, 123(1)*, 3-20.

Shipley, T. F. & Kellman, P. J., (1997). Spatiotemporal boundary formation: The role of local motion signals in boundary perception. *Vision Research, 37(10)*, 1281-1293.

Shipley, T. F. & Kellman, P. J., (2001). Temporal limits on visual integration. Manuscript in preparation.

Shipley, T. F., Cunningham, D. W., & Durgin, F., (2001). Monocular and binocluar contributions to spatiotemporal boundary and surface formation. Manuscript in preparation.

Sohmiya, T., & Sohmiya, K., (1992). Where does an anorthoscopic image appear? *Perceptual and Motor Skills, 75(3, pt 1)*, 707-714.

Stappers, P.J., (1989). Forms can be recognized from dynamic occlusion alone. *Perceptual and Motor Skills, 68(1)*, 243-251.

Steinman, R.M., Pizlo, Z., & Pizlo, F.J. (2000). Phi is not Beta, and why Wertheimer's discovery launched the Gestalt revolution, *Vision Research, 40*, 2257-2264.

Tarr, M. J., & Bulthoff, H. H. (1995). Is human object recognition better described by geon structural descriptions or by multiple views- comment on Biederman and Gerhardstein (1993). *Journal of Experimental Psychology: Human Perception and Performance, 27(6)*, 1494-1505.

Vierordt, K. (1900). Der Zeitsinn nach Versuchen: Scheinbare Verzerrung bewegter Gegenstände, 1868, 191 ff.; H. S. gertz, Untersuchen über Zöllner's anorthoskopische Tauschung, *Skandinav. Archiv. f. Physiol., 10*, 53-73.

Wallach, H. (1935). Über visuell warhgenomme Bewegungsrichtung. *Psychologische Forshcung*, 20, 325-380. (An English translation of this paper was provided by Wuerger, S., Shapley, R., & Rubin, N., (1996). On the visually perceived direction of motion by Hans Wallach: 60 years later, *Perception, 25*, 1317-1367.)

Wallis G. (1998). Spatio-temporal influences at the neural level of object recognition. *Network-Computation In Neural Systems, 9(2)*, 265-278.

Wallis G., & Baddeley R (1997) Optimal, unsupervised learning in invariant object recognition. *Neural Computation, 9(4)*, 883-894.

Wallis G., & Buelthoff H.H. (1999). Learning to recognize objects. *Trends in Cognitive Sciences, 3(1)*, 22-31.

Wallis G., & Buelthoff H.H. (2001). Effects of temporal association on recognition memory *Proceedings of the National Academy of Sciences of the United States of America, 98(8)*, 4800-4804

Wenzel, E.L., (1926). Die sukzessive Erfassung der Figuren, *Zeitschrift für Psychologie, 100*, 289-324.

Wertheimer, M. (1912). Experimentelle studien über das sehen von bewegung. *Zeitschrift für Psychologie, 61*, 161-265.

Yin, C., Kellman, P. J., & Shipley, T. F. (1997). Surface completion complements boundary interpolation in the visual integration of partly occluded objects. *Perception, 26*, 1459-1479.

Yin, C., Kellman, P.J. & Shipley, T.F. (in press). Surface integration influences depth discrimination. *Vision Research.*

Zöllner, F. (1862). Über eine neue Art anorthoskopischer Zerrbilder, *Annalen der Physic, 117*, 477-484.

AUTHOR INDEX

Abramov, I., 54, *66*

Adelson, E. H., 211, *240*, 486, 487, 488, *504*, *505*, 510, *525*, 565, *581*

Ahlström, U., 498, *504*

Ahlström, V., 498, *504*

Ahumada, A., Jr., 285, *288*

Aine, C. J., 149, *176*

Alais, D., 253, 256, 257, *261*

Albert, M. K., 191, *244*, 449, *457*, 532

Albright, T. D., 449, *458*

Allik, J., 124, 125, *139*

Allison, T., *480*

Allport, A., *146*, 173

Alpern, M., 125, *139*

Alter, T. D., 314, 325, *326*

Altoff, R. R., *478*

Andersen, E., 98, 102, *113*, 534, 539, 540, *553*, 570

Anderson, A. W., *479*

Anderson, B. L., 438, *454*, *457*

Anderson, G. J., 510, 513, 516, *525*, *526*, 576, *581*

Anson, R., 311, *328*

Anstis, S. M., 253, 255, *263*, 464, *478*, 561, *581*

Arndt, M., *395*

Arterberry, M. E., 44, 47, 50, 54, 55, 56, 57, 60, 61, 63, 64, *65*, *66*, *67*, *69*, 71, *115*, 534

Asada, H., 418, 428, *455*

Ash, M. G., 247, *261*

Aslin, R. N., 45, 46, 49, 50, 54, 55, 61, 62, 64, *65*, *67*

Atchley, P., 447, *454*

Atkinson, J., 561, *581*

Attneave, F., 250, 255, 257, *261*, 403, 409, 410, *454*

Averbach, E., 122, 127, 133, *139*

Bachmann, T., 124, 125, *139*

Baddeley, R., 558, *585*

Badenoch, M., 47, *68*

Bahnsen, P., 434, *454*

Baillargeon, R., 41, 43, 57, *65*, *68*, 79, *113*

Baird, L., *478*

Baizer, J., 494, *504*

Baker, C., 500, *504*

Baker, E., 91, *115*

Baldwin, D., 85, *113*

Ballard, D. H., 464, *478*

Bandera, C., 465, 476, *478*

Banton, T., 224, *239*

Barchilon Ben-Av, M., 491, *504*

Barclay, C., 497, *504*

Barenholtz, E., 405, 447, *454*

Baron, M. K., 498, *505*

Barrow, H. G., 193, *239*

Bartrip, J., 465, *479*

Basri, R., 198, *242*, 314, 319, 321, 324, 325, *326*, *327*, 524

Basso, G., 167, *174*
Baud-Bovy, G., 501, *507*
Bauer, P. J., 80, 82, *116*
Bauer, R., *395, 396*
Baumann, R., 377, *395*
Baumgartner, G., 207, *243,* 276, *292,* 360, *395, 400,* 524, *528*
Bavelier, D., 155, *180*
Baylis, G. C., 148, 152, 158, 159, 160, 168, *173, 174, 175,* 270, *288,* 333, *348,* 403, 405, 411, 412, 435, 442, *454, 455*
Beard, B. L., 285, *288*
Beck, J., 248, 256, *261, 290, 327, 350,* 438, *454, 458*
Becklen, R., 157, *178*
Behl-Chadha, G., 81, *113*
Behrmann, M., 146, 147, 148, 154, 155, 164, 165, 166, 167, 169, 172, 173, *174, 176, 177, 179, 180,* 268, 270, *288,* 405, 448, *458, 480*
Beller, H. K., 268, *288,* 337, *349*
Bellman, R., 472, *478*
Bellugi, U., 499, *506*
Bennett, B. M., 409, 433, *454*
Bennett, P. J., 268, 286, *289, 290*
Bennett, S. C., 403, 413, 414, 442, *459*
Benson, J., 12, *17*
Berkeley, G., 20, 25, 26, 27, 28, 29, 31, 32, 71, *554*
Bernardis, P., 537, 540, 543, 544, 549, 550, *553*
Bertamini, M., 237, *239,* 268, *288,* 337, *349,* 510, *525,* 534, 537, 539, 540, 543, 544, 545, 550, 551, 552, *554,* 570, *581*
Bertenthal, B. I., 44, 51, *65,* 391, *395,* 498, 499, *504*
Berti, A., 167, *178*
Berzins, V. A., 534, *556*
Beusmans, J., 417, *454*
Beutter, B. R., 268, *292*
Biederman, I., 75, 77, 80, 86, 99, 100, 108, 110, *113, 118,* 316, 319, *326,* 343, 344, *349,* 402, 407, 414, 415, 416, *454,* 558, *581, 584*
Bienfang, D., 500, *507*
Binford, T. O., 319, *326,* 407, *455*
Birch, E., 54, *66*
Bischof, W. F., 128, *140*
Bishop, P. O., 71, 491, *506, 554*
Bisiach, E., 167, *174*
Black, S. E., 169, *174*
Blake, A., 305, *326,* 517, 522, *525*
Blake, R., *261,* 498, *504,* 540, *553*
Bloom, L., 98, *113*
Bloom, P., 72, 80, 86, *113, 114*
Blum, H., 426, 428, 429, 449, 450, *455*
Bobes, M. A., *179*
Bonda, E., 500, *504*
Bonnet, C., 213, 216, *239, 504*
Bornstein, M. H., 41, 48, *65*
Boroditsky, L., 98, *114*
Boselie, F., 232, 233, *239,* 278, *288,* 332, 336, 337, 340, 345, *349, 350, 352,* 403, 405, *456*
Bosking, W. H., 358, 394, *395*
Boucart, M., *176,* 268, *289*
Bouma, H., 122, *139*
Bowerman, M., 95, 96, *114*
Boyes-Braem, P., 80, *117*
Boynton, G. M., *175*
Braddick, O., 500, *504*
Bradley, D. R., 536, 543, 546, *553,* 570, 571, *581*
Brady, M., 297, *326,* 418, 428, 429, *455,* 546
Braunstein, M. L., 405, 415, 423, *455,* 510,

525, 534, *553*
Bravo, J., *478*
Bravo, M., 540, *553*
Brehaut, J. C., 135, *139*
Breinlinger, K., 58, *69*
Breitmeyer, B. G., 124, 125, 127, 134, 135, *139*
Bressan, P., 449, *458*
Bridgeman, B., 127, *139*
Brookes, A., 434, *458*
Brooks, R. A., 464, *478*
Brosch, M., *395*
Broughton, R., 254, *262*
Brown, A., 85, *114*
Brown, C. M., 476, *481*
Brown, E., 47, *68*
Brown, J. M., 213, 216, *240,* 268, *288*
Brown, R., 80, *114*
Bruce, V., 411, *455,* 465, *478*
Brunn, J. L., 169, *174*
Bruno, N., 237, *239,* 266, 268, 270, 271, 275, 276, *288,* 337, *349,* 487, 510, *525,* 534, 536, 537, 539, 540, 541, 543, 544, 545, 547, 548, 549, 550, 551, 552, *553, 554,* 570, 574, *581*
Buelthoff, H. H., 558, 573, *581, 585*
Buffart, H., 278, *288,* 335, 336, 340, *349*
Bullier, J., 130, *139, 140, 395, 397*
Burbeck, C. A., 490, *504*
Burgess, A. E., 283, 284, *288*
Burr, D. C., 190, 206, 207, 220, *242,* 561, 563, *581*
Burt, P., 487, 494, *504*
Buswell, G. T., 464, 469, *478*

Campbell, F. W., 188, *239*
Campos, J. J., 51, *65, 395*
Carey, S., 73, *118,* 466, *478*
Carlson-Radvansky, L., 107, *114*
Carpenter, G. A., 386, *395*
Carpenter, R. H. S., 464, *478*
Casati, R., *455*
Casco, C., 565, *581*
Cassandra, T., *479*
Castet, E., 491, *504, 505*
Cate, A., 167, *174*
Cave, K. R., 133, *143*
Cavedon, A., *456*
Cecchi, G. A., *399*
Chan, E., 260, *262*
Chater, N., 345, *349*
Cheesman, J., 126, *139*
Chelazzi, L., *177*
Chen, Z., 159, *174*
Chitty, A. J., 500, *506*
Choi, A., 500, *507*
Chun, M. M., 134, *139,* 148, 442, *456, 479*
Cicerone, C. M., 510, 511, 513, 515, 516, 524, *525, 527,* 570, 577, 578, *581, 583*
Clark, E., 80, 83, 105, *114*
Clark, H., 72, *114*
Clark, J. J., 136, 137, *142*
Cobb, S., 127, *142, 327*
Cohen, J. D., 149, 167, *174*
Cohen, L. B., 41, *66*
Cohen, M. A., 355, 364, *395*
Cohen, M. H., 40, *67,* 237, *241,* 510, *527,* 535, 543, 545, *554,* 570, *582*
Cohen, N. J., 476, *478*
Colborne, B., 283, 284, *288*
Collard, R., 335, *349*
Connell, J., *480*
Cooper, E. E., 416, *454*
Cooper, G. F., 188, *239*
Corballis, M. C., 280, *288,* 411, *455*
Corballis, P. M.., 268, *288*
Coriel, A. S., 127, 133, *139*
Cortese, J. M., 510, 513, 516, *525, 526,*

534, 539, 540, *553,* 570, 576, *581*
Costes, N., 501, *504*
Cox, S. I., 126, *140*
Crabbé, G., 197, 223, *242,* 559, 560, 570, 574, *583*
Crane, H. D., 468, *478*
Craton, L. G., 43, 46, 53, 59, 60, *66, 69,* 534, *554, 556*
Creutzfeldt, O. D., 524, *528*
Crick, F., 367, *395*
Cristobal, G., 392, *398*
Crook, J. M., 524, *528*
Cruse, D. A., 99, 102, 109, *114*
Cunningham, D. W., 266, 278, 515, *526,* 532, 535, *554,* 570, 571, 575, 577, 578, 579, 580, *581, 584*
Currie, C. B., 136, *141*
Cutting, J. E., 316, *326,* 497, 499, *504, 505*

d'Ydewalle, G., 280, *292, 328*
Da Pos, O., *456*
Dale, A. M., *398*
Damasio, A. R., 130, *140*
Dannemiller, J. L., 54, *66*
Darrell, T., 476, *478*
Davi, M., 278, *288*
David, G., *17,* 19, 28, 29, 168, *177*
Davidoff, J., 95, *114*
Davidson, B. J., *178*
Davies, I., 95, *114, 176*
Davis, G., 268, 274, *289*
de Haan, E. H. F., *480*
de Weert, C. M., 438, *455*
Debner, J. A., 122, 126, *140*
Decety, J., 501, *504, 506*
Descartes, R., 19, 20, 21, 22, 24, *32, 140,* 247
Desimone, R., 145, 146, 149, 150, 151, 169, *174, 177,* 466, *478,* 494, *504*
Deutsch, D., 332, *349*
DeYoe, E. A., *395,* 500, *507*
Di Lollo, V., 128, 129, 131, 134, 135, 137, *140,* 562
di Pellegrino, G., 167, *174*
Diamond, A., 57, *66*
Diamond, R., 466, *478*
Dicke, P., *395*
Dinnerstein, D., 278, *289*
Dittrich, W. H., 498, 500, *504, 505*
Divita, J., 552, *555*
Dixon, P., 128, 134, *140*
Do Carmo, M., 409, *455*
Domini, F., 268, *288,* 337, *349*
Donnelly, N., *176*
Dosher, B., 95, *117*
Dougherty, T., 541, 542, 543, 544, 545, 546, *555*
Downing, P. E., 146, *178*
Drain, H. M., 472, *479*
Dresp, B., 213, 216, *239, 240*
Driver, J., 126, *142,* 148, 152, 158, 159, 160, 161, 162, 164, 167, 168, *174, 175, 177, 178, 179, 180,* 268, 270, 274, 283, *288, 289,* 333, *348,* 403, 405, 411, 412, 435, 442, 445, *454, 455,* 500, *505*
Duncan, J., 133, *140,* 145, 146, 148, 149, 150, 151, 157, 170, *174, 175,* 249, *262,* 270, *289,* 442
Duncker, K., 544, *554*
Durgin, F., 577, 578, 579, *584*
Dyer, F. C., 467, 471, 473, *478, 480*
Dziurawiec, C., 465, *479*

Ebel, B., 254, *262*
Eby, D. W., 253, *262*
Eckhorn, R., 386, 391, *395, 396, 399*
Edelman, G. M., 377, *396,* 524, *526*

Efron, R., 164, *175*
Egeth, H. E., 150, *180*
Egly, R., 148, 152, 153, 160, 164, *175, 179,* 283, *289,* 445, 447, *455*
Eimas, P. D., 81, 93, *114, 117*
Eizenman, D. R., 44, *66*
Elder, J., 250, 254, *262,* 306, 325, *326*
Ellias, S. A., 386, *395*
Ellis, S. R., 476, *481*
Engel, A. K., 391, *395, 396*
Enns, J. T., *66,* 128, 129, 131, 134, 135, 137, *140,* 255, *263,* 268, 272, 273, 274, *291, 292,* 562
Enroth-Cugell, C., 188, *239*
Epstein, W., 19, *32, 67,* 332, 334, 345, *349*
Eriksen, B. A., 152, *175*
Eriksen, C. W., 133, *140,* 152, *175*
Evans, A., 500, *504*

Fadiga, L., 501, *506*
Falk, R. J., 467, 471, *478*
Fantz, R. L., 41, *66*
Farah, M. J., 138, *140,* 148, 155, 156, 157, 163, 167, 168, 169, 170, *174, 175, 176, 179,* 472, *479, 480, 481*
Farell, B., 283, 284, *291*
Farroni, T., 391, *395*
Fazio, F., 501, *504*
Fei, X., *116*
Feldman, J., 405, 447, *454*
Felleman, D. J., 130, *140*
Fendrich, R., 268, *288*
Feroe, J., 332, *349*
Field, D. J., 192, 198, 201, 211, 213, 217, 218, *240,* 250, 254, *262,* 272, *289,* 301, *326,* 354, 388, 394, *396*
Filapek, J. C., 147, 154, *179,* 405, 448, *458*
Fillmore, C., 72, 107, *114*
Findlay, J. M., 469, *481,* 561, 563, 566, *583*
Finkel, L. H., 184, 192, 206, 210, 211, 212, 213, 214, 216, 218, 219, 221, *244,* 377, *396,* 524, *526, 528*
Fischer, B., 188, *240*
Fischl, B., *398*
Fitzpatrick, D., *395*
Fitzsimmons, C. M., 79, *118*
Fize, D., *399*
Flynn, C., 230, 233, *243,* 268, *291,* 337, *350*
Fodor, J. A., 76, *114*
Fogassi, L., 501, *506*
Foley, J., 520, *526*
Fonlupt, P., 501, *506*
Francis, G., 390, *396*
Franzel, S. L., 133, *143*
Frasinetti, F., 167, *174*
Freedland, R. L., 54, *66*
Freeman, T., *176*
Freeman, W. T., 211, *240,* 420, *455*
Freyd, J. J., 494, 495, 496, 501, *504, 506,* 562, *581*
Friedman, A., 476, *479*
Friedman, H. S., 127, *143*
Frien, A., 391, *396*

Gale, A. G., 469, *479, 481*
Gallese, V., 167, *178,* 501, *506*
Gallistel, C. R., 562, *581*
Gallogly, D. P., 202, *240, 396*
Gandhi, S. P., 169, *175*
Ganz, L., 125, *139, 140*
Garner, W. R., 250, *263,* 333, *349, 350,* 540, *554*
Garrett, M., 72, *114, 115, 116*
Gauthier, I., 466, *479*
Gaymard, B., *480*
Gazzaniga, M. S., *113,* 268, *288, 507*

Geiger, D., 297, *327*
Geisler, W. S., 202, *240,* 392, 393, 394, *396*
Gelade, G. A., 133, *142,* 147, 149, *179*
Gellman, L. H., 564, *582*
Gelman, R., 85, *118*
Gelman, S. A., 88, 89, 91, *114*
Geman, D., 303, 305, *326*
Geman, S., 303, 305, *326*
Gennari, N. N. R., 95, *116*
Gentner, D., 84, 85, 98, *114, 115*
Gephstein, S., 424, *456*
Gerbino, W., 267, 268, *289, 290,* 318, 322, *327,* 337, *349,* 434, 438, *455, 456,* 537, 541, 543, 544, 545, 547, 548, 549, 551, *554,* 570, 574, *581*
Gerhardstein, P. C., *118,* 168, *178,* 344, *349,* 558, *581, 584*
Gershkoff-Stowe, L., 79, 94, *118*
Gerstein, G. L., 130, *142*
Gettner, S. N., 170, 172, *178*
Ghim, H., 52, *66*
Gibbs, B. J., 272, *290*
Giblin, P. J., *526*
Gibson, B. S., 158, 159, 160, *175, 178,* 188, 194, 230, *243*
Gibson, E. J., 54, *66,* 97, 110, *114,* 553
Gibson, J. J., 54, 55, *66,* 190, *240*. 266, *289,* 461, 510, *526,* 534, 553, *554,* 557, 569, 570, *582*
Giersch, A., 268, *289*
Giesbrecht, B. L., 135, *140*
Gilbert, C. D., 169, *178,* 210, 211, *240, 241, 244,* 354, 358, *396, 398, 399*
Gilchrist, A., 551, *555,* 564, 565, *583*
Gilchrist, I. D., 168, *175*
Gilds, K. S., 162, 173, *175*
Gillam, B. J., 251, 252, 254, 255, 256, 258, 259, 260, *262, 263*
Girard, P., 130, *140, 397*
Girgus, J. S., 564, *582*
Gizzi, M. S., *505*
Gleitman, H., 44, *68, 115, 241, 479, 582*
Glicksman, M. L., *66,* 534
Gold, J. M., 268, 286, *289, 290*
Goldmeier, E., 280, *289*
Goldsmith, M., *175*
Goodale, M. A., 74, *117,* 464, *480,* 493, *505*
Goodenough, B., 258, 259, 260, *262*
Goodman, N., 16, *17*
Goodrich, S., 167, 169, *180*
Gordon, J., 202, *243*
Gore, J. C., *479, 480*
Gormican, S., 442, *458*
Gottschaldt, K., *263*
Gove, A., 366, 387, *396*
Gowdy, P. D., *525,* 570, 577, *581*
Granrud, C. E., 54, 59, 63, *65, 66, 67, 69, 530,* 534
Grant, T., Jr., 252, 255, 256, *262*
Grassi, F., 501, *504*
Gray, C. M., 386, 391, *396*
Gray, W., 80, *117*
Greene, H. H., 213, 216, *240*
Gregory, R. L., 524, *526*
Grenander, U., 297, *326*
Grezes, J., 501, *504*
Grimes, J., 136, *140*
Grimson, W. E. L., 297, *326,* 513, *526,* 546
Groner, M., 476, *479*
Groner, R., 476, *479*
Grose-Fifer, J., 54, *66*
Grosof, D. H., 276, *289,* 524, *526*
Grossberg, S., 202, 213, 216, 222, 225, *240,* 253, *263,* 272, *289,* 314, *326,* 355, 356, 357, 360, 361, 362, 363,

364, 365, 366, 368, 369, 371, 376, 378, 379, 386, 388, 390, 392, 393, 394, *395, 396, 397, 398, 399,* 525, *526, 527*
Grove, A. J., 524
Growney, R., 126, *140*
Grzywacz, N. M., 192, 212, *243, 399,* 487, *504,* 510, *530*
Gurvits, L., 297, *327*
Gutheil, G., *118*
Guttman, S. E., 197, 227, 228, 229, *240,* 266, 268, 270, 271, 272, 273, 274, 275, 277, 278, *289*
Gwiazda, J., 54, *66*
Gyoba, J., 47, 48, *67*

Haber, R. N., 561, 563, 566, *582*
Hadad, B., 155, *176*
Haglund, M. M., 127, *141*
Haimson, C., 146, *174, 176*
Hainline, L., 54, *66*
Haith, M. M., 12, *17,* 51, *65, 395*
Hake, H. W., *554*
Hall, D. G., 91, 92, *115,* 173
Halligan, P. W., 168, *175, 177*
Halper, F., 510, *528,* 552, *555,* 563, 570, *583*
Hamstra, S. J., 270, *291*
Hanazawa, A., 127, *143*
Hansen, T., 386, *397*
Hanson, A., 297, 307, *328*
Harmon, M., *478*
Harries, M., 500, *506*
Harter, M. R., 149, *176*
Hatfield, G., 19, *32,* 332, 334, 345, *349*
Hawken, M. J., 276, *289,* 524, *526*
Haxby, J. V., *479*
Hayes, A., 192, 218, *240,* 250, *262,* 272, *289,* 301, *326,* 354, *396,* 475, *480*
Hayhoe, M. M., 464, *478*
Hayward, W., 72, *115*
He, Z. J., 196, 202, 203, *240,* 268, 274, *289*
Heeger, D. J., *175*
Heider, B., 164, *176*
Heider, E. R., 95, *115*
Heise, D., 82, *117*
Heitger, F., 184, 190, 192, 206, 207, 208, 209, 210, 211, 213, 214, 215, 216, 217, 218, 221, 222, 224, *240, 241,* 314, *326,* 377, 378, 379, 381, 382, 384, 388, *397, 400, 527*
Held, R., 54, *66*
Helmholtz, H. von, 247, 272, *290,* 345, *352,* 559, 562, *582*
Hemenway, K., 280, *291*
Henderson, J. M., 300, 464, 467, 471, 473, 476, *478, 479, 480,* 557, 564
Henry, G. H., 130, *139, 395*
Heptulla-Chatterjee, S., 496, 497, *504, 506,* 567, *583*
Herbart, J., 335, *349*
Herskovits, A., 72, *115*
Hess, R. F., 192, 218, *240,* 250, *262,* 272, *289,* 301, *326,* 354, *396*
Hietanen, J., 500, *504*
Hildreth, E., 190, 220, 221, *242,* 485, *505,* 510
Hillyard, S. A., 170, 171, *176, 177*
Hine, T., 539, 540, *554,* 570, 576, 577, *582*
Hobbes, T., 92, *115*
Hochberg, J., 160, *178,* 332, *349,* 434, *455,* 564, *582*
Hoffman, D. D., 4, *17,* 57, *66,* 80, 99, 100, 101, 102, 109, 110, *115, 117,* 147, 154, *176,* 191, 197, *241, 244,* 315, 322, *326,* 403, 404, 405, 406, 407, 409, 410, 414, 415, 418, 420, 421,

424, 430, 431, 432, 433, 434, 435, 436, 439, 440, 441, 449, *454, 455, 456, 457, 458,* 461, 510, 511, 515, 516, 524, *525,* 570, 577, 578, *581*
Hoffman, J., 152, *175*
Hollingworth, A., 464, 467, 471, 476, *478, 479*
Horn, B. K. P., 304, *326*
Howard, R. A., 472, *479*
Hubel, D. H., 40, *68,* 188, 207, 210, *241, 397,* 484, 491, 492, *505*
Hulleman, J., 403, 405, 413, 414, 442, *456*
Hummel, R. A., 339, 374, 375, *400*
Humphreys, G. W., 133, *140,* 151, 163, 165, 168, *175, 176, 178, 262,* 268, *289,* 442
Hupé, J. M., 130, *140, 397*
Huston, T. A., 149, *174*
Huttenlocher, J., *17*

Imai, M., 85, *115*
Inoue, H., 47, 48, *67*
Isaak, M. I., 134, *141*
Ishai, A., 466, *479*
Ito, M., 211, *241, 398*
Ivry, R., 438, *454*

Jackendoff, R., 72, 73, 74, 75, 76, 77, 78, 87, 90, 104, 105, *115*
Jacobs, D. W., 198, *242,* 302, 306, 307, 308, 310, 311, 314, 316, 318, 319, 321, 322, 323, 324, *326, 327, 328,* 383, 384, 391, *400,* 524
Jacobson, A., 58, *69,* 152, *176*
Jacoby, L. L., 122, 126, *140*
James, A. C., 47, 71, 130, *140,* 247, 325, *397*
Jeannerod, M., 501, *504*
Jeffreys, D. A., 127, *140*
Johansson, G., 234, *241,* 498, 500, *505, 507,* 557, *582*
Johnson, D., 88, *117*
Johnson, E. C., 80, *116*
Johnson, M. H., 465, *479*
Johnson, S. P., 44, 45, 46, 47, 49, 50, 55, 61, 62, 64, *66, 67, 68*
Johnson-Laird, P., 72, 88, *117*
Jones, H. E., 130, *142*
Jones, M., 332, *349*
Jones, S. S., 79, 84, 85, 94, *116, 117, 118*
Jonides, J., 150, 171, *180*
Jordan, W., *395*
Joseph, J. S., 268, 282, *290,* 442, *456*
Julesz, B., 147, 150, *176, 179,* 190, 212, *241, 242,* 250, *263,* 301, *327*
Jusczyk, P. W., 44, *67*

Kaelbling, L., 473, 476, *479*
Kahneman, D., 124, *141,* 272, 281, *290*
Kanizsa, G., 39, *67,* 196, 203, 229, *241,* 267, 268, *290,* 297, 307, 318, 322, *326, 327,* 338, *349,* 381, 388, 390, *397,* 405, 438, 448, *456,* 536, *554,* 570, *582*
Kanwisher, N., 146, *178,* 466, *479*
Kapadia, M. K., 211, 212, *241,* 356, 357, *398*
Kaplan, G. A., 190, *240,* 510, *526, 527,* 532, 533, *554,* 569, *582*
Kappers, A. M. L., 416, *456, 458*
Karnath, H.-O., 168, *179*
Kato, H., 491, *506*
Katz, D., 532, *554,* 570, 577, *582*
Katz, N., 91, *115*
Kaufman, L., 57, *68, 239, 350*
Kaufmann, F., 50, 59, *67,* 534, *554*
Kaufmann-Hayoz, R., 50, 59, *67,* 534, *554*
Kavsek, M. J., 56, *67*

Kawabata, H., 47, 48, 49, 55, *67*
Kawaguchi, J., 233, *241*
Kawahara, J., 137, *140*
Kehr, H., *396*
Keil, F., 85, 86, 88, 89, *115*
Keil, M. S., 392, *398*
Kellman, P. J., 38, 39, 40, 41, 44, 45, 46, 47, 48, 49, 50, 53, 54, 55, 56, 59, 61, 62, 64, *67, 68,* 71, 78, 79, *115,* 184, 187, 188, 190, 191, 192, 195, 196, 197, 198, 199, 201, 202, 203, 204, 210, 214, 218, 219, 223, 224, 225, 227, 228, 229, 230, 232, 233, 234, 235, 236, 237, 238, *240, 241, 242, 243, 244, 245,* 253, 254, 257, *263,* 266, 268, 272, 274, 275, 277, 278, 280, *290, 292,* 310, 320, 322, *327, 328,* 336, *349,* 361, 366, 367, *398, 399,* 424, 449, *456, 457,* 491, *505,* 510, 513, 514, 515, 516, 524, *526, 527, 528, 529,* 532, 533, 535, 539, 543, 545, 546, 550, *554, 555,* 559, 565, 567, 568, 569, 570, 571, 572, 574, 575, 576, 578, 580, *581, 582, 583, 584, 585*
Kelly, F., 371, *398*
Kemmerer, D., 75, 76, *115*
Kennedy, L. J., 44, *67*
Kersten, D., 206, *242,* 268, *290*
Kim, J. S., 233, *241, 525,* 570, 577, *581*
Kimchi, R., 155, *176*
Kimia, B. B., 417, 420, 421, 422, 423, 425, 449, 450, 451, 452, *456, 457*
Klymenko, V., 535, *555*
Knill, D. C., 206, *242*
Koch, C., 367, *395,* 510
Koenderink, J. J., 416, *456, 458, 527*
Koffka, K., 19, 193, 247, 248, 255, *263,* 305, 332, *350,* 354, *398,* 434, 435, 437, *456*
Köhler, W., 315, *327,* 332, *350*
Kojima, H., 535, 539, *555*
Kojo, I., 237, *242*
Kolers, P. A., 124, 126, *141*
Komatsu, H., 127, *143*
König, P., *395, 396*
Kosslyn, S. M., *118,* 137, *141*
Kotovsky, K., 332, *351*
Kourtzi, Z., 558, *582*
Kovacs, G., 276, *290*
Kovács, I., 212, *242, 263,* 268, *289,* 301, *327*
Kozlowski, L. T., 497, 498, *504, 505*
Kramer, A. F., 152, 170, *176, 180,* 447, *454*
Krinsky, S. J., 48, *65*
Krüger, N., 392, *398*
Krumhansl, C., 494, *505*
Kruse, W., *395*
Kübler, O., 184, 206, 208, 209, 215, *240, 241, 397*
Kubovy, M., 298, *327,* 345, *350,* 424, *456*
Kuczaj, S. A., *114, 115*
Kumaran, K., 297, *327*
Kuniyoshi, K., 464, 465, *479*

Lamme, V. A. F., 130, *141,* 163, 172, *176, 177, 178, 180*
Lamy, D., 161, *177*
Landau, B., 72, 74, 75, 77, 79, 80, 84, 85, 86, 88, 89, 94, 95, 96, 97, 102, 104, 105, *115, 116, 117, 118, 241, 582*
Landman, R., 172, *176, 177*
Lavie, N., 161, 162, *177*
Lee, E. Y., 57, *66*
Lee, K., 536, *553,* 570, 571, *581*
Lee, S., *261*
Leeuwenberg, E. L. J., 230, *244,* 278, *288,*

292, 298, *328,* 331, 332, 335, 336, 337, 339, 340, 341, 343, 345, 347, *349, 350, 351*
Lemay, M., 500, *507*
Lesher, G. W., 191, 202, *242,* 356, 368, 382, *398*
Leslie, A. M., 7, *17,* 79, *116*
Levi, D. M., 224, *239*
Levin, D. T., *17,* 136, *141, 142*
Levine, S., *17*
Levinson, S. C., 78, 95, 105, 106, *114, 116*
Leyton, M., 86, 102, *116,* 298, *327,* 409, 428, 429, *456*
Li, C. C., 197, 204, 235, 237, *241, 242,* 569, *582*
Li, X., 491, *506*
Li, Z., 385, 386, *398*
Lichtey, L., 497, *506,* 567, *583*
Liebmann, S., 513, *527*
Liinasuo, M., 237, *242*
Lindberg, D., 19, *32*
Little, J., 573, *581*
Littman, M., 477, *479, 480*
Liu, A., 470, *479*
Liu, A. K., *398*
Liu, Z., 198, 206, *242,* 319, 321, 324, *327*
Livingstone, M. S., 40, *68,* 125, *141,* 211, *242,* 492, *505*
Locke, J., 20, 22, 23, 24, 25, 26, 29, *32, 33,* 247
Loftus, G. R., 476, *480*
Logan, G. D., 147, *177*
Lomber, S. G., 130, *140, 397*
Loomis, J. M., 253, *262*
Lorenceau, J., 251, 256, *263,* 268, *292,* 487, 488, 489, 490, 491, 492, 497, *504, 505, 506,* 565, 567, 577, *582*
Loukides, M. G., 202, 210, *241, 398,* 448, *456,* 543, 545, 546, *554*
Lovell, J., 285, *288*
Lowe, D., 297, 316, *327,* 407, *456*
Luck, S. J., 126, *141, 143,* 146, 151, 169, 170, 171, 173, *176, 177, 179, 180*
Lund, J. S., 358, *399*
Luppino, G., 502, *506*
Lutes-Driscoll, V., 499, *506*

Macario, J. F., 85, *116*
MacArthur, L. Z., 498, *505*
Mach, E., 280, *290,* 345, *350*
Machado, L. J., 197, 204, 235, *241, 242,* 569, *582*
Mack, A., 136, 137, *141*
Macknik, S. L., 125, 127, *141*
Mackworth, N. H., 476, *480*
Macnamara, J., 91, *115*
Magnasco, M. O., *399*
Mahadevan, S., 467, 471, 473, *478, 480*
Maisog, J. M., *479*
Malpeli, J. G., 130, *141*
Malt, B. C., 88, 95, 96, 97, *116*
Mandelbrot, B. B., 81, *116*
Mandler, J. M., 80, 82, 87, 93, *116*
Maratsos, M. P., 105, *115*
Marcel, A. J., 126, *141*
Marey, E. J., 498, *505*
Markman, E. M., 79, 80, 86, 99, *116, 117, 118*
Markow, D., 80, 87, *118*
Marlot, C., *399*
Marr, D., 75, 77, 80, 100, 106, 108, *117,* 190, 194, 206, 220, 221, 234, *242,* 319, *327,* 402, 406, 407, *456,* 510, *527,* 558, *582*
Marshall, J. C., 168, *175, 177*
Martin, A., *479*
Martin, J., 134, *141*
Martin, K. A. C., 358, *398*

Matelli, M., 502, *506*
Matin, E., 464, *480*
Mattingley, J. B., 168, *177, 179*
Mattock, A., 47, *68*
McAlister, E., 332, *349*
McCarthy, G., 466, *480*
McConkie, G. W., 136, *141*
McCourt, M. E., 130, *139, 395*
McDermott, J., *479*
McDill, M., 535, *555,* 570, 574, 577, *583*
McDonough, L., 80, 87, *116*
McGoldrick, J., 147, 154, *179,* 405, 448, *458*
McGrath, D., *262*
McKee, S. P., 192, 212, *243, 399*
McLeod, P., 500, *505*
Medin, D., 86, *117*
Mehta, Z., *480*
Mendola, J. D., 390, *398*
Mennemeier, M., 168, *178*
Mens, L., 335, *350*
Merikle, P. M., 126, *139*
Mervis, C., 80, *117*
Metelli, F., 255, *263,* 405, 438, *456, 554, 582*
Metzger, W., 510, *527*
Meyer, D. E., 126, *141,* 173
Meyer, G., *173, 241, 243, 262, 456,* 541, 542, 543, 544, 545, 546, *554, 555, 583*
Meyer, M., 390, *398*
Michaels, C. F., 124, *141*
Michotte, A., 197, 223, *242,* 532, *555,* 559, 560, 569, 571, 574, *583*
Mignard, M., 130, *141*
Miller, George A., 72, 88, *117*
Miller, Gregory A., 170, *180*
Milner, A. D., 74, *117,* 464, *480,* 493, *505*
Ming, C., 390, *398*
Mingolla, E., 191, 202, 222, 225, *240, 242,* 253, *263,* 272, *289,* 314, *326,* 355, 357, 360, 363, 364, 365, 366, 368, 369, 370, 376, 378, 379, 386, 388, 393, 394, *396, 397, 398, 399,* 525, *527*
Minguzzi, G. F., 571, *583*
Minut, S., 473, *480*
Mistlin, A. J., 500, *506*
Mitchell, T., 467, *480*
Mitchison, G. J., 320, *327*
Mix, K., 7, *17*
Miyahara, E., 513, *527,* 577, *583*
Moghaddam, B., *480*
Moore, C. M., 268, 283, *290,* 445, 447, *456*
Moran, J., 169, *177*
Morgan, M. J., 221, *244,* 411, *455,* 561, 563, 565, 566, *581, 583*
Morison, V., 47, 54, *68*
Morrison, S., 540, *553*
Morrone, M. C., 190, 206, 207, 220, *242*
Morton, J., 465, *479*
Moscovitch, M., 165, 169, *174,* 466, *480*
Motter, B. C., 169, *177*
Moulden, B., 192, *242*
Movshon, J. A., 391, *399,* 484, 486, 487, 488, 490, *504, 505,* 510, *525,* 565, *581*
Mozer, M. C., 146, 148, 155, 165, 167, 169, 173, *174, 177, 180,* 268, *288*
Muller, H. M., *176*
Mumford, D., 127, *142,* 297, 303, 304, 306, 307, 310, 311, *327,* 387, *398, 399*
Munk, M., *395*
Munnich, E., 95, *117*
Murakami, I., 127, *143,* 197, *244,* 268, *292*
Muri, R., *480*
Murphy, G. L., 102, 103, 109, 110, 111, 112, *117*
Murray, R. F., 268, 270, 271, 276, 277, 284, 285, 286, *289, 290*

Musatti, C. L., 510, *527*
Musselwhite, M. J., 127, *140*
Mutch, K. M., 534, *556*

Nadel, L., 72, *114, 115, 116*
Nagel, R. N., 426, 428, *455*
Nakayama, K., 196, 203, 228, *240, 242,* 268, 274, 282, *289, 290, 291, 292,* 442, *456,* 500, *507,* 510, *528,* 564, *583*
Nakazawa, H., 197, *244,* 268, *292*
Nanez, J. E., 44, 46, 49, 54, 61, 62, *67, 68*
Nathanson, L. S., 561, 563, 566, *582*
Navon, D., 346, *350*
Needham, A., 57, *68*
Nefien, A., *480*
Neisser, U., 147, 157, *177, 178,* 557, *583*
Nelson, K., 16, *32,* 98, *117*
Neumann, H., 364, 386, 387, 390, *397, 399*
Newcome, F., 466, *480*
Newsome, W. T., *505*
Nishihara, H. K., 100, 108, *117,* 402, 406, 407, *456*
Nissen, M. J., 445, *457*
Nitzburg, M., 297, 307, *327*
Noland, J. H., 510, *528*
Norman, J. F., *529*
Noton, D., 476, *480*
Nys, G., 168, *178*

O'Craven, K. M., 146, *178*
O'Regan, J. K., 136, 137, *328*
Ogden, W. C., 445, *457*
Ohtsubo, H., 47, 48, *67*
Oliver, D. C., 95, *115*
Olson, C. R., 170, 172, *178*
Ooi, T. L., 202, *240*
Oram, M., 500, *505*
Orban, G. A., 276, *290,* 491, *506*
Orne, M. T., 539, *555*
Ortony, A., 86, *117*
Ostry, D., 500, *504*
Ozog, G., 125, *143*

Palmer, E. M., 197, 233, 237, 238, *241, 242,* 268, *290,* 510, *528,* 565, 567, 568, 569, 570, *583*
Palmer, J., 274, *291*
Palmer, S. E., 152, *178,* 194, 195, 230, 233, *242, 243,* 249, 254, 255, *263,* 268, 269, 270, 271, 275, 280, *291,* 298, *327,* 333, 337, 343, 348, *350,* 402, 435, *456, 457*
Parent, P., 361, 366, 371, 372, 373, 374, 375, 376, 378, 385, 386, 387, *399, 400*
Parks, T. E., 540, *555,* 563, 564, 566, 568, *583, 584*
Pashler, H., 133, *142, 177, 180,* 280, *291*
Pavel, M., 251, *263,* 487, 488, 491, 497, *506,* 540, 542, 543, 544, 545, 547, 548, 551, *555*
Pavlova, M., 498, *506*
Payne, B. R., 130, *140, 397*
Pelli, D. G., 283, 284, *291*
Pentland, A. P., 407, *457,* 466, 467, *480*
Perani, D., 501, *504*
Perrett, D., 500, *504, 505, 506*
Perry, J. S., 202, *240, 396*
Pessoa, L., 364, *399*
Peterhans, E., 40, *68,* 184, 206, 207, 208, 209, 213, 214, 215, 216, 218, 222, 223, *240, 241, 243, 244,* 276, *292,* 360, 362, 377, 381, 390, *395, 397, 399, 400,* 524, *528, 529*
Petersik, J. T., 535, *555,* 570, 574, 577, *583*
Peterson, M. A., 72, *114, 115, 116,* 160, 168, *178,* 188, 194, 230, *243*
Petrides, M., 500, *504*

Petry, S., *241, 243, 262, 456,* 543, 546, *554, 555, 583*
Petter, G., 200, 224, *243,* 449, *457,* 543, 546, *555*
Pettet, M. W., 192, 212, 213, *243,* 388, 389, *399*
Piaget, J., 11, 12, 15, 16, *17*
Pierrot-Deseilligny, C., 476, *480*
Pinilla, T., *179*
Pinker, S., 86, *118, 326*
Pinna, B., 278, *288*
Pinto, J., 498, 499, 503, *504, 507*
Pizlo, F. J., 570, 577, *584*
Pizlo, Z., 570, 577, *584*
Poggio, G. F., 188, *240*
Poggio, T., *480,* 573, *581*
Poizner, H., 499, *506*
Polat, U., 198, 211, 212, 218, *243*
Pollick, F. E., *526, 528*
Pomerantz, J. R., 250, 256, *263,* 298, *327,* 345, *350*
Pook, P. K., 464, *478*
Posner, M. I., 133, *142,* 152, 169, *178,* 445, *457*
Pouget, A., 167, *178*
Pratt, J., 268, 283, *291*
Prazdny, K., 438, *454,* 570, *583*
Precup, D., 476, *480*
Prenter, P. M., 198, *243*
Price, M. C., 168, *177*
Pristach, E. A., 256, *263*
Procyk, E., 501, *504*
Puce, A., *480*
Puterman, M., 472, *480*
Putnam, H., 86, *117, 140*
Pylyshyn, Z. W., *17,* 90, 91, 92, *117,* 133, *142*

Quine, W. V., 4, 6, 7, 15, 16, *17*
Quinn, P. C., 81, 93, *114, 117*

Rabin, C., 138, *141*
Rabiner, L. R., *481*
Radvansky, G., 107, *114*
Rafal, R. D., 148, 164, 168, *175, 179,* 283, *289,* 445, *455*
Raizada, R. D. S., 369, *397*
Ramachandran, V. S., 127, *142, 179,* 253, 255, *263,* 311, 313, *327*
Rao, R. P. N., 464, *478*
Rao, S. C., 276, *292*
Rapcsak, S. Z., 168, *178*
Ratoosh, P., 272, *291*
Rauschenberger, R., 268, 273, 274, *291*
Rayner, K., 464, *481*
Redies, C., 524, *528*
Redolfi, M., 501, *507*
Regan, D., 136, 137, *142,* 270, *291*
Regier, T., 72, *117*
Reitboeck, H. J., *395*
Rensink, R. A., 128, 129, 131, 134, 136, 137, *140, 142,* 268, 274, *291*
Restle, F., 278, *288,* 332, 336, *349, 350*
Reynolds, H. N., 190, *240, 526,* 569, *582*
Rich, A., 256, *263*
Richards, W. A., 3, *17,* 57, *66,* 80, 99, 100, 101, 102, 109, 110, *115,* 147, 154, *176,* 315, 322, *326,* 405, 406, 407, *454, 455,* 574, *584*
Riddell, P., 54, *66*
Riddoch, M. J., 163, 165, 168, *175, 176, 178*
Riggs, L. A., 464, *481*
Rimey, R. D., 476, *481*
Ringach, D. L., 199, 202, 224, 232, *243,* 268, 270, 271, 284, 285, 286, *291,* 390, *399*
Rivaud, S., *480*

Rizzolatti, G., 167, *178,* 501, 502, *506*
Roberson, D., 95, *114*
Roberts, L, 297, *327,* 407
Robertson, L., 346, *350*
Robinson, J. O., 225, *243*
Rock, I., 136, 137, *141,* 194, *240, 242,* 249, 254, *263,* 311, *328,* 338, *350,* 510, *528,* 551, 552, *555,* 562, 563, 564, 565, 567, 570, *583*
Rockland, K. S., 358, *399*
Rodriguez, V., *179*
Roelfsema, P. R., 163, 169, 172, *176, 178*
Rogers-Ramachandran, D., *327*
Roldan, C. E., 280, *288, 455*
Romero, R., 167, *174*
Rorden, C., 168, *179*
Rosch, E., 80, *117,* 268, *291*
Rose, D., 54, *68*
Rosenfeld, A., *327,* 374, 375, *400, 458*
Rosenthaler, L., 184, 206, 28, 209, 215, *240, 241, 397*
Rosin, P. L., 431, *457*
Ross, W. D., 253, *263,* 363, 364, 369, 386, *397, 398, 399*
Rovamo, J., 237, *242*
Rubin, E., 40, 147, *179,* 194, *243,* 257, *263,* 431, 434, *457,* 564, *584*
Ruddy, M. G., 126, *141*
Ruskin, D., *327*
Rycroft, J. E., *526*

Saam, M., 391, *399*
Sager, L. C., 250, *263*
Sagi, D., 150, *179,* 198, 211, 212, 218, *243*
Saidpour, A., 405, 414, 415, *455*
Sajda, P., 524, *526, 528*
Salmaso, D., 268, *289,* 337, *349*
Samaria, F., 467, 475, *481*
Sambin, M., 278, *288,* 305, *328,* 550, *555*
Sampaio, A. C., 532, 535, *555*
Samuelson, L., 79, 94, *118*
Scheerer, E., 124, *142*
Schiller, P. H., *180*
Schofield, B., *395*
Scholl, B. J., 7, *17,* 90, 91, 92, *116, 117,* 137, *142,* 405, 406, 446, 447, *457*
Schrater, P., 268, *290*
Schveneveldt, R. W., *141*
Schwartz, R., 7, 16, *17, 117*
Schyns, P. G., 102, 103, 109, 110, 111, 112, *117*
Scott, T. R., *65,* 510, *529*
Sekuler, A. B., 197, 230, 233, *240, 243,* 268, 269, 271, 272, 273, 274, 275, 277, 278, 280, 283, 286, *289, 290, 291, 292,* 337, 343, *350*
Sekuler, R., 268, *291, 292,* 570, *583*
Senghas, A., 87, *118*
Sepp, W., 386, 387, 390, *397, 399*
Servan-Schreiber, D., 167, *174*
Seyranian, G. D., 418, 420, 424, *458*
Shadlen, M. N., 391, *399*
Shah, J., 303, *327*
Shapiro, K. L., 126, 134, 135, *140, 141, 142, 143*
Shapley, R. M., 199, 202, 224, 232, *243,* 268, 270, 271, 276, 284, 285, 286, *288, 289, 291,* 390, *399,* 524, *526, 584*
Sharma, J., 276, *292*
Shashua, A., 301, 313, *328*
Shea, S. L., 54, *65*
Shen, L., 268, *290*
Shepard, R. N., 493, 494, *506*
Shepperson, B., 10, *17*
Sheth, B. R., 276, *292*
Shi, M. Y., 95, *116*
Shiffrar, M., 251, 253, 256, *263,* 266, 487, 488, 489, 490, 491, 492, 494, 495,

496, 497, 499, 501, *504, 505, 506, 507,* 540, 542, 543, 544, 545, 547, 548, 551, *555,* 558, 564, 565, 567, 573, 577, *582, 583*
Shimojo, S., 197, 228, *242, 244,* 268, 282, *291, 292,* 564, 574, *583, 584*
Shipley, E., 10, *17,* 96, 97, *116*
Shipley, T. F., 38, 40, 41, 44, 46, 48, 53, 56, 59, 64, *67, 68,* 184, 187, 190, 191, 192, 195, 196, 197, 198, 199, 201, 202, 203, 204, 210, 214, 218, 219, 223, 224, 225, 228, 232, 233, 235, 237, 238, *241, 242, 243, 244, 245,* 253, 254, 257, *263,* 266, 268, 272, 274, 275, 277, 278, *290, 292,* 310, 320, 322, *327, 328,* 336, *349,* 361, 366, 367, *398, 399,* 424, 449, *456, 457,* 491, *505,* 510, 513, 514, 515, 516, 524, *526, 527, 528, 529,* 532, 533, 535, 539, 543, 546, 550, *554, 555,* 559, 565, 567, 568, 569, 570, 571, 572, 574, 575, 576, 577, 578, 579, 580, *581, 582, 583, 584, 585*
Shore, D. I., 268, 272, 273, *292*
Short, K. R., 44, 54, *67, 68*
Shulman, G. L., 160, *179*
Shuntich, R., 124, 127, 133, 134, *142*
Siddiqi, K., 417, 420, 421, 422, 424, 425, 449, 451, 452, 453, *457*
Sigman, E., 562, 564, 567, *583*
Sigman, M., 392, *399*
Sillito, A. M., 130, *142*
Silverman, G. H., 228, *242,* 268, *291,* 510, *528,* 564, *583*
Simion, F., *395*
Simon, H., 332, *351*
Simons, D. J., 136, *141, 142*
Singer, W., *395, 396*
Singh, M., 80, 99, 100, 101, 102, *115, 117,* 147, 154, *176,* 197, *244,* 403, 404, 405, 418, 420, 421, 424, 430, 431, 432, 433, 434, 435, 436, 438, 440, 441, 443, 444, 445, 446, 447, 449, *455, 457, 458, 459*
Singh, S., *480*
Sitton, M., 146, *177*
Skudlarski, P., *479*
Slater, A., 47, 49, 54, *68*
Sloman, S. A., 95, *116*
Smith, I. M., *66,* 534
Smith, L. B., 79, 82, 84, 88, 94, 97, 98, *116, 117, 118*
Snyder, C. R. R., *178*
Sober, E., 345, *351*
Sohmiya, K., 562, *584*
Sohmiya, T., 562, *584*
Soja, N., 73, 80, 85, 86, *118*
Sokolov, A., 498, *506*
Solomon, E. M., *262*
Somers, D., 386, *397*
Somers, M., 47, *68*
Sorknes, A. C., *66*
Souther, J., 413, 442, *458*
Spehar, B., 254, *262*
Spekreijse, H., 130, *141, 176, 177, 178*
Spelke, E. S., 31, 32, *33,* 39, 44, 45, 46, 47, 49, 53, 55, 58, 61, 62, 64, *67, 68, 69,* 73, 79, 91, 92, *115, 118*
Spencer, T. J., 124, 127, 133, 134, *142*
Sperling, G., 146, *179,* 487, 494, *504*
Spillman, L., 359, *399*
Stappers, P. J., *556,* 570, *584*
Stark, L., 476, *480, 481*
Steele, C. M., 468, *478*
Steinman, R. M., 570, 577, *584*
Stevens, J., 501, *506*
Stevens, K. A., 434, *458*
Stoever, R. G., 250, *263*

Stone, L. S., 268, *292*
Stoner, G. R., 449, *458*
Storm, R. W., 133, *142*
Stucchi, N., 501, *507*
Stucki, M., 59, *67,* 534, *554*
Stultiens, C. I., 438, *455*
Stumpf, P., 509, *529*
Subrahmanyam, K., 85, *118*
Sugarman, S., 12, *17*
Sugita, Y., 253, *263,* 268, 275, 276, *292*
Sumi, S., 498, *507*
Super, B. J., 202, *240, 396*
Supér, H., *176*
Sur, M., 276, *292*
Sutherland, N. S., 406, *458*
Sutton, R., *480*
Swinnen, V., *328*
Szasz, T. S., 280, *290*
Szeliski, R., 517, *529*
Szoc, R., 125, *143*

Takeichi, H., 197, 198, *244,* 268, 275, *292*
Talmy, L., 72, 74, 76, *118*
Tanaka, J. W., 472, *479, 481*
Tannenbaum, A. R., 449, 450, 452, *456, 457*
Tarr, M. J., 72, 86, *115, 118, 479,* 558, *584*
Taylor, D., 47, *68*
Taylor, M., 91, *114*
te Winkel, W., 403, 405, *456*
Temesvary, A., 233, *241,* 268, *290*
Tenenbaum, J. M., 193, *239,* 407, *458*
Terman, D., 194, *244*
Tham, M.-P., *176*
Thinès, G., 559, 560, 570, 574, *583*
Thompson, I. D., 484, *505*
Thompson, W. B., 60, *69,* 534, *556*
Thornber, K. K., 305, 311, 325, *328,* 384, *400*
Thornton, I., 499, 500, *507*
Thorpe, S., 390, *399*
Todd, J. T., 416, *458, 529*
Todd, R., 332, *352*
Todorovic, D., 364, 510, *529*
Tolhurst, D. J., 484, *505*
Tommasi, L., 449, *458*
Tootell, R. B. H., *398*
Town, C., 54, *68*
Treisman, A., 133, *142,* 146, 147, 149, *179,* 272, 274, *290, 292,* 413, 442, *458*
Tremoulet, P. D., *116*
Tresness, K. J., *457*
Trick, L. M., 255, *263*
Troost, J. M., 438, *455*
Ts'o, D. Y., 211, *244*
Tsal, Y., 160, 161, *177, 179*
Tse, P. U., 191, 204, *244*
Turvey, M. T., 124, 126, *141, 142*
Tyler, C., *327*

Uchida, N., 85, *115*
Ugurbil, K., 268, *290*
Ullman, S., 301, 304, 313, *328, 399, 454,* 488, *507,* 510, *527,* 546
Umilta, C., *395*
Ungerleider, L. G., *479,* 494, *504*

Vaina, L., 77, *117,* 500, *507*
Valdes-Sosa, M., 147, 171, 172, *179*
Valenza, E., *395*
Vallar, G., 167, *174, 179*
Vallortigara, G., 449, *458*
Van Bakel, A., 343, *351*
Van Dam, A., 520, *526*
van der Helm, P. A., 230, *244,* 278, *292,* 298, *328,* 333, 334, 336, 337, 339, 340, 341, 343, 345, 347, *350, 351*
van der Walle, G. A., 46, 53, 55, *69, 118*

van der Spiegel, J., *481*
van der Zwan, R., 377, *395*
Van Doorn, A. J., 416, *456, 458*
Van Essen, D. C., 130, *140, 395,* 500, *507*
Van Gool, L., 280, *292, 328*
Van Horebeek, J., *328*
Van Lier, R. J., 188, 230, *244,* 266, 268, 270, 278, 280, *292,* 298, 333, 336, 337, 339, 340, 341, 343, 344, 345, 347, *350, 351, 352*
Varzi, A., *455*
Vaughan, B., 268, 283, *290,* 445, *456*
Vaughn, H. H., Jr., 127, *143*
Vecera, S. P., 146, 147, 148, 149, 153, 154, 155, 156, 157, 162, 164, 168, 169, 170, 172, 173, *175, 177, 179,* 405, 448, *458*
Vermersch, A., *480*
Vezzani, S., 538, 550, *556*
Vico, F., *478*
Vierordt, K., 561, *584*
Visser, T. A. B., 137, *140*
Vitz, P., 332, *352*
Viviani, P., 501, *507*
Vogel, E. K., 126, *141, 143,* 151, 173, *176, 180*
Vogels, R., 276, *290*
Volkmann, F. C., 464, *481*
von der Heydt, R., 40, *68,* 127, *143,* 184, 206, 207, 208, 209, 213, 214, 215, 216, 218, 222, 223, *240, 241, 243, 244,* 276, *292,* 314, *326,* 354, 360, 362, 377, 381, 390, *395, 397, 399, 400,* 524, *527, 528, 529*

Wachtel, G., 99, *117*
Wagemans, J., 268, 270, 278, 280, *292,* 318, *328,* 339, 341, 343, *351, 352*
Walder, F., *479*
Walker-Smith, G. J., 469, *481*
Wallace, M., 168, *175*
Wallach, H., 253, *264,* 485, *507,* 510, *529, 530,* 559, 560, 565, 573, 574, 577, *584*
Wallis, G., 558, *584, 585*
Waltz, D., 407, *458*
Wang, D., 194, *244*
Wang, Y., 95, *116*
Ward, R., 126, *142,* 167, 169, *180*
Watt, R. J., 190, 221, *244,* 561, 563, 566, *583*
Wattam-Bell, J., 50, 54, *69*
Waxman, A. M., 510, *530*
Waxman, S. R., 80, 87, 88, *118*
Weber, T. A., 170, 171, *180*
Weeks, P. A., Jr., *479*
Weichselgartner, E., 146, *179*
Weiss, I., 514, 517, 519, 522, *530*
Weisstein, N., 125, *140, 143,* 268, *288,* 535, *555*
Wellman, H. M., 88, 89, *114*
Wells, N., 491, *505*
Wenderoth, P., 280, *292*
Wenzel, E. L., 561, 562, *585*
Werner, H., 125, *143*
Werner, J. S., 359, *399*
Wertheimer, M., 147, *179, 180,* 197, *244, 262,* 278, *289,* 332, *352,* 570, *583, 584, 585*
West, D. C., 130, *139, 142*
Westheimer, G., 211, *241,* 320, *327, 398*
Wheeler, D., 552, *555,* 569, *582*
Wheeler, K., 190, *240, 526*
Whitteridge, D., 358, *398*
Wiesel, T. N., 188, 207, 210, 211, *241, 244,* 358, *396, 397,* 484, 491, *505*
Willats, P., 75, *118*
Williams, C. K. I., 173, *177*
Williams, L. R., 297, 305, 307, 308, 310,

311, 325, *328, 329,* 383, 384, 391, *400*
Williamson, J. R., 371, 392, *397*
Winocur, G., 165, *174, 480*
Winston, P. A., 407, *458*
Witkin, A. P., 221, *244,* 407, *458*
Woelburn, T., *396*
Wohn, K., 510, *530*
Wolfe, J. M., 133, *143,* 146, 149, *180,* 403, 413, 414, 442, *458, 459*
Woodman, G. F., 151, 173, *180*
Woodward, A. L., 79, 80, 86, *118*
Wouterlood, D., 232, *239,* 336, 337, 340, *349, 352*

Xu, Y., 403, 406, 443, 444, 445, *459*

Yantis, S., 150, 171, *177, 180,* 268, 273, 274, 283, *290, 291, 293,* 445, *456*
Yap, Y. L., 490, *504*
Yarbus, A. L., 202, *244,* 464, 466, 469, *481*
Yeh, Y.-Y., *176*
Yen, S. C., 184, 192, 206, 210, 211, 212, 213, 214, 216, 218, 219, 221, *244*
Yin, C., 187, 196, 197, 199, 203, 204, 223, 224, 225, 232, 235, *242, 245,* 272, *290,* 320, 322, *328,* 580, *585*
Yin, R. K., 466, *481*
Yonas, A., *33,* 54, 56, 57, 59, 60, 61, 63, *65, 66, 69,* 510, *530,* 534, *554, 556*
Young, S., *66, 67, 116,* 475, *481*
Yuille, A. L., 487, *504,* 510, *530*

Zamostny, K., 332, *349*
Zeki, S., 130, *143,* 500, *507*
Zemel, R. S., 148, 155, 156, 165, 173, *174, 177, 180,* 268, *288*
Zhang, Y., *395*
Zhou, H., 127, *143*
Zhu, S., 297, 303, *329*
Zihl, J., 500, *505*
Zipser, K., 130, *141,* 163, *180*
Zisserman, A., 305, *326*
Zöllner, F., 560, 566, *584, 585*
Zucker, S. W., 250, 254, *262,* 306, *326,* 361, 362, 366, 371, 372, 373, 374, 375, 376, 378, 379, 385, 386, 387, 390, *399, 400,* 449, 450, 452, *456, 457*
Zweck, J., 310, *329*

Subject Index

Accidental viewpoint, 344, 347
Accretion and deletion of texture, 54, 59, 193, 533-535, 549, 571
Amodal completion, 195-205, 222-224, 226-229, 253, 257, 265-287, 295, 299-300, 306, 319-320, 322, 336, 385, 446, 533, 542, 559
Amodal continuation, 196, 203-204
Aperture problem, 484, 486-487, 502, 509-513, 542, 548, 565
Apparent motion, 253, 282, 494-499, 501, 503, 509, 566, 570, 574
Attention, 41-42, 44, 50, 54, 83, 85, 94, 119, 121, 127-128, 130, 133-138, 145-173, 183, 256-257, 270, 345, 401, 405-406, 434, 445-447, 453, 465, 539-540
Avoidance of coincidence, 340

Bayes' theorem, 181, 229-230, 345
Biased competition, 145-146, 148, 149-163, 172-173
Bipole icon, 355-360
Boundary assignment, 38-39, 187-188, 193-194, 210, 216, 222, 227-230, 567
Boundary flow, 60, 534
Boundary interpolation, 41, 184, 187, 190, 192, 195-202, 203-204, 206, 210, 213, 214-236, 307, 363-371, 448, 580
  common mechanism, 198-201, 222-224
  in depth, 204, 234-237
  tolerable misalignment, 198, 225-226, 235

Calculation efficiency, 283-284
Classification image, 286
Coding rules, 332
Computer vision, 297-298, 303, 464, 466-467
Context and grouping, 377
Contour integration, 184, 192-193, 201, 206, 210-214, 216, 219, 230
Contour junctions, 56, 188, 190, 192-193, 196, 222
  detection, 184, 187, 192, 206, 207-210, 213, 221
Convexity, 106, 159, 194, 295, 299, 303, 306-307, 315-325, 430, 434
Count terms, 6-7
Curvature
  in boundary interpolation, 197, 201, 218-219, 221, 275, 320-321, 546-547
  in contour integration, 211, 213
  in Markov models, 303-305, 309, 317
  in object segmentation, 57, 101, 154, 191, 409-426, 430, 432-433, 440-442, 447, 449-450, 452-453

Depth information, 38-40, 54, 188, 533-535, 560-561
in boundary assignment, 193-195
in edge detection, 185, 187, 190, 193, 213, 220, 235
in grouping, 247, 250-253, 255-257, 261
in infant vision, 45, 47, 50, 59-60, 64
in object segmentation, 437, 440, 448-449
in visual interpolation, 187, 198-201, 222-224, 235-237, 272, 275-276, 287, 580
Disunity, 61-63

Edge classification, 193-194, 220, 223, 546
Edge detection, 38-39, 131, 187, 188-190, 201, 206, 207-210, 213, 220
multiple inputs for, 190, 213
End-stopped cells, 207-210, 215-216, 364
External Structure, 337, 338, 339, 340, 343, 344, 345
Eye movements, 136, 169-170, 464, 476, 552-553, 577

Face perception, 463-465, 476-477, 564
Face recognition, 463, 466-467, 471, 473, 477
Figure-ground, 10, 15, 101, 131, 147, 151, 158-159, 163, 165, 172, 188-189, 192-194, 210, 216, 257, 322, 401, 404, 409, 435, 527, 564
Formalization of regularity, 332, 347
Foveated vision, 464-465, 467, 473, 475-477

Gaze control, 300, 463-465, 467, 472-473, 476-477
Genericity principle, 440
Gestalt principles, 6, 44, 147, 154, 196, 197-198, 202, 229, 249-250, 253, 299, 306, 354
Global completion, 230-234, 278-281, 335, 337, 340
Global simplicity, 345-346
Good continuation, 147, 152, 164, 196, 197-198, 250, 253, 256-257, 272, 277, 304, 307, 309, 317, 325, 332, 354, 405, 419, 423-425, 449, 532

Habituation, 41, 47, 51, 60, 63, 82
Hypothesis of salient figures, 434-435

Identity hypothesis, 198-201, 222-224, 232
Illusory contours, 37-41, 44, 48, 50-53, 55-56, 63-64, 168, 187, 191-192, 195-202, 213-224, 226-229, 232-233, 237, 276, 296-298, 300, 304-305, 307-308, 310-311, 368-369, 377, 383-385, 389-391, 394, 396, 398, 400, 424, 525, 527-530, 535, 538, 550, 570, 577
Information load, 334, 345
Integrative approach, 337, 343-345, 347
Internal noise, 225, 283-284, 287, 576
Internal Structure, 337, 340, 344-345
Intersection of Constraints, 486-487

Kinematic information, 40, 46, 50, 53-56, 61, 63, 190, 237-238, 548, 571

Lateral interactions, 211, 214, 216, 218-219, 229
Likelihood principle, 345
Local and global processes, 229-234, 278-281, 287
Local completion, 230-234, 280-281, 336-337, 340

Local symmetry, 405, 418-419, 421, 426-429, 450-453

Markov decision process, 463, 472-473
Markov models, 300, 303-308, 314, 317-319, 325, 467, 476
Mass terms, 6-7, 11
Microgenesis, 270
Minima rule, 101, 401, 405, 407, 409-418, 422-423, 426, 443
Minimum principle, 335, 345
Motion
human, 496, 501
integration, 483, 487-492, 499, 503, 509, 542
segmentation, 489-490
Multi-scale filtering, 192, 220-221, 549

Negative minima of curvature, 409-426, 430-431, 433, 442-443, 448-453
Non-accidental properties, 343, 346, 407

Object permanence, 11
Object recognition, 3, 23, 80, 86, 99-100, 105, 124, 155, 181, 188, 206, 234, 265, 287, 296-299, 314, 316, 319, 325, 345, 402, 466, 494
from partial information, 230-234
Object segregation, 145, 147-148, 151, 162-163, 169, 172-173
Object unity, 44-50, 52-53, 55, 58, 64, 187, 193, 205, 235
Object-based attention, 146-167, 169-173, 268, 283, 445
Occlusion, 12, 15-16, 26, 37, 40, 47-48, 64, 92, 181, 187, 190, 193, 195-205, 209, 216, 219, 222-225, 226-229, 232, 247, 257, 260-261, 265-287, 299, 306-307, 313, 336-337, 340, 344, 448, 461, 532, 537-538, 540, 544, 546-551, 558-559, 561, 571-572, 574-575
Ontology, 6-7, 15

Paired-preference paradigm, 41-42
Part salience, 401, 405, 433-436, 440, 447, 452
Part structure, 110, 295, 299, 319, 322, 402, 405, 414, 426, 430, 433, 442, 447, 450, 452
Part-based attention, 154, 447
Partly occluded objects, 37-41, 44-50, 53, 55-56, 61, 63-64, 187, 198, 202-203, 222-224, 232-233, 266, 269, 271, 275, 287
Perceptual complexity, 337, 340
Perceptual interpretations, 347, 542
Perceptual organization, 6, 35, 80, 147, 157, 163, 166, 181, 183, 265, 295-300, 302, 307, 314, 319, 325, 333, 345, 347
Perceptual set, 157-160, 162
Petter's rule, 199-200, 449
Pre-attentive processing, 147, 413, 442-445
Priming paradigms, 231-232, 268, 270, 274-275, 278, 281, 337, 343
Protrusion, 322, 431, 435, 450-452

Quasimodal completion, 223-224

Recognition by components (RBC), 100, 343-344
Regularity, 229-234, 260, 331-332, 334, 337, 339, 469-470, 486
Relatability, 38, 40, 46, 53, 61, 64, 187, 195-198, 200-204, 225-229, 232-238, 253-254, 257, 272, 274-275, 320-321, 360-362, 366, 370-372, 375-378, 424, 449, 528, 546-547, 550, 567, 569, 580

Response classification, 285-287

Sequential decision making, 472, 476
Shape representation, 86, 94, 187-188, 205-206, 229-234, 303, 402, 406, 412, 434, 449, 453
Short-cut rule, 419-423, 449
Simplicity, 112, 182, 229, 331-333, 335, 337, 340-341, 345-347
Single-cell recording, 222-223, 356, 466, 500
Spatiotemporal boundary formation (SBF), 59, 531-553, 571, 574, 577-578, 580
Spurious objects, 11, 16
Static information, 46, 50-51, 55-56, 59-60, 63-64, 566, 569, 571, 580
Stereoscopic depth, 54, 188, 190, 193-195, 213, 235, 254, 275-276, 287, 320, 417
Stochastic completion field, 308, 311
Structural Information Theory (SIT), 181, 278, 331-334, 337, 341-348
Subordinate structure, 342-343
Superstructure, 342-343, 347
Support ratio, 202, 224, 252, 367
Surface interpolation, 187, 195, 202-205, 225, 232, 235
Symbol series, 332, 334, 337
Symmetry, 51, 104, 124, 151, 164, 167, 188, 194, 229-234, 270, 279, 303, 315, 318, 333, 336, 343, 346, 404, 411-412, 418, 425-430, 434, 442, 452-453

Tangent discontinuities, 190-192, 195-198, 200, 203, 221, 227, 440, 446, 448
Terminators, 251, 257-259, 489-492
Top-down processing, 138, 145, 150-151, 154, 155-163, 170, 172-173, 188-189, 225, 229-230, 296
Transparency, 155, 198, 333, 401, 404-405, 433, 437-441, 453, 540, 577-578
Transversality, 407-408, 432
Turning angle, 433, 440, 446

Viewpoint independency, 344
Viewpoint invariant properties, 295, 299, 316, 318
Violation-of-expectation paradigm, 41-42
Virtual structure, 337, 340, 343-345
Visible regions, 185-187, 190, 194-195, 205-206, 221, 230
Visual form agnosia, 163-167, 172, 466
Visual interpolation, 38, 41, 44, 53-55, 190, 192, 195-206, 210, 214-237, 307, 354, 398, 448, 531, 535, 545, 547, 580
Visual search, 145-146, 149-151, 157, 165, 250, 268, 274, 401, 412-413, 442, 445, 453

FSC
www.fsc.org
MIX
Papier | Fördert gute Waldnutzung
FSC® C083411

Kolibri 360 GmbH
Ferdinand-Jühlke-Straße 7
99095 Erfurt, Deutschland
produktsicherheit@kolibri360.de